P9-DNV-974

the WASHINGTON *diaries* 1981–1989

ALLAN GOTLIEB

McCLELLAND & STEWART

Library and Archives Canada Cataloguing in Publication

Gotlieb, Allan

The Washington diaries / Allan Gotlieb.

ISBN 13: 978-0-7710-3385-8

ISBN 10: 0-7710-3385-0

1. Gotlieb, Allan – Diaries. 2. Washington (D.C.) – Social life and customs. 3. Canada – Foreign relations – United States. 4. United States – Foreign relations – Canada. 5. Canada – Foreign relations – 1945–. 6. Diplomatic and consular service, Canadian – United States. 7. Ambassadors – Canada – Diaries. I. Title.

FC631.G68A3 2006 327.710092 C2006-902166-X

We acknowledge the financial support of the Government of Canada through the Book Publishing Industry Development Program and that of the Government of Ontario through the Ontario Media Development Corporation's Ontario Book Initiative. We further acknowledge the support of the Canada Council for the Arts and the Ontario Arts Council for our publishing program.

Typeset in Minion by M&S, Toronto

Printed and bound in Canada

Index created by J. Barnard Gilmore.

This book is printed on acid-free paper that is 100% recycled, ancient-forest friendly (100% post-consumer recycled).

McClelland & Stewart Ltd.

75 Sherbourne Street

Toronto, Ontario

M5A 2P9

www.mcclelland.com

1 2 3 4 5 10 09 08 07 06

To Sondra Gotlieb,
who got it right:
"Maybe we should invade South Dakota or something."
Quotation of the Day, *New York Times*, page 1, July 8, 1982

"Keep a diary. Above all, you must keep a diary."

– Charles Ritchie to Allan Gotlieb, October 31, 1981, on the eve of his departure for Washington

PREFACE

During my more than seven years as ambassador to the United States, I recorded, usually on a daily basis, the events that, at the time, seemed significant in my life and that of my wife, Sondra. I described my endless (and often mindless) battles with the bureaucracy and ministers in Ottawa. I recorded our experiences in trying to run Canada's largest embassy and to reshape the profile of Canada on Embassy Row. I wrote about trying to understand the mysteries of Georgetown and social Washington and to penetrate the inner chambers where the gossip was always best. I chronicled my efforts in navigating the swamps and jungles of Congress and finding my way through the labyrinthine corridors of power of official Washington. And I wrote about my ambition to do something that the embassy had been reluctant to do before – practise public diplomacy.

Although the diaries were not written with publication in mind, it occurred to me some years after I left Washington that they might possibly be of interest to a few people in Canada other than my wife and myself. Not, for sure, because of the accounts of my bureaucratic battles. Nor of my squabbles with ministers over our policies towards the United States. Nor because of the party lists and conversations in the salons we tried to run on Embassy Row. Nor because of the tales of my misadventures in the offices of congressmen and senators. Nor of my pastoral visits to remote parts of the country preaching the Canadian gospels to bored audiences. No, none of these recurrent themes in the diaries would tell the reader that much about the challenge of representing Canada in the United States.

But the conceit occurred to me that in the case of the diaries, the whole could be seen as greater than the sum total of the parts, and so, when taken together, a picture might emerge of the enormity, if not the futility, of the task of promoting and defending the interests of Canada in a country which has so long taken us for granted.

In preparing these diaries for publication, a number of obstacles had to be overcome. In their entirety they contain in the neighbourhood of a half-million words. Reducing them for publication by roughly 50 per cent required the omission of a large number of entries, and the excision of parts of many others. This in turn required difficult questions of judgment and editing. Sondra's assistance in this difficult process was invaluable.

I wrote these diaries not just in the chancery or at the Residence late at night but on airplanes, in trains, and in the back of automobiles. All were written long-hand. The problem of typing them was greatly aggravated by my shockingly bad writing – so bad that at times it is a challenge even for me to decipher. I am particularly grateful to Lalaine Aquino for transcribing them into readable form, a project that took several years to complete. I would also like to thank Laura Madokoro, who also helped in their transcription and editing. She wielded a particularly sharp knife.

Special mention should also be made of Sulai Quach and Gordon Chan, who searched out biographical information for the footnotes – no easy task. I am very grateful for their assistance as well as for the help of Trena White of McClelland & Stewart, who is a superb editor. I would also like to express my appreciation for the valuable assistance of D'Arcy O'Brien in my editing of the book.

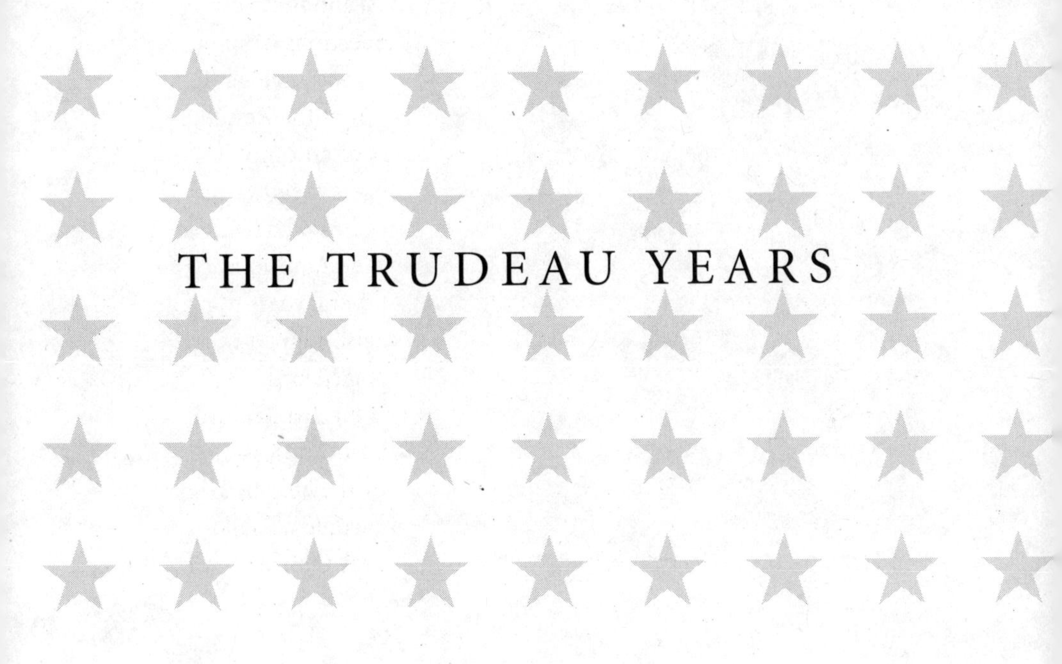

THE TRUDEAU YEARS

September 24, 1981 The prime minister informed cabinet today that he is appointing me ambassador to Washington. I always dreamed of being Canadian ambassador to the United States. I dreamed of it in Oxford. I dreamed of it in Berkeley. I dreamed of it at Harvard. I am dreaming of it now.

After almost five years as undersecretary, thirteen years as a deputy minister, twenty years as an Ottawa resident, and twenty-four as a bureaucrat, I've had enough.

On January 2, 1957, I came to Ottawa to work for External Affairs, just off the boat from Oxford, one of the seven most beautiful cities in Europe. I had seen the great neo-Gothic buildings on Parliament Hill once before, and I rushed to see them again. They were as I remembered: spectacular. But I was in a state of disbelief when I saw our national capital. The town looked like an unkempt, decaying village. Hideous telegraph poles leaning over the main street. A dismal place; to call it provincial would have been a compliment.

On my first anniversary in Ottawa, I scribbled a note to myself and put it in a sealed envelope and stuck it in a drawer at home. It read: "Allan, if the day comes when you say to yourself, 'I like Ottawa,' that's the time to leave. It won't be because Ottawa has improved. It will be because your standards have deteriorated."

I stayed. I began to like Ottawa. I remembered the envelope. I know it's time to leave.

October 7, 1981 The department sent me the following memorandum today: "The Head of Post Official Hospitality budget for 1981–1982 based on estimates submitted by Peter Towe[1] is $120,000. Approximately

---

[1] (b. 1922) Canadian representative to the Organisation for Economic Co-operation and Development 1972–1975; Assistant Undersecretary of State for External Affairs 1975–1977; Canadian Ambassador to the United States 1977–1981.

$30,000 covers costs for three personal servants including the cook and two maids. Three other members of the residence staff are on the locally engaged establishment, including the senior servant, the housekeeper and chauffeur." In our quarter-century of marriage, Sondra has never been able to stand having a live-in nanny or housekeeper. What's it going to be like having a crowd under our roof?

Sondra explained her apprehensions to an interviewer for *Ottawa Magazine*. "It's all the servants that are worrying me. You can't put your feet up on the tables or walk around naked, you have to make sure you look nice."

October 9, 1981 Al Haig[1] writes to "Dear Mark,"[2] informing him of his "increasing concern that our two countries are heading toward a confrontation." "The situation," he says, is "urgent and extremely serious." "Confrontation? . . . extremely serious?" This is Canada-U.S. relations? In the old days, states sent such communications just before declaring war.

October 13, 1981 Lunch at Ambassador Paul Robinson's[3] to discuss the deteriorating state of our relationship. Don Regan[4] and his chief aide on the international side, Marc Leland,[5] flew up for the meeting. Our side fielded Allan MacEachen,[6] Ian Stewart,[7] Mark MacGuigan, and myself. Robinson was charging like a bull, and Regan and Leland hit us on the whole span of our energy and investment rules.

The Americans have created a climate of near crisis over the NEP and FIRA – witness Haig's letter – and our visitors came here to reinforce that

[1] (b. 1924) National Security Advisor 1969–1970; Chief of Staff to President Richard Nixon 1973–1974; Secretary of State 1981–1982.

[2] Mark MacGuigan (1931–1998) Liberal Member of Parliament for Windsor-Walkerville 1968–1984; Secretary of State for External Affairs 1980–1982; Minister of Justice 1982–1984.

[3] (b. 1930) U.S. Ambassador to Canada 1981–1985.

[4] (1918–2003) Secretary of the Treasury 1981–1985; Chief of Staff to President Ronald Reagan 1985–1987.

[5] Assistant Secretary of the Treasury for International Affairs 1981–1982.

[6] (b. 1921) Liberal Member of Parliament 1953–1958 and 1962–1984; Secretary of State for External Affairs 1974–1976 and 1982–1984; Deputy Prime Minister of Canada 1977–1979 and 1980–1984; Minister of Finance 1980–1982.

[7] Deputy Minister of Energy, Mines, and Resources 1979–1980 and of Finance 1980–1981.

sense of crisis. Regan said "elements in Congress" think that our actions are anti-American and require retaliation.

I'm not sure what they expected to obtain from us when they came, but they did hear some important – and surprising – remarks from MacEachen. He informed them that "there would be no new NEPs" in the other sectors of our economy. That's quite an undertaking for a sovereign nation to make to a foreign power. Moreover, I am not aware of any previous discussion in cabinet or Parliament. No quid pro quo. MacEachen also went far in negating the statement in the Speech from the Throne that FIRA needs to be strengthened. That statement, he said, is under scrutiny as a result of U.S. concerns – a clear signal that we are unlikely to proceed.

MacEachen would never go out on a limb. He would not have made such far-reaching commitments without the knowledge that Trudeau would back him up. It's one thing for a politician to make such commitments in the domestic context. It is another to make them to a foreign power.

Thanks to MacEachen's skills and shrewd manoeuvres, we've gone some way towards showing Washington that we are not totally deaf to their concerns. But I still believe we are headed towards one of the most contentious periods in the history of our relationship.

October 20, 1981 The prime minister announced my appointment today. This ends a difficult period for us. We've been packing up, selling things (including our car), trying to rent our house, attending farewell parties, and during all this time, my appointment has not been officially announced. So I couldn't really tell anybody it was a done thing. In talking to the media, I've had to ask them to treat the appointment as confidential. The United States has granted "agrément," so I don't know why I've been placed in this ridiculous situation. It's public at last. The charade ends.

October 21, 1981 Pressure is growing on me to get down to Washington post-haste. Peter Towe has completed his four-year term and has been agitating to leave for months.

Peter was always aware that he wasn't my first choice for Washington. Trudeau was keen on Ivan Head[1] but recognized (with a big assist from me as undersecretary) that Washington was a stuffy, middle-class, moralistic

[1] (1930–2004) Canadian foreign-policy specialist and academic. Senior Policy Adviser to Prime Minister Pierre Trudeau 1968–1978; President of the International Development Research Centre 1978–1991.

town and probably would not take kindly to the fact that Ivan, having recently abandoned his wife, was living with his secretary.

I pressed Trudeau to appoint Klaus Goldschlag,[1] the best foreign-policy mind in the department. Don Jamieson[2] was convinced that the tall, cool, waspy Peter and his attractive socialite wife, Carole, would go down much better in Washington than a naturalized Jewish refugee from Berlin. He thus showed that he knew little or nothing about Washington. But Jamieson prevailed.

In fairness to Peter, I think he did a creditable job in Washington, particularly with the economic hands. He has a very good relationship with Walter Mondale,[3] going back to a previous posting in Washington, and he used it extremely well. But he seriously underestimated the depth of American anger over the NEP. As did we all.

October 22, 1981 Telegram received from our ambassador to Ireland, old friend Alan Sullivan.[4] Contents alarming. "On basis my experience, as new Ambassador you may wish to look into possibility of facial surgery guaranteed to keep smile on face for long fixed periods."

October 24, 1981 Lots of publicity about my appointment – more than I've ever received before and ever will again. Many comments in the papers: "Important elements in the U.S. Congress have gone on warpath against Canada." True. "American legislators – from both the Democratic and Republican Parties – are railing against a host of Canadian activities, ranging from the national energy program and foreign investment regulations to the fact that Canadian companies, aided by more suitable bank financing regulations, are outgunning American businessmen at their own game and buying up their companies." True. "There's also an export of acid rain across the border, U.S. studies of economic measures against Canada,

---

[1] (b. 1922) Canadian Ambassador to Turkey 1967–1971, to Italy 1973–1976, and to West Germany 1980–1983; Deputy Undersecretary of State for External Affairs (Political) 1977–1980.

[2] (1921–1986) Minister of Transport 1969–1972; Secretary of State for External Affairs 1976–1979; Canadian High Commissioner to the United Kingdom 1982–1985.

[3] (b. 1928) Democratic Senator from Minnesota 1964–1976; Vice-President of the United States 1977–1981.

[4] Canadian Ambassador to Ireland 1981–1982, to Austria 1982–1985, to Italy 1988–1991, to Libya 1988–1991, and to Malta 1988–1991.

the perennial thorn of the Garrison Diversion project, a failed fish treaty and the usual fears about Quebec separation." True, true, true. "Most Canadians do not know who their Ambassador to the United States is. Most people in the United States do not know who their Ambassador to Canada is. The neighbouring states who share the longest undefended border in the world are not at all that neighbourly." Standard refrain from people coming up to me in recent days: "You have your work cut out for you."

October 25, 1981 My mother in Winnipeg is very happy as a result of the big picture of me on the front page of the *Free Press*. My large head is imposed on the dome of the Capitol building in Washington. Two big domes.

I told the reporter, "I grew up in Winnipeg. As a young person you form impressions of what you want to do. It seemed to me then that the most interesting thing in the world one could do was to come to work for External Affairs." I really did feel that way. I still do.

I worry a lot about whether I'll be good at this job. I know that the way one measures success in an embassy is different from the way one measures success in the public service in Ottawa. Abroad, an ambassador is a salesman, promoter, public-relations operator, huckster, animateur, impresario, and lobbyist. But one thing he can't be: a bureaucrat or ruler of the desk. This is what I have excelled at.

October 30, 1981 I hear from Goldschlag, now our man in Bonn. As always, he gets it right. "You are assuming your post," he writes, "at a time of evident strain in our relations with the United States. We seem to find ourselves in a situation where strong ideological positions on one side confront increasingly ideological positions on the other." Of course, as Canadians we would never think of ourselves as "ideological."

October 31, 1981 The night of our farewell-to-Ottawa and hello-to-Sondra's-new-book party. Close to two hundred guests came to our house on Lisgar Road. Lots of media, Liberals, and writers mixed with members of Parliament, diplomats, and old friends. Mordecai Richler was here, along with Speaker Jeanne Sauvé[1] and her husband, Maurice; Gaby

---

[1] (1922–1993) Canadian journalist for the CBC, politician, and stateswoman. Elected Liberal Member of Parliament for Montreal in 1972; Speaker of the House of Commons 1980–1984; Governor General of Canada 1984–1990.

Leger;[1] Mark MacGuigan; and lots of colleagues from various stages of my career. Trudeau stayed a couple of hours and was, as always, the magnet who attracted all. My favourite Conservative was on hand, John Crosbie,[2] the only politician I know, other than Trudeau, who doesn't feel obliged to sail along comfortably in the conventional mainstream. Charles Ritchie[3] arrived in a taxi to stay a minute but was still here an hour later. "Keep a diary," he told me. "Above all, you must keep a diary."

Trudeau was very taken with Rebecca in her sensational 1930s red, white, and purple beaded art deco dress. He told her that she has to come, wearing the dress, to the opening of his newly acquired, Cormier-designed art deco house in Westmount.

November 2, 1981 My first interview as ambassador designate appears in the *Toronto Star*. They played it up (a page 1 story) because it fits in with their strong support of Trudeau's energy and investment policies.

The interview accurately reflects what my main role in the United States will be: public relations. I explain that the willingness of Canadians to allow the public sector to play a large role in our life doesn't derive from love of socialist principles, nor from ideological roots. It derives from history and necessity. The requirements of our nationhood have never really bothered the Americans before – not in a hundred years. Now, under the guidance of an ideological president, they do. Intervention is evil, or seen as evil, regardless of the context. U.S. parochialism: that is the root of the Canada-U.S. problem today.

But I have a problem, the *Star* says. I am reputed to be "unsociable," and "I don't like talking to people." I take exception. "I don't like a lousy party," I said. "I enjoy a good party. I hope to give a lot of good parties. I hope to go to a lot of good ones."

---

[1] Wife of Jules Leger, Governor General of Canada 1974–1979.

[2] (b. 1931) PC Member of Parliament for St. John's West 1976–1993; Minister of Finance 1979–1980; Minister of Transport 1986–1988; Minister of International Trade 1988–1991.

[3] (1906–1995) Canadian Ambassador to West Germany 1954–1958; Permanent Representative to the United Nations 1958–1962; Ambassador to the United States 1962–1966 and to the North Atlantic Council 1966–1967; Canadian High Commissioner to the United Kingdom 1967–1971.

November 10, 1981 I received a letter from another colleague today, the acute Peter Roberts,[1] former political officer at the Canadian embassy in Washington. "The problem for the Ambassador in Washington," he writes, "as it seemed to me when I was there in a lesser job, is one of access. Ambassadors are in the eighth or ninth ring out from the Sun King. The scramble towards the centre is rarely successful and always unseemly."

November 18, 1981 Part of the archaic ritual of the diplomatic corps is the farewell reception. Socially, diplomats in Ottawa see almost no one except each other. So when one leaves, for them it's a bit like losing a limb (or maybe a fingernail). As head of the department, it was inevitable that we would engage in the ritual. I count twenty-six farewell dinners and receptions in our honour since my appointment was announced, including several in the next two weeks (ridiculous that I should count them). Our friend Don McSween, head of the National Arts Centre, wit and bon vivant, had a mischievous idea. Instead of offering us yet another farewell reception, he and his wife, with two other couples who are also friends, the Johnstones[2] and the Kirkwoods,[3] would organize a surprise weekend for us. There was no hint of what it was. When the time came, we were picked up in a van, driven by David and containing the group, and were informed that our destination was Ogdensburg, New York. The idea was to expose the effete and elitist ambassador to the real America, the land of bowling alleys, diners, and sleazy motels. The van and its inhabitants soon reeked of alcohol, but amazingly, we were not stopped at the border or anywhere else. Sondra and I got so snockered we barely managed to survive the bowling alley. We have virtually no memory of the diner or the motel other than its name (the Oral – really).

It was a dumb idea. Imagine the headline: "Canadian Ambassador Arrested in Ogdensburg. Was in Alcoholic Stupor." A sensational beginning (or ending) of my assignment.

---

[1] (1927–2003) Press Secretary to Prime Minister Pierre Trudeau; Canadian Ambassador to Romania 1979–1983 and to the Soviet Union 1983–1985; Director of the Canada Council 1985–1989.

[2] Robert and Popsy Johnstone. He was Deputy Minister of Industry, Trade, and Commerce 1978–1982 and of International Trade 1982–1983; Canadian Consul General in New York 1984–1988.

[3] David and Diana Kirkwood. He was a long-serving deputy minister in Ottawa, including of National Health and Welfare 1983–1986.

November 20, 1981 In Toronto to call on Premier Bill Davis[1] and his ministers at Queen's Park, all of them relaxed and amiable – the contrast with tense Ottawa is striking. In the evening I met with a dozen hostile businessmen – a warm-up for the job, now only ten days off. Shell Oil was especially heavy. Some of these people hate the idea of an Ottawa bureaucrat (even worse, a "Trudeaucrat") representing them in Washington. I was pressed to explain my "long-term strategies for dealing with the Americans." I told them I didn't have any. For the time being at least, we had to formulate short-term policies. Deal with problems as they arise. Deal with them one by one. This struck them as somewhat perverse. Maybe it is, but I sure wasn't going to talk to this crowd about gaining greater control of our economy, trade diversification, and other grand strategies of Pierre Elliott Trudeau. I'll save that for American audiences.

November 23, 1981 In Regina to see the premier, Allan Blakeney.[2] We discussed uranium, potash, wheat. He said relations with the United States are good. I don't understand why there are no problems between the most socialistic region of the country and the most ideological American government ever.

It is clear from my provincial visits that I have to concern myself not only with Canada-U.S. relations but also Saskatchewan-U.S. relations, Ontario-U.S. relations, Alberta-U.S. relations, and so on. What happens if the interests of the provinces clash with each other? Answer not in rule book.

November 24, 1981 I call on fellow Winnipegger and premier-elect of Manitoba, Howard Pauley,[3] to discuss Manitoba's big foreign-policy problem with the United States: the conflict with North Dakota over the diversion of water caused by the building of the Garrison Dam. I tell him that the problem dates back to Roosevelt. He tells me to solve it.

I also attended a Hebrew University testimonial dinner in honour of my eighty-two-year-old mother. Everywhere I went tonight it was "Mr. Ambassador," and I am very puffed up.

---

[1] (b. 1929) PC Premier of Ontario 1971–1985.

[2] (b. 1925) NDP Premier of Saskatchewan 1971–1982.

[3] NDP Premier of Manitoba 1981–1988.

November 25, 1981 Late afternoon, a bitterly cold day. I take a stroll around the back of Parliament Hill, probably my last. I love looking at the spectral, bizarre Gothic shapes silhouetted against the dark grey winter skies. They give me a sense of empire and our great Victorian era. This is my era. This is my Canada.

I think of my most exciting and miserable moments on the Hill. Happiest with Trudeau, Lalonde,[1] Beetz,[2] and Pitfield,[3] working on the constitution, fighting the separatists, shaping our foreign policy. Least happy with Flora,[4] arguing over moving the embassy to Jerusalem and suffering petty indignities inflicted by her staff. Slamming shut my briefing books in a rage when she wouldn't listen to me and walking out of a cabinet meeting chaired by her.

In six days I'll no longer be Mr. Undersecretary. I've loved being at the command post, being Mr. Control. But I know I'm too satisfied standing on top on my own dunghill. And what is the point of hanging on? Is this an accomplishment?

"If anyone who wanders all day arrives towards evening, it is enough." Schopenhauer. I've had enough.

November 27, 1981 Among all the farewell receptions, the one hosted for me by Mark MacGuigan on the ninth floor of the Pearson Building was the most memorable. Thirty-six of the top senior officials were invited to lunch, seated at a single long table like in a church refectory. People were rather solemn, until the television monitors lit up. At MacGuigan's suggestion we watched reruns of *Yes Minister*. We all laughed, but he laughed hardest. A rare bird – a politician who respects officials, a politician without ego, who can mock himself.

---

[1] Marc Lalonde (b. 1929) Principal Secretary to Prime Minister Pierre Trudeau 1968–1972; Minister of Justice 1978–1979; Minister of Finance 1982–1984.

[2] Jean Beetz (1927–1991) Member of the Privy Council Office in the first Trudeau administration. Appointed to the Quebec Court of Appeal by Pierre Trudeau in 1973; Justice of the Supreme Court of Canada 1973–1988.

[3] Michael Pitfield (b. 1937) Canadian Senator and former senior civil servant. Clerk of the Privy Council and Secretary to the Cabinet 1975–1979 and 1980–1982.

[4] Flora MacDonald (b. 1926) Elected to the House of Commons in 1972 as the PC Member of Parliament for Kingston and the Islands. First Canadian female Secretary of State for External Affairs 1979–1980.

November 28, 1981 Last days in our rickety old Rockcliffe house. What will happen after Washington? I won't be there long. Trudeau is close to the end of his political career. The Conservatives will take over and won't want me. Joe Clark protected me from the talons of Flora. Not because he liked me. Far from it. It was simply that he liked Flora even less. The Tories will never believe I'm not a Liberal.

I remember Cardinal Newman's words: "I do not ask to see the distant scene; one step enough for me."

November 29, 1981 The telegram sent by MacGuigan to all posts abroad on the eve of my departure reads: "He set his stamp on an era of Canadian diplomacy." I didn't even draft it for him.

November 30, 1981 Last day as undersecretary before I leave for Washington. The prime minister invited me to lunch, tête-à-tête, at 24 Sussex. This might have been my last one-on-one encounter with him. I've had many over the past sixteen years, but for me he will always remain an enigma. One thing is clear: as I leave for Washington, I write finis to our close relationship. And in saying goodbye to propinquity, I say goodbye to power.

We spent most of the time discussing who my successor should be. My advice: "Beware of the people who put process over substance. In the bureaucracy, there is a whole new breed whose interest is how government is organized, not what government actually decides. Beware the process freaks." We barely talked about the state of Canada-U.S. relations.

I told the prime minister as we adjourned that he should know that some of his officials in the Privy Council Office were anti-American. "Every time you express exasperation with the Americans or utter some criticism," I told him, "these scribes immediately telephone around town, intimidating people, telling them that Trudeau was in a terrible snit about the Yanks and so we officials better be as tough as nails in dealing with them." I added that these officials ignored the helpful things he had done for Reagan as, for example, at the Ottawa and Cancun Summits; they use his occasional spontaneous remarks or acts of frustration to further their own anti-U.S. agenda.

Trudeau was reflective. He should remember, he commented, that he is prime minister and shouldn't allow himself the luxury of occasional outbursts.

After about sixteen years, I still find Trudeau unfathomable. He champions human rights at home but supports authoritarian regimes abroad and has no use for dissidents. He believes the Soviets can do no wrong but has steadily increased Canada's financial support for NATO. He proclaimed for years that foreign policy is an extension abroad of the national interest and ends up a *tiers-mondiste.* He champions the little states and weaker ones yet subscribes to nineteenth-century notions of Great Power spheres of influence. He is colour blind in his personal relations and is a philo-Semite but these days is consistently anti-Israel. He is anti-nationalist (Elie Kedourie's[1] influence) but embraces the narrow, inward nationalism of the Ontario anglos in his cabinet. He is a Quebecer and a French Canadian and all his peers are separatists, yet he is the most formidable federalist the country has produced. He loves American culture at its most superficial – the glitz, the glamour, the stars – yet the United States seems alien to him.

What makes this concoction so potent is that he holds to all his opinions with absolute conviction. He can never be wrong, so he defends them all to the considerable limit of his intellectual powers. His world of ideas collides. His relentless defence of his positions is what makes him so infuriating, yet it is also what makes him so fascinating.

What makes him great is his idea of one Canada and the conviction with which he holds to it. As de Gaulle said, a great leader needs to have only one great idea. Trudeau meets the test.

In the evening we attended a farewell party given for us by Paul Robinson and his wife, Martha, at their official residence. MacGuigan, Marc Lalonde, and a dozen or so others attended. It had the special distinction of being our last.

Martha had beautiful menus made, each decorated with hand-painted Canadian and U.S. flags. I looked around for the embassy's special signature: flowering plants from its greenhouses – oleanders, hibiscus, flowering maples. There were none. One of her first official acts, Martha recounted, was to fire the embassy gardener of seventeen years' standing. She likes only silk flowers.

Paul Robinson got up during the meal and made a farewell presentation. He handed me two dinner plates gilded with the American flag, removed

---

[1] (1926–1992) British historian of the Middle East. He was at the London School of Economics 1953–1990, where he became a professor of politics. He is well known for his 1960 book, *Nationalism.*

from the embassy's formal dinner service. I was startled, as were the other guests. I liked the plates but felt I was receiving stolen property.

The dinner was a nice gesture, but I can hardly forgive Martha's remark made to Max Yalden[1] at an earlier going-away dinner. "Don't you think it's appalling," she asked him, "that Trudeau is sending one of his homosexual friends to Washington?"

December 1, 1981 The morning of our departure for Washington, one of the coldest mornings in Ottawa in many years. My new assignment did not start auspiciously. Because of the atrocious cold, the pilot couldn't raise the landing gear on our early morning Eastern flight, so we had to return to Ottawa and start again. We were met at Dulles airport by the embassy's senior minister, Gerry Shannon;[2] the head of administration, Jack Hughes; and my executive assistant, Brian Dickson,[3] the chief justice's son, whom I met and selected for the job when I was on a trip to Romania, where he was our second secretary. U.S. Immigration and Customs came onto the aircraft and escorted us through the lines. I loved the special treatment.

At the Residence we were greeted at the door by all the servants, led by the Spanish butler, Rito, who has been here for several years and looks like he hasn't eaten for an equally long period of time. After making a tour of the house, I could stand it no longer. "So long," I said to Sondra. "I've got to go to the office." And off to the office I went. It's unbelievable. We're here. Exhausted. But here.

December 2, 1981 Day two. I can't describe my emotions as I sit behind this beautiful antique desk in one of the most ornate offices in one of the most magnificent mansions in Embassy Row. What a fantastic structure we occupy.

I had a Proustian recollection of an even more grandiose office, that of the

---

[1] (b. 1930) Canadian civil servant. Second Commissioner of Official Languages 1977–1984; Canadian Ambassador to Belgium and Luxembourg 1984–1987; Chief Commissioner of the Canadian Human Rights Commission 1987–1996.

[2] (1936–2003) Canadian Minister in Washington until 1982. Later, Canadian Ambassador to the United Nations, to the World Trade Organization, and to the General Agreement on Tariffs and Trade.

[3] Canadian Ambassador to El Salvador 1990–1993 and to Guatemala 1990.

Canadian High Commissioner to London, Norman Robertson,[1] who was chairman of the oral board that interviewed me for admission to the foreign service a quarter of a century ago. Nervous about appearing before the legendary mandarin, I had prepared for the interview by reading every book I could find on Canadian foreign policy, but he showed no inclination to quiz me on foreign affairs. "Gotlieb," he said, "I note from your curriculum vitae that your father was born in Hirsch, Saskatchewan. Jewish agricultural settlements were an important part of our history. I find them fascinating. What remains of the old community? Tell us about it." Taken aback, I explained that my grandfather left Hirsch for Winnipeg around 1895, and it had never crossed my mind to visit there. No village remained, maybe just a postal address. But Robertson was not appeased. "Surely, Gotlieb, in view of your roots, you would want to explore the cemetery and discover any remnants of your past." I squirmed and mumbled something like "great idea."

As I came into the chancery this morning, I stepped into the library on the ground floor, a long, dark, dismal room. Inserted into the mahogany walls are photographs of my predecessors, all eleven of them, who had served since Mackenzie King[2] purchased this building in the 1920s, our first embassy anywhere, acquired in the midst of a furious controversy over the pretensions and the price ($350,000 with furniture).

I counted the photographs of the Oxford men before me – Lester Pearson,[3] Hume Wrong,[4] Arnold Heeney,[5] Norman Robertson, Charles Ritchie, Ed Ritchie[6] – six out of eleven. But Canada is changing, and I might well be the last Oxonian to serve in this job.

---

[1] (1904–1968) Canadian diplomat and adviser to Prime Minister Mackenzie King. Undersecretary of State for External Affairs 1941–1946; Canadian High Commissioner to the United Kingdom 1946–1949 and 1952–1957; Canadian Ambassador to the United States 1957–1958.

[2] (1874–1950) Prime Minister of Canada 1921–1926, 1926–1930, and 1935–1948.

[3] (1897–1972) Canadian Ambassador to the United States 1944–1946; Secretary of State for External Affairs 1948–1957; Leader of the Liberal Party of Canada 1958–1968; Prime Minister of Canada 1963–1968.

[4] (1894–1954) Canadian Ambassador to the United States 1946–1953; Undersecretary of State for External Affairs 1953–1954.

[5] (1902–1970) Principal Secretary to Prime Minister William Lyon Mackenzie King 1938–1940; Clerk of the Privy Council and Secretary to the Cabinet 1940–1949; Undersecretary of State for External Affairs 1949–1953; Canadian Ambassador to the United States 1953–1957 and 1959–1962.

[6] (1916–2002) Canadian Ambassador to the United States 1966–1970.

December 3, 1981 Day three. Together with Sondra, we toured the chancery on Dupont Circle, all six floors, and shook hands with the staff. The building houses our political, economic, and administrative people, most of whom are squeezed into the corners and crevices of the building, if they are not in the basement. Then we toured the National Association of Broadcasters building and shook hands with our public-affairs and tourism staff. Yesterday we did the same at Sheridan Circle, the massive Stalinesque building that (appropriately) houses our military people and the RCMP. We are spread out all over, all three hundred of us, plus.

Will our new embassy on Pennsylvania ever get built? Not if our property managers in External Affairs have anything to do with it. They want to accord a higher priority to building new premises in Moscow and Peking.

December 4, 1981 Today I made my first calls on the administration, the two undersecretaries of state: Walter Stoessel[1] (political) and Mike Rashish[2] (economic). So bad has been the reaction to our investment and energy policies that retaliatory proposals are spewing out of the volcano on Capitol Hill. I count eleven legislative initiatives in Congress aimed at Canada. Trade Representative Bill Brock[3] has sent a sizzling critique of our policies, and Ottawa is stunned at its breadth and depth.

I urged Stoessel and Rashish to try to cool the tensions, because Ottawa has backed off plans to extend the reach of FIRA and MacEachen has now stated in his budget that the measures adopted in the NEP are "not appropriate for other sectors." But in reality, this does not make my task any easier. The Americans want us to rescind the NEP. They hate it. They regard it as confiscation. They don't give a damn about any supposed "sons of the NEP."

---

[1] (1920–1986) U.S. Ambassador to Poland 1968–1972, to the Soviet Union 1974–1976, and to West Germany 1976–1980; Undersecretary of State for Political Affairs 1981–1982; Deputy Secretary of State 1982.

[2] (1925–1995) American economist. Undersecretary of State for Economic and Agricultural Affairs 1981–1982.

[3] Republican Senator from Tennessee 1971–1977; Chairman of the Republican National Committee 1977–1981; U.S. Trade Representative 1981–1985; Secretary of Labor 1985–1987.

December 5, 1981 I know only three people in Washington: Harvey Poe[1] and Thad Holt,[2] both fellow students when I was at Christ Church, and now practising lawyers in town, and Bob Duemling,[3] former American minister in Ottawa. They are all worldly and intelligent. Last night we entertained them in our cavernous dining room, our first dinner party. It was a dull evening, because we talked about the old days. Why do people do this when the effect is always so depressing?

December 6, 1981 I like our official car and our driver, Jacques Helie, a crusty Quebecer with a bad heart who has been driving Canadian ambassadors here for decades. He will be a great mine of information about my predecessors. He already told me he used to drive Charles Ritchie to the movies in the afternoon.

The official car is an antique blue-black Oldsmobile, a mile long, very sleek, very quaint, and very anomalous in Washington. It looks like no other official car, because most of my colleagues drive new Mercedes and other fancy models. Jacques tells me that the administrative people at the embassy have decided to sell it. I will resist this as long as possible. This splendid antique gives me a bit of class, even if it is a little camp. It's the most distinctive diplomatic vehicle in town. Damned if I will be driven around in a humdrum new Ford.

The Olds has a car phone installed in it. I've never had one before, but it's also an antique. Jacques tell me I'll need it because I'll spend hours in traffic jams on the way to the Hill or State. The trouble is it's useless. You dial and dial, trying to find a free channel, which you never can. But having a car phone makes me feel important.

December 7, 1981 For a civil servant who almost never saw his name in a newspaper over a career of a quarter-century, it takes some getting used to, seeing my personality subject to regular dissection in the Canadian press. Apparently, the Montreal *Gazette* considers me to be a bookish, "somewhat Victorian gent" who collects prints and hand-carved ivories and

---

[1] Washington lawyer and distant cousin of the American writer Edgar Allan Poe.

[2] American lawyer and writer. Deputy Undersecretary of the U.S. Army 1965–1967.

[3] (b. 1929) Deputy Chief of Mission to the U.S. Embassy in Ottawa 1976–1980; U.S. Ambassador to Suriname 1982–1984.

"who entertains unabashedly liberal attitudes." Then the knife: "Sending an Allan Gotlieb to hold up Canada's side amid U.S. President Ronald Reagan's ranch-hands, the acid-rainers, the gun lobbyists, the budget slashers, the moral mafia, the friendly, altruistic folk from big Yankee oil, seems like sending Bertie Wooster to Dodge City in the heyday of the wild west." Bertie Wooster in Dodge City? We shall see.

December 8, 1981 I presented my credentials today, my first exposure to the Sun King. The experience was so sterile it was memorable. When I was undersecretary, I would attend presentations to the Governor General. The ambassador would bring his family, and there was always a reception after the ceremony in Government House. These were warm, personalized affairs, always one ambassador at a time.

Today I was one of a half-dozen ambassadors presenting their credentials, lumped together with the representatives of Gabon, Upper Volta, Tunisia, Ireland, and St. Vincent and the Grenadines. No doubt this was a mark of our special relationship.

I could bring only my wife. The ceremony was timed to take place at 4:58 p.m., and it did. It lasted precisely seven minutes. We were both whisked in magically as the previous zombie was whisked out. We were then quickly manoeuvred into a photo opportunity with the president. I mumbled a couple of sentences about better relations between Canada and the United States, and the president looked jolly and mumbled a few words in response.

The highlight of the affair was being driven in a stretch protocol car, with huge specimens of Canadian and U.S. flags flying on the hood, escorted by police cars with flashing signals, jumping the red lights and all that. The American way. Sondra loved it.

After the ceremony I gave a reception at the Residence for the embassy staff and Canadian media in Washington. My predecessor considered it Ottawa's job to brief the Canadian media; his task was to concern himself with the U.S. press. He was criticized by the media gang here for being secretive and reclusive. I've decided to try to open things up.

December 10, 1981 My first courtesy call on a cabinet secretary. I met with William French Smith,[1] Reagan's attorney general, who is said to

[1] (1917–1990) U.S. Attorney General 1981–1985.

be close to the president, being his former lawyer in Los Angeles. No serious business to conduct, but he will be a key contact for me. Descended from a president of Harvard, he is an elegant, sophisticated, mild-mannered man, not an ideologist. He has a precise sort of mind, like that of a New England solicitor. Not a firearm in sight. I don't think he's been to Dodge City.

Afterwards I dashed to Dulles airport to catch a flight for Paris to attend a meeting of sherpas preparing for next year's economic summit in Versailles. This is my last climb up the mountain. I'll miss being a member of the group of sherpas, a pack of egos all dropping the names of their illustrious principals: Schmidt,[1] Reagan, Thatcher,[2] and Trudeau.

I told the embassy to book me on the Concorde for my return. There is a direct flight to Dulles. Eyebrows were raised, but I need to get back in time to keep an appointment with the powerful Frank Carlucci,[3] deputy boss at the Pentagon, on a big procurement issue. I'll probably catch hell.

December 15, 1981 More about Bertie Wooster in Dodge City. A feature piece on me appears in *Maclean's* entitled "A Chess Player Moves to the Top," by Linda McQuaig.[4] It's snide and mean from beginning to end. Gotlieb "could well antagonize the rough-hewn anti-intellectuals who now populate Congress and the Reagan Administration." Gee, I haven't met any yet. "What's needed is someone who can stay up all night drinking Scotch with these guys, says one observer, who goes so far as to suggest that Reagan officials may take the Gotlieb appointment as an insult. If the Prime Minister had sent down their kind of person, the gesture in itself would have been appreciated. This way he's sending down an intellectual and essentially saying to the Americans, screw you."

I'll have to get someone in the embassy to find a rough-hewn, Scotch-drinking anti-intellectual in the administration, so I can drink with him all night just to prove the lady wrong.

---

[1] (b. 1918) Chancellor of Germany 1974–1982.

[2] (b. 1924) Prime Minister of the United Kingdom 1979–1990.

[3] (b. 1930) U.S. Ambassador to Portugal 1974–1977; Deputy Secretary of Defense 1981–1986; National Security Advisor 1986–1987; Secretary of Defense 1987.

[4] Canadian journalist, columnist, and non-fiction author. Business reporter at the *Globe and Mail*, then a columnist for the *National Post* before moving to the *Toronto Star*.

December 16, 1981 In a state of irritation, I draft a letter to Peter Newman.[1] A couple of weeks ago, I bumped into the distinguished editor of *Maclean's* on the Sparks Street Mall. He said, "Great article coming out about you, Allan. I read it and you'll be pleased." Did he have in mind McQuaig's quote that Canada has two kinds of public servants: those who work for the greater glory of Canada and those – me – who work for the greater glory of Trudeau?

December 17, 1981 The war continues. I send a stiff note, drafted by Ottawa and the embassy, in reply to Brock's harsh critique of our energy and investment policies. I inform him that I was "surprised and disturbed at the scope and tone of your letter." They zap us; they feel good. We zap them; we feel good. All words. No real discussions. There has to be a better way.

December 21, 1981 Yesterday I made a courtesy visit to the legendary Anatoly Dobrynin,[2] Dean of the Diplomatic Corps, at the magnificent Soviet pile on Sixteenth Street. In the presence of Cold War history, I was in awe. But I learned nothing. Much more instructive was my call today on Sir Nicholas Henderson,[3] the British High Commissioner, in his even more magnificent pile on Massachusetts Avenue. The son of a former warden of All Souls, he belongs to England's inner establishment and is the darling of Georgetown. Unkempt, dishevelled, leaning one way and then another, seeming to almost slip off his chair, he is reputed to be the best British ambassador to Washington in modern history. Our conversation was interrupted by frantic calls from his friend the defecting Polish ambassador. We talked about the complexities of Washington. The players are so numerous and dispersed, he said, you can never explain what actually happened. "If anyone tells you he knows where a particular decision was made in Washington, he is either a fool or a liar."

---

[1] (b. 1929) Canadian author and journalist who emigrated from Nazi-occupied Czechoslovakia to Canada in 1940. Former reporter for the *Financial Post* and editor of the *Toronto Star* and *Maclean's*. In 2005 he published *The Secret Mulroney Tapes: Unguarded Confessions of a Prime Minister*.

[2] (b. 1919) Soviet Ambassador to the United States 1962–1986 who served most notably during the Cuban Missile Crisis.

[3] (b. 1919) Joined the British diplomatic service in 1946. British Ambassador to Spain, Poland, Germany, France, and to the United States 1979–1982.

December 22, 1981 Our first dinner with our children in our new temporary home on Rock Creek Drive. It's a finely constructed, beautiful pre-war house but with a terrible mishmash of furniture (essentially haute Eaton's, reproductions of all ages selected by departmental decorators over the ages), a fading, dog-stained carpet in the main reception room, and a ghastly green boudoir-style carpet in the front hall covering up a huge, campy, inlaid maple leaf set into the marble floor. Sondra and I made our first decorating decision. We're going to dispatch the green carpet back to its second-floor boudoir and show off our marble maple leaf.

December 28, 1981 Access is easier than I anticipated. I've already seen Frank Carlucci, deputy secretary of defense, Chairman of the Federal Reserve Paul Volcker[1] (his very grunt suggests authority), Secretary of Transportation Drew Lewis,[2] Secretary of Commerce Mac Baldridge[3] (old-world courtesy), Secretary of Agriculture John Block,[4] Secretary of the Interior James Watt[5] (odd), Secretary of Energy Jim Edwards[6] (odder), and John Tower[7] of Texas, chairman of the Senate Armed Services Committee (oddest). From State I've seen Bill Clark,[8] deputy secretary of state and a close friend of the president; Larry Eagleburger,[9] in charge of Europe and Canada (thespian, funny); and Tom Enders,[10] the former ambassador to Canada, now running the Latin American empire (brilliant but scary).

[1] (b. 1927) Chairman of the Federal Reserve 1979–1987.

[2] (b. 1931) Secretary of Transportation 1981–1983; Chairman and CEO of Union Pacific 1986–1997.

[3] (1922–1987) Secretary of Commerce 1981–1987, when he died in a tragic rodeo accident.

[4] (b. 1935) Secretary of Agriculture 1981–1986.

[5] (b. 1938) Secretary of the Interior 1981–1983.

[6] (b. 1927) Governor of South Carolina 1975–1979; Secretary of Energy 1981–1982.

[7] (1925–1991) Republican Senator from Texas 1961–1985.

[8] (b. 1931) Member of the Supreme Court of California 1973–1981 (addressed in Washington as "Judge"); Deputy Secretary of State 1981; National Security Advisor 1982–1983; Secretary of the Interior 1983–1985. Close to the president, he became one of the most powerful political players in Washington.

[9] (b. 1930) Member of the U.S. foreign service from 1957. U.S. Ambassador to Yugoslavia 1977–1980; Assistant Secretary of State for European Affairs 1981–1982 (which included responsibility for Canada); Undersecretary of State for Political Affairs 1982; Secretary of State 1992–1993.

[10] (1931–1996) U.S. Ambassador to Canada 1975–1979 and to the EEC 1979–1981; Assistant Secretary of State for Inter-American Affairs 1981–1983; U.S. Ambassador to Spain 1983–1986.

Not a bad start – close to half the cabinet, many of the top players in State, and some of the top economic players.

My biggest shock was meeting with Energy boss Jim Edwards. A former dentist, he likes to say he was appointed to preside over the abolition of his department. He believes in the market – and nothing else. My impression was that until I mentioned it, he had never even heard of the Canada-U.S. Alaska Gas Pipeline project and the U.S. treaty commitments under it. Here, in a single container, is all the evidence one needs to prove that our two countries are ideologically out of sync.

December 29, 1981 I received a courtesy call from the ambassador of Sierra Leone, and I called on the ambassadors of the Ivory Coast and Belgium. Why?

December 31, 1981 New Year's Eve, no invitations. I sat in the library on the big black leather sofa with Marc in front of the fire and watched five Marx brothers movies back to back, starting at dinner and going on until well into the morning. Well cheered by Johnnie Walker Black Label, it was my most enjoyable New Year's Eve in twenty years. It was exactly that long ago that we gorged on caviar and pâté de foie in the apartment of our neighbour on Rue Crespin in Geneva, a Russian American of great intelligence and sophistication. It was only years later that we learned who Michael Josselson[1] really was: the secret agent of the CIA behind the Congress of Cultural Freedom and *Encounter* magazine. And an unsung hero of the Cold War.

January 1, 1982 New Year's Day, back on the black leather sofa, listening to Mozart, the best proof of the existence of God. I stare at my leather-bound books lining the room and my silver art nouveau photograph frames containing family pictures, spread out on the old oak refectory table against the wall. They look like they've been here forever. Thelma with the beautiful smile brings me coffee as I watch the fire. Who said about being a diplomat that it provides the consolations of old age in middle life?

[1] (1908–1978) Cultural-affairs officer for the U.S. War Department's Office of the Military Government in Berlin 1946–1949; public-affairs staff of the High Commission to Germany 1949–1950. Responsible for the "de-Nazification" of top German intellectuals and leaders, as well as the editing and dissemination of anti-communist propaganda.

January 8, 1982 The outgoing Israeli ambassador, Epi Evron,[1] whom I knew when he was ambassador to Canada, said the one man I have to meet here is Robert Strauss.[2] I listened, because when it comes to diplomats, there never was one more wily and cunning than Evron. This was said to be the assessment of Lyndon Johnson, who knew a thing or two about shrewdness. So when Epi offered to arrange lunch with Strauss, I was keen. The three of us dined today at the solemn F Street Club. It serves pretentious food but is a Washington favourite for some reason.

I met Strauss once before. He came to Canada when he was Jimmy Carter's[3] trade representative to discuss multilateral trade negotiations with senior officials. When Epi introduced us, Strauss professed to remember me, but I knew he was faking. In Ottawa I couldn't see why everyone thought Strauss was so special. I began to understand today. It's the mixture, I think, of a lot of different qualities: a world-weary sense of humour, a cunning political mind, a virtuoso anecdotalist, a genius for one-liners, a connoisseur of human folly.

Strauss raised my spirits. He told me not to be misled by all the Trudeau bashing that goes on among the Reaganites. Trudeau has a big profile in the country, maybe bigger than any other foreign leader (except for Margaret Thatcher), and is much respected for his intelligence and integrity.

This evening I had my second meal in the F Street Club – a black-tie dinner given by the patrician Elliot Richardson[4] in honour of Tommy Koh[5] from Singapore, president of the Law of the Sea conference, whom I knew from my UN days. It was a forlorn affair, more a wake than a dinner. To Reagan's crowd, the Law of the Sea convention is a communist accomplishment, and they came to bury it.

---

[1] Israeli Ambassador to Canada and later to the United States 1979–1982.

[2] (b. 1918) Chairman of the Democratic National Committee 1972–1977. He was U.S. Trade Representative under President Carter who successfully concluded the Tokyo Round of Multilateral Trade Negotiations 1977–1979. He served as last U.S. Ambassador to the Soviet Union in 1991 and as U.S. Ambassador to Russia 1991–1993. A founding partner of the law firm Akin Gump Strauss Hauer & Feld LLP.

[3] (b. 1924) President of the United States 1977–1981; Nobel Peace Laureate in 2002.

[4] (1920–1999) Secretary of Health, Education, and Welfare 1970–1973; Secretary of Defense 1973; U.S. Attorney General 1973; U.S. Ambassador to the United Kingdom 1975–1976; Secretary of Commerce 1976–1977.

[5] Singapore's Ambassador and Permanent Representative to the United Nations 1968–1971 and 1974–1984; Ambassador to the United States 1984–1990.

January 9, 1982 Pat Gossage,[1] newly appointed head of public affairs at the embassy, arrived yesterday. The idea that Trudeau has planted his press secretary to watch over me is, of course, ridiculous. So ridiculous that the press believes it's true. Gossage wanted out and I wanted Gossage. That's the whole story.

January 11, 1982 Called on the vice-president in the magnificent, restored Old Executive Building. Unlike Reagan, George Bush[2] knew what country I came from. He was knowledgeable about Canada and uncannily adept at putting one at ease. Then had dinner with an old contact, Tom Enders. I don't recall Tom being such a hardliner when he was U.S. ambassador to Ottawa. I wonder if the hawkishness in Washington is infectious or if, more specifically, it's the Haig influence, or if he is trying to prove himself to the Reaganauts. He outclasses his new political masters intellectually. They will not forgive him for it.

January 13, 1982 We gave a dinner, our first real dinner party, to say farewell to George Elliott, departing head of public affairs. He has lots of friends because he's been the Liberal Party's man in Washington for years. It was literally a disastrous evening. There was a snowstorm, an Air Florida plane crashed in the Potomac, killing all on board, the subway broke down, the storm paralyzed Washington traffic, and a number of guests did not arrive. Some spouses worried about their absent mates, those who came worried about getting home, and the host and hostess just worried the whole evening. A bad omen for us?

January 15, 1982 I received Adele Hurley[3] and Michael Perley,[4] executive coordinators of the Canadian Coalition on Acid Rain. Fancy titles for lobbyists. The difference between these lobbyists and other lobbyists is that

---

[1] Press Secretary to Prime Minister Pierre Trudeau 1976–1982; Minister of Information at the Canadian Embassy in Washington 1982–1986.

[2] (b. 1924) Vice-President of the United States 1981–1989; President of the United States 1989–1993.

[3] Co-founder of the Canadian Coalition on Acid Rain in 1980, which worked on a successful campaign aimed at bringing amendments to the U.S. Clean Air Act, and on regulations to reduce pollutants from large Canadian emitters.

[4] Canadian lobbyist who began his public-interest advocacy work with the Canadian Environmental Law Association in 1978.

these are *our* lobbyists, which means they are virtuous and on the side of God. They provide cover in our manoeuvres to persuade the Congress that acid rain is evil. We need all the help we can get. I don't know if they are effective on the Hill, but reports we receive are positive.

January 16, 1982 Paul Robinson gave me some advice before I left Ottawa: "If you want to get anywhere on acid rain, be nice to Anne Gorsuch"[1] – the EPA's reputedly fearsome boss lady – "Use your charm, lay it on thick. Above all, avoid John Roberts's[2] rhetoric and extremism." I called on her at the agency headquarters, determined to demonstrate my winnable ways. I put on my sweetest manner, speaking softly about our concerns on acid rain, about our long history of working together, and of American leadership in protecting the environment. The meeting was a farce. She was Perry Mason, cross-examining me at the bar. A pugnacious, small-town lawyer who wasn't going to give an inch. And didn't. So much for pillow talk.

January 18, 1982 Called on Cap Weinberger.[3] Very courtly and not at all the ogre that the Canadian media make him out to be. Tomorrow I see Don Regan, which will complete my courtesy calls on the top cabinet officers.

Tonight we hosted our first dinner, black tie, for a visiting Canadian minister – the solicitor general, Bob Kaplan,[4] and we had a crowd of spooks, including FBI boss Bill Webster,[5] the deputy attorney general, and some thirty-odd intelligence types. Sondra and I agreed afterwards that we need a new chef. Ibrahim, our big, beefy, amiable Turkish chef, cooked for the King of Jordan, but he seems better trained to feed an army than the privileged few.

---

[1] (1942–2004) Member of the Colorado House of Representatives 1976–1980; First female Environmental Protection Agency Administrator 1981–1983.

[2] (b. 1933) Liberal Member of Parliament for York-Simcoe 1968–1972 and for St. Paul's 1974–1979 and 1980–1984; Secretary of State for Canada 1976–1979; Minister of the Environment 1980–1983; Minister of Employment and Immigration 1983–1984.

[3] (1917–2006) Secretary of Defense 1981–1987 (second longest-serving defense secretary, after Robert MacNamara).

[4] (b. 1936) Liberal Member of Parliament for Don Valley 1968–1974 and for York Centre 1974–1993; Solicitor General of Canada 1980–1984.

[5] (b. 1924) Director of the FBI 1978–1987; Director of the CIA 1987–1991.

I think I'll suspend judgment as to whether giving dinner parties for visiting ministers is what diplomats should be doing. Probably depends on a combination of factors: the influence of the minister, the importance of the issues, the state of the relationship. Yes, entertaining is a way of making contacts and developing relationships. The question is with who and for what purpose?

January 19, 1982 Another black-tie ministerial dinner, this one for Mark MacGuigan. Up to a few days ago, we thought we would have a disaster on our hands. We were not getting any responses to our invitations, even though MacGuigan's a foreign minister. Part of the difficulty was that it was a non-visit. MacGuigan wasn't making an official or even a working one, just a "private" visit to a private friend who is on my staff.

The earth started to move late last week. Sondra's social secretary, Pat Thomas, was floored to receive acceptances from the two archrivals, Al Haig and Cap Weinberger, within an hour of each other. Do they tap each other's phones? To get these two together at a small dinner is said to be unheard of around this town. Then we got an acceptance from the U.S. ambassador to the United Nations, the formidable Jeane Kirkpatrick.[1] Then acceptances from other officials – and media – poured in.

Highlight of the evening. Sondra to Weinberger when he walked in early: "I'm your hostess. Who are you?" Weinberger replied, "Madame, I'm your guest of honour." Other highlights. Ben Bradlee's[2] astonishment on seeing Weinberger and Haig under the same (our) roof when he arrived with his wife, Sally Quinn.[3] The courtly Weinberger bad-mouthing Haig at one table and the intense, virile Haig bad-mouthing Weinberger at another. Ben Bradlee was immensely pleased, and the *Washington Post* will be even more pleased tomorrow morning when Bradlee relates all.

Sondra looked smashing in a new violet dress with a brilliantly multicoloured sequin collar.

---

[1] (b. 1926) U.S. Ambassador to the United Nations 1981–1985. Started her career as a Democrat but eventually left the party to join the Republicans in 1985.

[2] (b. 1921) Managing Editor of the *Washington Post* 1965–1991; Vice-President of the newspaper 1968 to present.

[3] Author, journalist, and reporter for the *Washington Post.*

January 23, 1982 Columnist Joe Kraft[1] and his wife, Polly,[2] gave a supper at their Georgetown home on P Street. Earlier this month Gaetana and Tom Enders did invite us to a party (in our honour, she said), but to our surprise, the only other guests were the Krafts. This was our first exposure to social Washington. Sondra had met Joe in Ottawa when he covered the economic summit for the *Washington Post*, but my first contact with him was at the Enderses'. He is widely considered to be one of America's most brilliant political columnists. We talked about the Reagans. "What are they all about?" Sondra asked. "Social climbing," he replied. Was he serious? I think so.

It was a high-powered crowd at the Krafts' tonight. Sunday brunches and dinners in Georgetown are where the mighty meet – and clash. The hardliner Judge Clark was there, as was the liberal Ben Bradlee and Sally Quinn. And so was Kay Graham.[3] The idea that weekends are for rest is a preposterous one in Washington. The media swarm these parties like bees. I got into a heated argument with columnist Clayton Fritchey,[4] ancient husband of limo-liberal socialite Polly Fritchey[5] and limo-lib himself. He told me, in a semi-apoplectic state, that Paul Volcker should be shot for causing all those high interest rates. I told him he should be deified. For the rest of the evening, we glared at each other.

January 24, 1982 The department filed replies to question 3571 from the exceedingly nasty Tom Cossitt,[6] MP, no friend of A.E.G. "On December 15, 1981 [Mr. Gotlieb] had to travel by Concorde from London to New York because of an urgent 5 p.m. appointment that day with the Deputy Secretary of Defence. The cost of this standard of travel was $865.00 more

---

[1] (1925–1986) Nationally syndicated columnist for the *Washington Post* and other newspapers and a regular contributor to the *New Yorker*.

[2] American painter who studied at the Corcoran School of Art, Washington, D.C., 1963–1967.

[3] (1917–2003) Head of the Washington Post Company for more than two decades. She was de facto publisher (her husband, Philip Graham, head of the *Washington Post*, died in 1963) of the newspaper from 1963 onward, formally assuming the title in 1979, and chairman of the board from 1973 to 1991.

[4] (1904–2004) Pentagon spokesman 1950–1952; Director of Public Affairs for the United States Mission to the United Nations 1961–1965; wrote a syndicated column for *Newsday* until his retirement in 1984.

[5] Prominent Washington hostess, formerly married to the late Frank Wisner, a high-ranking official of the CIA.

[6] (d. 1982) PC Member of Parliament for Leeds, Ontario, 1979–1982.

than the regular economy fare but Mr. G. as Ambassador to the U.S.A. had authority to travel first class. The additional cost to use the Concorde was only a surcharge of $65.00."

Mr. Cossitt must have been very disappointed with this reply. The issue in my mind is who in the embassy is feeding him the questions.

January 25, 1982 I called on Lane Kirkland,[1] chief union boss in the United States. A rather taciturn man. We talked generalities. Someone I didn't expect to like, I liked him enormously. Southern, civilized, urbane, well-read, a deeply committed, partisan Democrat. And a hardliner. We talked about labour in our two countries. I detected no warmth for our union leaders up north.

January 26, 1982 I attended the State of the Union speech by the president. The whole diplomatic corps was escorted onto the floor of the House of Representatives, where we served as props to a grand American event – sort of like the Fourth of July celebrations or the Rose Bowl. The president walked in and the crowd went wild. Congressmen leaped to their feet hollering partisan sentiments, surging forth, cheering, banging, and shouting, in an outpouring of rah-rah emotion, everyone totally unselfconscious, the whole affair resembling an assembly of adolescents in the presence of the divine Elvis. Reagan's personality filled the room. Seeing is believing.

January 27, 1982 We went to New York on my first official visit, where I gave a luncheon address at the Waldorf to the Pilgrims of the United States, an old upper-crust organization devoted to promoting British-American relations. I wore a sporty tweed suit. The other several hundred, mostly solemn Wall Street types, wore dark suits. I tried to act insouciant, as if I wasn't embarrassed. I was.

I explained that while Canada and the United States are great friends, we have different histories, policies, and maybe destinies. The audience wasn't expecting a defence of FIRA and the NEP, but they got one. Jeremy Kinsman,[2] a skilled writer, worked on the speech with me, and it had plenty of zip.

---

[1] (1922–1999) President of the American Federation of Labor and Congress of Industrial Organizations 1979–1995.

[2] (b. 1942) Minister to the Canadian Embassy in Washington 1981–1985; Canadian Ambassador to Italy 1996–2000 and to the European Union in 2002.

Citing dismal statistics relating to foreign control of our energy and resources, I spoke of the strategic underpinnings of the new energy law. Then I stressed the need for "nation building" in Canada and a strategic approach for achieving it. It was a high-tone rationalization of the Trudeau policies. Received politely, not warmly.

I'm going to be doing a lot of this in the months ahead. I have to do it. But, *in pectore*, I believe the energy program was poorly conceived, poorly put together, poorly rationalized, poorly explained. It was developed in secrecy by a handful of officials – Marshall Cohen, Michael Pitfield, Robert Rabinowitz, and Edmund Clark – without regard to the international impact and in total isolation from the government's foreign-policy advisers (in particular, me). As undersecretary, I was informed of the initiative only the night before it was announced and instructed to develop a plan to sell it in the United States after it was cast in concrete (that is, after it was unsaleable).

Ken Taylor,[1] the hero of Tehran, gave us a dinner party at his Park Avenue residence. It is widely thought that Ken should have been appointed ambassador to Washington. But Trudeau had reservations, believing – wrongly, in my opinion – that Taylor personalized a broad institutional effort to save the hostages. If Ken thought he should have gone to Washington, he certainly doesn't show it. MacGuigan believed Ken's celebrity was worth more in the United States than anywhere else, although Ken could pretty well have had any post he wanted in Europe. Ken declined to go to Los Angeles, where he would have been sensational. So as undersecretary I persuaded my friend Jim Nutt, consul general in New York, to accept a transfer to Los Angeles to make room for Ken in New York, where he was willing to go. Taylor seems happy enough here, but he is so cool he is difficult to read. There is this vacant air about him, this sort of aw-shucks, Li'l Abner quality that makes him very appealing and makes people interested in knowing what is going on beneath the surface. One mustn't be deceived. He is very shrewd.

January 28, 1982 Today at a lunch at the American Association of Exporters and Importers in New York, I attacked the notion of "reciprocity" in trade, which has become popular in Congress and forms part of various bills on telecommunications. I was nervous, because I was criticizing the

[1] (b. 1934) Appointed Canadian Ambassador to Iran in 1977; Canadian Consul General in New York 1980–1984.

U.S. Congress on U.S. territory. I think this was the first time anyone has publicly criticized the reciprocity concept and exposed its fallacies.

Back in Washington, we attended a ball-breaker black-tie dinner at the Luxembourg embassy, in honour of Charles Percy.[1] The host and hostess performed duets until 9:30 p.m., he playing the piano, she singing lieder, neither of them very well. A scene out of *Duck Soup*. Dinner wasn't served until the concert ended, and then we got speeches and listened to the stentorian tones of Senator Foghorn Percy.

January 29, 1982 Called on the youthful, handsome Max Baucus,[2] Democratic senator from Montana. He doesn't seem to like Canadians too much, no doubt because he's from a border state. Our cattle versus their cattle. Our hogs versus their hogs. Our wheat versus their wheat. Gotlieb's new theorem: the closer a U.S. politician's constituency is to Canada, the less favourably disposed he is towards us.

January 30, 1982 In Palm Beach for the Red Cross Ambassadors' Ball. Organized by our escort, the Baroness Stackelberg[3] (whoever she is), it's the one activity that my cautious and conservative predecessor, Peter Towe, recommended without reservation. Well, nobody's perfect.

The escapade was full of hazards. We almost missed the private charter transporting our small band of adventurous ambassadors because I forgot my white-tie outfit, and Jacques Helie had to defy the laws of the District of Columbia to race back to the embassy and bring it to me just as the plane was about to take off without us. We found ourselves staying with a pleasant, elderly couple in an unreal house, one of the dozen or two that "face both ways" – the ocean and Lake Wirth. The house is all white and marble from beginning to end. M. Palladio is everywhere present in his most degenerate form.

At breakfast we announce that we want to go for a beach walk. Our host and hostess look uncomfortable and try to convince us to walk on the road, despite the heavy traffic. "We'll go on the beach, don't worry," we reply.

---

[1] (b. 1919) Chairman of the Bell & Howell Corporation 1949–1964; Republican Senator from Illinois 1967–1985.

[2] (b. 1941) Democratic Senator from Montana 1978 to present.

[3] (1910–2005) Washington socialite and long-time Washington correspondent for the *Palm Beach Daily News*. Married Baron Constantine Stackelberg of Estonia.

We come back an hour later with our feet covered with tar. Locking ourselves into the great marble bathroom off our bedroom, surrounded by furry white rugs with three-inch piles, we try to get the damn tar off. I'm covered with sweat and I'm panicking. There is tar everywhere. On the sink, the bath, the marble. I manage to get Sondra reasonably clean, and she goes out of the bathroom and asks for turpentine. It is our host's turn to panic. It takes me another forty-five minutes to get every last speck off the floor and fixtures. I'm exhausted and a half-hour late for lunch at the Bath and Tennis Club, a precinct whose portal Jews do not normally cross.

Tonight we were presented at the "White Tie, Decorations, and Tiaras" Red Cross Ambassadors' Ball, attended by many ridiculous people, including ourselves. Another lunch tomorrow and then a concluding dinner hosted by the large Mrs. Sue Whitmore,[1] Listerine heir, whose prerogative every year is to be chairman of the ball.

As we leave Palm Beach, Sondra quotes Goethe: "Once a philosopher, twice a pervert."

January 31, 1982 Peter Newman writes to say he is "very upset" by my letter to him about Linda McQuaig's hatchet activity and fully understands my feelings. "Unfortunately, the story went through in my absence, though I must claim responsibility for it." This from the man who told me he read it in advance of publication and that I would be very pleased.

February 3, 1982 I was invited to lunch to brief the mighty *Washington Post* editorial board. There were about a dozen senior editors in attendance, who were all very solemn. In what was said to be a signal honour, the lunch was hosted by Katharine Graham herself, the heroine of Watergate, high priestess of Washington's political world. She led the questioning in a very heavy-handed manner and opened with zingers about Canada's cultural policies as they affected broadcasting and foreign publications such as *Time*, *Reader's Digest*, the *TV Guide*. She cited an article in Walter Annenberg's[2] *TV Guide* condemning Canada for being unfair and discriminatory.

---

[1] (1914–1993) Socialite and philanthropist, and great-granddaughter of Dr. Joseph Lawrence, inventor of Listerine.

[2] Publisher, philanthropist, art collector, and a close friend of Ronald Reagan. President of Triangle Publications 1940–1969; U.S. Ambassador to the United Kingdom 1969–1974; His wife, Leonore (Lee) Annenberg, was Reagan's Chief of Protocol 1981–1982.

The atmosphere was tense. The poor little Canadian ambassador did not expect the assault, but he figured he might as well give as good as he got. The United States was itself not exactly lily-white, he said, in its own investment and trade policies. There were restrictive, nationalistic clauses in the U.S. Communications Act of 1934, the Civil Aviation Act, the Jones Shipping Act, and many more. The counterattack surprised them. The ice broke. Mrs. Graham softened and the atmosphere got lighter and even gay at the end.

It's a revelation to see how unpopular Trudeau's investment policies are even in the inner sanctum of liberal circles.

February 4, 1982 Sondra was interviewed by Stephanie Mansfield of the Style section of the *Washington Post*. I'm extremely nervous about how the *Post* will treat her. I seem to be having a lot of revelations in this town, but none greater than the importance people attach to the Style section of the *Post*. Everyone reads it and talks about the scandals du jour. I find it inexplicable. One would think it very parochial if Washington weren't the political centre of the world.

February 5, 1982 In Ottawa to attend the second meeting of the Group of Foreign Policy Advisers, a body I created when I was undersecretary. The new undersecretary endorses the group as a "permanent institution," which means it could last a few months. Yesterday we spent the day talking about disarmament.

Trudeau joined us for lunch on the ninth floor of the Pearson Building. He was gripped by the discussion and stayed till after 3:00. I was surprised at how worked up he was over the recent criticisms of his stand on Poland. Listening to him justifying himself in a long and rambling discourse, I thought of how uncharacteristically he was behaving. He was being emotional. What he said boiled down to a few old-fashioned thoughts about spheres of influence, his respect for the Monroe Doctrine, and about why the United States should respect the Soviet sphere of interest. Were the Americans, he asked, trying to rewrite Yalta? It was all rather vintage Trudeau *realpolitik*, except that when he talked about the Soviet sphere of influence, he threw in Afghanistan!

I spoke about what I called "the new orthodoxy" in Reagan's Washington: the superiority of the Western capitalist system and the conviction that the communist empire will decline because it is deeply inefficient. History is therefore on the side of the West. We should help history by denying the

Russians our investment and technology. The Soviets can afford an arms race a lot less than we in the West, so we should have one. Our technological superiority will give us ascendancy, and the costs will hurt a stagnant and immobile society. And above all – no deals. You can't trust the Soviets.

The group seemed shocked by this account. I was surprised at how poorly they grasped the changed attitude in Washington. Did I have to tell them that Jimmy Carter was no longer president?

February 8, 1982 Ken Taylor informed me in New York the other day that during his upcoming two-day stint in Washington celebrating the Hockey Legends All-Stars, he would be attending a lunch at the White House. Rather casually, I mentioned this to Pat Thomas, our social secretary. In a fury, she called up Nancy Reagan's social secretary, and an hour before the lunch began, I received a hand-delivered invitation from the president and an apology from Mabel (Muffie) Brandon.[1]

I found myself seated next to the president. Aside from a couple of hockey officials, the others at our small round table were Bob Hope (I felt like asking him for his autograph), Wayne Gretzky (ditto), Gordie Howe, Phil Esposito, and Speaker Tip O'Neill.[2] How absurd for me to be among the hockey greats.

During most of the lunch, the president and I exchanged jokes, mainly about the Russians. His outnumbered mine four to one. The only serious moment was when he said, apropos of sports, that at heart he thought Russians and Americans wanted the same thing: a good life, family, and home.

The president told me that when he was in hospital recuperating from the attempt on his life, he wrote in his own hand to Brezhnev, making this very point and appealing for peace. He got a curt, bureaucratic, typed reply. Still, he thought he would like to talk to Brezhnev face to face. Maybe this could produce some sort of understanding. He seemed very sincere. Then he got up to speak. More jokes.

Gretzky never said boo during lunch. I pointed him out loudly to the president, saying what a super-superstar he was, the greatest man in hockey history. Gretzky blushed. Reagan made no comment.

---

[1] White House Social Secretary 1981–1982. Wife of Washington correspondent of the *Sunday Times* (of London) Henry Brandon.

[2] (1912–1994) Democratic Representative from Massachusetts 1952–1987; House Majority Leader 1972–1977; Speaker of the House of Representatives 1977–1987.

The *Wall Street Journal* carries a page 1 story on reciprocity in trade citing my speech. I hit pay dirt in New York.

February 9, 1982 *Toronto Sun* headline: "Snafu Averted in Nick of Time." Thanks to my last-minute invitation to Ronald Reagan's lunch, "an embarrassing international incident was averted yesterday." International incident? Where? In Alice in Wonderland?

I called on Tip O'Neill. I was escorted into one of the grand chambers of the Capitol building and waited with more than a dozen and a half other individuals standing around in small groups chatting self-consciously. After a while, the large and portly Speaker walks in and starts shaking hands and receiving members of the groups. He works the room, and when he comes to me, he pumps my hand. I tell him who I am (on the correct assumption that he would not remember me from yesterday). He smiles, graciously tells me what a great country I represent, and moves on. The interview lasted thirty seconds. This was one of the more ludicrous encounters in my diplomatic career. Some congressmen behave as if they are great satraps whose role it is to receive petitions from supplicants – and sometimes gifts as well.

February 10, 1982 The Style section of the *Washington Post* carries a banner article about Sondra that no amount of money could buy. There are 103 column inches of newspaper space about her personality, her wit, her recent book, and a huge, wonderfully sympathetic half-length photo of a smiling Sondra. Stephanie Mansfield describes her as "deliciously offbeat." This follows Sondra's interview last week on the *Today* show. She is awash in publicity.

February 11, 1982 Dinner at the White House for half of the diplomatic corps. Sondra had an encounter with a reporter from San Diego who covers the Washington social scene. During an interview with her yesterday at our Residence, Sondra was asked what she would do to create a sensation with her dinner parties and rival the divine Swedish countess Ulla Wachtmeister (who made a miniature tennis court out of glass as a centrepiece for her table). She laughed and said maybe she'd have to use a bashed-in baby seal. When the reporter began to write it down, Sondra said, "Don't, I'm just joking, of course. If you report it, that will send the seal lobby after us – they'll picket the embassy and the house." The reporter agreed not to, and then we heard through the grapevine today that she would. When the San Diego reporter came up to Sondra at the White House during cocktails before dinner, Sondra accused her of betraying her. The woman fled. We went home crossing our fingers that tomorrow we won't be picketed.

February 12, 1982 We look at the papers nervously. Nothing about bashing in baby seals. Great relief. But Pat Thomas tells us the lady from San Diego is very angry about the encounter in the White House.

February 13, 1982 The *Washington Post* feature on Sondra is being reprinted in articles across the country. The Southam chain in Canada writes, "It was Canada's biggest splash here since the so-called Canadian caper, when Washington practically went bonkers toasting the Canadian diplomats in Iran who helped free six trapped Americans out from under the Ayatollah Khomeini's nose."

February 14, 1982 The pace of our social activities is stepping up with remarkable velocity. We were invited to two A-list Sunday brunches, one in honour of Sandra Day O'Connor.[1] We went to both. We see "le tout Washington." Sondra is a celebrity. I am her companion. In the words of José Ortega y Gasset:[2] "What is happening to us is that we don't know what is happening to us, and that is exactly what is happening to us."

February 15, 1982 Nicko Henderson, alas, now departing from Washington, asked us to lunch with Isaiah Berlin,[3] along with Joe Alsop,[4] Kathleen Darman, Larry Eagleburger, and a couple of others. Lunch in the cavernous Lutyens mansion was pure high table, with Berlin in remarkable

---

[1] (b. 1930) First female Associate Justice of the Supreme Court of the United States 1981–2006.

[2] (1883–1956) Spanish philosopher and essayist. Well known for his 1929 publication *The Revolt of the Masses.*

[3] (1909–1997) President of Wolfson College 1966–1975; President of the British Academy 1974–1978; Fellow of All Souls College, Oxford. Described by Sir Nicholas Henderson as the "most renowned Oxford figure since Benjamin Jowett, rivalled only by Maurice Bowra as the greatest wit in living memory."

[4] Newspaper columnist with his brother Stewart 1945–1958 and alone 1958–1974. Author, art historian, and social arbiter of Georgetown.

form. Most of lunch we played a game suggested by Berlin: name a warm Englishman. There was agreement on only one person – my suggestion – Maurice Bowra.[1]

After coffee in the garden, I asked Berlin if he would inscribe his recently published book *Washington Dispatches*, which I praised effusively. He said he didn't much like the book.

February 17, 1982 The rounds of courtesy calls on other ambassadors continue. It seems to be the custom in this capital to perform the ritual as couples, so we added the Germans today, having recently knocked off the Egyptians and the Swedes, both of whom have been here for close to a decade. The Swedish ambassador, Count Willie Wachtmeister,[2] is one of those worldly Europeans who makes one feel uncivilized. Plays tennis with George Bush on the embassy's well-maintained courts. Knows Ted Kennedy[3] well. An ambassador for all seasons, a role model for us all.

February 19, 1982 My rounds on the Hill continue, and while I am received with courtesy and sometimes courtliness, I am struck by how widely it is acknowledged that our relations are strained. There is the attitude that Canada is not playing fair, that we are putting one over on Uncle Sam, trying to take advantage of our friends. In essence, the criticism is that we are not being friendly. This is a result of our actions directed against the U.S. communications industry, the U.S. oil industry, and U.S. investment generally. The attitude is: attack my corporation, attack my flag.

The media are doing a lot to contribute to this perception of confrontation. Some headlines of recent vintage: "The Chill from Dear Canada" (*New York Times*); "Canadian Brass" (*Wall Street Journal*), describing Trudeau's attempts to "hijack the Canadian investments of American oil companies"; "Friction with Canada" (*U.S. News & World Report*). When I said that U.S. retaliation against Canada would hurt the United States and not just us, the *Wall Street Journal* rejoined: "Perhaps the Ambassador should instead warn

---

[1] (1898–1971) Warden of Wadham College, Oxford, 1938–1971; Professor of Poetry 1946–1951; Vice-Chancellor 1951–1954.

[2] Swedish career diplomat who served as the Swedish Ambassador to the United States 1974–1989, latterly Dean of the Corps.

[3] (b. 1932) Brother of assassinated president John F. Kennedy and former U.S. attorney general and senator Robert F. Kennedy. Democratic Senator from Massachusetts 1962 to present.

his Premier [*sic*] that the days when American administrations acquiesced in assaults on American interests ended last November."

People here don't know what to make of this new situation, even less than we do in Canada. The incumbent of the Mackenzie King Chair at Harvard suggests that because Congress is now linking issues and threatening retaliation, we'll have to counterlink ourselves. This means we'll have to make trade-offs within Canada between regions and issues. Can you imagine? "You fix your acid rain, we'll fix our pollution of Glacier National Park." If we do this, we'll be in very deep waters. Link for link, the Americans can outlink us any day. In a modern democracy driven by organized purveyors of collective preferences, it is impossible to sacrifice the interests of one for the gain of another.

February 26, 1982 I called on Jennings Randolph[1] of West Virginia to lobby him about acid rain. He is a stout eighty-year-old senatorial workhorse from a coal-polluting state. The ego walls were completely covered with bronze testimonial plaques. There wasn't an inch to spare.

"Senator," I say, "I've come to pay a courtesy call and tell you about a problem." "Ambassador," he says with great courtesy, "please sit there a moment," pointing to a chair in front of his desk. The senator then gets on the phone for twenty minutes to some crony in West Virginia. Then, "Ambassador," he says, again with great courtesy, "I've got a problem. My friend loves Canada. He has a cottage on a lake somewhere up there in Quebec, I think. I don't know where exactly, but – you won't believe this – someone stole it. Stole it from under him, stole everything – the whole building, the wood, the windows, the doorknobs, everything." He's very upset. "Can you help?" he asks very gently. I reply, "That is an unbelievable story, Senator. I'd be glad to look into it, sir, glad to look into it."

"Ambassador, I've got another problem. My poor wife died just last year. I want to name a lake after her, the one in Canada where we honeymooned – she loved Canada. I can't remember where the lake is – in Quebec, I think – but I carved her name on a tree and want to name the lake after her. Can you help?" I reply, "Senator, that's very touching. I'll try. I'll do my best, but it could be a matter of provincial jurisdiction." (Quick thinking on my part.)

Then me, moving quickly to gain advantage: "Senator, those lakes up there, where your friend's cottage was stolen and that your good wife loved,

[1] (1902–1998) Democratic Senator from West Virginia 1958–1985.

they're dying – acid rain is killing them. Can you help?" "George," (pathetic assistant) "give the ambassador a rundown on the cleanup in West Virginia." Senator reads newspaper during five-minute rundown by George. Me: "Well, Senator, thanks a lot. I've got to be going. It's been a privilege, but I've taken up too much of your time."

"Nonsense, Ambassador, sit right here." Picks up phone again, and then to secretary, "Get my friend in West Virginia, the state senator, the one who used to have the cottage up in Canada. Ambassador, sit right here, sit right beside me." (Points to chair beside him behind his desk.) I move beside him. Five minutes later the phone connects. "Is that you, Sam? Do you know who I have here in my office, sitting right in front of me? You won't believe this. It's the Canadian ambassador. He is very anxious to talk to you about your cottage." Then me on the phone. Then long description of the situation by him that makes no sense. He doesn't own the land on which the cottage sits. Doesn't know who does. Built the house anyway. Then friend double-crossed him and sold the house or stole it or something. "Yes, sir," I tell him, "that's a shocking story. I'll be pleased to look into it. I'll get in touch with the Quebec authorities. Do my best. Write me the details."

I back out of the office, almost tripping over two large bronze testimonial plaques on the floor. "Thanks, Senator. No, I won't forget about your wife and the lake." And I'm out. A harrowing encounter in the service of my country.

February 27, 1982 Black-tie dinner last night at the Residence in honour of Attorney General William French Smith and his wife, Jean. Sondra's idea – she proposed it to Jean, with whom she has become friendly. Jean then got her husband to agree. I wouldn't have had the nerve to ask French Smith directly.

We discovered our first rule of Washington entertainment: it takes an American to catch an American. The cast was star-studded: Sandra Day O'Connor, Elliot and Anne Richardson, Richard and Kathleen Darman,[1] Charles and Mary Jane Wick,[2] Eugene Rostow,[3] Bill and Helene

---

[1] (b. 1943) Richard Darman was Assistant to the President of the United States 1981–1985; Deputy Secretary of the Treasury 1985–1987; Director of the Office of Management and Budget 1989–1993.

[2] (b. 1917) Charles Wick was Director of the U.S. Information Agency 1981–1988.

[3] (1913–2002) Dean of Yale Law 1955–1965; Undersecretary of State for Political Affairs 1966–1969; Director of the Arms Control and Disarmament Agency 1981–1983.

Safire,[1] Joe and Polly Kraft, Susan Mary Alsop,[2] Senator Larry Pressler,[3] Tom and Gaetana Enders, and many others. *People* magazine taking photographs. Everyone very animated. Some of the Reaganites didn't know the big-feet media. We introduced them.

March 2, 1982 We went to a dinner given by Laughlin Phillips,[4] director of the Phillips Collection, and his socialist-leaning, wonderfully wicked wife, Jennifer, at their large pseudo-Arts-and-Crafts-decorated house on O Street in Georgetown. In the Alice Roosevelt Longworth[5] tradition, she is one of the more interesting hostesses in Washington because she is willing – more than willing – to be indiscreet. We were told by our social secretary that the dinner was in honour of the Venezuelan ambassador to Washington. We accepted not just because our hosts are well-known Georgetown thoroughbreds but in order to see a few masterpieces on the wall.

Speaking no Spanish, we geared ourselves for a boring dip dinner with a pack of Venezuelans. Surprise – no Venezuelans there, no Spanish spoken. At first we couldn't figure it out. Then we realized we'd gotten things reversed. The event was for Bill Luers,[6] U.S. ambassador to Venezuela, and his very socialite (not socialist) wife, Wendy. The Georgetown set was out in force. Sondra said – to the amusement of all – she was surprised by Bill Luers's excellent English.

March 4, 1982 Eat, receive, visit, call, show up, eat, speak, receive, eat, drink, speak, call. A typical day in this profession.

---

[1] (b. 1929) Bill Safire was an author, columnist, journalist, and presidential speech writer for Richard Nixon. Long-time syndicated political columnist for the *New York Times* and a regular contributor to "On Language" in the *New York Times Magazine.*

[2] (1918–2004) Washington hostess, wife of journalist Joe Alsop, and author of several books, including *To Marietta from Paris: 1945–1960* (1975), one of the best portrayals of Paris during that period.

[3] (b. 1942) Republican Representative from South Dakota 1975–1979; Senator from South Dakota 1979–1997.

[4] Director of the Phillips Collection in Washington. Son of Duncan Phillips.

[5] (1884–1980) Only child of President Theodore Roosevelt and his first wife, Alice Hathaway Lee. Married Nicholas Longworth, representative from Cincinnati, Ohio, who became Speaker of the House.

[6] (b. 1929) U.S. Ambassador to Venezuela 1978–1982 and to Czechoslovakia 1983–1986; President of the Metropolitan Museum of Art in New York 1986–1999.

Breakfast at the Residence with the executives of Rogers cablevision, including Mr. Cable himself, the lean but not hungry-looking Ted Rogers[1] and his number two, the very smart Phil Lind. They are worried about pressures in Washington and in state capitals for "mirror legislation." They are concerned that the Americans could do unto us what we have done unto them: prohibit the foreign ownership of TV cable systems. What chutzpah on the part of the Americans. As one of the largest U.S. cable operators, Rogers now seems to understand they are a target. They have a lot to be worried about.

March 5, 1982 Weekend in New York. Had lunch at the Côte Basque with Dan Rather.[2] For a man who earns $1.6 million a year, he doesn't argue too much about who picks up the tab (I did). We were in agreement about Canada-U.S. relations. He views the U.S. response to our policies as an overreaction. Or so he says. Will he repeat these views on television? Of course not. I tried to stimulate his interest in doing more Canadian stories. His eyes glazed over.

After lunch I called on another *gros légume* of the media, Seymour Topping[3] of the *New York Times*. I had the same mission in mind, but with a greater sense of optimism, because Topping's father-in-law is the radical, very eccentric, very aged, very distinguished Canadian diplomat and carrier of secret messages to Hanoi, Chester Ronning.[4] Alas, I found Topping to be a man without strong Canadian convictions and uninterested in our agenda.

March 8, 1982 Visited Bill Davis and his minister of environment at Queen's Park. My message: Don't lobby independently in Washington on acid rain or any other front. Keep your visiting officials on a tight leash. The Americans will triangulate for sure, and Canada will be the loser.

I briefed a group of top Canadian businessmen at dinner at the

---

[1] (b. 1933) President and CEO of Rogers Communications Inc. 1986–1999.

[2] (b. 1931) Journalist and broadcaster. Anchor of *CBS Evening News* 1981–2005.

[3] (b. 1921) Joined the *New York Times* in 1959. Editorial Director of the New York Times Company's thirty-two regional newspapers 1987–1993. Administrator of the Pulitzer Prizes and Professor of International Reporting at Columbia University's Graduate School of Journalism 1993–2002.

[4] (1894–1984) Member of the United Farmers of Alberta who served in diplomatic posts in China, India, Norway, and the United Nations, including as Canadian High Commissioner to India.

Rendezvous restaurant, arranged by Jim Coutts.[1] I gave them my "new orthodoxy" message on U.S. foreign policy. The guests, including an intelligent banker, Ced Ritchie,[2] moaned about Reagan, Reaganomics, and the hard line. When they look south, Canadians turn blind.

March 10, 1982 I took care of a different kind of duty last night. I was invited, along with five other ambassadors, to be a judge at the Sixth Annual Congressional Chili Cooking Contest. The chefs were ten congressmen who had never cooked the stuff before. A brilliant colleague in the embassy shoved a mimeographed sheet of paper into my hand just as I was getting into my car to attend the event. It contained a half-dozen rules for judging chili – chunks of beef, not crumbling particles; no foreign objects (beans, tomatoes, etc.); good reddish colour; no fat on top; garlic taste. So I left an ignoramus and arrived an expert.

Not one of the dishes met any of the criteria. The chili was absolutely awful. I have always hated chili, and as a bonus, I had heartburn even before I arrived. The other ambassadors were entirely clueless. My instant expertise made me the leader. I was treated with great respect and authority. I helped the hapless lot select the winners. I wore a raccoon hat.

March 13, 1982 Jack McClelland,[3] the Great Canadian Publisher, arrives in town to discuss a book he is proposing Sondra write: *The Canadian Female Establishment*. Sondra's agent arrives from New York. Ten minutes before our proposed rendezvous at the Residence, Jack calls from the Madison. "I'm sick," he says. "I'm heaving, I'm feverish, I can't come." We sit around stupidly and wonder what to do. An hour later Jack calls and says he is coming. Four hours later we are all very drunk and incoherent. I never in my life saw a man smoke more in one evening.

March 14, 1982 I flew to New York on this Sunday afternoon to join MacGuigan at a meeting with Al Haig, on the margins of a foreign-ministers' meeting on the Caribbean Basin Initiative. Haig was in a benevolent,

---

[1] Appointments Secretary to Prime Minister Lester Pearson 1963–1966; Principal Secretary to Prime Minister Pierre Trudeau 1970–1976.

[2] Chairman and CEO of the Bank of Nova Scotia 1974–1995; Chairman of the Business Development Bank of Canada 2001 to present.

[3] (1922–2004) President of McClelland & Stewart 1961–1985.

pro-Canadian mood. He was appreciative of the support he has been getting from Trudeau and MacGuigan on El Salvador. When either MacGuigan or I would raise a point about a problem in our relationship, he'd turn to an official in his entourage and bark, "Good God – I can't believe it. Get me an answer by Thursday." Or, "I've got the same problems with those people." Haig is forceful in a group like this and appears decisive and professional.

March 15, 1982 Lunch today at the Cosmos Club as a guest of Joe Sisco,[1] former Kissinger[2] aide, world-class troubleshooter, indispensable former State Department ace. I accepted his invitation because I admired him in his glory years. Under persistent questioning, he extracted from me every bit of knowledge I had about the current political situation in Canada. In return, I extracted from him that he was preparing to brief some client about Canada. The lunch was very long. I expect he is paid by the hour.

In the evening we gave a black-tie dinner for Donald Sutherland,[3] whose *Don't Look Now* is being shown at the American Film Institute. Three hundred guests: three cabinet secretaries, one senator (Nancy Kassebaum),[4] one undersecretary of state, Kay Graham, Scotty Reston,[5] Joe Kraft, Hans Blix[6] (old friend and now director general of the IAEA), and a slew of Hollywood folks – Goldie Hawn,[7] Norman Jewison,[8] Rosie Shuster,[9] and

---

[1] (1919–2004) Assistant Secretary of State for International Organization Affairs 1965; Chief U.S. Mediator in the Middle East in 1968; Assistant Secretary of State for Near Eastern and South Asian Affairs 1969–1974; Undersecretary of State for Political Affairs 1974–1976; President of American University 1976–1980.

[2] (b. 1923) National Security Advisor 1969–1974; Secretary of State 1973–1977; Nobel Peace Laureate in 1973.

[3] (b. 1935) Canadian actor with a film career spanning over forty years.

[4] (b. 1932) Republican Senator from Kansas 1978–1997.

[5] (1909–1995) American journalist. Associate Editor of the *New York Times* 1964–1968, Executive Editor 1968–1969, and Vice-President 1969–1974. He wrote a nationally syndicated column from 1974 until 1987, when he became a senior columnist.

[6] Swedish Minister of Foreign Affairs 1978–1979; head of the International Atomic Energy Agency 1981–1997 and of the UN Monitoring, Verification, and Inspection Commission 2000–2003.

[7] (b. 1945) American film actress.

[8] (b. 1926) Canadian film director, producer, and actor. In 1988 he founded the Canadian Film Centre. Nominated for the Best Director Academy Award on a number of occasions.

[9] Canadian-born writer, producer, and actress who worked on the NBC television series *Saturday Night Live*. Daughter of comedian/writer Frank Shuster.

others. An unusual cocktail of Reaganites, Hollywood types, socialites, oddballs. Ms. Hawn arrived with a French boyfriend wearing black tie and running shoes. He was apologetic. She and the boyfriend insisted on sitting next to each other at dinner.

After most of the guests left, we sat around in a small group in the library. Sutherland became very talkative. He denounced cocaine as a horrid evil, turning people yellow, twisting their faces into pulp. All his friends were going around with plastic nostrils, he said. Later, when everyone had gone, he turned to Sondra and said, "You know, I bet they all take cocaine." At that point, I got up and said, bravely, "Let's knock it off. It's late." And we all went to bed.

March 16, 1982 Introduced myself today to two powerful players at opposite poles of the ideological spectrum, Bill Casey,[1] whom I called on at Langley, and Ted Kennedy, idol of my staff. On greeting me, Kennedy stuck out his hand and said in a rather perfunctory manner, "Nice to see you again, Mr. Ambassador." I had never met him before.

In the evening, another crowd at the Residence, this time for Arthur Erickson.[2] I had sent a message to Erickson that I wanted to see him privately. At our meeting today, he seemed ill at ease, expecting, perhaps, that he was going to experience the External *froideur*. Instead, I told him I was thrilled with his appointment (I avoided any reference to the method of his appointment) and assured him that he would have my enthusiastic support. I said I believed his building near the Mall would be the most important image Canada would carry in the capital for the next hundred years and that he could count on me to fight the bureaucracy, if necessary (and it probably would be) to get the building up. He seemed both pleased and astonished.

I asked Arthur about my project to preserve the chancery at Dupont Circle. He agreed that it would be unthinkable to dispose, in a commercial way, of Canada's first embassy anywhere – the home of Vincent Massey,[3]

---

[1] (1913–1987) Lawyer and close confidant of President Ronald Reagan. Director of the CIA 1981–1985.

[2] (b. 1924) Internationally celebrated Canadian architect, known for his Museum of Anthropology, B.C. Courthouse, and Simon Fraser University in Vancouver, among other buildings.

[3] (1887–1967) Canadian Minister Plenipotentiary to the United States 1927–1930; first Canadian-born Governor General of Canada 1952–1959.

Leighton McCarthy,[1] Loring Christie,[2] Lester Pearson, Hume Wrong,[3] and a historic architectural site inside and out.

March 19, 1982 The Governor General, Ed Schreyer,[4] and his party – wife, Lily; sons Jason and Tobin; companion, Nancy; Martha Ryan and a Miss Wilmot, ladies-in-waiting – arrived in Washington on a "private" visit. Their Excellencies are staying with us at the Residence. We met them and the entourage at Andrews Air Force Base. They are accompanied by the chief of protocol, an aide-de-camp, the deputy secretary of the Governor General, an RCMP inspector, the chief of staff of Government House, and his spouse. We went from Andrews to the house in a five-car procession. The tiny band is making its way (slowly) to Palm Beach to attend a Canadian cultural event. How big would the group be if this were an official visit? Of course, the Americans would never agree to such a thing.

Amidst great effort, we got Lily, the nanny (Lily's socialist, jogging friend), and Georgina Butler to tour the White House at 8:45 this morning. I took the Governor General and Lily, Jason, and Tobin on a mini museum tour. We knocked off five institutions in the tour before their Excellencies' caravan moved off to Florida. The Governor General was uncommunicative during the tour.

After entertaining about 150 Canadians at the Residence in their Excellencies' honour, we had a small dinner for them, *en famille*, with Jeremy Kinsman and a few other officers from the embassy. We toasted Tobin on his seventh birthday. We did not invite Americans, figuring the draw would be modest.

A last-minute attempt to get the Bushes or the Mondales to join us for lunch tomorrow failed utterly. The problem is that Ed has no power and no suitable title. Here, Governor General may as well be a term for senior prison guard. If Ed had a real title, like "the Marquis of Schreyer," snobby, anglophile Washington might have taken note.

---

[1] (1869–1952) Independent Member of Parliament for Simcoe North 1898–1911; Envoy Extraordinary and Minister Plenipotentiary to the United States 1941–1943; Canadian Ambassador to the United States 1943–1944.

[2] (1885–1941) Minister Plenipotentiary to the United States 1939–1941.

[3] (1894–1954) Joined the Department of External Affairs in 1927. Canadian Ambassador to the United States 1946–1953.

[4] (b. 1935) Premier of Manitoba 1969–1977; Governor General of Canada 1979–1984.

Just before departure, His Excellency handed me a pair of large silver cufflinks carrying, in the form of a medallion, a double profile portrait of himself and Lily posing like Roman proconsuls, cast by the Royal Canadian Mint. He added that he had a smaller gold pair he meant to give me, but he left them in a valise that was, alas, sent on ahead. I'll dream about them.

March 22, 1982 I have been brooding all day about a surprise package from External Affairs. Tom Cossitt, the Tory MP, has returned to the charge with more Parliamentary Questions. Did Michael Pitfield write to me as undersecretary on May 18, 1981, authorizing first-class travel for heads of post in Washington, Paris, and London? What date was my name "unofficially" submitted to Washington for approval, and when was I first aware I was being considered for this post? Did I ever discuss first-class air travel with Pitfield, and if so, when, and was it before or after I was aware of my posting?

He forgot to ask, "What time did you go to the bathroom on the morning of May 18?"

"If you sit by the window long enough and watch the river, you'll see the body of your enemy float by." Chinese proverb. I'll be sitting by the window and watching.

March 24, 1982 In Palm Beach again. The National Ballet of Canada is performing a "Tribute to Canada." Ed and Lily here – their destination after Washington. Will he dig out the gold cufflinks from his luggage, to which he has presumably been rejoined?

Party yesterday in their honour at the home of one Leonard Davis, whom I have not heard of but is said to be phenomenally rich and "close to" Senator Jackson. (Sondra calls all these allegedly closely connected people one meets in Washington and elsewhere "close-tos.") Tonight it was another reception for Ed and Lily at the home of a Montreal mogul, Robert Cummings, who, like Leonard Davis, is Jewish in spite of the name. Davis built a large wing off his palace for Jackson, to serve as the Palm Beach White House in case Jackson became president. He didn't show it to us.

Many prominent members of the Canadian Jewish community were present, but I knew very few. Charles Bronfman,[1] very polite, asked me, "How does it feel to be a line manager in External Affairs?"

---

[1] (b. 1931) Canadian industrialist and philanthropist; majority owner of the Montreal Expos franchise from the team's formation in 1968 until 1990.

In a short time we've tasted all three Palm Beaches: the blue-blooded Red Cross Ambassadors' Ball, with the Sue Whitmores and WASP remittance crowd, the Palm Beach that is Judenrein; the wealthy Jewish and French-Canadian and more arriviste crowd; and the West Palm Beach and Singer Island Folk, represented by Sondra's aunt and uncle, who have a modest apartment in West Palm, home of the ordinary middle class. We paid them a brief visit, in order to rejoin our roots.

We returned to the capital in time to attend a party at the home of Elizabeth Drew,[1] Washington correspondent for the *New Yorker*. We were anxious not to miss this, because she is known to be very well connected, especially among powerful Democrats on the Hill. I've already learned: you want to meet a senator, dine at the home of a journalist.

We were not disappointed. A small party packed with big names: Bill Bradley,[2] star of the Senate and possible president someday; Bob Packwood,[3] Republican chair of the Senate Finance Committee; Millicent Fenwick,[4] who is running for the Senate, Ben Bradlee and Sally Quinn, and more power. An extraordinary opportunity for a foreign agent (I was the only one) to make connections. I made them.

March 25, 1982 Attended a dinner for Conrad Black[5] given by Tom Enders and socialite Ina Ginsberg. Had a chance to ask Enders about the recent mission of General Walters to Cuba. He gave me bullshit. "He's not in my territory," he said. "I don't know anything." I said we were tired of getting significant information from the newspapers instead of from our friends in State and to whom, as we were being told, we were being so helpful over El Salvador. He opened up a little. It was unpleasant to have to be so unpleasant.

---

[1] (b. 1935) U.S. writer and journalist. Washington correspondent of the *Atlantic* 1967–1973 and of the *New Yorker* 1973–1992.

[2] Democratic Senator from New Jersey 1979–1997. A presidential candidate in the 2000 primaries and a former All-American Basketball player.

[3] Republican Senator from Oregon 1968–1998; Chairman of the Senate Finance Committee 1985–1987 and 1995.

[4] (1910–1992) Republican Representative from New Jersey 1975–1983.

[5] Newspaper magnate and biographer. In the 1990s his company, Hollinger Inc., owned or controlled over four hundred newspaper titles, including the *London Telegraph* and the *National Post*, which he started up.

At the same dinner, I met Zbigniew Brzezinski[1] for the first time. A brilliant man, but very much eclipsed in post-Carter Washington. Despite being a former Canadian, he didn't show much interest in this Canadian. But when I said to him that he and Kissinger had summed up nicely the whole dilemma of foreign-policy-making in modern democracies, he warmed up and became talkative. (Kissinger said foreign policy was all nuance, and Brzezinski said you can't explain nuances on television.) Brzezinski said the United States was not really in an isolationist mood but a unilateralist one. Unilateralism in the 1980s was not accompanied by unkindness [*sic*] nor lack of generosity [*sic*] but characterized by bitterness and a sense of betrayal. The United States was mad at Canada, mad at Japan, mad at Europe, the Third World, everyone. Beware.

March 26, 1982 Dinner with Democrats from another era at Abigail McCarthy's,[2] an amiable woman who said nothing all evening. Some of the other guests were also of a different (the Democratic) era. It was a bit like visiting Washington in a time machine. The dinner was in honour of Dear Abby, also an amiable woman, with whom we swapped Winnipeg-Minneapolis tales. Edmund Muskie[3] made stentorian sounds: "I have no desire to become a senator again, but I would indeed like to be secretary of state once more." He said critically of his former colleague Zbigniew Brzezinski that he entirely dominated the National Security Council's deliberations and would allow no debate. When he, Muskie, was appointed, people in the NSC told him that debate occurred there for the first time – there were even inconclusive meetings.

March 27, 1982 Norman Jewison invited us down to the set at Tysons Corner (ugh!) to watch the filming of *Best Friends*, a new movie he is producing. We met Goldie Hawn again and also Burt Reynolds.[4] At a break during the shooting, we went back to Reynolds's trailer to have a cup

---

[1] (b. 1928) National Security Advisor 1977–1981. Born and educated in Canada, his father served as Polish consul general in Montreal during World War II.

[2] (1915–2001) Author, political activist, and wife of Senator from Minnesota Eugene McCarthy.

[3] (1914–1996) Democratic Governor of Maine 1955–1959; Senator from Maine 1959–1980; vice-presidential nominee in 1968; Secretary of State 1980–1981.

[4] (b. 1936) American actor. An Oscar nominee and Golden Globe winner for *Boogie Nights* (1997). His other well-known films include *Deliverance* (1972) and *Smokey and the Bandit* (1977).

of coffee with him. He told us that he was invited a few nights ago to dine at the White House with Ronald and Nancy Reagan. Just the three of them. He said he had not met the president before and was a bit surprised by the invitation, as he had voted Democrat and told Reagan so that evening.

Burt Reynolds said he found the president energetic but forgetful. For instance, at one point in the evening he tried to show Reynolds a secret door but was unable to locate it. "Look here, Burt, at this secret door. Nancy, where is the secret door? I can't find it." Apparently, Reagan is exercising vigorously and has added three inches to his chest since the assassination attempt.

Reynolds described how, after dinner that evening, the president and he looked out the window of the White House at the Washington Monument and stood there silent for over a minute, both imbued with a sense of awe. "It was," Jewison said later, "power meeting power. Both are number one."

Despite a worsening cold, I attended the white-tie-and-decorations Gridiron annual dinner. Only a handful of ambassadors are invited, but the Canadian ambassador is included because of a tradition that he is a guest of one of the moving spirits of the Gridiron, Alan Emory[1] of the *Watertown Times*. The entire Washington establishment – the president and the first lady, the Supreme Court and half the Senate – sit down to a five-hour dinner to get insulted by the media. There was a sense that everyone there believed – just knew – they were at the centre of the universe. The highlight of the evening was Nancy, wearing a big hat and looking forlorn, performing in a takeoff about her "second-hand clothes." Out came this rack of terrible old clothes, and suddenly out of nowhere also came Nancy Reagan. The president looked astonished as she began to sing "Second-Hand Rose." It electrified this very jaded group.

I was placed at the endlessly long head table, separating the Saudi and the newly arrived Israeli ambassador. The former did not talk to the latter, so my head had to jerk from side to side to make conversation with both. The Israeli, Moshe Arens,[2] was very hurt by the Saudi's snub. Arens is smart but bloodless. He'll do well in Washington.

---

[1] (1922–2000) Reporter for the *Watertown Daily Times* 1947–1990. Recognized as the Dean of the New York Press Corps in Washington.

[2] Israeli Ambassador to the United States 1981–1983; Defence Minister 1983–1984; Foreign Minister 1988–1990.

March 29, 1982 We paid a ritual call on the very smooth Saudis, our neighbours. The bodacious, glamorous Mrs. Saudi, Nouha Alhegelan,[1] lionized in the media, told us she has loaned their official Residence eight times in the past two months to various Washington charities. Sondra and the splendid Mrs. Saudi spent an hour talking about the art of inviting the bitchy social reporters to diplomatic functions – which ones you have to invite, which ones you dare not invite, whether to invite only for cocktails before dinner or for dinner too, etc. Valid subject for discussion, because if your affair doesn't exist in the newspapers, it doesn't exist.

March 30, 1982 A call on Eagleburger. It seems ridiculous to say that a diplomatic call can be an enjoyable event, but a call on Eagleburger is an enjoyable event and I enjoyed it. I spoke to him alone about Mark MacGuigan's interest in becoming secretary-general of NATO. He had heard of it from Al Haig, whose reaction, he said, was sympathetic. (Eagleburger always knows everything.) "Al likes Mark," he said. But Eagleburger didn't think the Europeans would go for a Canadian. "You are only slightly more acceptable than we are," he said gleefully. How Canadians would hate to hear that!

In the evening we attended an elaborate dinner party at the French embassy given by the new French ambassador, Bernard Vernier-Palliez[2] (former head of Renault). The hosts sat everyone according to protocol (typical for the French). Congresswoman Millicent Fenwick, that silly woman, jumped to her feet at a strategic moment to salute – fulsomely, of course – the French and British ambassadors. No mention of the poor little Canadian ambassador. Joe Kraft pointedly rubbed it in after dinner – it was insulting to Canada. I didn't need to be reminded. Nothing that an ambassador hates more than a snub. It's not just personal, it's his country that is insulted. Humbug. It's all ego.

March 31, 1982 In the afternoon I called on Senator George Mitchell,[3] Democrat of Maine, a strong supporter of Canada on the anti–acid rain

---

[1] Wife of Sheikh Faisal Alhegelan, Saudi Arabia's Ambassador to the United States, and President of the Arab Women's Council.

[2] (1918–1999) President of Renault Auto 1975–1981; French Ambassador to the United States 1982–1984.

[3] (b. 1933) Democratic Senator from Maine 1980–1995; Senate Majority Leader 1989–1995; Chairman of the Walt Disney Company 2004 to present.

front and a rising star in liberal America. Friendly, courteous, plausible. This is senator number nine in terms of my calls on the Hill this month. My antique Oldsmobile is getting to be a familiar sight in the precincts of Congress.

My predecessor and mentor Marcel Cadieux[1] warned me that the most demeaning part of his job was trying to get an appointment with a senator, or waiting around to see him, or trying to get him to the house for dinner and coping with the seating plan when he, as so often happens, cancels his acceptance at the last minute. It's true. In any case, as Joe Alsop told me the other night, "no important senator dines out."

These Senate calls are very time-consuming. The senators invariably keep you waiting, the calls are almost always interrupted by something (a vote, an urgent phone call), and there is usually an air of expectancy on the part of the senator. An attitude of "What are you asking me to do for you today?" One always feels as though he is begging. One is. The challenge: how to beg and keep one's dignity.

April 1, 1982 There was a great crowd at the annual Christian Herter[2] lecture at John Hopkins University's School of Advanced International Studies in Washington tonight. Hal Sonnenfeld,[3] Sol Linowitz,[4] Willis Armstrong,[5] and many other former officials as well as academics, adversaries, and media were in the audience. I've been working on my speech for days, weeks.

I delivered the Ten Commandments of Canada-U.S. relations – the old set and the new. It was a superb opportunity to express a number of personal convictions, such as that there was no longer much use for secret

[1] (1915–1981) Canadian foreign-service officer from 1941. Undersecretary of State for External Affairs 1964–1970; Ambassador to the United States 1970–1975 (first francophone to hold the position).

[2] (1895–1966) Republican Governor of Massachusetts 1953–1956; Secretary of State 1959–1961.

[3] Director of the Department of State's Office of Research on the Soviet Union and Eastern Europe 1952–1969; Senior staff member, National Security Council 1969–1974; Counselor of the Department of State 1974–1977.

[4] (1913–2005) Prominent Democratic lawyer, diplomat, and businessman who helped negotiate the return of the Panama Canal to Panama in 1977 under President Jimmy Carter and served as his special envoy to the Middle East.

[5] (1912–1998) Director of the Department of State's Office of British Commonwealth and Northern European Affairs.

diplomacy in our relationship, that we are two different nations with different public policies, that we are diverging in important respects, that we are not simply two clone nations with one – us – occasionally suffering from aberrant policies, and that the time has come to exercise public diplomacy – the open discussion of our differences that sometimes couldn't be bridged, although they could be much better understood. The new, ascendant role of the Congress, a body whose deliberations were public and that increasingly operated in broad daylight, and the growing role and power of the media made public diplomacy all the more necessary and timely from a Canadian point of view.

No doubt I'm being immodest, but I don't think anyone has spoken about diplomacy in this town in this manner before. It marks a rupture with past thinking about Canadian diplomacy and, if I'm not boasting, about diplomacy generally.

April 2, 1982 I am astonished to see my Christian Herter lecture carried over four columns on page 7 of the *New York Times*. They recognized its significance. The coverage makes me and the "team," particularly Gossage, Kinsman, and Marc Lortie,[1] walk on air at the chancery this morning. By God, Canada is in the news. We're relevant!

April 3, 1982 In Ottawa to attend the annual press gallery dinner as a guest of Richard Gwyn.[2] Very different from the Gridiron – more informal and spontaneous, less managed. Also more alcohol. In a word, more Canadian. Tom Axworthy[3] told me Trudeau said, "I'll come if I can insult the press." He came and he did.

Bill Hopper[4] of Petro-Canada approached me and said his contacts in Washington told him I wasn't doing a bad job. "This was good news," he added, "because they were all expecting a socialist freak."

---

[1] First Secretary at the Canadian Embassy in Washington in the 1980s.

[2] (b. 1934) Canadian civil servant, journalist, and author. National affairs columnist at the *Toronto Star* 1973–1985 and international affairs columnist 1985–1992.

[3] (b. 1947) Principal Secretary to Prime Minister Pierre Trudeau 1981–1984.

[4] (1933–2006) Assistant Deputy Minister of Energy Policy in the Department of Energy, Mines, and Resources under Pierre Trudeau; Chairman and CEO of Petro-Canada 1979–1993.

April 4, 1982 Sunday brunch in honour of Sir Brian Urquhart,[1] political undersecretary-general at the UN, given by Evangeline Bruce.[2] She is not a woman of style. She is style. Her Georgetown house is decorated with taste as good as I've seen in this town. She radiates disdain.

We are being taken up by the Georgetown set. It's a snobbish group, much disposed to defining the "ins and the outs," liberal in slant, decidedly Democratic, admiring anything English, anyone famous.

I remember Charles Ritchie telling me the one thing he didn't like about social Washington: this snobbish and rather cruel game of dividing "the ins and the outs." In his time, Joe Alsop was the grand referee. As he is today. Susan Mary, who is very fond of Charles Ritchie, told me not long ago that Joe knew Charles from the days before he married Sylvia and liked him but, it seems, did not approve of Sylvia and barred the couple from his Georgetown salon.

Sol Linowitz warned me, "Beware the Georgetown set – don't get too close." I'm not sure why. Maybe we'll find out.

April 6, 1982 I sent Arthur Erickson a copy of the laudatory piece about him by Benjamin Forgey[3] of the *Washington Post*, to whom I introduced Erickson on his recent visit. He quotes Arthur: "When asked to describe what form the building might take, he demurred. 'I think the most dangerous thing is to have ideas before it is time to have them.'"

This attitude explains perfectly why Arthur bombed in the famous (infamous) External Affairs competition: he submitted no specific plans or models. The committee, headed by an illustrious predecessor of mine, Ed Ritchie, decided this was but another example of Arthur's arrogance and a sign that he thought he had the contract all sewn up. So he had to be punished. Ridiculous.

April 8, 1982 We spent the evening at Susan Mary Alsop's exquisite Georgetown home (covered with eighteenth-century monkey pictures) at a black-tie dinner in honour of Henry Kissinger – his first "coming-out" party

---

1 (b. 1919) Undersecretary-General of the United Nations 1974–1986. Widely regarded as the pioneer of the modern concept of international peacekeeping.

2 (1914–1995) Prominent Washington hostess. Wife of the late David Bruce, former U.S. ambassador to Britain, France, West Germany, and China.

3 Architecture critic and long-time observer of Washington architecture and urban design.

since having bypass surgery. A small affair, a mixture of past and present official Washington and bluebloods with names like Peabody. Sondra and Evangeline Bruce were placed on each side of Kissinger, presumably so he could be amused. Sondra said to him that to many he was known as the "King of the Jews." This pleased him, as his ego had not, it seems, been treated to this expression before.

At my end of the table, Susan Mary – the most attentive hostess I have ever known – kept a four-way conversation going among herself, myself, Caspar Weinberger, and Brent Scowcroft.[1] The banter was bright and brilliant, but I can't remember at all what it was about. "The idea of a good conversation: when neither party remembers a word of what was said afterwards." (Culled from *Geoffrey Madan's Notebooks*, a copy of which Evangeline Bruce gave me.)

Susan Mary toasted her guests, first at our table and then at the second table in the inner room. The new French ambassador jumped to his feet at the second table, where he was sitting, and replied to her toast. Evangeline began to shout that he should come over and do the same at our table. A couple of weakish voices were heard to say no, the Canadian ambassador should reply. After suitable importuning, I stood up, and Evangeline shouted, "No, let's hear the French ambassador." Humiliated, I slunk downwards into my chair. Bernard Vernier-Palliez then came over and gave another passable toast, to which Kissinger made a beautiful response.

Kissinger said the making of peace was a long journey, he had gone down the path, and now the baton was being carried by others, such as Weinberger and Eagleburger (also at the dinner). They were doing so bravely and intelligently, but would get no thanks. It was a handsome salute to these two officials, Weinberger in particular beaming in appreciation.

The speeches were over. At this point, Evangeline, perhaps conscious of her mildly insulting behaviour, began calling on me to speak. After more importuning, the poor little Canadian ambassador graciously decided to respond. He said he had long admired Kissinger's insights, but one in particular had served him over and over: that in foreign policy, there are no breakthroughs, only hundreds of nuances. The tragedy of a modern democracy was that the media allocates only seconds to explain the infinitely complex and that this contradiction between medium and message was

[1] (b. 1925) National Security Advisor 1974–1977 and 1989–1993; Chairman of the President's Foreign Intelligence Advisory Board 2001–2005.

becoming deeper, more difficult to cope with, and alarming for the exercise of democratic principles. Kissinger seemed pleased.

April 13, 1982 Jean Chrétien[1] and his wife, Aline, flew in from Ottawa for the day. I arranged a meeting with Attorney General French Smith in addition to a press lunch and a press briefing. There was absolutely no rapport between the two justice ministers. Nor any real rapport between Chrétien and myself. But what a great visit! Nice and short. Chrétien came in at 10:00 a.m. and left six hours later. All ministerial visits should be so brief. My impression of Jean Chrétien remains unchanged: an instinctive politician, a man who doesn't read and doesn't listen. But politics being what they are (instinct trumps intellect), he should continue to do well.

April 14, 1982 I continue my rounds. Don Regan, treasury secretary, still very unhappy with the Canadian economy; Bill Brock, still very unhappy with our trade policies; and John Block, not unhappy, because there are no agricultural issues to fret about. One thing cabinet secretaries all have in common: huge, impressive offices, mostly pre–World War I and Depression-era public works. The offices announce the power of proconsuls in the new Rome. But that's misleading. As appointed officials, these cabinet secretaries have only limited power. Even among the appointed, it's become clear to me that their power ranks well behind the White House quadrumvirate: Meese,[2] Baker, Deaver,[3] and Darman. The education of a Canadian diplomat in Washington.

April 16, 1982 First visit to the great American interior – Houston and Dallas. We arrived late yesterday afternoon, just in time to attend a welcome ceremony for us at something called the Kellum-Noble House in Houston. The welcome consisted mainly of women running around in the

---

[1] (b. 1934) Minister of Industry, Trade, and Commerce 1976–1977, of Finance 1977–1979, of Justice 1980–1982, and of Energy, Mines, and Resources 1982–1984; Deputy Prime Minister of Canada and Secretary of State for External Affairs 1984; Prime Minister of Canada 1993–2003.

[2] Ed Meese (b. 1931) Headed Reagan's transition effort following the 1980 election, then became counsellor to the president. Member of the cabinet and the National Security Council 1981–1985; U.S. Attorney General 1985–1988.

[3] Mike Deaver (b. 1938) Deputy White House Chief of Staff 1981–1985.

most peculiar costumes. I was presented with a huge (ten-gallon?) cowboy hat, in exchange for greetings I brought from the great northern plains.

I spoke at lunch today to a thin crowd about foreign investment and, to applause, announced the opening of a consular office in Houston. Our consul general, Frank Jackman, told me the speech had been sponsored by the Houston Chamber of Commerce, the Houston Committee on Foreign Relations, the Houston World Trade Council, the Institute for International Education, the Port of Houston Authority, and the Canadian Club of Houston. What about the humane society? The audience was so small I wondered if each of the sponsoring groups commandeered two of their members to represent them.

Dinner was in our honour at the huge home of one James Elkin, chairman of First City Bank Corporation. Various rich and important locals were in attendance, plus – alas – oil, gas, and investment people (how they hate us), plus Oveta Culp Hobby,[1] president of the *Houston Post* and one of America's filthiest-rich women. People were all kind, but I couldn't wait until it was over. Chekhov observed: "The most intolerable people are provincial celebrities."

April 17, 1982 Up early to have breakfast with Republican Governor Bill Clements[2] in his great Governor's Mansion. En route, I read the lead editorial in the *Dallas Morning News*, entitled "A Royal Mess." It was the most anti-Canadian diatribe I've seen in this country. That's quite an accomplishment. Even this did not prepare me for my ordeal with the governor. While insisting that there was no anti-Canadianism in the United States (I've got to get used to the idea that there's such a thing as anti-Canadianism), the governor proceeded, in an aggressive, bullying manner, not only to denounce our energy and investment policies but to speak of such disaffection in Canada that "there could be riots in the streets of Alberta."

Riots in the streets? In Canada? That was certainly a new one for me. Again and again he repeated, "Trudeau is ruining the country." The amazing thing about these arrogant American politicians is they try to tell you they know more about your own country than you do. Clements particularly

---

[1] (1905–1995) Newspaper publisher from Texas. Secretary of Health, Education, and Welfare 1953–1955, when she became President and Editor of the *Houston Post*.

[2] (b. 1917) Republican Governor of Texas 1979–1983 and 1987–1991; founder of SEDCO, the world's largest offshore drilling company.

enjoyed citing the number of Canadian émigrés in Texas as proof that we are rushing to hell in a fast cart.

The much-abused Canadian ambassador struck back. I told him his comments were a tissue of myths, distortions, and exaggerations. The crusty old buzzard seemed to half enjoy my fighting back, so the breakfast didn't end all that badly. As we parted, Clements even began discussing ways to promote better understanding and suggested meetings between the ten governors on his governor's task force (on something or other) and the Canadian premiers.

In the evening we attended the Dallas Mayor's International Ball. Yes, another ambassadors' ball, white tie, no less. And how I hate to dance. There were about a dozen ambassadors from Washington in attendance, a star-studded group that, in addition to myself, included my colleagues from Algeria, Liberia, Nigeria, Costa Rica, Morocco, and other points south. Herbert Hunt[1] and his wife picked us up at our hotel and drove us to the Fairmont, where the ball took place. His car, an old Mercedes sedan, reeked of gasoline and made me want to retch. His wife joked about it and told us to be sure to keep the windows open. "He loves this old wreck," she said. Very amusing for a man worth more than a billion in his own right, along with the billion owned by his brother Bunker and the extra billion by his sister.

We sat at Herbert's table and everyone in his group except us were Hunt employees. Their role was to laugh when Herbert or his wife made a joke – and they made plenty.

The young lady next to me was wife of the employee next to her. We had ice cream for dessert served in a full goblet, and after eating a portion of it, she drove her long spoon into the remains so that it stood splendidly upright, like the American flag planted on the moon. An appropriate gesture, as there were flags to be seen everywhere and we all had to sing a patriotic song from each of our countries, assisted by a forty-piece orchestra.

Hunt made insulting remarks about Canada throughout the evening, albeit in a teasing or jocular manner. At one point he started telling me how in the Canadian West, people were strongly opposed to the new constitution. I told him Premier Lougheed[2] was fully behind it. "Oh sure, him, yeah, but not the people of Alberta." The minds of the Texans are being poisoned by Canadians pissing on Canada.

---

[1] (b. 1929) Participant in the attempt to corner the world silver market.

[2] (b. 1928) PC Premier of Alberta 1971–1985.

April 22, 1982 I take my wares to the West Coast. It's my first time in Los Angeles since 1949. I flew first class with Sondra, which will make everyone mad at us in Ottawa. I tried to sleep so as to be in good shape for the very hectic next few days. I told a stewardess nattering endlessly with an older man and younger wife in front of us to shut up. It turned out this couple are two of Ron and Nancy Regan's best friends, members of the kitchen cabinet. I strike another blow for Canada.

April 23, 1982 I met with Mayor Bradley[1] in the morning. I could see why he is regarded as one of the nation's rising black leaders. I praised him for lowering the crime rates in the city during his term of office. "Why don't you publicize this, take credit for it?" I asked. "No way," he replied. "Figure it out. The crime rate goes down, I claim credit. The crime rate goes back up, I get blamed. Truth of the matter is, I have little influence over these things."

April 24, 1982 Yesterday I addressed city council in its art deco palace, talked to the intelligent and well-informed *Los Angeles Times* editorial board, did radio interviews, and attended a dinner given by our consul general – standard ambassadorial fare, I guess. Today was different. Norm and Dixie Jewison gave us a lunch at their beach house in Malibu, with a large chunk of the Canadian Hollywood community attending. Donald Sutherland and his pregnant wife, Francine; John Kemeny,[2] who just made the unspeakable *Quest for Fire*; Alan Blye from Winnipeg; the ancient idol Alexis Smith;[3] novelist Brian Moore;[4] Ted Allan; Bernard Slade;[5] Arthur Hill;[6] non-Canadians Art Buchwald,[7] "Dear Abby" (why?), and a few dozen others. I sat on the deck overlooking the beach and ocean under the dazzling sun, seized by a strong sense of unreality.

---

[1] Tom Bradley (1917–1998) Mayor of Los Angeles 1973–1993, the first African-American mayor of a major U.S. city.

[2] (b. 1925) Hungarian-born Canadian film producer.

[3] (1921–1993) Canadian-born actress in Hollywood.

[4] (1921–1999) Novelist and screenwriter. Immigrated to Canada in 1948, where he worked as a reporter for the Montreal *Gazette*. Published twenty novels.

[5] (b. 1930) Canadian-born playwright and television writer.

[6] (b. 1922) Canadian actor appearing in British and American theatre, movies, and TV.

[7] (b. 1923) Widely syndicated humour columnist and Washington insider.

Donald Sutherland and his wife took us to Ma Maison for dinner, where we had the best meal since arriving in the United States. Sondra and I sat next to Sean Connery.[1] We found him heavy-going. Hate to think how he found us. Sutherland arranged to have menus with a mounted Canadian flag before each person and with little Canadian flags spread all over the table. At the next table sat comedian and ex-Winnipegger David Steinberg,[2] who waved to me. I waved back. In this make-believe land, I find it easy to pretend I'm a somebody.

April 28, 1982 In Sacramento with our two consuls general in hand, Jim Nutt from Los Angeles and Jim McCardle from San Francisco. In the spectacular Victorian-style capital building, renovations just completed, I undergo the now familiar "capital waltz": welcome resolution from the Assembly, welcome resolution from the Senate, following inedible lunch, then formal speeches, everyone on automatic pilot. I talk about the terrible terrors of acid rain, now ravaging California lakes. (Thank God for acid rain.)

We sped back to the fusty Hotel Cliff in San Francisco, where we have a lush suite, to meet with Governor Jerry Brown.[3] He has a reputation for not showing up, so I was stunned when he did, and on time. I never liked the idea of him very much (trendy, like Trudeau) but was struck by the electric energy that he radiates. We talked about the environment and Canada-U.S. relations. He left me feeling a bit like how I feel sometimes when I leave Trudeau's presence – exhausted, relieved, and not particularly enlightened. He stayed for an hour and a half, and Sondra was locked up in the bedroom the whole time. It was rather primitive of me to keep her out of sight. I'll pay for it.

April 29, 1982 Chancellor "Mike" Heyman's[4] reception for us on the terrace of his home benefited from one of those perfect Berkeley afternoons – slight breezes, thin sunshine, cool air. Heyman announced in his welcoming remarks that he exercised one of his few presidential prerogatives

---

[1] (b. 1930) Oscar-winning Scottish actor, the original cinematic James Bond.

[2] (b. 1942) Canadian-born Hollywood comedian, actor, director, and writer.

[3] (b. 1938) Governor of California 1975–1983; Mayor of Oakland, California, 1998 to present.

[4] (b. 1930) Chancellor of the University of California, Berkeley, 1980–1990; Secretary of the Smithsonian Institution 1994–1999.

by drawing my academic file, to discover that in my two years at Berkeley, I had broken a perfect record of As to get one B. He asked me to tell the truth now and explain the story of the mysterious and disgraceful B. I was immodest enough to do so, to the consternation of the guests, and at some length.

We left just in time to watch the Montreal Expos play the Giants in Candlestick Park. We were guests of the owner in his box, along with that baseball maniac Donald Sutherland, who flew in specially for the game. I threw the first ball. Naturally, it didn't even reach the plate. The Expos were annihilated. I acted gravely disappointed.

April 30, 1982 Another day in San Francisco. Got socked by the president of the Bank of America for our nasty nationalist policies. Then spoke to the Commonwealth Club – my best audience so far and my best delivery. Even Sondra thought I was okay. We had no commitments this afternoon, so we wandered around the city. Great joy. And tomorrow we are taking the whole day off, which seems almost unimaginable. That will end our voyage of discovery to the far West. I seem to be getting over my *rage de voyager*. And as for my engagement in public diplomacy, I think I'm suffering from nimiety. The day after tomorrow, it's the Beltway again and the corridors of Congress. I never thought I'd miss them.

May 5, 1982 The unpopular (around here) minister of the environment, casual John Roberts, arrived in town, and I arranged a schedule (mostly on the Hill) that keeps him away from gorgon Anne Gorsuch at the EPA. It is not safe territory for him. The lady turns a rich purple colour when his name comes up in conversation. He is, for her, the *Antichrist*.

May 6, 1982 My day started by signing a book of condolences at the Algerian embassy, as required, I'm told, by protocol, although nowhere is it written or decreed. We lunched with the new senator from South Dakota, then Sondra received a visit at the Residence from the Ladies Auxiliary of the Kitchener-Waterloo Art Gallery, no less, and then we attended – why, I know not, as it is nowhere written or decreed – a reception by the Indian ambassador in honour of something called, ominously, "Parliamentarians for World Order." Finally, we went to dinner at the home of a Washington rabbi, whom, no doubt, I'll never see again. It was to honour Moshe Arens, who certainly was not sent to Washington to dine with me.

May 7, 1982 I had a breakfast this morning at the Residence to brief the Canadian press. Interest seems high about what I am trying to do. I set it all out in very plain language. My approach is to acknowledge differences, instead of pretending publicly that they don't exist. It involves lobbying the Congress to advance our interests, a practice not followed by Canada or even allowed by us until very recently. It involves public diplomacy. The basic aim is to increase understanding in the United States that we are a country with our own policies and purposes – we are not simply misguided Americans. I emphasized that we are both a foreign and a sovereign country, which means discretion over the securing of national interests that inevitably are not identical for both countries.

The Canadian press is eating this stuff up. They love the ink in the American press that my campaign has been getting. I worry that they love it too much.

May 9, 1982 I write to the number one Canada-basher, Big John Dingell[1] of Michigan, chairman of the House Energy and Commerce Committee, one of the satraps who rule the Hill. He wants to weaken air emission controls. The auto industry fiddles and he dances. In an aggressive mood, I tell him his criticism of our acid rain record is full of holes. It galls me that I have to defend the Canadian commitment against the attacks of a congressional strongman. There are a number of them on the Hill, but he has no equal.

May 14, 1982 Dinner tonight in Washington at the large, countrified home of Sargent Shriver,[2] brother-in-law of President Kennedy. The affair was in honour of the "originator of the aerobic dance program," so naturally, my presence was a necessity. I didn't know anyone there, and I didn't talk to anyone other than to exchange a few banalities. I went, however, to be seen. "Visibility" is much prized in this media-dominated town. "Visibility" in turn leads to "access," and "access" leads to "influence." That's the theory, and it corresponds perfectly to the Washington reality. But you can't mine for information at many of these affairs. Lots of dry holes and I was in one tonight.

---

[1] (b. 1929) Longest-serving member of the House of Representatives, representing a district in the Western suburbs of Detroit since 1955.

[2] Robert Sargent Shriver Jr. (b. 1915) Married Eunice Kennedy (sister of John F. Kennedy); U.S. Ambassador to France 1968–1970.

May 16, 1982 In Chicago with Sondra to accompany Trudeau to Notre Dame University. He is being awarded an honorary degree by the Reverend Theodore Hesburgh.[1] Trudeau was delighted to be at Notre Dame and was in an upbeat mood all day. A certain Buddha-like calm and serenity overtakes him when he is the centre of attention. He acquires a glow. He seemed to enjoy the rah-rah atmosphere of the convocation exercise and all the shouting, cap tossing, and high antics of the graduating class.

Trudeau's demeanour took me back five years, to when I invited him to Oxford for the day, when I was a visiting fellow at All Souls. He wore a white suit and the habitual rose in his lapel, and as we walked down the High Street, he glowed in the delight of recognition by the strolling students. When we dined at All Souls in the evening, he was mellowness and serenity itself. That most cynical and reactionary homosexual Warden John Sparrow[2] (I admired him greatly) was bewitched by Trudeau. As the warden told me before and after, he expected to dislike Trudeau, because he could not abide trendy people. And if he could melt John Sparrow, who is immune? Not the crowd at Notre Dame. The old charisma surrounded him.

Trudeau's speech on East-West relations and arms control was exactly the speech he should not have given. I did try, without much success, to moderate the tone and content. It was not, so to speak, an anti-Reagan speech, but it amounted to that because it was anti-hardline on dealing with the Soviets. There's nothing deplorable about that – it's a point of view and certainly reflects Trudeau's traditionally soft approach to the Soviet Union and on East-West issues generally. But what bothers me about the speech is that Trudeau managed to inject into it the old "moral equivalence" theme – the two superpowers are both bad boys, endangering world peace by their arms race.

This is a mistake. The Americans, and not just hardliners, don't like the notion that they and the Soviets are equally responsible for world tensions. That really was the message in Trudeau's speech, and he sort of rubbed their noses in it. His theme will appeal to some in the United States, particularly the arch-anti-Reagan left. But it offends many American policy-makers and the large community of the American elite that they influence – people we can't allow ourselves to alienate.

---

[1] (b. 1917) President of University of Notre Dame 1952–1987. Holds the *Guinness Book of World Records* title for Most Honorary Degrees, having been awarded 150. Member of the U.S. Civil Rights Commission from 1957; Chairman 1969–1972.

[2] (b. 1906) Warden of All Souls College, Oxford, 1952–1977.

May 17, 1982 My calls on the Hill continue. There are so many significant players they could go on forever. I visit Senator Henry "Scoop" Jackson,[1] the great warrior. Peter Lougheed told me there is no one in Washington as knowledgeable about Canada, and he was right. There is no continuity of experience in the U.S. administration. In that part of the government they seem to worship discontinuity – and have done so now for a couple of decades, as each new president runs against Washington, the establishment, and the inside-the-Beltway crowd. The first thing the president does after taking office is to fire everyone. It's only an enormously rich country that can afford such inefficiency.

I have learned that one has a better chance of finding knowledge and experience about Canada on the Hill, where a number of congressmen and senators go back a long way, like Bill Frenzel[2] of Minnesota and Sam Gibbons[3] of Florida in the House and Jackson and Moynihan[4] on the Senate side. They have a perspective, some sense of history about our country, that is very hard to find in the cabinet or among top officials. One shouldn't get carried away by this thesis, because it's rare to find elected politicians whose outlook is not determined almost entirely by parochial or regional considerations. The Senate was supposed to be more than an aggregate of baronies fighting for local interests, but it certainly is not. Jackson was, of course, well aware of the growing tide of tensions in our relationship, and being a Westerner and close to Peter Lougheed, the arch-enemy of the NEP, I knew where his sympathies were. But he impressed me as having a far larger view of the Canada-U.S. relationship than one encounters in Washington these days.

May 19, 1982 The big piece I wrote in defence of our energy policies in last Sunday's *New York Times*, with the headline "Freezing in the Dark Not Our Style," gets an orgy of praise in Canada. "Thank God somebody is standing up to the Yanks" is the theme.

---

[1] (1912–1983) Democratic Representative from Washington 1941–1953; Senator from Washington 1953–1983.

[2] (b. 1928) Republican Representative from Minnesota 1962–1991. Congressional Representative to the General Agreement on Tariffs and Trade in Geneva for fifteen years.

[3] (b. 1920) Democratic Representative from Florida 1963–1997.

[4] Patrick Daniel Moynihan (1927–2003) U.S. Ambassador to the United Nations 1975–1976; Democratic Senator from New York 1977–2001; Chairman of the Senate Finance Committee 1993–1995.

The *Times* really gave my article a lot of space – there was a big picture of my big dome. But all these stories are making me nervous. What goes up must come down. Also, the stories worry me because they make me feel a part of some campaign – or a leader in a campaign – of U.S. bashing. I feel I may be catering to an anti-American streak in Canadians, or at least in the Canadian media. I sense that I am feeding the Canadian press colony in Washington with anti-U.S. fodder. They are eating it up and asking for more and more. Most of them are American-bashers at heart.

The thing is, I believe in what I say. I think I'm on the right track. But I worry that my diplomacy is feeding the anti-American mood in Canada, and this makes me uncomfortable.

May 24, 1982 John Turner[1] is visiting us from Toronto. He's still practising at McMillan Binch, still hungrily waiting in the wings for the big Liberal takeover. He's in town with his wife, Geils, and they're staying with us as house guests. It's an old Ottawa weekend in Washington, as the Kirkwoods and McSweens are also visiting us. Turner was in top form: warm, self-confident, insightful, incisive, ebullient, energetic in everything he said, including the banalities.

May 28, 1982 Tonight we gave a black-tie dinner for Bill Mulholland. Bankers are not exactly big draws in this town, and Canadian bankers – well, that's even less excuse to attend a dinner party. This takes some getting used to – the heads of banks are gods in Canada. But I worked my butt off and got an A-list turnout. No doubt I've gotten vain, but I know why people came (and it wasn't to see the Canadian ambassador or the Mulhollands). They came because they knew that, at the embassy Sondra and I run, they would mix with other powerful U.S. players in the political game, people they wanted to see, or were trying to see, and they were not disappointed tonight. It was a good night for the Mulhollands and a satisfying evening for us, marred only by the Mulhollands' rather perfunctory "Thank you" as they walked out the front door. I could have used a little effusiveness.

I've gotten to recognize that kind of thank you and understand what it means: "You're doing what embassies are supposed to do, and I'm a taxpayer, aren't I?"

[1] (b. 1929) Minister of Justice 1968–1972; Minister of Finance 1972–1975; Prime Minister of Canada 1984; Leader of the Opposition and the Liberal Party of Canada 1984–1990.

May 29, 1982 I'm out of sorts because of a fatuous feature in the *Toronto Star* about the "sumptuous" Canadian ambassador's Residence in Washington, with its huge rooms, extravagant decor, and all that (with monstrous supporting photo). Message in the article is: damn these people living in luxury at our expense, drinking from the public trough.

The *Star* also stirs up the Erickson controversy: "Irked Architects Propose Boycott over Embassy Fiasco." (How the media love the word *fiasco*.) The report recounts once again the tale of the eleven competitors, the four finalists, and the appointment of Erickson, who did not make the shortlist. Typical *Star* brew: a dose of envy, a dose of fiction, a dose of fantasy, a dose of malice.

May 31, 1982 Sondra, our two daughters, and I were invited yesterday to the large and comfortable summer home of Arthur Goldberg,[1] whom I had met at the UN some years ago. "Southwood," as he calls it, was a very long drive from Washington, and when we got there, we were close to heat prostration. Not my notion of the ideal way to spend a Sunday afternoon. Goldberg and his wife were courteous, she especially, but I had no idea that he was such a monumental egotist. He talked of his honorary degrees. He has, he told us, been awarded more than any other American – some five or six dozen, which he has piled up for everyone to see. And the conversation never got any better, as we ate pasta off paper plates. We couldn't get away fast enough, and anyway, we had a dinner invitation from Marion Burros,[2] food critic of the *New York Times*.

Our impatience to get away must have showed, because today there was a hand-delivered note to the Residence, addressed to Sondra from the distinguished ex-ambassador and ex–Supreme Court justice. It was abusive. How dare you come to my house and act so bored? For some reason he made Sondra his principal target, but he was gunning for me too. It left an awful taste in my mouth. That's the one thing I hate about this job: always on duty, never a private person. Always having to have a smile on your face. Always appearing to be interested and appreciative. How one longs to be rude.

---

[1] (1908–1990) Secretary of Labor 1961–1962; Associate Justice of the Supreme Court of the United States 1962–1965; U.S. Ambassador to the United Nations 1965–1968.

[2] *New York Times* restaurant/food reviewer from the 1980s until present.

June 4, 1982 There is a nasty dispute brewing over softwood lumber – one of our biggest exports. The U.S. industry has been hollering about our alleged subsidies, claiming that we charge next to zilch for our "stumpage." I've never even heard of stumpage before. Now it's getting to be a big part of my vocabulary. I wake up in the middle of the night mumbling stumpage, stumpage. It dominates my vocabulary when I call on Brock and Baldridge. We're lucky the Trade and Commerce cabinet portfolios are in the hands of these two pros.

Dined with the Strausses at the Jockey Club at the Fairfax Hotel, a favourite spot for the chic and the power-brokers. We sat in the front room, of course, it being the place to be seen. Indifferent food, best company in a long time. Funny that a Jew from Texas should be the most quintessential American I've met in this town.

June 7, 1982 In Delaware peddling Canadian wares. This giant business promotion involved a fifty-person Canadian trade delegation, and it was not very successful. When asked by the media why no deals had been developed, I told them (lying), "I'm not a salesman. I don't think the people came here with their order books and samples" (more lying). I was depressed at how some of our chamber of commerce emissaries – not least the chairman, James Doyle – were publicly bad-mouthing Canada's investment policies.

They harm themselves by playing up our domestic-policy debates before foreign audiences, and they exaggerate the policies' significance. They want people to do business with Canada but tell them, in effect, we are a banana republic. You don't catch Americans crapping all over their government when they are abroad.

June 9, 1982 I started the day receiving an Indian chief from New Brunswick.

Then a pack of MPs and MLAs from Manitoba descended on us to lobby congressmen about the Garrison Dam. Led by Lloyd Axworthy[1] and Al Mackling,[2] my task is to steer these folks around the Hill for a couple of days

---

[1] (b. 1939) Liberal Member of Parliament 1979–2000; Minister of Employment and Immigration 1980–1983, of Transport 1983–1984, and of Foreign Affairs 1996–2000.

[2] (b. 1927) Member of the Legislative Assembly of Manitoba 1969–1988; Attorney General of Manitoba 1969–1972; Minister of Consumer and Corporate Affairs 1969–1970; Minister of Natural Resources 1982–1985; Minister of Labour 1985–1987.

so they can try to twist arms. It's been a logistical nightmare from the beginning. No pre-clearance at Baltimore airport. Special bus got lost. Legislators went to wrong hotel. Wrong addresses for congressmen. Anyway, it was a boondoggle. I doubt if they will have any real influence, and moreover, the threat of the Garrison project seems to be receding. We gave a reception in their honour at the Residence for a couple of hundred schnorrers. No one important from the Hill or the administration showed up. We snuck out and attended a small dinner at the home of IMF chief Jacques de la Rosière.[1]

From dams to dollars. From an Indian chief to high-tech executives. That's what I love about this job: the quick and seemingly limitless changes in focus. And players.

June 10, 1982 Our favourable publicity seems to feed on itself. Michael Killian[2] of the *Chicago Tribune*, in his new book, *Who Runs Washington?*: "If you were to draw up a list of the brightest men in Washington, you'd quickly write down Canadian Ambassador Allan Gotleib [*sic*] and then wonder who's next to put in that league." I met Killian only once – when he was covering the economic summit in Ottawa. I know he has no basis for saying this. But in a town with 150 ambassadors competing for attention, can I complain?

June 11, 1982 MacGuigan flew into town from Bonn after the two European summits: NATO and the Economic Group of Seven. It was apparent from MacGuigan's demeanour in my private chats with him that he was disturbed about the summit meetings. He told me our leader constantly contradicted, refuted, and needled Reagan at the two events. And he was the only one to do it. He said his performance bordered on self-indulgence. My heart sank.

June 12, 1982 There is a disturbing Washington custom according to which charity organizers cajole the larger, richer embassies into opening their buildings for fundraising charity events. Jean French Smith,[3] acting at the request of the Opera Ball, asked Sondra to host a dinner, thinking we

---

[1] (b. 1929) Managing Director of the International Monetary Fund 1978–1987.

[2] (1939–2005) Long-time *Chicago Tribune* reporter and novelist.

[3] Wife of U.S. Attorney General William French Smith.

might be able to draw a good list of lucrative donors. We drew one senator – Mark Hatfield[1] – and a group of about two dozen other guests.

At my table was a bubbly, wealthy, charming, talkative Californian, a friend of the Reagans and French Smiths named Ginny Milner. She was holding forth in her effervescent, non-stop manner when another lady at my table who sat opposite her, the ancient and one-time celebrated Washington hostess Gwendolyn Cafritz[2] (I don't think she's been sighted in years), started to look glummer and glummer.

As Ginny chattered on, Mme. Cafritz broke in with, "Why don't you shut up?" The guests were stunned. Ginny Milner, lady to her fingertips, let it pass and continued to babble on. Mrs. Cafritz again: "Didn't you hear me – why don't you shut up?" After a pause and more silence at the table, Mme. Milner said, "Mrs. Cafritz, I've heard so much about you. I've wanted to meet you for so long. You've done so much – you're a wonderful woman." Mrs. Cafritz thrust out her already protruding lower lip and sat sullenly and silently through the rest of the dinner. The guests never recovered from the exchange.

As Mrs. Cafritz uses a cane, I had helped her into the dining room when she arrived. She took my arm and said, "I rarely go to embassy dinners – the food is always so terrible." "You won't be surprised tonight," I replied.

June 17, 1982 I'm recovering from the most tumultuous party we have given in Washington. We had seventy guests in honour of Ken Taylor. The idea behind it was simple. Whenever I travel, someone gets up and says thank you, Canada, for rescuing our hostages. The further I go into the heartland, the warmer and louder the thanks. The closer I get to the epicentre, the Beltway, the less often I hear them.

So the object tonight, what with all the problems weighing us down, was to remind the folks on the Hill, in the White House, and in the media that they should show some gratitude to Canada for saving their kin.

Four senators (four) cancelled at 7 p.m. because of a vote. A number of key administration husbands cancelled or didn't show up: Judge Clark, Bill French Smith – it's the Falklands, Middle East crisis, or whatever. It rained

[1] (b. 1922) Governor of Oregon 1959–1967; Republican Senator from Oregon 1966–1996.

[2] President of the Morris & Gwendolyn Cafritz Foundation 1964–1988, an independent grant-making foundation focused on the Washington community.

at 6 p.m., so all the tables outdoors, set up for a barbecue (a black-tie barbecue), had to be stuffed inside. Joe Alsop complained bitterly about being underdressed – he was wearing a pink shirt and dark suit. No doubt he had never heard, for good reason, of a black-tie barbecue.

Ibrahim the Turk barbecued Columbia River salmon (how do the salmon swim up the Columbia after we built all those dams there, quipped fisherman Paul Volcker), and shrimp and crab shish kebab à la Turco-Canadian. Maple-walnut ice cream moulds for dessert.

We had Canada's greatest comedian, David Broadfoot,[1] come down from Canada to do a routine. What a hilarious mistake. We should have known that Washingtonians like to eat and run, so as to be in shape for next day's power contests. And they ran. A quarter of the guests disappeared even before Broadfoot began. They missed his great opening line: "I'm just delighted to be at the home of the world's most responsible people – with everything that happens in the world, you always hear that Washington is responsible."

I spied one of the fitter guests dart through French doors into the garden and over the hedge. Another quarter slunk out during the joke routine. Kay Graham looked bitchy (she's good at it), fell asleep during the Broadfoot performance, and walked out before the end. But it was a grand guest list: Bill Bradley, Vernon Jordan,[2] Jim Schlesinger,[3] Elizabeth Drew, Fred Iklé,[4] Sol Linowitz, Eugene Rostow, and many, many more.

I sat next to the rather forbidding wife of the national security adviser, Bill Clark. We chatted amiably and talked about the press, of which she is not overly fond. I told her stories about how Trudeau stands up to the press. "I didn't know that about him," she said. "I admire him for it. I'm sorry he does not like the United States."

---

[1] (b. 1925) Canadian comedian known especially for his work as a member of the radio version of the *Royal Canadian Air Farce* 1973–1993.

[2] (b. 1935) American business executive. President of the National Urban League 1972–1981. Member of the transition team for incoming president Bill Clinton 1992–1993, as a personal friend and adviser.

[3] (b. 1929) Director of the CIA 1973; Secretary of Defense 1973–1975; First Secretary of Energy 1977–1979.

[4] (b. 1924) Director of the Arms Control and Disarmament Agency 1973–1977; Undersecretary of Defense for Policy 1981–1988.

I reacted urbanely, trying not to fall off my chair. "Nonsense," I said, lightheartedly. "Wherever did you get that idea from? He likes Americans – it's just that he has an independent way of thinking on many issues." No comment. This conversation makes me uneasy.

June 18, 1982 The manager of the Washington office of the Canadian Coalition on Acid Rain, Adele Hurley, called on me to discuss progress in our efforts to get Congress to tighten emission controls. As a private organization, the coalition can engage in some visible and direct lobbying on the Hill without triggering the kind of xenophobic reactions that can result from direct interventions by a foreign government. The position of the embassy on this issue is not easy. We have to lobby *against* the U.S. government, the issue involves *domestic* legislation, this is an ideologically excited town, and Canada wins no popularity contest in Washington. So we must lobby in a low-key way, and the coalition offers useful cover. I believe it is doing a good job of raising awareness. I respect Hurley's competence. But I wish some of the people involved were not so self-righteous. A condition all too common among the environmental crowd.

June 19, 1982 We had a dinner for Robert and Theresa Ford,[1] who are visiting Washington. He's left Moscow, and they are now living in their château near Vichy. He is one of the most remarkable diplomats that Canada has produced – and not just because he recently sent me a couple of bottles of 1934 Château Latour. I had no problem getting a distinguished group of political experts together to meet him, among them Scotty Reston, the Buckleys,[2] the Sonnenfelds. Ford is revered in Washington, and even more so these days, because his hardline, unsentimental view of the Russians is very much in tune with the prevailing attitude in this town. Ibrahim cooked his best dinner yet.

I spent a lot of time at the party talking to Eagleburger. This was the first time I had seen him since he returned from the NATO and economic

---

[1] (1915–1998) Joined the Department of External Affairs in 1940. Canadian Ambassador to Colombia 1957–1959, to Yugoslavia 1959–1961, to the United Arab Republic 1961–1963, and to the Soviet Union 1964–1980.

[2] Jim Buckley (b. 1923) New York State Senator 1971–1977; Undersecretary of State for Security Assistance 1981–1982; Federal Appellate Judge 1985–2000.

summits. It was also my first opportunity to chat with the exceedingly sharp Rick Burt,[1] who has just been promoted to the powerful position of assistant secretary of state for Europe and Canada.

Eagleburger came at me almost at once. I was most disturbed by our conversation. He told me that at a meeting yesterday of the National Security Council in the White House, Reagan presided and they took a decision to move to new extraterritorial measures designed to stop the trans-Siberian gas pipeline. (This will infuriate the Europeans.) At a particular point, Reagan made some negative comments about Trudeau's behaviour at the NATO Summit, particularly about Trudeau's complaint that there was no real discussion and give-and-take at the NATO Council meeting, just a lot of set speeches. At the NSC meeting, the president said something to the effect of "That's not right – I spoke out at the summits. I was spontaneous."

I told Eagleburger that Reagan was under a misapprehension. I was sure that Trudeau was criticizing Secretary-General Luns,[2] not the president. I knew for a fact that Trudeau was always highly critical of the formal and rigid way Luns runs the NATO meetings. He would complain about it every time NATO was mentioned. I also knew for a fact that Trudeau thought the president was the only leader (aside from himself) who did speak spontaneously. Eagleburger told me he would pass that on to the president. (If he thinks I believe that, he must take me for a chump.) Eagleburger added that Trudeau infuriated Haig at Versailles as well as a number of others. I also didn't get good vibes from the refreshingly candid Rick Burt. One of our embassy wives said he told her tonight that Trudeau was a nuisance at the summit.

So everything MacGuigan told me is confirmed. Trudeau must really have been kicking his heels on that trip. The question is what will be the costs.

June 21, 1982 Bingo. The *New York Times* covers my speech last week to the Harvard Law Association of Washington – and on its editorial page. "Outspoken Diplomat" is the title of the article. "Canada's emissary here has

---

[1] Director of Politico-Military Affairs in the Department of State 1981–1982; Assistant Secretary of State for European and Canadian Affairs 1982–1985; American Ambassador to West Germany 1985–1989.

[2] Joseph Luns (1911–2002) Secretary-General of NATO 1971–1984.

replaced his pinstripe suit with a pair of boxing trunks and has taken a series of jibes at Congress. It is unusual for a diplomat to criticize publicly the processes of government in the foreign country where he serves. But Mr. Gotlieb says he is calling it the way he sees it."

June 22, 1982 In Victoria to talk lumber, lumber, lumber. Everyone is worried sick about the growing pressure in Washington for a countervail action against our lumber. So my dire noises about the growth of neo-protectionism in the United States were received here by very keen ears. In Ottawa I act a bit like the ancient mariner. Here I don't have to tug at people's sleeves – they're onto the message already.

June 23, 1982 I met with a group of cabinet ministers in Edmonton and listened to feverish and highly emotional attacks on Trudeau's energy and investment policies. "The NEP has killed the investment environment in Alberta. . . . Ottawa is sacrificing the West for the East." Heavy stuff all the way. I heard a recurring question: how can we trust you as ambassador in Washington to press our interests when the federal government is the servant of Eastern interests and you are the servant of the federal government? I told them that was bunkum – but it wasn't.

Everyone was polite, as was Lougheed, who understands the United States very well, better than most people in Ottawa. He told me the NEP is radicalizing the U.S. perception of FIRA, and the growing attacks on FIRA are mainly a fallout of the NEP. I told him he's wrong on that. The Americans detest our investment policies in their own right.

In Edmonton, Bill Hopper and Joel Bell[1] of Petro-Canada had a dinner for me. They invited about a dozen energy heavies, including Jack Gallagher[2] of Dome and Bob Pierce[3] of Foothills, a very worried lot. My message: phone me in Washington. I'm your man.

We talked gas exports until I practically passed out.

---

[1] Principal Economic Adviser to Prime Minister Pierre Trudeau; founder and Executive Vice-President of Petro-Canada.

[2] (1916–1998) Canadian petroleum geologist who founded Dome Petroleum in 1950 and resigned as CEO in 1983.

[3] Chairman and CEO of Alberta Gas Ethylene and Novacor Chemicals; Chairman and CEO of Foothills Pipelines Group.

June 24, 1982 After flying back from Edmonton, Sondra and I went right to a dinner party offered by Tom[1] and Joan Braden[2] in honour of the Deavers. It was a beautiful night. As we stood on the patio of the Bradens' large Chevy Chase home (said to be a gift from Nelson Rockefeller[3] to Joan for services rendered), Mike Deaver seemed to be beckoning me with his eye to talk to him. You can't be in Washington more than a few minutes without learning that Deaver is the grand panjandrum of the White House, the not-so-invisible hand behind Ron and Nancy's every move. So I left Joe Kraft, with whom I was chatting, saying, "Duty calls. I'm being summoned."

Without wasting a minute, Deaver said, "You know things went poorly between our two guys at the recent summits." I said, sadly, "I know." He asked me if I read the recent cover article on Trudeau in the *National Review*. "You mean," I replied, "the one that says Trudeau is a communist dupe and agent." "Yes," he said. "It made an impression on the president." In a state of anger, I responded, "You mean the president read that garbage?" "Yes," he confirmed.

I explained to Deaver that it had been written by Lubor Zink,[4] who was a fringe journalist and paranoid about Trudeau. I told Deaver we couldn't really afford to let our relationship go sour. He agreed emphatically and said it was sad that after such a good start between the two leaders last year at the economic summit in Ottawa, the relationship should have so deteriorated. We can't just leave it that way, he added. I asked him if I could call on him to discuss what we could do about it. He welcomed this and suggested having lunch at my place with Bill Clark. I readily agreed.

Sondra had insisted I come back from the Canadian West in time to attend this dinner, but I had been reluctant. Thank God I did! With Deaver involved, I've got one of the top White House players onside. I can hardly believe our relations are in such a state.

---

[1] (b. 1918) Journalist, broadcaster, and television host.

[2] (1922–1999) Vice-President of public-relations firm Gray and Company. Department of State's Coordinator of Consumer Affairs 1976–1978.

[3] (1908–1979) American politician, philanthropist, and businessman. Governor of New York 1959–1973; Vice-President of the United States 1974–1977, and a leader of the moderate wing of the Republican Party.

[4] (1920–2003) Long-time Canadian right-wing newspaper columnist for the *Toronto Telegram* and the *Toronto Sun*.

We stayed late, Sondra dancing with Nicko Henderson and talking to Art Buchwald, I kibitzing with Larry Eagleburger, who came very late and seemed a little wild, even for him. I informed him of what Deaver told me about the president, and he groaned. "God, what can you do with a man who reads the *National Review*? Don't get too excited or upset. The Canada-U.S. relationship is too big and too deep to get easily derailed." Ha ha.

Tom Braden's toast to Deaver was typical Washington: he insulted him for five minutes.

June 25, 1982 The news rocks Washington – Haig has resigned. Now I understand why Eagleburger seemed so odd and distraught last night.

I wrote a personal and confidential letter to Pitfield, with a copy to MacGuigan, spelling out the awful truth about the Trudeau-Reagan relationship. I repeated my conversations with Joan Clark, Rick Burt, Larry Eagleburger, and Mike Deaver on the subject. It made depressing reading. Pitfield assured me he will show it to the PM. The results of Trudeau's antics at the summit were worse than anyone thought. As MacGuigan correctly told me, our leader's performance was one long act of self-indulgence. And the country is going to pay for it.

The *New York Times* publishes the second reference to my speech before the Harvard lawyers in Washington. It's under the caption "Required Reading." "Ambassadors today are increasingly being drawn into public debate over U.S. domestic policy. And this seems to violate one of the cardinal rules of international diplomacy, namely, thou shalt not interfere in the internal affairs of the host country." The editors seem to find this notion very intriguing.

June 26, 1982 It's interesting that all the sources I cited in my letter to Ottawa about Reagan and Trudeau came from people I talked to at parties. No information whatsoever from any official in his office. Proof, if I need it, of the value of the social connection. As Jane Austen wrote (Sondra's favourite quote): "Everything happens at parties."

June 27, 1982 Last night we dined at Joe Alsop's, the innermost of the inner sanctums of the Georgetown snobs. He had a very small crowd (it would be a "cozy" evening, he said – he loves that word): Kay Graham, Bob

MacNamara,[1] Meg Greenfield,[2] and Alsop's nephew Warren Zimmerman[3] and his wife. We ate caviar, drank vodka, and had a swell time. At dinner, in his gloomy lower-floor dining room with pictures of Roosevelts and his other ancestors lining the walls, Alsop dominated the table. "Remember," he said to me again, "any senator or congressman who accepts social invitations counts for nothing." Later, he expanded. "The first rule to remember is that no senator is important. The second rule to remember is that no congressman is important." Of Pamela Harriman,[4] whom the company cut up all evening (she was projecting too high a profile at the Democratic Convention today): "The only distinction of her English family, the Digbys, is that every hundred years they produce a courtesan of international standing."

June 29, 1982 The embassy staged a satellite feed of the Budget Night session for a skimpy group of embassy staff, media, and low-level Canada-watchers in Washington (all Canada-watchers are low-level in Washington). Surprise, surprise, the Canadian budget is not seen as a big deal here at the centre of the universe. That is, until they learn of the latest "anti-American" measures. They'll pay attention to us then and the howling and recriminations will begin.

July 1, 1982 Washington, unlike Ottawa, is not much of a town for National Days. As far as I know, my predecessors never bothered with a July 1 celebration. But this year Pat Gossage came up with an idea. He prodded me into holding a reception on the empty site of our new embassy on Pennsylvania Avenue, hoping to attract congressional staffers who work almost across the street. We served hot dogs to a crowd of guests. Among a throng of Canadians, I didn't notice any staffers and only a few stragglers from the administration. I don't see how this sort of thing advances our national interests – feeding hot dogs to Canadians.

---

[1] (b. 1916) American business executive. Secretary of Defense 1961–1968; President of the World Bank 1968–1981.

[2] (1930–1999) Editorial Page Editor of the *Washington Post* 1979–1999 and a highly regarded syndicated columnist appearing in the *Washington Post* and *Newsweek*.

[3] (1935–2004) U.S. Ambassador to Yugoslavia from 1989 to the country's dissolution in 1992.

[4] (1920–1997) A prominent Washington hostess who was married to Randolph Churchill (son of Sir Winston Churchill) 1939–1946. U.S. Ambassador to France 1993–1997.

July 4, 1982 I'm spending a lot of my time discussing strategies for dealing with the controversial Siberian gas pipeline, today's big issue. The Reaganites have gone out on a precipitous limb in trying to block the participation in the pipeline not only of U.S. companies but foreign subsidiaries as well. The Americans just love extraterritorial laws. They must rule the world. What they do, so must everyone else.

July 6, 1982 I completed my twenty-six-page masterpiece to MacGuigan, Pitfield, and the department on the growing mess in Canada-U.S. relations.

I analyzed what is happening in Congress, the sweeping protectionist attitude, the bills that could damage Canada on uranium, trucking, telecommunications, and so on. Only the White House has any clout in Congress, and this is why we have to keep on good terms with the presidency. I conveyed a picture of the revolutionary changes in Congress since Watergate, in particular the collapse of the seniority system and the weakening of party discipline. And I put forward about a dozen proposals to improve things. I threw out every idea imaginable.

But only a willingness by Trudeau to be more sensitive to the concerns of the Reagan administration can change things at this point. That's not going to happen. Trudeau's blown his relationship with Reagan, and it's dangerous times for us.

July 7, 1982 Mad day at the embassy. In the morning I was about to see Jim Buckley at State to deliver a note protesting the U.S. pipeline decision as being extraterritorial.

At 10:30 – a half-hour before my appointment with Buckley – I got the content of the note from Ottawa. Kinsman said it was too tough, far too tough. But MacGuigan, he said, thought it was too weak, so I shouldn't try to change it.

I read it and thought it a disaster. Its tone was not acceptable; in fact, it was insulting. I grabbed the telephone and thankfully reached MacGuigan in Ottawa at once. "The note is too strong," I say. "It's too weak," he replies. "I'll stake my reputation on my opinion that it's offensive," I say. "Let me make a few changes and send you the revision at lunch. I can give the revised version to Eagleburger this afternoon." MacGuigan says, "I'm doubtful, but I won't go against you."

In the afternoon Kinsman comes down to my office and says, "You are not going to like this one bit. The tough note you received this morning from Ottawa was not authorized. It's a damn good thing you stopped it. MacGuigan never saw it, let alone approved it."

The department instructed us to deliver the wrong note. We could have had a disaster on our hands.

So, thinks I, ambassadors and their intuition do have some function in life. I earned my salary today.

Later, I delivered the revised note to Eagleburger. We talked for a few minutes tête-à-tête after the meeting was over and his people were out the door. I told him Canada-U.S. relations are going to the dogs. Something must be done. I suggested we have lunch as soon as possible and put our heads together. He said, "Yes, as soon as this crisis is over." "Sure," I said, "but you're always in a crisis."

On the way out, Eagleburger was very critical of Reagan's foreign policy. "These people are blind," he confided. I mumbled something. "Come on, Allan, you know I'm right, don't you?" I nodded, sort of. I can't imagine a Canadian official being so indiscreet or scornful of his government's policies. That's one of the merits of the U.S. system: it produces strong and independent-minded personalities.

July 8, 1982 A fine, sunny day for the poor little Canadian ambassador and his wife. There is a big article on Sondra and me in the *New York Times*, very flattering, with a large oval photograph in which we appear to be lounging in bath chairs on a Mediterranean luxury cruise. What a headline: "Not Your Usual Ambassadorial Pair." Sondra made page 1 – the Quotation of the Day. "For some reason, a glaze passes over people's faces when you say Canada. Maybe we should invade South Dakota or something."

One wag said to me today that if she'd said "North Dakota," the line wouldn't have been half as good.

The author, Lynn Rossellini, really captured Sondra's style. For example, "When we came to the residence, we bought from the former Ambassador a stock of liquor, including a lot of bourbon, Jack Daniels, something like that, high-class bourbon. Nobody has asked for bourbon yet. If you would like a bourbon, I would be very happy to give it to you."

July 9, 1982 Through Sondra's connections, the French Smiths invited us to dinner *à six* with Ed Meese and his wife, Ursula, at the Jefferson Hotel, where the French Smiths live. I couldn't believe my good fortune, because I was aching to get at someone very close to Reagan to complain about Jesse

Helms's[1] outrageous invitation to René Lévesque[2] to address the senator's prestigious "Wednesday Club" and the Republican Steering Committee. Well, I couldn't have got any closer to the centre of power. During dinner, when Meese asked me about separatism in Canada, I unloaded. I told him I had it on excellent authority (Michael Killian of the *Chicago Tribune* told me) that Helms invited Lévesque to visit the Congress in order to get at Trudeau.

Meese and French Smith expressed great surprise. They kept saying things like "Jesse is a great guy, but sometimes he does funny things." "Very funny," I replied. But Meese said emphatically that he would ensure no one from the administration would be at the lunch. Big deal, I thought.

At the end of dinner, Meese also said he would have a word with Helms. I was pleased, although I doubt it will help. Both Meese and French Smith showed a remarkable (but unsurprising) lack of knowledge about Canada. French Smith did not even seem aware that Lévesque wanted Quebec's independence. Although Meese doesn't know beans about Canada, his face lit up when we talked about the RCMP. I must get him up to Ottawa for an event with the Mounties.

It was a privileged evening for us – dinner with the two cabinet secretaries closest to the president. Sondra and Jean French Smith have struck a rare rapport.

My colleague Peter Roberts wrote that "ambassadors are in the eighth or ninth ring out from the Sun King." We have penetrated the first circle.

July 12, 1982 "The Gotliebs: Popular and Unusual Diplomats." Headline in the *Cincinnati Enquirer*. The *New York Times* piece on us continues to be reprinted. This stuff is intoxicating. And addictive. What goes up comes down.

July 14, 1982 Bastille Day. René Lévesque visits Washington. And a black day for Canada.

Jesse Helms got about fifteen senators to come out to the lunch. Worse, his staffers made appalling comments to us about how Helms was right to invite Lévesque because Helms is a champion of ethnic minorities everywhere. It's absolutely disgusting. Naturally, no one from the embassy was

[1] (b. 1921) Republican Senator from North Carolina 1973–2003; Chairman of the Senate Foreign Relations Committee 1995–2001.

[2] (1922–1987) Founder of the Parti Québécois; Premier of Quebec 1976–1985.

invited to attend, nor were we officially informed of the proceedings by anyone in Congress.

According to reports, Helms's speech introducing Lévesque on the floor of the Senate could have been written by Charles de Gaulle himself. He mentioned the word *Canada* only once. Lévesque, he said, is an advocate of private enterprise and wants American investors to enlarge the private sector in Quebec! Then Helms blathered on about uniting the American people and the people of Quebec. Unbelievable! So by implication Helms contrasts Lévesque's warm and cuddly policies with the restrictive, nationalistic ones of Trudeau. Apparently, what Helms told Michael Killian of the *Chicago Tribune* is true: he is intent on getting even with "bastards" Trudeau, Mitterrand, and Schmidt.

After the *National Review* attack on Trudeau, the Jerry Falwell[1] attack on him, and now the Helms shenanigans, I'm beginning to believe in right-wing conspiracies.

July 16, 1982 On our way to visit the Krafts at their beach house outside East Hampton, I bumped into Bill Safire at the airport. It was not a pleasant exchange. He wasted no time talking about the summit: "Your guy really got his teeth into Reagan." I replied, "Oh shit, that's all exaggerated. Trudeau was just making a few of his usual points in the usual way. There was no big problem. Anyway, everyone was after your boy."

Safire retorted, "Come off it. I've seen the minutes of the Versailles meeting. The White House guys showed them to me. Your man went after Reagan in an aggressive way."

Showed him the minutes? Either he's the biggest bluffer or some people in the White House are mischief-makers and rogues.

Stretching out on the sandy beach with Joe, I jumped up every two minutes to shake hands with a famous person.

July 17, 1982 The Krafts had a dinner party, in our honour, I guess. They are splendid but not relaxing hosts. Sondra is a bigger wreck than I am. At dinner (so-called small, intimate) there was Felix Rohatyn[2] of Lazard

---

[1] (b. 1933) Fundamentalist Baptist pastor, televangelist, and conservative activist from the United States.

[2] (b. 1928) American businessman and investment banker. Chairman of the Municipal Assistance Corporation of the City of New York 1975–1993; U.S. Ambassador to France 1997–2000.

Freres and his wife, Liz, plus a Rothschild woman (French, genuine), the head of an international PR firm, and so on. Felix had just returned from Paris, where he lunched with Mitterrand (arranged by Joe). Incongruously, we spent most of the time talking about French foreign policy. Not my idea of a day in the country.

July 20, 1982 I'm walking down the street in East Hampton, and I bump into a Palm Beach face. He entertained us once, having been described to me (wrongly) as the seventh richest man in the United States. He says, "Trudeau sure isn't popular here, at least as far as the Jews are concerned!"

I thought he was talking about our energy and investment policies (Jews as investors), so I rose to the occasion, cursed my fate, and defended. "FIRA's not so bad; the NEP is not nationalization." He looked at me like I'm crazy. Only after I walked away did I realize that he was talking about Trudeau's criticism of the Israeli attack on Lebanon. The NEP and FIRA are insidious diseases that have entered my brain and made me feverish.

July 22, 1982 MacGuigan sent me a message endorsing my proposals for ameliorating our relations with the United States. He specifically approved all my basic suggestions: using more public diplomacy, placing more emphasis on media relations, encouraging U.S. business with interests in Canada to exert influence in our favour, being willing to retaliate to show Americans that toughness can work two ways, hiring more lobbyists and lawyers on some issues, cleaning up FIRA, and so on. I don't think I have ever worked with a minister who has been so supportive. But unless Trudeau is willing to modify our energy and investment policies, the road to better relations won't be travelled in his time.

July 24, 1982 We fed Count Grafstein,[1] wife, and son, and talked about a troublesome subject: why Trudeau seems so anti-Israel.

We began by conceding that he is definitely not anti-Semitic, and I emphasized my belief that he is colour blind. I think Trudeau's anti-Israel feelings emerged as he evolved from *realpolitik* to *tiers-mondisme*. They were, I said to Grafstein, given a giant boost by his antipathy to Menachem Begin.[2] Curiously, Trudeau at first liked and admired Begin, particularly his

---

[1] Jerahmiel Grafstein (b. 1935) Liberal Senator from Ontario 1984 to present.

[2] (1913–1992) Prime Minister of Israel 1977–1983. A member of the Likud Party.

tough stance on terrorists. That was the impression I got personally from Trudeau. After all, Trudeau heroically led the cabinet in banning the PLO from coming to Toronto for a UN conference on crime some five years ago (on the grounds that it was a terrorist organization). Trudeau told me that Begin wrote personal letters to him longhand.

So when Begin came to Ottawa in November 1979, Trudeau thought he was a gutsy, courageous man. Trudeau believed he got Begin's word that he would keep Jerusalem out of the forthcoming federal election. Of course, this proved not to be the case. Joe Clark[1] made his famous commitment, egged on by Begin and his advance team, and the rest is history (Canadian). When he returned as prime minister a year later, Trudeau felt double-crossed and refused for a long time to meet with any Canadian Jewish leaders.

With Trudeau there is no looking back – he has resented Israel ever since. Joe's Jerusalem caper resonates until this day.

July 27, 1982 I called on Senator Barry Goldwater[2] to try to talk him out of his cable bill. I'd rather have talked to him about his place in history, but that would have been an indulgence. His retaliatory bill would zap Canada by imposing on us the same foreign ownership rule we impose on the Americans. The nerve. I arrived to be greeted by television cameras. The point, big surprise, is that it's show business. Barry Goldwater needs to be seen on the tube telling the Canadians to stop screwing around with American investors. Diplomacy as a photo op.

I chose to take the offensive. I said to Goldwater, "Look here, Senator, you can't do unto us what we did unto you." "Why not?" he asked. "You have a huge balance in your favour in this sector," I told him. "We're open and you're closed. Tit for tat is dangerous because with your surplus, you have more to lose than us."

He didn't buy it. No doubt he has a constituent who fears losing out to Rogers in some cable-franchise war.

July 30, 1982 Dinner at the Lion d'Or with Dick Darman and his wife, Kathleen. We managed to get them to dinner alone. Surprisingly, Darman

[1] (b. 1939) Prime Minister of Canada 1979–1980; Secretary of State for External Affairs 1984–1991.

[2] (1909–1998) Republican Senator from Arizona 1953–1965 and 1969–1987; Republican Party presidential candidate in 1964.

has shown great interest in Canada-U.S. affairs. This is my third breakthrough with the White House (Deaver first, then Meese).

Darman got the message across to me straight off that his role was to get to Reagan the pragmatist before other advisers got to Reagan the ideologue. He told me not to be overly worried about the poor Reagan-Trudeau relationship. After all, he observed, Reagan is a secure man. The president was not really upset by the fact that Trudeau said he was an imbecile.

I couldn't believe my ears. I held my breath for a moment. "That's impossible," I said. "Trudeau would never say a thing like that. It would be totally out of character – he is respectful of fellow leaders." Darman looked mildly surprised. He then went on to make the obvious point that the devoted aides surrounding Reagan got a lot more upset by criticism of the president than the boss himself did.

At the end of dinner (best food in town) he suggested I call on him next week in the White House and give him a complete list of irritants on both sides of the border. He is convinced, he said, that some of our difficulties can be ameliorated. Darman, of course, is not someone, anyone. He is the most skilful manipulator in the White House.

As we drove home, Sondra asked, "Do you really think Trudeau would be indiscreet enough to call Reagan an imbecile?" "Never," I replied. "He may think it, but he wouldn't say it."

July 31, 1982 I learned from a source in External that at a private dinner in Ottawa two nights ago, Helmut Schmidt gave Trudeau some very negative American impressions of Canada that he had gleaned at the Bohemian Grove in California. He found American businessmen uneasy about Canada. There was a pervasive sense of uncertainty about us. He heard concerns about nationalization, and he sensed pessimism about our economic future. At the dinner with Schmidt, Trudeau, it seems, entered into a spirited defence of his policies. That would be expected from Trudeau, because he never admits to being wrong. But I'm glad Schmidt spoke to him, because of all leaders, Trudeau respects him the most. He would be unlikely to dismiss his report. In 1978, at the Bonn Summit, he talked Trudeau into an austerity program.

The two men have something in common: both are pariahs in the White House.

August 1, 1982 I sent MacGuigan a personal and confidential letter. I described in detail Darman's observations at our dinner at the Lion d'Or about Trudeau and our relations. I can't believe I've managed to open up these channels into the White House. With Deaver and Darman, two of the innermost four, I've managed to open up key windows into the president's thinking and attitudes. My letter allowed me to get down on paper insights I would never in a millennium get from the functionaries at State.

Much trumpet-blowing on Darman's part, but he did give me some ideas that I might be able to convert into a plan of action to break down the gulf between Reagan and Trudeau. His comments on trilateralism provided the most useful insight into the Reagan mind as it affects Canada. "Trilateralism," Darman said, "call it the trilateral accord, or relationship, or summit, or whatever, is deeply embedded in Reagan's thinking." "It is," he added, "close to the heart of some of his principal aides (including myself)." Trilateralism was the one and probably only route to any kind of relationship with Reagan, as he deeply believes in the idea of the separateness – the separate destiny – of North America. At Camp David meetings of the president and his top advisers last February, it had been unanimously agreed that trilateralism should be given a top billing in the president's foreign policy, but for unexplained reasons it slipped off the agenda.

Darman intimated it was thought here that Trudeau had cooled to the idea of a trilateral summit, and this may have been the reason why there was no follow-through in Washington. Even more important is that State is opposed to trilateralism in any and all of its forms, not just incidentally but inherently and structurally. "For them, it has no place or priority in the foreign-policy agenda. They are completely wrong."

Darman explained why there was no point in our counting on State to be helpful. As long as State treated Canada as an appendage of Western Europe, it would misconstrue the true nature of the relationship; it would perceive us as marginal to the main East-West and West-West trends in the world. State would not play a more dynamic role vis-à-vis Canada until it changed its whole philosophy towards North America or, more particularly, the trilateral concept. It should create a North American bureau. Canada would get far more attention if it did.

I told Darman I was well placed to discuss Trudeau's personal thinking on trilateralism. The idea of a trilateral summit originated with Trudeau, I said. I admitted there was no enthusiasm for the idea at the bureaucratic level in External Affairs Canada. As the French say, it went against the grain, *à rebours*. But I thought Trudeau was personally intrigued by the notion of trilateral summits to discuss common issues, such as immigration, crime and law enforcement, environment and pollution. The reason Trudeau hadn't canvassed the idea of a trilateral meeting recently was because of the anomalous position of President Portillo[1] (his term expires soon). This has virtually excluded a get-together during 1982. So don't cool off the idea of trilateralism, I emphasized, because you think Trudeau is negative. He's not.

August 2, 1982 I spoke to MacGuigan in Ottawa about the fact that Trudeau seemed to be planning to turn down the long-standing invitation from the B'nai B'rith to be the principal speaker at their world conference in Toronto this autumn, the first ever held outside the United States. MacGuigan did not know of this but thought it just as well, since Trudeau was in a terrible anti-Israel mood. In cabinet the other day, he was accusing the Israelis of genocide in Lebanon. Jack Austin[2] was so upset, Mark said, that he was thinking of resigning from the cabinet.

It's a messy situation up there – Toronto versus Montreal, English versus French, now maybe Jew versus Gentile. Trudeau seems obsessed by the whole Middle East business and on an anti-Israel binge.

MacGuigan said he was calling a press conference today to announce what he was going to do at his first meeting with Shultz[3] tomorrow in Washington. I told him this was unwise from almost every standpoint. He replied, "Well, Dick MacDonald, my new press adviser, says I've got to make it clear before I go down there that I'm my own man. No more of this 'Al's pal.' I've got to change my image."

I called on Howard Baker[4] in the afternoon, the Senate majority leader and probably the second or third most powerful person in the capital. He lives up to his reputation as the most decent man in Washington politics, the natural leader of a small band of sane and balanced denizens of the Hill.

August 3, 1982 MacGuigan's first meeting with George Shultz. The political context for today's encounter is set by a front-page story in the

---

[1] José Lopez Portillo y Pacheco (1920–2004) President of Mexico 1976–1982.

[2] (b. 1932) Minister of State 1981–1982; Minister of State for Social Development 1982–1984; Leader of the Government in the Senate 2003–2006.

[3] George Shultz (b. 1920) Secretary of Labor 1969–1970; Director of the Office of Management and Budget 1970–1972; Secretary of the Treasury 1972–1974; Secretary of State 1982–1989.

[4] (b. 1925) Republican Senator from Tennessee 1967–1985; Senate Minority Leader 1977–1981; Senate Majority Leader 1981–1985; Chief of Staff to Ronald Reagan 1987–1988.

Washington Post. Front-page story in the *Post*? That alone speaks volumes about how the relationship is being perceived. The great non-story is becoming a story. The headline was to the point: "U.S.-Canadian Relations Worsen Seriously on Range of Issues." Picture of Trudeau looking tough above the caption ". . . Canada 'economically dominated.'" Reference to Bill Brock calling Canada "a developing country."

Shultz was impressive. In that Buddha-like pose he strikes, with the impression of weight he casts, his presence is strongly felt. I sense him to be a sort of dominant being. He seems, by his bearing, conscious that many of his friends in power in other Western countries are looking to him to be the voice of sanity amidst the cackle and confusion of the ideologues. Throughout the meeting Shultz said little, listened well, communicated sympathy and interest, and conveyed a strong impression of caring about the state of the relationship. I thought he lacked the flair, sense of wickedness, and electrical charge that radiated from Haig, but I also felt that here was a more serious person.

There were the usual officials present – but also one unseen person, John Turner. The first words to roll off MacGuigan's lips were "John Turner is a great admirer of yours." "I am of him," Shultz replied.

I fear MacGuigan may have come on too sharply at his press conference at the chancery after the meeting. When we discussed the tone he should adopt with the (largely Canadian) group of reporters, I suggested he not gloss over issues – that the media were too well informed for that, wouldn't believe him, and would think he was pulling his punches with Shultz as he allegedly did with Haig. But unfortunately, the theme of confrontation emerged more starkly and dramatically than he intended.

August 4, 1982 John Turner telephoned to give me his take on Shultz. "Understands Canada's problems and priorities," he said. "Knows our business community. Knows as much about Canada as any Canadian cabinet minister." According to Turner, Shultz "thinks our present government is an aberration." Turner added, "Shultz is a great friend of mine. One of the most substantial men I've met in my life. And I was part of a group that wanted to make him president."

August 5, 1982 I called on Darman at 5:30 p.m. in his office in the West Wing of the White House. We met alone. I went with a single piece of paper listing all the complaints that each country had against the other, the Canadian grievances in one column, the U.S. ones in another.

We focused on each item and went on for over an hour. This is the first time I've been able to get someone, anyone, on the domestic side to focus on the actual issues. Darman is the most skilful player in the White House, working with his alter ego Jim Baker.[1] We'll see what he can do. I'm excited. More than that – exhilarated. I've got a real interlocutor inside the skunk-works.

I gave him a copy of the list. I dream that it will circulate far and wide, up and down in the White House and the administration.

August 6, 1982 We attended a farewell reception for Count Roland de Kergolay, the European Economic Community's top man in Washington. Sondra has got to know the countess and, in a deft move, has arranged for us to hire her butler and senior servant at the Residence. She is a tiny Philippine woman named Teodora, very dynamic. We need her badly to replace Rito, who is overwhelmed. The demands of the Residence (our demands) have being growing furiously, and we are barely keeping up with ourselves.

August 7, 1982 I keep thinking about what Darman said to me the other day as I was leaving his office: "You know, for us in the White House, there is good news and bad news. The bad news is that Reagan really can't say no to the Canadians. The good news is you guys are too stupid to realize it." The sad reality is he's right.

August 8, 1982 Chatted recently with Rick Burt, now assistant secretary of state for Europe and Canada, former defence correspondent for the *New York Times*, and chief of the politico-military bureau at State. He is committed, he says, to managing things better in his new empire. He hinted strongly that I should deal with him and not Eagleburger. Shultz, he says, is hands on and will deal directly with the assistant secretaries. Burt seems to be a very effective sort of guy. But of course, I'm not going to stop dealing with Eagleburger. Also, there are rumours that Burt is headed for the chop. He is said to have been too close to Haig and a "leaker."

---

[1] (b. 1930) Chief of Staff to President Ronald Reagan 1981–1985; Secretary of the Treasury 1985–1988; Secretary of State 1989–1992.

Gotlieb: "I'm happy to deal with you, but are you for the chop?"
Burt: "What have you heard?"
A typical Washington conversation. And so it goes.

August 9, 1982 In Campobello to attend a seminar on the state of Canada-U.S. relations. I spoke in favour of more openness about our relationship. This didn't go down well with the State Department people. One of them, the number two at the U.S. embassy in Ottawa, warned against "a more public confrontational way of managing our relationship in high-profile diplomacy." Zap. Translation: the United States doesn't like to be criticized. Therefore, stop criticizing us. What a joke. Paul Robinson, his boss, craps all over our policies almost every day of the week.

August 11, 1982 Newfoundland days. Brian Peckford[1] gave me a lunch yesterday. During our three-hour meeting, he pressed me hard on the U.S.-Argentia base in Newfoundland, and I promised I'll talk to the Americans about it personally. The Americans have a ninety-nine-year lease, and the Newfoundlanders want to use part of the land. I told him Americans are better than wilderness.

Tonight I dined with John and Jane Crosbie at their summer place on Hogan's Pond. He has the distinction of being the only Conservative who has any time for me. Generically, they hate my guts.

"Peckford thought well of you," he said. What a tom-tom network they seem to have here – word passes so fast.

August 18, 1982 On the plane to Ottawa, I read with pleasure my press clippings from the St. John's newspapers. I am a hero. According to the headlines, I'm going to get a better deal for Newfoundland on Argentia.

In Ottawa, Pitfield wanted to talk about Canada-U.S. relations. He asked me to see him in his office at 2:30 p.m. I absolutely hated myself as I sat in his waiting room until 4:00. Never since Creation has God made so unpunctual a man. The only appointments that matter in his mind are with Pierre the Great.

Finally, the big talk. Can we arrange a trilateral summit – Canada, the United States, Mexico? When I told him that we cannot do it this year because of the changeover in Mexico's leadership, Pitfield suddenly lost

[1] (b. 1942) PC Premier of Newfoundland 1979–1989.

interest. "We must have a bilateral summit, Reagan and Trudeau, this fall, before Trudeau goes to Europe." I was taken aback. I quickly surmised that the Keith Davey[1] and Tom Axworthys, the Jim Couttses and Mike Kirbys,[2] and other Liberal masterminds were writing in their little red survival book that Trudeau better be seen talking to Ronnie and getting along with him. And so I found Pitfield in a sort of pro-American mood. Was this to be 1976 all over again, when, thanks to the separatist victory in Quebec, cozying up to Uncle Sam was all the political rage among the Liberals?

I gave Pitfield the bad news: Reagan would not want to see Trudeau, would find excuses for not seeing him, unless it was a guaranteed good-news event. His handlers would insist on that. And how could it be a good-news event? Were we going to begin to back off on FIRA and the NEP (as I had recommended the night before the MacEachen budget)? Our conversation ended up, as it always does, at some ill-defined point in the air. "Trudeau wants to have lunch with you and a few others to discuss where we are going. There must be a paper." Always a paper.

August 19, 1982 At a lunch with the deputy ministers in Ottawa, I talked about U.S. trends. It was like giving them the news from Mars. "The United States is becoming more inward looking and protectionist. This is not an aberration, it's a long-term trend, based on far-reaching demographic and economic trends. The United States will adopt trade laws and policies that could hurt the rest of the world. The question is what will happen to Canada? Do we continue to rely exclusively on multilateral diplomacy? Are multilateral institutions going to prevent us from getting beat over the head? Should we begin to think of an 'exceptions' approach? Should we pursue the notion that we should be treated as an exception, because we are a special case, because of our North Americanness?" (This is how I slipped in a small dose of the trilateral idea.)

I told them I was tired of hearing how the United States wants "a strong and united Canada." "What horseballs! The United States wants a weak and

---

[1] (b. 1926) National Campaign Director of the Liberal Party of Canada in the 1960s; Liberal Senator 1966–1996.

[2] (b. 1941) Assistant Principal Secretary to Prime Minister Pierre Trudeau 1974–1976; Secretary to the Cabinet for Federal-Provincial Relations and Deputy Clerk of the Privy Council 1980–1983; Chairman of the Task Force on Atlantic Fisheries 1982–1984; Liberal Senator from Nova Scotia 1984 to present.

divided Canada. Wouldn't we, if we were Americans? If Canada happens to fall apart, more than a few Americans might think it's not such a tragedy, and they'll pick up a few of the choice pieces, like Alberta and Newfoundland, where the oil is."

No shock, it seems, at my statement about real U.S. attitudes to national unity. Consternation about my reference to an "exceptions policy," with its echoes of continentalism and free trade.

August 20, 1982 I returned from Ottawa to find awaiting me a message to call Secretary Shultz. After a few hours of effort, I managed to connect. "I'm calling you about a fellow countryman of yours. Hal Sonnenfeld told me Robert Ford knows more and thinks more about the Soviet Union than any other Westerner. I would like to meet him and talk to him. Also, I'd like to receive his views in writing, if he were willing to submit them. What does he see as the main trends in the U.S.S.R., internally? How does he see Soviet policy evolving towards Europe, the United States? What policies does he think we Americans should follow? Can you make contact with him and make the arrangements?" I told Shultz, "Yes, absolutely. I will get hold of him in his château in Vichy, where he's living in retirement. He's in a wheelchair, but I'm confident he will make a special trip to Washington."

Shultz is an unusual person. Not many foreign ministers, overwhelmed as they are by daily, hourly pressures would ask to conduct a seminar with a former foreign diplomat with no power or authority.

I wonder what Ottawa's reaction will be to this invitation. They clearly can't refuse to go along with it. After all, Ford is retired, although on contract (thanks to my beating the department over the head for a year to get it). Many in Ottawa don't like Ford's hardline views. But they are pygmies and jealous of him. They're also wrong about him. His assessments are hard-nosed, but they are profoundly realistic, and he does believe in co-existence. And he does believe, as he told me many times, in the necessity of treating the Soviets with civility and not threatening their legitimacy.

August 22, 1982 In an act of desperation, I telephoned Tom Axworthy in Ottawa about Trudeau and the B'nai B'rith affair. I told him the B'nai B'rith had been trying to get Trudeau to appear at their world conference in Toronto in October for some nine months. They could get absolutely no reply. Zilch. Then, when I was away, my secretary got a message from the department that the reply was negative. Plain no. When she relayed the information to the organization's executive, he was outraged. "There will be repercussions," he commented. I said to Axworthy, "failure to make even a brief appearance at such a huge gathering, Jewish grassroots as it is, strikes me as kind of insulting to the Jewish community. Can't Trudeau drop in for ten minutes, say a few positive words, and then disappear?"

Axworthy replied that he didn't think the matter was a serious political one, but he would speak to the prime minister tomorrow.

To be frank with myself, I don't really understand why I have been busting my ass over this B'nai B'rith invitation. I've never belonged to B'nai B'rith, even as a kid. Maybe I just don't like being ineffective.

August 23, 1982 In Knoxville, Tennessee, for the official opening of Canada Week at the Knoxville World's Fair, so-called, or Energy Exposition. I felt ashamed of our pavilion; it looked third-rate next to Australia's (which looked second-rate). A luncheon was held in my honour. I made a little speech. I wandered through the pavilions in the mucky, torrid southern air, looking at human specimens more than at the lifeless energy displays – robots and buttons and gizmos everywhere. Who could tell the difference? I attended the official Canadian flag-raising ceremony and opening. The flag was already raised. The Canadian entertainment was unspeakable. I wandered through a sea of unknown faces, repeating to myself, "You are the Canadian ambassador to the United States. Be polite. Be dignified. Smile. It's worthwhile."

August 25, 1982 I have now spent two days on the telephone trying to reach Tom Axworthy on another matter. I need to tell him that Scotty Reston of the *New York Times* wants to see and interview Trudeau this weekend. I am getting nowhere. "The prime minister is at the lake. . . . The prime minister has the Korean president visiting." This reaction after a shocking editorial on Canada in Reston's newspaper. More evidence of a political death wish?

Finally, I decided to try Pitfield. He said, "Agreed. I'll get you your appointment with Reston." There's authority for you. I called Reston to tell him and asked him to talk to Trudeau about Canada. "Don't spend all your time on the PLO." Reston replied, "I'm not going to talk about the PLO. The letters stand for 'perfectly lousy organization.' I want to talk about Canada, the U.S., the hemisphere. I'm getting to be an isolationist."

August 27, 1982 Saturday and no briefing prepared yet in External on the Reston interview. Everybody flipping. What should Trudeau say? One of the divisions has been instructed to prepare the briefing document. I shudder at the thought of what they might produce.

August 29, 1982 Trudeau's appointment with Reston is for 5:00 today. Briefing received from External at noon. Fowler[1] called to say it was a disaster. I said I know, the guy who drafted it called and read it to me, and I wept.

At 4:50 the prime minister calls me. "Allan, what do I say?" Although the White House doesn't like the *New York Times*, or Reston for that matter (too liberal), they'll see this column. What better opportunity to send a message to the White House and the administration?

So I take an absolutely unambivalent line with Trudeau. "Reston likes you and he likes Canada. He believes in the relationship. Take an upbeat line with him. It will be a new tack, try it. Say that relations aren't really as bad as the press makes out. In fact, the two governments are getting along pretty well, and things have improved recently. Reagan and the White House have been helpful (lay it on). Our joint problems are borne of the recession and the protectionist congressional mood." We then touch on the main outstanding issues. Finally, I say, "Talk about your idea of the trilateral summit. Reagan likes it." Trudeau says fine.

I press my luck. "Joe Kraft wants to interview you at the annual IMF meeting in Toronto next week. He admires you." Trudeau: "I like Joe Kraft."

August 31, 1982 The Reston interview was a marvel. Trudeau gave an upbeat evaluation and praised Reagan. He was positive about a trilateral summit and said relations are really okay. This is a man you can brief! What did I learn from this? What I always knew: the importance of being the last one to give Trudeau advice. Or nothing propinques like . . .

I continue my effort at public diplomacy – a C-Span interview yesterday and lunch with the highly influential Bill Safire today at the Maison Blanche. Big surprise: Safire was not interested in Canada. His eyes glazed

[1] Robert Fowler (b. 1944) Executive Assistant to the Undersecretary of State for External Affairs 1978–1980; Assistant Secretary to the Cabinet for Foreign and Defence Policy 1980–1986; Deputy Minister of National Defence 1989–1995; Canadian Ambassador to the United Nations 1995–2000 and to Italy 2000–2006.

over. Canadian potatoes are too small for him? I tried flattery. I remarked, correctly, that he was the first important U.S. journalist to emphasize the potential significance for the United States of Quebec's separation from Canada. "How come," I asked, "now that the referendum is lost and the separatist danger is behind us, you can't point that out or emphasize the importance to the U.S. of stability on its northern borders?"

Silence. Canada breaks up – news. Canada doesn't break up – no news. It was a no-news lunch.

September 3, 1982 When I travel, I hear more complaints about FIRA than anything else about Canada, even the NEP. Businessmen in particular object to its lack of transparency. Stuff seems to go into Herb Gray's[1] drawer and never come out, never any explanation. Yesterday he announced important new changes, but we got no advance communication. I sent a sharp letter of criticism to the powers that be in Ottawa, and today I got a long letter of explanation, apology, justification. Advance notice, I was informed by the head of the agency, was not possible or appropriate. But as for lack of simultaneous communication, "it was a deplorable, if not 'inconceivable' omission."

Not, I suppose, surprising that the least transparent of agencies should send me the least transparent of explanations.

September 6, 1982 Bob Fowler in the PCO called to say everyone is mad as hell at me because I committed Trudeau to see Joe Kraft in Toronto today. A year ago – six months even – I would never have dreamed of how important journalists are in Washington. My views were shaped by twenty years in Ottawa dealing with the semi-educated press corps there. In Washington, journalists, being part of the elite, profoundly affect the way the educated class sees the political players. There are few journalists more influential than Reston and Kraft. They are insiders' insiders and dine with the great. Though both are the old-style print-media men, focusing on analysis, evaluation, interview, and the like, they influence the broader media community, especially in this town, where the tube follows the print.

---

[1] (b. 1931) Canada's first Jewish cabinet minister (1969). Minister of Industry, Trade, and Commerce 1980–1982; President of the Treasury Board 1982–1984; Solicitor General of Canada 1993–1997; Deputy Prime Minister of Canada 1997–2002.

September 8, 1982 The Kraft interview was as good as Reston's. I am amazed. Trudeau repeated the same positive remarks about Canada-U.S. relations that he made to Reston. And then he made them a third time, to Toronto journalist Betty Kennedy.[1] I'm going to take excerpts of all three interviews and send them to Darman, Deaver, and Shultz.

September 9, 1982 Robert Ford is in town to see George Shultz at his request. Shultz received him and myself in his boardroom on the top floor of State, accompanied by Eagleburger, Stoessel, and Wolfowitz,[2] head of policy and planning at State. Ford in a wheelchair radiates more dignity and authority than any Hollywood actor could do in his prime. He led the group through the highlights of his paper, and then Shultz and the others posed questions for an hour. I find it most impressive that Shultz should ask Ford to come here to brief him, receive him so quickly, and then organize a seminar around him involving his top experts. Not, definitely not, something a Canadian foreign minister would do, but Trudeau would.

Ford's message: "Don't humiliate the Soviet Union, and don't expect rapid change. The period ahead will be dangerous. Push arms control and disarmament, because the U.S.S.R. needs it – they're in bad economic shape." For sure not the message Ronald Reagan would want to hear but definitely in line with Shultz's thinking.

As the meeting ended, I said to Shultz, "I bring greetings from Allan MacEachen, our newly appointed foreign minister." (I lied; I hadn't had any such request from MacEachen.) Shultz had not heard of his appointment. He was extremely pleased at the news – positively happy. They went to MIT together, he told me, and then he invited me into his office alone. "Let's phone Allan now," he said. "It will be a big surprise." "Great idea," I said, "he'll be delighted. He was just sworn in at Government House a few hours ago, so we can reach him in Ottawa."

While waiting for Shultz's assistant to place the call, I handed Shultz three golden nuggets from Trudeau's recent interviews with Reston and Kraft. He looked at them for a few minutes and said, "They are remarkable.

---

[1] (b. 1926) Canadian broadcaster, journalist, and author. Panelist on the CBC Television show *Front Page Challenge* 1962–1995.

[2] Paul Wolfowitz (b. 1943) Director of State Policy Planning 1981–1982; Undersecretary of Defense for Policy 1989–1993; Deputy Secretary of Defense 2001–2005. Currently President of the World Bank.

They certainly do not reflect the general view of our relations. I will make sure the president sees them." Bingo.

Shultz's secretary came in. "I can't reach Mr. MacEachen." A slightly befuddled goodbye to Shultz, and I went back to the office to try to find out why the hell MacEachen couldn't (wouldn't) answer the phone.

September 10, 1982 I received a courtesy call from Sir Oliver Wright,[1] the new British ambassador, who replaces (Sir) Nicko Henderson. Very tall, very English, holds his head up high, shirts sensational – too much so. Turned down an appointment as head of a Cambridge college to accept Thatcher's invitation to be ambassador here. Every British ambassador who comes to Washington is a knight. Not the Canadian way, but would that it were. I also envy the British ambassador because the Reaganauts adore Thatcher, and the Georgetown snobs adore the English. But Wright won't find it easy to do what Henderson did: become the darling of Kay Graham, Evangeline Bruce, Polly Fritchey, and all the other Georgetown ladies who lunch. Henderson was easily the smartest of my colleagues. The longer I'm in Washington, the more I recognize the truth of his observation when I first called on him: "Gotlieb, anyone who tells you that he knows where a particular decision was made in Washington is either a liar or a fool."

After nine months in Washington, I can say, "That's all ye know on earth and all ye need to know."

September 13, 1982 MacEachen finally telephoned Shultz. As far as I am aware, the reason MacEachen didn't call Shultz back on Friday was that he simply didn't feel like calling him on Friday. Nor on Saturday or Sunday. The old mysterious bachelor, elusive as ever.

September 14, 1982 I keep up my contact with Sol Linowitz. A Democrat, he is out of office but is enormously influential. We don't breed this type in Canada. Increasingly, I seek his insights into the top players, such as Shultz and Weinberger. He seems to talk to them almost every day. He has become my personal guide to the perils of Washington. And he is no mean anecdotalist. At breakfast recently he told me of a gathering of Jewish leaders

---

[1] (b. 1921) British Ambassador to the United States 1982–1986.

dealing with the impact of the Lebanese wars on the Jewish community. He mentioned Max Fisher,[1] whom I had met earlier this year in Palm Beach. "Is that the man who is called or calls himself the King of the Jews?" I asked. "The same," he said. "Once," Linowitz recounted, "when I was with Begin on assignment from Jimmy Carter, Max Fisher was waiting to see Begin. Begin said to me, 'What do you think of Fisher?' I said, 'I'll tell you later.' Begin replied, 'I agree with you.'"

September 17, 1982 Called, with Kinsman, on Gary Hart,[2] star senator from Colorado. My trendy colleague has been excited by the anticipation of this call for some time. Hart is seen, people tell me, as a new kind of liberal, draftsman of a new American dream. I was more impressed by him than I expected. He engaged us in unhurried discussion and wanted to talk issues, not platitudes. An unusual occurrence when visiting a denizen of the Hill.

September 20, 1982 Attended a dinner at the Watergate tonight to hear several senators and congressmen speak on the mood of Congress. If they accurately reflect the mood of that body, the Congress is in deep trouble, as is the United States, as is Canada, and probably the whole world. The anti-foreign attitude was palpable and made me very uncomfortable. I was particularly surprised to hear the former chairman of the Senate Foreign Relations Committee, Charles Percy, making comments that were very hard on the Japanese. With the benefit of his powerful voice, using the most modulated tones and well-chosen words, the distinguished Senator Foghorn from Illinois managed to scare the hell out of half the audience. As the recession deepens, the obsession with Japan grows and the United States seems to fall more deeply into the hands of the protectionist monster. No one calls the monster by that name. Of course, it's all about "playing fair." It is disguised in a cloak of "reciprocity," "equity," and the "level playing field," but the disguise hides nothing.

---

[1] (1908–2005) Prominent realtor, businessman, philanthropist, and leader in the Detroit Jewish community and national Jewish scene. Served as chairman of United Jewish Appeal (U.S.A.) and many other Jewish congregations.

[2] (b. 1936) Democratic Senator from Colorado 1975–1987. Was seen at the time as a strong Democratic candidate for the presidency.

September 23, 1982 One of my diplomatic colleagues said to me, "The first year at a post, you do everything, accept everything, and then you learn to say no. You become much more selective." For some reason, I'm still in the first phase. Three large receptions at the Residence, two diplomatic lunches, and a couple of nondescript dinners.

A few weeks ago, Sondra received a beautiful handwritten note from Jim Baker's wife, Susan, asking if we would host a dinner at the Residence for a charity she was sponsoring (youth, drugs, the usual) and attend the fund-raising ball afterwards at the Organization of American States. Thinking it diplomatically prudent to do so – given the source of the request – we agreed. I didn't even know the names of the crowd who ate at our table. When we went into the huge, magnificent OAS building to attend the ball, we were submerged in a vast throng of revellers. Through a stroke of luck, I managed to catch a faraway glimpse of the Bakers as they majestically descended a staircase. We waved strenuously. They waved back. Mission accomplished in twenty minutes. We exited at once.

Definitely phase one.

September 24, 1982 "The New Diplomacy," Elaine Dewar's[1] article in *City Woman*, is out. Dewar began her fawning ten-page tribute with a quote from *First Lady, Last Lady*, which Sondra published just before we came down here: "Why on earth would you want to become Ambassador? Give Washington to the Belknaps. Stephen and Moira can play bridge with the Congressmen and run after the Senators. That's what Ambassadors do. All prestige and no power. Let Moira give the tea parties and burst into tears when the Cabinet wives don't show up."

I can't believe Sondra wrote that. How uncannily prescient. How dismally accurate.

September 27, 1982 Yom Kippur. We attended Bill Safire's annual "Break the Fast" dinner in his large Chevy Chase house. It's for Jewish movers and shakers, Jewish being very loosely defined. The rule is, to be invited you have to be a Jew or have a Jewish spouse. A lot of people, including us, were walking around staring and whispering to one another, "I didn't know he was Jewish." Also comments on who was not there – the tell-tale sign of being a crypto-Jew. There is no shortage in Washington.

---

[1] Canadian journalist and author of non-fiction works.

Safire devoted his attention to the most politically important of his guests – working his sources – all the time, while ignoring the others.

September 30, 1982 I'm in Boston to address the first meeting of the Canada–New England Business Council. My message: Canada and the United States may be sliding backwards to beggar-thy-neighbour protectionist policies, reminiscent of the 1930s. I tell them there are or have been fifty or more bills before Congress this session that are protectionist or trade restrictive.

October 1, 1982 Had lunch with Kenneth Galbraith[1] at Lochober's, as guests of Tom Winship, the editor of the *Boston Globe*. Galbraith was talkative, so I asked him, "Is there going to be a recovery soon?" "No," he said, "there won't be a recovery at all, until we get rid of Reagan. His economic policies are disastrous." "What should Canada's policies be?" I asked. "Don't follow the U.S. leadership when it is wrong. Protect yourself as much as possible against U.S. economic policy. Lower interest rates, put on exchange controls. Insulate yourself." Enjoyable lunch, scary talk.

I won't tell Lalonde of Galbraith's views when he comes here next week. He'll tell Trudeau and then we'll be in the soup.

October 2, 1982 Trouble continues on the trade front. A congressional report from the Ways and Means Committee hits my desk. It's on "Fair Practices" (of course) in trade in automotive products. There were some extraordinary comments inside. Bill Brock said, "I don't see how the [Canada-U.S. automotive] agreement could survive the bill." Congressman Gibbons (Mr. Free Trade) stated, "Our U.S.-Canada relationship is probably at the worst level it has been in my service in Congress." And these are serious men.

Reagan is signing the law restricting transborder trucking. I told a conference on foreign investment in New York: "This is the first occasion that Congress has imposed a form of reciprocity in retaliation against another country's laws in trade or services. The U.S. runs a massive surplus in services. Will it use the threat of barriers to force regulatory change in other countries?" If so, "Canadians won't take it lying down."

---

[1] (1908–2006) Canadian-born economist. Served in the administrations of Franklin Roosevelt, Harry Truman, John F. Kennedy, and Lyndon Baines Johnson. Professor of Economics at Harvard 1949–1975; U.S. Ambassador to India 1961–1963.

October 3, 1982 Pitfield arrived on my doorstep. We talked for seven hours and I killed a Sunday. To my surprise, he told me the advice Trudeau was getting in the PCO was too anti-U.S., too anti-Israel, and he hinted that officials (and a certain official in particular) had too much influence on Trudeau in these areas. I told Pitfield that I warned Trudeau of this just before I left Washington. But I am sure Trudeau's views are pretty much his own and not simply those slipped over on him by advisers. Anyway, some advisers tell him what they believe he wants to hear.

Pitfield asked me how it feels to take a lesser job in the public service than the one I had previously occupied. Like wanting to bite, I said, but lacking teeth.

October 4, 1982 Old friend Marc Lalonde, tough guy, now minister of finance, arrived in Washington to do the rounds. Lunch at Treasury with Don Regan was desultory. On the bad economy, the staggering interest rates, and the like, Regan took a banal line. We must hold to the course. He gave nothing away. Then he bolted. Didn't even finish his meal. Had to go to the White House. To have good chemistry with this cold, unsympathetic man, one would have to be an alchemist.

October 5, 1982 I spoke to the Council on Foreign Relations, then met with the editorial board of the *Cleveland Plain Dealer*. Publisher-owner Thomas Vail opened with a punchy line: "Is Canada in an economic mess because Trudeau's a socialist, or is there some other reason?"

Vail mentioned John Turner's name reverentially several times. The much berated Canadian ambassador waited for his moment. Then he said, "Oh, John, yes, he telephoned me this morning here in Cleveland. Sends you his best regards. Great pal of mine. Oxford chum, you know."

The Turner network in the United States is remarkable. If I want some respect in Cleveland, all I have to do is pretend he is prime minister. He will be.

October 6, 1982 Back in the office, I read the umpteenth Canadian article on the new Trudeau ministerial lineup and the new Trudeau policy vis-à-vis the United States. Reston's interview is the bible of Ottawa's new spin. "Trudeau Goes Out of His Way to Woo Washington," says the page 1 headline in the *Globe and Mail*. According to the media, the "conservative" business side dominates in the battle in cabinet. MacEachen and

Lumley[1] triumph. The soft line wins. Trudeau is cozying up to American economic relations. Reference made to such Trudeau nuggets as "Reagan is a man who seems to have encapsulated the mind of the American people. . . . I have no quarrel with the U.S. administration. . . . Reagan is like Churchill and Roosevelt in articulating the concerns of the day. . . . Relations were worse during Nixon's time." Lalonde was moved out of Energy. Gray was relieved of FIRA.

Immodestly, I think to myself, maybe my personal letters, telegrams, and briefings have had some effect back home. Whether true or not, the Liberal scribes are rewriting the little red survival book. Perhaps they have some secret polling data. Perhaps the great Canadian unwashed think Trudeau is screwing up with the Yanks.

October 10, 1982 End of B'nai B'rith story. Ted Johnson in the PMO tells me it's dead in the water. Trudeau is convinced that if he goes, he'll get harpooned on Israel. I've learned my lesson. I should not stick my neck out on such inconsequential issues.

October 14, 1982 Day trip to Toronto and back to Washington for dinner in honour of the French Smiths. Spoke off the record to a group of about sixty chief executives put together by the Business Council on National Issues. I offered eight rules on what the private sector should do to promote its interests in the United States.

The Rules: (1) use your own eyes and ears; (2) get more involved in U.S. trade issues; (3) help promote a better image of our country – stop bad-mouthing Canada in the United States; (4) play a more direct role on the Hill – use lobbyists; (5) mobilize U.S. subsidiaries/parents; (6) mobilize/align with U.S. interests benefiting from the Canadian connection; (7) treat every issue as a micro-issue; and (8) adopt Canada Inc. stance abroad.

My remarks seemed to bewilder some of the group. They expect the government to hold their hands and look after them abroad as it does at home.

---

[1] Ed Lumley (b. 1934) Liberal Member of Parliament for Stormont-Dundas, Ontario, 1974–1984; Minister of State for Trade 1980–1982; Minister of Industry 1982–1983, of Regional Economic Expansion 1983–1984, and of Communications and Regional Industrial Expansion 1984.

October 15, 1982 Lunched with Hyman Bookbinder,[1] doyen of Washington lobbyists. He's been influencing Congress on behalf of the American Jewish Committee for a donkey's years. He's supposed to be the best in the business but, curiously, I don't think I learned anything new from him, which shows I must be an old hand already. Many Canadian Jews are in town to attend a Hebrew University dinner. We went. I'm definitely still in stage one.

October 16, 1982 Last night I got into a dogfight on television. On the weekly show *It's Your Business*, the moderator, Meryl Comer,[2] kicked off a panel involving me, Bill Brock, the American Chamber of Commerce president, and a couple of others. She referred to "Canada first" investment restrictions and our policy "to nationalize the oil and gas industry." I immediately assailed her for "a misinformed and inaccurate indictment of Canadian policies." The other panelists jumped in to support her. Brock declared the NEP to be "absolutely incredible," "nationalist," and "confiscatory." It was a brawl, the worst encounter of my assignment.

October 19, 1982 In Ottawa to attend a meeting between Trudeau and a group of top U.S. businessmen – some twenty-one of them – sponsored by the Niagara Institute. Sixteen corporate jets at the Ottawa airport. Big names here, including the chief executive officers of American Express, Union Carbide, Bechtel, Westinghouse, and top officers of six major oil companies.

Trudeau walked into the conference centre and said to me as he passed, "I see you like to stand under your flag." I looked behind me and saw that I was standing under a large American flag. Good joke?

The idea of the meeting was to have an encounter with Trudeau to discuss the state of Canada-U.S. affairs. The executives were to ask questions, unload, get off what's on their minds. Strictly off the record. I was nervous about this initiative – unnecessarily. Trudeau, though plainly tired, was at his best. He demonstrated, once again, that he becomes most intellectually vibrant and alive when he is criticized or under attack.

---

[1] (b. 1916) Washington representative of the American Jewish Committee during the 1980s.

[2] Talk show host, moderator, and producer. Vice-President for Communications Development at the U.S. Chamber of Commerce 1987–1997.

Asked to predict the state of Canadianization ten or twenty years from now, Trudeau said: "I'm not an economic nationalist. I'm anti-nationalist in many senses. It's not good being more independent and more poor. I'm always leery of economic nationalism. I believe in the international division of labour and the free movement of capital. I apologize for FIRA's slowness, but it's not unjustified to have protected sectors such as financial institutions. As for forest products, you pose the question will we Canadianize this sector somewhere down the line? We'd be damn fools if we did. We'd be buying up the past, not the future. That's the only guarantee you have. But I'm on record as having opposed the nationalization of hydro in Quebec. And worse politicians in Canada are on my wavelength."

As for Reagan: "He's a very capable communicator. He's a good politician. I respect his role in Canada-U.S. relations. Most presidents have been friends of Canada, Nixon above all. But Reagan is dead wrong when it comes to his obsession on East-West problems. I'm not sure Reagan is doing his thing against Russia for domestic political reasons or because he believes the Soviet empire is collapsing. I don't think he believes that, but if he does, I disagree, because the Russians can only be pushed so far."

Back to Canada-U.S. relations: "France, Great Britain, Canada don't want to be pushed around by U.S. extraterritorial law. Our problems are with your Congress. They're with the protectionists in Congress. Our fisheries treaty was defeated by two senators and they were supposed to be enlightened Democrats."

American liberals would be deeply shocked by Trudeau's admiration for Nixon, the man who called him an asshole. He sees Nixon through Russian, Chinese, and European eyes, not American ones. Détente with the U.S.S.R., arms control, relations with China: these achievements are what counts, not Watergate. He wants Reagan to act like Nixon and has often told me so.

October 21, 1982 Notwithstanding Trudeau's crack at me and my flag, I got a welcome message from Pitfield today. Trudeau and I are still on the same wavelength. The PM particularly wanted me to know, Pitfield wrote, that he not only read my paper on Canada-U.S. relations "with interest in its substance but also much appreciated your careful reasoning from well-explained premises to clear, simply stated conclusions." Trudeau is exceptional in my experience in that he not only reads but grades the papers that are sent to him.

October 22, 1982 I gave a briefing to the U.S. press in the old library of the embassy. About twenty attended, representing the *New York Times*, the *Washington Post*, the three networks, and MacNeil-Lehrer – in other words, the quality press. They are accompanying Shultz on his trip to Ottawa in a couple of days, mainly so they can talk to him about the U.S.S.R., the Middle East, and other big foreign-policy areas of interest.

There's been an avalanche of news in Canada these days about the relationship. The new cover of *Maclean's* has the words "Friends Again" emblazoned on it. The point of its account is that "Ottawa is desperately trying to rebuild its battered relationship with Washington." The American press is not yet familiar with this new line Ottawa is trying to spread about. It's a good message, but far from credible at this point. It's the policies we have to change, not just the media message. No doubt the new line is being welcomed by the authors of the Liberals' little red survival book.

October 23, 1982 Back in Washington after a harrowing journey. I was invited to be guest speaker at the annual national meeting of the English-Speaking Union in Montgomery, Alabama. Just as I was getting on a plane yesterday afternoon, I was summoned to the State Department for an urgent meeting of the seven summit ambassadors with Eagleburger (the Siberian pipeline again). So I missed my air connections in Atlanta, but I managed to charter a small plane in Birmingham (Tom Cossitt, please note), which got me to Montgomery in time to speak. Through marvellous heroics, I arrived just as the guests were sitting down. A huge crowd, men in black tie, women in elaborate cocktail dresses, in an immense, cavernous room. The host, very blue blueblood Kingman Brewster, former president of Yale and head of the ESU, slightly snockered, was appreciative of my stupendous logistical efforts. More than I can say about the audience, who, from my distant head-table vantage point, seemed to be more than slightly snockered. In fact, everybody seemed pretty damn drunk. I delivered my platitudes over a very audible hum, dropped dead in my hotel room at midnight, rose again at dawn to get to Birmingham, to get to Atlanta to catch a flight to Washington. I still don't have a clue what the ESU does or stands for.

October 24, 1982 I sat next to George Shultz at a dinner in his honour in Ottawa. No one ever accused him of being a lively conversationalist, except perhaps when sitting next to a beautiful young woman. He's given to lengthy periods of silence – rather like MacEachen. While sitting next to me and before he got up to talk, he pulled out and reviewed a wad of notes that were all written in his own hand. When I expressed surprise and approval, he told me he likes to prepare his own speeches when he can. Not true of any foreign minister I have worked for. During his remarks, which were banal in content but effective because he seemed so sincere, he referred jokingly to the working meeting that took place today, just after his arrival in Ottawa. "Allan MacEachen," he said, "really likes to work people hard." I was sitting opposite MacEachen, and when Shultz made this light-hearted jab, MacEachen's body tightened and his expression turned into a scowl. I suspect he felt the bureaucrats talked him into a meeting today against his will.

Given my direct lines to Trudeau and the fact that my career path has not previously crossed MacEachen's, I'm not sure what kind of relationship I will have with him. I'm nervous.

October 25, 1982 Day two of the Shultz visit, and MacEachen conducted it skilfully. There was even a breakthrough of sorts: our side had the idea that the two foreign ministers and their officials should meet more often. The rationale behind this is that periodic meetings would help elevate Canada a little higher in the State Department's Euro-dominated agenda. Shultz picked up on this with lightning speed, and out of the discussion emerged the idea of regularly scheduled foreign-minister meetings, once a quarter or so. Shultz grabbed a pen and piece of paper and drafted a one-page document outlining the terms of reference – a sort of communiqué endorsing the plan.

This could turn out to be important in addressing the phenomenon Darman spoke to me about – that Canada is in the wrong bureau in the State Department. If Shultz delivers and treats the meetings as important, this will increase the focus of the State Department bureaucracy on Canada-U.S. problems – and God knows there is room for that. But I do have some misgivings. The main thrust of my recommendations to Ottawa has been the absolute need to bring about greater White House involvement in our affairs. More specifically, we should be encouraging summitry.

However, the idea of summits has not proved to be a winner with External Affairs, for the obvious reason that they would enhance the role of the Prime Minister's and the Privy Council Office and thus threaten to further downgrade External. The quarterly meetings will help keep the files in External's hands. In the bureaucratic world, turf explains all.

MacEachen hosted a small working lunch for Shultz at the National Arts Centre. Trudeau was invited but arrived an hour late. He announced he had been flying a CF-18 and had been at the controls. He seemed intoxicated by the experience, barely acknowledging his lateness. He then proceeded to bring up some point with Shultz that the Greek president asked him to raise when he was here recently. Why should Trudeau do the Greek dirty work? This is our number one issue?

But it was better than what followed. Trudeau went on about how the Bonn NATO Summit was useless and how the Versailles Economic Summit was unprofitable. He said Reagan had spent two hours talking about the marvels of the Chilean social security system when the seven heads dined alone in Versailles. Shultz got predictably defensive, noting how remarkable the Chilean system actually was, and Trudeau responded that he wasn't criticizing Reagan, only Mitterrand, for discouraging others from talking by arranging to have music played during the entire working dinner.

A decade ago Trudeau was preaching "the national interest" as the basis for Canadian foreign policy. Now his foreign-policy activity is directed less and less by Canada's interests and seems increasingly a matter of personal will and whim.

October 26, 1982 The word arrives from Ottawa: my old colleague, friend, sometime ally, opponent, and nemesis Michael Pitfield has resigned. Osbaldeston[1] replaces him.

The best political mind, the best political nose in Ottawa is gone. Also gone is the most complex, unfathomable, and devious person I've known in public life. In the twenty years of our relationship, I've never ceased to be amazed at the influence he has in Ottawa – at first on Pearson, then Trudeau. Too bad he became so obsessed with process, that is, personal control, in recent years.

---

[1] Gordon Osbaldeston (b. 1930) Deputy Minister of the Treasury Board 1973–1976; Deputy Minister of the Department of Industry, Trade, and Commerce 1976–1978; Undersecretary of State for External Affairs 1982; Clerk of the Privy Council and Secretary to the Cabinet 1982–1985.

October 28, 1982 Days of wine and PR. Dinner at the Enderses' yesterday, our dinner for Stoessel today, a reception by Reagan's new ambassador for culture, Dan Terra,[1] and interviews with the *Post*, *Newsweek*, CBC, *Le Devoir*. Lots of publicity, thanks to Big John Dingell, who is at it again with scurrilous attacks on Trudeau. He issued a report attacking Reagan for not cracking down on our "blatantly discriminatory economic practices." He has played "armchair politics" while the Canadian government "orchestrated a disastrous economic squeeze play against U.S. companies." "Reagan," he says, "is more interested in maintaining a facade of good feelings [*sic*] with the Canadian prime minister than in defending American interests." It's hard to believe that with a staff of a hundred or more, Dingell could be so poorly informed.

October 29, 1982 Another meeting in the State Department of the seven summit ambassadors on East-West issues, to deal with the infamous Siberian gas pipeline screw-up. Larry Eagleburger was his usual thespian self. No question, he's an actor, and a good one. He thinks, he laughs, he doubts, he intimidates, he snarls, he looks darkly ahead – all of this seems like a performance on a stage. And so it is. We got nowhere.

Dinner at the Krafts'. Sat next to Flora Lewis,[2] one of the few American journalists who understand the importance of Europe. She was drunk, but even then interesting. Talked to Evangeline about Joe Alsop's latest triumph, his opus on art history – *The Rare Art Traditions*. Talked to Nora Ephron[3] about her latest movie. Chatted with a publisher who, when she found out I was Canadian, told me she signed a contract with Mavis Gallant[4] for a book on Dreyfus nine years ago and is still waiting.

October 30, 1982 Shultz gave an immense black-tie national costume dinner and concert at State in honour of ambassadors on the

---

[1] (1911–1996) U.S. Ambassador-at-Large for Cultural Affairs 1982–1988. He founded the Terra Museum of American Art in 1980.

[2] (1921–2002) The *Washington Post*'s first female foreign correspondent (1965). In 1972 she joined the *New York Times* in Paris as its bureau chief, and in 1976 she became European diplomatic correspondent. Foreign-affairs columnist for the *New York Times* 1980–1990.

[3] (b. 1941) American film director, producer, screenwriter, and novelist.

[4] (b. 1922) Canadian-born author. Recipient of the Governor General's Award for Fiction for her collection of stories *Home Truths* in 1981.

occasion of UN day. (Everyone is there because duty calls.) We were all guests of some lobby or company. The poor little Canadian ambassador did not do well; he qualified for the Pneumo Corporation, whatever that is. The wife of an African ambassador sat opposite Sondra and had the prize seat – next to Larry Eagleburger. Sondra observed her as she dozed off at the table.

October 31, 1982 *Maclean's* calls me "the most visible Canadian ambassador to Washington since the Second World War." The *Vancouver Sun* says that if I raise my profile any higher, I'll "join the list of candidates for the prime minister's job." As someone who never got a line of publicity in Ottawa for twenty-five years, being a mere grey bureaucrat, I find this deeply unnerving. I fear I will become a target, and I won't be able to defend myself.

November 1, 1982 Travelled to New Haven to address the Yale Political Union. It sounded like a great initiative – a dream forum for a foreign diplomat. The embassy checked it out the best they could and everything sounded good. It was difficult getting there (driving from New York), and I had a tight schedule to meet in Washington before departure. It was a disaster, one of my worst performances. The audience at the union was so sparse my spirits went into the tank – there were no more than a few dozen students. Everyone made excuses – exams, etc. The reality is I'm not a draw. A useful and timely ego deflator.

November 7, 1982 I attended an excruciatingly boring dinner of judges at Chez Camille organized by old Wadham friend and pupil Judge David MacDonald, which he put together from his perch on the Court of Appeal of Alberta. I focused on only one thing: how to get out without being disrespectful to all these eminent judges (including Lewis Powell).[1] It took me until 11:30 p.m. to realize there was no way, so I just got up and walked out. Not very graciously, I'm afraid.

If you're in private life and want to be rude, you can – it's only you who is uncouth. But if you represent a country, the country is being rude. And you will read about it in the papers.

---

[1] (1907–1998) Associate Justice of the Supreme Court of the United States 1972–1987.

November 8, 1982 We gave a buffet reception in the evening at the Motion Picture Association building in honour of the mysterious, little-known Roosevelt–Campobello Park Commission, a Canada-U.S. body that looks after Franklin Roosevelt's old summer home. They are a cozy group of ancient Roosevelt hands and descendants who keep the flame.

We showed *Sunrise at Campobello*, and I was surprised by how good a movie it is. It lasted two and a half hours, and we had the buffet afterwards. The food was excruciatingly awful. Plastic ham, hard, turd-like meatballs, and that's about all. We co-sponsored the event with Senator Muskie, vice-chairman of the commission. Out of some seventy guests, fifty or so were old associates, friends, and hangers-on of the commission. But George Shultz surprised us by showing up, and he and his wife, Obie, stayed and stayed right through to the end. George loved the food, eating a mountain of meat-balls. Even more surprising, Averell Harriman[1] (ninety-one and in good shape) with his wife (and former mistress), Pamela, also attended and stayed.

November 12, 1982 A beautiful, warm Washington fall day. I started with a swim in seventy-five-degree weather. What Sondra and I both love most about Washington are the seemingly endless warm autumn days. I'm feeling good because a letter arrived informing me of my appointment as an officer of the Order of Canada. I've been wondering when, if ever, I was going to be appointed. To be named means nothing. Not to be named is an irritant.

Pitfield and de Montigny Marchand[2] called me from Bonn. They were with Trudeau. Should Trudeau go to the Brezhnev funeral? Yes or no? I said no. It's not, I said, a disaster if he does go, particularly since he dealt with Brezhnev personally over the years, but there are strong domestic reasons (Poland) and international reasons (the only summit leader) for letting the Governor General attend instead.

After the sixth meeting of summit ambassadors on East-West issues at State, I rushed like hell to give a talk to the Princeton Club in New York. It was a good speech (I slammed the Yanks). On the way back, it was pouring

---

[1] (1891–1986) U.S. Ambassador to the Soviet Union 1943–1946 and to Britain 1946; Secretary of Commerce 1946–1948; Assistant Secretary of State for Far Eastern Affairs 1961–1963; Under-secretary of State for Political Affairs 1963–1965. Harriman was one of the "Wise Men" who served under virtually every administration.

[2] Undersecretary of State for the Department of Foreign Affairs and International Trade 1989–1991; Canadian Ambassador to Italy 1991–1996.

rain and I couldn't get a cab, even in my black tie. An elderly lady standing in the storm who came to hear me offered to share hers. Looked like a bag lady of sorts, but a little better dressed. In the cab she said, "I'm Irene Roth – my husband was Cecil Roth."[1] I was stunned by the incongruity of it all. As a student I had dined in the museum-like home of the famed Jewish historian in Oxford a dozen or more times. In the cab with her I had a Proustian moment. I tasted the ghastly cold fried fish she served on Friday nights.

November 14, 1982 We were invited to a Sunday brunch at the home of Esther Coopersmith in Potomac, Maryland, a grand Washington Democratic hostess from earlier times, who teamed up with Republican PR expert Nancy Reynolds to co-host the event today. In snobby Georgetown, the rule is no speeches, or as few as possible. In the Coopersmith tradition, there were speeches, as many as possible. The large and imposing hostess, filling the room with her presence, saluted each and every one of us (and there were at least a couple of dozen) with words of praise about our personalities, accomplishments, and importance. We staggered out late in the afternoon. Three hours before the mast in the service of my country.

November 15, 1982 Roone Arledge[2] gave a reception for David Brinkley[3] at the Watergate. The purpose was to celebrate the first anniversary of *This Week with David Brinkley*. I debated whether it would be worthwhile going. What did I find? VIPs stacked vertically wall-to-wall. Senators stumbling all over each other. Only the media can draw power like this.

November 16, 1982 The stumpage issue stumps everyone. It occupies more and more of our time in the embassy. The U.S. softwood countervail is the biggest in history – against any country. Trees grow in every state, which means no limit to the number of senators who will keep the political pressure on Commerce. Fortunately, Baldridge has integrity, but the issue is going to be one big pain in the ass.

---

[1] (1899–1970) Jewish historian and educator. Editor of *Encyclopedia Judaica* 1965–1970.

[2] (1931–2002) Chairman of ABC News from 1977 until his death in 2002. Sports broadcasting pioneer and creator of *20/20* and *World News Tonight*.

[3] (1920–2003) Leading American television newscaster for NBC and later ABC. Co-anchor of NBC's nightly news program *The Huntley-Brinkley Report*; hosted ABC's *This Week with David Brinkley* 1981–1986.

Financial Times headline: "U.S. Trade Threat Deepens." Quotes my remark: "Canadians should know that there is a growing mood in this country that [the United States] is not getting a fair share. It is a broad mood."

Judging by the worried delegations of businessmen materializing in Washington, Canadians are beginning to get the point.

November 17, 1982 I left for Toronto to give the Ontario cabinet a confidential briefing on Canada-U.S. relations. The line I got from Davis and the ministers was: "Ontario is well liked in the United States. We have a fine image. The problem is Ottawa. Ottawa's image, Ottawa's policies – that's the problem. There's precious little we can do about Canada-U.S. relations. It's up to the federal government."

Good old complacent Ontario. They got a big surprise from their humble representative in Washington. "Look," I said, "you're wrong. Ontario counts. Ontario's making the headlines. Read this week's stories in the *Wall Street Journal*. The Chrysler strike – Ontario does nothing. The Cadillac-Fairview sale of apartments to Arab interests – Toronto intervenes retroactively. Look at softwood lumber – it's Ontario's and other provinces' stumpage rates. Look at trucking – Ontario started it all, turning down applications for licences from Yellow Freight and enraging their protector, Senator Danforth[1] from Missouri. It's Ontario Liquor Board practices that are making Washington yell and threaten Canada with GATT action. It's Ontario that levies a discriminatory land tax against foreigners. It's Ontario that is socialist, statist, interventionist, not just Ottawa, thank you."

November 18, 1982 Bob Andras[2] is dead. Best friend I had in the Trudeau cabinet. He had everything going for him in retirement. He organized it perfectly. Beautiful house in Vancouver, great job, fine business colleagues, financial independence at last. He was misdiagnosed. He had cancer of the prostate and didn't know until it was too late. "Man makes plans, the gods laugh."

---

[1] Jack Danforth (b. 1936) Republican Senator from Missouri 1976–1995; U.S. Ambassador to the United Nations 2004–2005.

[2] (1921–1982) Held various cabinet positions in the government of Pierre Trudeau. Minister without Portfolio 1968–1971; Minister of State for Urban Affairs 1971–1972; Minister of Consumer and Corporate Affairs 1972; Minister of Manpower and Immigration 1972–1976; President of the Treasury Board 1976–1978; Minister of State for Economic Development 1978–1979.

November 19, 1982 At last, we make yards in the annoying and almost unbelievable Sidney Jaffe case. MacGuigan and I pushed the United States long and hard to get some recognition that it has violated our sovereignty in the grossest possible way. Officials of the Florida government authorized bounty hunters to kidnap Sidney Jaffe off the streets of Toronto, and now he languishes in a Florida prison. The stuff of movies. Mr. Jaffe, alas, is not a sympathetic subject, but the behaviour of state officials goes against the most basic principles of sovereignty, not to mention civilized behaviour. Getting the Reagan authorities to intervene in the activities of the state members of their union is even more difficult than getting them involved in the market.

But French Smith finally delivers. He reluctantly agreed to intervene in the Florida courts. He wrote to Florida's attorney general: "We believe that the Canadian request for assistance merits our attention as a significant foreign policy matter, as we seek to maintain our long-standing relationship of close and warm ties between the United States and Canada."

I didn't think we'd get this far. Persistence pays. As do good personal relations.

November 20, 1982 In Windsor to receive an honorary degree, my first (or my last?). Arranged by Temple Kingston, with whom I was at Christ Church. I spoke on the occasion of the twenty-fifth anniversary of Canterbury College. In the audience were Paul Martin,[1] Mark MacGuigan, Eugene Whelan,[2] and Herb Gray. I felt like I was at a Liberal cabinet meeting. I returned to Washington feeling, well, important.

November 29, 1982 I should know better. I asked the embassy administrative officer to arrange with the weekend duty officer to have the Saturday *Globe and Mail* delivered at the Residence. Perfectly reasonable, no doubt, since I'm on duty twenty-four hours a day, seven days a week. But the request generated memoranda from the administrative officer detailing the arrangements to the weekend duty officer. Very complex instructions, in the worst bureaucratese. Someone at the embassy stuck a knife into me

---

[1] (b. 1938) Member of Parliament for LaSalle-Émard, Montreal, 1988 to present; Minister of Finance 1993–2002; Prime Minister of Canada 2003–2006. Prior to his public career, Paul Martin had a long career in the private sector, holding many positions within Power Corporation.

[2] (b. 1924) Minister of Agriculture 1972–1984; Liberal Senator 1996–1999.

and leaked the memoranda to Frank Howard of the *Citizen*, who devoted a long, pious column to it. So over two hundred thousand people in Ottawa can get outraged and ask themselves, "Why does Gotlieb need the *Globe and Mail* at home?" Or "Why doesn't he go to the airport and pick it up himself?" Or "How much is the taxpayer getting stung so this guy can read his paper enjoying his breakfast?" It makes me feel sick. How long does one have to be in public life to get used to this shit?

December 1, 1982 I lunched in Congress with Jim Oberstar,[1] Democratic congressman from Minnesota, an intelligent, youngish legislator. He knows Canada well, making him one of a rare breed. "You know," he told me, "I am a completely independent man in what I stand for and how I vote. The party cannot influence me; it has no hold over me. There are only two ways Tip O'Neill can do anything to affect me. He can decide where my office is and what foreign congressional delegations I can join. I don't give a damn about either. I vote as I want. I am my own man."

Oberstar is unusual in that he talks so bluntly about the new reality – the decline of party influence and the rise of the independent power of the congressman. Each can have his own domestic and foreign policy. This makes it a lot tougher for Canada, because the writ of a Republican president and a Democratic Speaker – presumably the two most powerful leaders in Washington – is often not honoured by their own teams.

December 2, 1982 Sondra hosted a lunch at the Residence for Jean French Smith, Ursula Meese, Marilyn Lewis,[2] and Mary Jane Wick.[3] You can't draw a better hand in Washington. I attended a reception given by Jack Valenti[4] at the MPAA and a viewing of Norm Jewison's *Best Friends*. I sparred with Valenti. I like him, but I'm not supposed to. Back home he is seen as the Great Satan. He is a remorseless critic of our cultural policies. I find him too aggressive, too black and white (we good, you bad), too hard, too much "no more Mr. Nice Guy." But I respect his intelligence and he does come to the point. And he can take as good as he dishes out.

---

[1] (b. 1934) Democratic Representative from Minnesota 1975 to present.

[2] Wife of Drew Lewis, Secretary of Transportation.

[3] Wife of former director of the USIA Charles Wick and one of Nancy Reagan's closest friends.

[4] (b. 1921) President of the Motion Picture Association of America 1966–2004. Creator of the MPAA movie rating system (1968).

December 3, 1982 I was called into the State Department by Assistant Secretary Malone, who is responsible for the Law of the Sea – curse words for the Reagan administration. The final act of the convention opens for signature this week. "We hope," he said, "that Mr. MacEachen, in his speech at the Law of the Sea Conference next week, says nothing that will undermine our view that the navigational articles of the treaty are customary international law. This is in our defence interests, as it is in yours." I told him I'll pass the message to MacEachen. A pretty routine affair.

Then I received a blockbuster. A few hours after I left Malone's office, he telephoned me and read me four passages from MacEachen's proposed speech that say exactly what the United States doesn't want us to say. I was extremely surprised. "You have the advantage of me," I told him. "I haven't seen the speech." I hated having to admit that. The worst thing in this business – the absolute worst – is a foreign government knowing more about your own country's position than you do.

I sent an irritated message to Len Legault[1] in the Legal Bureau in Ottawa. Why wasn't I informed? He was shocked. "How on earth did they get the draft? We certainly didn't give it to them."

But on the substance, I had to admit to Legault that I thought the Americans had a point. The Reaganites were making it all very clear that the United States was not going to be a party to the treaty, regarding it as the work of the devil. But they wanted to uphold its rules on innocent passage. We were going to use the very same arguments they were making in their favour, but against them. We will have to insist that the "Arctic exception" to innocent passage and the twelve-mile limit were customary international law and bound the United States, even though it isn't a party to the treaty.

December 5, 1982 Sunday night at home. I'm relaxing in our private upstairs study overlooking the garden, after two massive weekend receptions at the Residence. I'm well into half-slumberland, watching Benny Hill[2] reruns on the boob tube, when the phone rings. It's Allan MacEachen calling from Montego Bay. He's spooked by the fact that the United States has the advance text of his remarks. "How did they get it?" I reply, "From

---

[1] (b. 1935) Minister (Economic) and Deputy Head of Mission in the Canadian Embassy in Washington 1986–1990; Canadian Ambassador to the Vatican 1993–1997.

[2] (1924–1992) Comic British actor/singer, best known for his television program, *The Benny Hill Show* (debuted in 1955).

over the open wires, I presume. Really, Minister, every foreign-service officer in Ottawa knows that the U.S. has the capacity to intercept our phone calls and *en clair* telegrams." MacEachen: "I am profoundly shocked." He asks me to go to State and find out how Malone got a copy.

"Sure," I reply. "But it's a complete waste of time. They got it over the open wires. Malone will concoct some story. The only thing unusual in this case is that they were so open about it."

December 6, 1982 A day of intrigue.

I call Malone at State. I tell him we are taking some of his points but not others. Then I put it to him directly. "How did you manage to get hold of a draft of MacEachen's speech?" "Okay, I don't have a draft," he says. "Just some handwritten notes." "What's their source? Where do they come from?" I ask. "I don't really know," he replies.

Two chaps from Security and Intelligence in Ottawa fly down to see me. I've been wondering for months whether the United States has broken our code and is reading our confidential traffic. On a couple of occasions recently, American officials who fear they have been indiscreet have made me promise not to report their comments by telegram. If they are not reading our traffic, why would they say this to me? This Law of the Sea business now reinforces my worries. Pitfield and Black tell me it's technically impossible for any foreign country to read our encoded telegrams. But now the MacEachen affair has gotten them a little worried too. He must have asked for a new investigation.

So I cook up a scheme, a ruse, to try to smoke out the truth. I show the two security men a telegram to Ottawa that I propose sending. It would contain a phony secret message on a highly sensitive issue; if the Americans are reading our classified traffic, they will be beside themselves when they read this. I complain in the telegram that I was not consulted about a highly secret cabinet decision to declare Canadian sovereignty over all the waters of the Arctic Archipelago and to close them to all foreign navigation. The message is to go from me to Pitfield, urging him to make a final intervention to block the decision.

The spooks agree that my plot is a good one. The trap is set. If the Yanks are reading our secret messages, surely they will take the bait. Or will they? It is possible that the MacEachen-Malone affair has put them on their guard.

We threw another enormous reception, a buffet dinner for some seventy top businessmen who are in Washington to get a defence briefing from American officials. These events are wearing me out, they're wearing Sondra out, and they're wearing the staff out. We are being inundated by requests to come to the Residence. Every Canadian south of the North Pole wants to be entertained by us.

December 7, 1982 I met MacEachen in the first-class lounge at the airport in Montreal, en route to Brussels to meet with Shultz. A dapper man, dressed in a denim suit. He drank nothing while I got slowly plastered. A man of infinite tension and infinite control. A virtuoso violinist waiting to go on stage. Every encounter seems to call forth his innermost reserves. So he is a great conserver – he has no choice. He can survive no other way. We discussed the number one thing that seems to be on his mind: the mystery about the leak of his speech. He told me the U.S. ambassador says they got the draft from some junior officer in New York. No one believes him. I outlined my plot to catch the Americans codebreaking, if they do. He said nothing. Characteristically.

December 9, 1982 The last time I was in Brussels was three Decembers ago, when the Conservative government failed. Same hotel, same floor, and almost the same room. I hear again the wonderful words spoken to me at midnight from the other side of the door by Flora's fawning departmental aide: "Mr. Gotlieb, sir, the government has fallen." How I remember Flora the next morning, friendly and cordial for the first time, and her chief of staff positively chummy. How I remember the futile scramble to find Flora a plane to get her back to Canada for Joe Clark's suicide vote. There was even talk of chartering a 707 at a cost of seventy-five thousand dollars. Just three years ago. A lifetime ago. Never will I forget the joy of knowing that Flora might no longer be responsible for my fate.

December 10, 1982 MacEachen, Si Taylor,[1] and I met with Shultz and entourage in his suite at the Hyatt Regency. The ceiling seemed a mile high, the tall windows vibrated and rattled under the endless rain, and the wind never stopped whining. Brussels weather, as I remember it. Shultz

[1] J.H. (Si) Taylor. U.S. Ambassador to the North Atlantic Council 1982–1985; Undersecretary of State for External Affairs 1985–1989; U.S. Ambassador to Japan 1989–1992.

started off by mentioning the fine evening in Washington that we organized to see the old film on Roosevelt. Sondra said afterwards it must have been the meatballs that impressed him.

It was evident that Shultz had thought carefully about the agenda and the issues. "The technique of quarterly meetings is working," he said. "We are achieving results."

MacEachen hinted to Shultz that Robinson should cool it; his criticisms of our defence efforts were unhelpful. "The Canadian government," he said, "is undertaking a considerable political liability in ensuring that defence spending is rising faster than any other part of the government's spending. Moreover, Trudeau has committed his personal prestige to winning the support of his party for the cruise-missile testing agreement."

I think this was the first direct criticism of Robinson by our government. Shultz returned the point later, during the discussion on acid rain. "A man called Roberts," he said, should lay off lobbying the Congress. "It's our Congress, leave it to us." A message for me? I wondered.

Talking to Rick Burt at the preparatory breakfast last week, I had suggested that the two sides begin to discuss a bilateral treaty on extraterritoriality, now that the Siberian gas pipeline sanctions were lifted. Burt reacted cautiously. "You must understand how sensitive this is in Washington. Proceed with great care. You won't get far." To everyone's surprise, Shultz himself raised the issue in the meeting today. It was obvious he hadn't talked to Burt. "This is a problem I'd like to get at," he said. "When I was secretary of the treasury, I knew the difficulties we were experiencing. Let's look at this one. I'll get two broad-gauged lawyers, maybe Ken Dam[1] and Ed Schmults[2] over in Justice. You get two broad-gauged lawyers, and then we'll ask them to meet quietly and maybe have dinner with us when we meet in Washington next April."

A truly surprising move. Looks a lot like leadership to me.

December 11, 1982 In Paris. I called on Michel Dupuy[3] at his Residence to have breakfast with him. Dominating the room in which we

[1] (b. 1932) Assistant Director for National Security and International Policy of the Office of Management and Budget 1971–1973; Deputy Secretary of State 1982–1985.

[2] (b. 1931) Deputy U.S. Attorney General 1981–1984.

[3] (b. 1930) Canadian Ambassador to the United Nations 1980–1981 and to France 1981–1985; Elected Liberal Member of Parliament for Laval West in 1993; Minister of Communications and of Multiculturalism and Citizenship 1993–1996.

talked was a large oil portrait of himself. Nearby was a smaller oil portrait of a man who had the same job years ago – his father. The main drawing room has been regilded, and it looks gaudy. "It will last fifty years," Michel said proudly. He expressed apologies for not being more available. "I have official duties in the country," he said. "A frightful bore." We talked for an hour about Franco-American relations. Dupuy, as always, stiff, self-conscious. But not without talent, alas.

December 12, 1982 Back in Washington, I engaged in a first for me and maybe an all-time first for the embassy. I hosted a lunch at the Residence for a group of powerful congressional staffers. The idea of entertaining staffers, not just congressmen, was suggested to me by Dick McCormack,[1] a former staffer himself, who has now replaced Bob Hormats[2] in the key post at State of assistant secretary for international economic affairs. So I made McCormack the guest of honour, and he proved a powerful draw for the staffers. A perfect example of the wily Canadian strategy: use a Yank to catch a Yank.

I'll miss Hormats. He had three problems. He was too good at his job, he knew too much, and he had too much experience. So they fired him.

It was quite a lineup of the staffer kings at the embassy. We had the staff director of Dingell's Energy and Commerce Committee (to whom we owe the infamous Dingell report on our energy and investment policies), the minority staff director of the Senate Banking Committee, the chief legislative assistant to the spoiler Jesse Helms, four members of the Senate Oversight and Investigations Committee, staffers from the Senate and House Committees on Foreign Affairs, and more.

It's almost impossible for people in parliamentary systems to understand that there are no non-elected positions in our countries in which political power of a comparable sort can be exercised. These staffers are like politically appointed, partisan deputy ministers. I read them, politely, of course, and with great deference to their wisdom and authority, the whole megillah – all the irritants and problems for which Congress was responsible. This

[1] U.S. Ambassador to the Organization of American States 1985; Undersecretary of State for Economic Affairs 1989–1991.

[2] Senior Deputy Assistant Secretary of State for Economic and Business Affairs 1977–1979; Ambassador and Deputy U.S. Trade Representative 1979–1981; Assistant Secretary of State for Economic and Business Affairs 1981–1982.

took me through a tour of bad congressional bills and initiatives: U.S. domestic content for automobiles, now on the House floor (aimed at the Japanese but brutally side-swiping us), the Heinz-Moynihan amendment zapping telidon technology, various gas-pricing bills, activities fomenting agitation over the softwood lumber investigation, and so on through the lengthy list of threats and woes.

The staffers were very courteous and listened patiently. They came, ate, and fled.

December 13, 1982 I called on Don Hodel,[1] the new secretary of energy, a big improvement over the estimable dentist. Obviously, Reagan has given up on the idea of abolishing the department, and that is good. I came with a long agenda: the dreadful Corcoran bill that would freeze gas prices, suppress imports, and do all manner of nasty things to us; the cavalier attitude being shown to the Alaska Gas Pipeline; and the ongoing misrepresentation of our energy policies. As is often the case with expatriates or their offspring, the gentleman from Saskatchewan did not seem too sympathetic to Canadian concerns.

December 15, 1982 Shultz gave an intimate farewell breakfast for Sepulveda,[2] about to become Mexican foreign minister. A farewell breakfast must represent some new low in diplomatic practice – maybe as bad as a working picnic.

December 16, 1982 We gave a dinner party in honour of Larry Eagleburger. What a crowd. The Kissingers, Bill Clark and wife, the Art Buchwalds, the Scotty Restons, the Lane Kirklands, the Laughlin Phillipses, Meg Greenfield, and Susan Mary Alsop. Also Tom Axworthy, whom I had invited down from Ottawa. Eagleburger joked about everyone who was there and insulted a few. He said he was honoured that the greatest U.S. secretary of state in history was present at the dinner and then pretended to look around the room for Al Haig. He said he wasn't quitting and rumours to the contrary should be disbelieved, even though Tom Enders was measuring the

[1] (b. 1935) Secretary of Energy 1982–1985; Secretary of the Interior 1985–1989.

[2] Bernardo Sepúlveda Amor (b. 1941) Mexican jurist, politician, and diplomat. Ambassador to the United States 1982; Secretary of Foreign Affairs 1982–1988.

chair in his office. (The crowd loved that one.) He spoke firmly about Judge Clark's commitment to the president and praised him for it.

It was the most successful party we have given. Even Carter Brown,[1] the aristocratic director of the National Gallery – who loped through the rooms like a cross-country skier, gaunt and elusive – seemed impressed, if somewhat surprised. "What a crowd," he said when he arrived, and he should know. For me the evening was capped by Henry Brandon's[2] remark: "This was the best Washington party I've been to since the 1950s." The celebrated Washington correspondent of the *Sunday Times* of London is not known to be addicted to hyperbole.

Curiously enough, during all the speeches and toasts, I felt a bit like a voyeur at my own party. The only time Canada came into the scene was when Scotty Reston toasted Eagleburger and myself, invoking the contributions of Pearson, Wrong, Robertson, and other envoys of the past, in which tradition he somewhat romantically, if fictitiously, placed me.

December 17, 1982 I had Ed Meese for lunch at the Residence with Tom Axworthy from the PMO, not an easy get-together to arrange. Is Trudeau's star rising in this town? If so, I suspect it's because of the leadership he is showing on cruise-missile testing in Alberta.

Early in the evening, I dropped in for a few minutes at a farewell reception for the Chinese ambassador. As I was leaving, a considerable commotion was taking place close to the front door. Lots of TV cameras, booms, microphones, and reporters pushing and scuffling. The president? Impossible. He doesn't go to diplomatic receptions. The VP? Maybe, I thought, but why the fuss? No, it was Henry Kissinger. Then I understood. In this town, Kissinger is a celebrity. On Chinese territory, so to speak, doubly so.

December 18, 1982 The Bradens entertained the same crowd as at our place the other night: the Kissingers, Kirklands, Buchwalds, and so on. Substitute the Deavers for the Clarks. I sat on Joan Braden's right, and during the course of the long dinner, the bad food, and her sly insertions of chewing tobacco into her teeth, she suggested I have lunch with Bob

---

[1] (1934–2002) Director of the National Gallery in Washington 1969–1992.

[2] (1916–1993) Chief Washington correspondent for the *Sunday Times* (of London) 1950–1983.

Gray,[1] the most high-powered public-relations operator in town, who just happens to be her employer. I said sure. During the rest of the dinner, she kept repeating, "I invited you because I like you, not because we want your business. You know that, don't you?"

December 20, 1982 Our twenty-seventh wedding anniversary. I celebrated by flying up to Ottawa with Baldridge for a day's talks with Ed Lumley and Gerry Regan.[2] I pulled the gaffe of my life, and Lumley sadistically stuck it to me publicly.

Mac Baldridge was supposed to be picked up, courtesy of his Canadian hosts, by de Havilland's new super plane, the Challenger, which we are desperately anxious to peddle, although it's plagued with mechanical problems. No one told me that it was not the Challenger that arrived to pick us up at Andrews airport early this morning but an old crock of an American-made (and discontinued) Lockheed JetStar.

Naturally, I didn't know the difference. Once inside the aircraft, I performed my requested salesman's role, pointing out how remarkably quiet the airplane was, how wide the body, how large the capacity. Baldridge acted as though he was impressed, but Lionel Olmer,[3] his deputy, seemed dubious. "You can't get eighteen in here, as advertised," he said. "Sure you can," I said. "You just change the seating configuration." "Well," he replied, "maybe eighteen Japanese."

When we arrived in Ottawa, Baldridge told Lumley, on cue, how impressed he was with the Challenger. Well, Lumley practically rolled on the ground laughing. The Challenger, he said, was grounded for mechanical reasons (of course). Har, har, har. The old jet we flew in holds six passengers, not twenty. More har, har, har. Lumley liked the story so much he repeated it several times in the course of the morning to anyone who would listen and told it again in his speech at the lunch he hosted for about a hundred businessmen and press at the Pearson Building.

---

[1] Served as press secretary to President Eisenhower and worked on both of Ronald Reagan's presidential election campaigns. Founder of Gray and Company in 1981; executive at Hill & Knowlton, a U.S. public-relations firm.

[2] (b. 1928) Premier of Nova Scotia 1970–1978; Secretary of State for Canada 1981–1982; Minister of International Trade 1983–1984; and of Energy, Mines, and Resources 1984.

[3] Undersecretary of Commerce 1981–1985.

Later in the day, Lumley telephoned me in a state of some consternation. "Allan, the press are onto the story. They are going to print it. I'm shocked." Well, how naive can you be? He tells the "joke" to a hundred people and the media and is astonished when a reporter says he's going to run the story.

December 21, 1982 Canadian press story: "Not Plane Sailing for the Ambassador." Har, har, har. I hear Lumley laughing.

December 22, 1982 I get a last-minute invitation to go to the White House to attend a ceremony on the launching of the Caribbean Basin Initiative. The ambassadors from the region sit in the audience. The cabinet officers are all in a row. The media hangs from the rafters. One, two, three. Cameras on. Ambassadors line up. President enters. President speaks. Ceremony ends. Cameras off. President exits. Ambassadors escorted out. One, two, three. Life as a prop.

December 26, 1982 Boxing Day party at Elizabeth Drew's of the *New Yorker*. A very high-powered affair, people stretching their necks and looking over their shoulders to see who was there. Who wasn't? I told Walter Mondale that I have tried a dozen times to see him, always unsuccessfully, always brushed off by his office. He was apologetic, of course, and rattled off platitudes – how important Canada was to the United States, how personally concerned he was about Canada-U.S. relations when he was vice-president. "You have to work at the relationship continually," he said, "not just once in a while." I told him Shultz appeared to be doing just that. Mondale then made some very critical comments about FIRA and the NEP, saying they were disastrous policies. This from a liberal Democrat.

December 29, 1982 What a contrast with last Christmas and New Year's, when we knew no one. Muffie Brandon asked the whole family to the White House today for lunch and a tour of the place. Yesterday, Alan Fern, director of the National Portrait Gallery, took our family to lunch at his museum and gave us a tour of the magnificent structure where the gallery is housed. With two kids into art history and looking around at different schools, it could not have been a more opportune time for an art-history lunch. We dropped over to look at the Old Pension Building nearby, a spectacular Victorian construction. After one year, I am still seeing things in Washington for the first time.

Sondra's column, "Canada In or Out," appears on the *New York Times* op-ed page today, a first for her in that newspaper.

December 30, 1982 Tomorrow ends my first full calendar year in Washington. How many more will I have? How long will Trudeau stay on? One year? One and a half? His last year will probably be mine. If there is a change of government, I'll be for the high jump. The Tories will find it impossible to allow me to be their spokesman.

It's been a difficult year for Canada. We've had the Trudeau antics at the Bonn Summit, the growth of American protectionism, retaliatory measures aimed at our most advanced technology, vicious attacks on FIRA and the NEP, the impasse in civil aviation, paralysis in acid rain negotiations, the blossoming of Buy America, and softwood lumber at centre stage. Still, I think that our relations are better now than a year ago, at least marginally. Trudeau's stand on cruise-missile testing, Shultz's commitment, the new quarterly foreign-ministers' forum, the high-level review of extraterritoriality, the bottoming out of the recession have all helped.

I've learned a few things here. A little atmosphere of crisis is necessary to focus the administration. I've also learned that success in Washington means access, and access requires contacts. Here, the social event is the playing field where contacts are "won." Most importantly, no one here cares a farthing if a foreign country comes whining at the door. They do worry, however, if their own special interests whine. So to fight uranium import controls, alert the power utilities who will have to pay higher prices and urge them to lobby. To fight duties on subway cars, get the municipalities to squeal. To fight gas import controls, get the consumers to complain. They are worth ten ambassadorial calls.

Not the stuff of traditional diplomacy, for sure. But either you play the domestic game or you lose. The traditional ways of doing things don't work in Washington.

December 31, 1982 New Year's Eve party at Mel Elfin's, foreign editor of *Newsweek*. Our host's name really is Mel Elfin, and he looks just like a Mel Elfin should look: perky and elf-like. Bill Safire told Sondra there are only ten New Year's parties worth going to in Washington, and this was one of them.

I met Congressman Stephen Solarz[1] from New York, who said he wants to act as a "friend of Canada" in Congress and would be prepared to take up Canadian causes, regardless of their relevance to his voters. He seemed sober, so I asked him to lunch.

I got to talk to Mondale again. I discovered he has a sense of humour and likes Havana cigars. Two remarkable qualities in a presidential candidate that he has succeeded in hiding, for understandable reasons. Either could be politically harmful; two would be fatal.

January 5, 1983 We are spending a lot of time in the embassy thinking about how we can enhance our effectiveness in this town and particularly on the Hill. We need to separate attitudes towards Canada from the rising anti-Japanese and anti-European cast of congressional thinking. Do we need a Lloyd Cutler,[2] a Bob Strauss, a Sol Linowitz? Could we actually get any of these to work for a foreign power? Do we need a general-purpose Washington public-relations firm like Bob Gray's or Anne Wexler's? We've finally managed to get a request put forward to cabinet (I can't believe it had to go all the way to cabinet) for a figure of $650,000 annually to hire consultants. This kind of money is peanuts. It will give us about 3 to 9 per cent of what the Japanese spend annually. But it will be a start. The surprising thing to me is the wide support there is among my colleagues in the embassy for moving in this direction. Astounding, really. Six or seven years ago, officers of the embassy were not even allowed to work the Hill.

January 7, 1983 Sondra has a terrible cold, so I have to persuade her to go to a dinner given by one Steve Martindale, a young, debonair (unfashionable word) local lawyer. We met him as a result of his connection to Margaret Trudeau[3] (he acted as her book agent). We went to a very flashy restaurant in Georgetown called Pisces, lots of vulgar people and a few Washington glittering types. And Sondra was a star herself. She was seated next to an Englishman who was introduced to us as guest of honour. In a

---

[1] Democratic Representative from New York 1975–1993; Chairman of the Central Asian-American Enterprise Fund 1993–1998.

[2] (1917–2005) American attorney who served as White House counsel during the Democratic administrations of Jimmy Carter and Bill Clinton. Married to Washington socialite and painter Polly Kraft, widow of columnist Joe Kraft.

[3] (b. 1948) Married to Pierre Elliott Trudeau 1971–1984.

loud voice, he called Trudeau a horse's ass. Sondra protested volubly. This chap is a Tory backbencher who led a parliamentary committee that criticized Trudeau's efforts to repatriate the constitution. Sondra continued to protest, but he carried on until she got fed up with the distinguished Englishman. She decided to leave early and walked out, with me following after. "Did people think you were walking out in protest?" I asked her. "Maybe yes, maybe no," she replied.

January 14, 1983 I met with the Communications Task Force of the Canadian Softwood Lumber Committee, an assortment of Canadian lumber executives, all in various states of panic and trauma over the softwood countervail against Canada. With 65 per cent of Canadian softwood exports at risk, it's surprising they aren't even more traumatized. Last week the B.C. minister of forestry, Tom Waterland, was here, and I urged him to work in harmony with the other provinces. They all want to come to Washington to see Mac Baldridge, give press conferences, call on congressmen, and above all be visible. Of course, it's for home consumption. The only impact such uncoordinated activities have here is to annoy and confuse, create opportunities for triangulation on the part of our enemies, and stimulate countercoalitions to lobby Commerce and the Hill. The U.S. domestic lobbies outpower us on a scale of about a hundred to one.

January 17, 1983 I invited to lunch the lobbyists and Washington industry representatives working with us on the nasty border broadcasting dispute. There were seven of them, representing seven humongous American corporations, including *Time*, the *Times-Mirror*, *Hallmark*, GTE, and AT&T. They all say the same thing: Congress will be difficult, even more protectionist this year than last, and Canada ought to back down from its border broadcasting rules or face serious reprisals against our telidon computer technology.

The conversation should help Ottawa appreciate the real risks of doing nothing about our border broadcasting policy. It set our tourist industry back a couple of hundred million bucks, thanks to congressional retaliation. We've paid more than enough for a law that got us Peter Newman's success in life.

Networking with domestic interests is by far the most effective approach we can take to fighting protectionist actions against us in Congress. But it's a tricky form of diplomacy, bordering on interference in the U.S. domestic political process. The group today made it perfectly clear that it would not be useful to have it publicly known that we were working behind the scenes with the U.S. industry. In lobbying against the noxious Moynihan retaliatory amendment, they are emphasizing injury to U.S. corporate interests and eschewing completely the idea of "making a case" for Canada.

Canada has no "friends" in Washington, only "interests." This distinguishes us radically from some other foreign governments who have "friends" on the Hill – congressmen who espouse their position as a matter of their own political interests. Israel has a constituency, Italy has a constituency, Greece has a constituency; Canada has none.

January 18, 1983 We attended a black-tie dinner-dance at the Watergate hosted by Charlie Wick for his friend Rupert Murdoch.[1] It was an A-list crowd of about eighty, sitting at tables of ten. I saw Roy Cohen[2] amidst the crowd. Sort of like spotting Elvis. He looked weird. Thin neck, protruding coloured bow-tie, brown-coloured face, bulging eyes. Charlie sat him next to Sondra. What had Sondra done to deserve this? She even had to dance with him. Mac Baldridge, sitting on her other side, asked, "How could you dance with that man?" Sondra replied, "Because I've never danced with a really bad man before."

Wick told me he presented Murdoch to the president today (and Cohen). Wick is a very funny guy but gave an unfunny speech tonight. Content: Murdoch, you're rich and successful. We love you.

January 20, 1983 We threw a gourmet dinner party to celebrate Canadian food, cooked by a Canadian celebrity chef, Tony Roldan.[3] The guest list was first-rate for this sort of frivolous (by Washington standards) affair: Rowly Evans,[4] Jim Lehrer,[5] the Krafts, Marty Feldstein,[6] Rick Burt, the

---

[1] (b. 1931) Australian-born American media proprietor. Major shareholder, chairman, and CEO of News Corporation.

[2] (1927–1986) Controversial American lawyer who came to prominence during the investigations by Senator Joseph McCarthy into communists in government, for which he served as chief counsel.

[3] Corporate Executive Chef for Harbour Castle Hilton, Toronto, 1974–1977 and Third Generation Realty Ltd. (Sutton Place, Bristol Place Hotels), Toronto, 1977–1980.

[4] (1921–2001) American journalist best known for his decades-long syndicated column and television partnership with Robert Novak; congressional correspondent for the *New York Herald-Tribune*.

[5] (b. 1934) Established the *MacNeil-Lehrer Report* with Robert MacNeil in 1975; currently news anchor for the *NewsHour with Jim Lehrer* on PBS.

[6] (b. 1939) Chairman of the Council of Economic Advisers and President Ronald Reagan's Chief Economic Adviser 1982–1984. Currently George F. Baker Professor of Economics at Harvard University.

Enderses, and many more. I thought the food was indifferent except for the Montreal duck, which was very good indeed. The Lake Winnipeg goldeye was the worst I've eaten in my life, and I've eaten a lot of bad goldeye.

Jim White, food editor of the *Toronto Star*, said, "Goldeye is an increasingly rare whitefish, put into a brine and smoked with oak chips." Lehrer replied, "That's not a whitefish, that's a damn redfish." The worst line of the evening: "It's delicious," said Kay Evans, editor of the *Washington Journalism Review*, describing the New Brunswick fiddlehead ferns she had just consumed. "I thought it was pasta." Fiddleheads fared no better from Tom Enders. "Everyone eats them in Canada," he said, "except for New Brunswickers. That's where they come from." Harrison McCain[1] sent us a truckload.

January 21, 1983 I called on Paul Volcker at the Federal Reserve. The timing of my one-on-one was good. The situation is grim. New U.S. data reveal that last year the U.S. economy had its worse performance in thirty-six years – it contracted 1.8 per cent, which is peanuts compared to our own estimated decline of 4.7 per cent. It makes one wonder what is happening in Canada. Our businessmen are terrified. Is our economy collapsing? Meanwhile, the United States got its inflation rate down to 3.9 per cent, thanks, of course, to Volcker, whereas ours was a scarcely believable 9.3 per cent (in a depression!), with unemployment hitting 12.8 per cent.

Volcker has to be one of America's greatest gentlemen. He refrained from commenting that our economy was rapidly going down the tubes. But with the United States projecting a $200-billion deficit next year, and maybe $300-billion by 1988, Volcker seemed worried that the United States was headed in the same direction as us. I found him to be among the very best informed in town on the Congress, its doings and deliberations. He sees clearly the growth of protectionist forces on the Hill and is worried about them.

January 23, 1983 I pick up the *New York Times* this morning while eating my breakfast in the bamboo room, and I almost fall off the chair. There is a huge spread on us and on our Canadian food party. Marvellous publicity and all that (lovely photograph of Sondra and a cooing commentary

---

[1] (1927–2004) Canadian businessman. Co-founder, with brothers Andrew, Robert, and Wallace, of McCain Foods Limited.

by their Washington correspondent, Barbara Gamarekian),[1] but there I am, pictured with a larger-than-life Jim Coutts, tasting Canadian caviar. Just the two of us. Who needs a photo of him and me plastered across the *New York Times*? Now that Coutts is out of government, the Prime Minister's Office will hate it, Turner will hate it. Flora MacDonald will hate it, it will annoy the hell out of MacEachen, and my fate will be sealed in cement with the Tories.

January 27, 1983 Back to the Federal Reserve, this time to host a reception on the opening of the exhibition of my Tissot print collection. I was competing with a giant Saudi reception, a huge annual event at the National Gallery, and who knows what else. A typical Washington situation. But there was a turnout of about two hundred, not bad for a dead French artist in power town. Official Washington doesn't care a fig about art, notwithstanding all the museums in this city. Art galleries are merely places to hold functions or large political events hosted by lobbyists.

Washingtonians speculate where Deep Throat passed his or her Watergate secrets to Woodward and Bernstein. They speculate but I know. The meetings took place on Sunday afternoon in the Raphael room in the old National Gallery building. I've been there on a half-dozen Sunday afternoons to see what might be the greatest collection of Raphaels in the world. No one else is ever there. If you want to talk to someone in secret, this is the place.

The hanging of my prints was superb – they will never look better. The crowd was mildly curious. The entire Federal Reserve Board showed up, Volcker included. Also Energy Czar Don Hodel and the deputy director of CIA operations. A Canadian journalist [*sic*], Bogdan Kipling,[2] asked me why I didn't invite a visiting labour delegation from Canada. He told me my failure to do so was nothing less than scandalous. I wanted to tell him to fuck off, but I just walked away.

January 28, 1983 Earlier in the day, I called on Charles Percy of Illinois at his request. Another Washington rule according to Gotlieb: if a senator asks to see you, he's up to no good. I know why Percy called the

---

[1] (1926–2004) A reporter on the arts and Washington society for the *New York Times*. Press aide in the Kennedy and Johnson White Houses.

[2] Syndicated Washington columnist, currently columnist for the *Halifax Chronicle-Herald*.

meeting. It's so he can make a grand announcement afterwards. Our get-together will enable him to announce that he told the Canadian ambassador that Canadian gas is too expensive and he simply will not tolerate this situation.

During our meeting I explained that we are not a price leader, that the Canadian supply is marginal in a huge American market, that we don't know where the United States wants to go on pricing, and that the current price formula was introduced at U.S. request.

The senator didn't even listen, but he told me what a great friend of Canada he is, none, in fact, greater. The problem, he confided, is that he has an unfortunate "conflict of interest" – his words. His constituents think Canadian gas is too expensive. I hope he gets defeated.

January 30, 1983 Roy Faibish,[1] former close adviser to Trudeau, former boy wonder, former Conservative, now a mogul in the communications business in London, sent a letter to Sondra. Congratulations, he writes, for her courageous stand in what is now known in Canada – and Britain – as "the affair of the horse's ass." *Maclean's* played it up in vivid technicolour last week.

The gossip columnists picked up the story from the Martindale dinner and have called her early departure "a walkout in protest." It goes down splendidly in Canada. The embassy is not issuing any denials, simply a clever policy of "no comment."

The best and worst line in the affair of the horse's ass was a comment in the local press by Oatsie Charles,[2] a friend of Charles Ritchie in the old days and now a first-echelon Washington socialite. "It's true," she said, "that Trudeau is a horse's ass. But the man should not have said that to the wife of the Canadian ambassador." I like Oatsie Charles and her wickedness. But sadly, I'll have to strike her off our guest lists. I can just see the headlines: "Gotliebs Entertain Washington Socialite Who Insulted Trudeau."

January 31, 1983 Brilliant sunshine, fresh breeze – great is California. It's hard not to feel good to be alive. Stepping off the plane in Los Angeles, I

[1] (1929–2001) Canadian writer and producer for the CBC and former vice-chairman of the CRTC. Served as a consultant to Prime Minister John Diefenbaker.

[2] Long-time Washington social figure.

remember what Albert Camus said: "Every day not spent in the sun is a wasted day in life." I arrive at the Beverly Wilshire and the Canadian flag is flying everywhere. I'm bowed and grovelled into a splendid suite, and I feel like the Queen or like she should feel. A quick walk down Rodeo Drive, antiques, jewellery, and I want to be rich, rich.

Dinner at Ma Maison with Donald Sutherland, Brian Moore, John Kemeny, and a few others from the Hollywood Canadian clan. Sondra, in Washington, tries to reach me at the restaurant, but she can't. The number is unlisted. Only in Hollywood.

February 1, 1983 I gave my "Goodbye, Nelson Eddy" speech at the World Affairs Council in Los Angeles. Before I spoke, Jim Nutt warned me repeatedly that I may be talking down to the group – the most prestigious chapter of the council in the United States – but I think my speech hit it just right. The Hollywood's-goofy-image-of-Canada theme was perfect for the audience. Did they know that Hollywood made 250 feature films about Canada with a Mountie in them as the central figure? I used lots of one-liners, ones I've been polishing on the Gotlieb borscht belt. Like the one told me by Mordecai Richler: "What's the book title most likely to guarantee that a publisher goes broke?" Answer: "Canada, Our Good Neighbour to the North." Then the one about Big Chief Sitting Bull: "Buffalo meat taste same both sides of border." And then my Al Capone line: "Canada? I don't even know what street it's on." The folks in the audience might have been sophisticated, but I'll swear they never heard those cornball lines before. They liked them.

February 4, 1983 In Ottawa to attend the third meeting of the Group of Foreign Policy Advisers. The theme was the famous or infamous Third Option. I spoke of the need for the Prostitute Option – getting into bed with the United States. "Let's make special arrangements with our major trading partners; let's get whatever special deals we can. Forget the old clichés about multilateralism; if we aren't willing to scramble, we could be left out in the cold. Remember the scramble for Africa? This is going to be the scramble for markets. We're going to see a world of exploding competition, greater trade restrictions, and expanding preferential economic blocs."

Everyone managed to misunderstand me. One eminent colleague from the foreign ministry said, "But if we make special deals with the Americans, we'll lose respect in the Third World." I give him credit for the most fatuous statement I've heard in the Pearson Building (and I've heard plenty). MacEachen asked me, "Are you advocating that Canada abandon free trade, the international rules, and the multilateral system?" "No," I replied, "I'm advocating we not be the last member of the Boy Scouts Club." Trudeau said, inscrutably, "Well, if you are advocating integration with the U.S., we'll have to look at that as part of our contingency planning." Gerry Regan, the trade minister, was the exception – he was the only one to endorse what I said.

Michel Dupuy prepared a personal recollection of the origins of the Third Option. "With the wisdom of hindsight, the exercise seems to have faltered for three reasons: (1) failure to foresee the energy crisis; (2) failure to define in a credible way how it could be implemented; and (3) the strategy turned out to be an amalgam of ill-defined foreign and domestic objectives."

No one quoted Charles Ritchie, who is credited with a more colourful analysis: "It was fine as far as it went – there was a bridle, a saddle, but no bloody horse."

Trudeau looked tired. The only comment he made about the Third Option was that it was "far more than an economic strategy, it was a political one." Of course, that was the problem.

February 5, 1983 Back in Washington. MacEachen did not seem comfortable with the foreign-affairs advisers. The reason, I suspect, is that Trudeau always meets with the group and dominates the discussions. The prime minister enjoys the intellectual challenge, the debating club atmosphere. The officials devote their attention to boss number one, while MacEachen unavoidably is downgraded to boss number two. I'm not sure whether this bothered MacGuigan. If so, he never showed it. I'll bet my bank account that this will be the last meeting of our famous little group.

February 6, 1983 The plot of l'affaire Jaffe, our own North American B movie, continues to unfold. MacGuigan in Justice wants to file a writ of habeas corpus in Florida to get Sidney Jaffe out of the Florida pen where he is languishing. He may well belong there, for all I know, but the problem is he got there the wrong way – kidnapped off the streets of Toronto. The Justice officials in Washington seem to have passed the responsibility back to the Florida state prosecutors to investigate the affair. The idea of Florida officials investigating themselves is a bad joke. As Brian Dickson, now the legal officer at the embassy, put it to me (drawing from his Romanian experience, no doubt), "This appears to be a classic case of Dracula guarding the blood bank."

When you get into the U.S. legal system and see how it works, especially at the state level, and when you observe the behaviour of prosecutors, you realize how fortunate you are to be a Canadian.

February 7, 1983 In New York for *Newsweek*'s fiftieth-anniversary celebration. *Newsweek*, plaything of Katharine Graham. Two thousand five hundred members of the U.S. elite in attendance to witness an endless series of slavish tributes, mostly media loving media. In a strange way, we felt we were back in the National Arts Centre in Ottawa, as we must have known a hundred people or more at the party, or at least had previously met them, from Dear Abby and Jerry Brown in California to the Meeses, French Smiths, and Baldridges in Washington. It's hard for me to believe that people like Jimmy Carter, the Kissingers, I.M. Pei, senators, billionaires, movie stars, media stars, and the like would turn out for a magazine promotion. I can't imagine an equivalent Canadian event. Who could *Maclean's* or the *Ottawa Citizen* or *Saturday Night* get to turn out to an anniversary?

February 9, 1983 It arrives: an envelope for me by mail from Flora MacDonald. Contained within is the *New York Times* article describing our great Canadian cooking caper and picturing Jim Coutts and me tasting Canadian caviar. The following inscription was penned across the top of the page in Flora's own fine hand: "Allan, you were always so subtle about your partisan loyalties."

I also have another critic, it seems. Ed Lumley complained to MacEachen about my wasting government money – having dinners for frivolous purposes or something like that. "There must be a lot of fat in his budget," he said. Har, har, har.

The poor little ambassador reprimanded twice in the same day. And for the same reason: the success of our entertainment.

February 10, 1983 I'm becoming worried about the growing resentment back home at the attention we are getting for Canada down here. The attitude seems to be that I am engaged in self-promotion. Just the other day the *Citizen* played up a snotty letter about us – gave it a big spread and a cartoon – titled "Cocktail Party Winners." Its punchline was the Gotliebs are "becoming acknowledged as the 'Gretzkys of the Washington cocktail circuit.'" Oh Canada. Envy in its purest form?

February 11, 1983 Yesterday I manoeuvred myself into the office of the acting secretary of state, Ken Dam, in a furtive, secretive way, to sign our famous cruise-missile testing framework agreement with the Americans. I was instructed to keep the agreement a secret so MacEachen could announce it later in the House of Commons. Normally, one would give advance notice that Canada was signing such an important document, and the press would have been present – in droves. When I met with the Canadian press after the announcement in Parliament, they hooted and jeered at me because of this silly stunt.

February 12, 1983 Breakfast at the Hay-Adams with the worldly Sol Linowitz, who reinforced my anxieties. He repeated that we are becoming too pally with the Georgetown set. Also beware of the press, he said. They'll screw you. This advice served as a counterpoint to his peons of praise about our diplomatic triumphs – we are, he said, the most successful diplomatic couple in Washington.

February 14, 1983 Washington's worst storm in memory and the day we have a dinner party for Marc Lalonde. I blew up in the morning when I arrived at 1746 Massachusetts Avenue. The embassy was empty except for the security guards, after an administrative officer instructed it to close. This on a normal day in Ottawa, insofar as snow is concerned! I ordered the embassy reopened at once, which no doubt will add greatly to my popularity. I just don't think an embassy should close, short of being struck by a national disaster.

The Volckers, President of the World Bank Tom Clausen, the Baldridges, Brinkleys, Strausses, Restons, and Kirklands had all accepted our dinner. First to cancel was Strauss. He called me in the afternoon and begged me to let him off the hook. I yielded reluctantly. Then they went down like tenpins. All day long I debated – should I cancel or not? Should I let everyone off the hook? If I don't cancel, will anyone show? I held fast. Only two American guests showed – but they were Paul Volcker and Mac Baldridge. Both had four-wheel drives. The storm gave a sense of accomplishment to those who came, and it turned out to be one of the most enjoyable evenings we've had. And a marvellous opportunity for our ebullient minister of finance to get to know one of the most powerful people in America and one of the most powerful people in the administration.

February 23, 1983 Another long session at the embassy to develop strategies for dealing with Congress. I then attended a reception to mark the opening of the Washington office of Ed Muskie, a partner of Chadbourne, Parke, Whiteside and Wolfe, a law firm I've never heard of. I went for a few minutes because Muskie was a good friend of Canada both as senator from Maine and then secretary of state under Carter. How impressed I was when I watched him perform at a NATO foreign-ministers' meeting in Ankara just a few years ago. He radiated power, authority, self-confidence. Now I see a minor Washington lobbyist, scrambling for a living.

Why do former Washington powers linger on in this town, where they so rapidly become nobodies? The invariable rule in Washington is that people lose their power the day they lose their office.

Our host for dinner tonight at the F Street Club, Bob Strauss, is the exception. In my experience in Washington, he is unique. He has truly animal instincts when it comes to understanding how to survive as a political player. But I forget. Kissinger is another example of a former office-holder avoiding nobody status.

February 24, 1983 I tried to conduct a day's normal activities. Lunched with David Peterson,[1] new Liberal leader of the Opposition in Ontario. Nice guy but no political future. Gave a press interview with Don Oberdorfer[2] of the *Washington Post* and a reception at the Residence for some investment and trade seminar.

In the midst of all this, we are experiencing a crisis over an Air Canada seat sale to Los Angeles and some other U.S. cities. The sale is to go into effect tomorrow, and Canadian tourists were all set to go when the Civil Aeronautics Board decided to disallow the sale. Thousands of hysterical Canadian customers (fifty-five thousand, to be exact) are displaced, and they

---

[1] (b. 1943) Leader of the Ontario Liberal Party 1982–1990; Leader of the Opposition in the Ontario Legislature 1982–1985; Premier of Ontario 1985–1990, the first Liberal premier of that province in forty-two years.

[2] American journalist for thirty-eight years, twenty-five of them with the *Washington Post*.

are all screaming in unison at Jean-Luc Pépin.[1] In turn, everyone in Ottawa is screaming at me. Do something. Like exactly what? This is Washington: one operational crisis after another. Everyone passing the buck. In this decentralized town no one seems to know where the authority really lies. Is it in the CAB, Transport, State, NSC, the domestic side of the White House? Or is it, alas, in the hands of Continental Airlines, the complaining competitor of Air Canada? Another example, I fear, of Washington run by special interests.

February 25, 1983 To launch a madcap day, I gave a live interview to Peter Gzowski[2] on *Morningside* on protectionism, acid rain, cruise-missile testing in Canada, the Air Canada seat sale, and a new irritant in our irritable relations: the branding of National Film Board films as propaganda. Canada-U.S. relations follow the celebrated ODTAA theory of history: it's One Damn Thing After Another.

This, after being up all night. Jean-Luc Pépin woke from his political stupor and telephoned me at 2 a.m. to discuss the breakdown in the negotiations over the ticket sale. In the course of the morning, I managed to negotiate a delay in the U.S. suspension of the sale – this just minutes before the suspension was to take place.

Then the volcano erupted again. Some incredibly dumb American official in Justice requires three NFB films, two on acid rain and one on the arms race, to be labelled political propaganda. What a farce. This is surely one of the stupidest decisions taken in this administration. I immediately tried to reduce the visibility of our intervention, because I figured we'd have a better chance of getting rid of the ridiculous decision though U.S. domestic pressures. John Roberts, our unpopular (down here) minister of environment, seized the moment and shot off his mouth. Unfortunately, he was visiting New York at the time. Not a good idea for a foreigner to attack U.S. policies when on U.S. soil.

In the late afternoon, I got a telephone call from Pat Moynihan. I have been trying to see him for months to talk about our border broadcasting dispute (he is the scourge of Canada when it comes to this issue, thanks to a Buffalo broadcasting constituent of his), but I can never get an appointment

[1] (1924–1995) Canadian academic and politician. Member of Parliament for Ottawa-Carleton 1979–1984; Minister of Transport 1980–1983.

[2] (1934–2002) Hosted the CBC Radio program *This Country in the Morning* in the early 1970s and *Morningside* 1982–1997.

to see him. His office always stalls, finding some excuse to say no. And there he was, on the line. "Ambassador, I'm shocked. I'm ashamed." He explained that last year he had personally endorsed the films on acid rain and invited his senatorial colleagues to see them. So he was mightily embarrassed. If they're on your side, they are nice to you, and if they are not, the hell with you.

Actually, I find it hard to get excited about this decision. If the Americans want to make fools of themselves, I think that's their problem.

February 26, 1983 "U.S.-Canadian Relations Take a Testy New Turn," says the *New York Times* this morning in a headline on the top of page 3. I think the headline overdid it. The relationship has been improving, imperceptibly, marginally, but improving nonetheless. Signature of the "umbrella agreement" on missile testing has made a difference, "no new NEPs" has made a difference, and so has the appointment of Shultz. There is a better "tone" in the relationship, and in foreign affairs "tone" is important. It means more courtesy, less anger, and greater willingness to listen.

The reporter, David Shribman,[1] showed real insight when he wrote that "the state of relations between the two nations rises and dips with a rapidity that is sometimes astonishing." The eruption of the latest two disputes – on air fares and political propaganda – illustrates beautifully the reason for this. Our disputes often arise out of the management of U.S. domestic issues and actions by uncontrollable agencies. They have absolutely nothing to do with the foreign policy of the United States. This doesn't make our task easier, but it underlines that we have to develop contacts and relationships with the domestic agencies themselves, that we have to ally ourselves with friendly U.S. domestic interests.

Moynihan, our scourge on border broadcasting, has become a superb spokesman for us on the acid rain issue. "For two years," he said, "I have been trying to impress upon this administration that we are heading for a major foreign-policy crisis with the most important other country in the world on the issue of acid rain." Not bad, not bad at all. Right there in the *New York Times.*

What's more, we've even got the bibulous Ted Kennedy on our side – again not a Canada-lover. (He was responsible, in part, for sinking our fisheries treaty.) But there he is, in the *Times*, denouncing the Justice decision

---

[1] Reporter for the *Wall Street Journal*; Washington Bureau Chief for the *Boston Globe*; Executive Editor of the *Pittsburgh Post-Gazette.*

on our NFB films and demanding that Bill French Smith be called before the Senate Judiciary Committee "to explain this inexcusable action by the department he manages." Meanwhile, I formally asked the Justice Department to reconsider its decision.

February 28, 1983 So ends my fifty-fourth year. Seat sales, propaganda, kidnapped Canadians languishing in state prisons – these are the matters pressing on my mind and my nerves. Yet it's not the silly season, just another few weeks in the life of Canada-U.S. relations.

These crises come out of nowhere and can affect the lives of thousands or the sovereignty of foreign states. Crises caused not by the foreign policy of the United States but by the actions of assholes occupying obscure positions in obscure agencies. And who do you discuss the crises with – the assholes who caused them? High officials in the administration who have no control over them?

"In this country it isn't a question of how much you can do; it's a question of how much you can stand." Thus spoke Lord Lyons,[1] sometime British ambassador to the United States. I'm not there yet. I love this country. Notwithstanding my bitching, I love this job. But is it a question I might be asking myself before long?

March 7, 1983 In Boca Raton resting up for a few days before speaking here tomorrow to the College of American Trial Lawyers. The embassy telephoned from Washington and shattered my peace of mind during the only vacation I've had in a year. "Your foreign minister," I was informed (much smirking), "has rejected your recommendation that Vice-President Bush not be invited to visit Ottawa."

I had advised MacEachen that we should not press for a vice-presidential visit now, at the tail end of his European disarmament tour. I thought we should invite Bush to make a special visit to Ottawa later, to discuss both Canada-U.S. relations and the international situation. "MacEachen thoroughly disagrees with your advice," the embassy told me, "and he's so mad he's organizing the trip through Paul Robinson in Ottawa." No one in External headquarters has a clue about what's going on. He's talking to Shultz directly. The State Department and External are also against a visit now, but MacEachen is determined to prove his point.

---

[1] British Ambassador to the United States 1858–1865.

The poor ambassador is in the doghouse. But I still think "me-too diplomacy" is not good for Canada. The mentality is "Big Daddy goes to Europe to talk to all the Big Boys, so why does he neglect little Canada? He has to come here. Otherwise it will be seen as a snub, a signal to the world that Canada is not important."

So it's the same old story – our sense of inferiority leads to us whining after the Americans, begging them to treat us as the equal of the Europeans, which is humiliating. It stands as proof that we are not. The Darman critique scores. The State Department, he says, sees us as an appendage of Europe. So what do we do? Reinforce our image as an appendage.

No doubt the Bush visit is also mixed up in MacEachen's complex mind with his strategy regarding the cruise missile. He was supportive of signing the cruise framework or "umbrella" agreement, but I am not sure whether he actually wants Canada to test the damn missile. If he wants to be the next Canadian Liberal leader, he may well want to avoid alienating the vocal, activist anti-cruise, anti-U.S. faction in the cabinet and caucus led by the Reverend Obadiah Slope[1] Lloyd Axworthy.

March 8, 1983 What an awful place is Boca Raton. We are on the top floor of a spectacular new hotel in a grand corner room with views all around of the ocean and the waterways, and not a single window opens. We're sealed in a tomb in the sky. They don't specialize in hotel-keeping here, they specialize in crowd control. There are fifteen hundred trial lawyers, three hundred of whom listen to me speak on extraterritoriality and watch Warren Burger[2] hand Bora Laskin[3] a scroll.

Yesterday the premises were crawling with futures – pork-belly types and commodity exchangers, hundreds and hundreds of them. There were precisely twelve congressmen and senators in attendance to pay obeisance, including Tip O'Neill. The congressmen all seem to be mainstreeting and grandstanding and having free vacations for themselves and their families in exchange for a few words that pass as speeches. I doubt if any of them are not collecting fees for their visitation. Fees from special interests. It's pretty obvious that this is a corrupt system.

[1] A fictional character found in Victorian-era works by English novelist Anthony Trollope.

[2] (1907–1995) Chief Justice of the Supreme Court of the United States 1969–1986.

[3] (1912–1984) Chief Justice of the Supreme Court of Canada 1973–1984.

Hurrah. Splendid news flash from Washington: we won the lumber countervail action. The preliminary finding was that our stumpage is not a subsidy. Common sense wins. Protectionism loses. We played this one masterfully. Baldridge deserves great credit for standing up against the tide of protectionism. Reagan even visited Oregon lumber towns yesterday. Good for the administration! The best news we've had in months.

March 9, 1983 I called on Governor Bob Graham[1] in Fort Lauderdale, as arranged by Lloyd Cutler. He is reputed to be something of a rising star, with Florida being the sixth or seventh most populated state, and perhaps even more important, Governor Bob is Kay Graham's brother-in-law. After an outrageous fifty-dollar taxi ride, I found myself at our rendezvous, scheduled for 6 p.m. at the Marina Bay Beach Club. I was expecting a ritzy place, like the Bath and Tennis Club in Palm Beach or something like that. Instead, I found a bar, a blonde, and sleaze everywhere. Why would the governor of Florida be meeting me at some place straight out of Raymond Chandler or the *Rockford Files*? After waiting in those lurid surroundings for about half an hour, I figured I had to have gone to the wrong address.

Just as I was panicking, a flunky aide showed up and escorted me down a hallway and across a courtyard to a floating motel room(!). There, in this American version of Ukiyo-e, stood the governor himself. He extended his hand. "Delighted to meet you, Mr. Ambassador." The governor and I exchanged pleasantries before he got up, made some excuses, and disappeared into an adjacent room "to make an important telephone call." I waited another twenty minutes for the governor to reappear. When he did, he announced, "Someone has leaked a report that in the event of a nuclear holocaust, the population of northern Florida is to be moved into Alabama." (Sounds to me like a splendid plan.)

We spent five minutes talking about the Jaffe kidnap. I congratulated him on his admirable decision to appoint a commission of inquiry (although I suspect that it will be a whitewash). We then discovered that we had nothing more to talk about except trying to estimate how many million Canadians were visiting Florida at that very moment. We figured about two and a half million.

---

[1] (b. 1936) Governor of Florida 1979–1987; Democratic Senator from Florida 1987–2005.

March 12, 1983 A Saturday, the best time of the week to call on Eagleburger, as he is usually less hurried. Our Saturday morning tête-à-têtes are sheer enjoyment for me as we joust over policies and differences. I love to watch this man perform, and I mean perform. He listens impatiently, wheezing and spraying his nostrils with some sort of contraption and tapping his feet; he shakes his head and becomes agitated and then holds forth for a half-hour or so, non-stop, covering each hot spot on the globe, appearing to be indiscreet but giving little away while making it clear that he regards the Reagan team as a pack of unvarnished amateurs in foreign policy.

I tried to find out if the United States intends to make a move soon in the INF talks. Are they planning to move off the zero option? It seems not. The United States will stand firm and let the Soviets make the next move. This is not, I believe, the strategy of the State Department, but it is of the Reagan administration. Perle über allies.

March 13, 1983 "The United States, through its President, has more often than not displayed the most callous ignorance of the feelings, views, interests and sensibilities of the leaders of the country with which we are closely linked economically, politically and geographically. We have been so unheeding that Sondra Gotlieb, wife of the Canadian Ambassador to Washington, once remarked to the *New York Times*, 'For some reason, a glaze passes over people's faces when you say Canada. Maybe we should invade South Dakota or something.' We are the 800-pound gorilla in the hemisphere and, more often than not, we have acted it."

The dean of political journalists, David Broder,[1] in the *Washington Post*. Public diplomacy pays off.

March 18, 1983 Called on George Bush to brief him before his official trip to Ottawa next week. I also saw Marty Feldstein in order to learn about his recent European trip with Bush. They are peddling the latest U.S. enthusiasm: restrict the sale of oil and gas equipment to Russia as a major potential supplier.

This is the kind of thing the ideologists in the Reagan administration keep coming up with, always adding new strains to our relations. Given

[1] (b. 1928) Widely read syndicated columnist on domestic affairs for the *Washington Post* for many years until present.

their lousy state, maybe the Bush visit to Ottawa will do some good, but I still think it should come later, after the cruise issue has been settled one way or another.

When I called on the vice-president in the Old Executive Office, I found him extremely courteous, as always, making me feel very welcome and at ease. I briefed him about the political situation in Canada, especially as it affects the issue of cruise-missile testing. Unlike the rest of the Reaganauts, Bush likes and admires Trudeau. But what influence does he have on the president and his advisers? We know the answer to that.

March 23, 1983 Sondra and I accompanied Vice-President Bush and his wife to Ottawa. Barbara seemed delighted to be along, and for some inexplicable reason, thanked me warmly. She seems to be a very unpretentious woman.

Through the next five hours or so I experienced the tribulation of being an ambassador. Should I go here or there, be at this place or another? At the "private" meeting between Bush, Trudeau, and MacEachen (plus officials), some snotty clerk stopped me from entering the meeting room. "Your name is not on the list," he said. I pushed him out of my way and went in. Hard as I tried the rest of the day, I couldn't find the son of a bitch who excluded me from the list.

On the flight up to Ottawa, Barbara told us of their experience in China when her husband was the ambassador there. She recounted how much she had enjoyed knowing John Small,[1] who was the Canadian ambassador to Peking at the time. "Poor John," she said, "he was so humiliated when Trudeau, during his official visit, went in to see Mao alone, without taking him." (No doubt he took Ivan Head instead.) But for my pushiness, I could have found myself in the same position as Small.

The timing of the vice-president's visit turned out to be remarkable, although not by design. Bush informed us of Reagan's announcement, almost taking place at the very same time, that the United States intends to develop anti-missile defence systems in space. Trudeau seemed quite shocked about the implications for the Anti-Ballistic Missile Treaty, and for his part Bush was vague and rather wobbly and confused. I think he was poorly briefed, if he was briefed at all. It was far from clear to any of us whether Bush had any advance notice of the speech, let alone any input into

---

[1] (1919–2006) Canadian Ambassador to China 1972–1976.

it. The timing of Reagan's blockbuster was obviously pure coincidence, as far as the Bush visit was concerned.

MacEachen arranged a meeting of Bush with a number of his cabinet colleagues, including, surprise, surprise, all the opponents of cruise-missile testing – Obadiah Slope, John Roberts, and Don Johnston,[1] who also speaks and looks like a high-minded Anglican clergyman. The members of the anti-cruise squad peppered Bush with objections to testing, using the old device of quoting a worried or irate constituent in their ridings. MacEachen sat impassively, or rather, passively, while Obadiah, in his righteous manner, pursued his prey. I suspect the whole affair was staged by MacEachen so he could woo and win the support of the anti-cruise squad for his leadership of the Liberal Party.

An excellent example of the masterful MacEachen style. The hesitancy, evasiveness, and unwillingness to lead are not really these things at all. They reflect his desire to turn around the "radical" wing of the Liberals without actually alienating them at a time when the party is going through an unannounced, and indeed, secret leadership race.

Remarkably, Trudeau stepped into the debate and showed impatience with Axworthy's and Roberts's line of reasoning. He was annoyed and started debating with his cabinet colleagues himself.

Meanwhile, throughout the day the question remained whether Trudeau would use any of the successive drafts written for his remarks tonight at the banquet in honour of Bush.

I was pleased beyond all expectation. At the big banquet Trudeau, without using a note, gave a speech, addressed not at Bush or the Americans at all but at Canadians and his own colleagues. He says the choices are, in effect, test the cruise or get out of NATO! An amazing statement. A powerful debating point. He was really saying why stay in NATO if we don't have the courage to play our role. I shot up to Trudeau to shake his hand. Among the several hundred blue-ribbon guests was the Soviet ambassador, my former neighbour and Trudeau's pal, Alexandre Yakovlev.[2] He was all smiles – Trudeau went out of his way to say the Soviets wanted peace.

---

[1] (b. 1936) President of the Treasury Board 1980–1984; President of the Liberal Party of Canada 1990–1994; Secretary-General of the Organisation for Economic Co-operation and Development 1996–2006.

[2] (1923–2005) Russian economist and governmental official, called the "godfather of glasnost." Soviet Ambassador to Canada 1973–1983 and latterly Dean of the Diplomatic Corps.

March 25, 1983 Back from speaking to investors at the blue-blooded Bullock Forum on Wall Street and being charmed by the octogenarian Hugh Bullock.[1] At the airport I met MacGuigan, who is in Washington, this time wearing his minister of justice hat. We met with Bill French Smith to discuss the dismal Jaffe case.

Driving in from the airport, MacGuigan told me that the rainmaker, Keith Davey, wants Trudeau to run again. The insiders pushing this scheme include Tom Axworthy, Jim Coutts, and Bob Murdoch. Obviously, MacEachen plays no part in it. They had a daring plan: have Trudeau say no to testing the cruise. He would then become "the man who refused the cruise," an instant Canadian hero and a world hero, a super-peacenik sticking it to the Yanks. A truly extraordinary tale. Hence, no one in the audience during the Bush visit could have been more surprised at Trudeau's passionate defence of the cruise than the cabal, several of whom (Coutts included) were sitting right there. I guess these strategists forgot to tell the prime beneficiary of their schemes, and he screwed it up royally for them. They must be in shock. This group adheres to the Liberal rule: govern at all costs. Power over principle.

We gave a black-tie dinner for MacGuigan with a terrific guest list: the French Smiths, Sandra Day O'Connor, the Meeses, Bill Webster, Lane Kirkland, Roger Mudd,[2] Vernon Jordan, the Haigs, the Wicks, Joe Alsop, Meg Greenfield, and more. We invited Arthur Erickson, who was in town, and naturally, he charmed everyone. At lunch with him today, we discussed how to get the construction of the embassy off dead-centre. I was told by an embassy officer that the property officials down from Ottawa are furious with me for showing "favouritism" to Arthur. I could have vomited on them.

March 26, 1983 I attended the Gridiron Club annual dinner, my second, as a guest again of one of the club's stalwarts, Alan Emory of the *Watertown Times*. He has a mortgage on me. I felt very puffed up this morning when Joe Kraft told me that "bidding" on me was heavy when the selection was made. Only about a half-dozen ambassadors were invited.

I sat next to Pat Moynihan, who has been cordial of late (that is, he

---

[1] (1898–1996) An investment banker and pioneer in managing mutual funds. President or director of several investment funds, including Calvin Bullock Ltd. and Bullock Fund Ltd.

[2] (b. 1928) U.S. television journalist. Co-anchor of the *NBC Nightly News* 1982–1983 and NBC's *Meet the Press* 1984–1985; political correspondent with the *MacNeil-Lehrer Newshour*.

recognizes me). Through the various alcoholic slurs, I could, with difficulty, detect the point he was making – the only capitals in the world where this type of theatre occurs are Washington, Ottawa, and Albany. At the pre-Gridiron *New York Times* reception yesterday, Jim Schlesinger, whom I have tried but not succeeded in getting to know, was, for him, excessively cordial (that is, he recognized me).

March 28, 1983 After attending a reception given by the – believe it or not – American Concrete Pipe Association, I proceeded to the home of Ivan and Nina Selin,[1] who invited us to a caviar party. Chatted at length with Bob MacNamara and Richard Perle.[2] MacNamara told me that Cap Weinberger was personally responsible for Reagan's Star Wars speech last week and Edward Teller[3] was a major influence.

April 5, 1983 Day of the opening game in Chicago between the Cubs and the Montreal Expos. Someone had the brilliant idea that the ambassadors of the host countries of the two teams should throw the first ball at the season's first game. I fly to Chicago at 10 a.m., in time for the big event. The stadium is packed. The sky is dark. The national anthems are played. The game officially begins. We are summoned to the plate. We await the signal. We wait and we wait. It starts to rain, lightly, then a downpour. We wait some more. I don't throw the ball. The game is cancelled. I fly back to Washington, arriving at 7:37 p.m.

Among my papers are briefing notes for my long-awaited call tomorrow morning on the Senate's leading intellectual, Patrick Moynihan. There are three memoranda: "Canada-U.S. Potato Trade"; "Fresh Yellow Onions Imported from the U.S."; "Importation [*sic*] of Hard Red Apples into Canada." Nothing on peace. Nothing on war. Nothing on benign neglect.

April 6, 1983 Moynihan cancelled.

Jean Chrétien, minister of energy, mines, and resources, came to town again, and we gave him and his wife, Aline, a large dinner tonight.

---

[1] Ivan Selin (b. 1937) Founder and Chairman of American Management Systems Inc. 1970–1988; Chairman of the Nuclear Regulatory Commission 1992–1995.

[2] (b. 1941) Assistant Secretary of Defense 1981–1987; Chairman of the Defense Policy Board Advisory Committee 2001–2003.

[3] (1908–2003) American nuclear physicist known as "the father of the hydrogen bomb."

Jean-Luc Pépin, minister of transport, came to town with his wife, and we are giving them a large dinner tomorrow.

Andrews Air Force Base, my home.

I perform a balancing act, accompanying each to see his ministerial counterpart and Senate and House figures, providing them with briefings, participating in their press conferences, and so on.

This was the first meeting of Pépin with his opposite number, Elizabeth Dole.[1] A very odd couple. Pépin was at his most solemn and earnest, trying to explain to Mme. Dole why the Canadian airlines were inherently, permanently disadvantaged in competing for U.S. air traffic and hence why it was impossible for Canada to agree to allow unrestricted competition.

Pépin really did try, I'll give him that. He tried and tried. He leaned forward in his armchair as he explained the deeper, structural factors and forces that do not allow us to move to the U.S. position on a competitive North American air traffic environment, and he stayed there. The more he tried, the more dazed Elizabeth Dole looked, the frozen smile revealing only incomprehension. Her reaction reminded me of Samuel Johnson's comment to Oliver Goldsmith when Goldsmith was trying to get him to see a point. "Sir," said Johnson, "the more you explain it, the less I understand it."

Tomorrow Pépin tries again with the almost equally polite and charming Nancy Kassebaum, the most influential senator on matters of air transportation. I doubt he will do better. The Americans simply do not understand our line of argument: we're big, we're empty, we can't afford open competition.

Sondra went to a tea hosted by Barbara Bush at the vice-president's house, we attended a book launch for Zbig Brzezinski's new work *Power and Principle*, and we hosted our dinner for the Chrétiens. It's close to midnight. I'm going upstairs to our sitting room for the last and best part of the day: watching reruns of *Benny Hill* on the tube.

April 10, 1983 The Shultz dinner was a remarkable affair – remarkable that it took place at all. Everyone at State said that this intimate dinner that George and Obie offered Allan MacEachen was most unusual, a privileged event, a mark of recognition of their friendship since student days. It was held at Shultz's very modest and undistinguished suburban home in Bethesda. There was myself and Sondra; de Montigny and Rick Burt were

---

[1] (b. 1936) Secretary of Transport 1983–1987; Secretary of Labor 1989–1990; President of the American Red Cross 1991–1999; Republican Senator from North Carolina 2003 to present.

the only other guests. The idea of the evening was to get a lead, in a relaxed atmosphere, on tomorrow's agenda on Canada-U.S. and global issues.

Shultz set the tone by first getting us to guzzle down his favourite drink, Manhattans, and then by walking over to the open fire and barbecuing big, fat steaks directly on top of the logs. He managed to perform this feat, which Sondra and I had never seen done before, by laying a thick layer of salt directly on the burning logs and then positioning the steaks on the salt. The steaks were not only edible, they were delicious.

MacEachen had it in mind that he was going to express some concerns to Shultz about U.S. policy in Central America, especially in El Salvador and Nicaragua. Possibly he was inspired by de Montigny to do this, or perhaps it was simply a matter of knowing that the Canadian press would nail him if he didn't say he told Shultz that Canada disapproved of U.S. actions in Central America.

When the discussions finally got going, the two ministers sitting in easy chairs facing each other in the living room close to the fire, MacEachen broached the Central American topic with the utmost delicacy and deliberation, expressing himself in an even more rococo fashion than is normal for him. I knew where he was trying to go, but without my insider's knowledge, I would have been at a loss. It was evident that he did not want to offend Shultz on his first meeting with him on U.S. soil and dining, as he was, under his own roof. He worked his way around the subject like he was designing a pretzel. His analysis reached new heights of subtlety and obliqueness, even for the master himself.

During this hesitant monologue of some eight or ten minutes' duration, Shultz sat absolutely impassive (Shultz in his Easter Island–statue pose). For a while I wasn't sure Shultz was able to decipher the hermetic message that MacEachen was trying to convey. After he finally ended his exposition, Shultz continued to remain silent for what seemed an inordinately long time. Then he looked at MacEachen, who was rather unnerved, and said, "I see, Allan. What you are trying to tell me is that you don't care if we lose the Panama Canal." Full stop.

April 12, 1983 The denouement to our black-tie event for MacEachen last night. At the dinner we had, among others, the Shultzes, Paul Volcker, Scoop Jackson, Ethel Kennedy,[1] and Susan Mary Alsop. For some reason,

[1] (b. 1928) Member of the Kennedy family by marriage (1950) to Robert F. Kennedy.

Susan Mary, as she was leaving, became exceedingly effusive and gushy about the dinner, the host, hostess, and guest of honour and said she would be delighted if we could bring MacEachen to lunch tomorrow at her Georgetown house. This morning I rather perfunctorily asked MacEachen if he might be interested in dropping in at Susan Mary's for a bite of lunch, and to my great surprise he said he would. The old bachelor appeared intrigued by the lady.

Sondra telephoned Susan Mary to say we were coming. This caused panic on the part of Ms. Alsop, who professed to have no recollection of her insistent invitation last night and complained of a horrid headache and feeling quite ill. After much debate we went, bringing in tow the grub, the foreign minister, and Sandra and Richard Gwyn, who are visiting us from Ottawa.

Susan Mary, restored, it seemed, to health, welcomed us warmly. We entered into her room with the monkey paintings, and inside we noted a wispy, elderly man who turned out to be her house guest, A.W.L. Rowse, visiting historian from Oxford. For the next two hours, Rowse, the Cornishman, held forth non-stop in his high-pitched, shrill voice, mesmerizing MacEachen the Scotsman.

Only with difficulty did we extract him from Susan Mary's drawing room and the Cornishman's hand from Richard Gwyn's knee.

April 13, 1983 Washington is talking about the prominent article in the *Wall Street Journal* entitled "Canada Tries to Organize Lobby in U.S." Describing how our cement industry was blindsided by a restrictive provision buried in a gas-tax bill, the *Journal* article points out, correctly, that the days of our relying on the State Department and the White House to fight our battles are now over. The authorization by cabinet of our famous $650,000 is mentioned, and I am quoted as saying "foreign countries require a whole new level of sophistication if they are going to succeed in defending their interests in Washington." We must have allies in our battles. "The cast changes," I said, "as the issues change."

The attention being paid to our new strategy is gratifying but mystifying. What we are planning to do is something the Japanese have been doing for some time and on a far grander scale. So why the news? Maybe because in the American mind, Boy Scouts don't lobby.

April 14, 1983 Walter Gordon,[1] éminence grise of the Canadian nationalists, called on me at his request. I had not met him before. I was curious to know why I was to receive this great honour, but it turned out he had no agenda. He just wanted to gossip about the U.S. scene and the state of the relationship. I think this is the first time I've ever been graced by the attention of one of the founding fathers of our modern nationalist movement. I'm worried about this visitation. Do they see me as one of them? Am I becoming acceptable – or useful – to this cabal?

April 15, 1983 Sondra plans a luncheon for Alice Munro.[2] It's hard work. Washington is not New York or London. It's easier in this town to draw guests to meet a second-rate American politician than a first-rate foreign writer.

April 18, 1983 We held a meeting in the chancery library of all our consuls general in the United States. Officials from the U.S. Bureau in Ottawa came down for it. These U.S. heads-of-post meetings are always held in Ottawa, largely because headquarters is very turf-conscious and wants to make the point that our network of consular offices in the United States reports to the bureau in Ottawa and, heaven forbid, not to the ambassador in Washington. This time, under pressure from me, Ottawa relented and we had the meeting in Washington. The Ottawa officials are nervous and ill at ease.

My pitch was that the primary function of the consul general is public relations. Their job is not to sell widgets, it's to sell Canada. We made big strides. These people were delighted to be told that their jobs are important. It's been a long time since they've heard that from Ottawa. They were delighted to hear that they're not merely consuls but diplomats who should be stars in their communities and putting their country on the map. They particularly welcomed my encouraging them to cultivate the congressmen in their regions. It's far easier, I told them, to establish a personal relationship with a representative and his staff on their home turf than in Washington.

---

[1] (1906–1987) Elected Liberal Member of Parliament for Davenport, Ontario, in 1962; Minister of Finance 1963–1965; President of the Privy Council 1967–1968, when he retired from politics.

[2] (b. 1931) Canadian short story writer, widely considered one of the greatest short story writers in modern literature.

April 22, 1983 Al Mackling, Manitoba's minister of natural resources, is coming to town. His fellow Manitobans have just finished burning the American flag in their fair province, and I'm told he wants to repair the damage. The Manitobans have done the crusade against Garrison a lot of harm. If he wants to repair the damage, he should stay home.

April 23, 1983 Another weekend with John and Geils Turner as our house guests. Craig Oliver[1] invited them and us to attend the White House Correspondents' Dinner tonight, so when we heard that John had accepted, we asked them to stay with us.

I thought about it a lot and finally decided I would try to put Turner in touch with George Shultz. Shultz has such an enormous regard for Turner that I knew he would enjoy seeing him. Despite Trudeau's feelings towards Turner (personal animosity, which is reciprocated), I went ahead anyway because Shultz is more important for the relationship than any other American. So I asked Shultz to the Residence on Friday for a drink or even a bite of dinner, but he was doubtful. The invitation came at a very bad time, he said, because of the international situation and the recent massacre of the Marines in Lebanon. Then I got a last-minute call that he and Obie would come for an early dinner.

We rushed to set up a small table in the library at the Residence. It was ironic because I had just escorted out the advance men for Trudeau's visit here next week. The outgoing prime minister's men exit; the next prime minister arrives. We dined by the fire in a very intimate atmosphere. Turner knew that for Shultz to come at a time like this was an act of loyalty and friendship. But the conversation was extremely difficult. Shultz was tired. He gave the impression of a man submerged under the tide of events. The horrendous acts in Lebanon have created a ghastly personal burden for him, and although his strength is often compared to that of an ox, this was a melancholy man who seemed resigned to the course of events, whatever they may be.

After the early departure of the Shultzes, we sat around by the fire for a long time. We sensed that Shultz might not survive in the job, that his legendary strength and reserves may no longer be in play, and that perhaps foreign affairs may not actually be his thing, coming to the political aspects as he has, so late in life.

---

[1] (b. 1938) Joined the CTV television network in 1972; CTV's Ottawa Bureau Chief and Correspondent 1975–1981; Washington Bureau Chief 1981–1988.

April 24, 1983 We gave a small Sunday brunch for John at the Residence, to which we invited the Kirklands and Krafts. Kraft is one of the few American journalists interested in what's happening outside the United States (almost the last of the breed), and Kirkland has some (slight) interest in Canadian labour matters – mainly he can't abide our union chiefs. But he is deeply interested in politics. John, in top form, peppered the two men with questions about U.S. domestic politics and foreign policy. I was impressed with how easily Turner got on with the guests and how he sensed what he could learn from them. Both Kirkland and Kraft told me after lunch that they thought he was, well, prime ministerial.

Turner and I talked of his plans. He was cautious, noncommittal. I know he wants to succeed Trudeau, but he is deeply skeptical about the likelihood of Trudeau stepping down soon.

April 25, 1983 Two days to go to the Trudeau visit. Not a formal, official one (no chance of that) but a working visit to discuss the upcoming Williamsburg Summit. Last day for Sondra and I to agonize over the guest list. Can you imagine – Reagan speaking the same night as our dinner? Baldridge cancelling. Chief Justice Burger cancelling. Bush declining to drop in. Moynihan ringing up and saying he's too tired to come. I managed to add two more cabinet secretaries at the eleventh hour (Block, Hodel). This business of fortifying the guest list is a horror. I tried to persuade Judge Clark to attend – I said the absence of the president's national security adviser will be noted by the press. But he said he is with the president. I feel like calling Eagleburger and protesting. I don't. What could he do? I suppose it will be all right. The good news is that the turnout of the Washington media will be terrific. Trudeau asked us to invite Margot Kidder.[1] The Vancouver lady will add glamour and a dose of Hollywood radical chic.

April 26, 1983 A sad day in Washington, and one feels the shock and dismay everywhere. I attended the memorial service at the Washington Cathedral for the hundreds of Americans killed in the U.S. compound in Lebanon. The president and Nancy were there, as was everyone else in official Washington. There was a sense in the cathedral of pointless death, of the irrational triumphant. There is a sense of a Great Power that is

---

[1] (b. 1948) Canadian-born film actress of the 1970s and 1980s, best known for her role as Lois Lane in the 1978 movie *Superman* and its sequels.

powerless, of Gulliver lying prone, bound by invisible tapes. Perhaps only a Great Power could achieve such heights of ceremonial solemnity.

April 27, 1983 Trudeau winged into Andrews Air Force Base in the morning, where I met him, and we proceeded to a lunch at the Madison organized by the PMO for Canadian businessmen in his entourage. What a lunch. What a bunch. A dozen respectable businessmen such as Ced Ritchie and Charles Bronfman and a pack of PMO groupies. After this non-event, the prime minister had a relaxed meeting with Bush – arms control all the way.

Our black-tie dinner for about eighty exceeded all our expectations. We were competing with the president's address on Central America to a joint session of Congress, but that didn't distract the guests at all. The fact that so many American officials were playing hooky seemed to add piquancy to our event. Reagan spoke just before the dinner began. Trudeau watched his speech on the tube sitting in the library at our Residence. He seemed thunderstruck at the brilliance of Reagan's presentation. I couldn't believe it, but it was the first time he'd seen Reagan on television. The guests came early to watch the president's address, and they stayed late. As a result of my last-minute Herculean efforts, we ended up with three cabinet secretaries, three powerful senators (Moynihan, Stevens, and Laxalt),[1] and a broad array of movie and media stars.

We ate under a large tent, and it was noisy and cold. Jimmy Symington[2] sang songs from the thirties, Noel Coward[3] et al. Trudeau did the Charleston. I gave a short, solemn toast to Trudeau, and Bill French Smith gave a breezy, joking response that enraged the Canadian Hollywood celebrities (Christopher Plummer,[4] Donald Sutherland, Norm Jewison). The presence of Alan Pakula[5] (*Sophie's Choice*), Mort Zuckerman,[6] Ethel Kennedy, and Roone Arledge added to the sense that this was a glamorous

---

[1] Paul Laxalt (b. 1922) Republican Lieutenant-Governor of Nevada 1963–1967; Governor of Nevada 1967–1971; Senator from Nevada 1974–1986.

[2] (b. 1927) Washington lawyer and politician. Democratic Representative from Missouri 1969–1977.

[3] (1899–1973) English actor, playwright, and composer of popular music.

[4] (b. 1929) Canadian theatrical, film, and television actor and winner of many awards.

[5] (1928–1998) American film producer, writer, and director.

[6] (b. 1937) Canadian-born American magazine editor, publisher, and real estate magnate. Current Editor-in-Chief of *U.S. News & World Report* and Publisher/owner of the *New York Daily News*.

event. Barbara Walters[1] sat next to a noisy fountain and did not appreciate it. Susan Mary Alsop was gushing. After opportuning on my part, Trudeau invited her to visit and write up his art deco mansion for *Architectural Digest*. Kenneth Galbraith towered over all the crowd, except Volcker, and fended off idiotic questions from the press about whether he would like to replace him. Eagleburger and I sparred all evening. Charlie Wick played piano (badly, according to Deaver), Mike Deaver played the piano (well, according to Deaver), and everyone danced. Christopher Plummer, when asked if he was intimidated by all the powerful jobs surrounding the actors and stars, said, "Heavens, no, usually they are intimidated by us."

Much gossiping throughout the evening about the fact that one of our "propaganda" films, *If You Love This Planet* (the one starring Dr. Helen Caldicott,[2] anti-nuclear crusader), won an Academy Award. French Smith took credit for his department giving the film so much publicity. "We aim to please," he said.

Fresh Newfoundland halibut, Quebec maple surprise (called Bombe Ibrahim, after our chef), Manitoba whitefish caviar, New Brunswick fiddleheads (inedible), Alberta vodka. No Canadian wines. (I'll get flak.) A Canadian event with high Canadian flavour. A glamorous night, as glamorous, I think, as this town has seen in a while. What made it so? The mysterious magnetism of Trudeau, the high Washington officials, the mighty Washington media, the touch of Hollywood, and the knowledge that in the midst of the frivolity, the players in Washington count as in no other capital in the world.

April 28, 1983 I called on Trudeau at the Madison at 10 a.m. He looked tired. Out all night or in all night with Margot Kidder? We met in the Oval Office, four on four (Reagan, Bush, Meese, Robinson against Trudeau, Marchand, Fowler, Gotlieb). We talked arms control. Trudeau pressed Reagan for more initiatives, more proposals, more flexibility. Reagan handled himself well.

There followed a banal discussion on the Williamsburg Summit at an enlarged meeting and the lunch at the White House for a couple of dozen. When we gathered around a table in the larger group, there was a big

[1] (b. 1931) First female network news anchor, on ABC News starting in 1976. Known for her years on *20/20*, she became the show's sole host from 1999 to 2002.

[2] (b. 1938) Australian physician and anti-nuclear advocate. Actively involved with Physicians for Social Responsibility.

surprise in store for everyone except Trudeau. After the usual pleasantries and presidential anecdotes, Trudeau made an astonishing statement. With a view, I suppose, to reducing the tension in the room, he said, "I too have a joke to tell."

The Canadians were amazed – none of us had ever heard Trudeau tell a joke before. And, believe it or not, it was a Newfie joke. A zoo in Newfoundland, he recounted, placed an ad in the papers stating that there would be an award of ten thousand dollars for anyone volunteering to sleep with the zoo's rare white gorilla, who was not reproducing. Only one man answered the ad – a Newfoundlander – who was then interviewed by a panel and awarded the job. "Not so fast," said the Newfoundlander. "Before I accept, I have three questions I want answered." "Go ahead, ask," said the panel. "Number one. Do I have to kiss the gorilla?" The panel responded no, not if you don't want to. "Number two. If I'm successful, can the offspring be brought up a Catholic?" No problem, the panel replied. "Number three. Do I have to pay the ten thousand dollars before I sleep with the gorilla or can I wait until after?"

Reagan and the whole group of Americans – including Bush, Shultz, Deaver, and Meese – burst into almost uncontrollable laughter, which went on and on. I thought Reagan would roll out of his chair. Needless to say, we Canadians laughed too.

Trudeau amazed the Americans (and us) again by saying how much he was impressed by Reagan's speech last night, that it was statesmanlike, that the United States is a Great Power, has vital security interests in Central America, and that Canada understands this. (A very different line here from his own foreign minister's, again.) Trudeau then played the bad guy. Will you really push for a peaceful solution in Central America? Will Reagan really push the Reagan plan in the Middle East?

Reagan seemed to take the pushing and implied message (the United States and the Soviet Union should recognize each other's vital concerns) with equanimity. Meese looked relaxed, as did Bush (he always seems relaxed). But Judge Clark never stopped scowling throughout the lunch, except when he was looking shocked. Chatting with the media, Trudeau was supportive of Reagan on arms control and the Williamsburg Summit, so the White House gang are pleased. They were very nervous about the press conference. Trudeau showed he can be a statesman, but personally, I thought that throughout the visit he was a little wobbly and not at his best. But I've seen him a lot worse.

On the way to the airport, I took Trudeau to the embassy site and fired him up about the endless delays in getting a contract for Erickson. He was very disturbed by this. I didn't blame anyone in particular, just a combination of diplomatic glue and mud. We did a quick unscheduled stop at I.M. Pei's East Wing of the National Gallery. This was the first time he'd seen it. Trudeau adores architecture and was stunned by the building, saying that, along with the Anthropology Museum in Mexico City, he thought it was one of the two finest modern museum buildings in the world.

An easy visit. Trudeau was relaxed. Now I can be too.

April 29, 1983 We get many bravos for the dinner. The *Washington Post* covers the stars, Deaver playing the piano, Margot Kidder dancing, Don Sutherland (allegedly, inaccurately) sulking. Jack Valenti says it was the best Washington party in ten years.

April 30, 1983 The parade of visitors to Washington continues, MPs, the mayor of Quebec City, and on and on. Marc Lalonde is now in town, making him the sixth federal cabinet visitor within a month (not counting Trudeau). A curious thought occurred to me this afternoon: if I stay in Washington long enough, is there anyone important in Canada who will not make the pilgrimage? Will I meet everyone who is politically active in every region of the country? What draws them all to the American capital?

More questions. How long will my allowances last? How long will the embassy staff last? How long will the staff at the Residence last? How long will Sondra last? How long will I last?

May 1, 1983 In Minneapolis on my first visit to Minnesota since my appointment and since I was a university student in dry Winnipeg in pursuit of a wet weekend. Very handsome old market square in St. Paul. Stayed in the renovated Hotel St. Paul, run by a Canadian, and a very fine building. The city has a certain quality, a human scale that reminds me of downtown Winnipeg in the old days.

I spoke at the Humphrey Forum to an audience of several hundred. As the late Herbert Humphrey[1] was the most impressive American politician I ever met (it was in Geneva many years ago), I felt good about speaking

[1] Republican Senator from Minnesota 1949–1964 and 1971–1978; Senate Majority Whip 1961–1965; Vice-President of the United States 1965–1969; presidential candidate in 1968.

there. I held a press conference, snuck into a local museum, gave a TV interview at PBS, and got a visit from a slow-witted cousin of mine, whom I had not previously known existed. Then Governor Rudy Perpich[1] gave a grand dinner in my honour at his Residence. A beautiful northern spring night, a lovely old mansion, some sixty or seventy guests, musicians, enormous quantities of quite decent food, short speeches, and many pleasant encounters. It doesn't get any better.

May 2, 1983 I gave an address to a joint session of the legislature in Minnesota in their magnificent capital building designed by Cass Gilbert,[2] who also did the fabulous Library of Congress. It was a very solemn occasion – the first time in years that they held a joint session. I spoke on the evils of acid rain, and since Minnesota is a victim, it was very well received.

The address was, for me, the climax of a memorable day that began at a very early hour in the Old Russian Cemetery. As a result of some remarkable sleuthing by a friend of our fine consul general, I was able to locate the gravestone of my great-grandfather Jacob in St. Paul. I learned from his gravestone that he died here in 1906 (after coming down from Hirsch, Saskatchewan). And I learned that the name of his father, my great-great-grandfather, was Moshe, and my great-great-grandfather's name on the maternal side was David. The gravestones were remarkably unworn (no acid rain on this patch).

In that rather desolate old graveyard, I had the feeling, ever so corny and ever so moving, of being incredibly privileged to be Canadian, born in a land of opportunity.

May 4, 1983 In a rotten state of mind, I kicked off the day with a working breakfast for Peter Lougheed at the Residence. I sweat when I think of him being my official responsibility for four days. He's been planning this visit for months, mastering every last tiny detail.

I asked Lougheed, as I did on the telephone last week, not to visit senators and congressmen on the Hill without me or someone from the embassy

---

[1] (1928–1995) Lieutenant-Governor of Minnesota 1971–1976; Governor of Minnesota 1976–1979 and 1983–1991.

[2] (1859–1934) U.S. architect. His works include the Minnesota State Capitol, St. Paul, 1895–1905; Woolworth Building, New York City, 1913; and the United States Supreme Court, Washington, D.C., 1932–1935.

accompanying him. After all, I explained, our energy policies (particularly gas prices) are the biggest current issues we have with the States. His effectiveness as a communicator and his official position mean that his visit is important. I failed utterly to persuade him. "They will be more frank without a federal presence," he declared, "but I have no objections to your coming to Senator Jackson's lunch, since he invited you."

The visits of Lévesque and Lougheed signal that we are a divided country. I worry that we are inviting opportunities for the gentlemen of Congress to play off one level of our government against the other.

May 8, 1983 I was awakened this Sunday morning by an early call from Lougheed in Canada, who read me a letter he is sending to senators and congressmen and consulted me on some difficult passages. So I made some headway in convincing him that I work for Alberta in Washington and not just Ottawa. But I think he still harbours the curious constitutional view that the embassy is "accredited" to the administration (so I could accompany him to see the energy secretary) but not to Congress (so his people must make the appointments and he must see them alone). Aside from his belief in this unfortunate doctrine, I found him to be one of the most effective Canadian politicians to walk the corridors of Congress.

May 9, 1983 The long-planned "Acid Rain Dinner," inaugural event of the Movement Against Acid Rain, took place at the Sheraton Centre in Toronto. It was sponsored by the Muskoka Lakes Association. Never heard of it before, which is a comment on my ignorance. Over eight hundred people attended at a hundred bucks a head. The concern of the environmentalists has become the cause of the establishment.

The mixture of sulphur dioxide and nitrogen oxide that produces acid rain is a curious phenomenon. There may be doubts about its environmental effect, but there certainly can't be any doubt about its political effect – the crusade to reduce acid rain is the most unifying force in Canada today. Witness our head table tonight: David Peterson – Liberal; John Fraser[1] – Tory; John Roberts – Liberal; Doug Creighton[2] – arch-conservative;

---

[1] (b. 1931) PC Member of Parliament for Vancouver 1972–1993; Minister of the Environment 1979–1980 and of Fisheries and Oceans 1984–1985; Speaker of the House of Commons 1986–1994.

[2] (1919–2004) Veteran journalist and founding publisher of the *Toronto Sun* in 1971.

Bob Rae[1] – left-winger; Abe Rotstein[2] – socialist; Margaret Atwood – nationalist heroine; Izzy Sharpe[3] – businessman. Also the president of the *Toronto Star*, the bishop of Toronto, and the mayor of Toronto. All representatives of "Toronto the Good." All enemies of acid rain. I'm sure they all own cottages on the Muskoka lakes. A beautiful union of patriotism and the pocketbook. Everyone loved each other tonight – and hated the Yanks.

May 10, 1983 I called on Paul Nitze,[4] accompanied by Kinsman. I was impressed by this sinewy, cold, arrogant, intellectually tough septuagenarian. They don't get any more hardline than he. We got into a pretty stiff argument about whether the United States can better explain why the French and British nuclear forces need not be taken into account in the INF and START negotiations. This is a point that bothers Trudeau a lot. After raising it in his talks with Bush a couple of weeks ago, he's still very hot on it. He believes the Soviets are making yards in the propaganda wars because of our failure to explain our position. (It's not clear to me what the evidence is for his opinion.) I got nowhere with Nitze, and he got irritated. At least five times he asked if I had read Eagleburger's article on the matter in last Sunday's *Washington Post*. Wasn't I impressed by it? Not really. I tried to explain. I didn't succeed.

Dinner given by Lucky Roosevelt[5] for Oscar de la Renta at the F Street Club. On my left, Evangeline Bruce complained about how awful the food was. I agreed wholeheartedly. On my right, Elizabeth Dole extolled the quality of the cuisine, and I agreed with her wholeheartedly. Keeping in shape in a duplicitous profession.

May 11, 1983 Dinner again at the F Street Club, the favourite hangout of the Washingtonians. This one was given by Elliot Richardson in honour of Jim Baker. A great crowd of senators, journalists, and socialites.

---

[1] (b. 1948) Member of Parliament for Broadview-Greenwood 1979–1982; Leader of the Opposition in the Ontario Legislature 1987–1990; Premier of Ontario 1990–1995, the first leader of the Ontario New Democratic Party to serve in that capacity.

[2] Canadian economist and co-founder of the Committee for an Independent Canada.

[3] (b. 1931) Canadian businessman and founder, president, and CEO of Four Seasons Hotels and Resorts.

[4] (1907–2004) Secretary of the Navy 1963–1967. Chief Negotiator of the Intermediate-Range Nuclear Forces Treaty 1981–1984. Special Advisor to the President and Secretary of State on Arms Control 1984. Helped shape Cold War defence policy over the course of numerous presidential administrations.

[5] U.S. Chief of Protocol 1982–1989.

Jim Baker told me he was impressed by reports of Trudeau's open letter on cruise-missile testing. When I offered to send him a copy, he said he would give it to the president. Trudeau has made big yards in this town with his defence of the cruise. They just can't figure this guy out. Welcome to the club.

I asked Baker why, according to opinion polls, the American public did not seem to accept that vital American security interests were at stake in Central America. He said he was mystified and didn't know the answer. He asked me if Canadians realized what were the demographic implications for Canada if Central America went communist. We could not, he said, insulate ourselves from the northward pressures.

I congratulated Bill Ruckelshaus[1] on his appointment as EPA administrator. It's hard to believe that Anne Gorsuch has gone down in flames. I talked to him about our concerns over acid rain, and he replied, much to my astonishment and pleasure, that progress had to be made in this field. He had already talked to the president about this, he added. Unlike his previous boss, Nixon, Ronald Reagan, he said (again, to my astonishment), had an open mind.

Trudeau respected in the Reagan White House? Progress on acid rain? The dawn of a new era? Am I dreaming?

May 12, 1983 My successor in Ottawa, Marcel Massé,[2] is in town. We called on Eagleburger, who was in outstanding form and extremely frank about the Soviets and his recent discussions with Dobrynin about the Middle East. Eagleburger said he is very unimpressed by Dobrynin – he ranks him in the lower half of the diplomatic corps, in terms of ability. I find that extraordinary. Eagleburger doesn't believe the Soviets will enter into any agreement on missiles until our deployment actually takes place. He fears that if things go badly in Central America, an isolationist tide could sweep the United States that will last for years.

I asked Eagleburger about Trudeau's concern with regard to counting the French and British nuclear forces in the INF negotiations. He referred me

---

[1] (b. 1932) First Environmental Protection Agency Administrator 1970–1973 and again 1983–1985. Director of the FBI 1973. In a 1973 event known as the "Saturday Night Massacre," Ruckelshaus and his boss, Elliot Richardson, resigned their positions within the Justice Department rather than obey an order from President Nixon to fire the Watergate special prosecutor, Archibald Cox.

[2] (b. 1940) Clerk of the Privy Council and Secretary to the Cabinet 1979–1980; Undersecretary of State for External Affairs 1982–1985.

to his article in the *Post*. I told him (gently) that I thought it was too long and not very effective. Eagleburger confessed, "Nitze wrote it. He couldn't sign it, so he asked me." Now I understand why Nitze was so impressed by it.

May 13, 1983 Kay Graham called on me at the embassy yesterday. She came with Mark Edmiston, the president of *Newsweek*. They told me *Newsweek* is planning to print its magazine in Canada, or at least the Canadian edition – a big difference, I said – and thereby create jobs in our country. Graham and Edmiston were very aware that *Time* is doing well up north and explained that what the *Post* and *Newsweek* want is for us not to eliminate postal subsidies for foreign periodicals, as it was rumoured we were going to do. Eliminating the subsidy would cost *Newsweek* about half a million a year. Kay said it would be most upsetting if the *Time* subsidies were grandfathered and *Newsweek* did not get them.

I found it rather amusing to see the most powerful woman in America and perhaps the most powerful person in Washington outside the White House acting as if she were an advocate in a Coke-Pepsi war and engaging in unvarnished lobbying.

Discriminatory media policies are a pain in the neck. They create more bad public relations than almost anything else we do. It won't make me popular in Ottawa, but I'm going to advise Trudeau and MacEachen to give very careful thought to grandfathering *Newsweek*, if we remove the subsidies.

May 15, 1983 Sunday night dinner at Marshall Coyne's[1] for Eva Gabor.[2] The connection between the ancient hotelier and ancient movie star is unknown and unexplained. A beautiful night and we ate a barbecue on the terrace, jutting out from the museum of ancient oddities and curiosities that fill his house. There were a couple of dozen Washingtonians at dinner, but Bernie Kalb,[3] who has just returned from the Middle East, where he accompanied Shultz on his triumphant tour, was the star of the evening. The media are always the stars in Washington. Shultz, he said, was very impressed by Begin.

---

[1] (1911–2000) Builder and owner of the Madison Hotel in Washington, which opened in 1963 and has hosted every U.S. president since.

[2] (1919–1995) Hungarian-born American actress.

[3] (b. 1922) Journalist, media critic, and author. Assistant Secretary of State for Public Affairs and a spokesman for the State Department 1984–1986.

We ate at the same table as Bob and Helen Strauss. Strauss seemed in low spirits, which was unusual for him. People are urging him to run for the presidency, including a group of businessmen who offered to set up a large fund – about 15 million – to help him do so. "So why not run?" I asked. "You'd make a great president." He didn't answer, but the truth is that despite his awesome political sense and unrivalled understanding of how to broker the zillion interests in the country, he stands no chance. He's Jewish. Even if he is from Texas.

May 16, 1983 Joe Kraft dropped over for tea. He asked me about the *Washington Post* report of Trudeau denouncing Reagan as fanatically anti-Russian. Is it true? I got the same question several times last night. It's rough working for this man. One day I walk tall, getting kudos from the Bakers of this world, and the next I'm on the defence, explaining that Trudeau is not really questioning the sincerity of Reagan (that's the best way I could put it).

May 18, 1983 On a few hours' notice, I got invited to the Old Executive Office to attend the swearing-in ceremony for Bill Ruckelshaus as EPA administrator. The president was there, cabinet secretaries, senators, congressmen, family members – and myself. The only ambassador. I was given a front-row seat. It seemed someone had decided that on this occasion I could be a useful prop.

The president gets up, welcomes Ruckelshaus back to his old job under Nixon, when he was first EPA administrator, calls him "Mr. Clean," and then says: "There are many areas of immediate concern, but let me single out four that I would like you to address as quickly as possible in your new post. First, many of us, both here and in Canada, are concerned about the harmful effects of acid rain and what it may be doing to our lakes and forests. So I would like you to work with others in our administration, with the Congress, and with state and local officials to meet this issue head-on."

This is Reagan speaking? Or is this Reagan, the actor, reading his lines? Ruckelshaus must have written those lines. Obviously, he laid down his conditions for accepting the appointment as administrator. And Reagan, or his advisers, agreed to them. But why? Is this for real? Or is this show business, a let's pretend we're serious and thus disarm our environmentally minded critics?

There are also Darman fingerprints on Reagan's text. Ruckelshaus would never have got that statement out of Reagan without the plotting and manoeuvring of Darman. Is it possible that my discussions with Darman on this issue played a role?

Dealing with Ruckelshaus will be heavenly after Anne Gorsuch. Under any circumstances, it would be a pleasure to deal with him, an American in the best tradition of this nation's governing elite.

May 19, 1983 The day started with a novelty. In Washington, a senator calling on an ambassador is the rarest of rare events. According to U.S. protocol, when a U.S. cabinet secretary or any official other than the president or vice-president wants to see a senator, he's got to call on them on the Hill. Even if the senator wants to see the secretary, the secretary goes to the Hill. And when an ambassador wants to see a senator, he, of course, goes to the Hill. And, of course, waits around.

So I was surprised to get a telephone call the other day from the legendary senator from Louisiana, Russell Long,[1] nephew of the Kingfish, Huey, saying he wanted to call on me at the embassy. I responded, "Senator, I'll be happy to come and see you." "No, sir," he replied, "it's my pleasure to call on you." Well, when Russell Long wants something, he goes out and gets it – that's his reputation. Bob Strauss told me that Huey's nephew, as senior minority member in the Finance Committee, is perhaps the most powerful Democrat in the Senate. He gets people in debt by doing them a favour and – wham – collects at the right moment.

The senator wanted something badly, and it didn't take long for him to come to the point – it's a Canadian pavilion at the New Orleans World Fair next year. This will be a world-class crummy affair but if we want a U.S. pavilion in Vancouver in 1986, we had better recognize the connection. The jolly senator – and he was all chuckles – made absolutely sure I recognized this. My problem will be to find a way to make Ottawa understand his personal power to make or break U.S. participation in Expo '86. And U.S. participation in Expo, or lack of it, will make or break the fair.

In the evening Polly and Joe Kraft threw a party in honour of Sondra at their Georgetown house. The occasion was the publication of the U.S. edition of Sondra's book *A Woman of Consequence*. A great mixture of Democrats and Republicans showed up: the French Smiths, the Brandons,

---

[1] (1918–2003) Democratic Senator from Louisiana 1948–1987; Chairman of the Senate Committee on Finance 1965–1981.

Cattos, Phillipses, Brinkleys, Stevenses, Fritcheys, Schlesingers, among others. And the *Post* was covering the event. We are awash in ink.

May 22, 1983 Trudeau received Gorbachev[1] in Ottawa a few days ago and had a one-hour private dinner in his office and a ninety-minute conversation at lunch. It was, according to my sources, a spectacularly interesting couple of meals. Gorbachev (while being officially responsible for agriculture) talked without notes in a remarkably assured and well-informed way about the current state of play in arms negotiations and everything else. Trudeau defended our right to test the cruise, making the point that the Soviets were testing it. He made it clear that the Soviet deployment of the SS-18 was a major factor in Western determination to proceed with its own deployment. He also told Gorbachev that while he found Reagan's rhetoric distasteful, it would be a mistake to believe the president doesn't reflect public opinion. Look what happened to Carter, he said, after America's humiliation over events in Iran and Afghanistan. Trudeau the hardliner. Go figure.

May 28, 1983 Jacques Helie drove me to Langley Air Force Base to meet Trudeau on his arrival in Washington to attend the Williamsburg Economic Summit. The prime minister was resplendent in a snappy brim-down straw hat, extremely well-tailored brown suit, and long-collared yellow shirt. He was very conscious of his dandified appearance, the image of studied spontaneity. He seemed excited, but in a low-key, controlled way, about his imminent appearance on the world stage. I am wondering whether he is going to treat this summit as theatre, in the best Trudeau tradition at international diplomatic events. (Got a banister, anyone?)

We had a briefing shortly after his arrival, and immediately I worried about his tone and attitude. He opposes any references to features of our common negotiating position in the proposed summit declaration on security and arms control. He is adamant. He simply wants a call for peace. He is insensitive to the British and French demands to exclude their nuclear forces from the negotiations, and he will refuse to agree to any declaration that endorses their position. I asked him if the type of statement he has in

[1] (b. 1931) General Secretary of the Communist Party of the Soviet Union 1985–1991. Awarded the Nobel Peace Prize in 1990.

mind wouldn't simply increase public pressure on ourselves in the West, rather than on the Russians. He didn't reply. He doesn't see my point or he doesn't agree with it.

May 29, 1983 Day two of the Williamsburg Summit. I hate this cutesy place. Artificial and didactic. More sitting around. More ego diminishment. I'm angry at my colleagues. I had to push so hard to get into the summit. If the Americans hadn't invited the summit ambassadors to the social events, I doubt I would be here. I had to push to get a room, and then I had to push to get into their briefings of the PM. For all this I think I have to credit my two good colleagues, neither of whom would be in their jobs if it weren't for me: de Montigny Marchand and Bob Fowler. Ah well, what is gratitude? Samuel Johnson defined it accurately: a lively expectation of favours to come.

At the main Trudeau briefing today, we learned about his dogfight with Thatcher and Reagan. Our prime minister, true to form, is playing the bad boy. I'll concede that he's probably sincere in his peace-loving role, but I don't understand his lack of acknowledgement of the limitations on Canada's interests in all this. He is battling not just the Americans but the British and French – and even the Germans, although I'm not sure he fully appreciates this. Maybe he thinks he is just tweaking the nose of the negotiator, Uncle Sam. But in fact he's telling the European leaders what is good for their national interests and public opinion. He is playing a rather immodest role and one that doesn't seem to be grounded in Canadian interests. Ah, where is the Trudeau of yesteryear, the champion of the national interest in foreign policy? There is so much in his performance that now smacks of personal indulgence. MacEachen is nervous but not helpful. Members of the Canadian team make little cracks about Reagan, in the characteristic Canadian manner of looking down one's nose at the Americans.

By the afternoon it was clear that the national positions on the arms control declaration were six against one, the one being Canada. Trudeau rather nervously asked MacEachen and Lalonde what are the Canadian politics of being isolated. Lalonde characteristically gave a quick, simple answer. Bad. MacEachen, *à sa façon*, gave an immensely convoluted answer that amounted to almost (but not quite) the same thing. I get the impression that Mr. Theatre has had his theatre and is backing off. The word is Trudeau and Thatcher had a slinging match. (Trudeau said that at dinner last night she addressed all her hawkish arguments directly at him, but he thought this might have been because he was the only leader other than Reagan who was at ease in English.) Ron, it seems, was shouting at Pierre, and the French and Germans just couldn't understand the Canadian position.

In the evening, after the separate dinners of the summit heads and of the foreign ministers, we gathered in the PM's cottage (cozy, cutesy, of course) to debrief him, MacEachen, and Lalonde on the evening's events. MacEachen told a bizarre tale. At the foreign-ministers' dinner, Hans-Dietrich Genscher[1] temporarily took the chair while Namibia was being discussed. After comments by four members of the Contact Group (everyone other than the United States), Shultz exploded. He took their comments to be a criticism of U.S. leadership. He said he was fed up with criticism of the United States, with the infighting among France, Britain, Germany, and Canada and that this was the worst day of his life. And he walked. The chairmanship of the meeting then devolved to MacEachen, who terminated it forthwith.

While MacEachen gave the account, Trudeau had a big grin on his face, about the widest I've seen him wear, the mischievous grin of the bad boy at the party. We discussed this performance by Shultz as well as his extraordinary paean of praise for his leader in the closing moments of the summit meeting today, which apparently took everyone aback. I opined that it derived from a feeling of loyalty and the need to protect his master. This is typical of the overprotectiveness of Reagan's team.

Late at night I returned to my hotel exhausted. I received a vintage Burt blast. "You guys blew it. And MacEachen has blown his relationship with Shultz." I said to Burt, "Cut it out. What are you fussing about? Trudeau's comments weren't even directed at the U.S. They were aimed at the Europeans." "Three things," he replied. "Your guy is reopening the NATO two-track decision. He's completely out of touch with politics in Europe and especially Germany. And he was implicitly criticizing U.S. leadership. Shultz is very upset. He's been busting his ass for Canada. Why the hell should he do that now?"

May 30, 1983 A new day dawns and the darkness dissipates.

MacEachen, reading the writing on the wall, was clever and helpful in suggesting to Trudeau that he praise Reagan's leadership at the conclusion of the summit today. Trudeau did just that. He praised Reagan's role in fulsome

[1] (b. 1927) Foreign Minister of West Germany 1974–1992. Member of the Free Democratic Party.

terms. "You did it, Ron, you gambled on an unstructured summit, and you won. It's what I wanted at the Ottawa Summit and couldn't get." Well, this went down marvellously. I chatted with Jim Baker and Dick Darman, and they were purring. I said to them, without being specific, that I had received some negative vibrations yesterday from other well-placed members of the U.S. delegation. "Not true," they both said, "we're very happy."

Trudeau repeated the same congratulatory message to Reagan at the closing press conference this afternoon. He performed beautifully. He was self-confident, joking, plainly well satisfied with himself. It was as if this time he did his pirouette inside the conference rather than in public view.

Notwithstanding Burt's comments and Trudeau's jousting with the Europeans over the arms control declaration, I don't think any harm was done to our relations with the Americans. All the U.S. team really cares about is Reagan's image, and it came up just fine, as far as they're concerned, thanks in part to Trudeau's closing intervention. So Pierre played the game, the Reagan team knew it, and they appreciated it.

May 31, 1983 I flew with Trudeau in the helicopter to Langley Air Force Base, and we talked about the summit and his relations with the Americans. I told him his praise for Reagan's performance earned him much goodwill in the White House. He said it was good that he and others stood up to Reagan's pressure to rubber-stamp the declaration on security. "I wouldn't be upset if they were upset with me," he said, "but I acknowledge it would have been a lot more difficult for you." A deft twist of the Trudeauvian stiletto.

June 3, 1983 The day after "Haute Canada" – our maple-leaf fashion show and gala dinner-dance. It was Sondra's idea to produce this extravaganza. She, Beverley Rockett, and Pat Gossage have been working at it for a month. It's been a huge undertaking and has produced huge tensions.

First there was a lunch for more than a dozen Canadian designers and an even bigger crowd of models, along with buyers from the women's retail stores and reporters from the *New York Times*, *Washington Post*, *Vogue*, and *Woman's Wear Daily*.

Then a black-tie sit-down dinner for 120. It was a gorgeous night, with gorgeous models, pink and white flowering dogwood exploding in the garden, guests dining at small tables al fresco, dancing around the pool, photographers and reporters everywhere. The dinner guests were highly animated: Bill Casey and wife, the Wicks, Brinkleys, Ben Bradlee and Sally

Quinn, the Shrivers, the Haigs, the Krafts, the Baldridges, the Eagleburgers – all the usual suspects. The party was still going strong at midnight – unheard of in Washington.

The only problem was there were so many models, handlers, and assistants that we had nowhere to seat them. As the evening wore on, we realized even feeding them was a challenge. Adding to the difficulties was that we hired no outside chef or caterers; everything was done by our personal staff.

But when I opened the *New York Times* this morning, I was exhilarated. It gave the event more than a half-page of ink. Headline: "Canadian Fashion Takes a Bow in Washington." Underneath there is unvarnished hype. This was promotion on a grand scale. The phones have been ringing off the hook today to locate Alfred Sung,[1] Wayne Clark,[2] and other designers. This business has taken hundreds of hours, with many nasty quarrels, tensions, tempers, and explosive scenes. But I doubt we'll ever generate more publicity for any Canadian product, even if we stay here a century.

June 4, 1983 A tale of diplomatic misadventure. The organizers of the Red Cross Waterfront Festival, whatever that is, in Alexandria invited the magnificent Canadian schooner *Bluenose II* to pay a visit during their celebration (of something or other). They asked that notorious sailor the Canadian ambassador and his wife to join them on their yacht, *Finished Business*, as it met the arrival of the *Bluenose* just outside the harbour. I said okay but extracted an undertaking that I wouldn't have to consecrate (that is, waste) more than half a day at the ceremony. "No problem," the organizers said, "you'll be back in D.C. by late morning. Guaranteed."

With our hosts, dignitaries, and media aboard, our ship sails out on the Potomac during the bright, clear morning, but unfortunately, we can't find the *Bluenose*. We go farther and farther out to sea, make many false spottings on the distant horizon, and get lost. Panic sets in. After more than two hours of searching, the mysterious Nova Scotia schooner is sighted. Unrestrained jubilation. The spoilsport, me, insists on holding the organizers to their time commitment. I didn't have a tantrum but came close to it. After much persuasion, our hosts finally hail a passing motor launch, the crabby ambassador and his calm wife disembark, they graciously wave us

---

[1] (b. 1948) Canadian fashion designer, producing apparel and perfume for men and women. Born in Shanghai and raised in Hong Kong.

[2] A Canadian-born fashion designer based in Toronto.

off, the scribblers scribble, and we are back in Washington by early afternoon. Another day before the mast in the service of my country.

June 6, 1983 After months of discussion and planning and weeks of hesitation, I finally committed: we will take our holidays in France. What's persuaded me to go offshore is the realization that as long as I'm on American territory, I'm Mr. Ambassador. Ergo, I'm on duty. I'm in the mood for self-indulgence. All praise to nimiety. After three weeks of exposure to France's greatest kitchens, in Auch, Eugenie-les-Bains, and the Perigord, I'll try to follow in the steps of Talleyrand, who spent an hour every day with his cook.

June 15, 1983 We leave for Paris at 6:40 p.m. Sondra and I have never been so exhausted, thanks to the social vortex we seem to have fallen into. Our social calendar defies belief. A year and a half ago, we knew no one. Our modest success then began to feed on itself. We are asked to more and more places we cannot afford, or we cannot afford to refuse, by more and more people we know, or don't know and want to know.

July 1, 1983 C-Span celebrates Canada Day with twelve hours of programming and an interview with me before my departure. In a stroke of great good fortune, I get to use an old line about Canada that I haven't yet been able to deploy on the Gotlieb borscht belt. Asked about the Canadian character, I reply: "As a nation, we tend to shy away from extremes. As some wit put it, 'Canadians are like vichyssoise: we are cold, half French, and difficult to stir.'"

July 10, 1983 Back in Washington after the grand gastronomic tour of France. Sondra's mother and mine arrived from Winnipeg to visit us for a few days. My mother is eighty plus, and Sondra's is not far behind. They both require a lot of attention, but it's my mother who is high maintenance. If you have to attend to mothers, there's no place like an embassy. Comfortable bedrooms overlooking the garden in glorious bloom; courteous, thoughtful staff to give them breakfast, lunch, tea, and dinner; a chef to cook their favourite dishes; and big, comfortable salons for them to sit in and watch television. No complaints from my mother, the world's most accomplished complainer. No household chores for Sondra's mother, the world's most self-effacing helper. We marvel at how the mothers get along. One dominating, wilful, the other agreeable, even saintly, they meld in perfect harmony. We invited David and Susan Brinkley to meet them on Sunday, and the mothers could not believe they were in the presence of living television.

July 11, 1983 While I was away, the *Los Angeles Times* gave prominent coverage to an interview I gave to one of its top reporters, Stanley Meisler. "Americans just do not see us as different from themselves. You know, one hamburger, one hot dog, one culture, one boundary. There is a good side to this. If the U.S. goes around bashing someone, they don't bash us. But there is a negative side. When we do something different, Americans feel betrayed. They don't see us as foreigners but as perverse Americans."

July 12, 1983 I attended, as a head-table guest, a luncheon at the National Press Club in honour of Ken Taylor. I counted less than a hundred in the audience, at least half of whom were embassy staff, Canadian press, and other Canadians. It doesn't take long for this town to forget. If we had any money in the bank resulting from the great Canadian caper, the Washington branch has closed the account.

July 13, 1983 What I've been fearing most has happened: a congressman has accused me of interfering in U.S. domestic affairs. He has even complained to Shultz. It's a ridiculous tale. Thomas Luken[1] from Ohio attacked Canada's record on acid rain on the floor of the House. His statement was full of gross errors, so I wrote to him in early June to correct it, and I concluded my letter by saying, "In the interest of fairness, I would like to ask you to insert my comments in the congressional record."

Not a big deal when you know all the garbage they throw into it. But the congressman was deeply offended, or so he says. In a letter to Shultz, he referred to my "brazen request" that he enter my comments into the congressional proceedings. He "and others," he said, have questioned the propriety and efficacy of my aggressive lobbying campaign, and my letter "raises questions as to protocol and appropriate conduct by emissaries to this country." The distinguished representative is clearly sizzling. Amazingly, he did read my letter into the record, but at the same time wrote to Shultz virtually inviting my reprimand or recall. And he read that into the record too. I hope this business doesn't get out of hand. I'm not ready to be deported.

---

[1] (b. 1925) Mayor of Cincinnati 1971–1972; Democratic Representative from Ohio 1977–1991.

July 15, 1983 I have had a brilliant idea – or maybe not so brilliant. I have been thinking about writing a political letter to Ottawa, a format for departing from the standard telegraph form of reporting, which lends itself all too well to bureaucratic gibberish. My inspiration is Isaiah Berlin's recently published political dispatches, written when he was first secretary at the British embassy during World War II. I'm hoping my reports will get more attention if they are composed in the form of a political letter, well constructed, chatty, written in a personalized style, and addressed only to a limited group of politicians and senior officials. I know from my print-collecting obsession that a limited edition is accorded a much higher value than an open run.

It's probably just a huge conceit on my part. I've always worshipped Berlin, so now I dream of a similar role for myself. But this isn't World War II, and I'm not Berlin. Moreover, he told me he didn't particularly like his letters. But the hell with it – I'm going ahead anyway.

What I'm now finding is that it takes a long time to write such a letter. My first one is twelve pages, double-spaced, and the only officer who's got the range and style to help me is Kinsman.

I chose as the theme the struggle taking place within the inner circles of the Reagan team, as the town drops into a summer lull and preparations begin for a presidential election year. Jim Baker and Bill Casey represent the two competing schools: the pragmatic, moderate one and the hardline, ideological view. So a struggle between the two men represents, in a sense, a struggle over the control and direction of the administration, the '84 campaign, the second-term agenda, and the future of the presidency, if not the future of the world itself. (I am getting carried away.)

If Reagan wins a second term, as I believe he will, and re-election is no longer an issue, the arch-conservatives and ideologues will be in a stronger position and will try to dominate the pragmatists. The conflict takes place on what one writer calls a "political fault line." But it won't succeed without an earthquake. And it won't happen under Reagan.

July 16, 1983 It's the dog days of summer. A party today at Senator John Warner's[1] place, Atoka Farm, in Middleburg, and that's about it. The distinguished senator, former husband of Elizabeth Taylor, told me I should

[1] (b. 1927) Republican Senator from Virginia 1979 to present. He was also married to banking heiress Catherine Mellon.

be proud that the most fabulous paintings by Sir Alfred Munnings[1] are to be found in Canada. I told him I've never heard of Munnings. He grimaced and told me he is the greatest painter of horses since Stubbs.[2] I apologized for my ignorance, but this ambassador has lost face.

July 22, 1983 The chauffeur we like the most, Lyle Thivierge, has left the embassy after fourteen years to seek a better life. Saturnine but warm-hearted, he drove regularly for Sondra and me. We would have preferred him to the mercurial senior driver, Jacques Helie, but there is no way Jacques would step down. He drove Peter Towe, Jake Warren,[3] Marcel Cadieux, and even some of their predecessors. A Quebecer with the most irascible temper, he's slowly killing himself because he gets so angry at all the stupid drivers he encounters on the road. But he knows everything and anybody and drives well when he's not apoplectic.

The long-serving local Canadian staff – and there are many of them at the chancery, such as top maintenance man Glen Bullard – provide the only real continuity at the embassy. They know the past, and they know a lot of secrets. And they are not noted for keeping them.

August 1, 1983 I sent headquarters my definitive recommendations for hiring professional consultants and counsel. I proposed that we engage three professional firms in addition to those we now use in specialized areas (acid rain, anti-trust). Their functions: early warning and political intelligence, general counsel, and advice on energy matters. My argument is that Congress does not respond to Canada's representations per se. Our economic interests are protected only when they correspond to influential U.S. domestic interests. Therefore, the objectives of the embassy must be to obtain information and influence the administration and Congress to our advantage.

What I wrote amounts to a primer on how the U.S. system works, even though it shouldn't be necessary to give one. The problem in Ottawa arises from two conditions: the sheer disbelief that the president, administration, and State Department can't solve the issues themselves (they should stop "hiding behind the Congress") and the practical experience of many in

---

[1] (1878–1959) One of England's finest painters of horses. President of the Royal Academy 1944–1949.

[2] (1724–1806) British painter, best known for his paintings of horses.

[3] Canadian Ambassador to the United States 1975–1977.

Ottawa who served in Washington in the old days (a decade or two ago), which taught them that the president is the almighty, the imperial power, the Sun King. All we need do is to look to him and his administration and – presto – our problems will be solved.

There is almost no understanding of how profoundly the workings of the political system have changed. They think a strong president would solve all our problems. "Ford was a klutz. . . . Carter was weak. . . . Reagan is dumb," and so on. They think everything that has happened in Washington in recent years is an aberration.

August 5, 1983 In Newport to see the Canadian team competing for the America's Cup. Bill Davis, in a very congenial frame of mind, his wife, Cathy, and entourage are in attendance. And I am attending too – on Bill Davis. It's ridiculous, my being here. I know nothing about boats. I don't like boats. I don't like people who talk about boats. But where the premier goes in the United States, there go I.

I thought I would give him the bad news right off. I told him about a congressional fiasco yesterday. During a legislative conference on the Hill, the army's procurement program for six hundred light-armoured vehicles was erased – deleted in its entirety from the budget. The vehicle happens to be made mostly in London, Ontario, and the deal was worth about $300 or $400 million to General Motors Canada. I called Cap Weinberger and Jim Baker personally and tried frantically to get the decision reversed at the last moment, but it looked like my efforts failed.

"Think of the jobs involved in Ontario," I said to Davis, all worked up. I added that I was in constant touch with Washington, trying every possible angle to reopen the decision, which was taken against the wishes of the military. I was disappointed that Davis didn't seem all that concerned. Is this a facade? Or is he simply the most relaxed politician in the world? Am I the one who is running for election in Ontario?

In the evening we attended a dinner given by the Aga Khan[1] and his wife, the beautiful Begum, the Princess Salimah, in their Newport home. Having read about her (the former model Sally Croker Poole) in the popular press, I was surprised to see that she is as smooth and sophisticated as he. The Aga Khan is a sponsor of the Italian boat, and he knows Davis because of the large Ismaili community in Toronto. I debated with the premier before

[1] (b. 1936) The current (forty-ninth) Imam of the Shia Imami Ismaili Muslims, since July 11, 1957.

dinner whether or not we'd be allowed to drink and smoke. That was stupid. The evening was wet and smoky, the conversation light-hearted and witty. Our host did not reveal to Davis that he and the Begum had just spent two weeks on a yacht in the Mediterranean with their very good friend Pierre and his kids.

August 6, 1983 Still in Newport. Gave a brunch for 150 for the Canadian team and syndicate backing them, at some yacht club or other. Unbearably hot. The party came off because for unknown reasons the Aga Khan and the Begum came. The reception was well organized by Sondra's new social secretary, Connie Connors, an American who used to work at Protocol at State. She fell afoul of someone there but seems pretty good. We learned – it took a while – that one needs an American for this kind of job.

I was encouraged to learn that I wasn't the first Canadian ambassador to do so. Joe Alsop told me a sad tale at dinner at his place the other day. Long ago, he was a great friend of one of my predecessors, Loring Christie, whom Mackenzie King sent to Washington as head of legation shortly after the outbreak of World War II. Christie was brilliant, the only Canadian to be editor-in-chief of the *Harvard Law Review* and, as adviser to Sir Robert Borden,[1] the architect of Canada's separate adherence to the Treaty of Versailles in 1919. It was his idea that Canada sign the treaty separately from Britain under the heading of "British Empire."

At that time, our heads of mission lived upstairs at the gloomy chancery at 1746 Massachusetts Avenue. Christie hired an American social secretary, a friend of Joe Alsop, married her, and on his wedding night, in his wedding bed at the chancery, died of a heart attack. Joe Alsop swears by the story. His coda on the tale: the Canadian government refused to give her a pension, not a nickel's worth. Joe said he tried for years to get the government to give her something. He failed.

Flying back from Newport, I ask myself, is all this socializing and entertaining worthwhile? I have to reply yes. If it weren't for the after-hours life, I wouldn't have been able to get through to the two absolutely key players on the General Motors light-armoured vehicles contract, which happens to be the biggest deal in our history. I connected with two of the hardest men in Washington to reach – in a matter of minutes, Weinberger; in a couple of hours, Baker.

[1] (1854–1937) Conservative Prime Minister of Canada 1911–1920.

August 11, 1983 I sent my second political letter from Washington, this time about the ascendancy of Judge Clark, who now plays a primary role in U.S. foreign policy. As evidence there is the transfer of arms control management from Shultz to Clark personally, his assumption of the management role over foreign policy in Central America, and the appointment of his own deputy, Bud McFarlane,[1] to be Middle East negotiator. While Nitze and McFarlane both formally report to Shultz, there is little doubt the formal arrangements are but a fig leaf to hide the reality of power.

My letter dealt with the big worry in Washington: because Clark is part of the president's "family," his mistakes, even costly ones, won't count. What, then, does the future hold? Official and unofficial Washington regard Jim Baker, backed by Darman, as the key White House operator, the most sensible and effective aide, to whom Reagan owes a great deal for his success. But as Baker told his good friend Bob Strauss, "I can't go against Clark or Weinberger once they have the ear of the president."

August 15, 1983 Back in Washington after a socially wrenching weekend at Kay Graham's cottage on Martha's Vineyard. The house sits in isolation on the wild south shore of the Vineyard, separated from the ocean by acres of abundant high flora, through which a long path winds down to the sea. We were in a large room of our own in a separate wing of the house. In spite of our hostess's injunction of no ties ("This is not Edgartown") and her protestations about "informality," it's impossible to imagine a more formal style of summer holidaying. There were typed lists in our rooms providing the names of the guests at each lunch and dinner. Only for breakfast were we given the option of eating in our room.

On our first day I decided to exercise that option and have breakfast in bed. Sondra, however, had breakfast with Kay and her social secretary, Liz, who is permanently on duty. Sondra told me afterwards that Kay was annoyed. "Where is Allan?" she asked a couple of times. But for Sondra it was a riveting meal, as Kay recounted to her the story of her husband's terrible death by self-inflicted gunshot.

Organized activities throughout the day. Cocktails and elaborate lunches and dinners. Revolving guests from the Vineyard, the Hamptons,

---

[1] Robert McFarlane (b. 1937) U.S. Marine Corps Lieutenant Colonel who served as National Security Advisor 1983–1985.

Georgetown, New York (mostly liberal, for example, Bill Styron,[1] his wife Rose, the Rohatyns). Earnest conversations and eastern-establishment high seriousness. We left stuffed, talked out, exhausted. And anxiety-ridden. Were we being tested? Did we pass? I was happy to learn that Mrs. Graham is less intimidating on her own anthill than on those of others.

August 17, 1983 The lugubrious, immensely sincere, socialist MP from Winnipeg David Orlikow,[2] whom I have known for a long time, came to see me in Ottawa some years ago when I was undersecretary to ask that the Canadian government get the United States to accept responsibility for the brainwashing activities of the CIA in Canada after the war. His wife, Velma, suffered cruelly from such experiments ("psychic driving") at the Allan Memorial hospital in Montreal, carried out by its then chief neurologist, the American Dr. Ewen Cameron.[3] This was the era of the *Manchurian Candidate*, and "brainwashing" was believed to be a potentially vital tool in Cold War propaganda battles. As the CIA seemed unwilling to accept any responsibility for the Canadian experiments – which would have, in their view, occurred with or without CIA funding – the Canadian government, under my prodding, has agreed to consider helping the victims get compensation.

But Ottawa has been reluctant for me to raise the matter with the State Department pending the results of their in-depth review of the case, as they say it would be premature. Meanwhile, Orlikow has been complaining bitterly about CIA stonewalling. So I decided to raise the case on my own initiative with Rick Burt and told him that the delay in the CIA's response was really quite unreasonable. Burt knew nothing about it and was noncommittal. Even wary, I would say.

August 24, 1983 Back home in Ottawa with Sondra. I'm on "consultations," which means a few days of home leave. I called on Gordon

---

[1] (b. 1925) American novelist, best known for *The Confessions of Nat Turner* (1967) and *Sophie's Choice* (1979).

[2] (1918–1998) NDP Member of Parliament for Winnipeg North 1962–1988.

[3] (1901–1967) Scottish-American psychiatrist who was president of the American Psychiatric Association and head of the Montreal Neurological Hospital involved in experiments in Canada for MKULTRA, a "mind control" program in which the CIA was involved.

Osbaldeston, now ensconced as secretary of the cabinet. We talked about Trudeau and MacEachen. The prime minister, he said, is very deferential to the deputy prime minister and vice versa. MacEachen, he said, has manoeuvred Trudeau away from the Department of External Affairs. "Nothing now goes forward from External to the Privy Council by way of advance copies, pre-communications, or such activities." It's completely different now, he said, from when I was undersecretary. At that time, a day didn't pass when I was not engaging in back channels. Osbaldeston, of course, knows that.

I sensed he was trying to tell me something. "Are you?" I asked him. "Well," he replied, "not really, but whatever you do, don't go around MacEachen. Don't deal directly with Trudeau. He'll never forgive you."

Since the time I accompanied Trudeau to Washington on the occasion of the signing of the Panama Canal Treaty, I've seen first-hand how Trudeau spooks MacEachen, and how MacEachen has to work in the shadow Trudeau casts over foreign affairs. But after all the years I have worked with Trudeau, I cannot change my ways.

September 4, 1983 Back in Washington after ten days in Ottawa and Quebec City. The embassy staff have been practically living at the State Department, dealing with the crisis over the Soviets' shooting down of the Korean airliner. They have done an excellent job without me. At times I wonder whether an embassy really needs an ambassador. Maybe it does, just to make contacts, open doors, get hold of the big shots, and enter precincts forbidden to lower ranks. All prestige and no power, as Sondra wrote in *First Lady, Last Lady*.

MacEachen gave a major news conference in Ottawa announcing airline sanctions against the U.S.S.R. I called Judge Clark to convey the good news. We walk proud in Washington today (for a change).

September 8, 1983 Charles (the *nudnik*) Caccia[1] is in town to discuss environmental problems. I set up appointments with Jim Watt in Interior, Bill Ruckelshaus, and some players on the Hill. The good news is our new minister of environment is less outspoken and quick off the mark than John Roberts. The bad news is he has a one-track mind. He was personally responsible for large chunks of the Immigration Act, so persistent

[1] (b. 1930) Liberal Member of Parliament for Davenport, Ontario, 1968–2004; Minister of Labour 1981–1983; Minister of the Environment 1983–1984.

was he on behalf of his constituents (Italians in Toronto). His efforts led to greater recognition of the family class at the expense of the independents. He almost drove me out of my mind when I headed the Department of Immigration.

We learned from the press (no communication to us from the administration) that Ruckelshaus and the EPA are considering options on acid rain controls. Speculation has focused on one approach that interests us the most, the so-called Northeast option. It would focus on reducing emissions in New England, and as a result, we would be a beneficiary. However, at our meeting with Ruckelshaus, he refused to be drawn out. He doesn't want to discuss ideas with us before he has put anything forward to the White House.

September 9, 1983 Derek Burney[1] is in Washington, new assistant deputy minister in charge of U.S. affairs. More aggressive than his amiable predecessors, he will be more effective, provided he restrains himself from rolling over and squashing people, as he has a tendency to do. We called on Bill Brock to review Canada-U.S. trade problems, and there's a mountain of them. The U.S. decision to impose quotas and tariffs on specialty steel, including ours (even though they export more of the stuff to us than they import), the cancellations by U.S. companies of contracts with Canadian gas-exporting companies, the possibility of sectoral free-trade negotiations – all were discussed. Brock is sympathetic towards our concerns.

September 11, 1983 Congressman Pat Schroeder[2] of Colorado invited us to a small dinner at her home, about a half-dozen people, in honour of Edgar Kaiser[3] of Vancouver (who also happens to own the Denver Broncos). She is a very passionate Democrat. One has to admire her outspokenness. It's not often that a member of Congress entertains at home, and I feel privileged. It's a weekend for liberals, as tonight we mingled with many at a cocktail party given by the *Post*'s highly respected defence

---

[1] Canadian foreign-service officer. Chief of Staff to Prime Minister Brian Mulroney 1987–1989. Canadian Ambassador to the United States 1989–1993.

[2] (b. 1940) Democratic Representative from Colorado 1973–1997, the longest-serving woman in the history of the House.

[3] (b. 1942) Grandson of American industrialist Henry John Kaiser. President of the former Bank of British Columbia and of Kaiser Steel.

correspondent, Walter Pincus.[1] Like so many of Ben Bradlee's people, you know where Pincus is coming from politically. Most of the crowd was press, and more specifically, *Post*. Why the group is somewhat trying is not that they are liberal. Even I have some tendencies in that direction. But alas, they tend to be: (1) self-righteous, (2) certain in their outlook, and (3) predictable. Dinner after with Joe and Polly Kraft was an antidote. Joe is an independent thinker who follows his own star, and predictable he is not.

September 12, 1983 In Halifax to be the speaker at Portday (yes, Portday) '83. What a crowd – about seven hundred people in the audience. I was scheduled to speak at 8:30 but took the podium at close to 10:30. By that time just about everyone, including the sixty-odd people at the head table, was either drunk or asleep or both. I had a dense text on the woes of protectionism in shipping. The noise from outside the dining hall and from those still awake inside was so great I could barely hear myself speak. I gave the bastards what they deserved. I read the whole speech slowly. And it was long and technical.

September 13, 1983 Sondra attended a luncheon given by Jane Weinberger in honour of the wife of the British minister of defence, Michael Heseltine.[2] Would Jane Weinberger give a luncheon in honour of the wife of the Canadian minister of national defence? No. The reasons lie not in strategy, geopolitics, or good relations. They are to be found in a curious snobbism that breeds in Washington. Anglophilitis is prevalent in Georgetown, and a little bit on Capitol Hill. Cap and Jane Weinberger have it bad.

September 14, 1983 Called on Jim Medas at State in the afternoon. He has just been appointed deputy assistant secretary for Canadian affairs, a triumph for George Shultz. Thanks to him, Canada is now the only country to have a full-time officer at that level in the State Department. Almost equally unexpected, Shultz got the European Bureau to change its name to the Bureau of European and Canadian Affairs. (How the Europeanists at

---

[1] Journalist and staff writer who joined the *Washington Post* in 1966, specializing in national security issues. Executive Editor of the *New Republic* 1972–1975.

[2] (b. 1933) British Conservative politician and businessman. Member of Parliament for Henley 1974–2001; Secretary of State for Defence 1983–1986.

State must hate that.) I don't know how Shultz managed to do this, but it is a significant step forward in the management of our relationship.

Medas is an attractive, youthful guy (he is thirty-nine). When he was in the White House, he was responsible for relations with the states. Is this suggestive of how our own status is perceived? Medas sees acid rain and natural gas imports as priority problems. He's right about that. But he knows squat about Canada.

September 15, 1983 Farewell reception for the Saudi ambassador, Alhegelan, and his Lebanese-American wife at the spectacular building of the Organization of American States. He is being recalled, it is said, because his wife, the glamorous Nouha, is too westernized and high-profile. There were more than a thousand guests in attendance, maybe double that. It was the largest reception of its sort I have seen. When we drove up, there were enormous lineups to greet the couple, extending up and around the massive stairway, so we decided to turn around and go home. While standing on the front steps waiting for our driver, Jacques, Cap Weinberger (on his way out) approached us, and we described our predicament. Ha, he said, use the back stairway, which we then did, led by Sol Linowitz, and found ourselves perfectly centred in the midst of an abundant supply of food being gorged upon by hungry Washingtonians. How they are drawn by the mystical power of the Saudis – or the not so mystical power of oil.

September 22, 1983 Breakfast with Maurice Strong[1] and the very rich and ultra-liberal Congressman Jim Scheuer[2] of New York (he wants us to sue the United States in the World Court over acid rain), a call on Paul Volcker (interest rates), lunch with Larry Eagleburger (the world), then flew to New York at the invitation of Bill Casey on his government aircraft, to attend, as a head-table guest, the William J. Donovan Award dinner honouring Sir William Stephenson,[3] the Man Called Intrepid.

---

[1] (b. 1929) CEO of Petro-Canada 1976–1978; Chairman of the International Energy Development Corporation 1980–1983; Undersecretary-General of the United Nations 1985–2005.

[2] (1920–2005) Democratic Representative from New York 1965–1993.

[3] (1897–1989) Canadian soldier, airman, businessman, inventor, spymaster, and senior representative of British intelligence for the western hemisphere during World War II. Best known by his wartime intelligence codename, "Intrepid."

I was alone with Casey in the cabin of the aircraft and thought it would be a marvellous opportunity to pick his mind on Central America, the Middle East, Afghanistan, the KAL, and whatever. I was very eager and excited. After all, I had him captive. But I found him incomprehensible. When I posed a question, which I did repeatedly, he talked freely and at length, but I could not for the life of me follow what he was saying. He seems to swallow not just words but whole sentences, even paragraphs. He has mastered the technique of obfuscation.

Before dinner I met privately with the eighty-six-year-old Stephenson (he lives in self-imposed exile in Bermuda). What did I get from my private chat with the enfeebled spymaster? He hates Trudeau. Believes he is a communist.

September 24, 1983 David Silcox[1] arrived to try to win concessions from Jack Valenti in favour of more distribution of Canadian films. Of course, we got nowhere. Negotiating with Valenti is like negotiating with Stalin.

September 27, 1983 The town is crawling with bankers, here for the bankers' world fair. Tomorrow Roland Frazee, czar of the Royal Bank, is coming to lunch. It's good to be an ambassador. Back home, when a mere civil servant, I'd be lucky to have an introduction to the local bank manager.

September 29, 1983 We gave a dinner party for thirty Washingtonians. Putting the list together was a terrible pain. It's always the same in Washington: you get started, get a few good names, and then you realize you are competing with some damn official event that you don't know about. This time it happened to be a "return dinner" hosted by Sir Oliver Wright for Margaret Thatcher, who's in town on an official visit. We realized eventually that our party would consist largely of journalists. We had the Safires, Krafts, Elizabeth Drew, and a number of other media stars plus a Democratic congresswoman (Pat Schroeder), a Democratic senator (Leahy),[2] the Strausses, and a few others. We were gnashing our teeth for days before the

[1] (b. 1937) Canadian art historian and administrator. Assistant Deputy Minister of Culture in the federal Department of Communications 1983–1985; Deputy Minister in the Ontario Ministry of Culture and Communications 1986–1991.

[2] Patrick Leahy (b. 1940) Democratic Senator from Vermont 1975 to present.

dinner because the journalists were not going to meet any important officials at our place. So it would be a flop, we decided. When Sandra Day O'Connor cancelled at the last minute, we even debated whether we should cancel. No, we decided. It turned out to be one of the best parties we have given. I learned something from the experience. Journalists believe they are the real players. If they are present, who else matters?

September 30, 1983 Contrary to my custom, I dropped in on a National Day at noon, my first in a few months. It was the Chinese Day. I decided to go because I like the new ambassador (he invited me to his dinner for his foreign minister) and because I hoped to get lots of Chinese goodies at the lunch table. As I was entering the main hall, there was a major commotion – lights, guards, people shoving – and the great man walked in. From my last visit, I knew it must be Henry Kissinger. He stopped. "You, your wife certainly impressed Kay Graham at Martha's Vineyard last month," he said. "I want to come and see you about your famous commission," I said. "Why?" he asked, with a huge grin. "You are not part of Central America." I stammered and flubbed and then responded, "But damn it, we are part of North America." "Okay," he said, "you can come and see me." And I will.

October 1, 1983 I rushed to Evangeline Bruce's in Georgetown, who was giving a small lunch for Princess Margaret. Yes, Princess Margaret. A prized invitation, as always a premier locale for the exchange of gossip. Rowly Evans asked me, "Did you hear the story about Ken Dam? He was supposed to be the official greeter of Margaret Thatcher the other day but completely forgot. They had to run around trying to hand her a letter of apology." This is what passes for gossip at Georgetown lunches. Chatted with the superbly maintained Claudette Colbert,[1] then with the princess about her trip to Winnipeg years back. ("They have the same accent there as in Minneapolis, don't they?")

October 5, 1983 I was summoned to the White House for a second time to mark the celebration of the Reagan administration's Caribbean Basin Initiative. The Congress has now authorized tariff reductions for some Central America and Caribbean countries to take effect next January.

---

[1] (1903–1996) French-American actress, appearing in such films as *It Happened One Night*, for which she won an Academy Award for Best Actress.

As on the last occasion, I came, I lined up, I stood, I sat, I witnessed, I listened, I shook hands, I was photographed, I was televised, and I left.

October 6, 1983 Last night we gave a small dinner in honour of no one, for a change. No competition from "big event" Washington. We had Joe Alsop, Meg Greenfield, Evangeline Bruce, Jean French Smith, Marc Leland, and the Kinsmans. Alsop held forth and displayed his remarkable knowledge of diplomatic history and his astonishing memory. We speculated on what was happening to Andropov,[1] who hadn't been seen in weeks. Joe's recitation of facts and events in Soviet history was a feat that had us gasping, but his thesis that there is a prospect of an imminent military takeover of Soviet authority was not convincing.

October 26, 1983 The United States has inconveniently invaded Grenada. It has thus delivered a fatal blow to our planned pastoral visit to Arizona and California today. The president has sent in seven thousand troops and, wonder of wonders, never consulted Trudeau, never even alerted him. On instructions, I called on Ken Dam at State (in charge today) and formally communicated Canada's position. Canada very much regretted that the United States had undertaken this military intervention, I told him. "Based on the information available to us, it does not appear to be justified." More particularly, "you did not frankly and adequately consult with us and inform us of your intentions before undertaking the operation."

Dam reacted in his usual cool, low-key, easy manner ("the Joe DiMaggio of public policy," Shultz calls him). They did not consult with us because of the absolute need for secrecy. More precisely, Canada was not consulted by the U.S. government "because of concerns on the security side that the invasion shouldn't be too widely known."

When I left State, I was stormed by the Canadian hack-pack hanging out in front of the building. I gave them a very explicit briefing, repeating what Dam had told me. It sounded stupid, but what else could I say? It was impossible for me to cook up a more ridiculous excuse for not consulting us. Obviously, Dam's remarks will lead directly to the inference that they don't trust Trudeau. This will invite a great deal of acrimonious debate back

[1] Yuri Andropov (1914–1984) Soviet politician. Head of the KGB 1967–1982; General Secretary of the Communist Party of the Soviet Union 1982–1984.

home about who was informed and when (when was Thatcher informed and when were the other Commonwealth leaders informed?).

The Canadian media spin will be right. The administration doesn't trust Trudeau. They think he would have objected. But I'm not so sure. He would have to struggle with the fact that, in his worldview, Grenada is part of the U.S. sphere of influence. Trudeau sees the United States as having a special position in the hemisphere and the Caribbean. It's called the Monroe Doctrine. I doubt the apologist for the Soviet presence in Poland and Afghanistan would have been openly critical of the U.S. decision to remove an unfriendly regime, had he been consulted.

What's galling for Canada is that we regard the Caribbean as an area where we have real economic interests and special relationships, because of the Commonwealth connection. As my colleague Klaus Goldschlag put it, "In the Caribbean we have interests but no foreign policy. In Africa we have a foreign policy but no interests." Possibly the only bon mot ever coined about Canadian foreign policy.

October 27, 1983 Trudeau's new peace initiative is being launched today. He's speaking at a conference at Guelph University on "Strategies for Peace: Security in the Nuclear Age." It's the culmination of a lot of planning in the PMO and PCO to get Trudeau back on centre stage and combat his decline in the polls.

When I was summoned to Ottawa a couple of weeks ago to attend a deep strategy session with Trudeau and his closest personal advisers at Meech Lake, I thought he seemed rather reluctant to engage in the "peace" initiative that was being urged upon him by his entourage. He asked, more than once, "Why me?" His advisers all described his unique qualifications, his credibility abroad, his status as an elder statesman. But he seemed skeptical. I replied that although I thought there could be a role for him to play in reducing world tensions, he was not in a unique or special position to do so. So I thought Trudeau would say no to the idea of being leader of a big peace mission, but I was wrong.

My role today was to brief the U.S. and Canadian media in Washington on the initiative. Predictably, the reaction of the Americans was pretty ho-hum. But the Canadian media were hyper – almost hysterical. My briefing followed pretty well the content of Trudeau's letter to Reagan of October 24, which caused no joy here.

According to the letter, the West is attempting to manage its relationship with the U.S.S.R. largely in a political vacuum, devoid of any real high-level political dialogue. There is an evident mutual loss of confidence in one another. "The East at a distance may misread, misinterpret, or miscalculate our true intentions." There is therefore an "urgent requirement" for Western leaders to apply themselves to "the task of arresting the downward trend line in relations." The letter suggested (reflecting Trudeau's personal fixation on the need to include the British and French arsenals in disarmament negotiations) that "all five nuclear weapons states" engage in negotiations on global limits on their strategic nuclear arsenals. Then Trudeau said he plans to take up the subject personally with Kohl and Mitterrand in Europe and maybe even in Moscow.

The final sentence read, "I would particularly welcome the opportunity at an early date to discuss this subject personally with you in more detail in Washington at a brief private meeting if our mutual calendars would permit." Thank God for that line. I had told Trudeau when he asked for my views at the Ottawa meeting that I thought by far the best chance he has of making a contribution to peace is to convince Reagan to move.

Trudeau is playing with other people's marbles. And the idea of involving all five nuclear powers in negotiations is dynamite. The Russians will hardly rejoice at the idea that they should bring their mortal enemy, the Chinese, into the negotiating arena. As if they don't have their hands full with the Americans. And one can imagine the French reaction. They'd never participate in any forum from a position of great disparity and weakness.

October 28, 1983 Met again with the admirable Canadian Coalition on Acid Rain. I had to tell them that, according to my intelligence, it now appears certain that neither the House nor the Senate will pass any bill before the year's end. The congressmen are quarrelling with each other, with Democrats Dingell (con) and Waxman[1] (pro) being practically at war. So tense is the situation that Waxman does not want us to lobby his committee at this time. As for the EPA, I told them there has been no indication of movement since Bill Ruckelshaus met with Stockman, Meese, Baker, and Deaver last week. The meeting was described to me as "informational," but I understand it did not go well. Ruckelshaus's Northeast option is proving to be a chimera.

---

[1] Henry Waxman (b. 1939) Democratic Representative from California 1975 to present.

October 30, 1983 Lots of fussing throughout the weekend about Grenada, the Canadians still on the island, and our interests or involvement there. An unconfirmed news report has it that a convoy of Canadians was fired on by snipers. This has energized Ottawa, so I am now living on the phone. I told Ottawa that if we are supporting the idea of a Commonwealth peace force, I'd better get onto Eagleburger fast, so the United States won't be taken by surprise and blow it away. MacNeil-Lehrer want an interview with me. This is a first for me on the big-time tube, and no doubt I'm being asked because Canada is being critical (albeit mildly) of U.S. behaviour. Gossage urged me to accept. Kinsman contra.

November 1, 1983 November kicks off with the arrival of Allan Fotheringham[1] as a weekend house guest (he came pickled, he left pickled) and then the culminating event, a dinner that we gave at the Residence in honour of ABC's new anchorman, Canadian Peter Jennings[2] and his wife, Kati Martin.

Jennings had the glow of someone on the threshold of fame and success. There is some annoyance in Canadian circles about his recent comment that he will apply for U.S. citizenship, but as one of my colleagues at the embassy put it (albeit somewhat crudely), "We honour any Canadian, past or present, who is just terrifically important."

We drew in a star-studded crowd of about forty guests. Roone Arledge, head of ABC News and Sports (who looks even more Canadian than Peter, although he isn't), Kay Graham, Senators Pat Moynihan and Nancy Kassebaum, Mac Baldridge, Bob MacNamara, Meg Greenfield, Dick Darman, Lane Kirkland, Bill Ruckelshaus, Paul Volcker, Canadians Robert MacNeil, Lloyd Robertson, and plenty more. It doesn't get more A-list than this.

Among other things, we served crepes filled with golden Manitoba caviar. Washingtonians love these eggs. They are not Iranian and they are not caviar, but they are good.

November 7, 1983 Entertaining again tonight for the Aga Khan and the Begum. The party was to be in honour of Bill Davis, but in his best

---

[1] (b. 1932) Columnist for the *Vancouver Sun* and then Southam News Service and *Maclean's* magazine. Southam Washington correspondent 1984–1989.

[2] (1938–2005) Canadian news anchor for *ABC World News Tonight* for over two decades, until his death in 2005.

political style of "now-I'm-coming-now-I'm-not," he cancelled on very short notice, so at Davis's suggestion we made the Aga the guest of honour. As he predicted, this did wonders for our party. Sondra recently hired a brilliant young French-Algerian chef, formally sous-chef at the British embassy, and today was his twenty-first birthday. We brought him to the table, saluted him, and everyone including the Aga and the Begum sang happy birthday.

Tomorrow we are giving a reception for over a hundred members of Ducks Unlimited, allies on acid rain. The leader of the Senate, Howard Baker, is coming, and he is one hard duck to get to fly our way.

November 8, 1983 Sondra's "Letter to Beverly" is spread out on the op-ed page of the *Washington Post* – right down the middle. What a huge hunk of space it occupies in the most important real estate in the country! In it she tells the tale, in a stylized, comical way, of her arrival in Washington as wife of the ambassador and then of our credentials ceremony. It will create a sensation in Washington, which is good, and a sensation in Canada, which is not so good. The Canadian press in Washington will hate it. Most of all, I can hear them asking, "How can an ambassador's wife have the chutzpah to think she can be a journalist?" And how come I never got a column in the *Washington Post*?

November 10, 1983 Another "Dear Beverly" bursts onto the op-ed page of the *Post*. Washington is highly amused, even slightly agog. Sondra is flooded with calls. United Press files a story, repeating large chunks of the first article: "The column, laced with observations on protocol, people and power, is witty, elegant and tart." Meg Greenfield is quoted as saying that Sondra is "a perceptive observer of Washington. She is acute, funny and says something about life."

Meg is the godmother of the column. After a couple of Sondra's pieces appeared in the *Post*'s magazine, she started to press Sondra for something to appear on her editorial page. Sondra had written a few "Beverly" columns with a view to publishing them in a book after she left Washington. She told Meg she had some material but doubted strongly that Meg would be interested or that her readers would. Meg kept on pressing, Sondra relented, Meg was ecstatic, and the rest is history.

No doubt people are going to ask me whether I "approve" or not, or whether I think Sondra should be writing at all. I haven't had a moment's hesitation. These columns will do more to put Canada on the map than all the calls I will make, even if I stay here a generation. They will open endless doors for me, particularly on the Hill. When you are talked about in this town, people want to meet you, even the congressmen, and that means you can get into their offices and strike up a relationship and make your case. After all, I'm a lobbyist. And why should a politician want to see a lobbyist? His interest has to be aroused. Sondra has hit a home run.

November 12, 1983 We are very pleased with our talented new chef, Yves Safarti. But as he is very young and speaks only French and can't communicate with the staff, Sondra worries that he is lonely and might quit. Someone told her there is a church in Georgetown where French-speaking people gather. She suggested he go to the church. He resisted. Sondra pressed him to go in order to meet people. He still resisted. "Why won't you go?" she asked. "*Madame*," he replied, "*je suis juif*."

November 15, 1983 Another "courtesy" day in the embassy in Washington. The fatal function of representation. The dreariness wears us all out or drives us to drink. A "courtesy" call by a member of the National Film Board, a "courtesy" call by the Japanese judge on the International Court, then received, with Sondra, a joint "courtesy" visit by the new Brazilian ambassador and his wife, then, as a "courtesy," co-hosted a reception on the "Art of Living" featuring National Film Board work, then represented Canada at the Wilson Center at the Smithsonian on the "Fiftieth Anniversary of U.S.-Soviet Relations." Any warm body could have done it, so long as it was called ambassador.

One knows that whatever one does, it is "official." If one says, "No, I won't go" or "No, I won't give you an appointment to see me," it's an official response. It's not A.E.G. who is saying no, it's the ambassador of Canada. So one does one's duty. Or overdoes it. And has a drink.

November 16, 1983 Jean-Jacques Blais,[1] our minister of national defence, is in town on an official visit. I spun off to call this morning on Jack Valenti. The purpose was to cool him off about a recent decision by FIRA to disallow the establishment by Orion Pictures of a distribution outlet in

---

[1] (b. 1940) Liberal Member of Parliament for Nipissing 1972–1984. Held several cabinet posts in the Trudeau government, including Minister of National Defence 1983–1984.

Canada. Jack was blazing hot and breathing fire. Question: What is the principal task of the Canadian ambassador in this country? Answer: Calming down Jack Valenti.

November 17, 1983 Endless whining in the press in Canada, led in particular by one Thomas Walkom in the *Globe and Mail*, about the Great Snub. Why didn't the United States inform us in advance or consult us about their Grenada invasion? When were we actually informed? Did the States deliberately keep us in the dark? Were our efforts to get advance intelligence stonewalled by Uncle Sam? Was there a conspiracy to mislead us?

These are vintage examples of the Canadian National Inferiority Complex. The U.S. failure to consult us about their Caribbean escapade is the best evidence we've had in a donkey's age that we have an independent foreign policy. The United States would certainly have consulted us if they regarded us as their satellite, ready, ever ready to bless their every action. They figured we would not have approved. Then, having consulted us, they would have ignored our advice. And that would have been far more "humiliating" for Canada and for Thomas Walkom et al. than our being ignored in the first place. The Americans were smart not to consult us. We were lucky, on this occasion, that they were smart.

It's bizarre that my modest contribution to this episode has earned me the compliment of "displaying dazzling candour." This is because when I met the Canadian media in Washington after whining to Ken Dam, I couldn't think of anything to say, so I told the truth.

November 19, 1983 I received the Outstanding Achievement Award of the Public Service for 1982. My good feelings are seriously diluted by what's going on in External Affairs regarding Sondra's columns. Some people in the bowels of the Pearson Building are alleging that I have a conflict of interest. They wish to deny her the right to write.

November 20, 1983 Dinner last night at the Brinkleys' and tonight at Joe Alsop's, my two favourite tables for dining out. David Brinkley has seen it all but still looks forward to tomorrow. He is completely free from illusions about his fellow humans but is invariably courteous to all. Behind the mask of skepticism, even cynicism, there is passion and strongly held ideals. Not only does he have an unsurpassable knowledge of American history, he is American history.

Joe Alsop provides the only high table in Washington, right up there with the best of Oxford, All Souls, or Wadham with Maurice Bowra presiding on a good night. Conversation is supreme. There are rarely more than eight or ten guests for dinner, and in a few hours at Alsop's table, American history, art and high culture, Washington intrigue, and base gossip all fuse into one great roaring conversation. Hands on his cheeks, elbows on the table, bowed with drink, he talks of his family (the Roosevelts), his friend Jack Kennedy, of Oriental art, of collecting, of English society, of everything and anything with equal authority, all the while barking, denouncing, contradicting, or confounding you with his timely revelation of some obscure fact. You know that if you never come back to his table, you'll never again experience the same kind of intoxication that you did that night.

November 21, 1983 After addressing the Washington Foreign Law Society, I got back to my office to receive a bombshell. A member of the embassy who was visiting Ottawa purloined a copy of a departmental briefing note to the minister about Sondra's column and bootlegged it to me. It was drafted by David Elder in personnel, devoted assistant to Flora MacDonald in the bad old days, and by Manfred von Nostitz of the U.S. Bureau, a descendent of Bismarck, who would not be proud of his progeny. They have spun a bizarre theory of conflict of interest.

The briefing declares, "Her column is not appearing in the women's or social sections of the paper [zounds!] but on the op-ed page" (good God, it can't be true!). They continue, "Undoubtedly op-ed editor Meg Greenfield's interest in Mrs. Gotlieb comes from the perception that she is writing on the basis of information acquired during the course of official duties, which information is not generally available to the public. There will undoubtedly be pressures on Mrs. Gotlieb to deliver petty material which has the potential of embarrassing the Administration or the Congress."

Then, "The Conflict of Interest Guidelines for Order-in-Council employees state specifically that they 'do not formally apply to spouses,' but they add that officials have an individual responsibility to prevent conflict-of-interest situations in property and other dealings of their spouses."

An insidious piece of work. A combination of humbug, malice, and sexism. After allowing my blood pressure to boil, I called Derek Burney in Ottawa, who is supposed to be in charge of the U.S. Bureau. I let him know exactly what I thought about the note and his responsibilities. "You didn't like it?" he asked. "You should have seen the first draft!" But he undertook to prepare a new briefing note, more accurate, less nasty, and send it to me in draft for comment.

November 22, 1983 I get Burney's new draft. It is a vast improvement, although not perfect. It points out that "Mrs. Gotlieb is an established Canadian author in her own right." It also makes the point that the columns are "intended essentially as a humorous insight into the travails of diplomatic life in Washington." The note adds, "We are not confident of the basis on which the Department could discourage Mrs. Gotlieb from pursuing her literary career in this manner." Now that's an admission! And then, "We are satisfied that Mrs. Gotlieb's activity is consistent with her diplomatic status in Washington."

But a warning: "We have confirmed with the Ambassador the need for discretion in the selection of content of material." I could hardly object to the contents of most of this note, because it states the obvious. But I find it hard to believe it was necessary for officials in Ottawa to conduct such a silly activity.

November 23, 1983 Allan MacEachen is eclipsed by Trudeau's disarmament capers. The wily Trudeau has stunned him. He has made MacEachen more or less irrelevant in the context of Canada's biggest foreign-policy initiative in years. And he has marginalized him in Shultz's eyes.

I think MacEachen is fairly critical of the whole peace mission. Aside from the fact that it elevates Trudeau to the rank of world player, because of his global junketing, and aside from the fact that it lowers MacEachen's profile to the same degree, MacEachen is smart enough to understand that this initiative is poorly thought out, inspired by domestic considerations, and cannot succeed. A Nobel Prize Trudeau will not get.

November 24, 1983 A lot of people are quoting Fotheringham to me these days, particularly his zinger about Sondra in *Maclean's*: "Wives of Canadian Ambassadors are not supposed to act like a cross between Lucille Ball and Dorothy Parker."[1]

November 25, 1983 I continue my discussions with Soviet experts in Washington, but now with those of more conservative bent, such as Jim

[1] (1893–1967) American writer and poet known for her caustic wit.

Ambassador Allan Gotlieb with Prime Minister Pierre Trudeau.

Allan, Sondra, and their children, Marc, Rachel, and Rebecca, in the Roosevelt Room of the White House on Sondra's birthday, December 30, 1982.

The ambassador and Sweetpea, the Gotliebs' Tibetan terrier, in front of Tissot prints hanging in the library of the Residence.

The Gotliebs reclining in the library prior to a reception.

The staff of the Residence with the Gotliebs in September 1983. Clockwise from the back: Allan and Sondra Gotlieb; Rachel Gotlieb; Janice Thorvaldson, the ambassador's executive assistant; Rebecca Gotlieb; Thelma Cafe, the upstairs maid; chef Ibrahim; Teodora Batacan, the only female butler on Embassy Row; and Naomi, the kitchen maid.

Dennis Desprois, courtesy of the San Francisco Giants

Throwing the first ball in Candlestick Park, San Francisco.

The plaque senator. In the office of Senator Jennings Randolph of West Virginia.

Discussing world affairs with Vice-President George Bush in his office, 1982.

Ty Cobb and Rick Burt, two of the principal advisers to Ronald Reagan, as he welcomes Pierre Trudeau at the White House. Allan MacEachen, Canada's secretary of state for external affairs, looks on from the left.

The ambassador with Christopher Plummer and Donald Sutherland at the Residence.

Kenneth Galbraith and his wife at the Residence, with Pierre Trudeau.

Pierre Trudeau and Margot Kidder dancing after a dinner at the Residence.

Reagan breaking up with laughter at Trudeau's gorilla joke in the White House, 1983.

Henry Kissinger at the Residence.

courtesy Shaw Festival

John Turner, Allan Slaight of the Shaw Festival board, Allan Gotlieb, and Geils Turner, in Niagara-on-the-Lake at the opening night of Thornton Wilder's *The Skin of Our Teeth*, May 24, 1984.

Billington,[1] Peter Reddaway,[2] Robert Tucker,[3] and Hal Sonnenfeld. The perception is of a state dominated by hardliners of the Stalinist era, repressive in character and beset by serious domestic problems and international challenges. But it is nevertheless essential, in the view of most of them, to establish a better type of dialogue with the Soviet leader, one that does not threaten their legitimacy, one that the leaders will see as based upon a mutuality of interest. This is the line Trudeau should take when he sees Reagan.

November 28, 1983 Bill Ruckelshaus, in a highly candid conversation, told me he is finding it difficult to get the White House to accept the priority that the acid rain issue merits. He thinks it is unlikely he can get the Northeast option past Stockman,[4] because the budget director is convinced that a narrow option will balloon into a bigger and more costly one. So Ruckelshaus has come up with a new thought. He is looking increasingly at an "international option," one where U.S. treaty obligations to Canada would define limits for a possible congressional program.

To me, this means we should take a highly active political stance and argue vigorously for action. This could provide some weight, even if modest, to Ruckelshaus's arguments. Let him play the foreign-policy card. It's probably all he's got.

November 30, 1983 Saw Langhorne Motley[5] at State, and Richard Stone,[6] Reagan's special envoy to Latin America. I'm trying to run down rumours (picked up by a Canadian minister visiting Latin America) about an imminent invasion of Nicaragua, possibly by Honduras, Guatemala,

---

[1] (b. 1929) Director of the Woodrow Wilson Center 1973–1987; Librarian of Congress 1987 to present. Accompanied Ronald Reagan to the Moscow Summit in 1988.

[2] Author and academic in political science and international affairs. Served as a consultant to U.S. government departments on Russia and directed the Kennan Institute for Advanced Russian Studies.

[3] A Sovietologist at Princeton University. Served as an attaché at the U.S. Embassy in Moscow 1944–1953.

[4] David Stockman (b. 1946) Republican Representative from Michigan 1977–1981; Director of the Office of Management and Budget 1981–1985.

[5] (b. 1937) Ambassador Extraordinary and Plenipotentiary to Brazil 1981; Assistant Secretary for Inter-American Affairs 1983.

[6] Democratic Senator from Florida 1975–1980; U.S. Ambassador-at-Large and Special Envoy to Central America 1983–1984; U.S. Ambassador to Denmark 1992–1993.

and El Salvador with U.S. backing. Since we were caught with our pants down in the Grenada invasion, everyone in Ottawa is hyper-nervous about yet another embarrassing surprise. I get assurances that there is no situation in the hemisphere today comparable to Grenada last October. Do I feel reassured? No.

December 3, 1983 At lunch today I asked Rick Burt what would be the most effective approach for Trudeau to take when he sees Reagan. Trudeau, he replied, should encourage the president to express his own views on Soviet relations. Get him to reveal his own thinking. Above all, Trudeau should avoid putting Reagan on the defensive by lecturing or hectoring him. If he starts to preach, members of the Reagan team will intervene and the president will withdraw from any real discussion. Excellent advice. I've heard over and over that Reagan disliked Helmut Schmidt because the chancellor lectured him.

Burt told me serious thought is being given at State about what it can do to improve communications between the United States and the U.S.S.R. A recent conversation between Hartman[1] and Gromyko[2] in Moscow suggests the Soviet leadership has been shaken by the administration's rhetoric, seeming, as it does, to question the legitimacy of the Soviet state. Burt believes the initiative in Washington now lies with Shultz.

December 4, 1983 I've organized a lunch next week with Stephen Bosworth,[3] chairman of State's Policy and Planning Council, and other State Department Soviet experts. This is in follow-up to all the meetings I've been having with Soviet experts, or so-called, of which there are whole platoons in this town. From State I expect I'll get the official line, but Bosworth is smart and I'm trying to leave no good mind unpicked in preparing for Trudeau's upcoming private visit to see Reagan. It will be one of the most important meetings of his career.

---

[1] Arthur A. Hartman (b. 1926) U.S. Ambassador to France 1977–1981 and to the Soviet Union 1981–1987.

[2] Andrei Gromyko (1909–1989) Soviet Minister of Foreign Affairs 1957–1985; Chairman of the Presidium of the Supreme Soviet 1985–1988.

[3] (b. 1939) Member of the National Security Council during the first Reagan administration. U.S. Ambassador to the Philippines 1984–1987 and to Korea 1997–2001.

December 5, 1983 Monday morning, sitting in my vast and runic cavern, drawing breath. We're being mightily entertained these days. Lunch at the Maison Blanche with the owner of Hallmark cards. Sunday lunch with the Brinkleys, Saturday dinner with Muffie and Henry Brandon, Friday dinner at Susan Mary Alsop's in honour of the wife of Baron Elie de Rothschild, Friday lunch with Gerard Smith,[1] former arms control negotiator, Friday breakfast, U.S. media briefing. This week, dinner at the Alibi Club hosted by the Stoessels, another by Elliot Richardson, a brunch at the Krafts', a Christmas reception at the Wachtmeisters', a dinner at Tom and Joan Braden's in honour of the Brinkleys.

We are much criticized in the Canadian press these days for being overactive on the party circuit. Nothing new here. But how do I explain that many of these events are of immense political value to me? How tiresome diplomatic life would be if we were not part of the social life of so many exceptional people.

December 12, 1983 Roy Pfautch[2] had a Christmas party at the Folger Library. A big, big crowd, including a horde from the White House. An "in" event for the Reaganites. We were about to rush off after the dessert when Midge Baldridge said, "You can't go, Sondra is getting the good girl award." The crowd gathered around the podium and Ed Meese came out dressed as Santa Claus, and a very convincing one at that, given his naturally red face. Jean French Smith, Midge Baldridge, and Carolyn Deaver were the chorus line. "Good boy," "good girl" awards were given to a bizarre assortment – one was given to the commandant of the Marines, in honour of their actions in Lebanon and Grenada, and another to Sondra for her "Dear Beverly" columns. She was presented with a long ribbon with fake medals. High camp and all very silly for grown-ups. But we felt good, against the background of Sinclair Stevens's[3] vicious attack on Sondra in Parliament.

---

[1] Strategic Arms Limitations Talk Agreement (SALT I) Negotiator 1969–1972; U.S. Ambassador-at-Large for Non-Proliferation Matters and for Nuclear Power Negotiations.

[2] Republican public-affairs consultant and lobbyist in Washington.

[3] (b. 1927) Elected PC Member of Parliament for York-Simcoe, Ontario, in 1972; President of the Treasury Board 1979–1980; Minister of Regional Industrial Expansion 1984–1986.

December 13, 1983 Tonight we changed planets again. It was dinner at Kay Graham's in honour of Averell Harriman. There were in all about ten guests, among them Scotty and Sally Reston, Joe Alsop, and Averell's wife, Pamela, the descendant of Jane Digby, the *grande horizontale* of an earlier century. In his nineties, Harriman's marbles are going. Pamela patiently repeated remarks to him, but even then he seemed unaware of what was going on. She was his nurse. I admired how solicitous she was, tending to him in a soft and affectionate manner. One wants to give her credit for that, but it's hard to suppress the thought that there's already plenty of credit there – maybe $50 million worth or more.

Today was typical of what makes Washington so fascinating. One minute you're into asbestos, steel, and protectionism. The next you're into a Georgetown dinner with history, politics, high gossip, and the celebrity world.

December 15, 1983 The most important day in the calendar of Trudeau's peace initiative. He sees the president at 11 a.m. The Canadian press is in a frenzy.

I rose early to accompany the prime minister, MacEachen, and Fowler on the Challenger to Washington for the working visit with the president. I have never found Trudeau more difficult. During the hour or so allocated to briefing him, he jumped down my throat several times, was very sharp and at times impossible. The atmosphere was heated. Trudeau put his hands over his eyes and seemed to go into a sort of trance-like state a couple of times. I concluded he was tired from the endless travels on his long crusade, very nervous about seeing Reagan, and just downright overbearing and arrogant.

I pressed very hard during the briefing. "You must engage the president in a dialogue. You mustn't let him pass the ball to the others. You must come at Reagan from Reagan's vantage point or perspective." Then I suggested to him my "signals scenario." He should tell Reagan that most of his signals were being received in Moscow and by our Western publics – that the United States was going to have a strong defence, that it was going to correct the arms imbalance, and that we in the West were united and could not be divided. But what was not getting through were his peace signals, that he, Reagan, was a man of peace and wanted peace, a man who believed nuclear wars were not winnable and shouldn't be fought.

Trudeau followed the line and presented it to Reagan with almost perfect pitch. "You are a man of peace," he emphasized, "but your peace signals are not getting through." Trudeau was cool, relaxed, and showed no signs of nervousness. He embellished the theme brilliantly, even saying to Reagan, "You had no choice, you were dealt a bad hand, you didn't invent the two-track strategy, you didn't weaken the West's defence, you didn't cause the humiliation of the U.S. in Iran."

Reagan responded to all this saying, with some emotion, "You are absolutely right. The press has distorted my image, and I can't do anything about it." He cited how his "peace" speech to the Japanese diet was ignored by the media. The discussion went marvellously and lasted twice the allotted time. Bush, Shultz, Weinberger, and McFarlane seemed disarmed by Trudeau's remarks.

Shultz offered a lunch at the State Department, which was disappointing. He made almost no effort to talk to Trudeau, asked him virtually nothing about his recent trips, and was short on grace, probably because he had no sympathy for his global peace mission. In contrast, the Bush dinner at the Alibi Club was a delight. The Baldridges were there and the Ruckelshauses, among others. Bush gave a touching toast to Trudeau, in essence saying that he admired and approved of what Trudeau said in the Oval Office.

At the end of a long and energy-draining day, I told Trudeau that Sondra and I had been invited to a dinner-dance at the Madison Hotel given by Washington socialite Buffy Cafritz[1] but wouldn't attend unless he might be interested in going with us. I could see the reaction of his entourage: they were all exhausted and they were all dead-set against his attending. Surprise, surprise. Trudeau responded enthusiastically. I thought he would. At four o'clock this afternoon, he asked Sondra, in an excessively courteous gesture, if she would mind his using the phone at the Residence, where he was resting. He called Lacy Newhouse and asked her to meet him after the vice-president's dinner. So we picked her up and the four of us went to the Cafritzes' dinner-dance. We made a grand entrance. Trudeau was beaming and radiating charm and absolutely delighted to be stared at and the centre of attention. He was almost purring as he greeted the well-wishers. But he was beat at the end of the dance. The proof? He asked me to take Lacey Neuhaus home.

December 16, 1983 I joined Trudeau at his hotel early this morning to go to an ABC Television interview. He was very pleased with his meeting with Reagan and felt he had accomplished something, but the

[1] Washington socialite and trustee of the John F. Kennedy Center for the Performing Arts.

coverage in the U.S. press was miserable – buried inside the *New York Times* and *Washington Post*.

Afterwards, on the drive to the airport, he talked enthusiastically about the new embassy and questioned me at length on what I wanted to do in the future. I gave him no clue (I don't have any).

Sondra and I then did our duty and went to a diplomatic dinner at the State Department hosted by Shultz. I asked him, when passing through the reception line, how he felt the Trudeau visit went. He replied, coldly, "All right." Trudeau chills him out.

What a relief that Trudeau and MacEachen are gone. Having either one on a visit is difficult, but having the two at the same time is excruciating. MacEachen came on this trip because Shultz wanted him to. He thinks MacEachen is on his side and Trudeau is not. I think he's right.

December 19, 1983 Gossage briefed me for my post-mortem on the Trudeau visit with the Canadian media tomorrow. They are not, he warned me, in a great mood. They feel somewhat "betrayed" (Gossage's word) by the prime minister's willingness to embrace the president as a man of peace! I have no sympathy with this posse. Their problem is that they are anti-American. When this prime minister actually makes some headway persuading Reagan to alter his rhetoric, they turn against him. All they want to hear is that Trudeau dumped on Reagan.

At dinner at the Residence, I discussed with Eagleburger U.S. intentions with regard to UNESCO. For Canada, our chief point of concern is U.S. unilateralism. Eagleburger responded with relish. "Haven't I been telling you for two years now that unilateralism is the mood of the United States?"

December 20, 1983 I spoke to the Canadian press in Washington about the Trudeau peace initiative. There is great support in Canada, led by prominent Canadian intellectuals such as Walter Gordon, James Laxer,[1] and Margaret Atwood. But the Canadian press is very disappointed that Trudeau did not castigate Reagan when he saw him here. Where are the results? I tried to explain that the prime minister's initiative won't yield instant results. "It was diplomacy," I said, "and diplomacy deals in nuances." "Diplomacy," I added, "is not rhetoric. It's an effort to achieve objectives

---

[1] (b. 1941) Canadian political economist and professor. In 1971 he came in second for the leadership of the federal NDP and was unsuccessful when he ran for Parliament in 1974.

in the most effective way and not necessarily and not ordinarily overnight."

Then I reached for it. "Here you have one leader in particular who has made a strenuous effort to talk to every significant leader in the West and many in the Third World and China. If you detect a changing climate shortly after those efforts start, then I think you have to strain a little to find no relationship."

What I didn't tell them is you have to strain more than a little to find that there is a relationship.

December 21, 1983 The Bradens had us to a dinner for George and Obie Shultz. Due to a very nasty ice storm, the Eagleburgers, Brinkleys, and Kirklands didn't show up. A hostess's nightmare. That left the hosts, us (intrepid Canadians), the Shultzes (security brought them in a four-wheel drive), Joe Alsop, his niece, and her husband, Warren Zimmerman, currently number two at the U.S. embassy in Moscow. A small crowd on a snowy night, but the dinner was not cozy. From the beginning to the end, I had a running argument, or a series of running arguments, with Shultz – from Vietnam to the Vatican. I questioned the will of the United States, after Vietnam, to use force in a major conflict. He was very dismissive of my arguments. He was in a quarrelsome state of mind. I said, "The U.S. should have consulted its allies before deciding to pull out of UNESCO." Shultz: "We are fed up with consulting." And so on.

When we left, Sondra was upset with Alsop for always siding with Shultz in a sycophantic manner, mad at Shultz for being hard and rough, and mad as hell at me for being obnoxious and continually arguing with him.

December 22, 1983 Carl Mollins files a CP wire report that says Eagleburger stated off the record that if Trudeau thinks the United States would support his peace initiative, he must be smoking pot or something. Ottawa is wildly upset, to say the least. My instructions are clear: "Do something."

I got through to Eagleburger three times. He told me the report was "a distortion" and "an absolute outrage." He also denied that he called Trudeau "an erratic leftist" and added (not too logically) that, anyway, his remarks were made in jest. (Hard to see the joke.) He admitted, however, that he did say off the record something to the effect that whoever thought the United States would support certain Canadian proposals had to be smoking something pretty funny. Some denial. Eagleburger fully recognized that his comments were unfortunate and offered "humble apologies." He repeated several times that he had been jesting. He was obviously very embarrassed.

We discussed whether he should issue any personal statement, and he asked for my advice. I said that if he thought his remarks and respect for Trudeau were being misrepresented, then he ought to issue a personal statement to that effect. Jim Medas told me later in the day that he and his colleagues in State considered the report of Eagleburger's remarks to be serious and unfortunate, given his position as top-ranking diplomatic professional. Medas emphasized the irony that Eagleburger was known in Foggy Bottom as "Canada's best friend."

December 23, 1983 I called on Eagleburger to make formal representations about the U.S. decision to pull out of UNESCO. I got nowhere. What was most disturbing, I told him, was the willingness of the United States to turn its back on the principle of universality. Putting together these UN organizations was the greatest post-war co-operative enterprise. Does the United States believe it is the only country that cares about freedom of information and the press or about human rights? Eagleburger was courteous, but it became obvious that the decision had already been taken and I was just passing wind.

Eagleburger was still troubled by Mollins's story, but he hasn't lost his sense of humour. He said with an impish grin that since the report of his remarks about Trudeau appeared, he had received several job offers from big Canadian corporations. I'm not sure he was joking.

December 24, 1983 Rebecca and Rachel arrived to spend Christmas with us. They were astounded when a little brown shaggy puppy ran up to greet them. He is a Tibetan terrier that Sondra bought after I quarrelled with Shultz at Joan Braden's dinner party. She didn't sleep the entire night after the party, got up at 6 a.m., read through the dog ads in the *Washington Post*, and went out and bought the dog for consolation. Since George Shultz was the cause of the purchase, she thought she would name him Shultz, but when the dog peed on the carpet on coming into the house, she called him Sweetpea.

December 25, 1983 Last night we went to the Kirklands' annual Christmas Eve dinner, an intimate affair held at their suburban house in

Chevy Chase. I argued intensely with Leonard Garment,[1] no slouch as a hardliner, about the U.S. decision to quit UNESCO. All of the people at the dinner, Lane, Bill Safire, Suzanne and Len Garment, and others, are all so hardline that I'm tempted to be a contrarian. I do agree with their strong anti-communist views, but they don't like the world the way they see it, so they want to turn their back on it and damn the consequence. Scotty Reston said to me the other day, "I've never seen the U.S. in a more isolationist mood."

December 26, 1983 At Elizabeth Drew's annual Boxing Day party, I had a discussion with Bill Safire about the UNESCO decision. He was jubilant. "Best thing Reagan has done since he ditched the Law of the Sea treaty." I knew better than to argue with him. So we talked about Haig, and I supplied him with some more examples of "Haig-speak" for his word column in the *New York Times*: *round table* used as a verb and *conclusion* turned into an adjective, as in "Let's round table it, but let's not be conclusionary." Bill used my earlier report to him about Haig's comment at the Ottawa Summit: "Snakecheck this draft right away."

December 31, 1983 New Year's Eve at Ben Bradlee and Sally Quinn's Georgetown home. Casual, buffet-style. Journalist groupies in attendance, the types who are pleased to be themselves, to be on the right side of history (meaning the left side), and above all, pleased to be entertained by Ben Bradlee. Sally said to me at the Krafts' the other day that the Gotliebs were in a rut – spending too much time with the Georgetown set. "You'll see a different crowd at our New Year's party," she said. Maybe so, but who is more Georgetown than blue-blooded Ben with his house on N Street?

January 2, 1984 Sondra and I took a long walk and talk about the Reagan phenomenon. People we see in Washington dislike Reagan, or profess contempt, because he is not an intellectual. They see him as a second-rate monarch, undermining social democracy and leading the country towards isolationism. But the fact is he has fouled up little. The land is strong and more self-confident. The U.S. domestic scene is at peace, and Americans sense that they stand taller in the world, after Carter, Iran, and Watergate. He

---

[1] (b. 1924) U.S. attorney who served as Special Counsel to President Richard Nixon 1972–1974.

is what the country needs now, a genuine conservative and a self-confident, optimistic man. Americans look at his broad smile, listen to his anecdotes and homilies, and believe that tomorrow the sun will shine.

January 4, 1984 My old nemesis Doug Fisher[1] poisons me in the *Toronto Sun*. He writes that he asked Bogdan Kipling, the Bulgarian stringer here in town, how I am doing in Washington. "Bogdan," says Fisher, "believes Gotlieb is a walking disaster of arrogance and insensitivity." Good old Bogdan. Whenever I see him, I'm always courteous and patient. This has been partly due to the fact that he tells me he is a friend of my old friend Larry Zolf.[2] I have thought of him as a harmless flatterer with a screw loose. Bogdan could have added to my list of faults that I'm a poor judge of people.

Sondra says I'm becoming obsessed with what the press writes about me. She won't discuss anything that's written regarding myself. She refuses to read the press clippings.

January 5, 1984 End of three-day visit of fellow Winnipegger the Reverend Lloyd Axworthy, minister of transport. Took him to lunch, held a working dinner for him at the Residence, went with him on calls on Elizabeth Dole and others, and gave him altogether special treatment, knowing how critical he can be of officials. I am surprised at his lively interest in deregulation, given that he is such a strong nationalist and deregulation is so much a part of the right-wing, Reagan way. But he probably sees some attractive populist theme in the offing – cheaper fares for grandma and the little guy. No one ever said he wasn't a good politician.

January 10, 1984 Back from the heads-of-post meeting in Ottawa. The very able Derek Burney, now big cheese of the U.S. Bureau, shows he is in command. He kicked off with a long prepared statement on "the view from Ottawa" and then invited me to follow with "the view from Washington," which was followed in turn by a "view from the consulates."

All the consuls general complained about lack of support for their operations, lack of funds, lack of information, lack of appreciation by Ottawa

---

[1] (b. 1918) Member of Parliament for Port Author 1957–1965. Columnist for the *Toronto* and *Ottawa Sun* newspapers, becoming Dean of the Parliamentary Press Corps in Ottawa.

[2] (b. 1934) Canadian journalist and commentator. In 1962 he joined the CBC and became a host of its controversial current affairs show *This Hour Has Seven Days*.

and the embassy in Washington. In short, lack of everything. Substance rarely gets discussed at these meetings, or if it does, there is virtually no participation from the consulates. The consuls general continue to act as glorified trade promoters.

In Washington I received a group from the steel industry who are worried about the current political situation. There is a very damaging quota bill before Congress and the growing possibility of a trade action that would limit imports of Canadian steel products. Our big companies, who have always believed they are an integral part of a single North American industry, are in shock. They rightly think we should be exempt from the impending quota because – remarkably enough – we don't subsidize our steel industry. Wonder of wonders, it stands on its own feet and is very competitive.

The U.S. industry has engaged high-powered Washington lobbyists to mount a massive effort to win congressional and public support for the bill. The Canadian companies, dues-paying members in good standing of the U.S. steel association (which is financing the lobbying), feel utterly betrayed. No wonder they are angry. They are paying for the advocacy of laws to restrict their own access to the U.S. market.

January 16, 1984 We staged a dinner for Ed and Ursula Meese. A record six cabinet members under the Canadian roof: Meese, Casey, Weinberger, Hodel, Brock, and Clark. (Half the ministers in the court of the Sun King.) Also in attendance: Kay Graham, George Will,[1] and Meg Greenfield, among others. The Meeses stayed until 1 a.m. At my table Kay Graham nodded off (a touch of narcolepsy) amidst a vitriolic argument between Will and Casey on Claire Sterling's allegations of a CIA cover-up in the papal assassination plot. I put Will up to this theme, and he responded with relish. He tortured Casey verbally (the most articulate of journalists pitted against the least articulate of high officials).

I had to work very assiduously on my toast to Meese, having regard to the grotesque "how-to-cook-a-Meese" theme current in the Washington press. (There-are-no-starving-people-in-America Meese.) I said I liked and admired him, which I do. I toasted the success of Reagan and his team in restoring the dignity of the presidency and its standing in the land.

[1] (b. 1941) Conservative American columnist, journalist, and author. Joined the *Washington Post* Writers Group in 1974, writing a syndicated, widely circulated, twice-weekly column.

January 17, 1984 Old Oxford chum Thad Holt, who practises law in Washington, had us to a small dinner at the Metropolitan Club with Bud McFarlane and his wife, Jondra. As I don't know the powerful McFarlane very well, I was delighted with the invitation. Once you get over his grimness and solemnity, he's not difficult to like. I mentioned the speculation about Trudeau's departure, to which he responded (surprisingly) that Trudeau's leaving office would be a real loss. He was especially complimentary about Trudeau's recent meeting with the president in Washington. George Bush's counsel and buddy, the affluent Boyden Gray,[1] also at dinner, told me the right word to describe the acid rain situation is *gridlock*. Total and complete, he said.

Our very civilized host, whose interests run to history and literature, seemed irritable at the endless Washington shop talk. But alas, there are no salons in Washington. Every party is primarily a forum for trading information and gossip.

Geoffrey Pearson[2] is in town in his new capacity as director of Canada's institute on peace and disarmament. We agree on little, but the Oxford bonds continue to hold (though barely), in spite of his anti-Zionist sentiments.

January 21, 1984 Limousine-liberal time in New York. In addition to Trudeau and glitz at the Metropolitan Opera, it's the crusade for arms control and disarmament, "the third rail," "the big peace initiative" on which rides the Liberal government's hopes for re-election.

I accompanied Trudeau in his call on the *New York Times* editorial board. We were in the heart of the eastern establishment – Punch Sulzberger,[3] Seymour Topping, and a crowd of editorial writers attended. Trudeau talked about his initiative. Rather black and white in his analysis and dogmatic in his comments, yet he elicited an approving response from the *New York*

---

[1] (b. 1943) Counsel to George H.W. Bush when he was vice-president; White House Counsel 1989–1993.

[2] (b. 1927) Son of Prime Minister of Canada Lester B. Pearson and Maryon Pearson. Canadian Ambassador to the Soviet Union 1980–1983; in 1983 he was appointed Special Representative of the Prime Minister for Arms Control; first Executive Director of the Canadian Institute for International Peace and Security 1985–1991.

[3] (b. 1926) Publisher and President of the *New York Times* 1963–1992. Son of Arthur Hays Sulzberger, a previous publisher of the *New York Times*.

Times. Why? The *Times* hates Reagan. I then accompanied Trudeau when he received Mac Mathias,[1] the "good" senator from Maryland, Georgetown's favourite dinner guest. He's fair-minded but has no influence. As Joe Alsop always reminds me, no important senator dines out.

January 22, 1984 Met yesterday with Judy Erola,[2] minister of corporate and consumer affairs. Pharmaceutical issues are flaring, thanks to the pressures of Pfizer to extend their drug patents. They're making research and development in Canada (read Quebec) contingent on our ending our patent grabs. This issue could turn out to be even nastier than the broadcasting one.

January 24, 1984 How I loathe the working breakfast. In my book, there is nothing more uncivilized. But power town loves them. No breakfast, no contact. This morning I arranged one at the Residence with Marty Feldstein at a most ungodly hour: 7 a.m. Ungodly for me, but typical for him. The Conservative MP Michael Wilson[3] is in town and wants to meet him. I don't get too many chances to prove my usefulness to a Tory. Then I gave a lunch for David Smith,[4] minister for small business. We went to a book launch for author Felicia Lamport,[5] Judge Benjamin Kaplan's[6] wife. When he taught me at Harvard Law, he was the professor I admired the most. It was an unusual book party – no booze, no guests, and no book. (It turned out to be doggerel aimed at Reagan.)

Afterwards, we attended a dinner in our honour (so it would seem) given by Bill Ruckelshaus. There were a couple of superior senators at the

---

[1] (b. 1922) Republican Senator from Maryland 1969–1987.

[2] (b. 1934) Liberal Member of Parliament for Nickel Belt, Ontario; Minister of State for Mines 1980–1983 and for Social Development 1984; Minister of Consumer and Corporate Affairs 1983–1984.

[3] (b. 1937) Minister of Finance 1984–1991, of International Trade 1991–1993, and of Industry, Science, and Technology 1991–1993; Currently Canadian Ambassador to the United States (from 2006).

[4] (b. 1941) Liberal Member of Parliament for Don Valley East 1980–1984; Deputy Government House Leader 1982; Minister of State for Small Businesses and Tourism 1983–1984. Appointed to the Canadian Senate in 2002.

[5] (1916–1999) Political satirist and writer of light verse featured in newspapers and magazines such as the *Atlantic*, *Harper's*, and the *New Yorker*.

[6] Royall Professor of Law at Harvard and Associate Justice in the Massachusetts Supreme Judicial Court.

dinner (Alan Simpson[1] of Wyoming, Dan Evans[2] of Washington), a couple of congressmen, a few other dignitaries, and Elliot Richardson, stunned into sobriety by the pursuit of a Senate seat. Having had several Scotches myself during the long pre-dinner interlude, I had difficulty listening to a heavy disquisition by Ruckelshaus on acid rain. But I began to focus when I realized he was propounding a new theory: the threat is over. Those north-east lakes that are dead are dead, and those that aren't are stabilized and no further harm will be done to them by sulphur dioxide emissions.

I was appalled. Was he snowed by some new "scientific" report, or was he snowing himself? I recognized immediately a new and dangerous tack on the part of the EPA. All the more dangerous because, as Alan Simpson put it, "Bill Ruckelshaus is the kind of guy who could dispatch you to hell and persuade you that you were enjoying the trip."

January 27, 1984 Ken Adelman[3] sends me a U.S. Department of State "Information Memorandum" reporting on five Gallup polls taken in 1983 on attitudes of Americans to each country. "Canada Rated Most Favourably: Cuba Most Negatively," the memorandum reported. We need this reserve of goodwill. It must be pretty deep; it survived the Trudeau years.

January 29, 1984 Sunday brunch at Meg Greenfield's and then to the airport to meet Joe Clark, who is coming to Washington to discuss disarmament and do a report for Brian Mulroney.[4] Is this Mulroney's way of keeping him out of the country?

I've had little contact with Joe Clark since the Liberals came back in power. It's very difficult in our political system for public servants to have a relationship with members of the opposition parties. We officials are seen as "belonging" to the governing party; contacts with the other parties are a

---

[1] (b. 1931) Republican Senator from Wyoming 1979–1997; Senate Majority Whip 1985–1987; Senate Minority Whip 1987–1995.

[2] (b. 1925) Republican Governor of the State of Washington 1965–1977; U.S. Senator from Washington 1983–1989.

[3] Head of the Arms Control and Disarmament Agency 1983–1987. An early neo-conservative, he was a member of the Committee on the Present Danger. Under President George W. Bush, he was appointed to the Defense Policy Board.

[4] (b. 1939) Leader of the Progressive Conservative Party of Canada 1983–1993; Leader of the Opposition 1983–1984; Member of Parliament for Central Nova 1983–1984, for Manicouagan 1984–1988, and for Charlevoix 1988–1993. Prime Minister of Canada 1984–1993.

sign of disloyalty. In the U.S. system, political lines do not seem to constrain such contacts. While partisanship here is very strong – at least as strong as in Canada – the American system allows constant interaction of officials with the political parties.

This is one advantage to being at an embassy: there are more opportunities for officials to deal with politicians of all stripes. When opposition members travel abroad, the constraints that exist in Ottawa tend to fall by the wayside. It seems silly, in fact paradoxical, that the farther one is from the political community back home, the easier it is to widen one's contacts with them.

Still, I really haven't been looking forward to Clark's visit. My problem is I can't fathom the man. When he was prime minister and I briefed him for the first time – just before the Tokyo Economic Summit in 1979 – I was impressed with how articulate he was and, for someone with no background in foreign affairs, how quickly he caught on to the intricacies of the issues on the summit agenda. Here, I said to myself, is a man who understands, as Ernest Renan[1] said, that "*la verité est dans la nuance.*"

Then I discovered the paradox of Joe Clark: the more deeply he gets into a subject, the more superficial he seems to become. He is a man who shines on first exposure to light. But the greater the light, the duller the glow. As some British MP said of another many years ago, "He is very profound until he makes up his mind."

January 31, 1984 Sondra and I hosted a dinner at the Residence in honour of Joe Clark. We put together a first-order assemblage of notables in the disarmament field, including Paul Nitze, Paul Warnke,[2] Jack Matlock,[3] Jim Billington, the Krafts, Steve Bosworth, and many more. I learned shortly before the party that Flora MacDonald was in town. Should I invite her or not? I couldn't make up my mind, so I decided to ask Clark's advice, and he said, "Invite her." I was confident she would not come. She came. Grant Reuber, ill-fated deputy minister of finance in Clark's ill-fated government,

---

[1] (1823–1892) French philosopher and writer.

[2] (1920–2001) Chief Strategic Arms Limitation Talks Negotiator and Director of the Arms Control and Disarmament Agency. Assistant Secretary of Defense for International Security Affairs.

[3] (b. 1929) U.S. Ambassador to Czechoslovakia 1981–1983 and to the Soviet Union 1987–1991; Special Assistant to the President for National Security Affairs and Senior Director for European and Soviet Affairs on the National Security Council staff 1983–1986.

called to say he was in town, so I invited him too. This meant I had three key members of the last Conservative government.

I gave a handsome toast to Clark, who replied in a droll, if slightly bitter manner. He pretended to look around the room, spotting Grant Reuber, and alluded to how Grant had brought down his government with the famous petroleum tax, and there he was, now president of the Bank of Montreal. And there was Allan Gotlieb, now ambassador to Washington. But neither he nor Flora had jobs. Very jolly. Even Flora grinned at this point.

So far so good. But then Joe gets more expansive. He intimates, semi-tongue-in-cheek, that he rather expected sympathy tonight because of all the former office-holders (read has-beens) in the room. This "from-one-loser-to-the-other" theme created a slight chill.

What Joe just doesn't get is that in the U.S. system these people are not part of the "outs." They are somebodies. They are waiting to be "in" and contributing to the debates in the meantime. Clark was extrapolating from his own Canadian experience where once you are out of office, you are a nobody.

February 1, 1984 The highlight of Clark's visit was a lunch at the Kennan Forum of the Woodrow Wilson Center, headed by James Billington. Jeremy Azrael, of the Policy Planning Council at State, spoke brilliantly on the Andropov regime. It was high-table conversation about Soviet affairs and the best political discussion I've heard on this subject since I came to Washington. My very smart colleagues at the embassy, Jeremy Kinsman and Ralph Lysyshn,[1] seemed less impressed. They intimated that the group is right-wing.

I said goodbye to Clark after his three-day visit, which left me wilted. You have to like this man. And I do – sometimes. There is something about him that is human and appealing. Maybe it's his self-deprecating, self-mocking manner. Maybe it's his genuine sense of modesty. Maybe it's deserved modesty, but he is an appealing figure nonetheless. At the end of the day, I urged him to ask Mulroney to use me and the embassy for any visit to Washington. He told me he would speak to Mulroney. We shall see.

Clayton and Polly Fritchey had a dinner in our honour tonight. There were selections from the Georgetown set plus Paul Nitze and the eminent

---

[1] Canadian foreign-service officer since 1972 serving in Moscow, Lagos, Washington, and Brussels. Minister-Counsellor at the Canadian Mission to NATO 1990–1994; Ambassador to Poland 2002–2006 and to Russia 2006 to present.

Michael Howard,[1] visiting from Oxford. Sat next to the right-wing Lally Weymouth,[2] Kay Graham's daughter. She lets you know if you're not on her screen, and she let me know. I talked to Howard about our discussions at lunch. "Is the institute right-wing?" I asked. "Anyone who says that," the professor replied, "is making a political statement. If you had to call it anything, you could say it was centre-left, like myself."

February 3, 1984 Some buzz in Washington about our diplomatic boo-boo at the dinner for Joe Clark. We invited the two eminent arms control negotiators, one current, Paul Nitze, and one former, Paul Warnke. We seated Mrs. Warnke next to Paul Nitze. Little did we know, the Ns and Ws hadn't spoken to each other in a half-dozen years. It seems that in a congressional hearing, N. called Warnke a traitor. Mr. W. did not take kindly to that epithet. We were not aware – a failure of intelligence – that they had not been on speaking terms since then. Everyone else at the party seemed to know it.

Sondra told me today that she became aware of the boo-boo at the end of the dinner. Mrs. W. said to her on the way out, "When I saw Paul Nitze, I wasn't going to stay. But my husband said, 'Have a Scotch, relax, and say what you like.' I did. Now I feel better."

February 5, 1984 We invited a blue-ribbon group to see the Edmonton Oilers (including Gretzky) and the Washington Capitals play hockey: George and Barbara Bush, the Deavers, Dick Darman (I got Gretzky to sign a hockey stick for his kid), Sandra Day O'Connor, Paul Volcker, Rowly and Kay Evans, and Rick Burt with his new girlfriend, Gahl Hodges,[3] Nancy Reagan's social secretary. Bush was affability itself, Deaver was silent, while Rick Burt was doing his usual thing: crapping on Trudeau.

Burt drew me aside several times during the game to moan about Trudeau's misbehaviour in Davos a week ago. Trudeau's public speculations at Davos on the credibility of NATO's defence doctrine and his expressions of doubt about the U.S. commitment to defend Europe were striking at the

---

[1] (b. 1922) Chichele Professor of the History of War and Regius Professor of Modern History at Oxford University 1980–1989.

[2] (b. 1943) Journalist and daughter of the late Katharine and Philip Graham. Currently Senior Editor of *Newsweek*.

[3] Nancy Reagan's Social Secretary in the White House 1983–1985.

heart of the alliance, said Burt. "They were upsetting the Europeans, subverting Western solidarity, and comforting the Soviets."

"That's all?" I asked. I suggested to him that he was overreacting. But he came down no harder than the State Department boys who called me in the other day to blast me about Trudeau's behaviour both in Davos and East Germany.

February 6, 1984 We attended a dinner given by Kay Graham in her mansion on R Street for Lauren Bacall.[1] Sixty guests had to stand around for an hour and a half in overheated rooms waiting for the chef to pronounce himself ready. But it got better. I had a seat of honour between Kay and the worldly Marietta Tree.[2] In fact, it doesn't get any better.

February 8, 1984 I met with John Allan, President of Stelco, to discuss the worrying congressional attack on Canadian steel. The good news is that the Canadian steel industry is getting off its ass and is lobbying on the Hill. The embassy is working with them closely – sort of Canada Steel Inc. After much persuasion on my part, Ottawa has agreed that the embassy employ a trade counsel, Dick Rivers from Bob Strauss's firm, and we're strategizing regularly. He is the best in town, Bob says (big surprise). I then met with Bob Pierce of Nova Gas. He comes from one industry that understands the congressional threats to their interests. The gas people know the U.S. players and the U.S. system. I can't teach them much.

February 9, 1984 I took Bill Davis to see Mac Baldridge and chat about autos and free trade. Davis presented to him a favourite theme of his about how much better off the United States would be if it switched to a parliamentary system. Baldridge looked at him uncomprehendingly. I explained to Davis afterwards that this theme of his is not a winner. The last thing the Americans want to do is change their constitution. They worship it, and they love its checks and balances.

At night we gave a dinner in honour of Davis for thirty-six people. We tried very hard to make it an A-list dinner. A provincial premier, even one

---

[1] (b. 1924) American film and stage actress and a former model. She is a cousin of Shimon Peres, prime minister of Israel 1984–1986 and 1995–1996.

[2] (1917–1991) Socialite and U.S. delegate to the United Nations Commission on Human Rights in 1961. Recipient of Susan-Mary Alsop's letters published in *To Marietta from Paris: 1945–1960*.

who has governed half of Canada for a decade, cuts little ice in Washington. We managed to bag one senator, two congressmen, the chairman of the president's Council of Economic Advisers, the undersecretary of state for economic affairs, and the rest were lesser lights. Of all the premiers, Davis is the least pretentious, and I enjoy his company the most.

February 10, 1984 The premier and I called on John Heinz,[1] the fabulously rich, handsome, humourless, protectionist senator from Pennsylvania, and we got a cold blast on steel. Then I lunched with Senator Mark Hatfield of Oregon, chairman of the all-powerful Appropriations Committee. We dined alone in his gorgeous Appropriations Room in the Capitol building, which he personally helped refurbish and of which he's enormously proud. Rightly so – it's dazzling. When he invited me to lunch with him solo, I thought he wanted to talk about Trudeau's initiative on arms control. Wrong: he wanted to talk about FIRA and a pending application that was upsetting a powerful constituent. Gotlieb's rule of Washington behaviour: when a senator invites you to lunch, beware.

Jim Medas told a visiting Canadian academic that the Americans were fed up with Trudeau. They think he's gone out of control and is being used by the Russians. Further evidence, as if any were necessary, of how unpopular Trudeau has become (again) in this town.

February 16, 1984 I met with Gerry Regan, who is scheduled to have discussions with Bill Brock on our sectoral free-trade initiative. The Liberal initiative is not likely to go anywhere, but it marks a historic turning point. It's an admission by our trade policy community and by the Liberals that our beloved GATT is not strong enough to shield us against creeping U.S. protectionism. Even if we could negotiate sectoral free-trade agreements with the United States, how we could get them past GATT is a complete mystery to me. For some reason, the Ottawa crowd doesn't seem to want to worry about that.

February 17, 1984 Jim Schlesinger asked us to a cocktail buffet at his home in Arlington, a prized invitation. Out of power, out of sorts, he's still one of the best minds in Washington. For some reason, I want to

[1] (1938–1991) Republican Senator from Pennsylvania 1977–1991. Died in a plane crash with a helicopter dispatched to assist his aircraft, which was in difficulty.

compare him with Bob Strauss. Both equally shrewd, Schlesinger obsessed with issues, Strauss obsessed with human nature, Schlesinger with ideas, Strauss with results and how to make things work. I love going to Mel Krupins or Duke Zeibert's with Strauss and eating their pseudo-Jewish food. Strauss draws the entire lunching population to his table. I can meet more players in an hour than I can in a month of house calls. The only downside? Terrible smoked meat.

At Schlesinger's, I summoned up my courage and asked him if he was worried by the mounting U.S. foreign debt. No, he said. Why not? I asked him. "If it gets too high, we'll cancel it," he said. "On what grounds?" I asked him, rather shocked. "National security," he replied.

February 18, 1984 We attended a benefit for the Princess Grace Foundation at the old Department of Labor grand hall. Washington is full of these magnificent chambers. Dozens and dozens of luminaries, including the president and Cary Grant.[1] Yes, Cary Grant. Ten thousand dollars a plate, but a freebie for us. We sat with a group from the fashion industry.

I was all set to have a good time when Rick Burt espied me and came up. "You bastards," he said. "Don't you know you guys are up to your asses in the Orlikow affair? It was your own brainwashing program that the CIA was participating in."

After catching my breath, I had the wit to ask him why, if this were true, it took five years for the United States to come up with this bit of information. No one had ever mentioned a Canadian government program. "You mean you guys didn't even know of your own involvement?" Burt asked. "Of course not," I said.

"Well," Burt replied, "because you are such a great guy and a friend, I'm going to call my deputy and tell him not to leak this information, as I asked him to do yesterday."

"Gee, thanks, Rick," I said. "You are really a friend of Canada."

If this information is reliable, the shit is going to hit the fan (the RCMP fan) in Canada. *If this information is reliable.* With these guys, you never know.

February 19, 1984 We attended a Sunday brunch at the Krafts' home in Georgetown in honour of Brian Urquhart, UN deputy secretary-general.

---

[1] (1904–1986) English-born American film actor whose well-known work included *The Awful Truth* and *The Philadelphia Story*.

Meg Greenfield said to me, "You must be happy about our editorial today on the Orlikow case. We really attacked the CIA for doing such terrible things to Canada." I thanked her warmly, turned, winced, and went on to the next famous person. I'll bet Burt is pissed off that he told Medas not to leak the story about the (alleged) Canadian involvement.

February 23, 1984 I am en route to Atlanta for a two-day visit. Before leaving, I called on Bill Schneider, undersecretary for security affairs, to deliver a hard protest note on acid rain. Schneider was the most senior officer available, but he knows zilch about acid rain. I blasted him. He didn't know what hit him, but that's what the diplomatic business is all about – dealing with things of which you're totally ignorant. I expressed our "deep disappointment" with the administration's decision "to do nothing" in the foreseeable future about acid rain. I told him we were dismayed that the United States had switched positions on the most difficult and important issue between us. Talking to reporters afterwards, I said there were emerging general principles of international law under which the United States has a duty, as we do, to protect the North American environment.

February 24, 1984 Atlanta was a "full-treatment" exercise – address a black-tie dinner on Canadian foreign policy, call on the governor, visit Michael Graves's[1] new High Museum (splendid white palace, nothing inside), call on the president of Coca-Cola (*de rigueur* for visiting foreign officials), TV appearance on CNN's *Day Watch*, dinner at the consul general's residence with Georgia businessmen, visit to the University of Georgia in Athens (surprisingly beautiful campus) to address Dean Rusk's[2] seminar, lunch hosted by the academic vice-president, meeting with Ted Turner,[3] president of CNN. Another two days like these and I'll be terminally incapacitated.

My meeting with Ted Turner was memorable, to say the least. He was excited (hyperbolic) about the prospects of technology and satellite communications, wanting to bring Canadian programs into his new network.

---

[1] (b. 1934) Award-winning U.S. architect. Professor of Architecture at Princeton University since 1962.

[2] (1909–1994) U.S. Secretary of State 1961–1969.

[3] (b. 1938) American media mogul and philanthropist who founded TBS and CNN. In 1997 he pledged $1 billion to the United Nations.

All the talk about business was punctuated by tales of his recent trip to Cuba and interview with Castro. "Where's the tape of my conversation with Castro? Where's the tape? Where's the tape?" he shouted to his hapless aide. (Fortunately, it could not be found.)

All the while he was jumping up and down, hopping in and out of his chair, and spitting into a spittoon on his desk. He simply couldn't stop spitting. Comment – spit, comment – spit, comment – spit. And they were big spits. Whoppers. It was absolutely revolting. I felt nauseous and was desperately anxious to get out of his cavernous office.

February 26, 1984 The *Los Angeles Times* carries a major story on our acid rain protest. My quote to them may not go down too well in Canada: "Environmental damage is close to the Canadian psyche, if we have a psyche." Also: "I don't know what we could have a debate on, in the way of retaliatory measures. You're a big country."

February 28, 1984 My fifty-sixth birthday, a frightening anniversary, as Maurice Bowra used to say. I remember him roaring at dinner at a Wadham high table on his fifty-sixth: "The most dangerous year. Julius Caesar, dead at fifty-six. Shakespeare, dead at fifty-six. Nietzsche, dead at fifty-six." And then he ticked off a long list of other great men dead at fifty-six. "If I get through this one," he said, "I'll be fine. I'll be good for years. But the coming year – a dangerous time."

February 29, 1984 Trudeau has announced his resignation. He took a walk in a blizzard last night, heard the wisdom of the winds, and decided to quit. His timing is good. When a political leader strives more and more to perch himself on high moral ground, when he undertakes a solemn international mission to save the world, it is indeed time for him to go.

March 1, 1984 I had a sleepless night. Of course, I've known that Trudeau was going to go sooner or later, but I didn't really expect him to decide to resign in the midst of his peace initiative and rising polls. He made a landmark decision, and for him it was the right one. Yes, for him a landmark decision. And for me too. Canadians are so sick of the Liberals I'm sure we'll see a great Tory victory. And a Tory victory spells lights out for I know who.

My first visit to Philadelphia. City of my mother's birth, she says. Everywhere I went I got questions on three subjects: pharmaceuticals, pharmaceuticals, and pharmaceuticals. This is the drug manufacturing capital of the United States, and the industry – all of it – absolutely abhors the drug legislation the Trudeau government introduced in 1968 ("confiscated our patents"). They have clout, really big clout, because they do most of their manufacturing and research in Quebec. And in cabinet Quebec has clout, really big clout. Canadian nationalists, stay tuned.

March 8, 1984 Congressman Tom Corcoran of Illinois issues a statement denouncing our diplomatic note. "It would appear," he says, that "Canada is more interested in promoting an acid rain publicity effort than in developing an acid rain mitigation program." Big John Dingell managed to get the letter he sent me last month on the "practise-what-you-preach" theme reprinted in the press. This seems to be the strategy at the heart of the congressional counterattack, along with questioning the propriety of my public diplomacy.

Our opponents are not stupid in criticizing us for failing to do enough ourselves. We're vulnerable here, no question. Recognizing this, we have finally announced a commitment to reduce emissions 50 per cent by 1994. It's the best possible thing we could have done, a lot better than over-reliance on lobbying. The coal industry and their friends on the Hill want to make Canada the problem, not acid rain. Up until now, they have been succeeding.

March 15, 1984 I had a long meeting with the embassy staff to discuss the new protectionist assaults on Canadian interests: the section 201 investigation on carbon steel and section 201 investigation on copper. The steel case was especially worrying, as it could devastate our industry if we are placed under a quota. To make matters worse, Senator Heinz and a colleague in the House have bills to limit all steel imports. We are witnessing the classic pincer movement – one is caught between a trade-restrictive action and legislation, the latter being pursued as a fall-back if the former doesn't succeed. The purpose of the bills is to politicize the investigative process.

March 24, 1984 Today's *Globe and Mail* features a picture of Sondra under the headline "Parody of Post Column Doesn't Tickle Everyone." The

Globe got hold of a scurrilous "memorandum" and "letter" circulating in the department, the letter purporting to be written by the wife of the Canadian ambassador to Bulgaria. Since they had a copy of the "letter," they should have seen at once that it was rife with anti-Semitic and libellous references, for example, Pitfield, Coutts, and myself sitting around discussing what more we could do to help Israel; Ed Schreyer and I schmoozing in delicatessens in Winnipeg, eating corned beef; and I as undersecretary, giving orders to the department to purchase large quantities of Sondra's latest book. The *Globe* also refers to Marcel Massé's order to conduct an investigation into the document. ("Several officials have been called in to be grilled.") I told Marcel not to undertake an investigation, as it would go nowhere and now it's an embarrassment.

That there is trash in External who would write this sort of thing, I can more or less – with effort – understand. But how a reputable newspaper can reprint it and describe it as good clean fun is beyond me.

March 25, 1984 Sondra continues with her columns, and Washington continues to love "Dear Beverly," even if the bureaucrats in Ottawa do not. The *Washingtonian* magazine runs an admiring, sympathetic piece: "Ambassador's Wife Defiant: She's Seen but Also Heard." It gives some delicious samples: "The Residence functions as something between a private home and a public drinking place. . . . It's like living in a small hotel with the 'wife of' as manager." For this, says the author, "she has been denounced on the floor of the Canadian Parliament."

March 27, 1984 After speaking in Vermont about acid rain and before getting on the plane taking me back to Boston and Washington, my hosts handed me two very heavy chunks of marble, Vermont marble, they explained, which were in the form of bookends. I lugged these things on my lap all the way to Washington. I could have dumped them, but the truth is they were handsome slabs and I wanted to keep them. Reminded me of a tale involving a predecessor, Lester Pearson. He was speaking somewhere in Illinois. As he was getting on the aircraft to take him to Chicago and Washington, the ladies he spoke to handed him a large homemade cake as a token of their appreciation. He had to carry it back with him on his lap, but when he got to the airport in Chicago, he dumped it in a garbage pail.

March 28, 1984 More criticism for lobbying Congress. Jake Garn[1] of Utah, chairman of the Senate Banking Committee, complained sharply about a letter I wrote to legislators on a bill extending the extraterritorial reach of U.S. law. My letter was hard-hitting but fully justified. Garn made a speech on the Senate floor entitled "Ambassadors Should Not Be Lobbyists" and entered it into the congressional record. "It seems to me inappropriate," he said, "for the ambassador of a nation that is here by our courtesy to take an active part in the political deliberations of the host country." He did not think the U.S. government directed its ambassadors to lobby other Parliaments' members on specific legislation. Is he kidding? How could a serious political figure be unaware that the United States intervenes and lobbies every other day against policies they regard as inimical to their interests?

Traditionally, the United States never even sought to justify its positions. Hence the wording of their famous diplomatic notes: "The U.S. Embassy has the honour to present its compliments to the Government of [fill in the country] and wishes to inform it that its proposed policy is contrary to the best interests of the United States." Full stop. Period. Finis. How could Garn not know how the U.S. ambassador and his staff cultivate and seek to influence legislators as a virtual way of life? If they didn't, they would be fired. Garn is a donkey. In the Bible it is said that when an ass spoke, it was a miracle.

March 29, 1984 Eagleburger summoned me to the State Department to deliver an official protest on a trivial matter. U.S. baseball is wildly upset because our Olympic Sports Pool Corporation is planning to use U.S. baseball scores in its lottery. We haven't heard a peep from the National Football and National Hockey Leagues, whose games will also be part of the lottery. But there is a problem for us. The fear in Canada is that the U.S. reaction could jeopardize the chances of a National or American League baseball team being located in Vancouver. Now that's a big deal. This is a little cameo of our problems with our giant neighbour. They can always out-link us, out-retaliate us, and therefore out-screw us. But I felt like telling Eagleburger (à la Dingell and Garn) that the United States should stop interfering in Canada's domestic policies.

---

[1] (b. 1932) Mayor of Salt Lake City 1972–1974; Republican Senator from Utah 1974–1993. Garn was the first member of Congress to fly in space, in 1985.

April 3, 1984 The United States hits us. We hit them. We're preparing a stiff note on the Garrison Diversion. The administration's proposed financial appropriation for the dam is a whopper. We keep trying to kill this damn dam, for years and years, and it just won't die. The two North Dakota senators, thanks to their seniority in Congress, wield enormous power. And they link up with the Corps of Engineers, which loves these massive projects. We've not been effective in killing the project – no surprise. Our main hope now is that U.S. domestic interests will succeed in accomplishing what we haven't been able to do: bury it. The project is preposterously expensive, so a combination of U.S. budget cutters and environmentalists might prove our salvation. We have to work more intensively with these allies.

April 4, 1984 Yesterday, an awards dinner for Nancy Reagan and a meeting at Andrews airport with Allan MacEachen, who was en route to Central America. It's a good idea for him to go there, since Trudeau has hogged disarmament, arms control, NATO, Western security, and East-West relations. He has taken over centre stage.

MacEachen's visit here is one of the few, very few ministerial trips to Washington that are slated in the coming months. Everyone in Ottawa is waiting for the Liberal leadership contest and then the election. The politicians don't want to be away from home, to my most excellent fortune.

April 9, 1984 I've come a long way in my thinking on how to manage Canada-U.S. relations. When I spoke in Lansing, Michigan, a few weeks after my appointment to Washington, I expressed great doubts about the role of binational institutions. I regarded them as constraining and undesirable. My views were very much in line with the prevailing orthodoxy in External Affairs. In a speech I gave today at Brookings, I turned full circle. The increased meshing of our economies is giving rise to more and more conflicts between special interests on opposite sides of our border. These conflicts arise from policies that emerge from equally staunch democracies. There is no way to resolve the conflicts, because elected politicians cannot be seen to subordinate the interests of their constituencies to foreign ones. This is why we need mediation, arbitration, and judicial settlement. In two words: bilateral institutions.

April 15, 1984 Sondra spoke to the ladies at the Women's National Democratic Club. Beverly was there. That was the name on the place-card at the head table. There was no one in the chair, but a Styrofoam head wearing an *outré* red hat was placed on the tablecloth in front of the empty seat. Sondra got a much better turnout than I am accustomed to when I speak.

April 20, 1984 Another farewell to Eagleburger. In Washington the senior government cadre is in a perpetual state of departure, hence the town is in a perpetual state of saying goodbye. This farewell was given by Reagan's cultural ambassador and remarkable collector of American art, Dan Terra, a likeable man. It was at the Georgetown Club, which has the distinction of being an even more lugubrious place than the F Street Club. There is absolutely no joy in this. The people at the party don't want him to leave. No one wants Eagleburger to leave, least of all myself. He is an irreplaceable interlocutor. And I don't really think that he wants to leave, but his health is rotten and he is broke. Eagleburger is known in some circles as being rather critical of Shultz, but he's in a minority. Moreover, Shultz's reputation in Washington is slowly beginning to rise (again). Shultz has staying power.

April 25, 1984 A nasty new problem has arisen out of nowhere. For close to a half-century, customs combine harvesters have been moving freely across our border every autumn, helping farmers gather their crops. The agreement allowing this was signed by Franklin Roosevelt and Mackenzie King. Now we have the sad story of protectionism eroding the benefits of an open border. Some unnamed senators have been demanding labour certification, which means the end of the agreement. By the time that process would be completed, it would be too late to harvest. Demonstrating the truth of Nicko Henderson's dictum, I have been utterly unable to put a name to the legislators pressing the INS for this change in the historic practice.

I called today on Bill French Smith to express my outrage, because the attorney general is responsible for the immigration service. He listened politely, sympathetically and shared my sense of outrage. He then told me he could do nothing. "Call on Labor," he suggested. This I will do, with predictably nil results.

April 27, 1984 I received a very significant phone call from Derek Burney. Brian Mulroney will be in Washington in June, and Mulroney would like me to arrange meetings for him with Shultz, Regan, Volcker, Brock, and

Senator Don Riegle[1] of Michigan, whom he met some time ago. Bravo. I'm euphoric. Unlike certain premiers, Mulroney is using the embassy. Given that I'm supposed to be a big Liberal, this is an achievement. I think Bill Fox[2] must have had a little (or a lot?) to do with getting Mulroney to handle this thing the right way. He is acting like he expects to be prime minister, probably with justification.

April 29, 1984 More good news. Mulroney responded positively to my suggestion that Sondra and I host a dinner for him and his wife on the evening of June 21. I am told he is "keen" on it. Mila will come if I think it is appropriate. He wants to hear my suggestions for a guest list.

May 2, 1984 Days of guerrilla warfare in Central America and bureaucratic warfare between Ottawa and me. A couple of days ago, I addressed a forum at the Woodrow Wilson Center on differences between Canada and the United States towards Central America. I spoke in the morning and wound up the conference later in the day. I walked a thin line, given the tender state of our relations with the States (Headline in yesterday's *Los Angeles Times*: "Canadian-American Relations Labor Under a Dark Cloud of Contention.") I said we were worried by the increased militarization of Central America. Canadians viewed the upheaval in the region "as a primary function of chronic social injustice and not primarily as a function of communist expansion." (We always manage to make ourselves more high-minded than the Americans.)

My participation led to a foolish contretemps with Ottawa. Burney, in full bullying mode, sent me a message today complaining that I was "authorized" to speak only once, not twice. I called him on the telephone and hollered, "I don't need your authority to speak in the U.S. or Canada, and it so happens that both my statements were approved in the Latin-American Bureau."

There seems to be a fuss back home on another Central American matter. When I saw Langhorne Motley last month to raise the issue of possible American involvement in the mining of Nicaragua's harbour, he assured me there was no American involvement. Now Allan MacEachen

---

[1] (b. 1938) Democratic Senator from Michigan 1976–1995; Chairman of the Senate Committee on Banking, Housing, and Urban Affairs 1989–1995.

[2] Prime Minister Brian Mulroney's Press Secretary and Director of Communications 1984–1987; formerly the Ottawa and Washington Bureau Chief of the *Toronto Star*.

has implied publicly that the CIA was involved. This, plus the fact that MacEachen decided not to go to El Salvador on his recent trip to Central America, has angered people here. State Department briefers seem to be citing MacEachen's avoidance of El Salvador as another example of Canada's unreliability as an ally.

May 5, 1984 Yesterday I called on Jack Matlock in the NSC, the most sensible interlocutor on Soviet affairs in the administration. You get a straight analysis from him, no ideological crap. After hosting a huge reception for Mario Bernardi[1] and the cast of *Rinaldo*, we went to Willie Wachtmeister's party for himself, celebrating ten years as Sweden's ambassador to Washington.

Ten years as ambassador to Washington. I can't imagine such a thing. I think he's lasted so long because he hasn't offended anyone either in Washington or, more importantly, in Stockholm. We ate at tables set in a tent in his garden. Many Democrats prominent in earlier times were there, including the epicene Claiborne Pell.[2] If the Democrats regain the Senate, this man becomes chairman of the Foreign Relations Committee and that undistinguished body plunges deeper into obscurity. Florid Ted Kennedy walked in. He waved to the assembly, stayed fifteen minutes, and left.

May 6, 1984 We attended a small dinner given by Marc Leland, now financial adviser to the Getty Trust. From Treasury to the Getty Trust. Nice progression. I repeated the remark Charles Ritchie's ancient aunt made to him when she learned he had just been appointed Canada's ambassador to Germany. "Charlie," she said, "you sure got your ass in a tub of butter now."

May 7, 1984 This was a beautiful, cool, sunny day in Washington, and since business at the office wasn't all that pressing, I decided to do something unusual. I asked Jacques Helie to pick up Sweetpea and bring him to the office at lunchtime so that we could go for a short walk, a modest attempt to stretch my – and Sweetpea's – legs.

---

[1] (b. 1930) Canadian conductor and pianist. The founding conductor of the National Arts Centre Orchestra in 1968, he was also conductor of the CBC Radio Orchestra 1983–2006 and the Calgary Philharmonic Orchestra 1984–1992.

[2] (b. 1918) Democratic Senator from Rhode Island 1961–1997; Chair of the Senate Committee on Foreign Relations 1987–1995.

We had a lovely outing down Massachusetts Avenue, past the embassies and the mansions, but when I returned Sweetpea to Jacques, I found him standing on the street in Sheridan Circle, next to our official vehicle, white and shaking. He stammered, in a wildly upset way, that while he was waiting a car pulled up to our Olds and paused. Two men were in the front seat and one of them yelled "Hold it," drew out a gun, and fired two shots at Jacques and the car. They then sped off at top speed, but miraculously, Jacques managed to get the licence plate of the fleeing vehicle.

Not long after, thanks to Jacques's presence of mind, the police got the car and arrested the two men not far away, at Wisconsin and M. It seems that traffic got snarled for over an hour. It turns out the gun that one of the men brandished and "fired" was a toy gun, a plastic one, that looks just like a real one and fires rubber projectiles. The two men, both under twenty, were charged with possessing a prohibited weapon.

That was the whole tale, or so I thought. But a local radio station picked up reports, initially from the police, about an attempt on my life and broadcast the news that two shots were fired at the Canadian ambassador. This then got repeated as an assassination attempt on my life (although I was nowhere near the car when the incident occurred). Maybe the story got credence because the Residence has been under the constant protection of the U.S. Secret Service almost since our arrival. (Canada has been a target of the Secret Army for the Liberation of Armenia.) The local reports were then picked up and carried across Canada by the CBC, and telephone calls started to pour in to our press section from all over. Within an hour I got a call from a hysterical mother – mine, in Winnipeg.

May 8, 1984 I spent a large part of the day talking steel with the Canada steel gang and discussing the new embassy with Arthur Erickson. I'm impressed with how sensitive Erickson is to the embassy's immediate environment. He is not a big-ego architect seeking to impose his image on the Mall. Instead, his concept is to adapt to the basic features of the public buildings in the area – or as I put it, to the "New Rome." He's going to salute the pillar culture of Washington by introducing pillars into his open structure. No one has done this for years.

May 9, 1984 The *New York Times* and the *Washington Post* trumpet the design of the new Canadian embassy. Marvellous pictures. Marvellous write-up. "It's a marvellous spot," I am quoted as saying. "We will be at the axis of two of the most important streets in the world." There is a great irony here: the building goes up as Trudeau, its great champion, leaves the scene. But will it go up? I very much fear that if the Tories win the upcoming election, they will not let the embassy go forward without further delays or even starting over. They hate Erickson, referring to him always as "Trudeau's friend," as if he had no legitimacy as an architect.

May 11, 1984 Sondra dined at Joe Alsop's, and I attended a dinner of the Canada-U.S. Chamber of Commerce Advisory Committee and gave the opening address. A more agreeable activity than speaking, as I do in a few days, at the Metric Conference. The Americans regard the metric system as an invention of the devil. But I'd rather speak about metrics than asbestos.

May 16, 1984 Colour photo of Sondra on the front page of *USA Today*. "Foreign Service Fun" is the caption and the story is about her thirteen columns in the *Washington Post* "lampooning diplomatic life in the capital of the free world." When I think of this story being carried in cities and small towns across America, I can scarcely believe it. It's awesome.

May 24, 1984 John Block assured me he's not too excited by Senator Jepsen's[1] anxiety over the recent surge of our live hogs and pork exports to the United States. I assured him (sticking my neck out) that our production had peaked and was beginning to decrease. "I, for one," Block said, "am not going to get too excited about hogs." I, for another.

May 28, 1984 We've just returned from the Shaw Festival in Niagara-on-the-Lake, where we were the guests of honour at the opening production of Thornton Wilder's *Skin of Our Teeth*. It was a beautiful late afternoon when the founding president, Calvin Rand, gave a pre-theatre reception on the lawn of his large house, dotted with magnificent ancient trees. In the centre of the crowd stood John and Geils Turner. John looked majestic. He was drawing people to him as if he were some powerful electromagnetic force. He was certainly radiating something – confidence, I believe. The confidence that he has the Liberal leadership in his pocket. We chatted in a group for a few minutes, long enough to sense that Turner talks like a man who has, and knows he has, a rendezvous with history.

---

[1] Roger Jepsen (b. 1928) Republican Senator from Iowa 1979–1985.

May 29, 1984 Bill Fox, now Brian Mulroney's chief press aide, and George Stratton, Tory party treasurer, called on me at the chancery to discuss Mulroney's upcoming visit to Washington. I was keen to talk to Fox, since I had learned that the president was holding a fish fry at the White House, honouring the Congress, on the same night as our proposed dinner for Mulroney. This, I told him, constituted a triple whammy: the top White House people, the cabinet, and congressional leaders were unlikely to be available. I explained that I wanted to change the date of our embassy dinner to the following night. Fox seemed very nervous about this. He said, "Mulroney might not understand," and I'd be well advised to stick to my current plan and do the best I could. My heart sank.

Why should Mulroney be upset at my proposal, given the special circumstances? After all, Mulroney is not exactly a household name in this town, and leaders of opposition parties visiting Washington are routine events. But I don't know Mulroney and Fox does, so I figured I should take his suggestion at face value. This means that I'm going to have to use every ounce of personal influence and every ounce of personal capital to produce an A-list crowd. Maybe I'll be lucky to get a B.

After our meeting Fox told me he wanted to speak to me privately, as he carried a message for me from Mulroney. He said his boss wanted me to know that he was very appreciative of my support and assistance in arranging his visit to Washington. I was deeply moved to hear this. I took advantage of the moment to explain to Fox why it was so important for Mulroney to allow me to accompany him on his calls, especially the one on the president.

Meanwhile, I gave a working lunch today for Allan MacEachen, here for a NATO ministerial meeting. The conjunction of the two events gave me a strange sensation, like working for both the assassins and their victims.

May 30, 1984 So much publicity for the Gotliebs. The *Star* does a favourable feature on my style of "public diplomacy" headlined "How Public Diplomacy Is Winning the Battle." A preposterous statement. The *Star* quotes Joe Kraft of the *Washington Post*: "There just isn't another diplomat in this town who's even close to being so well tuned-in to the power structure." Less preposterous, but is it doing us any good?

People say publicity like this helps our access to the decision-makers, and maybe they're right. This town feeds on myth. But it also brings loss of privacy. A *Citizen* article today: "Gotlieb Home for Sale; It's Become Too Big." It goes on: "Since they bought it about ten years ago, the Gotliebs' residence has been the centre of the social world of Ottawa, where prime ministers, ambassadors, and members of royal houses have been entertained." The hype seems to be feeding on itself. In all our years in Ottawa, where we allegedly entertained prime ministers and royalty, not one news article ever appeared about our social life. God, I feel nervous.

June 1, 1984 We attended a dinner given by the Turkish ambassador in honour of his visiting foreign minister. I was keen on going in order to get inside the magnificent *fin de siècle* Turkish marble palace on Massachusetts Avenue, not far from our own embassy. Looking at its pillars and undulating curves, one can almost imagine a sultan and his harem inside. It's the most magnificent pile of marble in the form of a house that exists in Washington, definitely superior architecturally to our own embassy, itself no mean pile. Washington can keep its monuments; it's the domestic architecture that is the glory of the city.

The most senior U.S. official to turn out for this staunch and important NATO ally was the deputy secretary of defence. Not one cabinet minister, let alone the secretary of state. The ambassador is much respected and has been here a donkey's age. Washington is a tough town.

June 8, 1984 I'll be getting a visit, on my return, from Mulroney's advance team to check everything out (including me) before his upcoming visit to Washington. Fox and Stratton will be accompanied by Bonnie Brownlee,[1] Mila's executive assistant. They are determined to get maximum mileage for Mulroney out of this visit, and I'm committed to making it a big, smashing success, even though it looks less and less like Mulroney is going to make it to 24 Sussex.

June 9, 1984 I'm busting my ass for Mulroney. I like what he is saying about the state of our relationship, but I'm rooting for Turner. I'm glad we are old friends, because another Liberal leader (such as MacEachen or Chrétien) would not be happy seeing me opening the doors of the power-brokers and media elite in this town to the leader of their Opposition.

June 11, 1984 Today's "Diana Hears," a gossip column in the *Washington Times*, reads: "Question: 'I'm worried, madame . . . with Pierre Trudeau's

[1] Press Secretary to Prime Minister Brian Mulroney and his wife, Mila, 1984–1987.

resignation as Canada's Liberal leader, must Washington wave goodbye to high-profile Canadian Ambassador Allan Gotlieb and his hooty writer wife of, Sondra?' Answer: 'Yup . . . if Conservative Brian Mulroney wins . . . and things look sunny for the Cons right now – the eighty-sixing of the Gotliebs will be swift, tough, rough and bumpy.' "

What else can I expect? The Canadian papers keep listing me high up on the Tory hit list. One even speculates on how unlikely it is that a Tory prime minister would want to work with "the architect of the infamous third option" [*sic*].

June 12, 1984 Pork again.

I call on Ed Zorinsky,[1] senator from Nebraska, at his request. "At his request." Those three words always signify the same thing: the presence of television cameras.

I enter his office. Sure enough: lights, cameras, action. I sit down among the aides and reporters. "Mr. Ambassador," he says, "the people of Nebraska are upset by your country's practices on pork. Pork is essential to the livelihood of Nebraskans, to their economic survival. Start playing fair," he admonishes me. "Stop subsidizing the export of your pork to our country."

I pause for ten or twenty seconds, look at him hard, and say, "Senator, don't you find it a bit strange, you calling me in here to lecture me about pork?"

The senator looks much taken aback. "Why?" he asks.

I reply, "A Jewish senator lecturing a Jewish ambassador about pork. That's not kosher."

At first the senator and his entourage seemed stunned. Then the senator started to laugh, and everyone broke up laughing. Great meeting after that, me explaining that we were the aggrieved and they were the oppressors. He didn't buy that, of course, but at least the meeting was pleasant and no longer confrontational.

Actually, I like Zorinsky. He has an excellent sense of humour. A small, unimposing-looking man, his favourite song is "Zorinsky for President." If you ask him, he will sing it for you without any encouragement.

June 13, 1984 Two more of Mulroney's staffers landed on me today. The preparation of this visit has been a major, major undertaking, especially

[1] (1928–1987) Democratic Senator from Nebraska 1976–1987.

the dinner, which I've been working on every day. The guest list is a nightmare, because I have the miserable fortune of competing with that damnable presidential fish fry at the White House. To make matters worse, a lot worse, it's in honour of Congress. I'm feeling sorry for myself. I'm having a difficult time getting acceptances for an unknown leader of the Opposition of a non-headline country. I'm beginning to feel like the poor little Canadian ambassador again.

Of course, I'm making all the calls personally. "You'll know who he is soon," I tell people. I wonder. The Liberals are rapidly rising in the polls. Official wisdom in this town is that Mulroney won't make it as a winner.

June 14, 1984 This evening we got a crowd together at the embassy to watch the CBC broadcast of the farewell to P.E.T. We were able to attract few Americans for the spectacle. Nobody is in mourning here. My own emotions are, I have to confess, mixed. I admired the man and especially his intellect. He was the most clearly committed federalist in the land. His vision of one Canada, with a strong central government, representing both English- and French-speaking peoples, was the only viable one for our country, but he stayed too long. His economic policies looked backward, not forward. He had fallen in love with his own image as a peacemaker. He had become a *tiers-mondiste*. And a Soviet apologist. He left us united but weak and full of false beliefs about ourselves. He was indeed a magician, because he sketched illusions against the Canadian sky.

But then – the illusions helped, perhaps, to keep us together. He despised ethnic nationalism. And unlike any other Canadian I have known, he had star quality. One could say of him what Hazlitt said of an English painter of his time: "Take him with all his faults and follies, we scarce shall see his like again."

June 16, 1984 At the embassy, we viewed the finale of the Liberal Convention with the usual forlorn Canada-watchers in attendance. I am grateful for the victory of my old Oxford friend John Turner, glad to see Trudeau go, he for whom foreign policy became a personal indulgence, and glad to see Chrétien defeated, an egotist, no man to lead a country.

Ever since I have known Turner, he has been sprinting and dashing. Now he crossed the line. He's come in first. The Turner era starts today.

THE TURNER INTERLUDE

June 17, 1984

I'm so excited I couldn't sleep. I've known Turner for a generation, and there has always been a bond between us. Whenever I see him in the presence of others, he always tells them that I won the Vinerian Prize at Oxford. He always flatters me, makes me feel good, more important than I am. He is strong, intelligent, principled, a Canadian nationalist, but pro-business, pro-American. He has the leadership qualities that can make us proud to be Canadians.

June 20, 1984 The first day of my life with Brian Mulroney. He and his party arrived at 1:15 p.m. The first thing Mulroney said to me was that he would not ask me to accompany him to see the president. He wanted me on the other calls, he explained, but not when he called on Reagan. The meeting with Reagan would be very "political," he explained. I would therefore find it awkward to be present, and he was sure I would understand. It was a pretty good con job. Of course I don't understand. The idea of a meeting with the president of the United States being too political for the presence of an accredited ambassador is horseballs.

I figured it would be stupid of me on my first encounter with Mulroney to start an argument with him, and he no doubt would have regarded me as being pushy and standing on protocol. But after all, as leader of the Opposition he does occupy an official position in Canada, he is not a private person, and I am *his* ambassador – at least until I am fired.

I briefed Mulroney on the guest list for tomorrow's dinner, going over the list one by one. I was deeply impressed by the fact that he seemed remarkably knowledgeable about the background and achievements of most of them. Very different from Trudeau, who knew little about individual Americans other than beautiful women in the entertainment field.

Mulroney had only one appointment today, with Mac Baldridge, and I accompanied him. For Baldridge, Mulroney was a vision of reasonableness. Mac has been very negative about Canada because of FIRA and the NEP. Mulroney heard out his criticisms, and he then made clear his scorn for these Liberal policies and his conviction that they were bad for Canada. He likened the NEP to holding up a gas station – it was a form of highway robbery.

Baldridge could scarcely believe what he was hearing. He has been beating his head against the wall with his criticisms for years. I could hardly believe my ears as well. I have to think that Mulroney is quite right in wanting to scuttle or reverse these policies. He's been saying this openly, so why shouldn't he tell the Americans? Still, I felt slightly uneasy. What if he doesn't deliver? His credibility here will then be seriously damaged. And will he be regarded in Canada as dumping these policies simply to please the Americans? The nationalists will lay political minefields for him on the road to change.

June 21, 1984 I went to Mulroney's suite at 9:20 a.m. to take him to the State Department. He had a 9:50 meeting with Rick Burt, who was going to escort him and his colleagues (Sinclair Stevens, Fred Doucet)[1] and myself to see Shultz at 10 a.m. Mulroney's advisers were not pleased about having to call on Burt. They are conscious of Mulroney's prestige and act as if he were prime-minister-in-waiting, which, after all, he is not. He's running well behind John Turner in the polls. In the car en route, I urged Mulroney to express his appreciation to Shultz for his commitment to managing the Canada-U.S. relationship and particularly for his initiating the quarterly foreign-minister meetings.

Mulroney followed the script, but Shultz said the credit belongs to the president for giving priority to Canada-U.S. relations (baloney, of course). Mulroney put a lot of emphasis on acid rain. "If the U.S. can put a man on the moon," he exclaimed, "surely it should be able to solve the acid rain problem." This line of argument, if you can call it that, did not cut much ice with Shultz. Once again, Mulroney spoke powerfully against FIRA and the NEP, which must have been heavenly music to Shultz's ears, as it was to Baldridge's. The NEP had no greater critic than Shultz. (He told MacEachen

[1] Chief of Staff to Brian Mulroney when he was leader of the Opposition 1983–1984 and Senior Adviser and Chief of Staff when Mulroney was prime minister 1984–1988.

some time ago that the NEP was "outrageous.") Mulroney was very "political" and not at all complimentary about Trudeau.

After calling on Don Regan in Treasury (same message), Mulroney returned to the hotel to have lunch alone (as I was told), and at 1:20 he left for the White House, to be met by a no doubt blissful Ty Cobb,[1] the Canada man in the NSC and a certified Trudeau-hater. I, of course, was not with him, this being a "political" meeting. I linked up with Mulroney after the encounter to accompany him during his call on the editorial board of the *Washington Post*, which he got through without mishap.

Mulroney was in ebullient form all through our embassy dinner this evening. He seemed to have an unlimited supply of confidence, which he radiated without interruption. The guests were scattered on the patio and the grass on an exquisite, cool Washington night. Round tables for eight or ten were placed around the pool, and the garden was lit by lanterns that Glen Bullard had spread everywhere. As the guests walked into the garden, Mulroney and I stood astride the garden door, and as I introduced them, Mulroney greeted each and every one with a few specially chosen words. He seemed to recognize virtually all of the guests, although they were, of course, strangers to him. He was carrying a mental file on everyone. It's as if he needed no introductions at all (another Lyndon Johnson in the making?). He and Mila made a brilliant impression. They dazzled the crowd.

Ben Bradlee sat at Mila's table, as per her request, and this hard-boiled egg was as soft as mush the whole evening. Ben kept asking me, with boyish enthusiasm, "Did she really ask for me at her table?" In fact, it was the only seating request she made, and it was a good one.

I kicked off my comments by saying that "there are moments in the history of a country when it senses that it is on the move and that a new chapter in its history is being written. The new leader of the Conservative Party will be playing a major role in the shaping of the destiny of Canadians for many years to come."

I then mentioned the presence of Supreme Court Justice Powell, the three cabinet secretaries present (Weinberger, French Smith, and Casey), the legislators (Dick Cheney,[2] Pat Schroeder, and Mulroney's friend Don

[1] Director of Soviet, Western European, and Canadian Affairs at the National Security Council 1983–1988; Special Assistant to President Ronald Reagan for National Security Affairs 1988–1989.

[2] (b. 1941) White House Chief of Staff 1975–1977; Republican Representative from Wyoming 1979–1989; Secretary of Defense 1989–1993; Vice-President of the United States 2001 to present.

Riegle), the White House folk (Deaver, Darman, McFarlane, and various other officials), Chairman of the Joint Chiefs of Staff General John Vessey, Paul Nitze, Mike Armacost[1] (Eagleburger's replacement), Ken Adelman, Rick Burt, and so on. Then the Strausses, Linowitzes, Schlesingers, Bob MacNamara, and the media crowd (and what a crowd): Ben Bradlee and Sally Quinn, Kay Graham, Meg Greenfield, Joe Alsop, the Brinkleys, Elizabeth Drew, Jim Lehrer, Rick Smith of the *New York Times*, Scotty and Sally Reston, and more. Then the chairman of the Republican National Committee, Frank Fahrenkopf,[2] and the chairman of the Democratic National Committee, Charles Manatt.[3]

A night to be remembered. There was a sense of expectancy, a sense of excitement, a sense of being present at a special moment.

If there is one thing that bothers me a bit about the dinner, it's the question of who should have replied to my toast to Mulroney. Justice Powell was the senior person and appropriately responded, but I really wanted Weinberger to say something as well. He was the senior person from the administration, and I considered it a faux pas not to ask him to say a few words. But Mulroney's people fretted endlessly and finally requested me not to invite Weinberger to speak. They were concerned about his image as a hardliner and what the press would make of it. Very nervous people in Mulroney's entourage. I hope this doesn't signal problems for the future.

June 22, 1984 A near miss at the embassy last night. The CP reporter in Washington, Carl Mollins, filed a wire report saying there were no members of the francophone press at the dinner for Mulroney last night. (I had invited only Joe Schlesinger[4] and Craig Oliver[5] from the TV networks and no press reporters and had so informed the Mulroney people some time ago.) During the dinner, members of the Canadian press, French- and English-speaking, hung around outside the gates of the Residence. So Mollins produced a tale about the francophone press being excluded.

---

[1] Undersecretary of State for Political Affairs 1984–1989; U.S. Ambassador to Japan 1989–1993.

[2] (b. 1939) Chairman of the Republican National Committee 1983–1989.

[3] (b. 1936) Chairman of the Democratic National Committee 1981–1985.

[4] (b. 1928) Canadian television journalist and author. He joined the CBC in 1966 and was a host on *CBC Newsworld* and a producer of documentaries for CBC *Prime Time News*.

[5] Joined CTV in 1972 and served as its Ottawa Bureau Manager and Correspondent 1975–1981; Washington Bureau Chief 1981–1988.

Snubbed. I learned this morning that Bill Fox, having heard about the report, went around to Mollins's house in the early morning with a view to beating up his former journalist colleague. It seems that he was restrained by Mollins's wife. Too bad. Of course, the whole Canadian media contingent was buzzing about this. Fearing press coverage, Fox then tendered his resignation to Mulroney, who, I was informed, declined to accept it.

Later in the morning, Mulroney, concerned about adverse comments from francophone reporters, insisted that Fox and I meet with them, explain what I had done, and calm them down. We did so. I took full responsibility for the guest list (which was only fair and appropriate, since Sondra and I selected just about every name).

The whole affair was exceedingly stupid. The Canadian press made asses of themselves – not difficult for them – and we made asses of ourselves by meeting with them and explaining our action. Mulroney should have ignored the whole thing. Trudeau would have held up his finger.

Sondra told me that yesterday's tea with Barbara Bush was memorable. While Barbara was entertaining Mila and Sinc Stevens's wife at her home, George Bush came into the room in shorts. Barbara asked the ladies, "Doesn't he look cute?" Both Bushes then praised Sondra's letters in the *Washington Post*. Sondra was amused that Mrs. Stevens heard this, given the nasty attacks by her husband against Sondra because of the columns.

We accompanied the Mulroneys to B.W.I. in the evening when they caught a commercial flight. This may turn out to be the last commercial flight they take in the United States. Then again, it might not. Both Mulroney and his wife looked sublimely happy, and they had every right to be. Mila brought me a present, an apron with recipes on it for crabcakes. She heard yesterday – from me – how much I dislike this Washington culinary passion.

June 23, 1984 The Mulroney visit was by any standard a remarkable success. But the Canadian press reports only one thing: l'affaire francophone. Today's *La Presse* headline: "*Une gaffe protocolaire ternit la visite de Mulroney à Washington.*"

June 24, 1984 Deaver to me: "Allan, as I was driving to your house the night of the dinner, I said to Carolyn, 'The poor Gotliebs, no one will be there tonight because of the president's fish fry for Congress.' I couldn't believe the crowd when I saw it. What an accomplishment." "I drew every chit I had," I told him, "including yours."

June 25, 1984 Notwithstanding the successful Mulroney visit and the beauty of his message in the eyes of the Americans, the White House is far from indifferent to the fortunes of our new prime minister, John Turner. Deaver told me that the White House, including himself, is enthusiastic about the idea of holding a great ceremony to commemorate the twenty-fifth anniversary of the opening of the St. Lawrence Seaway. In attendance would be the president, the Queen, and our prime minister. The actual dates of the anniversary are June 27 and 28, but the United States was suggesting July 17 for the ceremony. The Queen is scheduled to visit the States on her yacht, the *Britannia*, at about that time.

Such a meeting would be fabulous publicity and a dream political opportunity for John Turner to display himself as prime minister. His connections with the royal family would seem to make this all the more obvious.

In response to my very specific question, Deaver didn't think it would make a difference if we were in the middle of a federal election. Less surprisingly, he also saw no problem with the event occurring in the middle of the Democratic Convention. (He seemed to like it all the more so on that account.) I had a great thought. Why shouldn't they sign the Skagit River Treaty at the same time? The symbolism would be sensational, I said. The St. Lawrence Seaway on the East Coast, the Skagit River Treaty on the West Coast. One represents a huge co-operative project, the other fifty years of negotiation and a historic conclusion. Deaver responded enthusiastically.

June 26, 1984 Washington shows continuing interest in the idea of a St. Lawrence Seaway Summit on July 17. Sittman in the White House (Deaver's deputy) tells me the president is free and the Queen is free. What about Turner? If an election is called in Canada, this also is not a problem. Burt says the president saw Mulroney in a pre-election situation, so seeing Turner will balance it. The United States is thinking of Massena, New York, as the site, with a nearby Canadian counterpart. I can get no guidance from officialdom in Ottawa, aside from some mild expression of interest.

June 30, 1984 Since the Mulroneys left, it's been one dinner party after another for us. Fred Iklé's yesterday, our party for George Shultz the day before, preceded by a dinner at Elizabeth Drew's in honour of her filthy-rich uncle Tisch (she is very proud), before that a "Basque Bar" and "Shepherders' Fare" dinner given by Senator Paul Laxalt and Nancy Reynolds at her house in Arlington, and also an evening cruise up the Potomac on Marshall

Coyne's yacht, this time in honour of former Federal Chief Arthur Burns.[1] (We go up the river, we go down the river, and we die of the heat.)

Our Shultz party the day before yesterday was far from typical fare for us or Washington. Shultz once mentioned to Sondra that Fred Astaire and Ginger Rogers were his favourite Hollywood stars, and so she asked him whether he would like to see a screening of some of their golden oldies. He was enthusiastic, so we worked out a date and assembled about a dozen other guests with whom we knew he'd be comfortable. We imported the films from New York, Glen Bullard worked the old, very noisy embassy projector, and after dinner we watched the *Gay Divorcée* on a large screen set up in the living room, sitting in comfortable sofas and deep easy chairs. The noise of our ancient machine re-created the atmosphere of an old-time movie house. It was a gay evening.

July 5, 1984 Sondra and I are in Ottawa to honour a long-standing commitment to speak at a public-relations convention at the new Westin Hotel. In the evening we went to dinner at David and Diana Kirkwood's in their home in Rockcliffe. The Gwyns and McSweens were there at our request. When we arrived, we were surprised to see John and Geils Turner relaxing on the porch, John looking patrician and proconsular, holding forth. We kibitzed in a group for about three-quarters of an hour about nothing in particular. Turner was clearly at ease and in good form, sporting his English brown suede shoes.

When he got up to leave to go to another function, I bolted after him to have a private word. I told him that I needed to talk to him about the White House initiative to commemorate the twenty-fifth anniversary of the opening of the St. Lawrence Seaway. (I learned recently – to my amazement – that the prime minister was not going to accept the president's invitation.)

I managed to explain to Turner that the Americans were inviting him whether or not there was an election in Canada – Mike Deaver had made that clear. "It will be a high-profile event, having both an East Coast and West Coast PR dimension." I also told him that I thought the negative reply I will be asked to convey to the Americans would fail to reflect sufficient appreciation for the invitation. I stuck my neck out: "The White House is trying to be helpful to you."

---

[1] (1904–1987) Chairman of the U.S. Council of Economic Advisers 1953–1956; Chairman of the Federal Reserve 1970–1978; U.S. Ambassador to West Germany 1981–1985.

Turner's response was: "Allan, you've got it wrong. They didn't invite me whether or not there's an election in Canada. Wait and see what happens this week. Then you'll get your explanation. And you can pass it on to the Americans."

I replied that I was not wrong. Moreover, the Americans were very sensitive to a political gesture not recognized, nor picked up, nor even personally acknowledged. Turner said quickly, "I've got your message, I've got your message, I understand completely," and he drove off into the night.

Since I was assured that he was properly and fully briefed, I asked myself, is he being influenced by all those anti-American Liberals telling him to keep his distance from Reagan?

July 6, 1984 We flew to Winnipeg for my father-in-law's funeral. He lived for years with dreaded Alzheimer's, and his passing is a deliverance for his family. Over and under in twenty-four hours. The Jewish way.

July 10, 1984 It's Rachel's twenty-second birthday. Sondra is away, and I take her to the Jockey Club for dinner. We are seated in the chic front room. We eat and are about to leave when I see a woman waving vigorously at me from a nearby table (front room, of course) of about ten. I approach her table in time to recognize Ethel Kennedy, dining with her children and friends, including Art Buchwald. I introduce Rachel, who has no idea who they are, and Ethel asks me what we are doing this summer. She says, "You must come and see us at Hyannis Port." I mutter something to pass it off, and she says, "We'll expect you." I say, "Wouldn't you be astonished if we showed up at the gates." A couple of the guests start to laugh, and Ethel is silent for a moment. "Well," she says, "I'm serious. I'll call Sondra." I'll advise Sondra not to sit by the telephone.

July 14, 1984 We arrived at the St. Francis in San Francisco to attend the Democratic Convention as diplomatic observers. A boondoggle and I love it. The weather is glorious, the vast old hotel is like a crowded football stadium, and the streets are animated, awaiting the big gay-lesbian parade. Sondra intends to write a piece on the convention for the *Washington Post* (she'll have to walk an even thinner line than usual). Everyone is talking about getting invited to the right places and receptions. It's amazing how one gets caught up with all this social stuff. Bob and Helen Strauss asked us for dinner, and we went to an Italian restaurant along with his pal John

MacMillian and a few members of his family. My stock with Strauss went up when a beautiful woman approached our table and embraced me. It was Margot Kidder. She was sitting with Tom Hayden[1] and Patrick Caddell,[2] Gary Hart's pollster and adviser. All chic, very radically chic.

July 20, 1984 We left San Francisco, rather disillusioned. The convention was a media event. There was no drama, only lots of cheering and hyping of Ferraro.[3] A female vice-presidential candidate. The millennium. Mayor Feinstein[4] gave a reception in honour of the crowd of diplomatic observers idling their time (like me). As a way of life, it's amusing enough. But one feels irrelevant. One is.

July 23, 1984 I wish people at home would notice a couple of things about the Democrats. For some observers at least, particularly the Canadians, the notes of protectionism, patriotism, and isolationism to be discerned in the music Mondale was making need to be heard and not forgotten.

Another thing became very apparent in San Francisco: unity at the convention was achieved at a certain price – the continued projection of the image of the Democrats as a party of minorities and special interests. Even though Canadians don't like Reagan and the Republicans, the Democrats spell trouble for Canada.

July 24, 1984 At least one Canadian journalist gets it right. Diane Francis,[5] in the *Toronto Star*, took the line right from my mouth. "The most important function a lobbyist serves isn't to sell the Canadian point of view, but mainly to tap experience as to how to strategize," and strategies consist "of finding American allies." We diplomats are not salesman. We hire them. Nor are we advocates. We hire them too.

---

[1] (b. 1939) Social and political activist and politician, known for his involvement in the anti-war and civil rights movements of the 1960s. Served in the California State Assembly 1982–1992 and the State Senate 1992–2000.

[2] (b. 1950) American public opinion pollster who worked for Democratic presidential candidate George S. McGovern.

[3] Geraldine Anne Ferraro (b. 1935) Democratic Representative from New York 1979–1985; unsuccessful Democratic vice-presidential candidate in 1984.

[4] Mayor of San Francisco 1978–1988.

[5] (b. 1946) Canadian journalist and author, now Editor-at-Large for the *National Post*.

July 26, 1984 We start our visit with Jennifer and Laughlin Phillips at their large and pleasant house – or houses – in Martha's Vineyard. We occupy our own house on their grounds, very modern, comfortable, quiet, clean, air-conditioned, pleasing to the eye. This is the usual two-functions-a-day Martha's Vineyard visit. The theory is we are all relaxing, but in fact, we're working like hell. We started the ritual with lunch at the Phillipses' neighbour's, Milton Gordon, a rich collector of celebrities who talked only about the recent funeral of the Vineyard icon Lillian Hellman.[1] One man at lunch said nothing about Hellman. It was playwright Arthur Miller,[2] who, with his photographer wife, is a house guest of the celebrity collector. Later in the day we returned to Milton Gordon's to swim in his saltwater pool. While we were lounging by the pool, Miller began to speak very freely about Hellman – about how unkind and unencouraging she was to younger playwrights, how phony her efforts to protect human rights after the war, and how unimpressive and overrated she was as a playwright. Arthur Miller has a beautiful daughter, Rebecca, who was there along with her boyfriend, one of Felix Rohatyn's circle. The Vineyard is cozy. At the end of the day we remain totally unrelaxed, tensely poised, waiting for the next social challenge.

July 28, 1984 Lunch at Kay Graham's Vineyard estate, very informal – "no ties." Our second lunch at Kay's since we got here. Last time it was small, *en famille*, with the great cultural middleman Lord Weidenfeld,[3] who just changed coasts. At today's lunch there was, of course, Lord Weidenfeld, as well as the aged Walter Cronkite[4] and his mother (whom I took for his wife), Bob MacNamara, Meg Greenfield, Felix Rohatyn and wife (all regulars), and some dozen others, including Kay's son and rock-star friend Carly Simon.[5] Then some of us rushed off to swim at a private (otiose word)

---

[1] (1905–1984) American playwright.

[2] (1915–2000) American playwright, essayist, and author. Miller's best-known works were *The Crucible*, *All My Sons*, and *Death of a Salesman*.

[3] (b. 1919) British co-founder (1945) of the publishing firm Weidenfeld & Nicolson. Political Adviser and Chef de Cabinet in Israel to Dr. Chaim Weizmann 1949–1950.

[4] (b. 1916) Celebrated news anchorman on *CBS Evening News* for several decades.

[5] (b. 1945) American musician and winner of two Grammy Awards (1971 and 1990), an Academy Award (1988), and a Golden Globe Award (1989).

beach to which Ronnie Dworkin[1] has access. We've been at the same lunch or dinner as the Dworkins twice on this visit, and this doesn't add to my state of détente. The Oxford professor is the perfect model of East Coast radical-chic, well-dressed, well-to-do, leather jacketed, all-knowing. He explained that he must leave for Nova Scotia, where a congress of Marxist economists is discussing his philosophical contributions.

August 2, 1984 In New York, I'm informed of an urgent message just received in the embassy: Turner would like to meet Reagan on one of five or six dates in the next month. I'm blown away. Almost a month ago I urged Turner to reconsider the U.S. proposal for a summit. Now, of course, the Seaway anniversary date is far behind us, and the Canadian election is very close at hand. The Liberals must be panicking. I called Deaver to transmit the message, but he's out of town. So I got hold of Darman and suggested that the Skagit River Treaty ratification would offer a nice West Coast venue and environmental dimension to a get-to-know-you summit. Darman's reaction was unenthusiastic. "It's really pretty late," he said. "Reagan is campaigning, and the dates you're now suggesting are very close to your election date." (It's September 4.) "In these circumstances," he added, "a meeting could look like the U.S. is interfering in your elections." But it was "a nice idea and Reagan would like to meet Turner." The prime minister missed his opportunity.

August 4, 1984 At the Krafts' again, at their "cottage" in East Hampton. The weather is humid, misty, and hot. Polly has been talking the whole day about the party she is giving in our honour tonight. She mentioned it the first time a couple of months ago and told us she was having their close friends the Rohatyns, the Peter Jenningses, and Ben Bradlee and Sally Quinn. Today she was in tremendous spirits. We got, in addition to her pals, Beatle Paul McCartney and wife Linda (they insisted on sitting beside each other tonight and, it seems, on all occasions, no doubt for mutual protection), singer Paul Simon and friend, Nora Ephron and friend, the Eastmans,[2] and others. The affair was lightened by the odd memorable remark, such as

---

[1] (b. 1931) Professor of Jurisprudence at Oxford 1969–1998, jointly appointed at New York University Law School and Department of Philosophy.

[2] Lee Eastman (1910–1991) Show business attorney and father of Linda McCartney. He was Paul McCartney's business manager during the breakup of the Beatles.

Mrs. Eastman's: "Paul Simon's new wig is marvellous, don't you think?" And my conversation with the Beatle. "Come and see me sometime at my headquarters," he says to me. "Oh, sure," says I, "I'll just turn up, and they won't let me in." "Ha ha, that's right, they won't let you in. But seriously, come and see me sometime at 1 Soho Square." The invitation is then repeated, punctuated by more "ha has." The Beatle then told me that he and his wife had spent the day buying live lobsters in the fish stores and turning them loose back into the sea. The rich are very different from you and me.

August 5, 1984 We went to Ben Bradlee's restored East Hampton mansion for drinks. The Watergate-rich Ben is very house-proud – he showed us photographs before and after restoration. Formerly a derelict house filled with cats, it was inhabited by close but very eccentric relatives of Jackie Kennedy.[1] At Nora Ephron's, where we had dinner, we saw Ben Bradlee and Sally Quinn again and many trendy people, the Richard Cohens from Washington, Ken Auletta[2] (a rising financial journalist), various scriptwriters, producer-types. The Gotliebs are moving in two ideological universes, and we are more or less comfortable in both.

August 6, 1984 Mondale radio address: "I'd like to talk about how we can be the number one economy in the world – and how Americans can win. We must make the rules of international trade fair and make sure that everyone plays by the rules. Today foreign countries are not only getting a head start, their advantages are getting larger. We must have a president who stands up for American workers." Bravo, Fritz. Further proof – though none is needed – that the mood in the country is mean.

August 7, 1984 I sent an urgent message to de Montigny Marchand in Ottawa today concerning the plan to launch a made-in-Canada initiative called ASAT to ban anti-ballistic missile tests in the atmosphere: "Proposed course of action could have negative impact on Canada-U.S. relationship with potential fallout in other areas of bilateral relations at a critical time. I wish to inform you this embassy has reservations about your proposed course of action."

---

[1] The women and the house were the subject of a documentary film called *Grey Gardens*.

[2] (b. 1942) Journalist, columnist, and author. Wrote for the *Village Voice* and *New York Magazine*; weekly political columnist for the *New York Daily News* 1977–1983.

The truth is this relic of the Trudeau peace initiative is being pushed by External officials. And the truth is Chrétien would be most unlikely to stop it, even if he understood it, which I'm sure he doesn't. And the truth is the Liberals are desperate, and the bureaucrats are pushing their own agenda.

August 7, 1984 I hate fighting Ottawa over all their bad ideas. It's much more enjoyable to be constructive. I'm preparing an exciting proposal regarding the embassy project. The basic premise: the new chancery interior should be a showcase for Canadian design and manufacturing. Canadian producers should supply a substantial amount of furnishings of their own design and do so gratuitously. We should create a blue-ribbon committee of distinguished Canadians to oversee the project.

August 9, 1984 Telegram received from Ottawa. "Decision has been made to proceed with tabling of Canadian ASAT proposal in Geneva next week." The fools.

August 10, 1984 Met with Mssrs. Joe Rauh[1] and Jim Turner, counsel to David Orlikow's wife and other victims of the CIA brainwashing *Manchurian Candidate* experiments some decades ago. Tragic cases and we – and I personally – have tried to be helpful to the victims in urging Ottawa to get as much information into their hands as possible with regard to CIA operations, actual or alleged, on our soil.

Joe Rauh is a big man and a strange one. Courtly as possible when one talks to him directly, he puts a pen in his hand and it becomes a poison arrow. He hears the initials CIA and he turns from Dr. Jekyll to Mr. Hyde. I told him today I could not provide him with anything beyond what was in MacEachen's letter to David Orlikow last June 29 and what was said in our House of Commons at that time – that there is at least one member currently serving in External Affairs who recalls the oral transmission of regrets to Canadian officials by a U.S. embassy official. He is stunned at our refusal to give him more information.

Ottawa and the embassy are not on the same wavelength. In response to our urging authority for the release of more documents, the department has taken the view that they cannot (will not?) go beyond the Access to

[1] (1911–1992) Public interest lawyer. General Counsel to the Leadership Conference on Civil Rights and Chief Legal Counsel to the United Auto Workers.

Information Act and endanger intelligence relationships. Meanwhile, media interest is growing in the United States, thanks, I'm sure, to Rauh's PR skills. We recently advised Ottawa that the producers of *60 Minutes* are preparing for a show on this affair next autumn, that they are aware of the Canadian government's own involvement, and that they intimate that the manner in which the involvement will be portrayed will depend, at least in part, on the Canadian government's willingness to come to grips with this openly. A threat in the best (or worst) media tradition. Maybe this will concentrate their minds in Ottawa.

My differences with headquarters continue on a wide front. I composed one of the toughest, bluntest messages that I've sent during my time in Washington, on anti-satellite tests. I urged them not to table their proposal in Geneva (part of the dregs of the Trudeau initiative) to ban tests in high altitudes. I'm running out of time. I hope I get a response by tomorrow.

In the evening, some pleasant moments. We gave a barbecue dinner in honour of Larry Eagleburger for about thirty people. It was one of those hot, steamy, rainy Washington days, so we agonized over whether to eat indoors or out. Finally, we compromised and ate in but fetched our own food from the barbecue on the patio garden. It was a mixed crowd, the Carluccis, the Poindexters,[1] and other old colleagues, and we added the Brinkleys and Baldridges. Mac Baldridge drew me aside and told me he would go to the wall to get Canada an exemption on steel. He alluded darkly to people in Bill Brock's shop going for a global quota. This, he said, would eventually affect Canada. He would go to the president; he would fight to the end. Nothing bad will happen to Canada, he assured me. Baldridge is that rarity in the political world of Washington: a man of principle and a friend of Canada.

August 11, 1984 Nothing back from Ottawa in response to my latest blast on Canada's proposal to ban anti-satellite testing. I told them that, in the midst of two elections, their timing was awful, the U.S. administration would resent our initiative, it would cut across U.S.-U.S.S.R. arms discussions at this very moment, and would multilaterize what is a proper subject for superpower, not third party, negotiation. As for Shultz, our chief supporter in U.S. councils, he is "in particular given to emotional reactions to

---

[1] John Poindexter (b. 1936) Deputy National Security Advisor 1983–1985; National Security Advisor 1985–1986.

moves by allies against U.S. interests that he judges as feckless, inconstant, or self-serving." "We cannot," I added, "rule out the possibility that political capital and leverage at our disposal here will be reduced, at a time when we are in the middle of what may become our biggest bilateral dispute in years over possible administration action to restrict steel imports to the U.S.A." In other words, watch out for linkage.

On the trendy issue of a nuclear freeze, our new foreign minister, Jean Chrétien, is now toying with supporting it.

To summarize the Canadian style: exempt us on the one hand, screw you on the other.

August 12, 1984 I've been worrying about something Darman said to me the other day when I called on him to discuss steel. "Don't repeat any of my predictions by telegram. A lot of people read a lot of things around here. I don't know about your staff, but don't report by telegram." Are we being penetrated? I had convinced myself that my earlier fears were unjustified. But how can I explain Darman's remarks if our traffic is not being read? And last month, during a tête-à-tête lunch with Rick Burt, he aroused the same fears. We were talking about disarmament discussions involving himself and the Soviets. "Don't put this in a telegram," he said. I responded, "Really, are you reading our stuff?" "Oh," he said, "so much passes my desk that I can't remember. But don't put it in a telegram."

August 14, 1984 We're at something called the Pocono Weight Loss Center in the Pocono Hills, in the heart of Dutch country, Pennsylvania. It was recommended to Sondra by Ursula Meese, who said it was very cheap. Yes, it is. Crummy and cheap. Right on the highway, full of fat people living on three-day water diets, then sneaking out for *schnitz* and *knepp*.

I got interrupted from my main activity here – competing with other old geezers for one of the few aluminum deck chairs that have been arranged to watch cars zooming down the highway in front of this dump – by a telephone call from the embassy in Washington. The Americans have reacted with anger and disbelief at our intention (notified by Kinsman today) to table our anti-satellite proposal in Geneva. It will, they tell us, play directly into Soviet hands and diminish U.S. leverage. They are asking us to hold off.

August 15, 1984 Victory – of a sort. Ottawa has put its satellite initiative on hold for the time being. We inform the State Department.

What an issue to be grappling with in the middle of an election. Apparently, Chrétien remains for it. Surprisingly, so does Ed Lumley, arguing at a meeting of ministers that there is no connection between our position on satellites and the United States' on steel. Mind-boggling naïveté. The department has put the whole thing to John Turner in a memorandum in which my views are said to be contained. We'll learn something about the mettle of our new prime minister.

August 16, 1984 Flash. Instructions from Ottawa to Geneva: do not brief Western caucus today, do not brief Ambassador Issraylean (the Russian ambassador) today, do not deliver outer-space speech tomorrow in the conference, do not issue release, do not leave Canadian name on conference speakers' list tomorrow, do not, etc. Hurray.

The good news is, once again, accompanied by the bad. I received a communication from National Security Assistant Bill Clark: a nasty handwritten note accusing me of interfering in U.S. internal affairs because of the speech I gave on acid rain at the Northeastern Governors and Premiers Conference in Newport in June. He scribbled on the printed sheet of a State Department internal news report of my address: "Allan, I find the conduct of Mr. Caccia and yourself remarkable. No other country that I am aware of sends its representatives into a domestic foray [*sic* – it was an international conference] with this type of rhetoric on what is a basically domestic issue [*sic*] of the host country . . . Bill Clark."

Yipes. And Eagleburger told me at our party last week that Clark could well become chief of staff in the next Reagan administration, replacing Baker.

August 17, 1984 I saw the departmental memorandum on Canada's anti-satellite proposal. It's a five-page analysis intended for Chrétien's approval and for submission to Turner. The only reference to the embassy's views is a brief sentence stating, "Our Embassy in Washington recommends that the tabling of the proposal be postponed to allow Ministers to reassess the situation in the light of its possible implications for Canada-U.S. relations."

The memorandum is dismissive of the implications and reckless as to its consequences. "We are," it acknowledges, "in the middle of what may become our biggest bilateral dispute in years over possible Administration action to restrict steel imports to the U.S." – the action to be taken around August 24.

"While it is doubtful," the department opines, "that ASAT would have immediate derogatory impact on the principal players, namely Brock and Baldridge, a vindictive intervention by the White House cannot be ruled out, because the same political advisers around Reagan who are preoccupied with the formulation of the private and public diplomacy on arms control vis-à-vis Congress and the Soviets will also make the final decision on steel."

Bravo, they got the point. But the department, after this great insight, proceeds to recommend that we table the proposal in Geneva – full speed ahead and damn the consequences. Oh, professional diplomacy, where art thou?

August 18, 1984 I fear the only way I can stop this political aberration regarding anti-satellite testing is by going directly to the prime minister. I'm not clear in my mind whether I'll do this. I will wait to see how this little universe unfolds in the next few days.

August 20, 1984 Bad news. Chrétien has signed the department's memorandum to Turner recommending Canada proceed to table its anti-satellite tests proposal in Geneva. The wording of the document, which utterly fails to set out my views, stands as it is. I am finding it difficult to get information, because the bastards in External are closing me out. I'm in a frightful funk. The senior people at headquarters have been pushing this proposal, as have the disarmament gang. We Canadians must prove we're not Americans. Who cares about the consequences for our bilateral relations?

Chrétien is true to form in signing the document. He has already come out in favour of a nuclear freeze. I doubt he really understands the implications. I am sure the issue was explained to him orally, as he doesn't read documents.

August 22, 1984 I sent to Ottawa a hefty think piece on institutional arrangements in Canada-U.S. relations, which I prepared with Kinsman. Thirty pages long, it makes the case for developing new ways to deal with the increased fragmentation in the U.S. system, increased nationalism and patriotism, and the strengthened unilateral streak in American politics. It proposes creating new bilateral institutions and strengthening existing ones. This represents a major departure from our historic approach and a change in my own attitude towards managing the relationship.

I set out a number of ideas for new institutional arrangements: annual bilateral summits, joint meetings of periodic cabinet secretaries, new trade arrangements, joint economic commissions, targeted parliamentary missions, mixed legislative groups, standing legislative committees on Canada-U.S. relations, provincial involvement at the state level, more active public diplomacy, including the use of television and marketing tools, and the creation by the private sector of a Canadian economic institute in the United States or a joint foundation to help disseminate better understanding. My hope is that our new government – whether Liberal or Conservative – will pick up some of these suggestions.

August 27, 1984 Back from Dallas. It's hard for me to believe that the Republican and Democratic Conventions were held in the same country – the former so high-spirited, so emotional, so unified, so confident, so millenarian, the latter so fragmented in its voice, so defensive, so pessimistic, so backward-looking.

"Isn't it great to have a president who doesn't apologize for America?" Jack Kemp[1] put this question to the huge throng of delegates, and all you could hear for several minutes was a mighty roar of approval. His question was a dominant and recurring theme at an event that was more a celebration of Ronald Reagan and the Republican rebirth than a political convention to choose the presidential candidate. The atmosphere reflected the beginning of the post-Reagan era, permeated by intellectual populists of the right, single-issue conservatives, and earnest-looking, handsome young men and women, all responding to the invocation of God and religion, with the Olympic torch verbally carried through the chanting halls by the great Olympian himself.

The enthusiasm was heightened to a feverish pitch by the overpowering scent of success and the perceived weakness of Mondale, who was constantly portrayed as a liberal, vacillating, apologetic, pessimistic loser.

I report to Ottawa that the Republican Party was transforming "from the homburg to the stetson, from the business party to the party of small-town populist." Estimates are that of the 2,200 delegates at Dallas, close to 40 per cent may have been evangelicals or born-again Christians. "The convention had the atmosphere of a religious movement rather than a political rally."

"The Republican move away from middle-of-the-road policies to the shining city of private initiative, opportunity, conservatism, patriotism and

[1] (b. 1935) Republican Representative from New York 1971–1989; Secretary of Housing and Urban Development 1989–1993; Republican candidate for the vice-presidency in the 1996 presidential election.

privilege is probably irreversible." Question: "Does this indeed represent the world of the new majority in the U.S.?" Answer: "The Republican Party believes so and they may well be right."

Sondra and I had remarkable access to the Reaganites. We were invited to their private parties and boxes, always the only ambassadorial couple. I talked steel to Ed Meese, electricity to Don Hodel, and politics with everyone. Meese told me I could call on him at the White House after we got back to talk about steel quotas. This could be a breakthrough. Hodel told me that his recent spate of remarks on electricity exports were aimed at the U.S. industry, not Canada, against whom he had no complaints. He thinks the U.S. industry should import less or bargain with us harder. Thanks a lot.

August 28, 1984 I delivered Turner's letter to the president on steel to Dick Darman in the White House. He hinted that, as regards steel, Canada has little to worry about. My own interpretation is that, in all probability, the White House doesn't want to start off a relationship with either Turner or Mulroney with a huge dust-up on so critical a matter as our trade in steel.

We talked about the Republican Convention. Darman, as usual, gave me great insights. The insecurities of key political groups such as blue-collar workers, redneck voters, and lower-middle-class whites (numbering, perhaps, some 50 million) caused them to rally strongly behind the flag, religion, patriotism, and economic panaceas, but these symbols lacked content, and their content remained to be defined by the party as the decade unfolded. But in the meantime, the president's strength was that he symbolized these values without having to define them.

I got back to my office and resumed bureaucratic warfare. I received a message from Marcel Massé complaining about my not using proper channels in transmitting my Canada-U.S. think piece to Ottawa. It seems the bureau (Derek Burney) was all worked up because I sent copies of my paper directly to the deputy minister of finance and the clerk of the Privy Council. Shocking. The undersecretary seems never to have heard of the basic principle that the ambassador abroad is responsible to all ministers, not just the foreign minister. Not a word in his communication as to substance. That says it all. He demeans himself in sending this letter.

August 29, 1984 Another unpleasant communication, this time from my friend de Montigny Marchand. He too complains about my direct contacts with the prime minister and his office.

The functionaries in External are wildly upset about my directly advising Turner. So here I am in Washington, charged with representing my country, dealing directly with its government and legislators, promoting its interests in every aspect of our national life, and I'm not supposed to have direct contact with the prime minister or ministers or senior officials of other departments. The ban probably extends to my own minister. An utterly preposterous proposition, a power play, a flexing of bureaucratic muscles. The Canadian ambassador is supposed to be a puppet of the Ottawa bureaucracy. Never on my watch. But I have to face up to it. Officials in Ottawa want to cut me down to size.

August 30, 1984 After fuming all of yesterday, I dispatched a highly restricted message to Ottawa, addressed only to de Montigny and Marcel Massé, recording my direct dealings with Turner and his people during the past week:

1) John Swift[1] of the Prime Minister's Office called me in Dallas on August 23 on Turner's behalf. The Prime Minister wanted my personal assessment of the likely U.S. reaction to tabling our proposal in Geneva. I gave him the same negative assessment I gave Chrétien and the Department. I informed the Bureau of my conversation the next day.
2) The next day the Prime Minister himself called me in Dallas. He asked me for my personal assessment of the likely U.S. reaction to our initiative. He asked me to be frank. I told Turner that the U.S. might be even more upset about timing and process than the proposal. I urged him not to approve the plan.
3) The following day, Swift called me again on behalf of the Prime Minister. I went over the matter yet another time. Then I passed the gist of my conversation to the Department.

I was careful in my message to Marchand and Massé not to disclose what Turner said to me. I avoided any breach of the prime minister's confidence, while letting External know what I was doing and maintaining the principle that I had the right to do it.

---

[1] Principal Secretary in the Prime Minister's Office 1984 and Chief of Staff in the Office of the Leader of the Opposition 1984–1986.

But it doesn't matter. The anti-satellite proposal has gone down in flames. I killed their initiative, and it won't come back. It is better to win than to lose.

August 31, 1984 In Winnipeg with Sandra Day O'Connor, who is addressing the annual meeting of the Canadian Bar Association. I've worked like a dog to get her to come up to my native city, drawing on (wasting?) my reserves of personal goodwill. She interrupted her vacation back home in the Southwest to get here – a long, difficult trip. A very remarkable woman, a superior speech, and a poor turnout to hear her. She could be chief justice one day.

I got some good news. I learned that the department, in its memorandum to cabinet on Canada-U.S. relations, has embraced most of the proposals and ideas I put forward in the think piece I sent to External, Finance, and the PCO. The officials in the department must have gotten over their sense of outrage at my "bypassing" channels.

September 4, 1984 Election night in Canada. Interest in Canadian affairs in official Washington (and thus the media) is growing by leaps and bounds. We had a big crowd, perhaps as many as four hundred, including Rick Burt and a pack of journalists and lobbyists such as Bob Gray and Richard Allen,[1] to watch the CBC satellite signal. A Mulroney victory was a foregone conclusion before voting even began. But the full sweep of the victory stunned the watchers and me. While there was none of the excitement one gets with a race, there was a sense of this being a historic moment, an earthquake in the political life of Canada.

I'm happy to see a great Conservative victory, not least because the Liberals had become so cynical in their long reign. But on the personal side, I feel quite differently. I deeply regret seeing my old friend John Turner humiliated. It's true he ran a poor campaign, but the Canadian media treated him disgracefully, particularly in playing up the "bum-patting" non-episode on television. I would have loved to work at my post in Washington with him at the helm, but it is not to be.

I feel miraculously lucky that Mulroney came to Washington for a visit last June. I've asked myself before and especially tonight what kind of shape

---

[1] (b. 1936) National Security Advisor 1981–1982.

I would be in, what future I would have here, if he had never made that visit. He gave me a wonderful chance to do the professional, non-partisan thing, and I think I did it.

Trudeau should have handed over power to Turner a couple of years ago. What did he do in the meantime? He marched to the beat of clapping hands on the stage of the Third World. His feet left the ground as he pursued a mythological role as champion of equity for the masses of the Third World and as saviour of mankind from nuclear war. This behaviour and his late-blooming nationalist policies were his worst hours. Let's hope Mulroney doesn't get the missionary bug too.

September 5, 1984 In Toronto to speak at the *Financial Post*'s annual seminar at the Westin Hotel. When I arrived at the hotel to give my talk to the executives and businessmen, I noticed huge piles of this week's edition of the *Post*, with my photograph spread out on page 1 and an article saying I am going to be removed from office by the new government. I feel sick to my stomach.

September 6, 1984 Ed Meese received me in the White House to talk about steel. I was accompanied by John Allan, head of Stelco. I was surprised that Meese would see us, but he did. Allan was, I think, even more surprised. Most top White House folk won't receive ambassadors, let alone with foreign businessmen in tow. But when I asked Meese at the Republican Convention if I could call on him, I put him on the spot. He said he would see me and was true to his word. Allan made a good presentation on why Canada should be exempt from the pending steel quotas.

September 7, 1984 The dying days of John Turner's administration. Sent a personal message to him before he relinquished office. I wrote that when I saw Ed Meese recently, he told me that the president felt he had established a rapport with Prime Minister Turner, and a good relationship had developed. "The president," he said, "appreciated that Turner visited the reception at the U.S. ambassador's residence on July 4." According to Meese, the president also read his letter on steel. These comments echoed what I had heard at the NSC. The president, they said, appreciated Turner's courageous decisions in the areas of arms control and disarmament, and his willingness "to resist embracing certain positions in spite of public pressure." (The reference here was, no doubt, to the nuclear freeze.)

I'm struck by how much the Americans appreciate a gesture. Turner's attendance at the U.S. National Day reception was an agile move, and I'm even more impressed that the president should have been briefed on this point. Shultz must be at least partly responsible for the special goodwill towards Turner in the White House. The relationship is, alas, not to be.

September 8, 1984 Another voyage with rich hotelier Marshall Coyne, up and down, back and forth on the Potomac, and another opportunity to get drunk on the deck while having a privileged view of the Washington sewage works in one hundred degrees of heat. But who knows whom I might meet, buttonhole, lobby, persuade, cajole, or convert to a Canadian cause? Five hours before the mast in the service of my country.

September 11, 1984 I met with Jack Matlock and Ty Cobb at the White House this afternoon, and they told me something important: Reagan might want to meet Prime Minister Mulroney (still designate) before the U.S. presidential elections in November. They are thinking of an informal "get-to-know-you" meeting. In response to my query, the White House was very firm in stating that such an informal visit would not be a substitute for a major state visit next year.

The department's reaction will be predictable: Mulroney should not rush down to Washington. Appearances will be bad.

September 13, 1984 The Canadian press manages to squeeze a whole article out of the question "Will Gotlieb Stay in Washington?" They provide no answer, but I have one: "Just watch me."

September 15, 1984 Do I really want a second term? One of the great deprivations of this office is lack of downtime. Particularly wearying is having to entertain visiting groups on a Sunday night. This weekend it's a reception at the Residence for a hundred or more from the U.S. Junior Chamber of Commerce. The pattern is that big groups hit town on a Sunday so they can get their program underway early Monday morning. They usually approach the embassy nine or twelve months in advance, asking for a briefing or reception on the Sunday evening so their participants can get a good start. I look at my calendar, the days seem so far off, there is nothing booked, and I see some advantage to Canada in talking to or hosting the group. Also, I have to calculate whether if I don't receive the visiting Canadians or don't feed them, they'll run to the minister or PMO to complain. Then, in accordance with Earth's diurnal rhythm, the terrible date rolls out and we have to shatter the brief tranquility of a Sunday with hosting a draining event for a group of strangers. Even worse, we have to be polite and charming.

September 16, 1984 Brian Mulroney and his new cabinet get sworn in tomorrow. But the Mulroney era has already begun. Expectations are running very high in Washington that he will change Trudeau's policies on energy, investment, and the Cold War.

I fear the Americans will be disappointed. His team is inexperienced. His party is full of red conservatives (Clark, MacDonald). The bureaucrats will have great influence. In the Department of External Affairs, anti-Americanism runs deep and will not, cannot change. Part of the very grammar of the language they speak. Call it *deformation professionelle.* Will Mulroney be strong enough to resist the department's advice?

THE MULRONEY YEARS

September 17, 1984

On the first day in the life of the new government, it is fitting that I should deal with acid rain, a file where the Trudeau government made such little progress.

I had a long chat with Bill Ruckelshaus about our impasse, placing it in the context of Mulroney's great victory and Ronald Reagan's anticipated second term. As usual, he was frank and straight. As usual, the news was bad. He said that R.R. personally holds the key to any progress on acid rain; there is absolutely no chance of a program or commitment unless the president himself can be convinced of its necessity. R.R. was not well disposed towards environmentalists as a result of his experiences as governor of California (shocking news). Reagan is naturally skeptical and reacts enthusiastically to negative arguments. But – and this is important – his genuine scientific curiosity makes it possible for him to be reached. (This was real news to me.)

All strategies, Ruckelshaus said, should be directed to seeking to influence the president directly. The need to make progress for Canada's sake (the "Canadian connection") was our strongest card.

Ruckelshaus's message is clear: Mulroney has to make acid rain a top personal priority and get through to Reagan in a personal way, one-on-one. And in talking to the president, he needs to back it up with credible, convincing scientific facts.

September 18, 1984 The night of our big black-tie dinner-dance for ninety-six people on the occasion of the engagement of Rick Burt and Gahl Hodges, Nancy Reagan's social secretary. It's a good match – the brilliant, abrasive, acutely perceptive, high-spirited Rick and the warm, soft, discreet Gahl. It was a beautiful, warm night in Washington, one of those perfect evenings, like the one when we entertained the Mulroneys on the terrace in June. We were back on the terrace tonight. At Gahl's request, we kept it "informal" – open seating. There was a superb turnout: George Shultz and his predecessor, Al Haig, the Deavers, Susan Baker, Meg Greenfield, the Evanses, the Brzezinskis, the Perles, the Phillipses, Senator John Tower, the Wicks, the Helmses, George Stevens,[1] and on and on.

I stopped Deaver before he went into the garden and, standing on the great marble maple leaf embedded in the hall floor, recounted to him my tale of frustration in dealing with the NSC. They are proposing that at next week's lunch between Reagan and Mulroney at the White House, the U.S. and Canadian astronauts working on the recent *Challenger* flight be invited to attend. I explained to Deaver that putting the astronauts together with the president and prime minister at what is billed to be a small, private "get-to-know-you" lunch is ridiculous. It would undermine the very purpose of the visit and make Mulroney look stupid – flying all the way down to Washington to eat lunch with the astronauts. I told him the NSC response: "Piss off, please, Mr. Ambassador."

"Why don't they just have a three-minute photo op?" Deaver asked. I foamed. "That's exactly what I suggested, but your colleagues wouldn't hear of it." Deaver paused and then replied, "Okay, it's done. The astronauts won't be at the lunch." I was stunned. "That's it, then?" I asked. "I don't need to talk to the NSC again?" "No, you don't," Deaver responded. "It's been taken care of."

Mike Deaver at his best. The sanest man in the White House. But this no-nonsense style makes him enemies. He will make a few more after what he promised tonight. And so will I.

September 20, 1984 Canada wins on steel. After a midday cabinet meeting that divided the group between the protectionists and free-traders, the president decided to negotiate "voluntary" restraint agreements with a large number of steel-exporting countries. Canada is not one of them. Our industry is rejoicing. Administration officials are saying that our offer to monitor and consult with the United States (I made the offer to Baldridge at his invitation) was a wise tactical move. The idea behind it is that Canada won't exploit the opportunities created by the reduction of imports from other countries.

---

[1] (b. 1932) American producer, writer, and director of television and film. Co-founder/director of the Kennedy Center Honors in 1978.

September 21, 1984 I dropped in for a few minutes at a party for Al Haig's new book, *Caveat*. The Brinkleys then had a dinner in honour of Ronnie and Jo Carole Lauder,[1] a small affair with all of us sitting around one table in the Brinkley greenhouse–dining room. We dined exceptionally well for the simple reason that Susan is the best cook in Washington. Ron Lauder has a position in the Defense Department working for Perle. As Sondra says, he occupies the "donor's slot." An agreeable man, he's worth a billion dollars and likes art.

September 23, 1984 Washington anticipates the arrival of Brian Mulroney. There is great excitement among officialdom. I believe that the steel exemption may have been granted as a gesture to our new prime minister. While tensions are now lower, I'm still very concerned about the protectionist pressures in Congress.

September 24, 1984 The new prime minister arrives in Washington on his first visit in that capacity at 10:30 tonight. I came home in the early evening, exhausted from an empty day of running around from place to place during the World Bank/IMF meetings, attending a long luncheon given by Bill Mulholland in Georgetown and more than a few diplomatic receptions. I collapsed in front of the television, and both Sondra and I became very engrossed in an old movie, *The Thomas Crown Affair*. We got so caught up in it that we shaved our departure from the Residence a little too thinly. Jacques Helie had to drive like a bat out of hell to get us to Andrews on time. Due to unexpected traffic, he even had to put on his siren a few times, which he enjoyed quite a bit. We drove up onto the tarmac at Andrews just after the PM's plane had touched down. I think they waited a minute before the door of the craft was opened. We arrived just at that very moment.

As we rushed up, Lucky Roosevelt, the chief of protocol, was waving frantically at us and shouting, "Hurry, hurry, we didn't know what happened to you. You almost missed the arrival." Indeed we did – we had only seconds to spare. What a grand start that would have made in my relations with the new government.

I drove into town with Mulroney and went up to his suite in the Madison. The prime minister was in buoyant spirits, to say the least. Before we got into

---

[1] (b. 1944) Son of Estée Lauder, cosmetics manufacturer. Deputy Assistant Secretary of Defense for European and NATO Policy 1983–1985; Appointed U.S. Ambassador to Austria in 1985.

any substance, he talked about Joe Clark, who had been against his coming to Washington so soon after the election. He argued against Mulroney's accepting the president's invitation on grounds of unseemliness. Mulroney talked scornfully of this advice. Didn't he just win an election with a platform of "refurbishing" relations with the United States?

I have had several reports of the department advising against this visit. Sometimes I fear that the only bedrock policy of the officials of External Affairs is to differentiate ourselves from the Americans. Differentiation is all right if it results from legitimate policies but is not acceptable if it is the justification for developing our own. If we build our foreign policy on the basis of differentiation, we're going to have a foreign policy that is sometimes perverse and sometimes immoral. Worse than that, we will have a foreign policy that runs counter to Canadian national interests. To borrow a phrase from the Russians when they attack the West in the UN, these people in External behave like they are "divorced from reality."

Bravo to Mulroney for following his own instincts. A leader in command.

September 25, 1984 I briefed the PM in his suite at the Madison this morning, and at 11 a.m. we left for the White House in a motorcade, with two big Canadian flags flying on either side of the hood. At noon we proceeded to the president's private dining room, where an intimate lunch with four on each side took place (Mulroney, Doucet, Burney, and myself being the Canadian team). We sat below the beautiful John Singer Sargent[1] that dominates the room. As for the conversation, well, it was jokes, jokes, and more jokes. Reagan was amiability itself. The purpose of the function was for them to get acquainted. They certainly got to know each other's current repertoire of jokes. By 1:10 p.m. we were out of the White House and onto the helipad. Handshakes from the farewell committee, headed by acting Secretary of State Ken Dam (this time he didn't forget) and on to Andrews for a 3 p.m. departure.

These two Irishmen are going to get along like blazes. There is a special rapport between them, the rapport of two men who are not intellectuals but who are optimistic and confident, good communicators and fine storytellers, and very pro-business. The contrast with the Trudeau visit is stunning. There was no tension whatsoever. As events go, this was a non-event. Yet it was profoundly significant. They established a very special relationship.

[1] (1856–1925) Italian-born (to American parents) painter known for his portraits.

The prime minister was scrummed at the airport by the Canadian press. He was asked about my future. He announced that he informed the president that he has asked me to stay on in my post. He did.

September 26, 1984 I wake up at dawn, anxious to start the day. I feel like calling a press conference, inviting all my critics and detractors and those who have scored me high on the Tory hit list. I will announce, "Ladies and gentlemen, my second term begins today."

September 27, 1984 Lunch with Jeffrey Simpson[1] at the Metropolitan Club. We discussed the new government off the record. Simpson went on at length about how he expects Joe Clark to be a great pillar of strength and stability in cabinet, the rock on whom Mulroney will rely. It was as if the Joe Clark he was talking about was not the same Joe Clark who was prime minister from 1979 to 1980.

September 29, 1984 A bouquet of roses in today's *Globe and Mail*: "Gotliebs Shine in Washington's Swirl," by William Johnson.[2] I've never had such praise. It's intoxicating. "Those whom the gods wish to destroy they first raise high." The gods are smiling now. But tomorrow?

October 4, 1984 Bob Coates[3] is in Washington. A Mulroney buddy and now (amazingly) minister of national defence. Last night I held a working dinner for him and his entourage at the Residence. I gave them an overview of U.S. defence attitudes and the current political situation in Washington. The United States, I said, is facing a deficit of $297 billion. It is stressing burden-sharing by the allies and wants Canada to spend more on defence.

After my briefing we didn't do a stitch of work. Lots of jokes, drinks, stories, gossip, and clowning but no substance. It was an unbelievable atmosphere. It seemed like a bunch of guys on their way to a Rotarian convention.

---

[1] (b. 1949) The *Globe and Mail*'s national-affairs columnist since 1984, and winner of all three of Canada's leading literary prizes.

[2] (b. 1931) Canadian author and journalist writing for the *Globe and Mail*, the Montreal *Gazette*, and other newspapers.

[3] (b. 1928) PC Member of Parliament for Cumberland, Nova Scotia. Defence minister in the first cabinet of Brian Mulroney, he resigned in 1985 as a result of a minor scandal.

The phrase "down-to-earth" was invented for Coates. But he has, I fear, a feeble grasp of issues (I may be being charitable here). It was a pointless evening, unless "establishing a good atmosphere" among Canadian officials constitutes a useful end in itself.

At the Pentagon today, Coates was given full honours and then a lunch hosted by Weinberger. Cap and his team fell all over him, especially Ronnie Lauder. Coates loves Americans, that much was obvious, but alas, his performance was about the poorest I've seen on the part of any Canadian minister. His approach is to preside over his group of military and civilian officials but do virtually no talking himself, leaving all the interventions to the officials he urges to speak. He told me afterwards he likes to "give all the boys a chance to participate and do their thing."

The instincts are fine – pro-West, pro-defence, pro–United States. But where is the mind? He could end up agreeing to almost anything the Americans want.

October 5, 1984 I am disgusted to read about myself in the *New York Times* today. Tongue-in-cheek, the author of a snide little piece, a *Times* columnist, notes receipt of a publicity blurb from Gray and Company announcing that Mordecai Reichler [*sic*] was coming to town to give a talk at the Canadian embassy and that "Ambassador and Mrs. Gottleib [*sic*] will be lunching as guests of Art Buchwald on October 2 at Maison Blanche at 1 p.m. It occurs to me," the author wrote, "that we have a veritable round table of assorted wits and you might find a bit of humour in it."

This can make me a laughingstock in two countries. Never in my life would I authorize anyone to write a publicity blurb about me. Never in a million years would I use a PR agent to announce and hype my activities. I contacted Gossage in a state of apoplexy. He professed innocence. "Gray and Co. acted on their own," he asserted. "They were trying to get us ink." "Who told them to get us ink?" I asked. "Not sure," he replied.

I don't believe him for a moment. It's bullshit. He's covering for someone on his staff.

October 11, 1984 L'affaire Gotlieb-Gray continues. The *New York Times* carries an article entitled "Foreign Image-Making: It's a Job for the Experts," featuring me (alas) and Gray and Company. The article quotes their letter of September 19 announcing my lunches with Richler and

Buchwald. Humiliating. The Canadian papers have picked up this tale and are repeating it gleefully. My face is very red.

Last February we hired Robert Keith Gray to produce a program of satellite feeds and radio messages for local U.S. stations, promoting Canadian views about acid rain and the like. Gossage and his people worked on this campaign with Gray and Co. But somehow Gray and Co., or someone working for them (surely not Joan Braden?), decided to do a little promotion on behalf of the Gotliebs. Gossage continues to swear he was not *au courant*.

The whole affair is one huge embarrassment.

October 14, 1984 I leave for Toronto today to attend briefings for Joe Clark prior to his meeting with Shultz. I'm feeling very cross as I will miss a dinner party we are having tonight for Robertson Davies,[1] who just gave a lecture at the Library of Congress to a huge, enthusiastic audience of about six hundred. Sondra will host. I had looked forward to this dinner more than any other we've given. I admire Davies' writings immensely, and I've never met him.

October 15, 1984 The Clark-Shultz meetings in Toronto begin, starting with multilateral issues. This was their first "quarterly." To his credit, Shultz has been determined to carry on with the periodic meetings that began with MacEachen. I believe we do have a new "institution" in Canada-U.S. relations, to add to the very few existing ones. It may prove to be the most important tool for managing our relations with the United States.

Clark telephoned me before I left Washington yesterday to ask for my evaluation of Shultz and to discuss his attitude towards Canada. I sent him a record of conversation about Canada that Richard Gwyn had with Shultz when Richard was staying with us in April of last year. On that occasion Shultz came to dinner, and Gwyn got a chance to talk off the record with him about Canada.

Shultz told him, "Your problem is that you've politicized your economy. Politics now dominate all of your economic decisions. You've politicized your oil industry, and you've politicized provincial governments. Multiple interventions in the economy by the federal government have caused all the special interest groups and provinces to pursue political solutions to

[1] (1913–1995) Canadian novelist, playwright, critic, journalist, and professor.

economic problems." Shultz's view essentially came to this: "We favour the marketplace; you favour government intervention." An exaggeration, of course. But not so wide off the mark.

I briefed Clark on the various "irritants" in the Canada-U.S. relationship. He was affable but not all that comfortable with me, less so than when he was prime minister. Is this due to the fact that Mulroney confirmed or extended me, not him? It doesn't look like Mulroney even consulted him on my reappointment.

October 16, 1984 This morning, just before the meetings on bilateral issues were about to start, Derek Burney mentioned to me en passant that Clark planned to raise with Shultz the construction of the new Canadian embassy in Washington. He intended to tell him the Conservative government was not going to proceed with the new embassy – whether indefinitely or not for some time was unclear. I was furious that Burney had not informed me of this a day or two ago. Then I could have told Clark how incredibly stupid a decision that would be.

I dashed out to look for Clark before the meeting began and found him in the john as he was standing in front of a urinal. Undeterred, I started to urge him not to raise the embassy with Shultz until we could talk. Clark, in a jocular manner, replied, "You're too late. I've already spoken to Shultz." "What did he say?" I asked him. "He wasn't happy" was the reply.

I fumed about this the whole day. I can't get over the fact that Clark didn't have the courtesy to ask for my opinion. Same old precipitous Joe. At the airport to say goodbye to the American team, Shultz asked me to step aside. When we were alone, he said, "Allan, Joe mentioned to me his plan to defer the new Canadian embassy. I told him that if this was being done for economic reasons, it was a very short-sighted decision and a bad mistake."

October 19, 1984 Days of no consequence in Washington. Yesterday we attended a reception for author Dick Francis[1] at the Ritz-Carlton and a dinner at the new Regent Hotel given by Ginny Milner of the kitchen cabinet crowd. The Wicks and French Smiths were among the couple of dozen Reaganite guests. I like the Reagan crowd, but I'm tired of their patriotic hype. A typical example of this endless flag-waving was a ceremony in the National Archives to mark the opening of a special archive on Grenada,

---

[1] (b. 1920) British mystery writer and jockey.

an event co-hosted by no less than George Shultz. I gave it a pass. The Americans are still crowing about their great "victory." I can understand the U.S. desire not to have another Cuba. I can even understand their decision to get rid of a nasty group of radicals causing trouble in their backyard. But any country that needs the invasion of Grenada to restore its national pride is not too well.

October 23, 1984 I wrote a personal note to the department in Ottawa to complain that the briefing note that was sent to the minister on the planned deferral of the new embassy failed utterly to present my views about the political damage that would flow from any such decision. I was "totally taken aback" to learn that the new building was at risk. What is it about Joe Clark and embassies?

October 24, 1984 I talked to the prime minister about the disastrous decision to delay building the new embassy. I explained the damage to our image and our relationship. He understood immediately. He told me I can quietly and privately inform all the key players in Washington that the embassy will move forward. It will be built. There will be no undue delays. They have his word. Bravo, Mulroney.

October 27, 1984 Back in Washington after close to a week on the road doing God's work for Canada. Maybe if I were here as long as Count Willie Wachtmeister (Sondra's Baron Spitte), I might sense that I don't really have to do the travelling salesman bit. But the truth is I'm glad to go on the road. For one thing, it's a great opportunity to engage in public diplomacy. Secondly, so many U.S. cities provide real surprises – their public monuments, their museums, their commercial buildings, these are among the unacknowledged glories of the United States. Thirdly, if you don't get out of the Beltway, you lose perspective and you get cabin fever.

October 29, 1984 Sondra is giving a fashion show at the Residence for Lola Lehman, a promotional activity that enthuses her more than doing likewise for light-armoured vehicles from Ontario.

October 30, 1984 Burney wrote me a personal letter to assure me that my objections to delaying the embassy project were passed on to the minister. He had no idea that Clark intended to mention the chancery project to Shultz. Apparently, his superiors in External did, but they never told him. My points, he said, had been "registered prominently with Mr. Clark's senior political adviser." He confirmed that the idea had come from Clark, not the department.

The department confirmed another point that I already knew – per Fred Doucet – that the chancery project cuts are not simply a financial exercise. There is a strong political element in them. Last week the minister asked what the cost implication would be of releasing Erickson and choosing another architect. The answer, in excess of $5 million, dampened any enthusiasm for the idea.

October 31, 1984 I sent another message to Ottawa regarding the new embassy, each word carefully crafted by me. Given Clark's personal role in this exercise of deferral and dismemberment, I resisted my desire to send a copy directly to Mulroney. But I forwarded a copy to Fred Doucet, who will undoubtedly show it to the prime minister.

Canada was, I wrote, accorded a unique position as the only embassy adjacent to the Mall now and probably forever. Its site almost at the base of Capitol Hill is seen as a reflection of the special Canada-U.S. relationship. Erickson's model was exceptional and deemed worthy of complementing the dazzling East Wing of the National Gallery, designed by I.M. Pei. If Canada were to postpone progress without a hard commitment to begin on a specific date, critics of our privileged position would join with federal, congressional, and local authorities to fault us for holding up development of this special location. We own the property in trust and have a strong legal and moral obligation to proceed. We could be asked to relinquish the site and be reassessed for back taxes if the delay were open-ended.

"Cancellation would be a mistake of historic proportions for Canada. The privilege of building our new embassy on this special site is not one just for Canadians now but for future generations of Canadians. It will be Canada's signature in Washington in an area where virtually every American in his or her lifetime will visit and see. To forego this is to forego more than just an opportunity. It is to forego the requirement we have to project ourselves as a self-confident nation, optimistic about our future, conscious of our special destiny as North Americans, sharing a unique relationship with the United States, and proud of our culture, our artists, and our achievements."

November 4, 1984 As the Trudeau sectoral free-trade initiative fades into oblivion, Canada is beginning to show signs that it cannot simply stand on the slippery status quo. Maybe all my speech-making on the fractured U.S. system, the forces of protectionism, the power of the special interests, and the impact of U.S. processes on our own regulatory regimen has not been a waste of time. In elitist Canada one knows when an issue is emerging as an item of national concern: it becomes the subject of a little essay on the bottom left-hand corner of the editorial page of the *Globe and Mail*. This week, Jeffrey Simpson describes the new talk on trade policy and identifies myself, Sylvia Ostry,[1] John Crosbie, and Sinclair Stevens as advocates of full free trade with the United States. We are heading into a major, troubled national debate on free trade with the United States.

November 5, 1984 One of the Washington hostesses we really haven't gotten to know well is Polly Fritchey. Probably the most intelligent of the handful of celebrated Washington hostesses (including Kay Graham, Susan Mary Alsop, Evangeline Bruce, and Pamela Harriman), she is rather snobbish and gives smaller parties than her competitors. Her guest lists are more exclusive, more old-liberal establishment. So tonight we were excited to attend a dinner at the Fritcheys' Georgetown home on P Street in honour of the South African politician Helen Sussman.[2] The conversation focused entirely on South Africa, an unusual occurrence, as social Washington rarely shows an interest in foreign politics unless it concerns the Soviet Union. But tonight's conversation was imbued with domestic politics. When discussing South Africa, they were in fact discussing U.S. policy towards South Africa. In turn, this meant they were discussing black issues, which meant they were discussing the U.S. domestic agenda.

November 6, 1984 U.S. election night, at long last. We declined a slew of Republican, Democratic, and other bashes to stay at home and watch the results lying on sofas in our comfortable upstairs library. The big

---

[1] (b. 1927) Canadian economist and public servant. Head of the Department of Economics and Statistics of the Organisation for Economic Co-operation and Development in Paris 1979–1983; Deputy Minister of International Trade 1984–1985.

[2] (b. 1917) South African anti-apartheid activist and politician. Elected to Parliament in 1953 as a member of the United Party and served for thirty-six years.

Reagan victory is very satisfying from the standpoint of our national interest, although Canadians have difficulty understanding this point. All the protectionist forces (the unions, the depressed areas, the sinking industries, the pampered industries) threw their lot in with the Democrats, and they ended up with Mondale as their spokesman. So I say, more power to the Republicans.

On a broader plane, tonight has profound meaning for America and the world. To have a two-term presidency – such a rare phenomenon – means an end to the discontinuity that has so damaged U.S. interests. And it means experience, predictability, and greater prospects for coherence in U.S. foreign policy.

November 8, 1984 Joe Clark is about to announce a one-year deferral of the construction of the Washington chancery. I have been instructed to tell the State Department, on Clark's behalf, that this deferral and the decision to close our New Orleans consulate does not "reflect any diminution of the government's declared interest in refurbishing relations with the United States." Rather, it reflects the seriousness with which the Canadian government "is determined to deal with the deficit problem." What bilge.

A companion telegram of instruction says that in dealing with the press, I should "avoid saying anything which would tend to minimize the impact of the decision." More bilge.

November 9, 1984 Called on Paul Volcker in the afternoon to brief him on the new government's economic objectives (reduce the deficit, reduce government intervention in the marketplace, promote investment, competition, innovation, and make major changes to the NEP and FIRA), discuss our economic situation (Canadian unemployment running at 11.8 per cent versus the American 7.4 per cent), and get an insight into how he sees prospects for the U.S. economy, budgetary deficits, and interest rates.

In the evening we took Volcker and Dick Darman (with his kid) to see the Washington Capitals play the Edmonton Oilers at the Capital Center. I presented Darman and his kid to Gretzky. More hockey diplomacy.

November 10, 1984 On the current speculation about appointing an arms control czar, Adelman tells me he is the originator of the idea. He thinks a super-negotiator, especially Paul Nitze, could help overcome the rampant conflict within the administration. The problem is there is no consensus on what the U.S. objectives should be in disarmament negotiations with the Soviets. Shultz is completely opposed to creating an arms negotiation czar. Turf, no doubt. All this is mixed up with jockeying for power in the next Reagan administration. Darman tells me he thinks the idea of a czar is a good one and sees it as all the more important if super-hawk Jeane Kirkpatrick were to replace Bud McFarlane as national security adviser.

On the Republican agenda, Darman was most communicative. The White House strategy will be to go all out on the deficit in 1985. "We will," he said, "do all possible to maintain Reagan's popularity ratings as high as possible as far into 1985 as we can." After that the prospects for political success will be greatly reduced. So the ensuing years (1985–1988) will be foreign-policy years; the agenda will be overwhelmingly dominated by international issues.

November 13, 1984 Pierre Trudeau is in town to receive the annual Albert Einstein Peace Prize. Trudeau's speech at the luncheon where he was awarded the prize was critical of Reagan and the United States and was interspersed with predictable thunderbolts thrown at "nuclear accountants." It was appropriate for the liberal, anti-Reagan audience.

I offered Trudeau a dinner in his honour at the Residence, though I know full well that some of Mulroney's advisers would take a dismal view of this. Our dinner tonight for some fifty people turned out to be one big pain in the ass, the biggest social headache we've had since we got here. We have had to draw the invitation list from three disparate groups: the Chicago sponsors of the prize, Canadian Liberal colleagues of P.E.T., and the Washington political community (the last obviously being the most important). Things have gotten a little unpleasant the past few days, as I've had to tell some prominent former Liberal ministers who were inviting themselves (such as John Roberts) that we had no room to accommodate them.

In Trudeau's entourage there was Tom Axworthy, his peace initiative architect Maurice Archdeacon,[1] former aide Ted Johnson, Arthur Erickson, Stephanie Richmond (girlfriend), Teri McLuhan[2] (girlfriend), and a Hassan Yassin[3] and friend (connection to Trudeau mysterious and unknown).

---

[1] (b. 1934) First Executive Director of the Security Intelligence Review Committee 1985–1989.

[2] Film director and producer. Daughter of Canadian communications theorist/philosopher Marshall McLuhan.

[3] Head of the Saudi Information Office in Washington, D.C.

The Washington turnout was so-so – out of power, out of social favour. After much hard work we got acceptances, on the political front, from Democratic Senator Pat Leahy, Sol Linowitz, Bob Strauss, and former disarmament negotiators Gerard Smith and Paul Warnke. On the media side, Ben Bradlee and Scotty Reston came, and on the social side, Susan Mary Alsop, Donald Sutherland, and Margot Kidder (Trudeau girlfriend). The only acceptance from the administration was Ken Adelman. The refusal list was especially impressive: Jerry Brown, Mike Deaver, President Ford, John Glenn,[1] Peter Jennings, George Kennan,[2] Henry Kissinger, several senators (Dick Lugar,[3] Lloyd Bentsen,[4] Pat Moynihan, Sam Nunn,[5] William Proxmire[6]), Paul Nitze, David Rockefeller,[7] George Shultz, and more. Many, of course, had other commitments. Still, this is a town that breaks commitments.

Everyone had been invited for 8, but at precisely 7 p.m. the doorbell rang, and to my horror there stood four Einstein guests from Chicago, decked out in their evening clothes. I explained, perhaps too sharply, that they were exactly an hour early. One of the ladies spoke up and said my invitation said 7 p.m. This irritated me, because Connie, who was standing beside me, had told me specifically she'd called their hotel this afternoon to confirm the 8 p.m. start. One of the Chicago ladies took great umbrage and shouted, "If I'm not welcome, I'm leaving." She stormed out onto the front steps and refused to come back in. Ignoring my entreaties to stay, I got my

---

[1] (b. 1921) Democratic Senator from Ohio 1974–1999. Third American to fly in space and first American to orbit the earth.

[2] (1904–2005) American adviser, diplomat, political scientist, and historian. Known as the "Father of Containment" and as a key figure in the Cold War. Ambassador to the Soviet Union 1952 and to Yugoslavia 1961–1963.

[3] (b. 1932) Mayor of Indianapolis 1968–1975; Republican Senator from Indiana 1977 to present; Chair of the Senate Committee on Foreign Relations 1985–1987 and 2003 to present.

[4] (1921–2006) Democratic Senator from Texas 1971–1993; Democratic Party vice-presidential nominee in 1988; Secretary of Treasury 1993–1994.

[5] (b. 1938) Democratic Senator from Georgia 1971–1997. Currently co-chairman and CEO of the Nuclear Threat Initiative.

[6] (1915–2005) Democratic Senator from Wisconsin 1957–1989; Chairman of the Senate Committee on Banking, Housing, and Urban Affairs 1975–1981 and 1987–1989.

[7] (b. 1915) American banker, and the son and grandson, respectively, of oil tycoons John D. Rockefeller Jr. and John D. Rockefeller. Became Chairman of Chase National Bank in 1969, which subsequently became the Chase Manhattan Bank.

chauffeur to take her back to her hotel. The other three, embarrassed, conferred and decided to stay. The lady's husband, a key organizer of the prize, was disturbed and asked me to call her at her hotel and urge her to return. Realizing what a messy situation I was in, I agreed – reluctantly. She declined again, but the others did stay on, so total disaster was averted.

No doubt I'll hear more about this from the lady or the Einstein group. You're not master of your own house if it's an embassy residence. After three years in Washington, I still haven't learned this lesson. Moral of the story: a diplomat should never lose his cool.

November 14, 1984 Dropped in to chat with a couple of Mulroney's new ministers in Ottawa. When I went to see Coates, I was amused to observe what a disorganized office he had – visitors walking in and out, people kibitzing, joking, and taking photographs. His executive assistant was acting like a master of ceremonies at one big, fun event. Everyone seemed to be having a hell of a good time. I meant to engage in a conversation on defence policy with Coates, but we ended up having an extended photo opportunity.

Also called on Pat Carney[1] to brief her on energy prior to the arrival here tomorrow of Don Hodel, his deputy Danny Boggs,[2] and ERA Administrator Ray Hanzlik.[3] They are coming in the wake of a pack of positive announcements about energy in the Throne Speech last week (changes in the Crown share, movement towards world oil prices, and export-licensing amendments favouring buyer-seller negotiated gas prices). I said to Carney that all these positive news items from Ottawa were being so well received in Washington that it should make her meetings with her counterparts a love-in. What a revolution. I am sure some Americans, including George Shultz and Mac Baldridge, never thought they'd live to see it.

November 16, 1984 The Pentagon, Treasury, Congress, Democrats, Republicans, and just about everyone who counts in Washington would

---

[1] (b. 1935) PC Member of Parliament for Vancouver Centre 1980–1988; Minister of Energy, Mines, and Resources 1984; Minister of International Trade 1986–1988. Appointed to the Canadian Senate in 1990, serving until present.

[2] (b. 1944) Special Assistant to the President 1981–1983; Deputy Secretary of Energy 1983–1986; Chief Judge of the Court of Appeals for the Sixth Circuit 2003.

[3] (b. 1938) Administrator of the Economic Regulatory Administration in the U.S. Department of Energy 1981–1985.

welcome a reinforcement of our NATO brigade. I informed Ottawa that bringing it up to full strength would be one of those measures that both assists Canada-U.S. relations and contributes to international stability. What Canada does here will be seen by some Reaganites as even more important than what we do on foreign investment. Defence plays to the very top of the U.S. political agenda, as Shultz made clear to Clark in Toronto earlier this month. The gesture would serve Canada's interests in Washington like none other.

We attended a dinner tonight at Katharine Graham's in honour of Lord Weidenfeld. We were packed in tight – the intellectuals, the politicians, the snobs, all paying obeisance to Lord George and Lady Katharine, Queen of Georgetown. In any event, the jolly, corpulent, everybody-knowing, world-class raconteur and peer of the realm is one of the best excuses for a brilliant gathering of Washington's beautiful people.

November 20, 1984 I invited Bob Gray and Joan Braden for breakfast at the Residence. Sitting in our comfortable sunroom, I gave them the bad news. The embassy would not be employing their services in future. This was an awful task for me, because I like them both. I think highly of Bob's competence and Joan's enthusiasm, and they have become personal friends, but their unsolicited publicity blurbs about me and my activities were unacceptable.

November 22, 1984 In Toronto to be guest of honour at the opening of the Whistler print show at the AGO, organized by curator Kathy Lochnan.[1] My mother was in town, so she accompanied me. Radiant even at eighty-five, she was the centre of attention, competing effectively with Mr. Whistler. She came wearing a heavy mink coat, which she steadfastly failed to let go of. It was very hot at the reception, so she couldn't wear it, but it was so heavy she couldn't carry it either. She refused to let anyone check it (maybe someone would steal it), and I couldn't hold it because I was speaking. Thankfully, the president of the AGO, Fred Eaton[2] (CEO of Eaton's) came to the rescue. He carried the coat on his arm for an hour and

---

[1] Senior Curator and R. Fraser Elliott Curator of Prints and Drawings at the Art Gallery of Ontario.

[2] (b. 1938) Canadian businessman and great-grandson of Eaton's department store founder Timothy Eaton. Chairman and CEO of the T. Eaton Company 1977–1988; High Commissioner to the United Kingdom and Northern Ireland 1991.

a half. My mother kept an eye on him the whole time. She was appreciative but wary.

November 25, 1984 There is lots of speculation in Canada about Mulroney's appointment of broadcaster Bruce Phillips[1] to replace Gossage. I feel badly about Gossage. He was so anxious to stay on that he managed to convince himself he had a chance. His hope sprang in part from the fact that he used his influence – successfully – to keep Lloyd Axworthy out of Washington the day of Mulroney's visit last June. But that didn't buy him more than a one-way bus ticket to Ottawa.

December 1, 1984 This evening Fitzhugh Green gave a small dinner at his home for his boss, Bill Ruckelshaus, and Maurice Strong. Ruckelshaus and Strong know each other well and seem to like each other, drawn together, I suppose, by environmental causes. Ruckelshaus is the type who would spend several hours looking at every tooth in a gift-horse's mouth. Maurice Strong resembles an Iranian magician, extravagant, excited, always seeing visions. Ruckelshaus is going to give up the ghost at the EPA. He can't get anywhere with the ideologues at the White House. It's not clear yet what he plans to do, but most of the evening was spent with the three of us listening to Strong's exposition of a plan (or dream) to access the deep waters of the giant aquifer underlying his Colorado lands and exploit them commercially. The wealth to be attained would exceed the value of all the oil of Saudi Arabia. The usually cautious Ruckelshaus seemed mesmerized.

December 9, 1984 Met Mulroney at the airport in New York this morning and drove into Manhattan with him in his limousine, briefing him on the American scene. It was an unusual experience to be with a Canadian politician who delights in this country, who likes the United States and is not afraid to say so. He doesn't have an inferiority complex vis-à-vis the Americans. Maybe it's because he's from Quebec, not Ontario.

I spent the rest of the day sulking in Washington. I was irritated with myself for being irritated by Mulroney and Ross Johnson.[2] Ross, Mulroney's

---

[1] Minister of Public Affairs at the Canadian Embassy in Washington; Director of Communications for Prime Minister Brian Mulroney; Privacy Commissioner of Canada 1991–2000.

[2] (b. 1931) Canadian businessman. Vice-President of merchandising for the T. Eaton Company, President of Standards Brands Ltd., then President and CEO of RJR Nabisco in the United States.

biggest pal, is giving a black-tie dinner for him and Mila in New York tonight, at the Pierre, where they are staying. I hear that at least fifty people are attending and some from Washington have been invited (like Bob Strauss, who is not going). I feel very hurt. I don't understand why Johnson didn't have the courtesy to invite the ambassador of Canada to the first dinner given in the United States for the new Canadian prime minister. You don't need the mind of Spinoza to figure out that such an omission could fuel speculation about the future prospects of the absent ambassador.

December 10, 1984 The prime minister got the royal treatment at the *New York Times*. The publisher, Punch Sulzberger, presided over a rather elaborate lunch, attended by all their top people: Sydney Gruson (former Canadian,), A.M. Rosenthal[1] (said to be born somewhere in Canada, improbable as that seems), Seymour Topping (Chester Ronning's[2] son-in-law, strangely enough), Max Frankel,[3] and more. Our hosts were not too sympathetic to Mulroney, although of course they were impeccably polite. They see him as a conservative, friendly to Reagan and hostile to Trudeau. They don't like these traits.

I was out of sympathy with them for this reason. They should recognize a friend when they see one. But I suspect they have a touch of the liberal disease: anyone who hates Americans can't be all bad.

Later in the day Mulroney had what I think might have been his finest hour. The New York business elite were out in full force to hear him speak to the Economic Club at the Hilton. Corporate heavyweights were hanging from the rafters. Mulroney's buddy and the club chairman, Ross Johnson, presided, and GE boss Jack Welch[4] acted as an interlocutor. There were fifty people at the head table alone and a thousand at dinner in black tie and long dresses. The guests were falling all over Mulroney throughout the evening. Ross introduced him and sang his praises, but even with all the enthusiasm and expectation, no one could have anticipated how dramatic and important

---

[1] (1922–2006) Canadian-born *New York Times* Executive Editor and columnist 1987–1999; *New York Daily News* columnist 1999–2004. Worked for the *Times* for fifty-six years, from 1943 to 1999.

[2] (1894–1984) Ambassador to Norway and Iceland 1954–1957; High Commissioner to India 1957–1964.

[3] (b. 1930) Worked for the *New York Times* for fifty years, rising from college correspondent to reporter, Washington bureau chief, editorial page editor, and ultimately Executive Editor 1986–1994.

[4] (b. 1935) CEO of General Electric 1981–2001.

his speech would be. His Canada-is-open-for-business theme marked a historic change of direction for our country.

If he follows through, it will lead to profound changes in Canadian domestic and foreign policy. I was proud to have had a strong hand in preparing his remarks. In my twenty-five years of writing speeches for others, I've rarely had that feeling.

I couldn't help imagining, as the audience applauded, the speech that Trudeau might have given. He probably would have justified our NEP and FIRA policies and given the audience a dose of his "nuclear accountants" and "moral equivalence" themes.

I was happy to be a Canadian tonight. I am especially pleased about being from a country that can switch allegiance between political leaders so diametrically different from each other, yet both authentically Canadian.

December 11, 1984 Fred Doucet and Ian Richardson of the PMO arrived in Washington this morning from New York, where they have been accompanying Mulroney. Doucet was "in attendance" at Ross Johnson's special dinner at the Pierre the other night. It seems that wherever Mulroney goes, Fred goes too. They are here to start the planning for Reagan's visit to Canada next year. Mulroney is proposing a summit in March in Quebec City. I took Doucet to meet Mike Deaver, John Poindexter, and Dick Darman at the White House. We emphasized that the visit should be a substantive one, focusing on trade, environment, and defence (which the United States will push anyway). On trade, we mentioned the possibility of initiating negotiations on a treaty providing for enhanced and more secure access to each other's market. On defence, there was a possibility of signing an agreement on the new design of the north warning system. We stressed very strongly that it would be difficult to have a successful summit without at least some sign of movement on acid rain.

The boys from the PMO were warmly received. Considering that he has virtually no background in international affairs, Doucet seems to have absorbed the substance of the main files very well. He was effective, speaking quietly, with dignity and a sense of authority. He gives the impression of great sincerity, although there is something a little cat-like about him. He brings to mind Groucho Marx's comment "In politics, sincerity is everything, so you better be able to fake it." But I am probably being unkind.

Doucet revealed that he talks to Mulroney every day about the most detailed and even the most trivial aspects of the upcoming summit and our relations generally. When I am on the phone with Doucet (as I am several times a week), he invariably says to me, "Please hold. The prime minister is ringing on my other line." When I've been in his Ottawa office, it's the same thing. If he's not Mulroney's alter ego, then he is his devoted, loyal, worshipping aide. I have discovered on several occasions that this slave does indeed know his master's mind. That makes him both reliable and effective, an authoritative interlocutor of the new prime minister.

December 12, 1984 In the evening we attended a dinner at Gilbert and Margot Hahn's. He is a local businessman, she a well-known hostess plugged into Democratic and social Washington. Margot was a friend of Anita Cadieux's. It's astonishing how few links there are with one's predecessors. On one or two occasions, we have met friends of the Towes, never any of the Warrens, the Ed Ritchies, Heeneys, or others. The one exception is Charles Ritchie, who knew the Alsops, Oatsie Charles, and other Georgetown figures. But thanks to Joe, he was marginalized by the Georgetown set.

I find this lack of memory more than a little sad, because I know it will happen to us. In their day the Cadieuxs were a popular couple, and he was an effective ambassador. They were here just a short while ago (they left only six years before we came). But in this transient town we are all swallowed by anonymity, except for those exceptional few who make a mark of some sort on one of Washington's two permanent communities, the Georgetown crowd or the media.

December 17, 1984 I got a lift with Mike Deaver to Quebec City in his private government aircraft. He is "advancing" the president's official visit to Quebec City next March. On the ride up, I got a chance to brief Deaver on Canada's gripes and grievances and how they should be addressed at the summit. What an opportunity to influence the guy who probably has more sway on Reagan – and more importantly, Nancy – than anyone else in the White House or the world. But hell, I like the guy, even if some complain (I think unjustly) that he is arrogant. On the return trip later today, I continued our morning's discussion. "No progress on acid rain," I said, "equals no success at the summit." "Well, what do you have in mind?" he asked.

An idea came on the spot. I thought of the Marcel Cadieux–Lloyd Cutler ambassadorial exercise on the East Coast fisheries dispute during the

Carter-Trudeau era and suggested something similar to him. "Why not have the president and prime minister appoint two special ambassadors at the summit to conduct an independent review of the acid rain problem and report back personally to the two leaders in due course?" I added that "this wouldn't require a reversal of the U.S. position [which I acknowledged would be impossible at this time] but could create some movement and might even lead to breaking the impasse."

Deaver reacted quickly and positively to the idea. He thought maybe Bill Ruckelshaus could be appointed by Reagan. Who knows? Maybe I've thought of something useful here. Perhaps the special-envoys idea could provide a breakthrough. I feel excited. These things can make one's day – or career.

December 25, 1984 A quiet Christmas. We asked Joe and Polly for lunch today and are going to Elizabeth Drew's for her usual Boxing Day buffet tomorrow.

We said goodbye to the Gossages a few days ago. I was sad to see him go. I wasn't consulted on his displacement, but I have the slight feeling that he thinks I could have intervened on his behalf. I could not have saved him.

December 27, 1984 In a big huff about Les Gelb's[1] article in the *New York Times* today, I called on Rick Burt. Gelb engaged in obviously well-informed speculation about U.S. willingness to negotiate constraints on strategic defence systems in Geneva. I told Burt that, once again, I found myself in the unwelcome position of reading about U.S. intentions in the *New York Times* without any information or insights being passed to Canada by State Department officials.

Burt opened up and spoke frankly, if not indiscreetly. Gelb's report was based on a background briefing from Bud McFarlane in the NSC, but, said Burt, "it was impossible to decipher what McFarlane actually said. Thatcher, he told me, put remarkable pressure on Reagan when she saw him last week. She made a strenuous argument for the U.S. to be prepared to negotiate SDI constraints, and no one dared answer her except McFarlane. Thatcher then proceeded to demolish him."

---

[1] (b. 1937) Columnist, deputy editorial page editor, national security correspondent, and diplomatic correspondent for the *New York Times* 1981–1993.

Burt gave Mrs. T. personal credit for the president agreeing there would be no actual deployment of an interim strategic defence system without negotiations – a shift of some importance in the president's position.

January 3, 1985 Back from the Sea View in Bal Harbour, where we were guests of Bob Strauss and Dwayne Andreas.[1] Short, well-built, of Mennonite stock, Andreas works his grain and soybean empire from a telephone in his cabana while stretched out on a deck chair, D.K. Ludwig–style. The hotel is a monument to the era of the 1940s and 1950s. The long lobby has a huge saturated green carpet in the worst taste of the period; it looks like Astroturf – it's absolutely perfect. As you enter the lobby you expect to see a seedy Latin combo getting ready to strike up a tune.

Andreas owns a number of condos in the hotel, and over the years political and other friends of his – David Brinkley, Bob Dole,[2] Howard Baker, Bob Strauss, Tip O'Neill – have also purchased condos. So the Sea View is now perhaps the premier "political" hotel in America. This group of ultimate insiders is surrounded by trippers and tourists from Quebec, Germany, France, and Latin America, but there's no mixing. The Washington group barely notices the tourists; they are just part of the unattractive decor.

At Andreas's New Year's party in his penthouse suite, the beluga malassol was of the highest quality and, equally important, limitless. Dwayne just got the caviar in Moscow, where he was a guest of rising star Mikhail Gorbachev, the Soviet minister of agriculture, of whom Dwayne talked endlessly.

The Brinkleys gave a dinner on New Year's Day, and the next afternoon we helicoptered to the Everglades with Howard Baker and the Brinkleys to see the wildlife and the vegetation. Flying over the whole of Everglades National Park, we saw the old Florida, pre-strip, pre-franchise, pre-tourist, the land of the swamps and tropics, the alligator and flamingo. Whenever we stopped, we got the most unusual treatment. Unusual for me, but not, I guess, for celebrities. Baker has just stepped down as majority leader of the Senate and is probably running for the presidency. Everybody knows and

---

[1] (b. 1918) For thirty years he was at the helm of Archer Daniels Midland, the largest processor of farm commodities in America.

[2] (b. 1923) Republican Senator from Kansas 1969–1996. A former majority leader in the Senate, he won the Republican nomination for vice-president in the 1976 election and for president in the 1996 election.

recognizes Baker, and as for David Brinkley, he is probably the most recognized broadcaster in America. From the sky, we observed the two Floridas – the one pristine, mysterious, the other ugly, contaminated.

January 5, 1985 Lunch with Mike and Carolyn Deaver at the Jockey Club. They remain, along with the French Smiths, our best friends in the administration. Mike is, of course, a celebrity in this town and a preferred guest of the maître d' because he often lunches here with Nancy Reagan. Mike gave me the splendid news that Shultz (with whom he is close) is onside with the idea of appointing special envoys to address the acid rain problem.

Deaver wants to get out of the White House and do public-relations work. He's made a lot of enemies in this town (sometimes unnecessarily), but because he is so politically savvy and has a unique connection to the Reagans, he should do well, extremely well, in private life. His departure will be a tremendous loss for me. Thanks largely to him, I've had almost unparalleled access to the White House.

January 14, 1985 We conclude a week's stay in Mustique. Sir Rodney Touche of Calgary, our host, is a relaxed fellow with an excellent sense of humour, so in spite of the fact that he is at the vortex of society here, our stay managed to be almost relaxing. The universal subjects of conversation – Mick Jagger's new house and Princess Margaret's doings. Nothing else seems to matter. Mustique is paradise, except there is no conversation, and it is therefore a very boring paradise.

My spirits perked up when we called on Lord Glenconner, original founder of the island colony, who gave Princess Margaret her house here. Glenconner has built his Xanadu on this island, one of the most beautiful houses I have ever seen. Constructed entirely out of white coral, it sits on an exquisite promontory open to the sea all around. The house was designed in a manner that gives you the sense of being outdoors and indoors at the very same time. In the large white coral rooms, magnificent eighteenth-century Indian glass chandeliers hang, providing an astonishing contrast with the walls and the surrounding sea. Glenconner furnished the rooms (Oliver Messel[1] helped) with Anglo-Indian ebony, ivory, and mother-of-pearl furniture. In the middle of the sparingly furnished grand salon there

[1] (1904–1978) English-born interior decorator and designer. He is known for his international work on sets and costumes for opera, ballet, and film.

sits a stunning early twentieth-century grand piano made entirely of mother-of-pearl.

On the grounds, Glenconner is reconstructing an Indian temple, several centuries old, which he arranged to have removed, stone by stone, from India and shipped by sea to Mustique, along with two Indian artisans to reassemble it on the property in front of the house on a promontory overlooking the ocean. En route, the plans for the reassemblage were lost, so the two Indians have now spent about a year living on the estate, trying to rebuild the temple (a tale out of the Moonstones). The incomplete temple is an exquisite jewel. It was a brilliant inspiration of Glenconner to transport it (demonstrating that he would never let money stand in the way of a pleasurable experience). It seems that India's export-of-antiquities laws are very lax. Or so he says.

The future of the island and its legal status as a self-governing paradise are said to be in doubt, as its character will be reviewed in a few years' time. When I asked Glenconner about this, he seemed almost indifferent to the future of his Xanadu. He conveyed the impression that if the time comes, and when that time comes, that the island loses its status, he'll set sail and quit the emerald isle, leaving behind his exquisite coral mansion, Indian bijou-temple, and all the Indian ebony, ivory, teak, the mother-of-pearl, and coloured Venetian glass, and go wherever the winds will take him, abandoning his beauties to the new Barbars, whoever they may be, and he will start anew on some other far shore, without regret and without looking back. Am I being too romantic? Not while I'm in Mustique.

January 15, 1985 Back from our Caribbean vacation and onto U.S. soil. Now I am Mr. Ambassador again. If I feel inflated, I remind myself of a recent encounter with Rick Burt's friend the German editorialist and writer Joseph Joffe.[1] On being introduced by Burt, Joffe asks, "Do I understand you are the ambassador of Canada?" "Yes," I reply. "You mean you are the Canadian ambassador to Washington?" "Yes, I am," I repeat, somewhat puffed up. "That," he says, "is a very important job. It's like being Polish ambassador to Moscow." I congratulated him on his brilliant analogy.

January 16, 1985 The PMO is fully cognizant of the grave political risks for Mulroney if there is no movement on acid rain. Here's a leader

[1] (b. 1944) German journalist. Columnist and editor for *Die Zeit* weekly newspaper.

elected to refurbish relations with the United States, who has already agreed to address two of the Americans' biggest economic grievances against Canada, who has invited the U.S. president to be the first official visitor to Canada on his watch, and who, facing much criticism, flew to Washington immediately after being elected in order to put the whole relationship on a new footing. If Mulroney comes up blank on acid rain, the Liberals, NDP, and their media friends (in Canada this means just about all the media) will massacre the new government. But I advised Ottawa today that "prospects for near-term change in the U.S. administration or for an early breakthrough in Congress are remote."

I have been consistently saying for a month that the appointment of high-level personal representatives would be the most promising step forward we could take, and we should do all in our power to get the president to sign on to the idea. But there are a number of people in Ottawa who are not keen on the idea. They think another study would be difficult to sell politically in Canada, and I believe they are right. But the problem is they don't have a better idea.

January 18, 1985 Deaver has been sick in bed, one week after announcing publicly he will quit the White House later this year and three days before the inauguration, which he's organizing. I don't know what's the matter with him. No one seems to know. Some say it's his kidneys. Tonight Mike gave a birthday party for his wife at the New Glorious Foods Café in Georgetown. He managed to make it, but he did not look well.

January 19, 1985 Only back a week, and it was a whopper. We made up for lost time in Mustique. Calls on Paul Nitze and Rick Burt at State, Bill Casey at the CIA, lunch with Bud McFarlane, press breakfast with journalists, breakfast with Canadian MPs, lunch at the Residence for Leo Kolber[1] and his wife, reception for Judge Clark at Interior, dinner for the new chairman of Ford Motor Company, buffet lunch at Nancy Holmes's and lunch hosted by the French Smiths at Glorious Café, the Deaver party, reception honouring Art Buchwald, dinner at the Brinkleys'. We are so at home it's sometimes difficult to believe we haven't been here all our lives.

---

[1] (b. 1929) Canadian Senator from Quebec 1983–2004. Formerly president of CEMP Investments, a family holding company for the children of Samuel Bronfman; for many years, Kolber was the chief fundraiser for the Liberal Party of Canada.

January 21, 1985 The second Reagan inauguration and the coldest day of the year. The outdoor activities were completely annulled. We had bedecked our new embassy property with Canadian flags because the inauguration parade was to proceed right in front of it. This was a great disappointment to our staff, who set up the display and lost an opportunity to show off our new site.

I observed the inauguration in the Capitol building amidst a horde of officials and legislators. It was an exercise in push hard and shove. Lucky Roosevelt hosted a desultory lunch for the diplomatic corps, and later in the day we attended a cocktail-buffet hosted by Henry Grunwald[1] and Ralph Davidson[2] of Time Inc. In the evening, at the Kennedy Center, we squeezed into one of the half-dozen balls being held all over Washington in honour of the inauguration. It seems the president visits all of them (no doubt for a brief few minutes). The ball we attended was stuffed with party activists, contributors, and supporters, and again it was an exercise in push hard and shove. No grace, no elegance, no class. We stayed for half an hour, all I could stomach, and then went off to the Jockey Club to attend a small, rather chic party given by a couple known for giving small, rather chic parties.

Yesterday, pre–Inauguration Day, saw Washington inundated by hordes of party faithfuls who had to be amused. So there was a plethora of receptions, and we went to a couple of what we thought were the better ones – hosted by Don Kendall[3] and Mike Deaver. Then dinner at Henry and Muffie Brandon's.

I always thought that inaugurations were glitzy, exciting affairs, replete with impressive ritual, sort of like a coronation. I must have been overexposed to tales of the Kennedy inauguration. After today's event I know better, a lot better.

January 25, 1985 I'm under relentless pressure from Mulroney and the PMO, especially Doucet, to get the Americans to realize we must achieve something on acid rain at the Quebec Summit. They expect me to work

[1] (1922–2005) Managing Editor of *Time* magazine 1976–1987 and Editor-in-Chief of Time Inc. In 1988 President Ronald Reagan appointed him U.S. ambassador to his native Austria, a post he held until 1990.

[2] (b. 1927) Chairman of the board of Time Inc. 1980–1986.

[3] (b. 1921) CEO of Pepsi-Cola Company 1963–1986.

miracles. I am conducting a personal campaign to sensitize the White House and U.S. officials throughout the system. This has included McFarlane, Deaver, and Darman in the White House, Shultz and Burt at State and top officials at the EPA.

So far no consensus has emerged as to what they can do to break the impasse, given the profound hostility to any action against acid rain in so many circles in Congress, the administration, and industry. I'm convinced the White House really wants to be helpful to Mulroney and the new government. From the top down they appreciate the deep change of tone and attitude in Ottawa towards the international issues of principal concern to the United States.

January 26, 1985 Ruckelshaus's departure from the administration is painful for Canada and especially for me, as I have developed such a fine working relationship with him. I decided to have a last go-round with him to see if he had any thoughts on how we could move off-the-dime in Quebec City. His Northeast option, alas, is dead, thanks to the relentless opposition of Stockman[2] and his OMB gang ("give them an inch and they'll want a mile").

Reagan's mind isn't closed, Ruckelshaus maintains. He has genuine scientific curiosity, he is an outdoorsman, a nature lover and has no deep personal convictions on acid rain. I relayed to the PMO the message that how Mulroney personally handles the issue in Quebec will be of critical importance.

January 30, 1985 I continue my calls on newly elected senators. Saw Albert Gore Jr.,[2] Democrat from Tennessee, who is smooth, urbane, and waxen. You can just tell he was the president of his high school class. Doesn't seem to be quite real. Also called on George Mitchell, Democratic senator of Maine. A superior type and seems to know it. Has a strong intellect and a very gentle manner, if somewhat professorial. Ran them both through the Canadian agenda, especially acid rain.

---

[1] David Stockman (b. 1946) Republican Representative from Michigan 1977–1981; Director of the Office of Management and Budget 1981–1985.

[2] (b. 1948) Democratic Representative from Tennessee 1977–1985; Senator from Tennessee 1985–1993; Vice-President of the United States 1993–2001; Democratic Party presidential candidate in 2000.

February 1, 1985 Although the inauguration parade was cancelled, I've been receiving favourable comments about the array of Canadian flags flying on our new embassy site on that bitterly cold day. A letter from Senator Moynihan consisted of two brief sentences: "The cold snap denied the Avenue its day, but did not deter the *Washington Post* from printing my brief memoir. Great days." In his piece about the history of the redevelopment of Pennsylvania Avenue, he referred to "the best site of all, at the foot of the Hill, chosen by Canada for its new Chancery." Yes, but will we ever build it?

February 3, 1985 Weekend guest at the home of Mrs. Lamont du Pont Copeland, Bob Duemling's mother-in-law, at her grand estate in the suburbs of Philadelphia. Gloomy mansion, priceless early American antiques, mountains of orchids from the greenhouses. Toured Winterthur and Longwood Gardens. Black-tie dinner for twenty in our honour. No tension, no heavy-duty conversation, no brain damage. It's easy to be rich.

February 6, 1985 Mulroney is asked in the House of Commons whether the House will review the appointment of Bill Davis as Canada's new ambassador to Washington. He replies that he has confirmed me in my functions. He doesn't say for how long. Better to keep me on my toes.

February 7, 1985 I get the after-effects of last night's State of the Union patriotic orgy out of my bones and get down to work this morning by writing a long epistle to Lee Thomas[1] to tell him the good news about the Canadian anti–acid rain program. I inform him that our minister of environment and seven provincial premiers have signed on to a formula for achieving major SO_2 reductions to a level of 2.3 million tons annually, 50 per cent of the 1980 figure. "He who comes to equity must come with clean hands." Well done, Mulroney.

February 8, 1985 Last night, at dinner with Julia Taft, wife of the new deputy secretary of defence and a lively activist in volunteer circles, we got into the question of the succession to the present UN High Commissioner for Refugees. She told me some Americans believe Trudeau would be an ideal successor. She herself seems very keen on him. I reported the conversation to

[1] (b. 1944) Environmental Protection Agency Administrator 1985–1989.

the PMO with enthusiasm. If they are as politically astute as they seem, they should get behind this one.

February 12, 1985 The Washington press hypes the forthcoming Gourmet Gala dinner-dance next month: the Dan Rather Country Salad, the Tip O'Neill Scalloped Fish, the Michael Deaver Tomato Beef Curry, the Senator Fritz Hollings Charleston She-Crab Soup, the Sondra Gotlieb Parsley Scallops. Good company, good publicity.

February 13, 1985 Spoke to Weinberger to assure him there was really no more to the Coates resignation than meets the eye. That there was, in fact, no security angle. Trying to convince him was a tough assignment. I told him Mulroney simply didn't want a prolonged media focus on all of Coates's doings during his various peregrinations. Better to cut losses. Weinberger was at pains (right words) to express his keen regret about Coates leaving the cabinet, and he certainly was intrigued about the manner of his departure. He spoke very favourably of Coates and said his high opinion of him was shared by some four or five of his top-ranking colleagues in Defense. Weinberger simply couldn't understand the resignation. In this day and age no one, he remarked, resigns for simply going into a bar with stripteasers or hookers present. He found the whole affair very mysterious.

In the evening I attended a dinner at the King Edward in Toronto in honour of Kay Graham, given by Roy Megarry of the *Globe and Mail*. She speaks at the Canadian Club tomorrow. We found ourselves on the same flight from Washington to Toronto. One that is over two hours long with a stop in Rochester. It was an all-coach flight. "I don't mind flying coach," she said. "In fact, I always travel coach when I'm accompanied by *Post* people, as I am now, who are only authorized to travel that way." With Kay Graham, noblesse oblige. With a net worth of $500 million, you'd think she would charter a plane.

February 14, 1985 Medas told me we can expect some U.S. proposals on acid rain. He is now singing a different song since the last time I spoke to him. "They would be a package," he said, which would include an agreement to appoint high-level special representatives and commitments to move ahead on the tall-stack and regulatory fronts. He told me to protect this information very carefully. "It should not," Medas underlined, "be discussed with the EPA or any American officials." Whoopee.

February 15, 1985 Called in the afternoon on Will Taft, new deputy secretary of defence. Predecessor going to jail.

February 21, 1985 Joint session of Congress yesterday for Thatcher. She lays them in the aisles. American political theatre at its best.

Busy these days with calls on senators. Called on Senate Mitch McConnell[1] of Kentucky and Dan Evans, Republican senator from Washington. Latter new and impressive. Very reflective man, broad outlook, nuanced mind. Saw Paul Simon,[2] new Democratic senator from Illinois – liberal, pleasant, but seems a lightweight. Also Kerry,[3] Democrat from Massachusetts. Ditto. Then Tom Harkin,[4] Democrat from Iowa and Chafee[5] (Republican, Rhode Island). Then Lloyd Bentsen, Democrat, Texas – cool, haughty. Bob Strauss tells me he has one of the ten best business minds in America. Moynihan again. Brilliant as always, amusing, not quite sober.

February 22, 1985 The president and Nancy Reagan gave a buffet lunch for Bill and Jean French Smith at the White House for about thirty guests. The president only showed up at the end of the lunch to say a few words. Nancy hung by his side and never left it. No mixing. The Reagans and the French Smiths are supposed to be close. Is this Nancy's idea of closeness?

In the evening I dropped into the Cameroonian ambassador's Residence for a reception in honour of the French ambassador, "Bobby" de Margerie.[6] He's moving fast through social Washington, welcome everywhere. There were a dozen or so African ambassadors and their wives and virtually no one else. It was sad. The Africans are ghettoized in power town.

February 25, 1985 Rick Burt has had a great promotion. He will soon leave for Bonn to take up his post as U.S. ambassador. He gave me

---

[1] (b. 1942) Republican Senator from Kentucky since 1985; Senate Majority Whip 2003 to present.

[2] (1928–2003) Democratic Representative from Illinois 1974–1985; Senator from Illinois 1985–1997.

[3] John Forbes Kerry (b. 1943) Lieutenant-Governor of Massachusetts 1983–1985; Democratic Senator from Massachusetts 1985 to present; Democratic presidential nominee in 2004.

[4] (b. 1939) Democratic Representative from Iowa 1974–1984; Senator from Iowa 1985 to present.

[5] John Chafee (1922–1999) Governor of Rhode Island 1963–1969; Secretary of the Navy 1969–1972; Republican Senator from Rhode Island 1976–1999.

[6] (1924–1990) French Ambassador to the United States 1984–1989; Director General of the Museums of France 1975–1977.

some valuable advice about the Reagan administration and recounted for me the details of the White House meeting of February 10 on Canada, with the president and key cabinet secretaries participating.

Never had he seen cabinet officers so well prepared on a topic of discussion. Shultz was a powerful force at the meeting and helpful on acid rain but seemed to continue to harbour some doubts about Mulroney and the new government. According to Burt, Shultz thinks Mulroney may be trying to "exact a price" for his pro-American attitudes. He also seems to have doubts about Mulroney's attitude on defence spending and wonders whether he is equivocating. He is somewhat bothered by Mulroney's style. It raises questions in his mind about "candour."

I told Burt I was more than a bit mystified by Shultz's views. Mulroney had already made two courageous changes in policy on items of great and long-standing importance to Shultz: FIRA and the NEP.

But Burt urged me to be conscious of Shultz's reservations, whom he obviously respects. Shultz's influence, Burt pointed out, is greatly increasing in Washington in both the political and economic fields, and it's important he not be overlooked or forgotten amidst all this Reagan-Mulroney rapport. Canada has always been "Shultz's file" in the Reagan administration. It was important that we remember Shultz does not like to be sidelined. Being a "heavyweight," he is accustomed to dealing directly with heads of state and government.

February 26, 1985 I'm working on a report to Ottawa on Reagan's State of the Union speech. The theme of the dispatch: unilateralism and the mood of America. The central point of my message: "It is essential to understand that the administration tends to assess countries in terms of their degree of loyalty to the U.S."

February 27, 1985 Spent a lot of time recently on the Hill, trying to gauge the mood of Congress on trade and economic matters. I don't like what I see. Protectionism seems to be growing, finding expression in a sort of "blame-the-foreigner" posture on the part of many legislators. Concern about the U.S. trade performance has become more widespread and national in scope than it was when I first started working here. The trade deficit is seen as a major threat to American economic power and supremacy. Fortunately for Canada, many on the Hill seem to regard the deficit as almost uniquely of Japanese origin. One senior Democrat described the Japanese as "gluttonous" in their economic relations with the United States. While senators and congressmen have a fairly large list of complaints against Canada, there are no apparent anti-Canadian sentiments. The problem for Canada remains that if Congress passes bad trade legislation, whether of a procedural or substantive kind, it will almost certainly be general in character, and so we are vulnerable.

While there's no real anti-Canadian sentiment here, ignorance of our importance to the States is staggering. With Bruce Phillips, I've been giving thought to what we can do about this. It seems only sensible to examine if there's any way we could get across our messages better than we do now. So we met with a market research organization (Matt Reese) to get his ideas. I'm not too impressed.

February 28, 1985 My fifty-seventh birthday. For me it's been a good year. I never dreamed I would make the transition from the Trudeau to Mulroney governments so painlessly. I wanted a Turner government and never imagined it would collapse in two months. I never would have believed my relations with Mulroney would be so close, personal, and direct. I would not have believed my influence with the Reagan team would have grown as pervasively as it has. I would never have believed that Sondra and I would become embraced (I don't think that's too strong a word) by the Georgetown set and so at home amongst the all-powerful Washington media. I sense I'm at the height of my powers and effectiveness. I'm concerned, of course, that so many of my closest political contacts in the administration have left or are leaving – French Smith, Deaver, Eagleburger, Burt. But I have confidence now that no doors are closed to me in this town. It doesn't get any better. If this be vanity, so be it.

March 1, 1985 Had a long chat with Dick Darman, now at Treasury, to get his perspectives on Mulroney, the government, and the upcoming summit. Darman said the perception of the prime minister in the White House was a very positive one. Everyone welcomed Trudeau's departure. The president's view was that "Mulroney can do no wrong."

Darman told me he made the economic presentation at last month's cabinet meeting on Canada presided over by the president. He was positive about Canada, but there was skepticism within Treasury as to whether our new investment policy would change things very much. Since some 90 per cent of former investment proposals will no longer be covered because they fall below the monetary threshold, the result, they argue, is that the large bureaucracy in Investment Canada will have more time to scrutinize the really big ones – and thus frustrate the policy. Darman, however, believes the new act, which he has studied carefully, represents a significant liberalization of our investment policies. Again, there is enthusiasm for our new energy policies, the repeal of the NEP and all that, but the question being asked by some in the White House is the same: will the old bureaucracy undermine the new policies?

March 2, 1985 When you're hot, you're hot. *Vanity Fair*: "One night you can run into Secretary of State George Shultz and his predecessor, Al Haig, another night it will be Donald Sutherland, Margot Kidder, John Kenneth Galbraith and Mordecai Richler. . . . The Canadian Embassy in Washington is the only social hot spot on Embassy Row, where most people still use guest lists compiled three thousand years ago, during the Johnson Administration." The Gotliebs "have created what passes for one of the capital's very few salons. In a muted-blue reception room furnished with French side chairs and the requisite Oriental carpet, the Gotliebs collect the powerful, the correct and – strangely enough, given the singular drabness of the foreign-service circuit – the interesting. Those who usually wouldn't be caught dead at an embassy affair will always go to the Gotliebs', certain of meeting someone they know or need to know."

March 5, 1985 Burt telephoned me this morning about press reports that Mulroney may call Reagan to break the acid rain deadlock. He urged me to make a special appeal to Ottawa to hold off initiating any such action for a few more days. The issue was being pushed back up to the top, and they may yet be able to achieve something.

Paul Nitze will visit Ottawa to discuss disarmament and arms control. The central issue in Washington at this time is SDI, and Nitze's role is critical in determining its potential negotiability. According to the best insights I can gather, the president is profoundly committed to SDI and the elimination of all nuclear weapons. This is a "core" belief with him. Indeed, SDI has all the markings of a religious movement. The meetings in the White House of the eight or nine key presidential advisers, I told Ottawa, are unusually harmonious; dissent is not allowed. Shultz is adamant that there be no doubters.

March 9, 1985 Tonight we again have the Shultzes as guests of honour at the Residence. The purpose, again, was solemn: to see an old movie. Sondra worked this out with Shultz, who would ordinarily not be caught dead at an embassy dinner. The crowd of twenty-one was *convenable*, as we checked out most names with him. The one error we made was to listen to Rick Burt, who told us that Hitchcock's *Foreign Correspondent* was a wonderful film. It was terribly dated. In fact, it stunk. It lasted so long we lost half the guests (this being early-to-bed Washington) but not George and Obie. They stayed to the end, but we should have stuck with Fred Astaire and Ginger Rogers. Next time we will.

Much talk between Shultz and myself about how our mutual friend John Turner is faring.

March 11, 1985 At the personal request of an ebullient and enthusiastic Mulroney, who telephoned me to give instructions, I informed Shultz and Weinberger last night of the decision (to be announced today) to send more troops to Europe to bring our brigade up to full strength. I also told them about an increase in funds and timing – we want to be seen to be strengthening conventional deterrence on the eve of the Geneva talks.

I wasn't keen on disturbing Shultz and Weinberger at home on a Sunday night, but the prime minister was most anxious I contact them immediately. Shultz thought the news was "terrific" and significant. Weinberger, ditto. Weinberger suggested as an "off-the-wall" and entirely "personal" thought that perhaps the United States could help Canada execute the plan and, as a cost saving to us, assist in the transport of troop movements to further strengthen the Canadian presence. I told him I thought the idea was "not on."

Former CIA chief Jim Schlesinger told me today that Reagan is a deep believer in the astrodome version of SDI. In other words, total fireproof defence. It's personal with him. It is an apocalyptic vision, but he will not modify it. Moreover, he says, Nitze knows the astrodome theory is a myth and no SDI system could ever meet the president's two criteria of cost-effectiveness and invulnerability.

March 12, 1985 Another victory on acid rain. After a long day of haggling, Medas called to say the United States will accept our most recent suggestions for the operative parts of the summit declaration on acid rain. The special representatives, he said, must be called envoys, not ambassadors

(ambassadors require Senate confirmation – a no-no) and report at the next bilateral summit, not at a meeting of the leaders held in the margins of the economic summit. I told Ottawa it is still undecided whether the United States will want to announce the names of the envoys in Quebec. The State Department is also uncertain whether the White House will want to release the declaration after the tête-à-tête meeting of Reagan and Mulroney on the first day.

I spoke to Deaver about this, and he agrees with me that the document ought to be issued on day one. Deaver is always sensible. He sees the point: they meet by themselves on day one, they agree to appoint envoys, they issue their declaration, and they get the credit for it. Simple, obvious.

March 15, 1985 I'm up to my neck every day in summit preparations. This could go down as one of the most over-prepared events in history. But we are doing well on all fronts.

March 16, 1985 Just as I thought we'd finally got this summit all prepared and put to bed, I got an unexpected and urgent call from Fred Doucet requesting I get hold of Bud McFarlane to see if anything further could be obtained from the United States by way of concessions. The prime minister, said Doucet, doesn't think the language on the appointment of the acid rain envoys goes far enough; he'd like it to be more pointed and forward-looking, and he wants me to make a final appeal for more favourable language.

I told Doucet this was impossible to achieve, but he insisted I ask anyway, "so you can tell Mulroney you tried." In a way I'm caught by my own reputation for having so much influence with the Reagan team. I'm expected to perform miracles. I contacted as many Reaganites as I could. I got all barrels shooting at me from Ty Cobb and Bud McFarlane and so advised Ottawa.

I write this in a very matter-of-fact manner, but today was absolutely punishing.

March 17, 1985 Ross Johnson sent his Nabisco plane to pick me up in Washington, and I flew with him and his trophy wife to Quebec City. Ridiculous as it may seem, there was no way for me to get to Quebec City by commercial aircraft in time for the summit because of Mulroney's request that I stay in Washington yesterday in a futile effort to get further concessions from the Americans on acid rain. So I depended on Air Nabisco.

Just before dinner, the two leaders had a meeting at the Château Frontenac, attended by Shultz, Regan, Clark, myself, Robinson, Doucet, and Burt. It was a heavily anecdotal affair, Mulroney getting deep into the jokes, as did Reagan. There was great interest in Mulroney's impressions of Gorbachev, whom he had met at Chernenko's[1] funeral. "He reminded me," said Mulroney, "of Khrushchev[2] in a nine-hundred-dollar suit." The president and his group fell into a paroxysm of laughter. I told Burt immediately after we left the room that he better make damn sure that story doesn't leak. This is the kind of story that gets into the press. "Don't worry," he said, "no problem. That won't happen."

After the meeting, as pre-arranged, Mulroney and Reagan announced the appointment of the acid rain envoys. Reagan was more positive in his language at the press conference than expected – a gesture towards Mulroney. Drew Lewis and Bill Davis, the two envoys, were on hand for the announcement.

The state dinner at the Château Frontenac was the quickest official banquet I've ever attended. The idea was to get everyone out in time for the big televised gala later in the evening. At our table we had an unlikely mix, consisting of such ideological soulmates as René Lévesque and Ed Meese. Sondra sat between them. They both clutched at their soup bowls as the waiters tried to whisk them away. At the table of eight that Mulroney arranged for the Reagans and himself and Mila, he seated the Desmaraises[3] and the Ross Johnsons. I think I was the only Canadian official at the dinner. Mulroney evidently wanted to get as many business and political supporters as possible into the room.

At the rather brief reception before dinner, Jim Medas went up to Maureen McTeer[4] and asked her who the Canadian guests were, as he did not recognize most of them. She replied, "I'm not surprised you don't know them. Two-thirds of them are assholes."

The gala event following the dinner was huge and forgettable, with one exception: Ron and Brian on the stage crooning "When Irish Eyes Are

---

[1] Konstantin Chernenko (1911–1985) General Secretary of the Communist Party of the Soviet Union 1984–1985.

[2] Nikita Khrushchev (1894–1971) First Secretary of the Communist Party of the Soviet Union 1953–1964.

[3] Paul Desmarais (b. 1927) Billionaire Canadian businessman, the chairman and CEO of Power Corporation of Canada.

[4] (b. 1952) Author and lawyer, wife of Joe Clark, the sixteenth prime minister of Canada.

Smiling." This was totally unscripted. Both he and Reagan seemed to be in heaven. It was a splendid show of friendship and reflected, in a very personal way, a new era in our relationship. It left me with a warm feeling. I couldn't imagine Trudeau crooning with anyone, except maybe Barbra Streisand.

March 18, 1985 Day two of the summit. I got a call before 8 a.m. to go to Mulroney's suite. The boys were already there – Doucet, Fox, and the usual crowd of political staffers. Mulroney had all of today's papers spread out on the table – the *Globe*, *Gazette*, *Citizen*, and French-language ones as well. The acid rain envoys were headline news on all the front pages. Mulroney was in a high-spirited, ebullient mood. He was delighted, and you could hear it in his voice.

The past forty-eight hours proved the importance of summitry. Without the summit, discussions on salmon, legal assistance, north warning, and acid rain could have dragged on for years. The acid rain agreement was innovative and creative and a fine example of diplomacy at work. The north warning system was a landmark and possibly a turning point in Canada's willingness to shoulder responsibility for our sovereignty. The trade declaration, coming at a critical time, may prove the most significant of all. Altogether, I've never seen a more substantive meeting between leaders.

The only avoidable event was Reagan's very hardline, anti-Soviet speech during the large official lunch today. It's not that the substance was wrong, but Reagan should have saved that one for U.S. soil. Anyway, a great summit. So much is owed, on the U.S. side, to Mike Deaver. I wanted to tell him that, but I haven't been able to find him for the past twenty-four hours.

March 20, 1985 Back in Washington, I've received many bouquets on the Quebec Summit from officials here. Deaver thought it was "a remarkable and unqualified success." According to Don Regan, the summit was a "moving experience" for the president, giving him a sense of North American solidarity at a time of critical East-West negotiations. Shultz told me he thought the substance was "solid," much was accomplished, and the event was symbolically important. Brock commented that this was the "most substantive summit" he had ever participated in. He believes the trade program is awesome in scope and will provide a major challenge in months to come. Burt pronounced the summit the "most productive Canada-U.S. meeting in history." Measured against our joint objectives, he added, it was a solid success for both sides.

March 26, 1985 A day to remember and to forget.

I took Jeffrey Simpson to breakfast at the Metropolitan Club. We chatted about the Washington scene until Rowly Evans, also breakfasting in the vast dining room, as is his want (he almost lives at the Metropolitan Club), passed by our window table. He said, "Mr. Ambassador, I want to ask you something about the Reagan-Mulroney summit. It's urgent." I excused myself and stepped a few feet away from our table to talk to Rowly.

"I understand, Ambassador, that at the Quebec meeting, your man Mulroney told our man Reagan that when he saw Gorbachev at Chernenko's funeral, 'he thought he looked like Khrushchev in a nine-hundred-dollar suit.' A marvellous line. I'm putting it in my column tomorrow. I have it on very good authority. So I want to ask you a straight question and I want a straight answer. Did your man say this to Reagan?"

I hesitated a moment, in total shock, and replied, "No, he did not say that." Rowly shot back, "You're shitting me." Flabbergasted, and being within earshot of Simpson, I muttered, "I got to go, I got to go, I'll call you," and I fled.

I rushed back to the office and reached Rowly by telephone. I said, "Rowly, don't print that. Do me a favour, a big personal favour. I'm not confirming the story is true, but don't print it. It would be embarrassing to a friend of the United States."

It was a difficult conversation, one of the most difficult I've ever had with a member of the press. I engaged in a bald-faced lie, and he knew it. But after fifteen minutes of intense conversation about the new Canadian leader and how upsetting it would be if his open relationship with the president in a confidential tête-à-tête were to be violated, I managed to exact a half-commitment from Rowly that he would consider my request.

Since there were only a handful of Americans in the room at the summit meeting, I figured right away that the leak came from Rick Burt. So I asked Rowly, "Did Burt leak this to you?" Rowly emphatically denied it, so I said, "You're shitting me."

Burt and Evans are thick as thieves, but I was still pretty shocked at Burt's indiscretion. I was even more annoyed because I had told Burt that I was worried that the Khrushchev story, being a damn good one, could leak and that he should make every effort to be absolutely sure it didn't.

Meanwhile, I alerted Fred Doucet and Bill Fox in Ottawa, who were understandably upset. I then called Burt and, point-blank, accused him of passing the story to Evans. "Allan," he commented, "it wasn't me that leaked the story. It could have been one of several people. It might have been Paul Robinson. You know Paul's been in town the past few days." I said, "Rick, that's bullshit. Robinson doesn't even know Evans."

Then I dropped my own little bombshell. I told him I was under instructions to call Shultz and make an official complaint. The idea of me or Clark calling Shultz really shocked Burt. "You have one course of action," I told him, "call Rowly and kill the story. You've got huge leverage over him – you're one of his key sources. You leak everything to him. Every day. He can't afford to have you dry up. Use your leverage, kill the story."

Burt, shaken by my hardball but admitting nothing, said he would call Evans and see what he could do. Later in the day Rick called back to say that if Rowly does use the story, he won't attribute it to Mulroney. I told Burt, "Damn it, that's not good enough and you know it. Get us out of the soup you put us in."

Burt said he'd have another go at it. From this, I surmise the story will be axed.

Tonight we flew to New York with Shultz on his government aircraft to see the Oilers play. This was on my invitation, since he told me some time ago that he was a great admirer of Gretzky and longed to see him in action. On the way, I had a chance to discuss the recent Canada-U.S. summit with Shultz. He was amazed at the growth in stature of the prime minister between when he met him for the first time last June and when he saw him perform in Quebec. He greatly sympathized with the problems the prime minister was facing in dealing with the attacks of the Opposition and the attitude of some of the media. He expressed his disappointment at the policy positions being embraced by the leader, his old friend John Turner. A bizarre twist.

We watched Gretzky score a goal and make a couple of assists and then met him personally when he came up to the box to shake hands with Shultz (who was thrilled).

March 27, 1985 I introduced Arthur Erickson at a luncheon hosted by the Americas Society in New York on the occasion of the opening of an exhibition there of his architectural achievements. As I walked in, I saw Mrs. Bill (Pat) Buckley, former Canadian from Vancouver, and I said hello. She didn't have a clue who I was, although I met her several times and talked at length with her at Roy Cohen's reception in Dallas last August at the Republican

National Convention. She is the one who is said to have slipped a copy of Lubor Zink's scurrilous piece on Trudeau into Reagan's reading material.

Fotheringham tells me Bruce Phillips will be a mole under my couch.

April 3, 1985 We attended a reception at the Watergate given by Roone Arledge for Ted Koppel[1] on the fifth anniversary of *Nightline*, where all of power town was in attendance. Then we sped back to the Residence to host our black-tie farewell dinner for the Deavers. It was a brilliant crowd, A-list all the way. But Mike and Carolyn were not in a good mood. He seemed bothered by something. What, I don't know. Mike is riding so high these days. "Mike the Wizard" is all one hears since Reagan's mighty re-election. Mike, the guy responsible for the president's successes, the guy who could be White House chief of staff, the guy who is going to make millions in public affairs and lobbying.

April 4, 1985 The prime minister is furious about the release to the press of Cap Weinberger's letter at the NATO foreign-ministers' meeting in Luxembourg before it was received by the governments to which it was addressed. He instructed me to protest to George Shultz. Deaver and Burt both told me emphatically to make the demarche to Bud McFarlane, not Shultz. It would not be effective, they said, for Shultz to carry a protest about Weinberger to the president. So I conveyed Mulroney's concerns to Bud McFarlane. He told me, not very discreetly, that the White House view was that the handling of the SDI issue was inexcusable.

I am amazed at how strong the prime minister's personal reaction has been. He feels "blindsided" or "tricked" or personally let down.

April 5, 1985 My sources tell me Shultz heard about my protest and commented, "Too bad the prime minister didn't call the president."

April 22, 1985 Back from Palm Springs, where we were house guests of the Walter Annenbergs at Sunnylands, along with the Wicks and French Smiths. Sunnylands is one of the most magnificent estates in the United States. Annenberg's collection of impressionists is probably worth a couple of hundred million dollars. I spent a lot of time talking politics with him and

[1] (b. 1940) American journalist. Long-time lead anchorman for ABC's news program *Nightline* (1980–2005).

about Canada and the people we know in common. He is a great admirer of Reagan but not of all those around him. He is surprisingly down on Deaver. Perhaps this is because when Lee was chief of protocol, he believes Mike was not helpful to her.

Walter's attitude towards Canada is brutally negative. He believes his property there, the *TV Digest*, was confiscated by Trudeau. He is, understandably, much better disposed towards Mulroney.

Annenberg's first wife was a Canadian, a Dunkelman from Toronto whose mother was a friend of my mother. Annenberg talked freely about his Canadian family connections, but he showed no nostalgia for our country. He is a great admirer of Ken Thomson,[1] whom he got to know when Thomson's father, Roy, was in London and Walter was U.S. ambassador to the Court of St. James. Annenberg had an endless fund of tales about Lord Thomson and about how he wanted Walter to become a partner in his great North Sea Oil ventures and how insensitive Roy was to his son Ken.

Members of the kitchen cabinet, the Armand Deutsches,[2] the Jorgensens,[3] and several Annenberg sisters (each worth a half-billion plus), were in and out of Sunnylands throughout the weekend. Another house guest was Mark Thatcher, son of Margaret, Walter's heroine. The son was rather obnoxious and was treated dismissively by our host.

Back in Washington we attended a dinner at Evangeline Bruce's in her house in Georgetown. Ironic because there is such bad blood between the Annenbergs and Evangeline. The cause occurred years ago, but the bad blood continues. The Annenbergs, who replaced David and Evangeline at Winfield House in London, said publicly that they found the Residence uninhabitable, and then they brought in decorators to redo the whole place. If Evangeline is proud of one thing – and justly so – it is her beautiful and refined taste in clothes, design, and decoration. She never forgave the Annenbergs.

April 25, 1985 Mila Mulroney departed for Ottawa at 6:15 p.m. from Andrews Air Force Base, ending a hectic two-and-a-half-day visit to

---

[1] (1923–2006) Canadian businessman and art collector. Second Baron Thomson of Fleet and chair of the Thomson media empire. Son of Roy Thomson, First Baron Thomson of Fleet, founder of the Thomson Corporation.

[2] (1913–2005) The grandson of Sears, Roebuck and Co. chairman Julius Rosenwald and a film producer for MGM. He and his wife had a long-time friendship with Ronald and Nancy Reagan.

[3] Earle M. Jorgensen (1898–1999) U.S. steel magnate.

Washington. She came in response to Nancy Reagan's initiative (her idea?) to hold a "First Ladies' Summit" to combat drug abuse. There were about a dozen "first ladies" (what an expression) attending the meeting, at one time or another. We kicked things off by hosting a black-tie dinner in honour of Mila at the Residence, with sixty-two guests in attendance, A-list all the way.

At first there seemed some lack of enthusiasm for this trip among Mulroney's team, but the PM thought, correctly, that it was the right thing for Mila to attend. The worry, I believe, was that Mila might be seen as Nancy's sidekick and too closely associated with her campaign against drugs.

The opening of the "summit" was a very staged event: attractive young former addicts tearfully but skilfully recounting their harrowing experience in the drug world for the edification of the first ladies. Mila was given a highly favoured position at the luncheon, sitting beside Nancy, no doubt through the courtesy of Mike Deaver. After a late-afternoon reception at the Residence for the Canadian press (Mila asked for it), she spent the evening on "private time," having dinner with Allan Fotheringham.

Today I accompanied her and her party on a flight to Atlanta for more of the same. There were school bands, confessions, workshops, true-life stories, emotional tales. I had to confess to myself that Nancy Reagan and her handlers and public-relations folk probably did accomplish something with all this gimmickry. She contributed to raising the consciousness of Americans about the seriousness of the drug issue and to getting volunteers from all strata behind the efforts to address it. Politically, she has gained yards for Reagan and the Republican agenda by playing up the family theme.

Mila will be fortunate if she does as well with her own chosen disease: muscular dystrophy.

April 26, 1985 "Sweet Pea Gotlieb of Canada" makes the *New York Times*. "At the Capital Canine Follies and Fair (a children's museum fundraiser), Democratic dogs are competing against Republican ones in the 'Dog-Eat-Dog-World' class, while in the 'Ambassadoggeral' class the competition will be between such diplomatic dogs as Countess Chloé Wachtmeister of Sweden and Sweet Pea Gotlieb of Canada." I'm rooting for the commoner.

April 27, 1985 During my call on Daniel Patrick Moynihan, my hero, we had an amiable chat about Canada-U.S. problems – trade, environment, and all the usual suspects. As always, he was wonderfully cordial. As I walked out of his office, the senator said, "Oh, Mr. Ambassador, you might be interested in reading the analysis of America's trade woes that I wrote in my last newsletter to my constituents. Of course, I write these myself."

I thanked him in a rather perfunctory manner, as one does when receiving a political handout.

Some days later I picked up the circular from my desk and glanced at it. I then discovered that what the good senator was telling me during our chummy chat was rather different from what he was telling his constituents. After kicking off with "Dear New Yorker," he writes, "the time could come when about the only thing American below the hood ornaments of an American automobile will be a license plate made by prison labor." After that warmup and more, he gets to Canada.

"New Yorkers grow onions. Canadians grow onions. Not as good as ours, from say Orange County, but good enough, I'm sure. And sooner or later some food wholesaler in the Bronx discovers that for a dollar he can buy $1.37 worth of onions across the border. Result: Canadian onions start coming into this country much like Japanese cars. Last year our trade deficit with Canada was $20 billion. Comparing their 25 million people to Japan's 120 million, the per capita trade deficit with Canada is three times as great as with Japan . . ." Low blows, Senator, very low.

April 29, 1985 The prime minister telephoned this morning with one issue weighing heavily on his mind: "Allan, I'd like to try to find a way to help Reagan back off from the Bitburg mess." He suggested that he could propose that the economic summit in Bonn be extended half a day. If it were, then the president would have a visible "conflict" and hence a credible public reason to reverse his decision to go with Kohl[1] to visit the war graves in Bitburg. "Try out this idea on the White House," Mulroney said, "and let them know I'm willing to take the lead in being helpful." I told the prime minister I thought Reagan was not looking for a way to back down and would not back down, but I would, of course, pass on his offer to help.

I contacted Deaver and spoke to him a couple of times – appropriately enough, since Deaver was the architect of the plan to visit Bitburg and is now taking a lot of shit for not knowing about the Nazis buried there. Deaver did not seem inclined to pick up the offer. "Backing off," he said, is out of the picture. The president was not looking for a way to do so. "The storm will pass." The president would not want the summit extended.

---

[1] Helmut Kohl (b. 1930) Chancellor of Germany 1982–1998.

Reagan's not only got guts but realizes that yielding to media pressure would be seen as a sign of weakness and hurt him politically. Mulroney seems to have a more natural inclination to seek a compromise. Reagan understands the political benefits of standing firm. But Mulroney is shrewd in trying to be helpful to Reagan. It's lonely at the top, and the president will appreciate the gesture. So Mulroney's instincts are pretty good too.

April 30, 1985 Rick Burt dropped around to the Residence to dine with us last night and laid a blockbuster on me. Tom Niles[1] was nominated yesterday to be ambassador to Canada.

The nomination was virtually accidental. At a meeting at the White House dealing with diplomatic appointments, the State Department proposed Tom Niles as ambassador to Finland, but his name was rejected in favour of a political candidate. The view emerged at the meeting that Canada "deserved" a careerist. Ken Dam then proposed Niles, who had been left dangling as a result of the earlier excision. There being no dissent, the deal was sealed, the lucky winner was informed, and the State Department was delighted to learn that a professional foreign-service officer had nailed down a major embassy.

I called Burt today to tell him that I thought the appointment might not go down all that well with Mulroney. "You are being appointed as ambassador to Bonn," I exclaimed. "Your assistant is going to Ottawa. Niles is very able, but this says loads about how the U.S. positions Canada in relation to the Europeans."

In the past, I pointed out, when professionals were sent to Canada, they were top-ranking officials such as Livingston Merchant,[2] William Porter,[3] or Tom Enders. Obviously, Mulroney would have nothing against a career appointment, and no one would argue that Niles was less than fully competent. But appointing a relatively junior-level official to your top trading and defence partner?

---

[1] Career diplomat in the U.S. foreign service. Served in a variety of posts in Belgrade, Moscow, Brussels, and Washington, D.C., 1962–1981. Assistant Secretary of State for European and Canadian Affairs 1981–1985 and 1991–1993; U.S. Ambassador to Canada 1985–1989, to the European Union 1989–1991, and to Greece 1993–1997.

[2] (1903–1976) Undersecretary of State for Political Affairs 1959–1961; U.S. Ambassador to Canada 1961–1962.

[3] (1914–1988) Undersecretary of State for Political Affairs 1973–1974. U.S. Ambassador to Canada 1974–1975.

Burt's reaction was subdued. He would discuss the matter with Deaver as soon as possible. He called back a little later to say that the president had already approved the appointment. Burt said to me, "Allan, don't try to resist it. It's not likely the president will change his mind." He said Shultz was now in the picture and was very pleased with Niles's nomination. I'm not surprised. He'd far rather have one of his State Department officials in Ottawa than a high-profile figure whom he might not be able to control.

I pondered for a while if I should do anything with this sensitive insider information. What Burt said was probably true: the appointment should be regarded as done and more or less cast in stone. Nevertheless, I decided to inform Mulroney – in the interests of full disclosure on my part. I urged the prime minister to proceed with caution. He might, I suggested, discuss the appointment in a private, low-key way, in the margins of the Bonn Summit.

I'm probably playing with fire here. But I believe that Ottawa is as important to U.S. interests, probably more important, than London or Paris. Yet the Americans would never appoint someone as junior as Niles to either of these capitals.

I am sure the U.S. administration thought they would be doing the right thing by us, that we would be happy to see the good-natured but blustering political appointee Paul Robinson replaced by a competent, lower-key professional diplomat. But I believe the Americans fail to grasp the Canadian government's need to demonstrate in Canada that the new relationship delivers in terms discernible to Canadians – whether on acid rain, removal of trade restrictions, or the appointment of a high-profile confidant of the president as ambassador.

May 1, 1985 Lunched yesterday at the Residence with Arthur Kroeger,[1] who is conducting a special study for the cabinet on whether Canada should participate in SDI research and development. His is a good appointment because he's got lots of common sense. We agree that there is only one answer to this question. If we consider our true long-term defence interests in North America, the answer is an unqualified yes.

---

[1] (b. 1932) Deputy Minister of Indian and Northern Affairs 1975–1977, of Transport Canada 1979–1983, of Regional Industrial Expansion 1985–1986, of Energy, Mines, and Resources 1986–1988, and of Employment and Immigration Canada 1988–1992.

I had one of my periodic one-on-ones with Paul Volcker at the Federal Reserve. He's concerned about the still-growing U.S. trade deficit and the protectionist winds that are blowing increasingly strong. I presented him with the usual token of my homage: a single Cuban cigar.

In the late afternoon we leave for the Homestead in Virginia, where Sondra is speaking to the National Machine Tool Builders' Association. An incongruous duo.

May 2, 1985 The Montreal *Gazette* devotes the front page of its Food section to what we ate at our diplomatic dinner for Mila Mulroney last week: Crepes with Golden Manitoba Whitefish Caviar, Rack of Lamb with Thyme, Tomatoes Florentine, Potatoes Yves Safarti (our chef), Quebec Maple Success. Seeing it in print brought home to me the fascination diplomatic dinners hold for those fortunate enough not to have to sit through them.

May 3, 1985 More grand dinners. Last night we attended an intimate black-tie affair for eighty at the Watergate, in honour of the Annenbergs, hosted by the Wicks. Tonight an even grander affair, white, not black. Paul Mellon,[1] retiring as chairman of the board of trustees of the National Gallery, was honoured by a celebrity-studded affair at the gallery on the occasion of the opening of an exhibition by George Stubbs. We were greatly privileged to be among the few diplomatic couples in attendance. Billionaires and millionaires from across the land were everywhere to be seen. Mellon loves horses, many of the guests love horses, and Stubbs was the Michelangelo of horse painting. It was a perfect harmony.

After dinner we wandered through the exhibition with the marvellous Sidney Freedberg,[2] senior curator, great scholar, connoisseur, bon vivant, fantastic wit, and my favourite person in Washington. I stopped to admire a superb picture by Stubbs. Sidney agreed that it was a fine picture, but added, "Regrettably, it suffers from *le vice anglais*." "What on earth is that?" I asked, suspecting a deviation of some sort. "The necessity to tell a story," he replied.

---

[1] (1907–1999) Son of Andrew W. Mellon, Secretary of the Treasury 1921–1932. Chairman of the Board of Trustees of the National Gallery 1979–1985.

[2] (1915–1997) Professor of Art History at Harvard University 1954–1983; Chief Curator of the National Gallery 1983–1997.

May 4, 1985 The Bitburg storm continues. My sources are putting a lot of the blame for Bitburg on Kohl, but most feel that the president's decision to carry on with it goes to show he is his own man. I was told that at one recent NSC meeting everyone around the table except Bush urged the president to back off. However, he stood firm to honour a commitment he had made to Kohl, who has stuck to his promise to deploy missiles on German territory, against heavy opposition. What is especially interesting about the affair is it shows there is a real Reagan behind the bonhomie. Could this be the very reason why R.R.'s staff wrap him in a protective media envelope: to minimize the effects of his tendency to take a strong – and sometimes idiosyncratic – position on matters and then stick to them? SDI comes to mind.

May 7, 1985 Peter Lougheed is in town for one of his regular pilgrimages to the capital of North America. He loves these visits, plans them meticulously and works earnestly at accomplishing his purposes. These are: (1) meet as many influential policy-makers as he can over a period of two or three days and (2) get them to understand Alberta's (repeat: Alberta's) point of view. During this visit, he agreed that I should accompany him on his calls to the Hill (the embassy had set them all up), whereas during his last visit, during my tenure in the Trudeau years, he went alone. Was his very different behaviour based on the fact that there is now a Conservative government in Ottawa? Is it based on the possibility, as the Canadian papers speculate, that he will replace me here (and therefore erase a bad precedent)? Maybe the answer lies in both hypotheses. Anyway, we called yesterday and today on several cabinet ministers – Baker, Block, Baldridge – and a slew of people on the Hill: Danforth, Lugar, Helms, Gibbons, and more. Add to this a working breakfast for sixteen yesterday, a reception at the Residence last evening for forty, and a lunch at the Residence today for sixteen.

Two meetings were of special interest. The purpose of Lougheed's call on Jim Baker at Treasury was to assess Baker's attitude to a free-trade agreement between Canada and the United States. Responding to Lougheed's very intelligent question as to whether there would be, in the present climate, a reasonable chance of entering into such an accord, Baker said categorically yes; it would be tough, but it would make sense and could be done. He would certainly wish us to follow up. The United States, like Canada, prefers the multilateral path, but if the European Community doesn't get its act together on trade, a Canada-U.S. bilateral agreement would make even greater sense. Particularly since congressional legislation of a protectionist character would be across the board, he warned, and Canada would not be exempt.

The other highlight was the call on Jesse Helms. I had not called before on this notorious legislator and have had a conscience about being reluctant to do so. Unpleasant he may be, but there's no questioning his power and influence as chairman of the Senate Agricultural Committee. This was also the first time Lougheed had called on Helms, and he was anxious to meet him to discuss agricultural irritants. I was delighted at his initiative.

Lougheed made a few preliminary remarks, after which he moved into his well-oiled presentation about Alberta hogs, Alberta pork, Alberta beef, and Alberta's constitutional jurisdiction over natural resources. But during his presentation, Helms seemed not to be looking at him. He seemed to be focusing on me, glaring at me, in fact. Lougheed, alert as always, became conscious of this and, finally getting unnerved by Helms's seeming disinterest in his recitation, asked him if anything was wrong.

Helms paused but continued to fix his beady gaze on me. "Are you the ambassador from Canada?" he asked. I said yes. "Let me get this straight," he responded. "Are you *the* ambassador of Canada here in Washington?" Yes, I thought so. "Then, sir," he said, "you are the husband of the lady who writes a column for the *Washington Post*?"

Now beginning to sweat, I admitted I was. At that point his face relaxed, he seemed to melt, and he said, "Well, I can't tell you how much I admire your wife's columns. They are marvellous. I read every one of them. Tell her she has a great admirer in me."

I was thrilled to learn that the dour and severe Helms had this affinity for Sondra's satires. But I believe my surprise was somewhat less than Lougheed's, who nevertheless took this diversion from hogs and pork with excellent grace and who repeated the story several times during the day.

May 8, 1985 During the last couple of days, I have communicated with Joe Clark and the Prime Minister's Office on some sensitive points. Clark is showing a keen interest in the Central American region. I think he wants to carve out a foreign-policy profile for himself in this area. If so, I think he is making a political error. He will get no credit for enhanced Canadian involvement in this region from the small segment of our public that is interested in it, unless he attacks U.S. policies and attacks them vigorously. This he will find it politically inexpedient to do.

May 9, 1985 Stephen Lewis's[1] attack on the Heritage Foundation makes waves in Washington. The foundation has sent me a sizzling letter to forward to Mulroney. I worked out a response with External, Doucet, and Lewis and then called the vice-president of Heritage to try to contain the controversy. The Heritage people, who are closely linked to the Reagan administration, are deeply stung by Lewis's attack, which they think is unfair. There is no question that Lewis has made himself a hero in certain circles in Canada. The views he expressed had some element of justification, but vitriolic public attacks win us no friends in the administration. Mulroney should have distanced himself from Lewis.

May 10, 1985 Mulroney's new environment minister, Suzanne Blais-Grenier,[2] is in town on her first visit. I took her to see Lee Thomas at the EPA and Don Hodel at Interior and various others. An intelligent woman, but she seems weak. I'm surprised the Conservatives haven't yet learned what the Liberals knew so well: the environment ministry is a guaranteed success for a Canadian politician. All he or she has to do is knock the Yanks and accuse them of doing nothing about acid rain and he or she will receive praise on page 1 of the *Toronto Star* and the *Globe and Mail*.

The politician who understood this best was John Roberts. It's a portfolio, he told me, in which you can't lose. You just open your mouth, complain that the Americans are poisoning our lakes and trees and, bingo, you're on the networks and in the press. I'm glad Blais-Grenier doesn't seem to understand this. Poor thing.

May 13, 1985 After weeks of thinking about it, I sent the Prime Minister's Office a far-reaching proposal to use the new embassy to launch a special celebration of Canadian culture in the United States. I proposed that Mulroney personally create a "blue-ribbon committee" to take charge of this ambitious task. It now looks like construction will get underway this autumn. Without the personal support he has given, we would not have a new embassy in Washington.

---

[1] (b. 1937) Leader of the Ontario New Democratic Party 1970–1978; Leader of the Opposition in the Ontario Legislature 1975–1977; Canadian Ambassador to the United Nations 1984–1988; Deputy Director of UNICEF 1995–1999; subsequently Secretary-General's Special Envoy for HIV/AIDS in Africa.

[2] Minister of Environment 1984–1985; Minister of State for Transport 1985.

The blue-ribbon committee should have three purposes: (1) make the official opening of the embassy in 1988 an occasion to launch a cultural blitz in the United States of our finest cultural achievements. A program of events including paintings (Canadian masterpieces), architecture, theatre, ballet, artifacts, and Native art could have a powerful effect if we go about it in a major way. (2) make the interior of the new chancery a showcase of Canada's best and most innovative furnishings and designs; and (3) determine the disposition of the existing buildings in Washington. Our embassy off Dupont Circle is a protected historic building because of its architectural design and beauty. It was the residence of Vincent Massey, Loring Christie, Lester Pearson, Hume Wrong, among others. We should not sell a unique piece of Canadian history.

May 14, 1985 The softwood lumber situation gets more menacing by the day. The congressmen never give up. They are convinced that we are not playing fair. Don Bonker[1] (the appropriately named representative from Washington State) and about forty of his colleagues in the House slammed in a bill to limit our lumber exports to the United States. "The question," Bonker said in a speech today, "is no longer whether the problem of Canadian imports will be addressed, it's how the problem will be addressed. The entire U.S. industry is galvanized like never before, to take whatever action is necessary. There is widespread frustration within Congress, and a conviction that action is long overdue." Congress at its worst.

May 16, 1985 After breakfasting with Bob Strauss and lunching with Dick Darman, I met Mike Deaver in my office to discuss the possibility of his acting as a consultant for us. Mike has just left the White House, and Doucet has been urging me to get in there early before he gets "booked up." He's going to be in great demand. This guy's profile is about as big as the ones on Mount Rushmore. Rumours have it he is being pursued by mighty corporations and hungry governments. The PMO is anxious to recruit Deaver, primarily to advise us and help raise our profile here in the United States – a sort of general-purpose counsellor.

I offered Mike a retainer of U.S. $50,000 per annum, as suggested by Doucet, but this did not please him. He said he did not want a lot of clients paying him smaller amounts, just a solid group (the lucky dozen) that would

[1] (b. 1937) Democratic Representative from Washington 1975–1989.

each pay him $200,000 to $300,000 a year. I told Deaver this was definitely not on, but I would get back to him if we had any flexibility. I think the right figure is about $100,000 – he won't do it for less, and I don't think we should pay him more.

We attended a dinner in our honour held by Barbara Walters in New York. There were about a dozen attending, including Merv Adelson,[1] Henry Grunwald and his wife, Louise Melhado, and the head of Sloan-Kettering. We sat at a round table and had a single focus of conversation, an old-fashioned party that one could actually enjoy. Our hostess seemed genuine. Under the celluloid image, there could be a warm, intelligent human being. Or was she just faking it?

May 19, 1985 Joe Clark is in town with Maureen to attend the quarterly meeting of the two foreign ministers. Hard to believe that this new institution is still working; Shultz shows no sign of losing interest or enthusiasm, which is remarkable, given that the secretary of state invariably spends almost all of his time on crises. On the occasion of Clark's visit, we decided to give a buffet luncheon on Saturday in their honour. The weather was clement, so we were able to eat outdoors. A top-flight collection of Washingtonians attended, there was no *place à table*, it was informal dress, and the cuisine was excellent – it was an almost enjoyable affair.

The problem was that throughout the lunch, the host was distracted; he was worrying about what to do with Maureen McTeer. She was in a very sour mood, so sour that I figured the only reason she wanted to accompany her husband on this trip was to make him miserable. Joe, however, seemed to be having an excellent time, working the crowd and chatting amiably. He sat beside Senator John Tower's wife, Leila, who reported to Sondra how fondly Joe spoke of his wife during the lunch, commenting that he was very deeply in love with Maureen but couldn't guarantee there was a state of reciprocity.

In accordance with the custom to date, as established with Allan MacEachen, we had dinner at the Shultzes' modest home in Bethesda in the evening. He invited the Clarks and us, Gordon Smith,[2] the Burts, the Alan

---

[1] American producer and owner of Lorimar Productions 1968–1993. Husband of Barbara Walters 1986–1992.

[2] (b. 1941) Canadian Ambassador to NATO 1985–1990 and to the European Union 1991–1994; Deputy Minister of Foreign Affairs 1994–1997.

Wallises,[1] and Jim Medas. Maureen was seated at Shultz's table, and she lectured and hectored him on such matters as the rights of women, peace and disarmament, the inadequacy of U.S. foreign policy, and the U.S. failure to understand Canada. George Shultz managed to bear all the criticism with dignity but was relieved from having to argue with her because he couldn't get a word in.

May 20, 1985 I prepared a communication to the Prime Minister's Office in Ottawa proposing that it play a more direct role in our public-relations efforts in the United States. It's a risky proposal, but I am desperate to get authority and support for a major public-relations effort in the United States and I'll never get it from External Affairs. This is the only way I know to get the money to do the job.

We have arrived at a position, I told the PMO, where our public relations demand something much better than what we have had until now: they require a carefully designed, coherent, sustained, and well-managed program in which all elements are pulled together in one place and made to serve a common objective. Such a program needs a lot more than "the piecemeal, seat-of-the-pants approach which has characterized most of our work over the course of time." The PMO should, I told them, establish a mechanism reporting directly to it with sufficient authority to provide direction to all activities concerning the promotion of our public image in the United States. A radical proposal all right, but "it is the only way I know of providing the time-and-issue-responsive organization that is needed in the U.S., where the scene is constantly shifting, needs constant monitoring and the ability to make rapid tactical changes in support of long-term policy."

May 22, 1985 There is a story doing the rounds in the State Department about Maureen McTeer's aggressive behaviour towards Shultz the other night. Bogdan Kipling picked it up and called McTeer in Ottawa directly to ask about it. It seems she was greatly taken aback. At the embassy we denied the story, lying conscientiously for our country. Given Kipling's reputation for unreliability, I doubt the story will get picked up, which is just as well.

[1] (1912–1998) Undersecretary of State for Economic and Agricultural Affairs 1982–1989.

June 4, 1985 Our social activities proliferate. In New York we attended a dinner in our honour by Marietta Tree. It was held in her ground-floor apartment on Sutton Place with its French doors opening flush onto a garden on the East River. She had a dozen and a half guests, including the Gutfreunds,[1] Philip Johnson,[2] Kissinger, and various media types. After dinner the guests strolled through the garden down to the river under a huge sky illuminated by skyscraper lights.

Back in Washington we attended a wedding in Maclean given by Henry and Jessica Catto.[3] I've gotten to know him through his job as assistant secretary of defence, a solid guy, reliable, with the modest good fortune of being married to a woman of immodest wealth (a newspaper heiress from Texas) and something of a bohemian. Henry set up a marvellous tent on the grounds that I figured must have cost thousands to rent. "Would you believe twenty-five thousand dollars?" he asked. Le tout Washington was there, as the Cattos are very close to the Bushes and the Reagan crowd.

June 6, 1985 Fotheringham reports that the *Washington Post* is to send a full-time reporter to Canada instead of covering us out of their Chicago office. He is, says Fotheringham, Herb Denton, a Harvard graduate, French-speaking, black, Vietnam veteran, and personal friend of Donald Graham.[4] All very accurate.

I don't really know if this is good news or bad. I've been lobbying Kay Graham and Ben Bradlee since I got here to appoint a resident correspondent in Canada. I've told them it's better not to cover Canada at all than to pretend to cover it out of an office in the American Midwest. But I don't hear good things about Denton. *Per contra*: Jeremy Kinsman.

June 7, 1985 Sandra Day O'Connor and her husband, John, invited us to a buffet dinner at the Supreme Court tonight. It was the first time I have

---

[1] John Gutfreund. CEO of investment bank Salomon Brothers Inc. 1978–1991.

[2] (1906–2005) American architect. First director of the architecture department at the Museum of Modern Art (New York) in 1946. His most famous work is the Glass House in New Canaan, Connecticut, a transparent open-plan frame structure initially designed as his own home.

[3] (b. 1930) He was Assistant Secretary of Defense for Public Affairs 1981–1983; U.S. Ambassador to the Court of St. James 1989–1991.

[4] (b. 1945) CEO and Chairman of the Board of the Washington Post Company. Elected to the board in 1974, he was made executive vice-president and general manager in 1976 and chairman in 1993.

seen Rowly Evans since the episode of Gorby in the nine-hundred-dollar suit. He was cool towards me until I provoked him by saying that I was sure he had also lied and misled people at times. He howled in protest. "Never," he said. But I added, "What about the source of your story for Mulroney at the summit? Obviously it was Rick Burt, but you deny it. You're lying." He denied it again. So I said, "There you are, you keep illustrating my point. You know damn well he was your source, and I do too." After that exchange I think we will be able to return to our normal relationship.

June 10, 1985 I called on Sam Gibbons today to give him hell over his foolish natural-resource subsidy bill. He is "Mr. Free-Trader" and "loves Canada" but . . . He's inserted a clause that would leave foreigners wide open to anti-subsidy trade actions if their natural-resource costs happen to be lower than those of their U.S. competitors. This seems to be the latest salvo on the protectionist front. It's so stupid it may not go anywhere, but meanwhile we're being hit by Commerce on hogs, whacked by the International Trade Commission on raspberries and salt cod, and now there's talk of quotas on footwear.

June 12, 1985 I received a copy of the memo Doucet submitted to the prime minister:

> The enclosed letter from Ambassador Gotlieb recommends action on the following fronts:
>
> a) Setting sod turning date for new Washington Embassy for early 1986, tied to your official visit to the U.S.
>
> YES ☐
> NO ☐
>
> (Advantage here is this would add a colourful event to the Washington part of the visit's venue.)
>
> b) Creation of a blue-ribbon committee from the private sector to enhance the presence of Canada in Washington and in the U.S. generally.
>
> YES ☐
> NO ☐

If you agree to this concept then the mandate could include the following:

i) Advise on manner of disposing of existing buildings in Washington.

YES ☐

NO ☐

ii) Be responsible for making the interior of the Chancery a showcase for Canada's best and most innovative furnishing and fixture designs (with private sector donations).

YES ☐

NO ☐

iii) Use the moment of the official opening ('87 or '88) to launch a cultural blitz in the U.S. of Canada's cultural artworks, etc.

YES ☐

NO ☐

A real contrast to Trudeau's style. No lengthy analysis. A multiple-choice test. Am I complaining? Absolutely not.

The PM gave the right answers – yes all the way.

June 13, 1985 Strange affair earlier this week at the Residence. A tall, thin, black intruder surprised Sondra in her bedroom at 11 a.m. He walked in, lifted his cap, and said to her, "Power, madam" (thus leading her to think he was from the local power company). At first she thought nothing of it, but a few minutes later she asked a staff member why she wasn't informed of the appointment. At that point, everyone realized there was an intruder in the house. The police managed to arrest the person not far from the Residence. Now we learn he has been released on bail by the police. No matter that he broke into our house. No matter that he has been stalking Sondra when she walks Sweetpea. No matter that he's a suspect in a rape case next door.

He was released because of a "screw-up"; not even the prosecuting attorney was informed of his bail. It seems that the Secret Service (who swept through our house in droves) and FBI can't work with the Washington police. It seems that the American Civil Liberties Union posted bond for this individual. It is, one is told, automatic. The ACLU would have done this even if he had murdered Sondra.

Our security people are angry and alert, watching to see if the "power man" returns to his stalking position in front of our house.

June 14, 1985 Arrived back from Toronto in time to greet Solicitor General Elmer MacKay[1] (here to do the rounds at the FBI, Justice, and on the Hill) and host a party for departing embassy staff, to which we invited about 150 guests. Yesterday I spoke at an energy conference at the Royal York Hotel and the evening before briefed a blue-ribbon group of Canadian businessmen in Toronto on the U.S. scene. Gave them a harem-scarem account of the protectionist monster stalking the United States. Conrad Black was very pro-Reagan, an unusual stance for any Canadian businessman, and it warmed my heart.

My remarks up north reflected what's on my mind and agenda these days. I've been telling Ottawa that although the protectionist mood is not all that new – it's been growing since 1982 – what strikes me as rather different now is the apathy that seems to be affecting the administration's response. It has not developed any strategy to combat the fair trade–protectionist mood and pressures in Congress.

So far we haven't done all that badly as regards softwood lumber and energy issues (and possibly also regarding the dreadful health ban on our hogs – Meese is finally considering taking some legal action against the offending states). But there is now, to boot, a trade action on our hogs and pork production, we just lost two Trade Commission decisions on codfish and raspberries, the pressure on lumber is almost unbearable, and we are under a virtual de facto quota on carbon steel and a de jure one on specialty steel.

So how long can we coast along with our ad hoc, mano-a-mano, issue-by-issue operational approach? There are heavy costs in terms of political and economic uncertainty.

The irony is that we entered into a fancy high-flown trade declaration at the Quebec Summit, committing ourselves towards more free trade and fewer barriers. I suggested Mulroney call Reagan at some point and remind him of these great commitments. The president is out to dinner, and the administration is soft and spongy on this issue. In the meantime, Congress is doing a lot of harassing.

---

[1] (b. 1936) PC Member of Parliament for Central Nova 1971–1983; Minister of Regional Economic Expansion 1979–1980; Solicitor General of Canada 1984–1985; subsequently Minister of National Revenue and Minister of Public Works.

June 17, 1985 The "power man" continues to stalk. He sits across the street from the Residence, partly hidden by the bushes. He's been sitting there for several days. Our security people are very concerned, but nobody seems to be able to do anything about it. "He'll leave when he leaves," the police say.

June 19, 1985 Lunched today with Drew Lewis and Bill Davis and staffer Jack Svahn[1] and aide Mary Smith in the White House mess, the first time for me in this secret precinct. Subject: acid rain. Lewis startled the hardline Svahn and Smith by saying to us categorically that man-made sulphur dioxide and nitrogen oxide cause acid rain, and something should be done about it. A blockbuster of a statement. And not something I expected to hear from an American official. Another blockbuster: the report must be handed in by the end of the year, he said. Lewis was remarkably firm in the way he expressed himself. The United States must initiate some sort of program moving in the direction of Canadian concerns.

What a breath of brisk, non-acidic air! It was also clear that without Lewis's intervention, the White House would have been a lot softer on the matter of reducing emissions from tall-stacks. To say that Svahn and Smith were unhappy with Lewis's remarks would be a gross understatement.

In the evening I gave a stag dinner at the Residence to discuss the steel situation. We are under heavy pressure to reduce our steel exports, bad news indeed for our very competitive, non-subsidized, and integrated industry. Jim Kelleher[2] flew in for the dinner, as did the chief executives of the three largest Canadian steel companies and the source of most of our exports: Dofasco, Algoma, and Stelco. A long, heavy, tedious evening with too much food and too much inconclusive discussion.

June 20, 1985 A rather dismal day for me. Jim Kelleher and his laid-back deputy, Bob Richardson, decided they wanted to make some calls on the Hill – a very good idea and something rarely done by members of this cabinet or its predecessors. It seems to be a Canadian constitutional belief that for ministers to call on senators is rather beneath their dignity. Some

---

[1] (b. 1943) Domestic Political Advisor, Office of Policy Development in the Reagan White House.

[2] (b. 1930) Elected in 1984 as PC Member of Parliament for Sault Ste. Marie, Ontario; Minister of International Trade 1984–1986; Solicitor General of Canada 1986–1988. Appointed to the Canadian Senate in 1990, retiring in 2005.

dignity. It's curious that this is not the view of the provincial premiers. Peter Lougheed, Bill Bennett,[1] and others seem to understand the workings of the U.S. system better than our federal cabinet ministers and their bureaucratic advisers do. I've been screaming for years for calls on the Hill by ministers, but they never come down here for long enough or seem to want to walk the corridors. So I was pleased that Kelleher was willing to make an effort with the legislators. He is not without savvy, seems honest, conservative, and has some feeling for the business side of affairs.

I arranged calls on Sam Gibbons and Lloyd Bentsen and Jack Danforth, who in turn arranged for a few senators to drop into his office. Danforth is very rich (Ralston Purina), rather self-righteous, a man of the cloth who preaches weekly and officiates at weddings and funerals. A lean, hungry-looking, long-headed man, he reminds me of Louis Jouvet[2] playing an English bishop in a French farce.

Danforth's group of four or five senators were all well known to me, and I had called on Danforth several times and entertained him and most of the others. After a very weak selling job by Kelleher on the importance of Canadian trade and a few desultory exchanges, Kelleher then, in a rather formal way, apologized for our "ignoring" the Senate. This, he said, will not happen anymore. The Senate was most important to Canada and would no longer be neglected.

He told the senators if they had any problems, they should get in touch directly with his office in Ottawa, or with the head of the U.S. Bureau, Derek Burney (who was at the meeting). One senator had a particular question, and Kelleher responded by asking Burney to give the senator his card, which Burney did, as did Kelleher's assistant. Then Kelleher again called on the senators to deal directly with his office. The apologies and proposals for future direct dealings with the minister and his staff went on for about ten minutes, during which time I was getting redder and redder. Seeing the embassy undermined as a channel of communication, I finally blurted out, "You know, there is a Canadian embassy here too, so you can get in touch with us if you like. And incidentally, I hope none of you gentlemen feel that I have been ignoring you." Protestations followed from Danforth and the senators that I certainly had not been ignoring them, and then a weak murmuring sound emerged from Kelleher's lips about our embassy doing its best.

---

[1] (b. 1932) Premier of British Columbia 1975–1986.

[2] (1887–1951) Renowned French actor and producer.

The meeting broke up on a tense note, reflecting my high state of irritation. I walked out with Kelleher. When we got to the steps outside the Senate building, I told him I wanted to speak to him privately. "Not now," he replied, "I've got to get ready for my press conference." "Now," I said. "Oh, all right," he replied. "What is it?"

He knew damn well what was coming, and it showed on his face. I fired both barrels. "Don't treat me that way again in this town. Don't humiliate me or the embassy before my key clientele. Do that again and I'll resign so fast you won't see my back."

Maybe I overreacted – I probably did. But as I sit in the upstairs library, fiddling with the tube before going to bed, I'm still mad.

June 21, 1985 Visit today from some key executives of Gulf and Western to complain about our new book publishing policy. Gulf and Western bought out Prentice Hall Canada and have had an application pending before FIRA since last year. I heard a litany of complaints.

Cabinet has come out with a new anti-investment policy, treating foreign book publishing interests in a discriminatory manner and subjecting them to retroactive laws. The first I heard of the new policy was a phone call from Ottawa just after the discussion had taken place at a cabinet meeting at Baie Comeau – and immediately announced by Marcel Masse.[1] We were caught totally unawares, just like the good old NEP days.

I'm very mystified. The prime minister announces as a centrepiece of his foreign policy that "Canada is open for business" and rejects discriminatory practices and retroactivity. In order to sell the policy, Sinclair Stevens launches a major advertising campaign in the United States to welcome new American investment. Now his government totally confuses the message. I suppose I could say of myself that I can teach that the world is round or I can teach that the world is flat, but I can't teach it both ways at the same time.

If this legislation and the way it was adopted are to be hallmarks of the new Conservative government, it's going to be in deep trouble, fast. I know that our cultural lobbyists in Toronto are a powerful group (our equivalent to the National Rifle Association for clout). The Liberals never made this concession. Why should Mulroney? He has a far greater majority in Parliament and a much wider base across the country.

---

[1] (b. 1936) Minister of Communications 1985; Minister of National Defence 1991–1993.

June 22, 1985 At lunch yesterday Sondra and I were invited to brief the owner of the *Washingtonian* magazine, Philip Merrill,[1] and his wife and their staff on the ways of their hometown. I do like playing de Tocqueville, explaining America to Americans.

Then I called on Senator Spark Matsunaga,[2] Democrat from Hawaii and member of the powerful Senate Finance Committee. I extolled the virtues of Canada-Hawaii trade and tourism and could barely get a whisper out of him. But you never know when a senator's support might come in handy.

June 23, 1985 Spoke to Deaver the other day about the next U.S. ambassador to Canada. I indicated to him very privately that sentiments were being expressed in Canada that this person should be a senior envoy who has the close personal confidence of the president, so as to mark the attainment of a new relationship. The appointment of a competent but relatively junior official would therefore come as a disappointment in some quarters in Canada. Deaver told me that several weeks ago Reagan wanted to take another look at the appointment, but Shultz was pressing hard for Niles and regarded any attempt on Canada's part (my part?) to inject our views into the process as being plain interference in U.S. affairs. But I gathered from what Deaver said that the matter may not be entirely settled. For obvious reasons, I am laying low.

June 27, 1985 The end of Bill Bennett's exhausting two-day visit to Washington. I arranged a remarkable program for him: Baldridge, Block, Yeutter,[3] and Hodel in the administration; Wilson,[4] Danforth, Johnston, McClure, and Baucus from the Senate. He even met with the anti-Canadian-lumber coalition of congressmen led by the hot-headed Larry Craig.[5]

---

[1] (1934–2006) President and CEO of Capital-Gazette Communications, Inc. Counsellor to the Undersecretary of Defense for Policy 1981–1983; member of the Defense Policy Board 1983–1990; Assistant Secretary-General of NATO in Brussels 1990–1992; head of the Export-Import Bank of the United States 2002–2005.

[2] (1916–1990) Democratic Representative from Hawaii 1963–1977; Senator from Hawaii 1977–1990.

[3] Clayton Yeutter (b. 1930) U.S. Trade Representative 1985–1989; Secretary of Agriculture 1989–1991; Chairman of the Republican National Committee 1991–1992.

[4] Pete Wilson (b. 1933) Mayor of San Diego 1971–1983; Republican Senator from California 1983–1991; Governor of California 1991–1999.

[5] (b. 1945) Republican Representative from Idaho 1981–1991; Senator from Idaho 1991 to present.

Bennett's trip was lumber, lumber, lumber. He was an effective spokesman on the issue, but it is like battling a tidal wave. Breakfast this morning with Max Baucus was particularly futile – the man from Montana is the scourge of Canada. I wonder whether Bennett is being realistic in refusing to recognize that some accommodation of the Americans is going to be necessary. I spent considerable time talking to him about liberalizing B.C.'s policy on the export of logs. He wouldn't hear of it. But Bennett is shrewd and is beginning to grasp what a mess we are in.

Bennett also wanted to pitch lumber to Pete Wilson. I warned the premier that the senator from California is no friend of Canada. When we got to his office, he was waiting for us. He had a piece of paper in front of him criticizing provincial management practices in the industry. Bennett immediately recognized the paper and flushed with anger. He said to Wilson, "Ignore that. It comes from the NDP. They're wild men, they're communists."

Pauley from Manitoba will be here soon, wearing his NDP (communist) clothes. He will be pitching Canadian electricity to Wilson. Good luck to him.

July 1, 1985 Our National Day and a good time to send Ottawa some reflections on our precarious trade position in the United States. Protectionist pressures are turning into a stampede in Congress. There is an almost inexplicable atmosphere of anger over trade issues, and a substantial element now seems to be aimed at Canada. A meeting called by a relatively unknown congressman – Larry Craig – on the subject of Canadian lumber drew an unprecedented sixty congressmen and twelve senators. It was described to me by Max Friedersdorf[1] of the White House as the most hostile hearing on any issue that he has ever attended on the Hill. Baldridge speaks freely of a trade crisis and compares the situation to a runaway freight car without a brakeman. Don Regan and James Baker both told me that the White House trade strategy has failed, and Baker opines that Canada has become a prime target for the protectionists because of our trade surplus. Regan believes a proposal for a liberalizing comprehensive Canada-U.S. trade agreement would be a positive step but that the White House must have advance notice so as to prepare the way. Regan seems to share the view put to us earlier by Baldridge that the administration must

[1] (b. 1929) Assistant to President Ronald Reagan for Legislative Affairs 1981–1982; U.S. Consul General in Bermuda 1982–1983; Assistant to President Ronald Reagan and Legislative Strategy Coordinator 1985–1986.

get behind the least damaging congressional trade initiatives, since they cannot all be stemmed.

I warn Ottawa that "what hits the floor of the Congress first probably has the best chance of succeeding. . . . In this dangerous conjuncture, our own strategy becomes of great importance. Perhaps most significant will be if and when we indicate our willingness to explore a comprehensive trade agreement and what we are willing to discuss as part of such an agreement."

July 2, 1985 This morning I sent the PMO a note on the planning of the next summit in Washington. (It's still nine months off. This is ridiculous.) If Reagan follows through on his invitation to Mulroney to visit his ranch in Santa Barbara, this would make the visit a unique event. With the exception of Queen Elizabeth, no foreign official visitor (not even Maggie Thatcher) has visited there. There is strong opposition in the White House to the president encouraging such visits, for fear of creating a precedent for other visiting heads of state, and for fear of losing control over the president's privacy, and perhaps even the substance of the agenda.

I sense a real reluctance in Ottawa – both in External and the PMO – to go for the idea of a visit to Santa Barbara. Just like the Americans, Canadian officials fear a loss of control.

July 4, 1985 *Washington Post* story on the "re-entry" to California by Jean French Smith: "From the Corridors of Power to the Aisles of Safeway." She writes of compensations, "One of these has to do with ending a problem that my friend Sondra Gotlieb refers to as 'wife of.' The onset of the 'wife of' effect begins when we attend our first Washington party. We've polished our make-up, put on our best dress, practiced our most sparkling smile and read up on the achievements of the guest of honor. To our surprise, the newspaper accounts of this party note the attendance of the secretary of state, the attorney general and other notables. No mention is made of their little team-mates, who evidently stayed home. Be advised, however, that this invisibility does not confer immunity if we happen to say something silly in public."

July 5, 1985 In my call on Mike Armacost yesterday, we discussed the possible "neutralization" of the Beirut airport, in the context of the recent TWA hijacking. Armacost startled me by asking if Canada really wanted to be consulted in advance about the possibility of any U.S. unilateral action in the area. I answered, yes, we do. We would probably counsel restraint, I said, but out of consultation could come greater wisdom and possibly even solidarity. Recalling (vividly) our Grenada experience, I said it was better for a friend to disagree than to be ignored.

Armacost asked a good question. I gave him the correct diplomatic answer. But maybe not an honest one.

July 11, 1985 Conrad Black has been telling me for a year how much he'd like to meet David Brinkley. Conrad is a hero-worshipper and has apparently been worshipping David from afar for years. In addition to the Brinkleys we invited Dick Darman as well as Harold Evans, former editor-in-chief of the *Times* of London. Black was delighted, as he had not met any of them before. We sat at a round table and had a single focus of conversation throughout the evening. Brinkley came with a fever of 101 degrees. Susan told me that before dinner he was sick as a dog but insisted on showing up. Black lived up to my advertisement: he was expansive and brilliant, deploying his vast knowledge of English history, American history, and contemporary American politics. I know no other Canadian like him.

Conrad told me a story about Kissinger and myself. When he asked Kissinger about me at Bilderberg or somewhere, Kissinger said, "He's the only Canadian ambassador I've met with whom you can have a discussion about something other than migratory birds."

July 14, 1985 Rococo letter from Conrad Black thanking us for the dinner party a few nights ago. He asked me to follow up on invitations he sent to Chief Justice Burger and Richard Perle. "I wonder if someone from the Canadian Embassy could ask the Chief Justice's and Assistant Secretary of Defense's offices if they plan to accept or not the invitation that they encouraged me to send them. Such interventions would emphasize the sincerity of the invitation without conveying the impression that I was badgering the individuals concerned. Or to apologize again for seeming to involve you in my sporadic and rather trivial efforts at diplomacy with prominent American office-holders." Is he planning a political career?

July 18, 1985 An article in the *Post*'s Style section announces our dinner-dance tonight. We are "defying the season." The black-tie dinner was in honour of Charles Wick and Len Garment. Wick was at the piano and Garment at the saxophone. People danced into the late hours, on one of the finest summer nights this town has seen in a long time. Marked by the media, Charlie and Mary Jane Wick have come to be recognized even in this mean-spirited town as a generous, likeable, and distinguished couple.

July 20, 1985 News of Niles's appointment to Ottawa is out and is receiving a big ho-hum. They are happy that Robinson is gone and are fine with having a professional appointed to replace him. My instincts about the Canadian reaction were wrong.

Burt tells me Shultz is angry at me for intervening on this issue. He regards it as interference in U.S. affairs. Burt says John Whitehead[1] is going to call me in and reprimand me. I should have kept my nose out of the whole business.

July 30, 1985 Yesterday the *Wall Street Journal* published a front-page, above-the-fold, top left-hand-column article about me and Sondra that, as Allan Fotheringham says in a report today, "is so laudatory one would think [Allan's] mother had written it." David Shribman astounds me by praising us so much. Sondra is described as the "Alice Roosevelt Longworth of her time."

I am quoted as saying, "I am practicing a diplomacy that is thoroughly modern. It is different from traditional diplomacy. It is not in any books. It is not widely understood. And it is not practiced in any other country."

"Needless to say," notes Fotheringham, "our ambassador is a chap who believes in the John Kenneth Galbraith dictum that modesty is a highly overrated virtue."

July 31, 1985 Gulf and Western are in a state of continuous warfare over the threat to their Prentice Hall acquisition. Lautenberg[2] and Bradley of New Jersey wrote letters to Mulroney expressing concern. Shultz, Baldridge, and Yeutter are being lobbied furiously by the U.S. industry to "do something."

I got a call from Bob Strauss today, whose firm is acting for Gulf and Western. It was vintage Strauss. "Allan," he said solemnly, as if each word were worth a chunk of Fort Knox, "Gulf and Western say they will adopt a scorched-earth response if your government enforces their new book policy on them.

---

[1] (b. 1922) Deputy Secretary of State 1985–1989; Former Co-Chairman of Goldman Sachs.

[2] Frank Lautenberg (b. 1924) Democratic Senator from New Jersey 1982–2001 and 2003 to present.

They'll close down Prentice Hall Canada before they agree to a forced sale."

The new policy is going to give the Conservatives a massive headache. They'll have to reconsider, sooner or later. They should do so now.

August 4, 1985 We've just arrived back from a few days at Martha's Vineyard. Sondra and I were house guests of Laughlin and Jennifer Phillips and then, on the weekend, of Kay Graham. The Vineyard is an alternative workstation for Washington's and New York's establishment during the month of August.

All we had to do for several days, aside from walking on the rugged shore, was to stagger up to the large mother house owned and occupied by the Phillipses, to dine with their various literary friends such as William Styron and his good-works wife, and visit neighbours such as Arthur Miller. Kay Graham was a guest at one of the Phillipses' meals, along with the Deavers. Mike's presence signifies the likelihood of a visit by Nancy Reagan to the Vineyard in the near future, to stay with her new friend Kay Graham.

At Kay's, we occupied a large isolated wing of her house. Kay's social secretary, Liz, typed up lists of the guests at all the luncheons and dinners and placed these intimidating documents in our room. The other house guests were Warren Phillips,[1] publisher of the *Wall Street Journal*, and his wife, Barbara, Ed Ney,[2] a top officer of Young and Rubicam, and his wife, Judy, Arthur and Alexandra Schlesinger,[3] Felix and Liz Rohatyn, Bob MacNamara, Meg Greenfield, and Joe Alsop. At lunch we sat at a round table on the great terrace overlooking the ocean, enjoying light breezes, heavy food, and big political talk. Only the breakfasts were informal, but even on these occasions we were expected to eat together.

After spending three days with Kay, Sondra and I agree that we are fortunate to be included in her circle. She is impressive in her wide-ranging curiosity about the world. She is not arrogant, and power becomes her. She is a grand hostess in the classic tradition. The breed is near extinct.

I am basking in the glory of the puff piece on us in the *Wall Street Journal*.

---

[1] (b. 1926) Executive Editor of the *Wall Street Journal*. CEO of Dow Jones and Co. 1975–1990.

[2] (b. 1925) Chairman and CEO of Young and Rubicam 1971–1985; U.S. Ambassador to Canada 1989–1992.

[3] (b. 1917) He is an American historian focusing on the philosophies and policies of U.S. presidents, including Andrew Jackson, Franklin D. Roosevelt, John F. Kennedy, and Richard Nixon. Special Assistant to the President in John F. Kennedy's administration.

August 5, 1985 I've been thrashing about for weeks, debating the best way for me to get the government to understand the implications of their hastily put-together and ill-thought-out publishing policy. I decide to write a confidential letter to the "responsible" minister: Sinclair Stevens at Investment Canada. Clark can't regard my writing him as a circumvention of his authority, although he won't like it. Kinsman made some useful suggestions, toning my letter down a bit. But I kept in Bob Strauss's comment about Gulf and Western's threat to adopt a scorched-earth policy if we apply the law retroactively to them. This should focus their minds in Ottawa.

I emphasized for my Conservative masters that Trudeau and the despised, nationalistic Liberals never even tried to "Canadianize" the book publishing sector. Now the Conservatives are doing so and doing it retroactively.

August 6, 1985 Rumours are circulating in this town that I intervened in the U.S. political process by trying to get a high-level political appointee named as U.S. ambassador to Canada. There are also rumours that Shultz is personally irritated with me. It looks like the poor Canadian ambassador is in deep doo-doo. The irony is that it's in my own interests for the United States not to have a highly privileged channel in Ottawa. I should be a happy camper, thanks to Niles.

August 7, 1985 I put the finishing touches on an eight-page personal letter from me to Dr. Fred, for the PM's eyes only. The letter analyzes why it would be a grave political mistake to respond to the latest Northwest Passage brouhaha by trying to draw straight baselines around the waters of the Arctic Archipelago. The pressure to do so is coming directly from the prime minister and his people, so I've decided to go at them directly and Clark be damned. If they read my memorandum and if they're not politically brain-dead, they won't draw those baselines. Nobody, as I say in the letter, but nobody, is going to recognize them. So why behave like a banana republic?

We leave this evening for an extended vacation in Europe. Sondra and I have been planning this vacation for months. We will stay with friends in Brussels, Paris, and Siena. We rarely ever plan our holidays, so this one is going to be different. We're calling it "The Schnorrers' Odyssey."

August 29, 1985 The last day of our visit with Evangeline Bruce and Marietta Tree at Poggio al Pozzo, their villa in Monti San Marcellino in the midst of the Tuscan hills and wine country. This is the closest we have come to the sheer *douceur de vivre*. Eating delicious pasta made by two elderly Italian ladies, talking, reading, sunbathing, snoozing, swimming in a beautiful pool, with sheets of water running over the edges like extended waterfalls, taking meandering excursions in the Tuscan countryside – this has been our mode of existence for almost a week. It doesn't get any better.

The Nicko Hendersons were here when we arrived, but for the past week we've been the only guests, except for a British poet friend of Evangeline (a well-regarded poet, according to her) by the name of Charles Gardiner, who reads us poems, on occasion, at Evangeline's urging. Marietta has been tireless, organizing itineraries, proposing restaurants, arranging events, while Evangeline has managed to be magically elusive, even invisible. The only other guest we've seen at the villa is the curious British journalist Woodrow Wyatt,[1] who made me laugh when I was introduced to him by saying, "Canada, ah yes, a very interesting idea." Alas, we did not meet Harold Acton,[2] whose celebrated villa is nearby. He declined the invitation from the ladies because no car was sent to pick him up.

September 4, 1985 Back in Washington after the most memorable August I've had, thanks to the three great ladies: Katharine Graham, Evangeline Bruce, and Marietta Tree.

There are tremendous issues on our plate: SDI, free trade, our claims to Arctic waters. The most pressing issue in Ottawa is whether Canada should participate in SDI, as the Americans have invited us to do. I am urging a decision now, rather than let the pressure build up while the government prepares its white paper on defence. The Conservatives are wavering, afraid of being criticized for working with the Yanks, even though the other allies are doing so.

We gave a small dinner for Rick Burt and Gahl Hodges tonight. They filled us in on the "news" that we missed while we were away, mainly ridiculous rumours circulating about Bud McFarlane. They struck me as preposterous. What is not preposterous is that the knives are certainly out for McFarlane. Washington at its most evil, nasty, absolute worst.

---

[1] (1918–1997) British Labour politician, author, journalist, and broadcaster. Member of Parliament for Birmingham Aston 1945–1955 and for Bosworth 1959–1970; Chairman of the British Horserace Totaliser Board 1976–1997.

[2] Scholar and art connoisseur, probably most famous for inspiring the character of Anthony Blanche in Evelyn Waugh's novel *Brideshead Revisited* (1945).

September 5, 1985 I received a surprise telephone call from the PMO telling me the prime minister wanted to see me in Ottawa immediately. I explained that airline schedules being what they are, I couldn't get there today. The PMO said they would send an aircraft to pick me up – something they have never done before. When I heard this, I knew right away something important was going on, but I had no clue what to expect.

Arriving in Ottawa, I was asked to go to 24 Sussex Drive directly. Mulroney was alone, except for Dr. Fred. I sat down in an armchair in front of the prime minister, and he told me very deliberately that he had made three decisions of importance that the government would soon be announcing. These would significantly affect Canada-U.S. relations. He wanted to explain these to me personally and help me prepare for dealing with them in Washington.

I was struck by his gravity and his wish to brief me himself, without intermediaries. I felt a solemnity and seriousness of purpose as regards the United States that I did not experience in Trudeau's time.

First, he planned to propose a free-trade agreement with the United States. I was deeply surprised, because when I had talked to him earlier this summer, he was clearly going the other way. Mulroney said that he understood there were risks in this course, but he believed this was the right way to go. He spoke highly of Donald MacDonald[1] and his work on the Royal Commission. Both his report and recommendation for free-trade negotiations were courageous and groundbreaking. I said I welcomed his decision, it was a bold and courageous one, and I would work for it with great enthusiasm.

Secondly, Mulroney had decided that the government will not participate in SDI, although it will not object to our private sector doing so. I told him I was sure Reagan would be disappointed and there would be some fallout. Mulroney's comments then surprised me further. It was necessary and prudent, he said, for the United States to conduct SDI research. Reagan knew that he, Mulroney, was asserting this publicly and vigorously. But the Opposition, the NDP, the media, all the anti-U.S. elements in our society, would make SDI participation by Canada the endless focus of debate, hostility, dissent, and division. It was my job to ensure that the White

---

[1] (b. 1932) Member of Parliament for Rosedale 1968–1978 who held various cabinet positions in the Trudeau government, including Minister of Finance; High Commissioner to the United Kingdom 1988–1991.

House understand that the costs would be too high for the Conservatives, given that we could, in reality, contribute so little to the development of SDI.

I assured Mulroney that I would do all I possibly could to keep things cool in Washington and would start by calling on McFarlane as soon as I got back. But I thought to myself, thus ends a long debate on the wrong side.

The third initiative, the PM told me, would be to draw straight baselines around the waters of the Arctic, so as to assert our sovereignty. I immediately responded that it would be a mistake for Canada to act unilaterally. The United States would never recognize the legitimacy of our action. We'd end up painted in a corner and looking impotent. Trudeau, I said, never went that far. Much as the United States likes you and your government, I said, it won't recognize our claim. They believe that what is high seas belongs to them. They would rather share the freedom of the international straits with the Russians than see them under the sovereignty of a third party, even Canada.

Mulroney seemed surprised by these comments. He had no problem, he told me, in not proclaiming the baselines now but just announcing that we were going to do so and then negotiating on that basis. "Speak to Joe Clark about this," he said. I wasn't encouraged by this remark. He sees the method of proceeding with the baselines as a mere detail – appropriate for Clark to focus on.

I thought to myself as I left the Residence that the PM saw these three decisions as linked, political trade-offs among each other – one decision that would be very welcome by the Yanks, a second disappointing them, and the third antagonistic to their interests. I wondered whether he had exaggerated in his mind the likelihood of a positive reaction on free trade and underestimated the negative U.S. reactions on SDI and the Arctic. One thing I am sure of, he appreciates the risks and difficulties of obtaining a free-trade agreement with the United States. "We'll do our best on this one," he said. "I know we can't guarantee we'll get it."

Another thing I am sure of: he thinks broadly and strategically and sees the interrelationship of things.

September 6, 1985 The new German ambassador, Gunther Van Well,[1] whom I knew when he was my opposite number in Bonn, gave a going-away party for Rick Burt, who takes up his duties in Germany in a few days. He's going to put Germany on the map in this town. It was a warm

[1] West German Ambassador to the United States 1984–1987.

night and we dined outdoors. I chatted with both McFarlane and Shultz about developments in Canada, and I told Shultz I was concerned about certain trends in Canada-U.S. relations, suggesting I call on him to discuss them. Any time, he said. Unfortunately, State officials hate it if I go to him directly, and if I do, they surround him and it's difficult to have a frank, informal chat. The best approach is to steer clear of his office and continue to have him at our embassy. Then we can talk. I have to thank Fred Astaire and Ginger Rogers for providing the bait.

September 8, 1985 A busy Sunday in Washington. As a follow-up to my conversation with Mulroney earlier this week, I telephoned Joe Clark in Ottawa and urged him not to create a *fait accompli* by proclaiming our straight Arctic baselines. Even the great relationship with Reagan, I emphasized, will not lead the United States to act contrary to its national interest.

I didn't make much headway. Clark said he might agree to proclaim the baselines now but not have them come into effect until the end of the year. This is not really a satisfactory alternative – we'd still be locked in. The truth is plain: Joe likes unilateral action. This, after all, is the man who proclaimed that Canada would move its embassy to Jerusalem.

September 9, 1985 Had a tête-à-tête lunch with Ed Broadbent[1] the other day. Talked a lot about cruise-missile testing and free trade. Found his personality charming and his mind closed.

September 10, 1985 I've been talking to Alan Simpson about the Simpson-Mazzoli immigration bill, an important piece of U.S. legislation, and giving him pointers based on Canadian experience with enforcement. Simpson is not only extraordinarily witty, he's courageous. "Why not run for the presidency?" I asked him. "Impossible," he replied. "You can't do that with a political base in Wyoming."

September 11, 1985 Kay Graham and her new head of *Newsweek* dropped around to the embassy to tell me about *Newsweek*'s expansion plans in Canada and their (long overdue) decision to open a *Washington*

[1] (b. 1936) Member of Parliament for Oshawa 1968–1990; Leader of the New Democratic Party 1975–1989; Director of the International Centre for Human Rights and Democratic Development 1989–1996.

Post bureau in Toronto. *Newsweek*, they said, will also open an office in Toronto. I did not mention that I heard that *Newsweek* is making a pack of money in Canada, nor did I reveal that this was in part due to my intervention with Trudeau, advising him to avoid the imposition of retroactive measures in *Newsweek*'s postal rates.

We held a small dinner party tonight in honour of Philip Johnson. He came in from New York for the event. I was very excited. I invited Arthur Erickson, although I'm not quite sure what their relationship is. I sensed tonight that Johnson is slightly patronizing towards Erickson, regarding him as a promising architect who got stuck in modernism. In my toast I talked about Arthur's new embassy building, and Johnson replied, making some handsome comments about it. Later he told me that, on the basis of the plans he saw, it could turn out to be Arthur's finest building. He mentioned that this was the first time any embassy had given a dinner for him and how honoured he was. Pulling my leg?

During the course of the dinner, I praised I.M. Pei's East Wing of the National Gallery. The true masterpiece, he said, was John Russell Pope's[1] West Wing. Unsophisticated me. I always thought it was banal and rather ugly.

September 13, 1985 A troubling day for Canada in Washington. Mike Wilson,[2] who is attending the IMF/World Bank meetings, met with Don Regan and his opposite number in Treasury, Jim Baker. We got a very unwelcome earful from Reagan's chief of staff on the timing of our free-trade initiative. In a word, it was inconvenient. The trade situation in Congress was one of pandemonium, and the behaviour of congressmen was highly unpredictable. What a response to Canada's most important economic and foreign-policy initiative this century!

We were astounded by Regan's comments, but this understates our reaction to what we heard from Baker and Darman, who was with Baker. These two favoured postponing notification of our proposal to the president until after the American Thanksgiving (until the end of November), when Congress will be close to adjourning. It seems Baker might have other

---

[1] (1874–1937) American architect best known for his design of the Jefferson Memorial (completed in 1943).

[2] (b. 1937) Minister of Finance 1984–1991; Minister of International Trade 1991–1993; Minister of Industry, Science, and Technology 1991–1993. Currently Canadian Ambassador to the United States.

legislative priorities (such as tax reform) that he doesn't want to muck up. Later in the day I heard the same thing from Yeutter.

These men are all singing from the same song sheet, and the music is bad.

September 14, 1985 Yesterday was capped by a bizarre evening at the Kennedy Center. Bud McFarlane and his wife, Jondra, invited Sondra and me to a concert featuring Liza Minnelli. I looked forward to chatting with one of the most powerful men in the nation in relaxing circumstances. Seize the occasion. The only drawback was that I'd have to listen to Liza Minnelli.

Just as the curtain was raised, Bud got a telephone call and went to take it in the anteroom of the presidential box, where we were sitting. I followed him. I found him fidgeting in the anteroom, apparently not too eager to listen to Liza Minnelli's bellowing.

I decided that now was the moment for important business. I mentioned my worries about Don Regan's stalling tactics in seeking approval of our proposal for free-trade negotiations. Bud gave me a totally unexpected blast. "You're in a mess," he said, "and it's your fault for going to Regan. Regan doesn't know what a coalition is. You blew it. I told you to work with me and we'd get it through. But you went to Regan. You can see what you got. I can't help you. It's too late now."

I tried to placate him. I told him I had not deliberately tried to bypass him. The meeting with Regan was haphazard, since Wilson was in town and wanted to renew the contact. McFarlane backed off a bit. He would try to put humpty dumpty back together again, he muttered. But he was clearly trying to teach me a lesson. Deal with him or Regan but not both. And if I wanted results, deal with him.

I was thoroughly shaken. At intermission we all remained in the box, drinking New York State champagne from plastic goblets. Then we returned to our seats for round two, listened to the shrieks emerging from the stage, said our goodbyes, and escaped into the crowds. I did not raise the subject again.

Afterwards, I realized that McFarlane was right about our discussion with Regan. It's all about panic on the Hill. The congressmen are back from their summer visits to their home constituencies, where they found that the mood is rotten on the trade front. The populace want to zap the foreigners. They want the old playing field levelled. Regan reflected this new wisdom, priority, hysteria – call it what you will. He has no sense of design, strategy, history, or destiny. A small man in a big job. Woe to the administration.

September 18, 1985 Got a letter from Jim Schlesinger informing me of a report of the Atlantic Council of the United States saying that I have more clout than any other envoy in town. "It may well be that the Congress is hearing the Canadian view of many matters more clearly than the opinions of the Executive Branch." Schlesinger concludes: "Perhaps you had better not press your luck. 'Pride goeth before a fall,' as a humble American poet once put it."

September 21, 1985 A two-day visit to Washington from Premier Howard Pauley – the first of five premiers making pilgrimages to the capital of the universe, the others in the pipeline being Grant Devine,[1] Peter Lougheed (again), Bill Bennett (again), and David Peterson.[2] Beyond relief from the tedium of politics back home, I'm not sure these visits accomplish much. No value whatsoever in terms of the policies of the administration. Probably some value in building relationships on the Hill.

September 25, 1985 It's the evening of Yom Kippur day, and we gave a dinner at the Residence in honour of Ross Johnson.

I didn't know Ross before my Mulroney days, but I see him fairly regularly now because he is Brian's closest friend in the United States – or clearly seems to be. Ross is a very big man these days, a towering figure in business circles. His picture is a regular feature in business magazines as he climbs to the top of America's glorious corporate heights. Culture he ain't got, but energy, zip, shrewdness, boldness, self-confidence he possesses in abundance, along with a giant ego. He's the right man to head up the blue-ribbon committee to finance and run the Festival of Canada. He's the kind of guy who can pick up the phone and raise a few million dollars from a half-dozen Canadian moguls of industry – or so I hope.

We invited people Ross knows well, many of whom count for something around here: the Strausses, the Andreases, Vernon Jordan and his wife, Ann, the Mahoneys. It was a surprisingly good Washington turnout for a mere

---

[1] (b. 1944) PC Premier of Saskatchewan 1982–1991.

[2] (b. 1943) Premier of Ontario 1985–1990, the first Liberal premier of Ontario in forty-two years. Currently the Chancellor of the University of Toronto.

businessman, even one who happens to be running one of the world's largest corporations.

September 30, 1985 A hyperactive time. I conveyed to Dick Darman our extreme displeasure on being closed out of the information loop on all aspects of the G5 meeting in New York last Sunday at the Plaza Hotel. The government in Ottawa, supposedly so close to its soulmates in Washington, is highly embarrassed by its publicly displayed ignorance of what has been going on, not to mention its failure to be consulted. Darman said he understood our position and concerns. He gave me an insider's account of the deal struck at the Plaza and what led up to it, spending an inordinate amount of time explaining how vital it was to maintain absolute secrecy, how the U.S. cabinet was kept in the dark, how the outcome of the meeting was unknown until the very end, and how Baker went out of his way to call Wilson before he spoke to anyone in the U.S. cabinet except Shultz.

October 1, 1985 I had a tête-à-tête lunch at the Residence with the new deputy secretary of state, John Whitehead, today. My purpose was to get him engaged in Canada-U.S. issues, a task I figured shouldn't be too impractical, given that as co-chairman of Goldman Sachs he must have had plenty to do with Canada. This is a man I could like – cultivated, an art collector, direct, frank, and with that rare quality of "likeability."

I talked to him at length about his role as number two at State. I suggested to him that it was essential to convince Shultz to let him carve out a territory for himself, his own terrain on which he could stand, for the most part, on his own. "This is what Vance did for Christopher in the Carter years," I told him.

October 2, 1985 At long last I get a communication from Jake Warren about the origins of the site of our new embassy on Pennsylvania Avenue. The mystery of whose initiative it was is solved. It comes down to this: U.S. officials, in 1975, identified about six sites to External Affairs officials, and we liked two, one near the State Department, the other on Pennsylvania across from the National Gallery. Notwithstanding the serious security problems, Canadian officials, for symbolic and other reasons, came to prefer the Pennsylvania site.

As Jake put it, the question was whether the secretary of state for external affairs, the government, and most of all the prime minister would be willing to back the Pennsylvania Avenue option and stand up to possible nationalist critics that the location took us too close to the U.S. corridors of power. That green light came in due course, and the project was finally approved. It was somewhat reduced in scale and acreage from what had originally been proposed, and the idea of incorporating a park, which would have been Canada's gift for the U.S. bicentennial, had also fallen by the wayside for reasons of austerity. But enough land was left, and it was successfully purchased at a reasonable price.

October 9, 1985 I attended an address to a joint session of Congress by Lee Kuan Yew,[1] who denounced U.S. protectionism in very strong terms. It could, he said, totally undermine American strategic interests in the Far East. There was lots of clapping and cheering by the congressmen and senators, which was inexplicable behaviour on their part. I guess they get infected by the atmosphere that always prevails at these events – part football game, part political rally, part celebration in Rome when the barbarians come to pay obeisance at the Forum.

We then attended a dinner hosted by Vernon Jordan at the Ritz-Carlton in honour of Lena Horne.[2] It was probably the only evening we have spent in Washington where many blacks were in evidence – about one-fifth of the hundred or so guests. Other than Vernon and Ann, the only blacks we normally see in Washington are Bill Coleman,[3] Lasalle de Lefalle, Colin Powell,[4] Congressman Rangel,[5] and occasionally their wives. Blacks don't get invited to the power parties in Washington. It is a tale of two cities.

October 11, 1985 A memorable night in Washington. We attended Joe Alsop's seventy-fifth birthday party, given by Kay Graham at her home. It was a roster of Washington power, a mixture of office-holders, Georgetown elite, and the upper media (to borrow Sondra's phrase). Joe sat impassively through the long and tedious toasts, his head bowed and held between two

---

[1] (b. 1923) First Prime Minister of the Republic of Singapore 1959–1990.

[2] (b. 1917) American popular singer and Grammy Award winner.

[3] (b. 1920) Public servant, civil rights and corporate lawyer. Secretary of Transportation 1975–1977, the second African American to serve in the U.S. cabinet.

[4] (b. 1937) A professional soldier for thirty-five years. National Security Advisor 1987–1989; Chairman of the Joint Chiefs of Staff 1989–1993; Secretary of State 2001–2005.

[5] (b. 1930) Democratic Representative from New York 1971 to present.

clasping hands, elbows on the table. The best toast was given by Marietta Tree, who reminisced about growing up with Joe when her father, Endicott Peabody,[1] was headmaster of Groton. Joe was greatly under the influence, as is his wont. He did not reply to the toasts, which disappointed me, because he never fails to astonish, outrage, shock, and amuse when he talks, no matter how drunk he is. He says toasts are not appropriate in private residences. There is no one like Joe Alsop in Washington, with his extraordinary retentive memory, his pedantic manners, his peculiar accent, his snobbishness and affectations, his exuberance, his mercurial behaviour. I hope he lives forever.

October 12, 1985 Joe Rauh, Mr. Smear, is celebrated by Mr. Fotheringham. "Rauh," writes Fotheringham, "who has practised law in Washington for fifty years and knows where all the bodies are buried, notes that Canadian Ambassador Allan Gotlieb has hosted former CIA Director Richard Helms,[2] the man who had all the files on Dr. Cameron and his experiments destroyed." Fotheringham doesn't mention that when I "hosted" Helms, it was at a huge farewell dinner we gave for the Deavers, and Helms was on their list. Nor that Helms is a favourite of Kay Graham, Polly Fritchey, and others of the Washington left. Nor that Helms denies having had anything to do with the Cameron brainwashing experiment.

October 13, 1985 This week the *Wall Street Journal* published on page 1 the results of a poll that vindicates everything I have been saying about the need for a calculated and well-financed plan to disseminate the facts about Canada. Results of the poll: country with which the United States conducts the most trade? Answer: Japan – 62 per cent; Canada – 15 per cent. (Canada-U.S. trade last year – $113 billion; Japan-U.S. trade last year – $84 million.)

October 15, 1985 Lunch at the Residence with Max Friedersdorf, special assistant to the president. Since Baker, Meese, Deaver, and Darman left the White House, it's difficult for me to know how best to plug into the domestic side of that institution (no problem on the foreign-affairs side – McFarlane, Poindexter, and Ty Cobb are all very accessible). Don Regan is

---

[1] (1920–1997) Governor of Massachusetts 1963–1965.

[2] (1913–2002) Director of the CIA 1966–1973; U.S. Ambassador to Iran 1973–1976. In 1977 he was fined and given a two-year prison sentence for lying to Congress over CIA undercover activities.

friendly but not that easy to see, understandably. Jack Svahn, the domestic policy adviser, is easy enough to see but difficult to deal with. Now Friedersdorf is on the way out, but I asked him to lunch anyway. I tried to arouse as much interest as possible in our free-trade proposal. There must be some others on the domestic side of the White House whom I could work with, but I'm not sure where to turn. Mike Deaver has not been helpful in suggesting names. Maybe he's being realistic and doesn't want me to waste my time.

The Phillipses gave a book party for Sondra tonight at their mansion on O Street. *Wife Of*, a collection of her *Washington Post* columns, looks marvellous in its bright pink covers. A big crowd, about 150, with a heavy media turnout. Lots of Washington friends: the de Margeries, Duemlings, Mac Baldridge, Abigail McCarthy, Pat Schroeder, Evangeline Bruce, and Charles Fried.[1] There have been many newspaper articles about the book. Betty Beale:[2] "No ambassador's wife in memory has dared to poke fun at the city in which her husband is accredited." She adds, "That Mrs. Gotlieb does it without offending the sensibilities of the natives is a tribute to her talent, and the admitted reality of a political society when the position occupied cuts the ice, never the person in it." Precisely.

October 22, 1985 David Peterson is in town, and we are giving him the royal treatment. It's a pleasure to do so. Cocktail party tonight, lunch today, dinner last night, lunch yesterday. Alert, courteous, keen, always smiling, and sharply interested in anything to do with the United States and what's happening in Washington, he reminds me in some ways – surprisingly – of Mulroney, a less vulnerable Mulroney. Beneath all Peterson's smoothness, with-it-ness, glitz, and niceness, there is one tough, hard-nosed guy. Last night we got a stellar group to the Residence for dinner: Senators Chafee, Lugar, and Durenberger,[3] Bob Strauss, Lee Thomas, Lloyd Cutler, Tom Braden, Jack Valenti, and Lesley Stahl,[4] plus spouses. Peterson and his

---

[1] (b. 1935) Professor at Harvard Law School since 1961; U.S. Solicitor General 1984–1989; Associate Justice of the Supreme Judicial Court of Massachusetts 1995–1999.

[2] (1912–2006) Syndicated society gossip columnist with the *Washington Star* (defunct in 1981).

[3] David Durenberger (b. 1934) Republican Senator from Minnesota 1978–1995.

[4] (b. 1941) American television journalist. White House correspondent during the presidencies of Jimmy Carter, Ronald Reagan, and George H.W. Bush. Moderator of *Face the Nation* 1983–1991 and correspondent for *60 Minutes* 1991 to present.

equally appealing wife, Shelley, oozed charm from every pore. Sondra sat Pamela Harriman next to the premier. "*La Grande Horizontale*" seemed almost to fall in love with him, calling him a "young Kennedy." I heard the murmur of "Kennedyesque" among other guests at dinner.

October 23, 1985 I took Peterson on calls to Senators Bentsen, Baucus, and Durenberger, among others. He demonstrated on each occasion that he is a master at making a good impression. The meeting with Durenberger was especially interesting. The senator has been siding with the lumber crowd in their dispute against us, because he has been so fed up with the lack of progress in his dispute with Ontario over hunting and fishing licences. It's a nickel-and-dime dispute. But the tourist industry is depressed on both sides of the border, and in Minnesota, at least, the industry has clout. During the discussion, Peterson appeared to be reason personified and said sympathetically that he would personally review the situation. Durenberger was pleased that he was at least listened to, so I think we put a bit of capital into the bank. As for Baucus, he's got lumber on the brain. Bentsen, true to form, was courtly in manner, protectionist in attitude.

I was furious when the wire services reported a comment by Peterson about his unhappiness with the quality of information Ontario was getting from the Canadian embassy and that this was not surprising because we owed our loyalty to the federal government. (He never stops babbling to the Queen's Park media midgets.) I told Peterson in the plainest terms that I was flabbergasted by his remarks. He said he wasn't talking about me – I was doing a wonderful job, blah, blah, blah. It seems he was talking about another Allan Gotlieb.

October 24, 1985 I met the prime minister in New York and briefed him for his meeting with the other five heads of state participating in the economic summit (Mitterrand declined to attend) and for his bilateral meeting with Reagan tonight. Mulroney insisted I accompany him to the G6 meeting at the U.S. mission, which was restricted to heads and their foreign ministers. All the leaders had their foreign ministers with them, except Mulroney. I was embarrassed as I came in sports clothes, not expecting to attend the meetings.

The summit get-together was suggested by Reagan so he could hear the views of other leaders on his upcoming encounter with Gorbachev. Mulroney's comments were well prepared, but he went into a major digression, describing at length how he and Margaret Thatcher had told Mugabe[1] at the Nassau Commonwealth Summit that he was wrong to accuse the United States of imperialist behaviour. Reagan was beaming. Thatcher and Kohl sounded like Thatcher and Kohl. The surprise was Reagan, who read a prepared speech he said he'd written with his own hand. There were touches of the old hard line and evil empire, but he went on at length about how, in matters related to human rights, you had to avoid trying to embarrass or corner the Soviets through public condemnation or criticisms. Trudeau would have loved it. He sounded like Nixon. An impressive performance.

The bilateral meeting turned out to be a non-event – a fifteen-minute interlude before dinner. They talked a little trade, a little acid rain, and little else of consequence.

October 25, 1985 I met Drew Lewis and Bill Davis at the River Club in New York for breakfast. Lewis is convinced that acid rain is harmful and something must be done. That's good news. He wants a big, expensive technology commercialization program. The key question will be whether Reagan's people will swallow this. But I don't think anyone can turn Lewis off. He comes across as strong-minded and decisive. And a pain in the ass to the administration.

October 30, 1985 Washington is a long, colourful parade, and we are getting good seats to watch some of the marchers. Stay in Washington and see the world. I went to a lunch the other day for Adnan Khashoggi[2] given by Steve Martindale at the Four Seasons, and a dinner for anthropologist Richard Leakey[3] and his wife given by Nancy Reynolds in her log-cabin home in Arlington. Kay Graham and Marty Peretz[4] gave a book party for Washington's new star columnist, Charles Krauthammer,[5] and we also

---

[1] Robert Mugabe (b. 1924) Prime Minister of Zimbabwe 1980–1987; President of Zimbabwe 1987 to present.

[2] (b. 1935) Saudi international businessman most active in the 1960s and 1970s.

[3] (b. 1944) Paleontologist, archaeologist, and conservationist who discovered early hominid fossils in East Africa.

[4] Editor-in-Chief of the *New Republic* 1974 to present, and a part-time lecturer at Harvard.

[5] (b. 1950) Canadian-born syndicated columnist for the *Washington Post* and *Time* magazine, as well as other publications.

attended a celebration of the tenth anniversary of the *MacNeil-Lehrer Report*. Octogenarian Canadian journalist Bruce Hutchison[1] interviewed me in my office about Washington. I felt I should have been interviewing him. I attended cocktails for the new State Department legal adviser, Abe Sofaer,[2] and his wife, Marion, and also a dinner given by Sondra's gynecologist for four NIH doctors and their wives. Possibly the most valuable dinner I've attended in Washington, in terms of information obtained. All the doctors take Aspirin to reduce the chances of a heart attack.

November 1, 1985 Flew to Boston today to open the new Canadian consulate. It's in a modern office building, situated over a maze of malls, with endless caverns of corridors, leading down to a sunless sea. An office sans history, sans warmth, sans distinctiveness, sans anything. I don't know how anyone will find the damn place. The ceremonies were held outdoors in brisk weather. In the midst of the standing crowd, accurately described as motley, consisting mostly of hangers-on, walkers-by, schnorrers, curiosity seekers, and friends of Canada, there was the erect, towering figure of Kenneth Galbraith. He and his wife stood through the entire ceremony and came to the reception afterwards, a remarkable thing to do at his age. I invited him to the ceremonial groundbreaking of the new embassy in Washington in March. Galbraith told me he was asking the Harvard Coop to stock Sondra's new book.

Got back in time to attend the opening of the exhibition of the Treasure Houses of Britain at the National Gallery and a dinner at Evangeline Bruce's in honour of some of the noble British lenders. It was a sumptuous reception at the National Gallery, snobs meeting snobs from both sides of the Atlantic. The British contingent was so large that it filled a specially chartered 747. At Evangeline's I was seated next to the Duchess of Devonshire (Debo of Mitford girls fame), and we talked of the splendours of American cities. She was ecstatic about Trammell Crow's[3] colossal Infomart in Dallas, modelled after the Crystal Palace in London, an enthusiasm I share. I showed off by displaying my knowledge of how Crow came to construct it.

[1] (1901–1992) Canadian journalist and political commentator, and the author of seventeen books. Editor of the *Victoria Times* 1950–1963; Editorial Director of the *Vancouver Sun* 1963–1979.

[2] (b. 1938) U.S. District Judge in the Southern District of New York 1979–1985; Legal Advisor to the Department of State 1985–1990.

[3] (b. 1914) American real estate magnate from Dallas.

November 4, 1985 I'm in shock. My letter to Sinc Stevens on our publishing policy is plastered across the top of the front page of the *Globe and Mail*. It leaked, big time. "Taking a line that is sure to inflame Canadian cultural nationalists," the *Globe* states, "Canada's Ambassador to Washington has advised the federal government that it should reconsider its policy of increasing Canadian ownership in domestic book publishing." Nobody in Canada plays more dirty than our virtuous Canadian nationalists. Now I am their enemy.

Later in the day I accompanied Ed Meese and his wife, Ursula, on their trip to Ottawa, flying in a small FBI aircraft. The purpose of the visit is to conduct talks with John Crosbie. Working arrangements among law enforcement people on both sides of the border are outstanding, and we have few problems requiring high-level attention, but I've pressed Meese for an early trip to Ottawa, principally for symbolic reasons. Tomorrow Meese will be in the hands of the police most of the day. Meese loves cops. He can't see enough of them. Every time there is an RCMP reception or event at the embassy, he is sure to be there.

November 5, 1985 The book publishing story unfolds, and predictably, it's a textbook case of media fever. The *Globe and Mail*'s headline today: "Gotlieb's Letter on Publishing Policy Irks Nationalists." "I'm wondering if our ambassador remembers which country he's supposed to be working for." – Mel Hurtig.[1]

I get hit in the House of Commons, and who should lead the attack but my old friend John Turner. He turns the stiletto. "I think our ambassador to the United States, within the terms of the letter, was not only reflecting the reactions that he met in the United States but was also advocating a dilution of our cultural nationalism." Clark purports to defend me. He starts with a weak defence and then moves to a non-defence.

November 11, 1985 The Gotliebs are in the eye of the storm. Both of us are awash in publicity – mine bad, Sondra's mixed. The nationalist yahoos are screaming at me for my infamous letter to Stevens. The head of the Canadian Conference on the Arts wants artists to conduct a write-in campaign calling for my resignation. The Writers' Union is preparing a

[1] (b. 1932) Canadian author and politician, and publisher of the *Canadian Encyclopedia* in 1985. Founding Chairman of the Council of Canadians.

resolution asking for my recall. I've given these people a sense of purpose. Sondra's book has been receiving massive coverage in Canada and has been profiled in most of the dailies with large photos and the like. Most of the stories have been inclined towards the positive, but there is an edge, sometimes a wicked edge. Carole Corbeil[1] in the *Globe and Mail*, downright nasty in a satirical knock-off of a Sondra column, bites me with her nationalist venom.

November 13, 1985 Flora, now in charge of Employment and Immigration, arrived yesterday and we made several calls today. Not an easy visit, at least for me, and probably not for her.

I'm determined that there be no evidence of grudges and that everything be done correctly and be seen to be done correctly during her visit. I correctly went to the airport to greet her, correctly rode in with her and briefed her, and correctly gave her a dinner party for a couple of dozen guests. It was an excellent list that, hubris notwithstanding, no minister of employment of any country could bring out in this town on his or her own. My toast was generous, and I got it out without having to bite off part of my tongue. Sondra was a model of courtesy, although she will never forgive Flora for knifing me in the back.

I explained to Flora that Senator Alan Simpson is the nearest thing in the United States to a minister of immigration. We visited him on the Hill, and they hit it off like a ton of bricks falling on top of them. Unfortunately, they got on almost at once to the "sanctuary" phenomenon, whereby certain churches in the United States give illegal asylum to refugees or alleged refugees from El Salvador. Simpson thought the flouting of U.S. law abominable. Flora gave Simpson a lecture on U.S. policy towards El Salvador and Central America and intimated that if she had her way, she'd be giving these Salvadoreans sanctuary as well.

All this wouldn't have mattered very much if the purpose of our call had not been to further our efforts to persuade Simpson to find a way to stop the INS from imposing new barriers on our temporary workers. (Everyone from western harvesters to baseball umpires, judges at county fairs, musicians, bus drivers, and so on.)

---

[1] (1952–2000) Canadian novelist and arts and theatre columnist for the *Globe and Mail* and the *Toronto Star*.

November 15, 1985 At breakfast with Bob Strauss, we discussed the unfolding drama affecting Gulf and Western in Canada. Strauss believes that the publication of my letter in the *Globe and Mail* and the torrent of rage it's producing has cooked the GW goose. The Gulf people thought my criticism of the government's handling of the issue could be helpful to them, but Strauss disagreed. Reluctantly, I had to admit he was correct. What the leak has done is inflame the nationalists, brand me as a vendu, and further politicize the issue.

Don Mazankowski[1] is in town to speak at a luncheon at the National Aviation Club. He argued for our proposal to deregulate North American transborder air traffic and allow cabotage between cities in our respective domestic markets. It's amusing to see the Americans, the grand deregulators, squirm. When the competition is not obviously to their advantage, the ideology of the market becomes less persuasive.

We attended a dinner in honour of Peter Pocklington[2] given by Admiral Elmo Zumwalt,[3] a strange and unforgettable evening. Much flag-waving and patriotic demonstrations throughout the event. At the table we were all asked, one by one, to say something about ourselves and our aspirations. Each of Elmo's children and their spouses gave thanks to the admiral, each expanding on the meaning of what the other children had to say. They spoke emotionally and with patriotic fervour. There was something eerie about all the father-worshipping. Zumwalt, an attentive host, spoke about his tragically ill son and his fight for survival. That he was poisoned in Vietnam by Agent Orange and that the father played so prominent a role there made the evening dramatic for ourselves and the other guests, including Admiral Crowe,[4] new chairman of the Joint Chiefs of Staff.

No such event could ever occur north of the border. Absolutely inconceivable. Who says Americans and Canadians are the same?

---

[1] (b. 1935) Minister of Transport 1984–1986; Deputy Prime Minister of Canada 1986–1993; President of the Privy Council 1986–1991; President of the Treasury Board 1987–1988; Minister of Agriculture 1988–1991; Minister of Finance 1991–1993.

[2] (b. 1943) Canadian business owner who made his fortune in the meat-packing industry. Best known as the owner of the Edmonton Oilers and, as such, brought Wayne Gretzky to the team. They won five Stanley Cups from 1984 to 1990.

[3] (1920–2000) American naval leader. In 1968 he became Commander of Naval Forces in Vietnam and Chief of the Naval Advisory Group, U.S. Military Assistance Command, in Vietnam. U.S. Chief of Naval Operations 1970–1974.

[4] William James Crowe Jr. (b. 1925) Chairman of the Joint Chiefs of Staff 1985–1989.

November 18, 1985 Gave a speech in Oklahoma to the Economics Club. It was unmemorable in every respect: the trip, the city, the audience, the food, the speech.

November 19, 1985 We gave a dinner party for "Miss Manners" (a.k.a. Judith Martin).[1] It was intended to be a very small affair, but a couple of weeks ago, Sondra got a call from the guest of honour asking if we would mind if ABC televised the party and if we could make it black tie. It seems that Barbara Walters's *20/20* is doing a segment on Miss Manners and liked the idea of photographing her at an embassy party.

Sondra had a wicked idea. She decided to serve as a first course a type of pasta, each strip of which was about a yard long. We would not tell Judith but allow the TV cameras to observe how she would handle the challenge. The truth is Miss Manners did not handle it too skilfully – not nearly as well as Evangeline, who, after thrusting her fork into the pasta, held it as high as her long arms could reach and then popped it elegantly into her mouth. Everyone except Miss Manners was in on the secret, including the cameraman, but the lady took it with good grace. It was a high-spirited affair. We'll see what *20/20* does with it.

November 20, 1985 I continued calls on a slew of curators and museum directors to try to interest them in participating in our 1988 Festival of Canada. Today I saw the director of the Hirshhorn and the senior curator of the National Gallery, Sidney Freedberg. Freedberg and Carter Brown are both interested in an exhibition of masterpieces from the collection of the National Gallery in Ottawa, to celebrate the arrival of their Canadian neighbour on Pennsylvania Avenue – a marvellous idea that I am promoting furiously. I will also be seeing the director of the new National Building Museum to propose that he stage an exhibit to celebrate Erickson and Canadian architecture. Add to the list Laughlin Phillips of the Phillips Collection and the directors of the Corcoran and of the new Women's Museum and something might come out of all this, especially if we can produce some money.

November 25, 1985 Breakfast with Clayton Yeutter to discuss pharmaceuticals, book publishing, and "cultural sovereignty." So far as

[1] (b. 1938) American journalist, novelist, and etiquette authority. Since 1978 she has written an advice column carried in more than two hundred newspapers.

pharmaceuticals are concerned, the problem, as perceived here, is the lack of toughness in the Mulroney government. As for cultural sovereignty, no one here understands what that means, and insofar as they do, they regard it as a bogus concept, a protectionist cover, a transparent attempt to deny them access to markets in an area of their comparative advantage.

I tried to cover some new territory with Clayton. Mulroney, I explained, has all the right instincts, as does Clark. But the Conservatives have no tradition of governing, and this means they are a divided party. There is sometimes a lack of consensus in the party on key issues (such as cultural nationalism, where it's Masse vs. Stevens), and they don't have the experience of disciplined decision-making to deal with internal conflict. Also, their lack of tradition in governing means there is often an unwillingness to refer matters to the bureaucracy for analysis and recommendation. This has the effect of prolonging policy differences. So it is not ill will, lack of guts, or incompetence that leads to delays or failure to resolve conflicts. The United States would make a great mistake, I said, if it failed to be understanding and supportive of the Mulroney government. Yeutter listened politely.

November 26, 1985 Tom and Joan Braden gave a dinner party at their home in Chevy Chase in honour of Dwayne and Inez Andreas. I think they met Dwayne – the new Armand Hammer,[1] as he is wrongly called – at our house. The Bradens rounded up a distinguished group of Washingtonians: the Strausses, Brinkleys, and Kirklands, among others. Tom exceeded himself in the bad taste he exhibited during his toast. He alluded to Andreas's problems at the time of Watergate and made several other remarks that were either insulting or designed to embarrass him. This is the Braden style and is meant to be hilarious.

November 27, 1985 I had a long talk with Whitehead, and he assured me that at the Economic Policy Committee of cabinet yesterday it was made absolutely clear that there was no link between the U.S. proposals for talks on lumber (as communicated to Senator Packwood) and the FTA negotiations. However, the question of possible congressional linkage was another matter entirely. Of course, he's right. It's congressional linkage we

---

[1] (1809–1900) American industrialist and art collector. CEO of the Occidental Petroleum Company, an oil and natural gas exploration and development company.

have to worry about. The administration can hide very nicely behind that. But the fact is, suspicion remains high that the administration made some major concessions to the softwood lobby in order to buy the support of some of the senators. This is very dangerous stuff.

At the cabinet committee meeting, Whitehead said, Baker urged that notification to Congress of our free-trade negotiation be contained in the president's State of the Union speech around January 20 and played up as a principal goal in Reagan's second term. I told Whitehead we would be happy to see the Canadian initiative as a centrepiece in the address, but I was absolutely confident that a delay until then for notifying Congress would be unacceptable to Canada. There is now a serious asymmetry between us: we are committed to the proposal and the United States is not. Political problems, serious ones, are growing in Canada because of the vacuum created by the president's failure to act. I said early notification to Congress was the only option.

November 28, 1985 I met with Simon Reisman[1] in Ottawa today. We always got along reasonably well as Ottawa mandarins, probably because I have respect for his abilities – and his temper. I briefed him on the Washington scene and how I read attitudes on the Hill towards our free-trade proposal. He'll be a strong negotiator. That's what I told Mulroney when he called to ask me about Simon when he was considering appointing him as chief negotiator. I said that while my first choice would have been Donald MacDonald, I thought Reisman would be a good appointment. But I'm not sure how current Reisman is on the American scene. When he negotiated the Auto Pact, it was in the heyday of presidential power. The Washington of today cannot be seen through the prism of the imperial presidency in the pre-Watergate era.

December 2, 1985 Met with Don Regan in the White House to discuss acid rain. Both Drew Lewis and Bill Davis have been urging me to soften him up because he will play a key role. Surprisingly, Regan proved to be open-minded and optimistic that some progress could be made. I went away feeling better than I have in a long time about the chances of achieving something. Regan is loyal to the president and wants to do what the president

---

[1] (b. 1919) Chief negotiator in the Canada-U.S. Free-Trade Agreement. Secretary of the Treasury Board 1968–1970; Deputy Minister of Finance 1970–1974.

wants. I think he believes Reagan will not want Mulroney to leave the next summit empty-handed.

December 3, 1985 This morning I called again on Sam Gibbons, Mr. All-Powerful in the kingdom of trade. The Ways and Means Committee, he told me, will not block fast-track authority to negotiate a Canada-U.S. free-trade agreement. "That is unthinkable," he said. Very significant commitment. Let's hope he sticks to his guns.

December 4, 1985 I flew to Chicago this morning to meet the prime minister and his party. *Time* magazine arranged a speech by Mulroney at the University of Chicago, followed by a reception, to be followed by ample coverage by *Time*. Mulroney gave a good speech, was adept at handling the students and other questioners, displayed some nice touches of humour, and didn't put a foot wrong.

After the speech Mulroney was guest of honour at a dinner for about a dozen businessmen arranged by our consul general, where he spoke exceptionally well about his government's philosophy. The guests, including Donald Rumsfeld,[1] were impressed with his performance, as was I. If he could project on the big screen the way he does in a small room, he wouldn't be having problems at the polls.

After dinner Mulroney invited me up to his hotel suite, where Doucet, Fox, Richardson, and a couple of other personal assistants were present. He was in a relaxed mood and reminisced at length about his election victory. At a particular point, he rose and walked over to a table and picked up the telephone. He stood listening to something intensely, and after a while, I figured out what it was. He was getting a simultaneous briefing on the contents of the ten o'clock news in Canada. When the call finally ended, it was clear Mulroney did not want to engage in any substantive discussions. Previously, he was always keen to talk to me – pump me – about the American political scene and on "how we were doing," searching out every little detail. At this time, he seems deeply focused on his treatment by the Canadian media. I'm sympathetic to his concerns, because the press is being frightfully unfair to him.

---

[1] (b. 1932) Chief of Staff to President Gerald Ford 1974–1975; Secretary of Defense 1975–1977. Rumsfeld held various public posts during the 1980s, including Special Envoy to the Middle East 1983–1984 and member of the President's General Advisory Committee on Arms Control 1982–1986. Secretary of Defense 2001 to present.

December 5, 1985 The breakfast briefing with the *Tribune* editorial board went well. Mulroney gave a vintage performance. He did his McCormack routine when talking to the progeny of McCormack's old empire. He gave them the full shtick – how as a kid he sang for the old man in the backwoods of Quebec, how McCormack had given him fifty bucks and how he thereby became the first recipient of U.S. aid. Then Mulroney gave them hell for the second-rate coverage of his speech in the *Tribune* this morning. They were embarrassed, but what could they say – that his speech wasn't newsworthy? Still, he embarrassed them into agreeing they would publish excerpts in their Sunday edition. No question that in the give and take, Mulroney was in top form, and these guys left impressed by the great force of his personality.

December 8, 1985 At noon today the Residence resembled a busy French restaurant getting ready to receive the oncoming rush of fashionable eaters. And fashionable they were, all sixty-nine of them, attending our Sunday luncheon in honour of Walter and Lee Annenberg.

The Washington contingent ranged from Don Regan, Chief Justice Warren Burger, and Alan Simpson to a large chunk of the kitchen cabinet. The Hollywood contingent provided a surreal dimension, at least for me. I found it hard to get used to seeing Bob Hope under my roof.

Sondra did a lot of shifting of guests during the lunch, rotating some of the Powerful Jobs as the courses progressed. This only added to the nightmare of mixing politicians and entertainers. At Don Regan's request, she sat Meg Greenfield beside him. Soon thereafter, the subject of conversation became the departure of Bud McFarlane from the White House, the reasons for which have been a matter of frenzied Washington insider speculation. The table was rather shocked to hear Regan contribute to the rumour mill.

In the evening we dragged ourselves to the Kennedy Honors, where Bob Hope and Irene Dunne[1] were being honoured in the presence of the Reagans, most of the cabinet, a plethora of congressmen, media moguls, and top business executives from across the nation.

The evening confirmed for me the need to try to have a kind of "Canada Honours" to mark the opening of our new embassy. I have spoken to Norm Jewison about this, and he is very keen on being the executive director of such an event. It would, like the Kennedy Honors, be a mixture of film,

---

[1] (1898–1990) Film actress throughout the 1930s.

theatre, comedy, and music, all based on Canadian talent. It could be a spectacular event that would take place in the presence of the president, cabinet, and Congress and be televised live for both nations to see. Like the Kennedy Honors, it would be self-financed through the purchase of tables by corporate America and Canada. Jewison believes that if it's done right, it could make money, which could then be used to launch a Canadian film institute in Toronto.

December 9, 1985 I called on Paul Nitze this afternoon, the Grand Panjandrum of arms control and disarmament. Just a short while ago, we were guests together at a small lunch at Ronnie and Jo Carole Lauder's, but whenever I see Nitze, there is that steely glint of non-recognition. Not "Who are you?" but "It doesn't matter to me who you are." He deals with me because I am the representative of a foreign power. It is his job, as he sees it, to receive such people, but you know that it is the office he is receiving, not the person.

We discussed where the strategic arms talks are likely to go. "It depends," Nitze said, "on where the Russians want them to go." He believes they won't signal a serious interest in disarmament until they remove two roadblocks they have placed in the way of serious negotiations. One is their insistence on counting British and French missiles in the mathematics of the U.S.-U.S.S.R. balance, and two is their proposal to count "forward-based" or European-based American weapons in their calculation of strategic numbers.

On this occasion he was somewhat more informative, less flinty, and less rebarbative than usual. Anyway, Nitze was a mine of information compared to Ken Adelman, whom I chatted with a few days ago on the same subject. Ken talks, Ken philosophizes, Ken teaches like the old Jewish *melamed*, but he gives away little or nothing.

December 10, 1985 I'm in Brussels for forty-eight hours to participate in a meeting about disarmament and arms control, held in the margins of the NATO ministerial meeting. The gathering was Joe Clark's idea, so that expert officials from Ottawa and our ambassadors to NATO countries could discuss Canada's role. I've been working for Canada in and around its foreign policy for almost thirty years, and we are still searching for a Canadian role or, more accurately, the big Canadian initiative, the one that's going to win our minister, whoever he is, a Nobel Peace Prize.

The discussion today reminded me of the time I was the most junior of junior officers. In both 1957 and 1958, the Diefenbaker government canvassed each officer in External Affairs for initiatives that Canada could take at the UN or elsewhere in the international arena. The Conservatives were living in the shadow of L.B. Pearson, and now the Conservatives are living in the shadow of P.E. Trudeau. I urged Clark to concentrate on a verification role, the most valuable contribution third countries can make to the big game. I suggested we look at the possibility, along with other countries, of an independent satellite verification role, although this could conceivably make our American friends a little nervous (not to mention the Russians). Clark was keen on exploring the idea, and it was agreed we should do so.

Dinner was at the table of our new ambassador to NATO, Gordon Smith, his umpteenth job in a small number of years. A shrewd guy who has worked for some pretty dense ministers. An apparatchik *sans pareil.* Also a skilled escape artist.

December 13, 1985 The second of two large parties we are giving this month. The dinner tonight was in honour of ourselves. We decided to celebrate the completion of four years in Washington, a full posting! We tried to have the people we like best in this town. What means the most to us are the relationships that we have been able to establish with "permanent Washington," the people who remain here and yet still manage to play significantly in the power game, year in and year out. These people are the solid core of the capital. They provide the glue that holds the centre together, even though they may not exercise power in the way the word is used in most political systems. Among those I put in this group and who were with us tonight were the Brinkleys, the Strausses, the Kirklands, Joe Alsop, the Krafts, Kay Graham, and Meg Greenfield. To these we added the office-holders we like or admire, including the Volckers, the Wicks, and the Meeses. The Eagleburgers and Baldridges were out of town.

Many of the personal relationships we enjoy result from Sondra's contacts. In the case of the Kirklands, Brinkleys, Wicks, French Smiths, Deavers, Krafts, Bradens, and others, Sondra's rapport with the women was the key that unlocked the relationship. The same holds true for our relationship with Meg Greenfield. No mean achievement.

The past four years have been the most rewarding of my life. I have come into the daylight, so to speak, out of the basement or the backroom, a man who writes his own lines and not merely the lines of others.

For Sondra, it has meant recognition of her talent as a humorist. The more sophisticated understand she has perceived the absurdities in the social and political life in Washington and the effect of power on people, and this she has done with more wit than anyone in a long, long time.

December 14, 1985 *Life* magazine is still photographing our parties. Val Sears[1] of the *Toronto Star*, who is doing a feature on us, covered them as well. CTV took pictures of the guests as they arrived. It was like a circus.

December 19, 1985 Marcel Masse sends me a letter asking that I get behind the selling of his task force's newly issued report on the Canadian film industry. He writes: "Negotiations of one kind or another have been held with the American film industry since 1922 without much effect on our part, I believe, because our side has never shown sufficient solid resolve in clearly staking out our own interests." His message to me: "Get with it, man."

The reality is, proceeding with a film policy equivalent to or more radical than that adopted for book publishing would align the opposition of the foreign publishing industry with that of the film industry and make an even more disastrous brew.

December 23, 1985 We invited Joe and Polly Kraft to dinner by themselves, along with Polly's son. Joe has been very ill lately. He had a heart attack last summer and was hospitalized in New York. Then his health seemed to be restored and he seemed his old self again at our four-year-anniversary party earlier this month. But tonight at dinner it was clear that he is a very sick man. Polly convinced him to come out, just to pick him up a bit, but he was breathing heavily throughout the meal and was obviously in distress. We felt very sad. We may never see him again.

January 6, 1986 In pursuit of weight loss, we are at the Palm-Aire Spa in Pompano Beach, and we both hate it. The theory: I work off my diplomatic paunch before going back to my diplomatic pouch. The theory's not working. Everybody should know himself. I hate exercise, dieting, and not drinking. The only man in the gym with me is Claus von Bulow.[2] He introduces himself to the waitresses as Dr. Shapiro. The ruse doesn't work.

---

[1] Columnist and foreign correspondent for the *Toronto Star*.

[2] (b. 1926) British socialite accused of having attempted to murder his wife, Martha von Bulow, by an insulin overdose in 1980. A second jury found him not guilty on all charges in 1985.

January 9, 1986 A reporter working for CJOH in Ottawa says on its TV news program that I have used my official position in Washington, through the embassy's contact with Mike Deaver, to promote Sondra's book. A monster lie. I'll sue if they don't retract.

January 10, 1986 I appeared on Question Period to defend the envoys' acid rain report. I hit hard on my main point: if the president endorses the report, the United States "will have moved off the dime. No American pressure group, no American lobby, no American environmentalist group, no congressman or senator has been able to move the administration off the dime. That is a very big step."

January 11, 1986 In the debacle following the leak of my letter to Sinc Stevens on the Gulf and Western takeover, Marcel Masse has been my enemy. I have been trying to convince the PMO and PCO – Fred Doucet, Charles McMillan,[1] Paul Tellier,[2] and others – that Masse must be restrained, that his *dirigiste*, interventionist cultural policies, with their anti-foreign, anti-U.S. bias, could undermine our trade and investment policies. The result? A call from Doucet and now Mulroney himself asking me to meet with Masse. The message from the boss: you restrain him, you convince him of the error of his ways. Ottawa doesn't seem willing to fight its own fights.

My meeting with Masse in his suite at the Ritz-Carlton in Montreal lasted two hours, tête-à-tête. The first hour Masse summarized his views on Canadian culture: it must be protected and be seen to be protected as a matter of political necessity. He believes the Canadian communications industry needs to be restructured in a major way – hardware and software, films, video, books, records, everything. Not only for cultural survival but for economic prosperity. If we fail, we will end up as part of the United States. The recurring theme was that he is prepared to demonstrate the toughness necessary to achieve his objectives and that he must not be underestimated.

I told Masse, in my most diplomatic manner, that his film and other cultural policies were too ambitious and would not succeed, that he should aim

---

[1] Senior Policy Adviser to Prime Minister Brian Mulroney 1984–1987; currently Professor of International Business at the Schulich School of Business at York University.

[2] (b. 1939) Clerk of the Privy Council 1985–1992; CEO of Canadian National Railway 1992–2002 and of Bombardier 2002–2004.

for less and thereby accomplish more, that it was politically better to succeed in a minor task than to fail in a big one, that he simply could not succeed in restructuring so large a part of the Canadian industry as the culture and communications sector, that it was a political error to try to rely on ownership as the instrument of cultural enhancement, and that his objectives and those of the government in trade, investment, and refurbishing relations with the United States were incompatible.

Masse heard me, but it was obvious he did not agree. No real dialogue – two monologues, ships passing in the night.

January 12, 1986 A Sunday in Washington but not a quiet one. I spent most of the day answering a request by the prime minister for a full report of my conversation with Masse by tomorrow. This I did, in a seven-page memorandum that left little to his imagination. In essence, I said, "*dirigisme*" is the name of his game, disguising itself as "sovereignty." A fine program for Conservatives.

I added a very private piece of advice to Mulroney: Masse cannot be held back. He is not a team player, does not believe in cabinet solidarity, and has only one purpose in mind: to be seen as a big player and get a bigger job. As he said, "People think I have a junior portfolio. They should just wait and see. They will know I am someone to be reckoned with. They will take me seriously."

My advice to Mulroney was, if Masse is politically important to you, give him a bigger job, but in a less sensitive portfolio.

January 14, 1986 The memorial service for Joe Kraft took place at the Naval Chapel in Washington. There was nothing at all Jewish about it, just like there was nothing Jewish about Joe, only his personality, his taste, his looks, his manner of thought, his mind. Polly asked me to be an usher. Kay Graham gave a eulogy. I helped her with it, but it was an undistinguished performance.

After the event Kay held a reception or, more accurately, a cocktail party. The mighty mingled and joked, and everyone went on their way, back to the old cycle of gossip and more gossip, the trading of information, true and false. The friends were there, the family was there, the hypocrites were there, Joe's enemies were there, and we were there, feeling very sad and knowing no one will replace him as a companion, as a friend, and not least of all, a source.

January 16, 1986 An important day for me, one that I have waited for, for a very long time. We held a ceremony on the occasion of my signing the construction contract for the building of the new chancery on Pennsylvania Avenue. Victory, solid victory. I can't believe the day has come. After years of debate, political rancour, the vilification of Trudeau and Erickson, the change of government, the delaying tactics of Joe Clark, the pettiest politics imaginable, the scorn of bureaucrats, and their sometimes outright attempts at subversion, we are going ahead. I feel sad about only one thing: I probably won't be here when it is completed.

When my day is done in Washington, my contribution to the survival of the embassy project may be my most significant achievement. Tens of millions will march and drive past this building over the generations. They will see it as a permanent monument to Canada, a symbol of our nationhood, our neighbourly status, and our excellence. We owe this achievement to Jake Warren and the bureaucrats who went to bat to acquire the site. We owe it to Trudeau's arbitrary but justified handling of the architectural commission. We owe it to some U.S. senators who have been consistently supportive, such as Baker and Moynihan. We owe it to Mulroney's appreciation of the embassy's importance and his willingness to disregard the advice of Joe Clark and the manoeuvring of his backroom brokers. And we owe just a little bit, I think, to my role in helping to persuade Mulroney to give it the green light. And, of course, we owe it to Arthur Erickson.

January 20, 1986 In Ottawa to attend a meeting in Fred Doucet's office in the PMO to prepare for the Mulroney-Reagan summit on March 18 and 19 in Washington. It's to be a full-scale state visit, the first since 1977 for a Canadian prime minister. The meeting proved unsatisfactory. We spent a lot of time on formalities and none on substance.

There is a consensus that we wish to mark the Mulroney-Reagan relationship as special. I outlined three possibilities: (1) hold part of the visit at Camp David, which would be unique or almost so; (2) have Reagan attend the embassy during the return hospitality on the second night (this too would be unique or almost so); and (3) have Reagan and Mulroney officiate at a groundbreaking for the new embassy. There is some (limited) enthusiasm for one, not too much for two or three.

Fred was in and out of the room, until he left definitively. It's always urgent, there are always excuses, politely expressed, there is always an atmosphere of crisis. There is, on all occasions I am privileged to observe, a continuing condition of disorganization in the affairs of a PMO. This doesn't bode well for the summit.

January 21, 1986 Now it's the pharmaceutical people who are hounding me. Pfizer and Squibb, along with their Uncle Sam, are getting exercised about the failure of the Mulroney government to follow through with its promised changes to Canadian patent law. Mulroney and his ministers know well that the Canadian patent protection rules, introduced by the Trudeau government after its election in the late 1960s, are worthy of a Third World government – or perhaps not worthy of a Third World government. Of course, some Canadian drug manufacturers got very rich thanks to our legislation. Reform of our law has now been promised many times, almost from the inception of this government. If it doesn't deliver, its credibility will be strained in the United States. Every time the Mulroney government agrees to move on this issue, it seems to back off, always explaining itself with references to "timing."

January 27, 1986 In Toronto to meet with Ross Johnson to discuss the Festival of Canada idea. At the meeting, the first where we really have got our teeth into it, Mila showed up to signify the PM's interest. As I had proposed, there will be three dimensions to the initiative. The first is a kick-off event at the Kennedy Center in the spring of 1988, during the PM's visit, which would celebrate Canada's talent on the screen and stage. The second is to mark the opening of the new embassy by sponsoring, under Erickson's direction, an art and design competition for its interior, while at the same time establishing a continuing Canadian connection – probably through its use by the private sector – with our Dupont chancery, our first embassy anywhere. The third is the sponsorship of Canadian cultural events in the United States that year, in New York and Washington, involving the theatre, ballet, and visual arts.

Ross has unbelievable energy and throws out an idea a minute but unfortunately shows no interest in the third initiative. He doesn't see the payoff. Culture is not his shtick.

January 28, 1986 Called on two of the most impressive denizens of the Hill, Republican Senate Whip Alan Simpson and second-ranking House

Democrat Tom Foley,[1] to make a pitch for our free-trade initiative. Simpson was sympathetic but remote. Not much trade with Wyoming?

Simpson was much more anxious to talk to me about blue-tongue disease, whatever that is. I wasn't sure he knew either. "Ambassador," he said, "blue-tongue is an important issue. It is a matter of great concern in my state. We have to address it." He was immensely gratified by my assurances of our purity and our cattle's purity.

Immigration remains his biggest concern, and I spent some time picking up the pieces in the wake of Flora's call. Simpson and his wife have become regulars at our embassy dinners.

Foley was supportive of our initiative, being a real free-trader. He'll be a key player, and when the game gets tough, he'll be on our side.

January 30, 1986 The Stratford Theatre performed *King Lear* at Washington's National Theatre, its first appearance in Washington in my period, so we threw a dinner party after the event, at the National Press Club. We had over a half-dozen senators and congressmen, led by Pat Moynihan in tremendous form, leaping up and down, proposing toasts, and grabbing people as they walked by his table. Evangeline Bruce, while trying to escape early from the play, fainted in the hall. A successful evening.

January 31, 1986 I flew to Houston on a special flight for diplomats to attend the funeral ceremony for the astronauts who died in the crash of the *Challenger*. The president was in attendance and gave the funeral oration. In times of achievement and success (Grenada, for example), his popularity goes up, and in times of failure, national disaster, and distress (the Lebanese massacre, the *Challenger* accident), his popularity also goes up. He has managed to become the flag. He transcends politics, political as he is, and through his thespian qualities embodies the national mood, no matter what it is, transmitting it straight back into the hearts of Americans.

Gore Vidal[2] never spoke more accurately than when he said: "It's a great myth that Ronald Reagan was a B actor. He's an A actor who played in a lot of B films."

---

[1] (b. 1929) Representative from Washington 1965–1995; House Majority Whip 1981–1986; House Majority Leader 1986–1989; Speaker of the House of Representatives 1989–1993 and 1993–1995.

[2] (b. 1925) American writer of novels, plays, and essays.

February 3, 1986 In Palm Springs with the Annenbergs. Walter told me he admired my (all-too-well) reported stance on Gulf and Western. He added that Marvin Davis[1] also admired my "independent and courageous" stand. I underlined in the most emphatic way that what I was doing, I was doing because it was good for Canada, not Gulf and Western. (I didn't tell him I thought Gulf and Western was becoming a pain in the butt.)

February 9, 1986 It's Sunday. The PMO people are in town to prepare for the Mulroney visit, and the new Quebec premier, Robert Bourassa,[2] is in town to peddle hydroelectric energy. Bourassa believes in his product like his fellow Quebecers used to believe in God. Yesterday I gave him a very strong sell on the need for a comprehensive free-trade agreement. Bourassa seemed less well informed than I expected, given his economist credentials, and a little reticent in drawing the obvious conclusions from the deteriorating trade situation in the United States, but I think I made some headway.

I gave a lunch today at the Residence for the PMO team. Discussions were mostly on form and format. We want the PM to spend some time in Camp David during his two-day state visit. This would signal special respect for Mulroney, as would having Reagan come to the embassy for return hospitality, an idea the PMO now favours. There is no enthusiasm, however, for a ceremony at the new embassy site, such as laying a foundation stone. (No "visuals," they say.) They are also against the idea of Mulroney addressing Congress, even though Trudeau did so when he was here on a state visit.

It's agreed all around that I must apply maximum pressure on the White House to get Reagan to endorse the Lewis-Davis report. The administration remains divided; there is powerful opposition on the domestic, budgetary side.

Doucet asked me to arrange to get ten Canadian couples who are the prime minister's friends invited to the official state banquet at the White House. That, I told him, will be very difficult, probably impossible.

February 10, 1986 The PMO/External/embassy team did its rounds, seeing National Security Advisor Admiral Poindexter and others in the White House. Doucet spoke passionately and convincingly of Mulroney's

---

[1] (1925–2004) Billionaire former owner of Twentieth Century Fox, Pebble Beach, the Beverly Hills Hotel, and the Denver Broncos NFL team.

[2] (1933–1996) Liberal Premier of Quebec 1970–1976 and 1985–1994.

need for action on the acid rain report, the need for total endorsement. We pressed hard for a "privileged" meeting at Camp David, but we met a lot of reserve. No leader, they told us, has had a meeting with the president at Camp David (except Lopez Portillo of Mexico, very early in Reagan's first term, it seems). Moreover, the summit dates are on Tuesday and Wednesday, and the president only goes to Camp David on weekends. Hence, it will be difficult to arrange a meeting there. (Helicopters don't fly on Tuesdays and Wednesdays?) The White House discouraged the idea of the president attending a return dinner at the embassy. The NSC told us it's never been done by Reagan, and they were angry when I said it was done for Thatcher. Nicko Henderson brought it off with great success.

I continue to work on the request for a special Mulroney invitation list for the White House banquet, pushing hard at State, the White House, and the NSC, but – big surprise – I am having no success. It is the "invariable practice," I'm told, to limit the foreign invitations to the fourteen persons on the official visiting list. No one can believe I'm trying to get the Reagans to share the guest list with us. It's Nancy's personal prerogative, they say. They have no influence.

February 11, 1986 Major General Cheriton, our military attaché, advised me that his minister, Erik Nielson[1] ("Yukon Erik"), will be visiting Cap Weinberger in Washington February 20 to 21. Nielson wants to keep his visit "low-key, low-profile, no protocol." He will see me on the first day of his visit, in his rooms at his hotel (not the embassy) for a half-hour. The meeting with Weinberger is to be a "one-on-one." I get the message: I am not invited.

Does Nielson think the briefings are too sensitive and secret for a mere official? Or is it just the mind of the Great Paranoid at work? One can be sure Weinberger will be accompanied by note-takers and officials. Reports will be circulated immediately and widely in the administration on the content of the meeting. Equally certain, the only way the Canadians will ever learn about what Nielson agreed to (and he will agree to plenty) will be from the Americans. Old-style Tory distrust of officials.

---

[1] (b. 1924) Minister of Public Works 1979–1980; Deputy Opposition House Leader 1980–1981; Opposition House Leader 1981–1983; Appointed Deputy Leader of the Progressive Conservative Party in 1983; Deputy Prime Minister of Canada and President of the Privy Council 1984; Minister of National Defence 1985–1986.

February 12, 1986 I told Deaver about Mulroney's desire to invite friends to the White House dinner. He shuddered. "You're wasting your time," he said. "Nancy controls the list and won't let go of it for a second. You'll get nowhere." These words from as close to the horse's mouth as one can get.

February 14, 1986 Breakfast with outgoing State Department Legal Adviser Davis Robinson and lunch with Abe Sofaer, new legal adviser, to discuss Orlikow and related cases. I have been taking abuse lately from that McCarthyite of the left Joe Rauh Jr. He has been accusing me of "hobnobbing" with Dick Helms, who, according to him, is the dark force behind the whole experiment.

The virtuous June Callwood[1] has been repeating Rauh's attacks on me in her newspaper columns in Toronto. Of course, she has never phoned me to ask for the facts. Helms was at the Residence only once, at a going-away party last year for Mike Deaver – and at Deaver's request. Helms says he had nothing to do with brainwashing.

We have known for some time – since Rick Burt alerted me to it – that Canadian government funding was a major factor in the financing of Cameron's brainwashing experiments at the Allan Memorial. Sofaer told me that he had studied these files back to the 1950s at Shultz's request. I was shocked by what the eminent former judge had to say. He claims that the cases were without merit. There was no way anyone could establish cause and effect between the condition and the treatment. Moreover, Mrs. Orlikow was out of the program before the CIA funding even started.

We then discussed Sofaer's idea that, notwithstanding the lack of merit from the legal standpoint (in his view), Canada could offer an *ex gratia* payment in order to settle this longstanding matter and invite the United States to do the same. Perhaps a joint panel could be established to award funds in cases where a causal link could be found. Sofaer said the idea was a personal one and he didn't think it was so great, but if Canada, as "the prime responsible country," took the lead, the United States would have to consider doing likewise.

I think Sofaer's idea is a non-starter, but at least he is showing some ingenuity. But Ottawa is silent, and I don't know what to make of U.S. allegations that our hands are dirtier than theirs.

---

[1] (b. 1923) Canadian journalist, author, broadcaster, and social and anti-poverty activist.

February 17, 1986 The mood in the NSC regarding the prime minister's visit is not good. Cabinet secretaries and senior administration officials are unhappy about Canada for different reasons. Some influential advisers want to link U.S. discussions on acid rain with our defence spending (or lack of it). Their refrain goes: "They want us to spend money on acid rain; let's have something in return." I've been telling Ottawa that any backing off of our defence commitments in the next budget carries dangers on the acid rain front, as it plays directly into the hands of our opponents in the administration and on the Hill. Moreover, cutting back on defence spending is the one action that could influence the president negatively. It would hit ideological raw nerves.

February 19, 1986 More aggravation each day as the summit nears. I'm not getting too far in a number of our requests, but I've just received the splendid news that the president is inviting Mulroney to visit with him (and Mila with Nancy) on the Sunday before the summit. The suggestion is that they have a working session at Camp David with a few officials and travel by helicopter together back to Washington on Monday. The rest of the day would be private, and on Tuesday, March 18, there would be a meeting in the Oval Office, a large luncheon at State hosted by Shultz, the official White House dinner Tuesday night, followed by return hospitality by Canada on Wednesday night. The White House also suggests that the PM might want to attend a congressional farewell dinner for Tip O'Neill on Monday night, which will be attended by Irish prime minister Garret Fitzgerald,[1] here on a private visit, and probably by the president.

I relayed the great news to the PMO. They will be ecstatic. Talk about marks of favour.

February 23, 1986 How wrong can I get? The idea of a Sunday visit to Camp David is not agreeable to the prime minister. The PMO told me to explain to the White House that Sunday is the last day, the windup, for the Conservative Party Convention in Montreal, the first in two years and a day of extreme importance. It would be impossible for the PM to absent himself. I took a dark view of this news and told them the White House will be very surprised. I explained that Poindexter, Cobb, and Regan have all gone to bat

[1] (b. 1926) Prime Minister of the Republic of Ireland 1981–1982 and 1982–1987.

for this invitation, that it's a rare honour, a special mark of favour, all we ask for. But I hit a solid wall with the PMO.

My refusal of the invitation is reverberating in the White House and State. Equal dismay greeted my proposal, on instructions, to press for a Camp David meeting on Tuesday, March 18. They were incredulous in the White House. First the president offered the unique honour of a visit to his home in Santa Barbara, then a weekend visit at Camp David, and we have rejected both. Incredulity was accompanied by hostility and a fair amount of abuse. I went into flights of exaggeration, preposterous exaggeration, about how at the next election the government might fall if Mulroney isn't at the convention on Sunday. They didn't take me seriously. I'm not surprised – I myself can't figure out why Mulroney has to be in Montreal until midnight. Somebody is giving me bullshit. There has to be some other reason for his unavailability.

February 24, 1986 The PMO is unhappy about my report. Surely, I am told, I haven't emphasized enough the special political circumstances that make the Sunday visit impossible. Try harder, push more, plead more for Camp David on Tuesday. I'm becoming highly irritated, difficult to live with at home.

February 28, 1986 My birthday. Not how I like to spend it. I attended a Canada Day series of events in Atlanta. I was speaker at a huge ball – some seven hundred people. The nice hostess sitting beside me asked, "Mr. Ambassador, dare I give you a word of advice?" "Please do," I replied. "Don't be intelligent, be brief."

March 3, 1986 As the visit draws closer, my frustration level rises higher and higher. Everyone in Washington from Shultz on down is furious about our saying no to the Sunday visit to Camp David. My effort to get Mulroney's friends invited to the White House dinner was laughed out of court. But I had an ingenious idea. I suggested substituting these people for the official delegation of fourteen. Amazingly, Lucky Roosevelt, chief of protocol, and the White House staff accepted this suggestion. If that's what the prime minister wants, they say, then so be it. "But won't the official delegation mind being bumped?" they asked. Nope. There is none. Mulroney, to the surprise of the Americans, is not bringing any ministers with him, not even Joe Clark. So thanks to my inspired idea, Ross Johnson, Paul Desmarais, Moses and Jonathan Deitcher (father and son), and Robert Shea[1] from Boston, with their spouses, will all be there. Add the Mulroneys and the two Gotliebs (unless we're bumped), and that makes fourteen.

There is also a mountain of aggravation over Shultz's list for a luncheon the same day. He's having a large group, a couple of hundred, at State. After long negotiations with Lucky, I have secured twenty-four places for Mulroney's party, counting spouses. But the PMO has given me about fifty names, mostly Conservative Party stalwarts. There is much fuss and irritation about the whole process. Meanwhile, the delegation of officials was also bumped from the lunch, and neither State nor our officials are delighted.

Most challenging for me is the PMO request that as the Canadians accept the Shultz lunch, they automatically qualify for invitation to the official return dinner at the Residence on March 19. How will we be able to accommodate them all? We have never given a dinner even approaching the size they have in mind. I shared my worries with Sondra. She says we'll just have to cope.

March 6, 1986 Called on prominent Democrat Henry Waxman at his request so that he could denounce the special envoys' report. I knew he would say no to the report, because he will be introducing his own perennial bill in the House. And thus it was. I told him that we've been holding our breath for years and haven't seen an ounce of progress on his bill. The meeting was very strained. We might, I said, obtain more through "the Canadian factor" than through the efforts of all the professional environmentalists and lobbyists in Washington.

I pleaded with Jack Svahn in the White House yesterday for full presidential endorsement. He's no believer in the sins of acid rain, but he accepts that the summit will be a disaster without endorsement. The president cannot back away from Drew Lewis's recommendation.

The whole issue stinks of U.S. internal politics, but Waxman's criticism will be lapped up by the *Toronto Star* and the Canadian press, who bring little sophistication to the Washington political scene – and that's an understatement.

March 7, 1986 Joe Clark came to Washington to meet with Shultz and help plan the visit. One admires this man for his soldierly qualities. He shows

[1] Chairman and President of Shea Financial Group Inc.

the temper of the trooper. Mulroney drops him from the official delegation and he doesn't bat an eyelid – at least in public. Clark talked rather excessively and Shultz listened passively – the usual situation when the two meet.

Before the meeting I reluctantly briefed Clark about the Camp David fiasco. I had to because I thought it likely he would get a piece of Shultz's mind. Both Clark and his assistant, Jodi White,[1] were very surprised at what I told them. They said they were under the impression that the Tory convention was over on Sunday at midday. White went to make a phone call and returned with confirmation of this. I was thunderstruck. I had been deliberately misled by the PMO. I had been lied to. I was a diplomat sent abroad to lie for my country, but I didn't even know I was lying. Worse, the Americans must know I have been lying. They would undoubtedly have got a report from Tom Niles in Ottawa letting them know precisely when the convention ends. I am furious.

I asked Clark and White what might have prompted this charade. What was the point of this deception? White offered, with hesitation, an explanation. Mulroney's advisers seemed to be determined to keep him away from Washington until late Monday to avoid the Irish connection. It seems that the Mulroney-Reagan serenade at the Shamrock Summit in Quebec City last year didn't play well in Canadian public opinion. So the political imperative has become to keep him away from Washington on St. Patrick's Day. No one in the PMO squared with me about this.

That explanation seems far-fetched, but is there a better way to explain this bizarre behaviour? Any explanation is better than none.

March 8, 1986 Jodi White called someone in the PMO (Bill Fox?) to discuss whether Camp David was still possible. Her contact then raised it at a morning staff meeting. Fred Doucet exploded. He called me in a rage, accusing me of trying to reopen the matter. Should I explode or keep my temper? I kept it, with difficulty, remembering (to paraphrase Cicero) that he cannot control others who cannot control himself. I managed to explain calmly – and icily – to Fred that I had not recommended reopening the issue and had told Clark that even if we wished to do so, it was certainly too late. I spelled out that I briefed Clark because he had to know as much as Shultz did about the matter. Otherwise he might have been blindsided. Doucet

[1] Chief of Staff to the Minister of External Affairs 1984–1988; Chief of Staff to Prime Minister Kim Campbell 1993.

accepted my explanation. I am, however, annoyed and showed it. I feel my credibility has been undermined in Washington.

March 14, 1986 Planning the dinner at the Residence is driving me mad, and Sondra as well. We started with a suggested list for a dinner for about 100 to 125 guests, which is more than we have ever had at the embassy, or dreamed of having. We are now at about 220. We have spent weeks trying to find the right tent to put in our backyard. The only solution is to build a special platform over the pool and put the tent on top of the platform, at a cost of about fifteen thousand dollars. Today we received about the dozenth configuration for the tent. The PMO keeps adding names, in spite of Fred's firm promise to cut off the list. They are still flowing in like water at high tide. Until last week we were going on the basis of an absolute maximum of 160 (expanded by about one-third from the first ambitious plan). Every injection of new names means changing the size, place, and configuration of the tent. Also, the tent must be heated, but the heating can't be noisy. There is the problem of entertainment, and there is the ghastly problem of our super-list of American and Canadian notables being swamped by the party faithful. Every day, the phone rings and Fred is on the line with absolutely and positively the last name. The connection between the visit and the invitees gets more and more tenuous. We have even added all of a Canadian law firm associated with a Washington firm associated with a friend of the prime minister.

Another big issue is whether Bush will come to dinner. First his people told me no, then yes, for coffee and doughnuts, then yes, maybe for the whole meal, depending on what time he gets back from Pittsburgh (where he's giving a speech), which in turn depends on the headwinds.

The Bush people are invariably polite and helpful, and Bush is putting himself out enormously to come. I receive definitive word: no Reagans at the dinner. All in all, I don't believe I've ever been more exasperated by the trivia relating to diplomacy. The silly has become the important, and I am creating the most godawful pressures around town to get our way on a lot of minor things, not to mention the pressures I'm putting on Sondra.

March 16, 1986 Now it's the NSC that is upset about trivial points. They want the NORAD signature on summit day one and the press release on summit day two. This is impossible, because the wording of the delicate compromise Iklé and I worked out presupposes simultaneous signature and press declaration. It's hard to believe that I should be having midnight telephone calls with Iklé and Ty Cobb in the White House about this. I suffer the most abusive remarks of my career from the mouth of Ty Cobb, which I accept passively, so as not to foul up the possibility of our working out a deal with the Pentagon.

In this town patience has run out with Canadians. When they hear the latest Canadian demand or complaint, they lose it and abuse me.

March 17, 1986 Mulroney arrived in Washington in the early evening. I told him everything is in good shape for the summit, which is true enough, if all the costs are ignored.

I wondered all day if I should discuss with Mulroney his apparently dismissive handling of the vice-president's personal invitation to him and Mila last week to dine with Barbara and himself *à quatre* upon their arrival in Washington or, if he were too tired, to join them later for coffee. Both invitations were rejected. Fred asked me to say that the PM would be too fatigued and would in any event need to be briefing himself for the next day. Given that Bush is most likely to be the next president, I found the episode difficult to understand.

Was there again some explanation to be found amidst the fog of the Irish theory? I decided not to raise the issue. What was the point of raising it now? I kibitzed a few minutes with the PM at his hotel and went home to bed.

March 18, 1986 God knows what really happened in the half-hour or so tête-à-tête between Mulroney and Reagan before the main meeting. Probably nothing, but I suppose we'll never find out. At the principal meeting, with the full teams present, Mulroney was forceful, convincing, and moving as he explained what he had done to refurbish relations between our two countries and why. After an uneventful lunch at the State Department hosted by Shultz, Mulroney met with members of the Senate Foreign Relations Committee and was again in top form, fielding the questions easily and well. The senators were all extremely polite, except for the lightweight Larry Pressler of South Dakota. I'll never be able to figure out why Mulroney declined the opportunity to address Congress. I never got a good explanation, though I did get wind that the Mulroney team was worried that the seats in the chamber might not all be filled. This would have led the Canadian press to cackle about the Americans slighting Ron Reagan's best friend.

For the official dinner, we went in our limousine ensemble and were escorted to the Reagans' private quarters for an intimate cocktail. On all occasions when I meet the Reagans, I find her icy and him impersonal (although jolly and nice). I chatted with Shultz. No one, he said, can figure out why Mulroney left his cabinet ministers at home. Shultz seemed particularly amused by the fact that he didn't bring Joe Clark. I told him it was a Canadian tradition. Trudeau never brought his ministers in tow.

The dinner guest list was not appropriate for the first Canadian visit in close to a decade, but again all Nancy's choice, her exclusive choice, which meant dress designers, hairdressers, interior decorators, social figures, and actors (but no Canadian ones). The affair reflected neither the nature of the occasion nor the reasons for it.

After dinner, as we chatted and the guests danced, I looked around for the Mulroneys but couldn't find them. Yet, because I saw the president and Nancy dancing and mingling and chatting away, I assumed the Mulroneys were still there. I was wrong. In accordance with the invariable Reagan custom, the guests of honour and the Reagans leave together immediately after the conclusion of the dinner and before the dancing starts. What the protocol people didn't tell me is that the Reagans then come back to dance and socialize and have a good time.

March 19, 1986 Day two of the summit, and I suppose one of the worst day of our lives. We were both under tremendous strain all day, especially Sondra. A powerful windstorm threatened to blow our huge tent away, and there was endless uncertainty about the arrival time of the vice-president. Mulroney told me at the last moment that he did not want to be in the reception line to greet the guests (even though he and Mila were the hosts), and worst of all, there was a flood of last-minute cancellations that required massive shifting and reshifting of guests at the tables. My office did not keep Sondra well informed and up-to-date about the cancellations, even though she was doing the *place à table*, as she always does. I couldn't help – I was out of touch most of the afternoon, following Mulroney around Arlington Cemetery and attending his press conference before briefing the press myself.

Unfortunately, the seating for the dinner has been horrendous. There have been so many issues: the flood of last-minute additions from up north, the shifting requirements imposed by protocol, our practice of assigning husbands and wives to different tables, the need to avoid putting political enemies together, attempts to keep the press at bay from some of their victims, the uncertainty of knowing whether senators would be accompanied by companions, the problem of seating strangers next to each other, and of course cancellations.

Just before the Bushes arrived for dinner, Sondra slapped Connie Connors in the hall of the Residence, when Connie informed her for the first time that there were new cancellations and that tables would have to be redone. I was standing right beside Sondra when it happened. Connie ran down the front steps of the Residence and Sondra ran upstairs and I after her. In the blue bedroom, she was upset, then calmed down and ran after Connie to apologize immediately and demonstrably. They made up and the dinner went on normally, toasts were exchanged, and everyone was very convivial. No one seemed to have observed or to have been aware of the event. Connie continued her work at the party and seemed in good spirits.

Mulroney was not feeling well. He was somewhat dizzy at the reception and sweating profusely. Rather than mixing, as he did during the great dinner we gave him two years ago when he was leader of the Opposition, he asked to be taken at once into the tent after he arrived, because it was cooler and quieter. After the dinner the Mulroneys decided to linger a bit as the guests slowly filtered out, and they seemed to be relaxing with some of their old Canadian friends and supporters.

After everyone left, Sondra and I relaxed on sofas in the living room and chatted with Bruce Phillips and Connie, who lingered behind. The telephone rang around midnight. I went into the library and took the call. It was Fred Doucet. Did I know there were reports of a strange incident at the Residence during the party? What incident? I asked. A report of Sondra slapping Connie. He said Julie O'Neill of the Canadian Press had picked up the story. He asked me if there was any truth in it or did I deny it. I said I could not deny it. Doucet was upset. He told me the prime minister was upset.

March 20, 1986 I didn't sleep all night. Sondra dropped off about dawn. I got up at 6 a.m. to go to the CTV studio to appear on *Canada AM*. I did the interview and then went to the Madison, where Mulroney was staying. I asked to see him and speak to him in his room alone. He asked me whether the story was true or whether it could be denied. I said the slap was a totally unintended event, but it happened and could not be denied. I thought the story was bound to be printed soon. We discussed the possibility of my having to resign, but he wanted to see if the incident became the subject of discussion in the House of Commons. I asked him how he thought it would be played in that forum. He replied that the "character assassins" there would go after us. A few minutes later we heard that Julie O'Neill had filed a story with CP.

Later in the morning, after accompanying Mulroney to a meeting with the editorial board of the *Post*, I went home. I told Sondra the news. I also had to tell her of a change of plans. She was supposed to accompany me to the airport at midday to say farewell to the Mulroneys, but apparently, or so I was told, the PM thought it was best that she not go. On the tarmac Mulroney turned to me and said, "Allan, remember the old Indian saying John Diefenbaker used to quote: 'Big bear hunter going after moose doesn't chase rabbit tracks.'"

I thought it was very unfair not to include Sondra at the airport farewell. She was subject to such demands from me on every minute and trivial aspect of the visit, on every silly detail, especially about the seating at the dinner. These have been my obsessions. I placed her under such enormous pressures, it's no wonder that the steam erupted.

Sondra managed to attend a lunch that Buffy Cafritz was giving at her home. One of the not-so-nice guests phoned the *Post* to tell them Sondra was there. Big deal. A hand-written, hand-delivered note from Joe Alsop (who was at the dinner), says "Sondra, we all love you." I sensed that Joe, the old Washington pro, expects we are in for a rough passage. Kay Graham called, urging Sondra to make a statement and explain that she had been under great stress and pressure. I told her the Mulroney staff were insisting that we make no statement other than to repeat that Sondra had apologized to Connie and the apology had been accepted.

I learn that the *Toronto Star* has the story on page 1, and it's on CBC and other Canadian networks. Bob Strauss says keep cool, be strong. The story won't go anywhere – "it has no legs." It will flare for a while, subside, and die. Both of us are aware of the storm gathering and feel helpless.

In the evening we kept a commitment to attend a dinner at Rowly Evans's in his Georgetown home. People were sensitive and kind. We were emotionally exhausted, but the Burts insisted on coming back to the Residence for a nightcap. "You must counterattack," Rick said. "You can't let the press run over you. You must fight back. You must develop a strategy. I'll think about it for you," Burt continued, and came up with some ideas. "We'll get people to come out and support you. They can work for your survival." I don't think it will be necessary, I told him.

March 21, 1986 We are awash in bad publicity. Page 1 stories in all the newspapers and the top item on TV and radio news. Horrid front-page articles. Headlines such as "Slap Echoes Around Continent," "Slap That Reverberates in Two Capitals," "Slap Flap," "The Slapshot Summit." The *Washington Post* prominently placed a story on the top of page 1 of the Style section. Their reporter at the dinner must have been embarrassed that she missed the story and is no doubt trying to make amends. She filed a very nasty report.

Kay Graham called again and said Sondra must carry on and not run for cover. She must show strength, go everywhere, be herself. She should also find a way to say publicly that she is sorry. She heard that Sondra and I were hosting a reception for the Montreal Symphony at the Kennedy Center tonight. We must go ahead with it, she said. I told her Sondra couldn't really bring herself to go. She spoke to Sondra and urged her to, with some success.

Many other friends have called to say the same thing. It was tough, but Sondra did it.

Sondra was sleeping when I took a call from Barbara Bush. She was appalled, she said, at the *Post* story. The whole thing was blown out of proportion. The incident was human and understandable, and we should not be worried at all, we were both wonderful people. We should know that the vice-president, who was travelling, felt exactly the same way. Many letters came in today by hand that touched us deeply, but nothing touched us more than the call from Barbara Bush.

Less pleasant was a disinvitation I received today to attend Fred Doucet's wedding in Ottawa on Saturday. The wedding is to take place at 24 Sussex. Fred has urged me on a number of occasions to come. Given the continuing brouhaha in the Canadian media and the press reports alleging that Mulroney is furious, I asked Bruce Phillips to make a discreet inquiry as to whether I should still go to Ottawa for Fred's wedding. Bruce reported back that Doucet thought the decision to attend or not was entirely my own. On the other hand, said Bruce, the press people and others in the PMO thought it best if I didn't come.

Before the Montreal Symphony event, I went alone to the *New York Times* reception on the eve of the Gridiron dinner. I was in a grim state of mind, annoyed at the PMO distancing themselves from me, but many at the reception seemed to go out of their way to be helpful to us. In this category I do not put Ben Bradlee, who, leaning against a wall as I came in, beckoned to me and then uttered these immortal words: "Ambassador, keep your pecker up."

March 22, 1986 Saturday night at the Gridiron. Old warhorse Phil Geyelin[1] of the *Washington Post* was host, and he tipped off Meg that Sondra would be the butt of a couple of jokes – good-natured and harmless (of course). Geyelin was true to his word. We were the butt of his jokes.

Back in my beloved country, the yahoos are screaming for blood. More front-page stuff, gossip, ridiculous stories, inventions, fabrications, cracks, innuendos, and poisonous things about both of us.

March 23, 1986 We attended a brunch given by Carolyn Peachy for the Burts. Everyone knew each other and was especially warm, knowing what we're going through. We find it hard to go out and equally hard to stay at home. Sunday afternoons are always a time for family telephone calls. It was painful for us to talk to our aged mothers in Winnipeg. They are bewildered and appalled by the muck being hurled at us. There was even a call from Rachel in London. She saw a piece in the *International Herald Tribune* about the slap and was upset.

I appear on Canada's most popular public-affairs program: Question Period. Pamela Wallin[2] asks me about the "incident." I apologize again for Sondra and myself. The apology was repeated on the national television news.

A decent word spoken about us in Canada. John Turner on *Front Page Challenge*, pursued with leading questions by Pierre Berton, responds: "It was an unfortunate incident. She said herself she was devastated. I consider the issue closed." Will the print media report this? Not bloody likely.

March 24, 1986 At the office this morning, I received some appalling news. My executive assistant, John Siebert, informed me that at 7 a.m. the day after the Mulroney dinner, the husband of our precious Philippine housekeeper, Teodora, attacked one of our drivers with a kitchen knife. He was stopped from stabbing the driver only as a result of physical intervention by other staff members in the kitchen.

Sondra and I discovered for the first time that Teodora's husband has been threatening her recently, striking her in her apartment upstairs in the

---

[1] (1924–2004) *Washington Post* Editorial Page Editor 1967–1979.

[2] (b. 1953) Canadian television journalist. Joined CTV in 1981 and was named Ottawa Bureau Chief in 1985. She co-hosted the CBC's *Prime Time News* with Peter Mansbridge 1992–1994.

Residence, apparently out of mad jealousy over the driver. I consulted the most senior officers at the embassy, Jacques Roy,[1] Paul Heinbecker,[2] Bruce Phillips, and Lionel Lepage (who has replaced Jack Hughes as chief of administration), and we agreed – sort of – on a course of action. We will try to get Teodora's husband into the hands of a psychiatrist immediately. There is little else we can do. Her husband lives apart from her, but he has evidently been hanging around, so we will ban him from the premises immediately. We must find a way to enforce the ban. And we must hope for the best – for all of us.

Sondra spoke to the Women's Democratic Club in Washington. It was very difficult for her to keep this engagement. We've been debating for days whether she should or shouldn't. She did extremely well, according to all accounts. There was one question on the "incident." She said she was terribly sorry, devastated. I was told her statement brought lumps to people's throats.

March 25, 1986 Everyone wants to talk to Sondra, to hear from her about what happened at the embassy that night. Unfortunately, the PMO has put a lid on her. They don't want her to give her own account of events. For my part, I have been weak and wobbly. Rightly or wrongly, probably wrongly, I have supported the PMO line, or more accurately, I have not stood up to them.

Friends at the *Post* – Kay Graham and Meg Greenfield – have suggested Sondra bring her self-deprecating wit and humour to the situation and do a piece on herself and the incident. Sondra feels that if she could reveal herself a little, in a frank, disarming way, if she could put her own light on the happening, tell her own story, in the humorous style that has given her so wide a readership in this city, the result would be much better than that obtained by suppressing all comment. Reflecting the PMO's strategy, I have not encouraged her to do this.

---

[1] Canadian foreign-service officer. Minister and Deputy Head of Mission at the Canadian Embassy in Washington 1982–1986; Canadian Ambassador to Switzerland 1990–1994, to the European Union 1994–1996, and to France 1996–2000.

[2] (b. 1941) Chief foreign-policy adviser and speech writer for Prime Minister Brian Mulroney. Assistant Secretary to the Cabinet for Foreign and Defence Policy 1989–1992; Canadian Ambassador to Germany 1992–1996 and to the United Nations 2000–2004.

March 26, 1986 Michael Wilson is in town, and we called on Volcker, Baker, and the new president of the World Bank, Barber Conable. The days and nights continue to be long and difficult. The abuse continues in the Canadian press. I can't recognize myself amidst the slanders. All kinds of false things are being written – that Sondra hit Connie twice, that Connie has resigned, that I threw ashtrays at employees, that I pay slave wages. Yet, writes Dalton Camp,[1] the coverage of Gotlieb is "soft." The press is too beholden to us to be honest.

March 28, 1986 We learned that at a recent meeting of the staff of the *Post*'s Style section, the reporters were instructed to "get the Gotliebs." Never mind our close relationship with Kay, Meg, and Ben. The *New York Times*, in its "News Quiz," republishes the photo of Sondra and Connie standing together and smiling. When will all this stop? Bob Strauss thought the story would not last because it had "no legs." It's walking nimbly without them.

March 30, 1986 CJOH apologized to me for its fabrication that I used Mike Deaver and the embassy funds to promote Sondra's book. They wrote me a mincy letter of apology. Some consolation.

The press continues to quote "PMO sources" in reporting that Mulroney is furious at me. I'm not sure. I've had no word from him, or anyone in Ottawa, for that matter. Other than the original statement that the issue was "regretted and closed," no one in the PMO and External has publicly defended Sondra or me or our record. The only statement of support has come from the leader of the Opposition.

What makes the situation all the more frustrating is that although there is no defence from Ottawa, there is still no inclination to allow Sondra to explain herself. The *Toronto Star* offered to give Sondra a whole page to tell her story. Everyone wants to interview her, but we hear one unbroken record of advice: "Starve it, don't debate it, don't feed it. Say nothing. Let it die." Sondra, under pressure, has declined Meg Greenfield's persistent invitations to write about it.

April 1, 1986 Tonight Polly Kraft had a one-person exhibition of her paintings at the Fischbach Gallery in New York, with a reception afterwards

---

[1] (1920–2002) Canadian journalist, politician, and political strategist. A regular political commentator on CBC's *Morningside* and a political writer for the *Toronto Star*.

at the home of her friends the Eastmans. We went to the exhibit but didn't stay long, both of us being in low spirits. At the Eastmans' party we had an agreeable surprise because Sondra saw Alan Pakula, who said he wanted to do a movie based on her writings about diplomatic life and asked her to come up and discuss the idea with him soon. This was a lift for Sondra, a badly needed one.

April 3, 1986 Warren Phillips, publisher of the *Wall Street Journal*, took Sondra and me to lunch at the River Club in New York. "You can't win with the press," he told us. "If you fight back, you will only prolong the fight, and the story, and you will lose anyway. And you will lose more." One hates that kind of advice (just roll over and play dead).

April 7, 1986 We attended a dinner at the Japanese ambassador's Residence, in honour of John Block, retiring secretary of agriculture. Sondra was seated between the French ambassador and our host. As each successive Japanese course was gobbled up by an eager de Margerie – shrimp, seaweed, tempura – the Japanese ambassador ate nothing. The French ambassador kept saying, "*J'adore la cuisine japonaise, c'est extraordinaire, c'est une merveille*," while the Japanese ambassador pecked unenthusiastically at his plate. Halfway through the parade of courses, Sondra turned to her Japanese host and asked him why he wasn't eating. "I don't like Japanese food," he replied.

April 8, 1986 Claire Hoy[1] writes in the *Sun* that we work our staff on shifts to avoid overtime – an illegal practice. The *Globe and Mail* reprints an article appearing in the *London Observer*, entitled "A Feeling That Canadians Have No Right to Be Amusing." Never a word from my erstwhile friends, supporters, and admirers at the PMO. The *Washington Times* reports that "my recall is inevitable" and Ken Taylor will replace me. The bad ink begins to flow about my hiring Deaver to assist the embassy. "An Embarrassing Adviser" trumpets a Canadian headline, this time from faraway Winnipeg.

---

[1] Canadian author, columnist, and broadcaster. He has written regular columns in the *National Post* and *Law Times*, and weekly political syndicated columns. Co-hosted a nightly political debate show, *Faceoff*, on CBC *Newsworld* for five years in the 1990s.

April 9, 1986 I meet in my office tomorrow with Simon Reisman for another discussion about the U.S. political scene and prospects for getting a free-trade agreement with the United States. He seems to envision a scenario where a small group of key players can sit around a table and strike a deal.

April 10, 1986 When I was at the U.S. trade representative's office this morning, optimism prevailed. Everyone expects a positive outcome at tomorrow's meeting of the Senate Finance Committee, when the senators decide whether to give the president fast-track authority to negotiate a free-trade agreement with Canada. U.S. officials calculate that the negative votes will be tactical ones from the lumber boys, and their votes will be a distinct minority. They aren't opposed to a free-trade agreement with us, hell no, just as long as there is no free trade in lumber products.

We're also feeling pretty good at the embassy. The staff have actively worked the Hill, and the count looks okay. I personally have covered all the bases, and there are no goodies we can offer the lumber barons to buy their votes.

At the end of the afternoon, I received a call from the Hill. It was Senator Moynihan, and he had an alarming tip. There will be a revolt, he said, against the fast-track proposal. There is anger against the administration on many trade issues, and "the Canadian proposal might be the victim."

In a state of alarm, I called all senior officers to the embassy, and we did a quick canvas of congressional staffers that we were able to locate. No corroboration. Danforth's, Roth's,[1] and Heinz's people indicated that concerns may be expressed about softwood lumber, pharmaceuticals, and investment, but they can't believe fast-track authority will be denied. They are not aware of a revolt. At worst, the committee might attempt to put a few riders on the negotiating authority.

April 11, 1986 A fateful Friday. At around 10 a.m. I receive a call from Jim Medas at State, who, as the department's top Canadian man, was monitoring developments on the Hill. "Things are going very badly in the Finance Committee," he tells me, his voice shaking. "How badly?" I ask. "Very," he replies.

---

[1] Bill Roth (1921–2003) Republican Representative from Delaware 1967–1970; Senator from Delaware 1971–2001.

A few minutes later, Jim Judd[1] calls from the Hill. He says if there's a vote today, our initiative is dead.

When the senators met privately with Yeutter just before the hearing this morning, most of them attacked the administration's trade policy as weak, vacillating, and inadequate. At the actual hearing, ten senators then spoke against giving the administration fast-track negotiating authority. Of that group only the softwood lumber gang – Packwood, Baucus, Symons, Pryor,[2] and Long – specifically aimed their criticisms at Canada. (These five were the ones we had – accurately – counted as negatives.) But when the group gathered this morning and started comparing positions, they realized the naysayers represented a majority of the committee. United by grievances against the administration, they realized they could defeat the request for fast-track authority.

I explained to a skeptical Canadian press later in the day that a sort of "spontaneous combustion" occurred when these senatorial grandees got together.

What a ridiculous situation. Months of work down the drain. What an insult to Canada. We are being mowed down by firepower aimed largely at others. I cannot bring myself to believe that the Senate would be so egregiously capricious and stupid as to reject this historic initiative. I've been educating myself for years about Congress's parochial mentality, but I simply can't believe they can be as parochial as this.

April 12, 1986 Saturday morning at the embassy. We are in a state of shock. I debriefed the embassy officers and then advised Ottawa of my discussions with Jim Baker late yesterday. Baker told me he sees the Friday meeting of the Finance Committee as a terrible rebuff to the president by the members (a majority of whom are, of course, Republican). Clearly, he said, it would have been wise to delay seeking fast-track authority until after the negotiations were underway – a position he has always advocated, as he reminded me. (I needed no reminding: on this point he has been consistent.) The encouraging news, if one could employ so positive a term, is that

---

[1] (b. 1947) Counsellor and Congressional Liaison at the Canadian Embassy in Washington 1983–1987; Deputy Minister of National Defence 1998–2004; Director of the Canadian Security Intelligence Service 2004 to present.

[2] David Pryor (b. 1934) Governor of Arkansas 1975–1979; Democratic Senator from Arkansas 1979–1997.

Baker (unlike Yeutter) believes that a majority of the committee can be turned around. At this time, Baker counts eleven hard negative votes out of twenty. This leaves some space – not much, but some – for manoeuvre.

I told Baker that the prime minister expects the president to engage his full prestige. I then passed this same message to John Whitehead at State. Baker fully appreciated the necessity of this. He, at least, understands that what is at stake, beyond the free-trade initiative, is the president's prestige and authority in the whole field of international trade and probably beyond. I also told Baker – as I had done before – that Mulroney believed the idea of trying to negotiate a free-trade agreement between our two countries without congressional negotiating authority was not realistic, and he would not accept such a notion.

Then I got apocalyptic. While no cabinet decision had been made, my personal assessment was that the Canadian government would withdraw the request for negotiations if the Senate rebuffed fast-track authority. "In my personal opinion," I told Baker, "the senators must be left in no doubt that their behaviour has grave consequences. If they think for a moment that they can reject our proposal without prejudice to U.S. interests and without responsibility being assigned to them personally, they must be relieved of such a false impression." I hope my words sunk home.

At the embassy we prepared an overall assessment of prospects for a turnaround in the Senate Finance Committee. Unlike Yeutter, we concluded that there is a good chance the gap can be closed. It is probable that a combination of administration/embassy/third-party lobbying can produce a positive vote for fast-track authority. Obviously, it will be a close vote, thanks to the lumber barons. Of the mighty twenty, ten spoke out against, a few were clearly positive, and about seven were absent or unheard from. Our assessment:

Republican Chairman **Bob Packwood** (Oregon) – Lumber the principal concern. Up for re-election. Unpredictable. Unlikely to be turned.
Max Baucus (Democrat, Montana) – Lumber obsessed. Position fixed and impenetrable. No chance for a turnaround.
Steve Symons (Republican, Idaho) – Lumber all the way. No chance for turnaround.
Chas Grassley[1] (Republican, Iowa) – Lumber. Hogs. No chance.

[1] (b. 1933) Republican Representative from Iowa 1975–1981; Senator from Iowa 1981 to present; Chairman of the Senate Committee on Finance 2003 to present.

Russell Long (Democrat, Louisiana) – Ranking minority member. Lumber. Oil. Some chance.

Lloyd Bentsen (Democrat, Texas) – No major gripe. Unhappy with administration trade policy. Partisan outlook. Chance for turnaround.

George Mitchell (Democrat, Maine) – High-mindedness a pose. Lumber, potatoes, and fish govern his partisan agenda. Problematic.

Jack Danforth (Republican, Missouri) – Crypto-protectionist. Against us on trucking and telecommunications. Angry at White House trade policy. Chance of turnaround.

John Heinz (Democrat, Pennsylvania) – Protectionist. Steel dominates his thinking. Remote chance, at best.

John Chafee (Republican, Rhode Island) – Onside.

Patrick Moynihan (Republican, New York) – Onside.

Bill Bradley (Republican, New Jersey) – Onside.

Bill Roth (Republican, Delaware) – Onside.

Bill Armstrong (Republican, Colorado) – Probably onside. May demand a pound of flesh from White House.

Bob Dole (Republican, Kansas) – Senate majority leader. Key vote. Angry at administration over budget, tax, and trade: possible.

Malcolm Wallop[1] (Republican, Wyoming) – Should be onside.

Dave Boren[2] (Democrat, Oklahoma) – Oil and energy. Some chance.

Spark Matsunaga (Democrat, Hawaii) – Some chance.

April 13, 1986 We flew into New York last night to attend the Stassinopoulos-Huffington[3] wedding given by Ann Getty[4] at the Metropolitan Club. Not too clear why we were invited. It was a strange scene. A half-dozen or so aging bridesmaids, including Barbara Walters and Lucky Roosevelt, shuffled down the aisle in identical lavender dresses. The ceremony was bizarre. Kissinger said, "There was every kind of ritual except Aztec."

I chatted with the great Kissinger. "I am astonished," he said, "at how you get around." He was recently speaking to "an important Canadian" and told him "what an outstanding job" I was doing. "But," said Kissinger, "I can't

[1] (b. 1933) Republican Senator from Wyoming 1977–1995.

[2] Governor of Oklahoma 1975–1979; Democratic Senator from Oklahoma 1979–1994.

[3] Michael Huffington (b. 1947) Deputy Assistant Secretary of Defense 1986; Republican Representative from California 1992–1994.

[4] (b. 1952) American oil heiress, granddaughter of oil man J. Paul Getty.

remember whom it was I was talking to." Then a little later he commented to me, "Now I remember whom I was talking to, but I cannot tell you his name. All I can say is that the conversation I had with this person will be very helpful to you."

I thought afterwards, how very Kissingerian. He created a mystery and thus made himself very interesting. He also placed me, or at least this is the implication, in debt. This explains to me how Kissinger is Kissinger.

Back in Washington for what I hoped would be a quiet Sunday. I need downtime in the aftermath of the PM's visit and the crisis over free-trade negotiations, but I am not getting much. I spent a large chunk of the day discussing with Ottawa how to respond to the Senate revolt.

In the evening I kept a commitment to attend a small get-together with Malcolm Fraser,[1] former prime minister of Australia, in his suite at the Hay-Adams. This tall, haughty man is co-chairman of what is modestly called the Commonwealth Eminent Persons Group, charged with trying to create a dialogue with the government of South Africa and convince it to show some flexibility and movement. I was invited, along with Oliver Wright, to brief him and his co-chairman and staff on the Washington political scene. He seems convinced that there are real parallels between South Africa and Vietnam and has an apocalyptic vision of South Africa's future. The vision is simple and clear: the end is near.

I shocked him by saying that South Africa was not a great issue in Washington right now. This town is notorious for being unable to concentrate on more than one big political issue at a time, and at this moment it is not South Africa. But I promised to help open some doors for him on the Hill.

April 14, 1986 Don Regan, the White House chief of staff, admitted to me today that "the administration was caught way off base" on the free-trade issue in the Senate and was "totally unprepared" for what happened. Canada was a victim of a lot of senatorial anger aimed at others – the EEC and Japan. He assured me that the president would now become engaged. Regan asked me about postponement of fast track, but I told him Mulroney would never agree. Postponement would leave us negotiating with a gun (cannon?) at our head, to be fired at will whenever a contentious issue arose.

In further discussions with Yeutter, he too assured me that the president

[1] (b. 1930) Leader of the Liberal Party of Australia 1975–1983; Prime Minister of Australia 1979–1983.

will engage in lobbying, as will Shultz. On the basis of a collective political assessment just made by Yeutter, Darman, and White House chief congressional lobbyist William Ball, we on the Canadian side will focus our own lobbying on a selected dozen members of the Finance Committee.

We discussed a wider strategy at the embassy: inviting the advice and assistance of outsiders or non-committee members – Bob Strauss, Alan Simpson – and getting chambers of commerce, the NAM,[1] and consulates involved. Quite a challenge. The vote will likely be in three days' time. Three days to salvation or to hell. The *New York Times* and the *Post* have given the issue very little coverage to date. I raised the issue with the all-powerful Abe Rosenthal of the *Times* last weekend, but I'm not optimistic we can do much with the media profile in the United States.

Darman tells me the situation is bleak, but he thinks it can be turned around. After the cabinet economic policy meeting today, chaired by Baker, everyone is finally getting into the act. Postponement beyond April 17 is very unlikely. The sixty-day deadline for a fast-track decision expires April 22.

At the end of the day, the prime minister called and asked for my assessment and recommendations. As a result of my discussion with him, I now have the personal authority to tell key senators and administration officials that if the Senate rejects the fast-track authority, Canada will withdraw our proposal for a free-trade agreement and will not reintroduce it. Definitive stance.

April 15, 1986 Atmosphere of anxiety and even paranoia grows in the PMO, External, and the embassy. CP wire report out of Washington: "Canadian officials said privately a rejection would be a devastating blow to Prime Minister Brian Mulroney, who has made improved relations with the U.S., including a new trade deal, the centre piece of his government's agenda." This report is not received with joy in Ottawa. I get hell. Bruce Phillips and I agree it is probably a good example of reporters putting words in officials' mouths by making statements and not eliciting denials. We urged all embassy officials to exercise extreme care.

Yeutter and Whitehead briefed me on this afternoon's legislative strategy meeting at the White House. The president will meet tomorrow with Senate leaders Packwood, Danforth, Bentsen, and Heinz. A head count has eight on our side now. Eight down, two to go.

---

[1] National Association of Manufacturers.

After speaking to a number of senators today, I fear we are in a hostage-taking situation, with Canada as hostage. They regard concessions to them by the administration to be of critical importance. I learned something even more worrying from Heinz, more worrying than the vote against us that he said he will deliver in the committee. He signalled that the administration may attempt to buy off the lumber senators in order to ensure their votes.

Good news: Shultz has undertaken to lobby some senators personally. His own prestige far outweighs that of his department.

In the evening I learned that the vote in the Finance Committee will be further postponed – until Tuesday night, April 22. Also that twelve members of the committee, organized and led by Danforth (Senator Pious), have asked the administration to *withdraw* its request for fast-track authority and then *resubmit* it later with a commitment to work on a general trade bill and to provide evidence that key bilateral disputes with Canada were being resolved.

How preposterous can these guys get? And I picked up more troubling news about a lumber deal to wean a few of the senators away from their negative vote. The arrogance of the senators leaves me overwhelmed. Even after all I have witnessed here for four years, I am still in a state of disbelief.

April 16, 1986 Spoke again this morning to a number of senators on the Finance Committee. I'm slowly gaining the impression that many of them, possibly a majority, don't want to be tagged with responsibility for torpedoeing the negotiation. They want to put pressure on the administration and they want concessions from Canada, but they don't want to be responsible for killing our free-trade agreement. Whitehead confided to me that withdrawal and later resubmission of the request for fast-track authority would only happen as a last-ditch ploy to avoid rejection.

Yeutter gave me a bit of good news. The Finance Committee chairman, Packwood, is mightily pissed off about the letter from the twelve members of his committee asking for postponement and concessions from Canada. He's particularly annoyed at his Republican colleague, Jack Danforth, chairman of the Trade subcommittee, whom he regards as the instigator.

Yeutter said he is leaving tomorrow for an OECD meeting in Paris. I couldn't believe my ears. "For God's sake, don't go," I told him.

Later in the day, I called on Russell Long, who is pushing the withdrawal scenario. The conversation was memorable. Before meeting with him, I asked his close friend Bob Strauss if I should follow the tactic of trying to extract a favour from Long (a vote for fast track) for a favour I did him (got Canada to open a pavilion at the New Orleans World Fair). Strauss said, "You can try, but you don't stand a chance."

Well, I tried. "Remember, Senator, when you came over to the embassy to see me and told me how extraordinarily important it was for Louisiana that Canada open a pavilion at the New Orleans World Fair? Remember how I personally went to bat for you, got in touch with the cabinet and key ministers and pushed for a favourable result? Remember how everyone said ours was the best pavilion at the fair, save for the U.S. one? I did this for you. I did it for you personally. Could you now personally help Canada by supporting this proposal of ours, this fine free-trade proposal, which is also good for you and the good people of Louisiana, whom Canadians love very dearly?"

The senator smiled from ear to ear and, looking directly into my eyes, said, "No, son, I can't. You did me a favour, I grant you, and I appreciate it enormously. You went to bat. You got a Canadian pavilion in my home state. But I've already paid for this. I got a U.S. pavilion in the Vancouver World Fair coming up this year. Without my support, the U.S. wouldn't be there. So, son, now we're even."

Long will vote against. So will Bentsen. Two Democrats, one low-minded, the other high-minded.

April 17, 1986 Packwood's people confirmed we have eight positive votes. All we need is two more, because a measure to reject fast-track authority would require eleven votes out of twenty in order to pass. Packwood urged me to concentrate on Mitchell, Pryor, Symons, and Baucus(!). I think all four are lost causes. I recited the usual arguments to these people: no fast track, no free-trade agreement, no free-trade agreement, lumber is to blame.

Got a characteristic brush-off from Danforth. "Mr. Ambassador," he said politely, "the problem has nothing to do with Canada." Can you believe it? "The problem is the administration – its unacceptable position on trade policy. Don't lobby the Congress, lobby the administration."

Lloyd Axworthy and Don Johnston, representing the Liberal caucus, are in turn working the Hill, trying to defeat the initiative. Ironically, I got them appointments to conduct their unhelpful mission and briefed them with infinite care.

April 18, 1986 Had lunch today with Willie Wachtmeister at the Metropolitan Club. He's now dean of the corps, having succeeded the near eternal Dobrynin. The reason I asked him was really quite preposterous. A rumour has been circulating among the diplomats, it seems, that the reason Sondra slapped Connie is that she and I were having an affair. This is surely the most ridiculous tale to emerge (so far) from the incident at the Residence. The rumour was put about by a reporter from the gutter, Sandra McIlwaine, as she was "gathering material" for her article on Sondra, subsequently rejected, for *People* magazine. The rumour reached Connie's ears, and she became upset by it. If people believe this, she told me, it could hurt her career. I told her I didn't think anyone would believe this salacious gossip, since it was obvious to so many that there was no foundation to it whatsoever. But Connie wanted me to do something about it. She had some suggestions about how I might go about refuting the story, but the only one that was feasible was for me to tell Willie that if he and his wife ever heard such a rumour, they should deny it.

I talked to Willie about many things until I found an opening. It wasn't the easiest assignment of my career, but it might have been the most embarrassing. When I mentioned the alleged rumour of an affair between me and Connie, Willie didn't seem to get it. He just looked perplexed. So I repeated what I said. At that point Willie, who is rather staid, broke into laughter, which made me feel even more stupid. Returning to his usual solemn self, he assured me he would ask his wife, Ulla, to deny this vicious rumour if it were to come to her ears. So now I can tell Connie that Wachtmeister will take the matter in hand. Mission accomplished.

Some mission. Some accomplishment.

April 19, 1986 Mike Deaver is becoming a target on the Hill. John Dingell, the great non-friend of Canada, is getting more and more into the limelight with his allegations that Deaver engaged in illegal lobbying on acid rain. He's our number one opponent on acid rain controls and has stumbled on the fact that Deaver helped us, although certainly not in any significant or improper way. So "get Deaver."

Had breakfast with Sol Linowitz yesterday. More and more I regard him as my therapist in Washington, and a very good one at that. With the media pounding us over the "incident," with Congress behaving like idiots on free trade, and with the Deaver investigation beginning to spread its long, ghastly tentacles, I definitely can use a political therapist. With Linowitz, as with Strauss and also Cutler – that intelligent Jewish legal triumvirate – it's not a matter of their power or influence that leads me to them. It's their wisdom that I value, the special wisdom that comes with being a survivor in this town.

April 20, 1986 A change of scene for us and a change of pace. We escaped to Norfolk, Virginia, to crown the Azalea Queen at the Azalea Festival. We arrived late last night to what I expected would be a city drowning in azaleas. Well, I haven't really noticed too many, and those we have seen are nearly all ghastly pink (only white ones are said to be in correct taste), and anyway, I don't like azaleas. But I crowned the queen, a pleasant Canadian girl called Andrea Carter, and officiated at ceremonies celebrating Canada. Our "queen" is a nice person, well looked after by her mother, who is convinced that her daughter was chosen by an international jury of high NATO officials on the basis of her outstanding leadership and moral qualities. Highlight of the event was this morning's parade. Oh, how they love a parade in this land. All sorts of high school bands, marching legionnaires, Shriners in funny toy cars, and kitschy floats. A real hunk of Americana and a balm for our souls, so badly bruised in the Beltway.

April 21, 1986 Over the weekend I kept in regular contact with Darman, Cobb, and Murphy. Darman told me Packwood thinks he's got nine votes – still missing one. It's amazing how Packwood has shifted from leader of the opposition to leader of the supporters of fast track. It makes one more than slightly suspicious of hanky-panky on the lumber side, but we're told over and over that there is none. Packwood thinks he can hold off the vote until midnight tomorrow.

Yeutter called me later in the day to say he's optimistic he will get his tenth vote – maybe Armstrong or Pryor. It is difficult to credit (if one doesn't understand Washington), but all these chaps have a price. With Armstrong, he wants a commitment from the administration to ban trade with countries using slave labour (read the U.S.S.R.).

Mitchell's posture is more difficult to understand. He's intelligent, has Senate leadership ambitions, and comes from a state that benefits hugely from Canadian trade and tourism. There are parts of Maine that in summer are simply a southern exterior of Quebec, and the tourist dollars they drop must be enormous. Even more weird, he's been a supporter in Congress of the idea of creating a trade commission between our two countries to objectively investigate bilateral disputes and make recommendations. He has even read his proposal into the congressional record.

I decided to give Mitchell one more try. He suggested I meet him in the antechamber of the Finance Committee – he would step out of the meeting when I came. I sat with him on a comfortable sofa in a corner of the Senate anteroom and made my pitch.

"Mr. Ambassador, I have a problem," he explained. "The potato farmers in my state are going out of business because they can't meet the competition from your New Brunswick potato farmers, mainly on account of your devalued dollar. So I need help from the Department of Agriculture, which I'm not getting."

At that moment, Bill Bradley came loping by, paused, looked at us from his lofty height, and said to his fellow Democrat, "My God, George, you're not telling the Canadian ambassador you're going to vote against Canada-U.S. free trade because of a hundred potato farmers." Mitchell flushed deeply. He was speechless.

Bradley notwithstanding, the conscientious senator from Maine will not, I predict, be embarrassed out of his opposition. No potato money, no free-trade agreement. A man of principle.

April 22, 1986 Packwood called off the vote in the committee, after a two-hour discussion. He calculated the vote would go against Canada eleven to nine. The vote will now take place tomorrow morning, the ultimate deadline, and will allow time to lobby three possible swing votes: Matsunaga, Boren, and Armstrong. There is still a chance to win this one, and I so advised Ottawa. Reagan is supposed to meet with Armstrong this afternoon.

There are now three resolutions before the committee:

1) Packwood's proposal to oppose fast track, which he himself will vote against (very odd);
2) Danforth's resolution to invite the administration to engage in consultations with Congress and require a yes/no vote in thirty days; and
3) Dole's initiative, which calls for a non-binding Senate resolution expressing a number of senatorial concerns (that is, knock off Canadian subsidies and preserve U.S. trade remedies). In other words, a dirty launch.

In between the various skirmishes, I dropped in to see Sidney Freedberg at the National Gallery, one of the small band of cultured people in Washington (asked to explain his strange English accent, given his Brooklyn origins, he replied, "Sheer affectation").

In the midst of our visit, I was called to the telephone. It was Senator Matsunaga from Hawaii, he who could provide us with the critical but missing tenth vote. I have been trying to reach him for days, but he had not yet returned my call. In desperation, we cooked up at the embassy a rather far-fetched manoeuvre. I called our consul general in San Francisco, Jim McCardle (Hawaii is in his territory), and asked if he could telephone the governor. He would then say that we at the embassy simply could not understand how the senator could be so indifferent to the wonderful tourist trade that comes from Canada. All those fine tourists, especially from the Canadian West, would resent Matsunaga voting against a free-trade agreement with Canada; they would feel he was disregarding the sensitivities of all those Canadian friends. McCardle called the governor and made the point, the governor called the senator, and presto! the senator called the ambassador. He was profusely apologetic about not returning my phone calls. I gave him the same story, gently, softly, in deep sorrow, no signs of anger.

"Senator," I told him, "Canadians love Hawaii, maybe even too much, but they just wouldn't understand your rejecting Canada."

The senator then came to the point. "Ambassador," he replied, "I committed myself to Russell Long to vote against your proposal, but I am impressed by your comments. I will seek a release of my commitment to him."

Yet another example of how Washington works. Long seems to have more chits drawn on more senators than anyone in the Senate. "Hell," Bob Strauss told me the other day, "he's even got a chit on me."

Have we got the missing vote? If so, I will deserve a statue in downtown Winnipeg.

April 23, 1986 Victory, glorious victory. The Finance Committee approved fast-track authority. Ten votes in favour of denying fast track and ten in favour, so it passed. No written undertakings. A clean launch.

Before the dust settled on the bizarre battle of the senators, I composed a message for Ottawa saying that without the support of two Democrat senators – Bradley and Moynihan – we would not have succeeded in launching our free-trade negotiations. Both were consistent, courageous, and principled in their stance over several months. I've been in daily contact with both right up to last night. After consultations with the prime minister and just before the vote, I thanked both of them in his name for their stance.

Interesting that although both have grievances or complaints against us, no promises were asked for or made on any subject. Bradley's state is the home of the pharmaceutical industry, but he never raised their complaints against Canada in this context, while Moynihan good-naturedly referred a couple of times to onions and raspberries, and that's all.

I am told the president saw Matsunaga, and Matsunaga switched sides. We won by a whisker, but a win is a win. Some in town are saying that the Finance Committee contrived to be evenly divided. By so doing, there would be less risk of the administration missing the senators' message: "You are not listening to our grievances and criticisms on the broad trade front – against Japan, the European Community, Canada, and the newly industrialized Asian countries. You had better hear us, or we will come down on you like a ton of bricks."

April 24, 1986 Even as we enjoy victory, a dark mist rolls in, poisonous vapours from the territory of Chairman Dingell. A letter from him to me landed on my desk today. His subcommittee on "Oversight and Investigations" – what a sinister title – has got the General Accounting Office of the Congress to investigate whether Deaver has complied with the applicable post-employment laws and regulations. Dingell said in his letter that I have not responded to the committee's request to meet and discuss Deaver's activities on acid rain. "Mr. Ambassador," the courtly congressman writes, stiletto in hand, "this is a matter of grave concern. I am particularly pleased to be able to count you as a very able and distinguished friend." Wrong about that. I'm no friend. I am a country, and countries have only interests. But I respect his forceful and formidable personality.

To make matters worse, if that is possible, I received a call from yet another powerful person, the managing editor of the *Washington Post*, Jim Downey. He informed me that the *Post* possesses damaging information about Canada's role in the Deaver affair and wants to give me a chance to comment. Bruce Phillips called the gentleman, who said that their correspondent in Canada, Herb Denton, has reported that the ambassador and/or Canadian officials cut a deal with Deaver while he was still working in the White House. This Phillips denied emphatically, as did Bill Fox in the PMO to Denton.

I became aware recently that Doucet apparently made some kind of remark to Deaver, around the time of the Quebec Summit, about the possibility of his working for Canada. Before issuing the denial, Fox accordingly spoke to Doucet, who denied ever making such a remark or any proposal or offer to Deaver. He recalls making some joke about how wonderful it would be to have a guy like Deaver on one's side. But the comment was purely by way of compliment and without significance. So Fox felt comfortable issuing the denial, and this seems reasonable enough to me, given Doucet's explanation.

As for myself, I certainly never talked to Deaver until after he was out of the White House. I'm not that stupid.

Late at night I sat around the Residence, with Bruce Phillips working the phone, waiting for tomorrow's edition of the *Post*, which my driver picks up at its office around midnight. Sure enough, the story appears on the top half of the front page. The article is false and scurrilous; however, it makes no specific mention of me personally, referring more generally to reports of Canadian officials making a deal with Deaver while he was still in the White House. The inevitable inference, unfortunately, is that I made the deal, as it is well known that I am the only official who dealt with Deaver and I am close to him. .

A nasty situation is shaping up. Who is the source of this poisonous lie?

April 25, 1986 I've been trying to get away from Washington to attend the Bilderberg meeting in Gleneagles, Scotland. Conrad Black and Vernon Jordan were responsible for my invitation. I've already missed part of the meeting, but I plan to leave tonight to get there for the last day. I'm then planning to meet Rachel and Sondra in London and spend a few days there.

I spent most of today trying to figure out what secret deals, if any, White House officials may have entered into with the lumber senators. During the past forty-eight hours, I have been constantly assured by the NSC that there were no presidential letters and no promises. Yeutter told me the same thing and so did State. Yet it emerged today that there has been at least one letter sent and maybe more. Even after more than a full term here, it is a real eye-opener to me to learn that the NSC doesn't seem to know what they are doing across the hall in the executive offices of the White House.

The mystery continues about the identity of the leaking, lying Canadian official, the kindly person who told Denton of the *Washington Post* that the Canadian embassy (the reference had to be to myself) cut a deal with Deaver. Suspicions about the source of the leak focus on an embassy official who works for me or did so until recently.

Someone is lying to me. I think I know who it is, but I know damn well I'll never be able to prove it.

April 26, 1986 In Gleneagles but too exhausted to function well. Had to fly overnight to arrive here for the last day. I'm a bit shell-shocked. These past few weeks have been bruising – the "incident" at the official dinner, the ugly domestic staff affair, the free-trade battle, the Deaver investigation, the treachery at the embassy. Gleneagles is a long way from Washington, but not too far for me to receive a copy of the *Washington Post* page 1 story, "Canada Refuses to Aid Congress in Deaver Probe," a match for the *Toronto Star*'s "Canada Mired in Murky Deaver Affair." What fun awaits me on my return.

May 3, 1986 Dinner at Meg Greenfield's house in Georgetown. The other guests were Joe Alsop and Kay Graham. Something was on our minds: a reporter for the Style section of the *Washington Post*, Lois Romanow, is doing a piece on us. This we learned from several people whom she contacted. Given the amount of garbage the *Post* has already written about Sondra and me, another piece would seem superfluous, to say the least. All this is further evidence of the "Get the Gotliebs" operational directive at the *Post*.

At the end of the evening, Sondra, looking at Meg, asked her directly, "Why is the *Post* doing yet another piece on us? What's the purpose of it all?" Meg, embarrassed, did not shrug off the question but turned towards Kay and said to Sondra, "Why don't you ask Kay?" Kay's response was perfectly predictable. "Oh, I don't know – I simply never get into that kind of thing. I don't interfere in the running of the paper."

It all seems very odd – Kay and Meg are among our closest friends here, yet their newspaper is trying to drive us out of town. Well, thanks to Sondra, Kay and Meg are aware of this now.

May 6, 1986 While I was in Scotland, the "quality" newspapers here continued to hound me on Deaver. The *New York Times* ran a front-page story (can one believe it?) blaring out the words "Deaver Was Active on Canada Issue." Never to be outdone, the *Washington Post* carried on with its anti-Deaver crusade and reported the egregious lie (citing again "a Canadian source") that Deaver discussed the possibility of representing Canada before he left the White House. At least it also recorded Bill Fox's denial and his statement that the first contact with Deaver was by me and did not occur until six days after he left the White House.

During my absence in Scotland, the embassy and External Affairs collaborated on a letter of reply from me to John Dingell about Deaver. I went over the letter carefully and signed and dispatched it today. The key provisions are that my initial discussion with Deaver about a possible contract was on May 16, 1985, which was some days after he left the White House, and that all proper procedures were followed. I assured Dingell that any suggestion that the facts concerning the negotiation of the contract were otherwise was "utterly without foundation."

May 7, 1986 I slept well last night. In the morning I felt fairly good about getting that damn letter out to Dingell. It was clear from the beginning that there was no possibility of my appearing before a congressional committee. Everyone in Ottawa had the good sense to see that. Moreover, Canada has never agreed that a Canadian official be a witness before a congressional body, except, very exceptionally, on a technical matter when it was in our best interest to do so. And not at all in my time. So the letter was not a bad form of voluntary co-operation and should help us avoid some criticism here and in Canada. Anyway, I felt pretty "clean" about it. I told what we knew. And I made as clear as possible that the embassy was not involved in negotiating with Deaver while he was in the White House.

I came home for lunch and went for a swim. As always, I felt guilty about it. Leading the soft life of the diplomat.

While doing my laps, a worry began to gnaw at me. Is there any way in which I could be accused of lying to or misleading a congressional committee? That would be fatal for me. I thought not. I clearly described in the letter the embassy's involvement and the subsequent steps of the contract approval. But this didn't prevent doubts from creeping back on me. I got out of the pool and reread my letter. Yes, it looked okay. "Our initial discussion was on May 16, 1985." Yes, the antecedent to "we" was clearly this embassy. It was a strictly accurate statement. I felt better. I got to the office and resumed my work. Then the doubts came back. Why was I worrying so? I reread the letter yet again, and then again and again. It still looked okay. Yet, wait a minute. What's this sentence on page 2? "I can assure you that any suggestion that the facts concerning the awarding of this contract are other than those set out above is utterly without foundation."

But what about the Doucet-Deaver conversation? If the Dingell people already knew about it or if Deaver informed them, could I be accused of misleading the committee?

We ate at home tonight – a rare event. I mentioned my anxieties to Sondra, who thought they were unnecessary. They probably are, but I couldn't put my worries out of my mind. I could see myself becoming part of a *cause célèbre.* "Congressional Committee Deliberately Misled," the headline in the *New York Times* would read.

For the first time in many years, I couldn't fall asleep. I lay in bed in a state of anxiety and got up and wrote in my diary.

May 8, 1986 When I rose this morning, I was tense and confused. Why had I been so precipitate in signing that damn letter? After all, it was my signature on the document, nobody else's. What had happened to my political instincts, instincts that I have always believed very keen? Now it was too late. There was simply nothing I could do. I could not revoke the letter. It was on the record and could be in the public domain shortly, if it wasn't already. Surely Deaver had testified to that conversation with Doucet, trivial and meaningless as it was. Or surely Dingell's investigators had learned about it from someone else. Deaver might have mentioned it to Fred Fielding,[1] the White House counsel. If he did, Fielding would surely have mentioned it to Dingell's investigators. Why on earth had I failed to mention it too? Yes, I could argue that my letter was accurate, that it contained no false statement. But if it was regarded as incomplete, then would it be seen as misleading? Or at least alleged to be misleading?

I turned these questions over and over in my mind, and I had no answers. All I could think of was what fun the Star Chamber would have with this. Then I realized that perhaps I did have one course open to me. I could write a second letter to Dingell, supplementing my first. I could say that I had been turning the matter over in my mind and realized I had some supplementary information to add.

I called Phillips and Judd into my office and outlined my worries and my idea. They were appalled. My letter was accurate. Why worry? Anyway, Doucet was in China with Mulroney. He couldn't be reached and wouldn't understand the fine points of my reasoning. We discussed the matter for over an hour. Phillips went away to think more about it. He then telephoned back and said, "You are absolutely right. Let's move." Judd too got on board.

We spent most of the day drafting a letter to Dingell and trying to reach Doucet in Peking. Phillips finally got hold of him, and we both tried to explain the problem and the recommended solution. To say the least, this

[1] (b. 1934) Associate Counsel for President Richard Nixon 1970–1972; Counsel to President Ronald Reagan 1981–1986.

was not an easy thing to do, especially on the telephone. Fred was dubious. His remark to Deaver was not an offer but a jestful comment. I said we know this, but if Dingell was aware of the remark, trivial as it was, my letter would be regarded as misleading. Fred said he had not been consulted on my letter. He would discuss the problem with the PM and let us know.

We sent off a "flash" telegram, for immediate delivery in Peking, explaining the whole situation in detail and suggesting the text of a second letter.

May 9, 1986 I slept better last night but fitfully. I knew I had the right solution, the only solution. Send the second letter and there would be no problem. External Affairs was on board. Joe Clark was consulted last night in Vancouver and agreed. He saw the point immediately. But what if Doucet doesn't agree? What course of action is open to me? I went to the office worried. No word back yet from Peking. Doucet said last night he would see the PM early in the morning, so that means we probably won't hear until later today. I spend hours debating with myself. If Fred won't agree, should I speak with the PM directly? That would end my relationship with Doucet, of course. Yes, I would do this. What if the PM then upholds Doucet's position? Should I then resign? What consequences would ensue?

To make matters worse, the *Post* says today that Dingell will issue his report on Deaver's acid rain activities on Monday. I am standing on the edge of a cliff, facing the abyss, and about to take a giant step forward.

Another disaster of the day. I'm shocked by Bill Safire. In his much-read column in the *New York Times*, Safire, who has been leading the pack against Deaver, writes that this business was "the most serious allegation of Canadian-American governmental corruption in history." What garbage! I can't believe he would write this and not even call me about it.

Brian Butters of Southam interviewed me. He's a good reporter and a gentleman, but the tenor of his interview was painful. The "incident," the Deaver affair, the close free-trade vote, the asbestos leak – don't all these show you are on the decline?

At 5 p.m. Fred called me. "Go ahead with the letter," he said. We spent the next hour refining the text. I felt good. My letter said that the special envoy idea emanated from the Canadian side, not from Deaver (it was my idea). After elaborating on this, the key paragraph read: "The initial business with Mr. Deaver about a possible contract occurred on May 16, 1985, and any suggestions to the contrary are without foundation. At a time considerably after Mr. Deaver announced that he was leaving the White House, an official in Canada did make a light-hearted conversational remark to Mr. Deaver to the effect that the U.S. was indeed fortunate to have a person of Mr. Deaver's talent on its team, and how much we could use a good man like that. The exchange was regarded as so inconsequential by the Canadian official that he does not recall the precise time at which it was made but believes it was after the Quebec Summit. This was a remark made entirely as a light-hearted and jesting conversational filler, and it is hardly the stuff of negotiations or offers or proposals, of which there were none."

May 11, 1986 Sunday brunch at Evangeline Bruce's. The *New York Times*, page 1, has an account of my second letter to Dingell. I'm becoming notorious.

Evangeline's brunches are the most enjoyable social events in Washington. I didn't enjoy this one.

May 14, 1986 The Parliamentary Committee on Foreign Affairs decided today to conduct their own investigation into the Deaver affair. Bravo! Congress penis envy. They want to call me as a witness. Joe Clark, in talking to reporters, seemed to suggest he had no problem with that. I have.

May 16, 1986 The Reverend Lloyd Axworthy, commenting on the Deaver affair, accuses me, the embassy, and the government of participating in a breach of U.S. law. The *Post* says he is co-operating with Dingell's investigation. According to Lloyd, Deaver is guilty and I am guilty. A fine demonstration of due process. Is he turning himself into an assistant to the foreign investigators?

May 21, 1986 I had lunch with Bob Strauss at the Metropolitan Club today. He said that he and Helen thought of giving a party in our honour after the "incident" at the Residence but hadn't pursued it because he believed "the story had no legs." Now he has thought about it and proposes that he and Kay Graham host a party in our honour.

Bob told me Kay was disgusted with the article in the *Post*. Apparently, there will be an equally nasty one in *Newsweek* (also her magazine), in connection with the Deaver affair. It's extraordinary that she should want to co-host this dinner. Her own managing editor, Ben Bradlee, is as much responsible for the attacks as anyone.

Bob has been outstanding. He helped stop the *People* story, and he's the instigator of this dinner.

May 22, 1986 Another stormy day for Canada in Washington. We've been worried about a possible decision by the administration to put a tariff on our shingles and shakes. We sell about $80 million worth to the United States and have well over half their market. The shakes and shingles all come from B.C. The International Trade Commission, in a divided vote, ruled that our exports were injuring the U.S. industry. We've been lobbying the administration not to affirm the commission's findings, but today the president, in a ridiculous and ill-considered decision, upheld the ruling, with minor variations, and applied a 35 per cent tariff. We received no prior notice whatsoever.

I got a telephone call from the prime minister. I have never heard him more angry. "What's this about shingles and shakes?" I explained it to him in unvarnished language. "We are victims of a U.S. domestic battle. We are innocents struck down to prove a domestic political point. The president wanted to show that he was sensitive to lumber interests."

Mulroney was furious. "We must retaliate," he said. I told him that would be desirable.

Then he said, "I can't go forward with the free-trade negotiations." That, I said, would be a terrible error. The whole affair demonstrates the necessity of a new trade agreement, with new procedures to resolve disputes. The president's decision shows we need an agreement to avoid unilateral and protectionist action.

We spoke for half an hour. I wasn't sure where he stood on the free-trade issue when we finished. I think I talked him out of precipitate action. The clinching argument I used is that if he suspends or cancels the free-trade talks, he'll eventually be accused of having no steady policy.

I think what hurt him most was that the president gave Canada, and more specifically him, no advance notice.

May 23, 1986 Late in the morning, I learned from External Affairs that Mulroney sent a letter to Reagan. He never mentioned the idea to me last night. As far as I can tell, the letter was drafted by Doucet in the presence of the prime minister, with his personal input. One official from the U.S. Bureau in External was invited to participate in the exercise, and Joe Clark agreed with the text. All this must have taken an hour or so. The letter was intemperate. It should not have been drafted in anger, and it should not have been made public before the president received it. The letter should have been delivered through the Canadian embassy in Washington. It was not. I was not consulted and should have been.

May 24, 1986 The prime minister telephoned me again. I am virtually in constant communication with him. What was the reaction to his letter? Given his own involvement, I replied delicately. I told him the Americans certainly deserved a very strong reply. They got it and they didn't like it. They thought we were overreacting. I gently told the prime minister that whereas the content of the letter was appropriate, some drafting changes would have improved it. He asked me what I meant. Well, first and foremost, I replied, you should have used Reagan's first name in the salutation, as you always do. Instead you called him "Mr. President." The White House was taken aback by this.

The prime minister told me another letter was on its way, this one lauding the president for his speech attacking protectionism. He asked me to deliver it today.

I spoke to Ty Cobb in the White House, who told me the president was in Camp David and was writing his own reply to the prime minister's shingles and shakes letter. It was a very personal one, and he expected it to be ready Monday. Did I have the original of yesterday's letter from Mulroney to the president? Not yet, I replied. His question surprised me. What's so important about the original?

May 26, 1986 Cobb told me that the president's reply to the prime minister was now in hand. The letter was unusual. The president apologized for lack of advance notice, which he said was an oversight. Cobb told me, "The president of the United States never apologizes. We would never have recommended such a letter. Please don't make this public." I said I would relay his request.

Later in the day – big surprise – word comes out of the PMO press office that the president apologized for the lack of notice. They made it public.

Cobb told me the president again asked for the original of Mulroney's letter. What's on his mind? I think the president wants to see the salutation.

May 30, 1986 I'm in Halifax. The NATO ministerial meeting is being held here, along with a bilateral meeting between Clark and Shultz. Shultz made no effort to defend the shingles and shakes decision. He suggested that we each improve mechanisms to avoid surprises. A good idea, but we all know the U.S. system well enough to understand this will lead nowhere.

May 31, 1986 Yesterday, after the meeting with Shultz, the Canadians had a long discussion about whether we should retaliate for shingles and shakes. I argued the reverse of the view generally held in Ottawa. Retaliation might be unpopular in Canadian consumer terms (because of higher prices for some U.S. goods), but sometimes, such as now, retaliation was essential in the management of our relationship. We must show the administration that the government will stand up to unfair action. We must show the Congress that protectionism cannot be cost-free. Many congressmen are confident that countries will not retaliate against U.S. measures, and we need to correct this dangerous misconception.

The battle about whether to retaliate or not has been going on in Ottawa all week, with External Affairs itself divided. I hope I tilted the balance.

June 1, 1986 Bill Bradley gave me a nice bit of news. He said he called Mulroney to tell him I was the best ambassador in Washington. He was amazed to get through to the prime minister so easily; he just picked up the phone and got connected at once.

June 3, 1986 We had a dinner party in honour of Lane Kirkland and Lynn Williams,[1] the Canadian head of the United Steelworkers of America. Lane is very high on Lynn. We invited the Wicks, Baldridges, McFarlanes, George Will, and an assortment of other Washingtonians. Lane said to me, "Allan, I see you are taking retaliatory action against the United States. Some of my boys don't like that very much. I think you should give Mulroney some good advice about dealing with this country."

"What's that, Lane?" I asked.

"Something my pappy always told me. Never play leapfrog with a unicorn."

June 4, 1986 We went to a surprise birthday party for Mike Deaver, given by Nancy Reynolds. She's been planning this for weeks. "It's only for

---

[1] Canadian trade union leader. International President for the United Steelworkers of America 1984–1994. He has also served as an executive of the Canadian Labour Congress.

about a half-dozen couples," she said. "The Laxalts, the Wicks, you, and a handful of others." But when we got there, the crowd was large, and it soon got larger. There must have been fifty or sixty people, including most of Mike's firm.

As we were leaving, Mike called me aside. "Allan," he said, "my contract is expiring, and if it makes it easier for you, I can let it expire." I told him this was a fine gesture, it made some sense, and we should talk about it. I wanted to be gentle with him because he is in sad shape, and it was his birthday to boot.

I have been wondering for weeks how to tell Mike that I could not recommend extending his contract pending the results of the investigation. He took a load off my mind.

June 5, 1986 Charlie Wick said to me last night as he was leaving, "That was a fantastic party you had for two of the most powerful labour union leaders in the country. No diplomat in town could pull off an evening like that. Get hold of Mulroney and make sure he is aware of the guest list." I told him I could not do that. "Why not?" he asked. "I could not blow my own horn," I said. "It would look bad. Anyway, the prime minister knows about our contacts," I added. "You're making a mistake, Allan," Wick replied.

June 6, 1986 Malcolm Baldridge announced that the United States will accept a new petition of countervail against our lumber exports. Bad news for the Conservative government. Bad news for British Columbia. Bad news for Canada. And it's bad news for Canadian and U.S. consumers. One more example of the new form of protectionism: procedural harassment. One more illustration of what a rough experience it is to be the biggest trading partner of the United States, and one more illustration of the difficulties in executing a policy of close friendship with America. A country of a thousand players who can deliver a thousand wounds.

June 10, 1986 I returned early this morning from New York to join the vice-president's aircraft. We are going straight to Victoria; Sondra will meet us in Vancouver tomorrow.

Talked with Bush on the way up about the political situation in B.C., where an election is being held and feelings are running high on lumber and shingles and shakes. I urged him to try to have a heart-to-heart talk with the prime minister in Ottawa. Shingles and shakes and the lumber countervail are bruising events for a man who campaigned on the necessity of refurbishing relations with the United States and who delivered on his promises. He should understand the political cost in Canada of a posture of close friendship with the United States. He could make a personal contribution by demonstrating to the prime minister that the White House understands his predicament and will avoid aggravating matters further.

Bush said, "I understand. You have made a helpful suggestion."

June 13, 1986 Bush visited the Expo site and gave a splendid speech on our trade problems. He warned Canadians that "a protectionist juggernaut was stalking the United States." Bravo for telling the truth. I was glad that Canadians were hearing it from American lips, for a change.

I received an instruction from Joe Clark to drop out of the Bush party, remain in Vancouver, and address a meeting here tomorrow of all interested players concerning the softwood lumber countervail. This despite the fact that I am in *official* attendance during an *official* visit to Canada of the second-ranking American. But there is no point in arguing the fine points of diplomacy.

Had a breakfast meeting with Clark, Pat Carney, Jim Kelleher, and a few others before this morning's session with the lumber industry, unions, and all the provincial forestry ministers. I told them the country was going protectionist, so we better get inside the tent with them, and quickly, if we could. The meeting confirmed the only possible strategy we could follow: fight the countervail. Clark was deft in his handling of all the parties.

I received a call from Bruce Phillips, who is now in Ottawa, working in the PMO. There is a page 1 article in the *Toronto Star* by their new reporter in Washington, Bob Hepburn, who writes that I am shortly to be replaced by Peter Lougheed. The PM is annoyed by my derelictions and failures, and I am out. Clark told me that the report is false. Phillips told me that the PMO said the same thing.

June 14, 1986 When we got back to Washington this afternoon, I learned that yesterday, at his televised press conference, the PM was asked about the report of Lougheed replacing me in Washington. He said it was wrong. He stated clearly that I was staying in Washington, the first time he has personally said this (as distinguished from his office). Welcome news.

June 16, 1986 The night of Kay Graham and Bob Strauss's dinner party in our honour. It took place in Kay's grand house in Georgetown. Sondra has been terribly sick with a cold/bronchitis/pleurisy/sinus/allergies. She's been coughing and hacking for weeks, but she pulled herself together tonight to attend. It's well that she did. The crowd was absolutely dazzling. Shultz, Baker, Baldridge, Casey (basically one-third of the cabinet), Volcker, Grunwald, Bill Bradley, Lugar, Simpson, George Will, Joe and Susan Mary Alsop, Dwayne Andreas, the CEO of the *Times Mirror*, Sandra Day O'Connor, Charlie Wick, Brent Scowcroft, John Whitehead, the Fritcheys, Barbara Walters, Alan Greenspan,[1] Ben Bradlee and Sally Quinn, Vernon and Ann Jordan, Mike Deaver, and many, many more.

Some observed to me that this was probably the most powerful collection of people ever to pack into a private dwelling in Washington. An exaggeration, but I didn't argue the point.

Kay and Bob proposed toasts. Strauss was witty, as always. He apologized that all he and Kay could get together for this evening were members of the Washington B-list and that he himself could not stay until the end of the party because he had to rush to an A-list party in honour of the wife of the New Zealand ambassador.

He instructed me to keep my reply brief. I followed his instructions. This was easy, as I was almost speechless. For Sondra and I, this was an evening never to be forgotten. The solid core of Washington was there for us.

June 17, 1986 Kay and Bob's party is written up today in the Style section of the *Washington Post*. People tell us this is unprecedented. The betting was that it would not be reported. Kay never allows her parties to be covered by her newspaper.

June 21, 1986 Another Saturday shattered by a telephone call from Ottawa. Fred Doucet got me as I was doing laps in the pool in the hot noonday sun. "Did you see the article about you by Bob Hepburn in today's *Toronto Star*? It is absolutely awful." "What did it say?" I asked, trying to catch my breath. "Oh! It's just awful. The PM read it and is upset. They are trying to destroy us one by one. Read it and think what you can do about it."

I managed to get hold of the text. It was a long piece (for the *Star*) criticizing me for every failure imaginable. Entitled "Gotlieb's Fall from Grace

---

[1] (b. 1926) Chairman of the Board of Governors of the Federal Reserve 1987–2006.

in Washington," it was vicious from start to finish. I was shunned by the A-list, goofed on the Senate vote on free trade, and missed the boat on shakes and shingles. The embassy was a forlorn place no one wanted to go to, the Deaver affair was my fault, the Lewis-Davis acid rain report was an embassy mistake, the PM is angry at me, and Joe Clark is angry at me. And, oh yes, Flora MacDonald was snubbed by Sondra.

And, oh yes, Lougheed is replacing me.

All Hepburn's negative comments about me are based on only two sources he cites by name, one a consultant that the embassy let go, the other an academic in town whom I barely know. According to Phillips, Hepburn told the Canadian press he is out to get me. I guess he's as good as his word.

June 24, 1986 I go to New York to attend a B'nai B'rith dinner honouring Walter Annenberg at the Waldorf Astoria. The crowd is glitzy (ABC was a sponsor). Annenberg says to me, "Remember, Allan, life consists of ninety-nine rounds. That's what I always told Nixon." Then he repeats, "Remember, ninety-nine rounds."

June 25, 1986 I spent hours today, as I did yesterday and will tomorrow, writing a letter to the editor of the *Toronto Star* defending myself against Hepburn's calumnies. I wrote draft after draft, tearing most of them up or running the occasional one past Bruce Phillips. He hated them all. "Don't write," he said. I sent one of my drafts up to Fred Doucet. He hated it. "Don't send it," he said.

June 27, 1986 The government released their new pharmaceuticals policy today. This position will reintroduce us to the family of nations by making us pay our way – up to a respectable point – for the research of others. This issue has upset, divided, and splintered the cabinet for over a year and a half. Finally, the good guys won. Mulroney took this decision against massive opposition in the provinces and many of the journalistic yahoos who trumpet ignorance and fear.

The issue is important for two reasons. The first is the image of the Mulroney government in Washington. The view here seems to be that while the prime minister's instincts are excellent, he fears making unpopular decisions. This, of course, is nonsense. The second relates to what kind of a nation we are or want to be; are we a nation of consumers and borrowers? Or creators, inventors, industrialists, and intellectual leaders? Will we be at the forefront of technology or will we try to maintain our standard of living through importing, buying, and filching the work of others?

Mulroney gave the right answers to these questions. That took courage, and I admire him for what he has done.

June 30, 1986 The Parliamentary Committee on Foreign Affairs met in Ottawa before the recess and voted six-zero not to call me as a witness on the Deaver contract. No Liberals were present. I'm relieved. I believe Joe Clark's recent testimony on the contract was of great assistance (Judd did the first draft). He carefully set out why we use consultants and why we hired Deaver – not to lobby but to assist in developing better public-affairs programs in the United States.

At least I won't have this hanging over my head all summer. On the other hand, if Deaver gets indicted, Parliament could revisit the issue. Clark's letter to the committee made that point clear enough.

July 2, 1986 I spent more time on another draft reply to Hepburn's attack on me in the *Toronto Star*. I reduced a ten-page reply to a page. Phillips told me he hated it. I threw it away.

July 4, 1986 We started out at 6 a.m. with the "dip" corps to fly to Governors Island to witness America in its most patriotic stance. The Statue of Liberty ceremonies were so corny they were an embarrassment, but the weather was cool and bright, the tall-ships parade was magnificent, the hot dogs were delicious, the day was effortless, and everything was as American as apple pie. We were more relaxed than we have been in a long time.

But when we returned to the house, we were met with a new crisis. Only a few hours after we left this morning, Teodora's crazy-jealous husband comes to the Residence, although strictly forbidden to do so. The embassy driver threatens to kill the crazy husband. The crazy husband makes the (by now) usual crazy move for a knife, the chef throws the crazy husband out of the house, the driver calls the police, the police lock up the crazy husband, and the Gotliebs face the prospect of even greater notoriety and fame.

Lionel Lepage, the administrative officer, convinced the driver to withdraw the charge against the husband. Hopefully, we'll avoid confrontation in the courts and all the attendant publicity. We are stunned by the day's events.

July 5, 1986 A last attempt to reply to the *Star*. I reduced my draft to a single paragraph. I made it ironic, funny. Phillips hated it. I threw it in the wastebasket. I give up.

July 10, 1986 The big question in town: where is the administration going on East-West relations and disarmament? Called on Jack Matlock in the White House and lunched with Ken Adelman at ACDA and will shortly see chief negotiator Max Kampelman[1] and Paul Nitze at State, and Fred Iklé and Richard Perle at Defense. Trying to assess the U.S. position on arms control is one of the most intriguing aspects of my work; the task is Durellian. One has to analyze and compare the many perspectives in order to try to judge what the U.S. position really is, will be, or might be. I recall, once again, Nicko Henderson's comment "Anyone who tells you that he knows where a decision was made in Washington is either a fool or a liar."

July 12, 1986 In an attempt to find out what the U.S. thinking is on South Africa and what the president is likely to do and say in his forthcoming speech, I got hold of John Whitehead yesterday. He once again demonstrated his willingness to say something and not just hide behind evasions and clichés. He gave me a good feeling for Reagan's attitude, which I passed to the people briefing Mulroney for his meeting with Thatcher on Sunday. Most interesting was Whitehead's comment that Reagan is enraptured by Thatcher's recent pronouncements on sanctions: that they are wrong-headed, immoral, counterproductive, and harmful to black South Africans.

July 13, 1986 Had lunch with Ken Adelman the other day. He still does not believe in arms control or disarmament. He never did, he doesn't now, and he never will. Each time I see him, he reiterates his conviction: "If the president can avoid entering into a bad arms control agreement, he will go down in history as making an important contribution."

---

[1] (b. 1920) Ambassador and head of the American delegation to the Conference on Security and Co-operation in Europe 1980–1983; U.S.-Soviet negotiator on space and nuclear arms in Geneva 1985–1989.

July 14, 1986 I flew to Ottawa to discuss how we should respond to the request by the special prosecutor, Whitney North Seymour,[1] to interview me about Canada's dealings with Deaver. The group agreed that I should see Seymour strictly on the basis that I worked out with him, that is, in my office, one-on-one, no records, highly informal, no prejudice, no waiver of immunity.

Doucet called me aside to tell me the Mulroney-Thatcher meeting on South Africa in Montreal yesterday went badly. Mulroney would like to fly down to see Reagan in California this week, otherwise he would like to phone him. I said it was useless for Mulroney to try to get Reagan to twist Thatcher's arm over the sanctions issue. Reagan was swept away in the admiration for Thatcher's stand; he was totally opposed to sanctions against South Africa. Doucet said the PM was determined to call. In that case, I suggested Mulroney base his remarks to Reagan on the threat to the future of the Commonwealth (the United States doesn't give a damn about the Commonwealth, but it's a good peg).

July 15, 1986 Ty Cobb harangued me about the call I am trying to set up between Mulroney and Reagan on South Africa. "Mulroney should not call," he said. "South Africa is like Libya, a litmus-test issue for the president." (He loves that phrase.) Mulroney, according to Cobb, is grandstanding, playing for public opinion and trying to improve his standing in the polls. Cobb also thought Clark was being unhelpful in announcing sanctions just before the EC meeting last month, in a bid to influence the European position.

I told Cobb he should withdraw the message. It was offensive, wrong-headed, and unkind. I found the whole conversation distressing, as it demonstrated how little regard U.S. officials have for dialogue with Canada. They see us as "on the wrong side" and are quick to question the motives of our leaders.

July 16, 1986 I am trying to see Poindexter to brief him on the Mulroney call to Reagan, but I am getting the brush-off. I told NSC officials today it was monstrous that my request to see Poindexter should be turned down. I know they don't want Mulroney to call Reagan on the South African issue, but their behaviour is unfriendly and unfair. At dinner I received a call that I am to see Peter Rodman, Poindexter being unavailable. Isn't that great?

---

[1] (b. 1923) U.S. attorney. Partner at Simpson Thacher & Bartlett LLP in New York City.

We dined at the Brinkleys' with a lot of the usual crowd: Joe Alsop, Meg Greenfield, George Will, Kay Graham, the Helmses. We talked right-wing stuff, reverse discrimination, and American hypocrisy as evidenced by television coverage of the recent death of basketball star Len Bias.[1] I got back at 11:30 to find a message that Mulroney was waiting to speak to me – another of his regular nocturnal calls. We went over the groundwork for his telephone call tomorrow to Reagan about South Africa. I again explained how Reagan adores Thatcher, how he should avoid referring to her or giving any impression that he's trying to arrange a gang-up. Such an approach would backfire. Mulroney said he is in total agreement.

We chatted at length about the Canadian press. Mulroney said he talked to Trudeau the other day, and Trudeau commented, "Brian, I have an advantage over you. I had no respect for the press when I came to office, and I had no respect for them when I left. Unlike you, I had no friends in the press. Your mistake is you have a few."

July 17, 1986 Another call from Mulroney, this time just before he placed his call to Reagan. We spent another twenty minutes discussing his approach. I informed him that Ty Cobb told me that Reagan felt personally close to both leaders, Thatcher and Mulroney. "So remember," I commented, "that Reagan is in a sensitive position." It was also important, I said, to come on as a supporter of Reagan on Libya and East-West issues and to remind him of your defence of the United States in response to Mugabe's verbal onslaught at the 1985 Commonwealth meeting in Nassau.

July 18, 1986 I spent close to two hours yesterday talking off the record to Whitney North Seymour Jr. in my office. He is a big bear of a man, but I found him surprisingly polite. I gave him details about my contact with Deaver in the six-month period prior to Mike's resignation, both on the matter of a contract and the appointment of acid rain envoys. I told him there were absolutely no discussions between us on a contract until after Deaver left the White House, that we hired him to do PR, not lobby on acid rain or anything else, that I did not know until a year or more later of any discussions between Deaver and Doucet (proof of their triviality), that Deaver's role in preparing for the Shamrock Summit of March 1985 was one

[1] (1963–1986) All-American college basketball player who died of a cocaine overdose less than forty-eight hours after being selected by the Boston Celtics in the 1986 NBA draft.

of a helpful fixer or a master of ceremonies, that he was supportive and helpful on acid rain but not in a substantive way, and that on the whole we thought his role fairly marginal although supportive. I don't know whether I convinced Seymour of anything.

"I guess you will be happy when this is all over," Seymour said to me as he was leaving. "Think of it as an instalment in your memoirs."

July 20, 1986 In the Hamptons I walked on the beach, where I bumped into Kay Graham and her granddaughter. Earlier, I'd heard an interesting story from Marc Leland about Kay. At a lunch at Warren Phillips's, with Kay present, Kati Martin announced that on a trip to her native Hungary a few years ago, she discovered she was Jewish. She found that her grandparents were Jewish and her parents converted to Catholicism (leaving Hungary in 1957) and never told her that she was Jewish. At this point Kay informed the table, "I didn't know my father was Jewish until I was twenty-one."

Kay and I strolled together for half an hour or so, and she talked about her upbringing. She described how her mother made her feel insecure in all things. "Did you like to read?" I asked. "I loved to," she said, "but my mother ruined it all for me. I remember when I was about eleven, I was reading Dumas, *The Three Musketeers* or something. My mother said, 'When I was your age, I read that in French.' So I stopped reading." She went on about her mother's coldness, how she looked after her mother when she was an alcoholic, and how she became closer to her mother in later life.

The conversation was flagging, so I said, "I understand you mentioned the other day that you didn't know you were Jewish until you were grown up." She stopped cold. "You know I mentioned that to Kati yesterday. Today everybody is repeating it. Why is it people repeat everything I say? Why is there no privacy?" All I could say was, "Well, Kay, if you say something at a lunch party at the Hamptons, people will assume you are not treating it as a secret."

July 22, 1986 I got to the White House in time to hear the president's address to the nation about South Africa. A meticulously arranged event, of course, and we diplomats played our usual role as television fixtures. Reagan gave a poor speech, the worst I have heard from him. While his hardline position against sanctions was not entirely indefensible, he sounded complacent, unconvincing, and a bit like father knows best. You could see several hands in the script. I could identify them. It was like reading Isaiah and finding traces of Isaiah I, II, and III. Considering that the whole administration – Shultz, Whitehead, Poindexter, Buchanan – have been working on this for weeks, it was a pretty weak show.

July 24, 1986 The day after our farewell party for Jacques Roy, the second number two that I have had to say goodbye to. A loyal colleague and man of judgment, I hope he does as well as his predecessor, Gerry Shannon. More and more I sense how long I have been here. People arrive and depart; the summer season sees a vast parade of officers waving goodbye, and new, fresh faces come next in view. I feel old but determined and sense no weakness in my bones.

July 25, 1986 I've been trying to build a close relationship with Roz Ridgway[1] at State, who has replaced Rick Burt as top official for Europe and Canada. Recently U.S. ambassador to East Germany, Ridgway is said to be a favourite of Shultz, who regards her as a woman of iron. (Is East Germany a training ground for dealing with acid rain?)

For me, Burt will be irreplaceable. Notwithstanding the difference in our age, he has been a real *copain*, a pal who has helped me navigate the swamps of Washington. While occasionally at each other's throats, nobody has come closer than he to being a friend in this town. We're going to visit him and Gahl in Germany next month.

July 30, 1986 We absolutely must make more strenuous efforts to protest the ridiculous congressional plan to subsidize grain sales to the Soviet Union and China. This is a terrible initiative. The lack of interest and the passiveness in External Affairs and the PMO are inexplicable. They are all too busy endlessly discussing South Africa. For three days I've been cajoling, pleading, and moaning – get active. I told the PMO we must get a letter from Mulroney to Reagan as soon as possible – today.

August 2, 1986 I learned the White House has scheduled a telephone appeal from Mulroney on wheat subsidies, to take place an hour and a half *after* the U.S. decision would be announced! In a state of shock, I got hold

[1] Served thirty-two years with the U.S. State Department. U.S. Ambassador to Finland 1977–1980 and to the German Democratic Republic 1983–1985; Assistant Secretary of State for European and Canadian Affairs 1986–1989.

of Doucet at once and said the prime minister must drop everything and call immediately.

The next hour was one of extreme vexation. Although I tried on an "emergency basis," I could get through to no one responsible in the White House. Finally, Admiral Poindexter called the PMO to dictate some notes comprising a message from the president to the prime minister. The president said our views had been taken into account in the decision, which did involve subsidy to the Soviet Union but fell short of what the Senate wanted to do, and he had to go this far in order to block Congress.

Canadian interests overridden by domestic political expediency. As in shingles and shakes. As in softwood lumber.

August 4, 1986 Breakfast this morning with Rowly Evans at the Metropolitan Club. "Deaver," he said with gratification, "will be indicted."

This morning Joe Clark called to tell me things were going poorly at the Commonwealth gathering. It looked like Thatcher's opposition could not be overcome and the conference would terminate prematurely. He asked me to inquire what the U.S. reaction would be to a proposal that Mulroney and Rajiv Gandhi[1] come to Washington to discuss South Africa. Clark made it clear they wouldn't come unless the visit would be seen positively. Would it help Reagan in dealing with pressures from the Hill? He wanted an answer within two hours. Please perform miracles.

Again, the problem of getting a reaction out of Washington. No one was available in the White House. I finally got some reactions from John Whitehead, Roz Ridgway, and an official in the NSC. Whitehead said Reagan could see it as ganging up on Thatcher, and he wouldn't like that. Moreover, it wouldn't be helpful domestically. Reagan was serene, no, delighted with his speech last week, despite the criticism. He knew he was right in resisting sanctions. And why should Mulroney and Gandhi come together? Was that very friendly? Or was that ganging up?

I advised Clark within the time requested that the idea would not be well received here unless Thatcher was in favour of it. Which, of course, she is not.

August 5, 1986 Another issue is casting a dark shadow on our relationship: the potential voyage of the *Northwinds* through our Arctic waters.

---

[1] (1944–1991) Prime Minister of India 1984–1989. Assassinated in Sriperumbudur, India, in 1991.

Even though the United States would seek our authority for this, it would set off a furious response in Ottawa, and people would notice that we have yet to reach an agreement in the Arctic negotiations. "I sure would like to avoid this issue going upwards," I said to Ridgway, and I pointed up to the sky. Ridgway replied woefully, "I know exactly what you mean."

August 6, 1986 We arrived in Berlin to spend a few days as house guests of Rick and Gahl Burt, at their official Residence. We talked a lot about Deaver and Washington. It was Deaver, Deaver all day. The Burts had to receive both Dingell's congressional committee and Seymour's investigators.

Burt is surrounded all day by guards. He divides his time between Bonn and Berlin and lives like a viceroy. He presides over the largest U.S. embassy anywhere, and every time he breathes or opens his mouth, he is in the newspaper. Yet it is obvious to me he is not only underchallenged, he is underemployed. When I compare what he seems to do with his days to what I do, I conclude his job is kid's play compared to what the Canadian ambassador has to do in Washington.

August 7, 1986 PR maven Bob Gray writes to the *Financial Post* in Toronto: "Our firm represents neither Canada nor its Washington embassy. But once we did and in that relationship we formed the basis for our judgment that Ambassador Gotlieb is among the top five working lobbyists in Washington." I never dreamed, before I came here, that this is the ultimate compliment.

August 11, 1986 Sondra and I arrived in Salzburg today. We may as well be in Washington. The place is crawling with denizens of the Beltway.

Lloyd Cutler invited us two years ago to participate in a seminar about how the U.S. political system works. He also asked Joe and Polly Kraft. And Mike Deaver. It is a saddening thought. Joe is dead and Deaver is in disgrace. I feel like I'm participating in a "Dance from the Music of Time." Here is Lloyd Cutler, whom I dealt with in the late 1970s, when he was negotiator for the United States on our fisheries and boundaries problems. Warren Christopher[1] is also here. I dealt with him when the United States was planning sanctions against the Soviet Union following its invasion of

[1] (b. 1925) Deputy Secretary of State 1977–1981; Secretary of State 1993–1997.

Afghanistan. Richard Gardner,[1] former Oxford colleague, is also participating. He was Carter's ambassador to Rome in the late 1970s.

All these people have two things in common: they are all out of power, and they all dream of being back in power. A good chunk of the principal officers of the next Democratic administration might be gathered here in Salzburg.

August 12, 1986 John Brademas[2] gave a lecture today on the U.S. political system. A twenty-year member of Congress (until his recent defeat), he has a deep understanding of how Washington works. He spoke to the group of sixty fellows, almost all foreign, about why it was desirable for Congress to play a key role in foreign policy. He gave a vitriolic attack on Reagan's foreign policies and argued how fortunate it was for the world that Congress was frustrating these policies, citing South Africa, the Philippines, Central America, and arms control as examples.

It is a mistake for prominent Americans to attack their own country when they go abroad. All it does is reinforce the tides of anti-Americanism that are already running strong in Europe these days. Americans are so self-centred they can't tell the difference between a foreign and domestic audience.

But I have a high regard for Brademas's insights. He told me, "A chairman of a congressional committee or subcommittee, if he is persistent enough, and stays in his office long enough, can write the law of the land." If a foreigner understands any one thing about the U.S. political system, it should be this.

August 13, 1986 At a reception in Salzburg in the evening, I met the U.S. ambassador to Canada in the early 1950s, a strange experience. A very old man but obviously in great shape mentally and physically. We chatted about what Canada-U.S. relations were like in the era of Eisenhower and Louis St. Laurent. They were, he said, exceptionally harmonious. There were no real conflicts. The view about the minor trade issues of the day was that the market would take care of them. His biggest task was to promote the St. Lawrence Seaway. It was a little hard to believe we were talking about relations between our two countries.

---

[1] (b. 1927) Professor of Law at Columbia University; U.S. Ambassador to Italy 1977–1981 and to Spain 1993–1997.

[2] (b. 1927) Democratic Representative from Indiana 1959–1981; Senate Majority Whip 1977–1981.

August 14, 1986 I gave my lecture on "How an Ambassador Works the U.S. System," an eighty-minute *tour d'horizon*.

My main theme revolved around one key point: that all one's professional diplomatic training would be a positive hindrance to an ambassador promoting his country's interests in Washington today. The Vienna Convention calls for all official business to be transacted through the intermediation of the foreign ministry. Do this in Washington, I observed, and you are asking to be recalled.

The doctrine of the separation of powers has now evolved into the doctrine of the *sub*-separation of powers, with every other senator a chairman of his own committee or subcommittee. In the United States, governing is negotiating. As neither chamber can act without the other, and Congress cannot act without the administration in most important instances, and vice versa, the whole business of governing is an exercise in deal-making. A new national motto on the U.S. coat of arms should read "Let's make a deal."

I described the ambassador's role as the art of penetrating concentric intersecting circles of influence. At the centre there is the White House, which is an administration within an administration, then the fragmented cabinet, then the Senate and House of Representatives, then the lobbyists, who are the Third House of Congress, then the Fourth Estate – social Washington, intellectual Washington, the business world, and so on. An ambassador is paid to intervene in the domestic affairs of the United States. If he does it badly, he can get into trouble; if he does it well, he can get into an equal amount of trouble.

August 21, 1986 At breakfast today in Salzburg, Helmut Schmidt told me how nice a man Trudeau was. I questioned that. Trudeau was in some respects a great man, I said, but I cited Acton's famous dictum "Great men are almost inevitably bad men."

On the United States, Schmidt was very negative. It had not had good government for many years, he said. He was eloquent on what television has done to U.S. politics, and when I said the same would happen in Europe, he agreed. Yes, he said, "but as in the case of other diseases, it takes ten years for the contagion to spread from the U.S. to Europe." I mentioned to him the line from *The Great Gatsby* "The rich are different; if you get too close to them, you'll get bruised." "You must not like the Americans very much," he responded. To the contrary, I replied. "I am very pro-American. That is why we must understand how their system works and therefore what is realistic to expect from them."

September 6, 1986 I accompanied Mike Wilson on his call on Jim Baker yesterday. Baker has been standing too aloof from our free-trade initiative, justifying his stance on the grounds that his advice was not followed (we shouldn't have gone to Congress so early, and the president should have delayed the launch of the initiative until his State of the Union address in January).

Baker was gloomy about the prospects for a Canada-U.S. free-trade agreement. "Trade will be the biggest issue in the November mid-term elections," he said. "But I believe," he went on, "that next year when the big push comes, we will succeed in preventing the omnibus trade bill[1] from passing. It is, after all, the worst piece of trade legislation since Smoot-Hawley."

I asked him what price would have to be paid to prevent its passing. Baker snorted at this comment. "We had no choice in shingles and shakes," he replied. "There were six lumber senators whose votes would be lost on the free-trade agreement issue. Eighty million dollars is a small price to pay. But," he added, "you guys were right to retaliate. That helped us domestically in showing Congress that measures against our trading partners aren't cost-free." Wilson made a good pitch to Baker, urging him to get into the show and behind our efforts. Baker was confident the president would push hard for the agreement.

We're going to have a hell of a time getting a trade agreement past this protectionist Congress. At a lunch I arranged with Bob Strauss, he made that point crystal clear to Wilson.

September 9, 1986 A dim day in Canada-U.S. relations. On instructions from Ottawa, Heinbecker called on the Pentagon and said Canada would not agree to test the advanced stealth cruise missile, although we would continue to test the current one. This decision was taken by cabinet in Newfoundland last August, although we were unaware of it at the embassy until now.

When we received the instruction to deliver this message yesterday, I sent a telegram to Ottawa predicting an adverse reaction and recommending

---

[1] A Democratic initiative, originated in Congress, that would have introduced many new restrictive measures on U.S. trading partners. It was aimed at removing alleged unfair trading practices.

that we moderate its tone. (Provocatively, Ottawa has linked our decision to the U.S. policy to disregard SALT II.) In response, External sent a snarling message back to me saying this was a government decision and Joe Clark was fully behind it. I was told to carry out my instructions.

We did and the reaction was terrible. Cobb called from the White House, most urgently. "Tell me it isn't true," he said. "It is," I replied.

"You people are backing away from the testing agreement that Trudeau signed. People here are saying the Trudeau government showed more guts." And on he went. The "free-ride" argument, the "helping-the-Russians" argument.

The U.S. reaction seems to come down to this: if we don't support them on the big East-West issues, we are a disloyal ally.

September 10, 1986 The Woman of Iron took a hard line on our decision to avoid testing the advanced cruise. Her words were the hardest I've heard since I've been in Washington. Ridgway accused us of having a "lack of trust" in the United States. Do we have our own arms control policy designed especially for the United States?

I told the PMO again that we would be in a stronger position by just asking the United States to defer or withdraw their request without moralizing about it, as we are doing by tying it to our disapproval of their SALT decision. We should, I said, tie it to the political difficulties of the moment, treat it as a matter of delay by a government currently under pressure. Why, I asked, should we risk losing more political capital than we have to?

September 11, 1986 I had a long and difficult conversation with Perrin Beatty,[1] who is in town. He kept saying the Americans are "overreacting," that "our decision is not a big deal." He's been badly briefed, or misled, about the U.S. reaction. The nub of the issue, I said, was the reasons we gave for the delay. If we were trying to defer the test for reasons of timing, tactics, selling, and PR considerations, the United States could swallow this. If, however, our reasoning was that we disapproved of their foreign and arms control policy and their "breakout" on SALT, then the Americans will take this extremely badly. In other words, we should leave the pulpit at home.

---

[1] (b. 1950) PC Member of Parliament 1972–1993; Minister of National Defence 1986–1989; Minister of National Health and Welfare 1989–1991; Minister of Communications 1991–1993.

Beatty told me at the airport last night that Mulroney asked him to test the waters and report back. The main problem in dropping the link, it seems, is Joe Clark. He wants to stand on moral high ground.

September 12, 1986 Beatty went in to see Weinberger alone. I waited outside. After an hour, he called in his ADM, Bob Fowler, and they stayed locked up until lunch. After lunch, Beatty returned to see Weinberger alone. When it was all over, he didn't even want to tell me what had happened. I told him I had to know, that was my job. If he didn't want to let me know, he should have an ambassador they can trust, I said. I think he was in a state of shock from the way Weinberger came on with him – very hard, very tough, repeating his remarks over and over, without giving way. After first declining to withdraw the request, Weinberger finally did so, but on the clear understanding that the United States would resubmit it in December in order to allow testing next year. So we've postponed the crisis for a couple of months.

But I've little doubt what the outcome will be. We'll have to back off, or pay a decisive price in our relations with the United States.

September 13, 1986 At lunch at the Pentagon yesterday, guests were Senators Gramm,[1] Rudman,[2] and Lugar as well as Les Aspin.[3] Rudman, speaking across the table, said rather gruffly, "Ambassador, a lot of congressmen have mixed feelings about your embassy on Pennsylvania Avenue. We're glad it's not the Russians, but how did you ever get it? It's such a unique and special site."

"I will tell you the truth, but please don't spread it."

"Yes?"

"Bribery, Senator, we got it through bribery."

"That's the only sensible explanation I've heard," he responded.

September 16, 1986 We went to a memorial service for Averell Harriman at Washington Cathedral. Everyone is amazed that the ancient Averell is actually dead. It was a cold, dark service. Pamela was everywhere. There was virtually no mention of his previous wife or family. The party afterwards was very gay.

---

[1] William "Phil" Gramm (b. 1942) Democratic Representative from Texas 1978–1984; Senator from Texas 1985–2002.

[2] Warren Rudman (b. 1930) Republican Senator from New Hampshire 1980–1993.

[3] (1938–1995) Democratic Representative from Wisconsin 1971–1993; Secretary of Defense 1993–1994.

September 18, 1986 Received a telephone call in my office this morning from my son-in-law. Keith says Rebecca is ill, possibly gravely. I cannot believe it. She has not been ill a day in her life. I spoke to her physician in Toronto, and he thinks she has ovarian cancer. In shock, we will fly to Toronto with Rachel tomorrow.

October 3, 1986 We came back from Toronto yesterday after Rebecca's operation. We don't know what the prognosis is. We are not even sure of the diagnosis. It is hard, very hard, to resume work. It all seems so trivial, so unimportant.

October 4, 1986 We went to a black-tie affair at the British embassy on the occasion of the Washington horse show, which I thought perhaps could help distract us for a short while. The new British ambassador, Anthony Acland,[1] is an old friend – we were at Christ Church together. There will probably be a rotten little notice in the *Washington Times*, whose photographer and reporter were buzzing about, because Acland and I stood on the patio during the cocktail hour, talking forever to each other and not to the other guests. My obsession with the press is terrible. Am I getting paranoid?

October 6, 1986 Nice picture of Anthony, Sondra, and myself in the *Washington Times*. Commentary: British and Canadian ambassadors spend whole time talking to themselves at British reception. Ignore others. I'm not paranoid. I've got to know this town like the back of my hand.

October 8, 1986 Called on Ty Cobb at the White House. Like it or not, he is now the most authoritative voice in the White House, if not the administration, on Canada. Cobb is knowledgeable and committed, and as a director for Western Europe and Canada, with close to six years' direct experience behind him, he has an impressive personal knowledge of most aspects of the relationship. But he is emotional and at times erratic.

I was shocked and appalled – a popular phrase with me these days – when Cobb told me that there was no way Reagan would endorse full funding ($2.5 billion over five years) for the new program to commercialize new anti–acid rain technology. I asked how this could be, since Reagan

---

[1] (b. 1930) British Permanent Undersecretary of State 1982–1986; Ambassador to Washington 1986–1991; Provost of Eton 1991–2000.

announced his "full endorsement" of the envoys' report at last year's summit. Cobb said the president never intended that to mean full funding. I said that he must know, indeed the whole administration must know, that Mulroney could not go to another summit with Reagan unless there was solid evidence of his full support for the envoys' report.

Cobb responded that he always thought the annual summit commitment was a mistake, that the next summit should be postponed beyond March, and furthermore, that summits should just deal with multilateral topics. I was in a state of disbelief.

October 9, 1986 During our long discussions yesterday, Cobb gave me some insights into how the White House handles correspondence among heads of state and government. He said Mulroney's last letter on arms control was well received in the White House because it succinctly conveyed the hopes, best wishes, and faith of the prime minister on the eve of the Iceland Summit. The president does not see lengthy letters – they come summarized by an intruding pen. Given also the ideological biases in this weak and wobbly NSC, I can just imagine the kind of summaries they prepare. All this proves the point we make so often at the embassy: that most of Mulroney's letters to Reagan, drafted, of course, by some desk officer in External Affairs, are too long to be read and should never be sent in their current form. Trudeau would almost never sign letters longer than a page and a half – and those he rewrote extensively for grammatical and stylistic reasons.

October 10, 1986 Just as I got home for dinner, I received a very angry call from the PM. A ridiculous editorial in the *Washington Post* was a top item on the national news back home. It criticized Mulroney's leadership as weak and ineffectual and argued that Canada was too divided to enter into a comprehensive free-trade agreement with the United States. Mulroney asked me to contact Kay Graham or Ben Bradlee to get a rebuttal. I explained that Graham was in China, along with the editorial page editor, and Bradlee had no control over that page. I said I thought the editorial was no big deal down here, since few people pay attention to the *Post* editorials. This did not mollify Mulroney. He was convinced the *Post*'s piece would play in Canada for a week. He's probably right.

October 13, 1986 We went to Bill Safire's for his annual break-the-fast dinner, following Yom Kippur. This is the fifth time we've attended, and every year the crowd gets bigger, the wait to eat gets longer, the air gets stuffier, and getting a drink becomes more challenging. Safire herds his guests into the basement, picking out those he wants to talk to, and he ignores the rest. This year he sat upstairs in a cool room with Richard Perle, just back from Iceland, Len Garment, Abe Sofaer, and their spouses. The most interesting thing about this annual get-together is discovering which Jews are coming out of the closet. The rule is at least one spouse must be Jewish to attend. I counted 120 Jews, 57 crypto-Jews, and 40 compromised or assimilated Christians.

October 14, 1986 The end of an era? For the first time ever, Doucet broached the question of my future at the behest of the PM. I told him I'd stay until Mulroney wanted to move me, after which I'd quit. I had no further interest in the public service.

According to Doucet, Mulroney is appalled by the bad, unfair publicity we have been receiving. He doesn't think it will go away and the next bilateral summit could, in fact, give it further life. "Does that mean Mulroney wants me out before March?" I asked. "Not necessarily," he replied. Doucet seemed to be hedging, acting rather evasively.

He mentioned there were two people Mulroney dreamed of having in politics for the Conservative Party: Stephen Lewis and myself.

October 17, 1986 The softwood lumber decision was handed down yesterday. Fifteen per cent duty approved. It's all anticlimactic. Pat Carney called this morning. What's the reaction in the United States, she asked? I told her it's hard for me to tell her about official reactions in Washington, since the embassy has been bypassed on the lumber issue in a manner I have not experienced in five years. The whole situation in Ottawa is frantic and confused. Political assistants are running the show (or trying to), and External Affairs is fragmenting under a superfluity of bosses. Part of the trouble is friction between Mulroney's political aides on the one hand and permanent officials on the other. Another part is the secretive and somewhat erratic way Pat Carney runs her show, and still another is that the U.S. Bureau in External has become a black hole into which all issues, initiatives, proposals, and solutions disappear.

In Ottawa suspicion and friction between the political and official sides are increasing. Moreover, the prime minister's political advisers are, I fear, urging him to distance himself from Reagan and U.S. affairs.

We attended a dinner at Jennifer Phillips's at her Arts and Crafts home on O Street to meet Sir Lawrence Gowing,[1] the celebrated English art critic, who is staying with her and Laughlin. He may be a great art critic, but he sprays as he talks. The usual Georgetown crowd was there: Kay Graham, Evangeline Bruce, Meg Greenfield, Joe Alsop, Susan Mary Alsop, the Fritcheys, John Whitehead. But for interludes like this, softwood lumber would drive me mad.

October 29, 1986 I went to Ottawa for meetings in the PMO on acid rain and with Clark and Carney on Canada-U.S. relations. The acid rain meeting, chaired by Doucet, enabled me to alarm the group about the administration's lack of financial support for the envoys' report.

The next alarming piece of news on acid rain came from Tom MacMillan. Apparently, the Canadian funds ($180 million) previously announced to develop technologies to combat acid rain were never put in our own fiscal framework. There is no such money. In other words, the PM's policy of having "clean hands" is, at the moment, a sham.

Doucet announced that he wants to begin formal planning for the next Reagan-Mulroney summit in Ottawa. This is quite premature. It won't take place before next March or April. It's far too soon for the issues to be shaped properly. It also means a lot of unnecessary, gruelling travel for me, on the terrible Piedmont-Washington-Syracuse-Ottawa local.

October 30, 1986 Still in Ottawa, I attended a meeting with Clark, Carney, and a slew of officials to review Canada-U.S. relations. This was the first such meeting that has taken place in a long time.

I was surprised by the way Clark and Carney went on about advanced cruise-missile tests. Carney went so far as to say that if the government agreed to such tests, it would be defeated. A ridiculous statement. I told Clark and Carney that if a request were made to test the advanced missile and we refused outright, our relationship with the United States would deteriorate in headlong fashion and could even be as bad as under Trudeau. When Clark went on about the problems that the SALT II breakout would cause with the peace groups and that the United States had to be made to understand this, I told him the United States thought we were making more

[1] (1918–1991) Painter and art historian. Keeper of British Collections and Deputy Director of the Tate Gallery 1965–1967.

of a fuss about SALT II "compliance" than all the other allies put together. They were now comparing the government's lack of guts on this issue to Trudeau's stance on cruise testing.

Clark got angry. "Who says that?" he asked. I replied, the National Security Council, State, and Defense. "Don't shoot the messenger," I added, "but I'm here to tell you the truth." Carney then repeated, "We'll lose the election if we test." I said, "I'm not a politician, but I think you will assuredly lose the election, if, like John Diefenbaker, you can't manage the relationship with the Americans."

On the trade agreement, I informed Clark and Carney that Peter Murphy[1] was being intimidated by the congressmen, that he was too junior and weak to stand up to them, and that I feared he was overnegotiating. Shultz had argued for a high-powered outsider to be negotiator and was assuredly correct to do so. The Murphy situation is worrying and has to be watched closely.

Back in Washington, shaken by the travails of the day. I got into my black tie and went to a dinner at the National Gallery on the occasion of the marvellous exhibition of Matisse's paintings in the Nice period. This was indeed a soothing experience. I chatted with Shultz, Whitehead, Volcker, and others and sat between Pamela Carter Brown and Lucky Roosevelt. I was surprised by my capacity for distraction, having left Sondra home to stay with Rebecca and Keith.

October 31, 1986 In its widely read "Personalities" column, the *Washington Post* reprints the gist of a recent story in the *Star* claiming my allowances were slashed because of the slap incident (they weren't), that I overspent them (I did not), and that I took "unexplained" trips to New York and resort areas (unexplained only to the media). In the afternoon Kay Graham called Sondra and told her how disgusted she was by the piece. She said Ben Bradlee never told her and that she was sure he didn't even know. She said the abuse we were taking was awful. In the afternoon Bruce Phillips sent a letter to Bradlee and demanded a full retraction, prominently placed, in the same column as the lies appeared.

---

[1] (1948–1994) Head of U.S. delegation in Canada-U.S. free-trade negotiations. In 1983 he was appointed Deputy U.S. Trade Representative and U.S. Ambassador to the General Agreement on Tariffs and Trade in Geneva.

November 1, 1986 Lunch with Keith and Rebecca at Marc Leland's newly acquired grand estate on the Potomac in Virginia. The Kirklands were there, the Roosevelts, Vernon Jordan, and other familiar faces. Rebecca is convalescing after her twelve-hour surgery in Pittsburgh. I sat beside Kay Graham, but we did not discuss the *Post*'s treatment of the Gotliebs. I was amazed that we got a complete retraction in this morning's paper. The column, with the title "To Gotlieb's Defense," cited almost verbatim the External Affairs press release giving the lie to all the harassing falsehoods in the *Star*.

In the evening the Brinkleys took us to the Jockey Club for dinner, *à quatre*. David had said we would never get a retraction in a prominent place, the *Post* would never do it. And if it did, there would be a hooker in it. Smart man, who knows all about the media. He was wrong.

November 2, 1986 Claire Hoy, in the *Toronto Sun*, says it's no wonder the Gotliebs have so many friends – they spent $280,000 over the past two years wining and dining them. Then he repeats all of the *Star*'s mendacities, without even bothering to mention the External Affairs denial. He repeats his own former lie that we underpay our staff (we don't even pay them – the embassy does, in accordance with standard government scales). The whole thing is libellous and disgusting. Bruce Phillips says forget it – no one pays attention to Hoy. The hell with that. Enough is enough. I've decided to hire a Toronto lawyer to threaten a libel action unless I get a full retraction from both the *Star* and the *Sun*.

November 4, 1986 The U.S. congressional elections. Depressing results for Canada: the Democrats regained the Senate. A new page is turned in the chapter of protectionism.

Lunch with Jim Schlesinger to explore whether he might be interested in entering into a professional relationship with the embassy on energy matters. Just exploratory, I told him. "I don't lobby," he barked. "I'm not asking you to lobby," I barked back. "What we want is strategic advice on electricity, oil, and gas." I said I was sure we would see a big protectionist thrust in these areas in the new Congress. He was noncommittal.

November 5, 1986 We had a small dinner tonight at the Residence, the first since our return from Pittsburgh with Rebecca last week. We had

Edmund Morris,[1] now deeply at work on Reagan's biography, his spouse, Sylvia,[2] ditto on her biography of Clare Booth Luce,[3] Paul Volcker, Bob and Helen Strauss, Meg Greenfield, and Marc Leland. A successful mix, notwithstanding opposing political sentiments. Strauss was in high spirits because of the Democratic conquest of the Senate. He is close to Bob Byrd,[4] Lloyd Bentsen, and other Democratic senators as well as Republican Bob Dole. All sides seem anxious to get his political advice.

November 6, 1986 Pat Carney is in town to talk softwood lumber with Mac Baldridge. Her aides told me last night she was very confident about her planned presentation to Baldridge, but this morning she had a case of stage fright. She had forgotten her lines. I told her she should read out her briefing notes to Baldridge – that this was okay in international diplomacy. This relieved her enormously. She was on the point of a continual faint the whole day. I had to hold her by the arm on a half-dozen occasions. At lunch with Baldridge and the four provincial ministers who joined us to make the pitch, she seemed on the point of passing out.

November 7, 1986 I flew to Ottawa with Jim Judd to brief the deputy ministers, at their monthly luncheon, on the significance of the U.S. congressional elections earlier this week. I outlined the likely consequences of the Democratic and southern domination of the Senate, giving thumbnail personality profiles of Lloyd Bentsen (Finance), Bennett Johnston (probably Energy), Robert Byrd (probably majority leader), and others. I told the group the results were not good for Canada. They were bad for trade, bad for energy, and bad for the environment.

---

[1] (b. 1940) American historian, best known for his biographies of U.S. presidents. *The Rise of Theodore Roosevelt* won the Pulitzer Prize and the American Book Award in 1980. He spent several years as President Ronald Reagan's authorized biographer and published the controversial *Dutch: A Memoir of Ronald Reagan* in 1999.

[2] British-born American writer and biographer. Author of *Rage for Fame: The Ascent of Clare Booth Luce* (1997).

[3] (1903–1987) American editor, playwright, social activist, politician, journalist, and diplomat. Republican Representative from Connecticut 1943–1947; U.S. Ambassador to Italy 1953–1956. She fell seriously ill in 1956 from arsenic poisoning and resigned as ambassador.

[4] (b. 1917) Democratic Senator from West Virginia 1959 to present, currently the longest-serving member of Congress. President *pro tempore* of the Senate 1989–1995.

I walked with Paul Tellier to his office in the Langevin Block. We talked about my bad press, and especially the libellous attacks on me by Bob Hepburn of the *Toronto Star*. I said I thought the government's failure to defend me was a contributing factor. Tellier said, "This government would never defend you. They will never defend any public servant." His final words were ominous. "Don't trust anyone. Do you understand me? No one."

November 9, 1986 We dropped over this Sunday afternoon to have tea with Joe Alsop, who is ailing. Walking to his Georgetown house, we were bathed with sweat on this hot, humid day. It's hard to believe that back in my hometown of Winnipeg, the worst winter snowstorm in decades is raging. Listening to my mother go on about it on the telephone did not make it more believable.

We talked about George Shultz and whether he would resign over the Iranian fiasco. Joe thinks Shultz's credibility is greatly reduced. He should have stood up to Don Regan or whoever in the White House masterminded the arms-for-hostages deal with the mullahs. Alsop was confident Shultz would not resign, although he thought he should. Alsop says the argument one always uses in such situations is that "if I resign, it will only be worse."

We talked about John Sparrow. Joe described his decline in a manner highly descriptive of his own – "Drinks too much, gets mean and ugly, and does other unmentionable things."

November 12, 1986 Yet again, I called on Mac Baldridge to discuss softwood lumber. We had a hesitant conversation about what is called a "suspension agreement." He pointed out that if we had to go to "final determination," the precedent of finding a national resource to be subsidized could give them and us a lot of trouble downstream. We could avoid this through a suspension agreement, and we could keep the revenues, rather than let the Americans collect them.

In the evening we were invited to a party on the retirement of Lois Herrington, assistant attorney general, wife of John.[1] I had been trying to see this elusive man for weeks without success. He is the kingpin of the technology program on acid rain. Just before the dinner, I got a call from the Department of Energy saying Herrington would see me tomorrow.

[1] John S. Herrington (b. 1939) Assistant Secretary to the Navy 1981–1983; Secretary of Energy 1985–1989.

Again, proof of the efficacy of the social connection. If we were not going to see him socially tonight, I would not have been able to get an appointment to see him. There was a big crowd at the dinner – the Meeses, the Wicks, Pete Wilson, Jeane Kirkpatrick. We were the only foreigners at this very Californian–Reagan loyalist evening.

The new president of FERC told me the good news that we won't see action against Canadian gas next year and the bad news that we could see it on oil and electricity.

November 13, 1986 At my meeting with Herrington, he confirmed money was not available to implement the envoys' acid rain report. What's worse is that I learned that at the time of the Washington Summit, the administration knew monies were not available but gave full endorsement anyway, to get them off the political hook. The president endorsed the report knowing that it might never be implemented. All this goes some way to explain the astounding battles that took place within the administration at the time. I told Herrington the issue was not just acid rain but the good faith of the president and the credibility of Mulroney.

Herrington is sure we will face tremendous pressure for an oil import fee, with only a chance for an exemption for Canada and Mexico. We will face pressure on electricity and gas as well. So far as uranium is concerned, he gets calls from Senator Domenici[1] almost every day. "What's he want?" I asked. "To close the border to your uranium," he replied.

November 14, 1986 We went to brunch at Polly Kraft's in her new apartment on Connecticut Avenue, to which she moved after Joe's death. Mostly the Georgetown set: the two Alsops, Evangeline Bruce, Kay, Meg, etc. Two visiting Englishmen were in attendance, George Weidenfeld and Ronnie Grierson,[2] two of the most well-connected people alive, gossips of international standing.

Edward Morris told me he thinks that Reagan is personally responsible for the Iran caper. There will be a scapegoat, and it will be John Poindexter.

November 16, 1986 Tonight we hosted a monster dinner for the Washington International Horse Show – a sit-down crowd of 125 at the

[1] Peter Domenici (b. 1932) Republican Senator from New Mexico 1973 to present.

[2] (b.1921) Former Director of General Electric Corporation and of Warburg 1958–1986.

Residence. Poindexter was supposed to come, but not surprisingly, he cancelled at the last moment (Iran). It was one of the coldest nights Washington has ever experienced at this time of year, and our dining tent was vastly underheated. It was so cold under the tent that the guests had to wear their coats throughout the meal. Sondra gave me a great line with which to greet the guests: "Welcome to Canada." It was also her idea to hand out blankets and my socks to the crowd, so one of our maids went around with a huge basket of socks. Most of the guests turned them down, but when she got to a table consisting of a group of Polish breeders, they all grabbed them. I'm sure I will never see the Poles or the socks again.

I had determined on this occasion, as did Sondra, that we wouldn't worry about the party. There was a Canadian connection, the horse show people wanted it and said they would organize it, pay for it, arrange the great tent, etc. They hired Gretchen Poston[1] to do all the arrangements and protocol, so I decided to do an Oliver Wright – just come to my own party and not worry myself over the little details.

Result: a disaster. The embassy let us down. The supervisor of the Residence never came by to check the heating arrangements. No one knew how much power the electrical circuits could carry. Without supervision, the heating arrangements were totally inadequate, the power broke down, and the result was a frozen fiasco. The only good thing I can say is that the crowd was extraordinarily relaxed under the circumstances. No one left prematurely. But people were shivering – even with their coats on.

Highlight of the evening: Sweetpea peed on the trousers of the Soviet ambassador.

Earlier in the evening, I attended a well-publicized reception in honour of Mrs. Sadat to mark the anniversary of Anwar Sadat's historic trip to Jerusalem. Almost no "names" were there; what a cruel town this is.

November 17, 1986 I saw Baldridge alone to urge him to agree to an expedited review of a final decision against us on softwood lumber. If there is no quick review, U.S. customs will collect the countervailing duty, resulting in a transfer of wealth to the U.S. Treasury for possibly up to two years. We would be transferring about $600 million a year, and we wouldn't even be able to raise our own stumpage rates without hitting the industry with a "double tax." We sure have got ourselves into one hell of a box. All this because the

[1] (1934–1992) White House Social Secretary in the Carter administration.

previous government of B.C. was so pigheaded over the years, grabbing a larger and larger share of the U.S. market and not raising their revenues from industry. Baldridge said our request sounded reasonable and if he were in industry, he wouldn't hesitate to agree. He would do his best, within the limits that law and precedent would allow, but he couldn't promise anything.

November 18, 1986 I flew to Ottawa and back to participate in a federal-provincial ministerial meeting on softwood lumber chaired by Pat Carney. I have never seen the provinces so at war with each other. Before the meeting Carney asked me what we should do. I said we should probably go for a suspension agreement. If we don't, we'll probably lose the case. Moreover, we'll have a horrible legal precedent that will encourage all kinds of trade harassment cases against us on anything that comes out of the ground, and we'll transfer the revenue to the United States because we won't get expedited review. Too late, she said, Priorities and Planning just met, and they want to fight it all the way.

But at the federal-provincial meeting, we heard British Columbia, which exports most of our softwood lumber, pleading for a suspension agreement so they could raise stumpage rates. They were strongly supported by Quebec and Alberta, with Ontario playing a spoiler role. The B.C. forestry minister got so angry he asked the Ontario minister whether his province was ready to transfer to Victoria an amount equivalent to its loss of revenues. Nothing like the loss of a billion dollars to bring out the fisticuffs.

Got back in time to attend a dinner by former agriculture secretary John Block. Fred Iklé mentioned to me that Defense assumed everything was okay on the cruise-missile front. When I asked him what he meant, he said, well, we'll send up our proposal for testing and you'll agree. I told Iklé he was dead wrong. "Don't expect this government to approve the request. Clark is against it, linking it to your breakout from SALT II, and Carney thinks the government would never be elected again if it says yes." I warned Iklé that if the United States makes the request, it could precipitate a crisis in Canada and not even get an affirmative reply.

November 19, 1986 We had a breakthrough of sorts. Commerce Undersecretary Smart[1] (no friend of Canada) suggested a deal. If we raised

[1] Bruce Smart. Undersecretary for International Trade in the U.S. Department of Commerce 1985–1988.

stumpage 15 per cent, industry would withdraw the petition. I asked Smart, "Will you sell this hard to the U.S. industry?" He said, "Yes, it's a fair deal, and I will urge Baldridge to agree." Baldridge did so and I informed Carney. She thought this was the best approach, given the circumstances, and she is right. Baldridge and Smart want to avoid final determination. Theirs is a flawed decision, and they want to avoid taking it.

Later, I called on Lloyd Bentsen, who tomorrow becomes the chairman of the Finance Committee, and a man of enormous importance to Canada. I have been calling on him for years while he was in "opposition" (fortunately). Now that he is man of the hour, I have some standing. He is a close friend of Bob Strauss, a true Southerner, aristocratic in bearing, soft-spoken, highly controlled, and sure of himself and of America's place in the world. He is the most important and impressive of the Southern senators who have conquered the Senate. Strauss says he is one of "the two dozen most intelligent men in America." Intelligent he is, but surprisingly reserved, and in my opinion, rather hooded and possibly a tad hypocritical.

I raised the free-trade agreement, the possibility of an oil tax, and general trade legislation. His committee would be responsible for all three subjects. He outlined, very deliberately, his stand on all three. He was entirely in favour of a free-trade agreement, his principal observation being that the administration did not take the proposal seriously enough. His opposition to fast-track authority last spring had nothing to do with Canada; it was just a way of expressing dissatisfaction with the administration's approach to trade.

Unfortunately, he was also completely in favour of an oil import tax. Texas, he said, is going through a depression, not a recession.

November 20, 1986 I flew to Vancouver to attend the first-ministers' conference. The bad news was the presence on the same flight of Allan Fotheringham, at whom I am very angry for various sins and insults. The good news is I went first class, so I didn't have to sit close to him.

Whatever was on the agenda didn't matter much. It was all softwood lumber. I didn't think my presence before the federal ministers would serve much purpose, but it proved otherwise. The prime minister came into the holding room where I was sitting and asked me to explain why the latest Baldridge proposal on softwood was one we should accept. He then called me into the meeting with the premiers, without officials present. I explained in the most forceful terms why the course proposed, while bad, was the least bad for Canada. I ended up debating with Peterson, who, with 5 per cent of the export production, is playing a spoiler role.

November 21, 1986 At lunch I briefed the prime minister and premiers on the American political scene. My comments followed Reisman's on the state of the free-trade negotiations. I told them protectionism was getting worse, and the trend was bipartisan and irreversible. The news was also worrying on the energy front; we will face an assault on our oil, gas, and electricity exports. But I was more optimistic on the matter of our free-trade agreement than I was before the U.S. congressional elections. Bentsen was positive, Matsunaga as chairman of the Trade Subcommittee was a big improvement, and our basic bipartisan support on the Finance Committee remained intact – the Democrats Moynihan and Bradley, the Republicans Chafee and Durenberger. But taken in the round, the Democratic Congress was bad news for Canada.

Peterson talked at length on the need for a bigger antiprotectionist effort in Washington, a national effort, conducted by the embassy. I told him that was fine, but we had to realize that most of the protectionist efforts we were now fighting were not general ones hitting us accidentally, as was the case a few years ago, but measures targeted directly at Canada. So goodwill tours led by men of goodwill (Peterson suggested Bill Davis and Peter Lougheed) would not get us much. We needed to play the U.S. system, seeking out domestic allies. But we were nearing the point of diminishing returns in our ad hoc combats.

November 22, 1986 Mulroney told me he called the president after his Iran press conference. I said his instincts were good.

November 23, 1986 Sondra being out of town, I went to brunch myself at Nancy Reynolds's. She had Mike and Carolyn Deaver and their kids and me. An article appeared last week saying Deaver was in hospital in some secret place, implying he had a nervous breakdown or AIDS or something. But he looked well. Carolyn said she was going to have a New Year's Eve party for all the people who would be happy to see the end of 1986. Not a bad idea. She could have the Deavers, ourselves, the Colemans,[1] the Meeses,

[1] John Coleman (b. 1935) Owner of the Ritz-Carlton hotel in Washington.

the Regans, the McFarlanes, the Nofzigers,[1] the Poindexters, the Shultzes, and many others among the walking wounded.

We talked at length about Iran-Contra. Nancy Reagan is well plugged in to the California crowd, who are calling for the resignations of Don Regan, Shultz, and Poindexter. It seems Nancy is on the warpath and is determined to protect big daddy. No one seems to think Shultz's position is tenable.

November 24, 1986 After having breakfast at the Residence with Cobb and Hinckel to discuss Reagan's upcoming visit to Ottawa, we moved over to the White House for an expanded meeting, chaired by Poindexter and his deputy, Peter Rodman.[2]

The White House officials raised missile testing, making a hard sell. I gave them the same treatment I gave Iklé – don't press or you'll be unpleasantly surprised. I took Cobb aside and told him that it was ridiculous to hear this pitch from the White House when Shultz, in Ottawa last Friday, gave Clark the impression he had never even heard of the advanced cruise-missile testing. Shultz undercut my credibility and that of the embassy. Cobb, irate, said this was typical of Shultz. It wasn't because he wasn't briefed – he was. He was undercutting Weinberger on an issue of great importance to Defense.

Spoke to Mac Baldridge and told him that the prime minister, the Canadian government, and not least, myself, were hung out to dry on this softwood lumber problem. The country was exploding with anger, anguish, and anxiety about where the United States stood. He was the only one who could deliver the U.S. industry. If he didn't, it would be the biggest mess ever in Canada-U.S. relations, and the victims would be the free-trade agreement and Mulroney. I got his assurance that he would do everything possible.

November 25, 1986 One of those great, explosive days in power town. You know you are present while history is being made.

At 10 a.m. I attended a ceremony at State given by Shultz for Tom Enders to present him with an award on his retirement. Shultz arrived and left

---

[1] Franklyn "Lyn" Nofziger (1924–2006) American journalist and political consultant. Press Secretary to President Ronald Reagan and later his Assistant for Political Affairs in the White House.

[2] (b. 1943) Director of the State Department Policy Planning Staff 1984–1986; Deputy National Security Advisor 1986–1987; Special Assistant to the President for National Security Affairs 1987–1990.

before the ceremony, saying he was called to the White House. I was sure this was to present his resignation. John Whitehead's testimony before Congress yesterday seemed like the final nail in the political coffin. John defended Shultz, differed with the president over whether Iran was still a terrorist state, and criticized the operational activities of the NSC.

Later in the morning, I passed the guards at the chancery. They were watching TV and one of them shouted at me, "Poindexter has just resigned, as well as Colonel North."[1] As I walked to the Metropolitan Club to have lunch with Roy Denman,[2] several people I barely knew stopped me, asking, "Did you hear the news?" The disclosure of the diversion of the Iran arms sale funds to the Contras has ignited the city.

I feel that Poindexter and North are fall guys. Two experienced military men such as themselves would not have carried out such activities without higher authority. The balance sheet for this day: Shultz is saved by the bell to fight another round, and Don Regan will go, if not at once, then soon. The hounds are out for Regan's blood. Washington revels in a loser.

I regret Poindexter's departure. He was a solid, direct type. Now he joins the walking wounded. Mountains of shit will be heaped upon him. The New Rome turns thumbs down as the gladiator falls in its great amphitheatre.

November 27, 1986 I went to Thanksgiving dinner at Gerry and Eden Rafshoon's.[3] Just them, Elizabeth Drew, her husband, and myself. All four are, of course, big Democrats (though Elizabeth pretends to be neutral). The excitement over the Iran-Contra revelations is too much to contain. Washington is unrestrained in its enjoyment of the disaster that has befallen the Reagan administration. Of course, the catch phrase is "no gloating." "We're not gloating," said Elizabeth and Gerry, as they gloated.

December 1, 1986 John Herrington and our minister of environment, Tom MacMillan, met today. MacMillan made a good presentation, stressing that the good faith of the president and Mulroney's credibility

---

[1] Oliver North (b. 1943) Marine Corps Lieutenant Colonel assigned to the National Security Council staff in 1981. U.S. Counterterrorism Coordinator 1983–1986; subsequently Deputy Director for Political-Military Affairs.

[2] (1924–2006) British diplomat and trade negotiator. Head of the EC delegation to the United States 1982–1989.

[3] He was Assistant to President Jimmy Carter for Communications 1978–1980.

were both on the line, as well as the success of the next summit. Herrington made some encouraging noises on acid rain. Apparently the United States will spend $5.5 billion over the next five years on control technology for acid rain, and it will also seek new monies for the program.

December 2, 1986 The Regan-Meese television broadcast rivets all of Washington. I watched in my office, along with a number of officers and personal staff who gathered for a drink to celebrate the beginning of our sixth year in Washington. The appointment of Carlucci to replace Poindexter as national security adviser is welcome news. In times of crisis Washington behaves sensibly. He's a pro's pro.

This city is being compared to downtown Beirut. In all the years I've been here, I've never seen such a mess. Most depressing is the camera-hogging and publicity antics of the senators and congressmen and the posturing, smugness, and self-congratulation of the Democratic press.

At Roy Pfautch's annual Christmas party, the wreckage of the Reagan administration was everywhere to be seen. Even Mike Deaver came, as did another hit target, Lyn Nofziger (victims of the new Washington conflict-of-interest game). Ed Meese was there, along with a huge turnout of Reaganites: Baldridge, the Wicks, Herrington, and John Tower (who is now heading up the NSC investigation into Iran-Contra). I sat beside Ursula Meese and Mac Baldridge, who was this year's surprise Santa Claus. It is extraordinary how Roy, a bachelor lobbyist from St. Louis, has managed to turn this event into a Washington institution during the Reagan years. There was a special feeling of solidarity. When Meese, who announced the appointment of a special prosecutor today, got his "Santa" award, most people stood up and applauded.

December 6, 1986 Sweetpea is dead. He was hit by a car on Rock Creek Parkway. Apparently, some delivery man left the kitchen door open onto the street and out he went. He was such a mess the vet had to put him to sleep. We were both just wild about Sweetpea. I took Harry Truman's advice and bought a dog. Now I don't have a friend in Washington.

December 7, 1986 Bob Strauss had a big luncheon yesterday at the F Street Club for the powerful and mysterious Lew Wasserman.[1] It was a

[1] (1913–2002) Legendary Hollywood agent and film studio executive credited with creating the studio system.

quintessential Washington power lunch. Three presidential candidates were there – Howard Baker, Bob Dole, and Governor Robb[1] – along with Lloyd Bentsen, Jim Baker, Elizabeth Dole, Russell Long, and John Dingell, among others. I told Bob Strauss he had a great crowd. "A tribute to Wasserman," he said. "Bob," I said, "you would have had the same turnout if Wasserman wasn't here." "You're right," he replied.

Sally Quinn came up to me and said, "Poor Ben, he's getting so much grief from his statement that 'he hasn't had so much fun since Watergate.' The right wing is attacking him terribly."

I asked Howard Baker if the Iran-Nicaragua problem was going to get worse. He said the president has only one course of action. He has to get the news into the public domain before it is dragged out in the congressional committees or by the independent counsel. He has to get ahead of the story, stay ahead, and avoid surprises.

December 9, 1986 In Ottawa a delegation of U.S. senators has arrived to discuss free trade. Simon Reisman told me that the Prime Minister's Office was not planning to invite me to the prime minister's lunch for the senators at 24 Sussex. Simon said, "I told Burney this is ridiculous. Your role in Washington will be impaired if you are not there. If you're not invited and if I were in your shoes, I'd resign." Two minutes later, Burney called to say I would be invited and I would be the only Canadian official at the lunch. Doucet arranged it.

The senators – Bentsen, Matsunaga, Chafee, and Baucus – went immediately to a meeting with Canadian businessmen. This was, I believe, the most important Senate delegation ever to come to Canada. David Culver[2] of Alcan chaired the meeting and was impressive. Tom D'Aquino[3] produced graphs aimed at showing why a trade agreement was in Canada's interest, barely touching on why it was in the United States' interest. This was followed by a meeting with Clark, Carney, and Wilson, chaired by Carney, who

---

[1] Charles Robb (b. 1939) Governor of Virginia 1982–1986; Democratic Senator from Virginia 1989–2001.

[2] (b. 1924) Canadian businessman. Chairman and CEO of Alcan Aluminum Limited 1979–1989. He led the campaign in Canada's business community in support of the Canada-U.S. Free-Trade Agreement 1986–1988.

[3] (b. 1940) CEO and President of the Canadian Council of Chief Executives. A supporter of the Canada-U.S. Free-Trade Agreement and NAFTA.

was at her most erratic. Bentsen made a superb speech, coming on very positively about Canada-U.S. free trade.

Everything was going fine until Carney said, "Look here, there is one thing you have to understand, we don't control the provinces. They control the natural resource sector under our constitution, and there's nothing we can do about it." This played beautifully into Max Baucus's hands. While no genius, he was clever enough to understand this reinforced his main concern: Canada can't deliver the provinces in an FTA. I piped in to say Canada has ratified more treaties in provincial jurisdiction than the United States has in state jurisdiction and Baucus should have no fears on this score. I should have thought of saying that it is the resource provinces that so badly want an agreement, including B.C. and Alberta.

At Mulroney's lunch the discussions were gentle but not deep, which was just as well, because it's not in our interest to see the Senate get into the substance at this stage. The PM was very superior in his handling of the visitors. High-minded, courtly, even noble. He said the United States owes us nothing; it pays its dues in the world and so do we. And Canada wasn't going to misbehave and act like a juvenile delinquent if no deal was struck. We weren't going to pull out of NATO or pull back on defence, as some of the opposition members were calling for. The United States wanted a fair agreement. Well, so did Canada. There was a market for fairness in Canada.

After lunch I went to Question Period with the senators, who were introduced by the Speaker. We watched the proceedings from the gallery. Mulroney could not have paid the opposition parties enough to perform as they did. What a favour they did for Canada. Both displayed their deep anti-U.S. sentiment. Lloyd Axworthy, in particular, attacked the United States over nuclear submarines in the Arctic, their issuing exploration permits in the Beaufort Sea within Canadian territory, and so on. True nationalist paranoia was in evidence. Bentsen and his colleagues must have thought, God, we'd better deal with Mulroney, he's sane. Mulroney must have been very pleased.

December 10, 1986 Spent a quiet day in New York and in the evening attended a dinner at the 21 Club hosted by advertising executive Ed Ney. I sat between Patsy Preston, whose husband is head of the Morgan Bank, and Gayfryd Steinberg, a Canadian, and wife of financier Saul

Steinberg.[1] She was shocked when I asked her if she lived in New York. "Don't you know who my husband is?" she asked. No, I said. "I can't believe it," she replied. "Everyone has heard of Saul Steinberg."

She invited me to see his old master collection. "Has he been collecting a long time?" I asked. "Oh yes, for a long time," she replied. "Almost four years. He reads a lot of books. I do too. I'm reading a lot about the great religions. We both read every night before we sleep. We read the same book. We each have our own copy."

December 11, 1986 I was having breakfast at the Pierre with Ken Taylor, trying to revive interest in the sorely neglected Festival of Canada, when I got an urgent message to call Paul Heinbecker at the embassy. A story has broken that some Canadians were responsible for financing the Iranian arms deal. It seems Bill Casey testified to this effect on the Hill. At last, we're important. We're on the American agenda.

Ottawa is panicking for information. I tried to reach some contacts in Washington from my hotel, but this was massively frustrating. At the White House, Cobb could tell me nothing. He said everyone was under legal and administrative constraints, and in any event, no one in the NSC knew anything. I tried to reach the acting head of the NSC – unavailable. Then I tried to reach Bill Casey – unavailable, testifying. None of his deputies would return my call. Eventually, I reached Undersecretary Armacost, who also knew nothing. Stonewalled all around.

I got back to Washington late in the afternoon and managed to see the acting chairman of the Senate Intelligence Committee, Bill Cohen.[2] He couldn't tell me whom the witness had named, but he assured me that to the best of his committee's knowledge, the Canadian government was not involved. Cohen had suggested to the witness in question – a Mr. Furmark[3]

[1] (b. 1939) American businessman who acquired Reliance Insurance in 1968, a 150-year-old Philadelphia firm, and established Reliance Group Holdings, a financial services firm.

[2] (b. 1940) Republican Representative from Maine 1973–1979; Senator from Maine 1979–1997; Secretary of Defense 1997–2001.

[3] Roy M. Furmark. A New York business executive and former consultant to Ashland Oil Inc. who pleaded guilty for conspiring with Orin E. Atkins, a former Ashland chairman, to sell documents that would help the National Iranian Oil Company win a multimillion-dollar lawsuit against Ashland.

– that he call me. We shall see. A terribly frustrating day. Everyone is clammed up. We're in the dark.

In the evening I went to our annual RCMP reception. Bill Webster, director of the FBI, was there and we had a long chat about the Iran affair. He casually mentioned that he hoped we wouldn't be embarrassed by the covert assistance we had recently provided to the United States. But, he said, this might now be seen differently in the light of the Iran arms dealing and hostage links. He thought criticism of us would not be justified.

Covert assistance? Embarrassed? I didn't have a clue what he was talking about. But I sure wasn't going to tell him that. I fear the embassy's RCMP liaison officer, Bob Bell, has kept me in the dark about some Canadian undercover activity involving the Americans. I'm boiling mad.

December 12, 1986 I called Bob Bell into my office as soon as I arrived this morning and instructed him in plain language to brief me on the "covert operation" that Webster mentioned to me last night. The story he revealed is very worrying and shows foolishness on the part of the RCMP. Bell claimed that he personally and the embassy were not involved, although he was aware of the operation. It involved Canada providing cover in a high-risk caper in the Middle East. I gave him bloody hell for keeping me in the dark. Then I called Si Taylor in Ottawa and told him to brief the PMO on a potential major embarrassment to Canada.

Unfortunately, this is the kind of secret operation that could get the government into deep and murky soup. The RCMP should never have gotten involved with the FBI. So far as I can determine, only Jim Kelleher, the solicitor general, was aware of it at cabinet level. If he did not inform the PM or Clark, he should be reprimanded.

Back to the testimony of Mr. Furmark, whoever he is. I tried getting hold of Casey again in the morning but with no luck. Wonder of wonders, he returned my call this afternoon. We were in a terrible position, I said. The United States was not collaborating with us or telling us anything about the so-called Canadian connection. Would he authorize the CIA to provide information to us through official channels?

"No, I can't, Allan." he said. "I can't co-operate. Justice has put us under legal constraints. I can't tell you anything. Call me anytime."

Meanwhile, the Canadian media in Washington are going nuts over the "Canadian connection" in the Iran-Contra affair. So I called Meese and Webster. Webster told me the problem was that the president had announced the appointment of an independent counsel, and while waiting for his appointment, the FBI "was in a lock and could do nothing." But my plea had some effect. A short while later, Webster called me again, saying he and Meese have agreed to assist us to the best of their ability, within the existing legal constraints. They would not object to our talking to Furmark.

Later, I received a call from Mulroney. He was home with a cold and wanted to talk further about the meeting with Bentsen and the other senators in Ottawa. He was pleased with the outcome, as well he should be. Mulroney asked if I thought we were facing another Watergate. I told him we were seeing a badly deteriorating situation, and one that would continue to deteriorate for some time, but not a Watergate. Mila, he told me, had called Nancy, who seemed very low.

December 16, 1986 This morning I got a panicky message from Ottawa. "Call Furmark. Reach him. We look stupid. The FBI material hasn't come. Call Webster. Call someone. Do something." So I called Dave Durenberger, chairman of the Senate Foreign Intelligence Committee. (He was quoted in Canadian papers as saying a nervous Canadian ambassador called every member of the committee last week. Hyperbole. But it did show I was on my toes.) I asked Durenberger to ensure we weren't taken by surprise by any public report of the Senate committee issues. He promised to give me advance notice.

Durenberger then said, "Allan, the Iranians didn't get screwed in this arms deal, the Canadians did." He summarized the whole story in one pithy sentence: "You see what happens when amateurs start fooling around in the Middle East."

December 17, 1986 They took Bill Casey to the hospital this afternoon. A cerebral stroke or something equivalent. He's taken tremendous abuse, and I feel sad about this. Just last Friday, I was giving him a bit of a hard time myself. The diplomatic note I sent to State was extremely critical of his behaviour. I can't recall authoring a stiffer diplomatic communication in all my years.

Tonight we gave a Canada-U.S. friendship party at the Residence. I asked each Canadian officer to bring an American friend. It was a good formula, and it worked well. We had about 175 people for the buffet. Peter Murphy asked me why we were being so unyielding on investment. I gave him the best advice I could: "Don't overnegotiate; the best is the enemy of the good.

If you strip away all our constraints on investment, you will risk destroying the entire free-trade negotiation and for no real purpose."

Murphy seemed unimpressed by the Bentsen visit – the senators were playing politics.

December 18, 1986 Another dizzy day. More of the softwood waltz – deadlines set, deadlines past, negotiations ended, negotiations resumed, Carney this, Clark that, Mazankowski presiding with this and that in mind. Is Mulroney playing? Everyone in Ottawa is complaining about how badly the softwood issue has been handled. Subtext: Carney's fault? My fault?

Furmark came to the embassy in the midst of all this. It was staked out by an army of Canadian reporters. We had rehearsed with two RCMP investigators various scenarios to get him to talk, but as it happened, he wanted to sing like a bird and did.

In the evening we co-hosted with Jack Valenti a private showing of *The Decline of the American Empire* at the MPAA theatre. Garth Drabinsky,[1] the distributor, and now the largest owner of movie outlets in North America, flew in from Toronto, and we had him and Valenti for a drink at the Residence before the event. Drabinsky was walking in the clouds, because his film won the New York Film Critics prize for the best foreign film of 1986.

Valenti told me that he had called on Bentsen and Gibbons and warned them of our dangerous and deluded plans (as he saw them) to Canadianize or control movie distribution in Canada. "If you get away with this," said Valenti, "the industry will lose its market in Japan and Europe." He was breathing fire.

Garth's movie went over like a block of cement with the sixty assembled guests. Brinkley thought it was awful ("the worst movie I've seen in my life"), several walked out (including Rowly Evans), and the rest sat and slept or suffered through it. Paul Volcker brought his daughter – unfortunately. Who says Washington is a sophisticated town?

December 19, 1986 The RCMP came to town to talk to the FBI about Bill Webster's revelation regarding our involvement in an undercover rescue operation in the Middle East. They briefed me in the evening and looked pretty unhappy. I asked if there was an Oliver North connection. There was.

---

[1] (b. 1949) Canadian film and theatrical producer and entrepreneur, the founder of Cineplex and Livent.

December 20, 1986 The peace of the day was shattered when Steve Martindale asked to see me privately and anonymously about "the Canadian connection" in the Iran-Contra caper. Steve, whom we have known for years (he acted as Margaret Trudeau's book agent), told me an incredible story with a cast of characters out of an Eric Ambler novel.

He recounted how he had introduced two Canadians, a Mr. Fraser and a Mr. Miller, to Adnan Khashoggi and fronted for him. He says the Canadians made a lot of money from the deal (Furmark claimed they'd lost money), and their banks in Toronto and the Caymans and their companies in Vancouver were being used to receive illicit funds from Marcos's[1] New York properties (through Adnan Khashoggi). Martindale complained he had got no money from Khashoggi, "the Sultan," "the guru," or other strange characters he described as playing a role. He gave me names, bank account numbers, and other details, but mostly he was incomprehensible. I then met with the RCMP officer at the embassy and debriefed myself. Martindale claimed his motivation was to be helpful. I wonder.

I can't figure Martindale out. I can't figure out what he told me. But then I can't figure anything out with regard to this affair. When I read what I've just written, it's gibberish.

December 21, 1986 We gave a large Sunday lunch party for contacts and friends today. Considering the Christmas exodus, we had a fantastic turnout – three senators (Bradley, Lugar, and Durenberger – all big "newsmakers," as they say), Kay Graham, Warren Phillips, John Whitehead, Charlie Wick, Dwayne Andreas, the Brinkleys, Kirklands, Colemans, Deavers, Lehrers, Morrises, Susan Mary Alsop, Evangeline Bruce, and so on. Kay Graham complained to Sondra afterwards that she didn't understand why we had Arnaud de Borchgrave[2] at the lunch. (Sondra told her there were two newspapers in Washington.) All anyone talked about, of course, was the "affair."

In the evening we had dinner at the Gilbert Hahns' along with Joe and Susan Mary Alsop, Roger Mudd, Meg Greenfield, Evangeline Bruce, and more of the usual suspects, plus a couple of prominent lawyers and lobbyists. There is unadulterated glee all around at the anticipated fall of Reagan.

---

[1] Ferdinand Marcos (1917–1989) President of the Philippines 1965–1986.

[2] (b. 1926) Correspondent for *Newsweek* 1969–1980; Editor-in-Chief of the *Washington Times* 1985–1991 and subsequently Editor-at Large; President and CEO of United Press International 1999–2001.

December 22, 1986 Joe Clark keeps going on about the "sovereignty" issue in the softwood dispute, meaning the U.S. right to agree to what we substitute for an export tax. We have tried to tell him and cabinet that we can't offer 15 per cent and then claim the unilateral right to remove it the next day.

December 23, 1986 Further travails of softwood. This is the only negotiation in my experience where ministers are directing every word of the deal. Mazankowski, Clark, Wilson, and Carney sit in semi-permanent session with Shannon and Burney, passing on instructions about every nuance in the negotiations. Last night they went on until after midnight.

The prime minister called me in the midst of all this for a report. He said he doesn't want to lose this one, he doesn't want the Americans to remove our fig leaf (my language). I spoke to him earlier in the day about the political situation here. I told him that I thought Reagan might not fully recover, and it was most distressing to find out how many otherwise sensible people here don't want him to. There is no one home at the White House. I urged him to call Reagan in California to wish him a happy New Year. I have no doubt Reagan, who cannot understand the precipitous decline in his popularity, would welcome the call.

December 26, 1986 Casey is reported to be very ill after his operation to remove a cancerous brain tumour. It seems he is not recovering and is certain to be replaced shortly. I feel very shabby about that dreadful diplomatic note I sent to the State Department a couple of weeks ago. It was very unusual as it attacked him personally for keeping us in the dark about "the Canadian connection." We were a little hysterical, and the note haunts me.

December 27, 1986 There is a *Wall Street Journal* story on Bill Casey and Oliver North by John Walcott[1] in which he recounts a tale about the FBI and CIA being involved with Ross Perot[2] in trying to rescue a U.S.

---

[1] (b. 1949) Correspondent at *Newsweek* 1977–1986; national security correspondent at the *Wall Street Journal* 1986–1989; Foreign Editor and National Editor of *U.S. News & World Report* 1989–1997.

[2] (b. 1930) Billionaire businessman from Texas who was a presidential candidate in 1992 and 1996. Founder of Electronic Data Systems in 1962, Perot Systems in 1988, and of the Reform Party of the United States in 1995.

Walking down Pennsylvania Avenue with Prime Minister Brian Mulroney after visiting the site of the new Canadian embassy.

Mary Jane and Charles Wick relaxing at the Residence. The Wicks were among the Reagans' closest friends.

Rowly and Kay Evans with the Gotliebs at the Residence.

Sondra reading her "Dear Beverly" column in the *Washington Post*.

Evangeline Bruce and the ambassador aboard the *Intrepid* in New York harbour as guests of CIA Director Bill Casey.

The ambassador and broadcaster David Brinkley during one of their many conversations.

The ambassador at the Residence with Bud McFarlane, Ronald Reagan's national security adviser.

The prime minister talks to the president about an ambassador during his first official visit to Washington in 1984.

George Bush's farewell dinner at the exclusive Alibi Club for departing White House adviser Mike Deaver, 1985.

The ambassador aboard Air Force One, following the Shamrock Summit in Quebec City in 1985.

A meeting in the White House with the president, during an official visit to Washington of Brian Mulroney.

James Oesch Photography

Bob Strauss, Kay Graham, and Paul Nitze, three of Washington's power brokers, at the laying of the cornerstone of the new Canadian embassy on Pennsylvania Avenue.

The Canadian team behind the free-trade agreement (left to right: Allan Gotlieb, Stanley Hartt, Don Campbell, Derek Burney, Pat Carney, Gordon Ritchie, Michael Wilson, and Simon Reisman).

Allan and Sondra at the White House with the president and Nancy Reagan.

hostage in Lebanon. The effort was described as a scam, and the hostage was killed. There was no mention of Canada's role in this story. I got hold of the RCMP to warn them the story had come out, just as I had predicted.

December 29, 1986 Another day of tension as the softwood talks bog down further and further, and as our negotiating stance, or should I say, non-negotiating stance, gets sillier and sillier.

Luce, one of the staff at the Residence, has been ill again. Wasn't it Lady Diana Cooper[1] who said, "Servants should never be ill; it takes one's mind off one's own symptoms"?

December 30, 1986 I was up throughout the night as the softwood lumber talks reached their feverish last hours. There must be a "final determination" by midnight tonight. Our stalwart negotiator, Don Campbell,[2] is doing well, but our cabinet and prime minister have him on a ridiculously tight rein. They are obsessed in Ottawa with the "sovereignty problem." The polls show that the public believes the government is mismanaging the U.S. relationship, so they want to look and act tough – they think maybe this will work better for them. It won't.

This morning I got several frantic calls from Fred Doucet in Ottawa instructing me to reach Baldridge, who has top responsibility in the dispute. He is in hospital in Albuquerque with pneumonia, I told Doucet. "The prime minister wants you to reach him anyway," he said. "The public won't understand if we don't make a last-ditch appeal to him."

"Sure they will," I said. "Just say that he was incapacitated in the hospital."

"The prime minister wants you to try anyway," Doucet replied.

Groaningly, I contacted his office. "He's in intensive care and cannot be reached."

Miraculously, the negotiations concluded successfully. The Americans gave ground and eased the "sovereignty" issue. I suspect the industry got increasingly suspicious that final determination would not be to their complete liking.

---

[1] (1892–1986) Youngest daughter of the eighth Duke of Rutland. Married Duff Cooper in 1919 and served with him as the wife of the British ambassador to France during and after World War II.

[2] (b. 1940) Canadian Ambassador to Korea 1984–1985; Assistant Deputy Minister for U.S. Affairs 1985–1989; Deputy Minister for International Trade 1989–1993; Ambassador to Japan 1993–1997.

I've spent weeks planning a surprise fiftieth birthday party for Sondra tonight at the Sea View, where we are again guests of Dwayne Andreas. (The *Wall Street Journal* has just published a lead story on him, very praising, describing him as the new Armand Hammer. He'll hate that.) I have asked the Doles, Howard Baker, the Andreases, the Strausses, and the Brinkleys, and they accepted. I shipped down a case of champagne with Rachel earlier in the day and told her to tell Sondra (ever suspicious) that they were documents for Bob Strauss. I also bought a load of caviar. As I expected, Sondra wasn't very happy with the idea of the party, although it did come as a surprise to her. What with the sickness in the family, she just didn't feel we should be celebrating, but I thought it was the right thing to do.

December 31, 1986 At dinner in the kitschy Sea View dining room, the music and performers' voices were so loud there was very little conversation. In between noises, I talked to the Strausses about being Jewish. Mosbacher,[1] Bob said, is Jewish and admits it. Cutler is and doesn't. Schlesinger is (or was) and doesn't. Novak[2] is Jewish and anti-Semitic. Rowly Evans is a non-Jewish anti-Semite. I raised my eyebrows at this last one, but Strauss said that if I didn't know Rowly was an anti-Semite, I should be fired.

January 1, 1987 The beginning of a new year and the end of a ghastly one. I can't add up all the bad and nasty things that happened to us and our family last year. We are so glad to say goodbye to that awful year.

We spent the day in the warm Florida sun. No question, Albert Camus got it right. Then we attended Susan Brinkley's annual New Year's Day party at the Sea View, the third night in a row eating in its dismal dining room. I chatted with Howard Baker, who told me he would decide by February whether to run for the presidency. I hope he does, because he is a moderate, balanced man (with a very sick wife). His problem is raising money. He said he would have to attend an average of four money-raising events per day for the entire year if he is to raise sufficient funds to take a run at the presidency. So I think he will drop out.

Baker predicts, as does everyone, that Mike Deaver will be indicted.

---

[1] Robert Mosbacher (b. 1927) U.S. businessman in the energy sector. Secretary of Commerce 1989–1992.

[2] Robert Novak (b. 1931) American journalist and political commentator. Well-known columnist for several decades with Rowland Evans and a television personality who appeared in many shows for CNN.

Seymour has piddled around for seven months, so everyone thinks he's got to come up with something to justify his efforts.

January 2, 1987 Relaxing on the beach in Bal Harbour. Received a call from Washington. The softwood lumber deal is going down badly in Canada. All the press are attacking it as a sellout. The Americans have been very unhelpful, as Commerce and the U.S. trade representative sent letters to the U.S. industry interpreting the agreement in a manner unfavourable to us. The government in Ottawa is reacting very emotionally. This is also said to be true of the prime minister. They are very upset and even contemplated cancelling the agreement.

It's the same tale over and over again with the government. They don't get out and sell their message or explain their accomplishments. They got a good deal (considering the awful alternatives), but they can't explain it.

I was dumbfounded to learn that Carney is in Hawaii and Clark in Guadeloupe. The cabinet knew that December 30 was the date of the U.S. decision or alternatives, yet they had none of the principal ministers available to sell the message. I was told the prime minister had planned to call Reagan to wish him a happy New Year (and, as planned, make a pitch on acid rain), but under the circumstances decided not to call.

January 5, 1987 I flew eight hours, through New York and Syracuse, to get into Ottawa for an afternoon meeting with Doucet in the PMO. After the meeting he and Bill Fox asked me to talk to Jeffrey Simpson, who spooks them more than any other journalist. Fox sees his column as having almost canonical status, in terms of influence. So I spent over an hour on the telephone with Simpson trying to talk sense to him. The PMO also wants me to come back tomorrow to talk to the *Citizen*'s editorial board. I can't bear the thought. I told the PM's people they are wrong to be fixated on editorial writers. They should write their own ink, get news stories and reportage, get every member to go on radio and TV every day for a week. Oh, for a few professional spin doctors.

January 6, 1987 Before I left Ottawa yesterday, Doucet talked to me about my future. The PM thinks I have been in Washington long enough. After the next summit in April, Mulroney would like me to return to Ottawa and be his policy adviser (Charles McMillan is leaving), located in the PCO. I would be like Anatoly Dobrynin, returning to the big policy job. I would report directly to Mulroney and advise him personally on all aspects of the government's agenda.

I said no thanks in the politest way. I told Doucet I don't want to be, or intend to be, a backroom boy. Thirty years of civil service was enough. I had some offers, from universities, think tanks, and law firms in two countries. I wanted to be up-front in my life, to write, to make money. I thought the PM should keep me in Washington until next January, after the free-trade agreement is done or not done. I asked him to ask the PM not to bounce me out of Washington without notice.

January 8, 1987 Carter Brown has rejected the National Gallery of Canada's proposal to assemble an old master exhibition from museums across Canada instead of from the U.S. National Gallery. There wouldn't be time to put together such a substitute arrangement, and the quality would not be as good as the Ottawa collection's. Anyway, the whole point of the exhibition was to welcome the National Gallery's new neighbour, Canada, by celebrating its counterpart museum in Canada. I've never witnessed a more petty group of bureaucratic nigglers than the people at the National Gallery in Ottawa. The idea that they can't handle both a Washington exhibition and their own official opening at a later date is beyond belief. Anyway, I suggested to Sidney Freedberg that they propose an exhibition of drawings from the National Gallery in Ottawa in lieu of the paintings. He liked the idea, although it's obviously no replacement.

Also, Carter Brown is suggesting that his institution stage a Canadian film festival for two weeks. So perhaps we can salvage something. I spoke to Mimi Taylor, at the National Gallery in Ottawa, who is working for Phyllis Lambert[1] at her new architectural museum in Montreal. I suggested they try to stage an exhibition on Canadian architectural achievements in association with the National Building Museum. Mimi thought Phyllis Lambert would be enthusiastic.

January 9, 1987 It's sad to see the government in Ottawa taking such a beating. All these ridiculous allegations about selling out our sovereignty continue to be heard in the land of the intellectual baboons. Now the

[1] (b. 1927) Canadian architect. Founder and Chair of the board of the Canadian Centre for Architecture in Montreal. Played a key role in the selection of Ludwig Mies van der Rohe as architect for the Seagram Building in New York and the Toronto-Dominion Centre in Toronto.

cacophony is starting up on acid rain. I fear the administration has let us down on the envoys' report. All the billions they are talking about has only a remote or indirect relevance to the main recommendations for a $5-billion technology commercialization program.

This is a country run by special interests. We are beginning to act like one. That means we must raise the temperature, the noise level, the discomfort level.

January 11, 1987 I am brooding over the acid rain situation. I'm thinking about recommending dramatic action to Mulroney – postponing the summit – thinking that it might be necessary for us to create a crisis in our relations. Without it we are going downhill quickly. The United States is simply taking all our reactions for granted. We are being discounted every day. The acid rain situation looks potentially more embarrassing than the lumber agreement in political terms. On lumber the fact is we didn't do all that badly. On acid rain the fact is the Mulroney government is being screwed.

January 12, 1987 A red-letter day. I sent a message to headquarters recommending the government urgently consider postponing the Ottawa Summit with Reagan. Deferring the summit would be a political bombshell. It would be seen as out of character. It would be a diplomatic move rarely employed. For those reasons it would be effective in registering Canadian dissatisfaction on the U.S. political radar. It would also show Canadians that their government means business.

We were entertained at dinner by Clayton and Polly Fritchey. They know, have known, and will know everyone who is anyone in Washington. I like her but can never understand what she is saying, because she whispers in one's ear. She had the Georgetown crowd: Kay, Meg, the Helmses, the Newhouses, the Califanos,[1] Paul Nitze, and from New York, Marietta Tree. The dinner was held in our honour, she told us. Did she tell the others?

I sat next to Meg Greenfield, who asked me what I thought of a number of her columnists. I rated them for her. She was defensive.

I asked Paul Nitze if Karpov's removal and replacement by Vorontsov as chief Soviet arms negotiator had any significance. It was an attempt by the Soviets, Nitze thought, through their alleged "upgrading," to push him out as well as Kampelman. "They don't like either of us, that's pretty clear."

---

[1] Joseph Califano Jr. (b. 1931) Secretary of Health, Education, and Welfare 1977–1979.

January 13, 1987 Burney and I spoke on the secure line about the summit. He is opposed to my proposal to postpone it. His reasons are good, but his advice is wrong.

In the evening I attended a party given by Susan Mary Alsop for the warden of All Souls, Sir Patrick Neil, who replaced the admirable but dissolute John Sparrow. The warden, in his capacity as vice-chancellor, is here trying to raise money for Oxford. Appropriately, the ageless senator Fulbright[1] was at the reception. Again, I am in the presence of history.

January 14, 1987 At dinner at the Italian ambassador's, Jim Schlesinger, Tom Enders, and I chatted about the Canadian predicament. Schlesinger said, "Your problem is not with the Congress, it is with the administration. The administration didn't have to do the shingles and shakes trick, nor did they have to find subsidy on softwood lumber – you've got to stand up to Reagan."

January 15, 1987 The wimps of iron are behaving in character. The PMO called me this morning to tell me that the prime minister would indeed follow my advice to postpone the summit, were it not for the fact that he likes Reagan and the man is ill.

Fred Doucet then asked whether I thought Mulroney should try to see Reagan in Washington. I told him that would be a bad mistake. Mulroney flying down to the Court of R.R.? How would that be perceived? Doucet said the purpose would be to criticize him. "Sure," I said, "and I am sure he would do so. But it would be followed by a photo op with the two arm-in-arm, smiling. You know what the Canadian media will do with that. Recalling me will probably make it appear that I am being reprimanded, not Reagan."

Then I received instructions from the prime minister. He wants me to see George Bush at once, repeat, at once. I am to request a meeting between him and the vice-president for next Saturday. I called for an appointment and got it at once. I was told Bush left a meeting to receive me.

I put it to Bush that U.S. insensitivity was destroying the Canadian government. Mulroney had a foreign policy, which was to get along with the United States and be its friend. In return, the United States was giving us

[1] James William Fulbright (1905–1995) Democratic Senator from Arkansas 1945–1974; Chair of the Senate Committee on Foreign Relations 1959–1975.

nothing . . . other than tariffs on shingles and shakes and quotas on lumber and disregard for the envoys' acid rain report. Bush said he was concerned and would act as a conduit to the president. He would discuss the whole matter with him tomorrow morning.

I was pleased. But Ty Cobb wasn't. He called me excitedly in the middle of a reception we were hosting for Robert Bateman,[1] the painter, and asked, "What did you expect to accomplish at a meeting with Bush? You know we won't change our position. What was the point? Don't you know the president is ill? . . . Did you recommend this to Mulroney?"

"What I recommend is my own business," I told him, and added, "The U.S. was damn lucky they had a leader in Canada who wanted to talk and not act unilaterally. Mulroney was civilized, liked the president, and believed in dialogue. If the NSC wants to read about policy changes in the *New York Times* instead of talking, I'm sure Mulroney could accommodate."

Shortly after, Mulroney called to tell me about his just-concluded telephone conversation with Bush. I used the opportunity to be completely frank. The United States was pushing us around, I said. That was the perception in Canada, and it was not totally unjustified. He should react strongly and visibly.

January 20, 1987 In preparation for the vice-president's visit to Ottawa tomorrow, I gave Baker and Darman an earful on the administration's deficiencies on acid rain and trade. I told them the failure of the president to deliver was undermining Mulroney's credibility at home. Baker was surprisingly well briefed. He asked pointedly whether Mulroney's problems arose mainly from domestic perceptions about his uncertainty of purpose and leadership weaknesses. I rebutted those perceptions, as vigorously as possible.

The government sent a plane to pick me up, as I had to get to Ottawa in time for a briefing with Mulroney before the cabinet discussion about the state of the relationship. I saw Mulroney for about fifteen minutes before the larger meeting. Doucet, who arranged it, and Phillips, who accompanied me on the aircraft, were also there. I tried my best to explain the awful truth, that thanks to Iran-Contra, Reagan was barely governing or in command at this time. There was a sign hanging on the White House door – "No one home" – and there was no delivery service in the U.S. government. Mulroney said he understood my analysis, but can he can accept the implications?

---

[1] (b. 1930) Canadian artist known for depicting the natural world.

After the private briefing we went to the larger one in the cabinet room of the Centre Block. A lot of officials and executive assistants were there, along with Clark, Wilson, and Carney. Mulroney was in the chair. He asked everyone to say their say and then called on me. I gave them all barrels. It was a curious meeting. Everyone said his or her piece, but there was no dialogue.

Clark is angry with me for my messages and telegrams. So let them shoot the messenger.

January 21, 1987 This morning Mulroney and Wilson met with Bush and Baker for a couple of hours. There were no surprises. As he told me he was going to do, Mulroney played a specially prepared tape to Bush, consisting of excerpts of anti-American tirades launched in Question Period in recent months. Clever. Then we had a general powwow at Rideau Gate, followed by a lunch at 24 Sussex, where the discussions focused on South Africa, China, and Cuba. Bush asked how Canadians felt about American policy in Central America. Mulroney said they didn't believe the Nicaraguans were important enough for the United States to get itself overly implicated and involved.

At the press scrum afterwards, Bush responded to questions about acid rain. "Boy, did I get an earful," he said. This is very helpful to Mulroney, who, on the whole, had a good day.

January 22, 1987 Stuck in Toronto because of a huge snowstorm. I had dinner with Conrad Black alone in his home. We talked about what was happening in the United States to Reagan and his team and what was happening in Canada to Mulroney and his team. Black is well informed on U.S. affairs – better than most I know in External. According to Black, the prime minister is an incurable Irish optimist. Perhaps this explains Mulroney's apparent unwillingness to accept the dark news I have been conveying to him about the situation in Washington. But maybe history will prove him right for being an optimist and show me to be wrong.

January 24, 1987 Dinner at Kay Graham's for Brian Urquhart. A stellar crowd, including four senators. I sat between Kay and the wife of Bob Graham, Kay's half-brother-in-law and now senator for Florida. A rising star. I chatted with Saudi Ambassador Prince Bandur[1] about the Iran-Contra business – the main topic of conversation everywhere.

---

[1] Prince Bandur bin Sultan (b. 1949) Saudi Arabian Ambassador to the United States 1983–2005.

January 25, 1987 David Peterson arrived in the midst of yet another snowstorm. We had arranged a dinner of thirty-six guests for him, and it was a difficult task. First, it's hard to get people out on a Sunday night. Secondly, Washington is not interested in a provincial satrap, even one who governs half of Canada. Thirdly, it was the night of the Super Bowl. Bob Strauss, who regretted, said only a stupid Canadian would choose tonight for a dinner. But we got a couple of dozen guests, notwithstanding that it was the worst snowstorm in memory. The Clayton Yeutters came all the way from MacLean, and we had the Schlesingers, Rowly Evans, Elizabeth Drew, Mortimer Zuckerman, and Roger Stevens[1] – all in all, a good A-list.

January 26, 1987 An early start on the Hill with David Peterson, for a morning meeting with Heinz of Pennsylvania. The storm last night was hideous, and all the government offices are closed. I was astonished at the empty roads and the empty corridors on the Hill. There was virtually no one in sight. But Heinz was in his office and received us cordially. We had a charming conversation on a number of items of no consequence and touched briefly on steel. (No mention of his long-standing desire for a steel quota.)

As we walked out, his press aide handed us a release the senator had just issued on the subject of steel – "Heinz Denounces Canadian Ambassador and Ontario Premier on Steel." This is exactly what Heinz then did. He stepped out with us into the corridor and blasted us before the media. He validated his press release. Now I know why he showed up in his office in the aftermath of the storm.

Later we paid a number of other calls on the Hill, and at the end of the day visited Moynihan, who was in marvellous form, although slightly better for drink. He offered us Scotch, and we joined in his merriment. For an hour and a half, Peterson sat entranced. Moynihan had a lot of great lines: "The Republicans stole the flag in 1980, and the Democrats will try to get it back in 1988 with trade. . . . The U.S. defined its identity by the production of consumer goods such as trucks and cars [citing Daniel Boorstin],[2] and now the Japanese have stolen our identity."

---

[1] (1910–1998) Founding Chairman of the Kennedy Center 1961–1988 and of the National Council on the Arts 1965–1969.

[2] (1914–2004) Historian and writer. Librarian of Congress 1975–1987.

January 27, 1987 More calls with Peterson on the Hill, and everywhere we go, a busload of Toronto hacks follows us. Peterson gives an interview after each call as if each event was of consequence. This is the political strategy of Hershel Ezrin,[1] his top media manipulator. As we walk the halls, get in and out of cars, await the appointments, the cameras roll. There is something unpleasant about this pack, the way they talk, dress, and behave. They are *mouches à merde*. Peterson insisted I attend his final press encounter, no doubt to bolster the image of a successful and harmonious trip.

I'm feeling very saturated by two days of Peterson and paparazzi. He learned a lot. He got zapped by Heinz, zapped by Levin[2] of Michigan, who threw the book at him on the Auto Pact, and he also got some strong words from Bentsen.

Peterson had the temerity to suggest to Bentsen that the trade issue was a partisan one, so far as the Democrats were concerned. Bentsen acted like a true Roman senator. He gathered all his dignity together, paused for what seemed like a full minute, then got red and angry. "This is a national issue, not a partisan one," he said solemnly.

"You see that picture over there," he gestured and pointed to the credenza nearby, "that's my granddaughter. That's what it's all about – the future of our grandchildren, our nation, our capacity to defend the free world . . ."

He mentioned national sovereignty about a dozen times in a couple of dozen minutes, while discussing steel, energy, free trade, the deficit, and so on. I think for Peterson the truth has begun to dawn. This country is on a protectionist binge, and Canada, they are telling us, better shape up.

In general, I thought Peterson had not mastered his brief very well. He tried – and more or less succeeded – to charm his way through everything. But much to his credit, he did not criticize Mulroney to his interlocutors. The opposite was true. His message was more like "Give the guy a break."

In the afternoon, I said goodbye to Peterson and rushed to attend the president's State of the Union address. There was great interest in seeing how the president looked and presented himself, after his prostate operation and the Iran affair. The evening was very partisan, more than any other State of the Union address I can recall. Much rah-rahing by the Republicans, mock

[1] Principal Secretary to Ontario premier David Peterson; currently CEO of Government Policy Consultants International.

[2] Carl Levin (b. 1934) Democratic Senator from Michigan 1979 to present.

cheering by the senators, and similar silly antics. It was difficult for the diplomatic corps to know what to do. Do we jump to our feet with the Republicans or clap only when Democrats indulged? We watched the dean, Count Willie Wachtmeister, who decided to be restrained, so we were too. We were very conspicuous under the television lights in not applauding.

We were all lined up, according to custom, on the basis of seniority. I am about number ten. It was a strange feeling, being an antique after only five years.

January 29, 1987 Kay Graham invited me as her guest to attend a dinner where Jim Baker was the speaker. Luckily for me, we sat side by side at the same table, so we had a chance to discuss some current issues. Baker was confused by what Pat Carney had said to him in Ottawa on steel. I hesitated to tell him I was too. She blamed our increased exports on Korean transshipments or something. Baker told me he was worried we were intervening in foreign-exchange markets to keep our dollar down. I told him I'd speak to Wilson and get Wilson to call him right away, because that didn't correspond with what Wilson had told me. On acid rain he said, "Keep pressing." Interesting advice.

Later, I chatted with Craig Fuller, Bush's chief of staff. I asked him if Bush had any regrets about his visit to Ottawa, emphasizing how much we had appreciated it. Darman and Strauss mentioned to me earlier in the week that Bush had looked weak in Ottawa, thanks to his comment to the press "Boy, did I get an earful." According to the critics, he did not do his career aspirations any good in Ottawa.

Fuller said Bush knew exactly what he was getting into and was willing to take the risk. My own guess is Bush wants to get into the substance. Too much of the "you – die, I – fly" business. He doesn't have enough opportunities to do so and was probably glad to address some really important international issues.

February 2, 1987 This morning I called Doucet in Ottawa about preparations for his visit to Washington next week. Doucet, Mulroney, and his team just returned from Africa, to the accompaniment of welcome noises from the Canadian press, acknowledging, for once, Mulroney's role in fighting apartheid. It seems the PM made strong hints when seeing Mugabe about breaking off diplomatic relations with South Africa.

Doucet said he had not read any of the dozen or so messages I sent to Dakar or Harare. "The team," he explained, "was too small to allow time to look at any messages from home."

How can the Canadian Prime Minister's Office put itself out of touch for a week? They missed all the analyses of the fallout of the Bush-Baker visit. Inappropriate conduct for a country that wants to play in the big leagues.

We flew to L.A., a bad trip – lost luggage and cancelled connections.

On arrival, Jack Valenti called me breathing fire and brimstone over the telephone lines. "I'm going up to Ottawa Wednesday, and I want you to tell them that this idea of licensing film distribution is ridiculous. No other country has done it. I've studied your situation, and it has no merit. You have no economic justification – we're pouring millions in investment up there. You have no cultural justification – Canadians love our movies. Your theatres don't distribute Canadian films because you don't make enough of them. I'm talking to Bentsen, Rostenkowski,[1] Gibbons – we won't put up with this."

I told Valenti to calm down. "You know the justification. You've heard it from Masse, you heard it from Fox, you heard it from John Roberts, and if you don't understand, it's because you don't want to. My advice to you, Jack," I said, "is go up there and listen, speak softly, and don't carry a big stick."

We had dinner with the French Smiths at Chason's, along with Ross Barrett, a wealthy businessman and a friend of Reagan, and a highly successful movie mogul, Jerry Weintraub,[2] and his wife, a singer who once performed in Canada. The Weintraubs gave us a lift back to the Beverly Wilshire. We found ourselves slowly motoring down Rodeo Drive in a huge white convertible Rolls-Royce. Mr. W. said, "I came from a very poor background. In 1964 I was a failure and broke. I had five hundred dollars to my name, so I walked into a Rolls-Royce dealer in New York and put a down payment on one. The next day my luck changed, and I have driven a Rolls ever since."

I told Mrs. W. how thrilled I was to be in a white convertible Rolls-Royce.

"Our second Rolls-Royce is nicer," she said. "Unfortunately, it's in the garage for repairs."

---

[1] (b. 1928) Democratic Representative from Illinois 1959–1994. He was indicted on corruption charges in 1994 for his role in the congressional cheque-kiting scandal and was forced to step down from all congressional leadership positions.

[2] (b. 1937) An American film producer best known for *Nashville*, *Diner*, *The Karate Kid*, and *Ocean's Eleven*.

February 5, 1987 Jean French Smith gave a ladies' lunch in honour of Sondra and Lee Annenberg. Sondra said it was a fine lunch, attended by about twenty white-haired, wealthy ladies. The food was superb, and after lunch the ladies were entertained by a magician. Life's progression: from childhood to childhood.

February 9, 1987 We saw on TV just before dinner that Bud McFarlane tried to kill himself by taking an overdose. He has been hounded mercilessly by Congress and the media. When I think that not so long ago, the most powerful names in Washington – and among my best contacts – were Bud McFarlane and Mike Deaver, I can scarcely comprehend the change. Washington is unbelievably cruel. People are treated with inhuman contempt for any error, real or invented. There is no balance here, no wisdom, no compassion. Bud behaved with candour and dignity over Iran. Will he ever be able to live down this desperate act?

February 12, 1987 I received a blockbuster telegram. It informs the embassy that the government will announce a new film policy tomorrow. We henceforth will license distributors and distinguish between Canadian and foreign distributors.

We are changing the way business is being done in Canada. The firms affected have been operating in Canada for many years under one set of rules, and now new rules will discriminate against them. In changing the rules in the midst of a free-trade negotiation, we are placing a formidable obstacle in the way of our own initiative. We are misjudging the mood of Washington. The motion picture industry is the most powerful lobby in the United States – it has a direct line to the president. We are giving them no notice, although we screamed loud enough about the lack of notice on shingles and shakes.

I sent a personal emergency message to this effect to Joe Clark with a copy to the PMO and made telephone calls to the key players in Ottawa to tell them it was coming. My efforts are probably in vain. I'm sure, however, that they will increase my popularity back home, especially with Clark and the department.

I said at the outset of my message, forgive me for stating the obvious. I am not arguing for U.S. interests, I am arguing on behalf of Canadian interests.

Maybe a useless message, but I did it for my own conscience. Moreover, I bet the government will eventually back off, amidst much embarrassment, looking weak and indecisive.

February 13, 1987 I had a restless night. Am I overreacting in urging the government not to proceed with its new film policy? Why do I persist in making myself so controversial in Ottawa? Why don't I care that my critics think I am suffering from localitis? Why don't I care if they think I am acting as an agent of Uncle Sam?

I'm not sure I know the answers to these questions. I would like to believe, however, that if Norman Robertson were on this planet, he would not disapprove of my behaviour. As a very junior officer, he once called me into his office and criticized me for signing off on a memorandum dealing with Israel's passage through the Suez Canal. The memo took a restrictive view of Israel's rights. "Why did you do so?" he asked. "Because," I replied, "it's the government's policy." "Do you agree with the policy?" "No," I replied. "Then you were wrong to signify your approval," he said. "I'm surprised at your action, Gotlieb. A civil servant has a duty to advise the government honestly."

Robertson gave me that advice twenty-five years ago. In Washington I think about it all the time.

February 18, 1987 The end of a three-day U.S. heads-of-post meeting in Ottawa. Burney supported me in giving Arthur Erickson the task of designing the furnishings of the executive offices on the sixth floor of the new embassy. History will – or should – thank me – and Burney – for this.

February 19, 1987 Yesterday we sent replies to Whitney North Seymour Jr., in l'affaire Deaver. This morning I had a phone call from the man himself. "You were as good as your word. Your replies were timely, frank, and full."

I could have fallen off my chair. Praise from the devil. Then he said, "I am going to prosecute Deaver on a wide variety of fronts. On acid rain I'm prosecuting him for perjury, false testimony. I need you as a witness."

I caught my breath and replied, "I can't comment. We have to consider this carefully, bearing in mind what an important precedent it would be."

I told Sondra later that it looked like bad news for Deaver but tolerable news for Canada. Sondra pushed me vigorously to call Seymour back and ask for more details, which I did. He was surprisingly forthcoming. "I found no breach of U.S. law in his lobbying for you. But you'll see from my report, which I'll release next week, that his account of his activities in the White House prior to the Quebec Summit in March 1986 are not compatible with yours. He was giving false testimony. This is very sad, because he broke no laws lobbying for you."

I told Seymour I was astonished. Seymour said he was too.

I went to bed feeling that a heavy weight had been lifted from my mind, for the first time in close to a year. But I felt awful about Deaver. Just one year ago he was the star of Washington, on the cover of *Time*, with a $20-million contract with Satchi & Satchi. How could one fall so fast and far? What a town. Most ironic of all: he was the most helpful White House official to Canada. Now the U.S. prosecutor wants me to be a material witness in his prosecution.

I called on Cap Weinberger, along with Bob Craig at the embassy, to make a heavy pitch to allow the Martin Marietta Canada group to bid on the U.S. air defence system. Weinberger was surrounded by all the top brass. The contract is in the billions. I think I got somewhere – maybe it was a breakthrough.

We had Rick Burt for dinner – he is visiting Washington – along with David Abshire,[1] Rowly Evans, and Carolyn Peachy. All the talk was about "the decline and fall" of Reagan. Shultz is very depressed. Reagan is out of touch. People close to him say he doesn't comprehend what is happening. Being accustomed all his life to success, he is shocked by the sense of failure. Arms control is over. SDI wins. And on and on. Reality and myth intermixed.

February 20, 1987 As soon as I came into the office this morning, I called Seymour again. It seems to me that the only significant difference in my chronology, as compared to Deaver's, was that I listed having lunch with him on January 5, 1985, at the Ritz-Carlton hotel. I told Seymour that the lunch was a social one, as our wives were with us, at the Jockey Club. Seymour said, "That still doesn't account for his denying categorically that he had lunch with you that day."

In the United States you can go to jail for having lunch with someone and not remembering it.

February 21, 1987 We attended an event at the British embassy, hosted by the new British ambassador, my old fellow student from Christ Church days, Sir Anthony Acland. He had a superb brunch for eighty-eight, beautifully arranged, with excellent service and exquisite flowers from his

---

[1] (b. 1926) Member of the President's Foreign Intelligence Advisory Board 1981–1982; U.S. Ambassador to NATO 1983–1987.

own greenhouse. Upon arriving, I chatted with Elizabeth Drew and Ben Bradlee and Sally Quinn about the only topic of discussion in town: when does Don Regan quit, and who replaces him. Then we spotted Regan and his wife, Ann, coming towards us. Bradlee said to me, "We've been very rough on this guy. I am going to disappear," whereupon he and Sally rushed off to another room. Kay, on the other hand, was a brick. She asked Regan what was on the president's agenda that the press was missing, and Regan talked about his domestic priorities. I asked him about an arms control agreement; less than a fifty-fifty chance, he replied.

Regan said to me, "Keep in touch with Gary Bauer,[1] my domestic policy adviser in the White House. I've given him until March 15 to let me know what can be done about acid rain."

Claiborne Pell, now chairman of the Senate Foreign Relations Committee, was at our table during the dinner. I said to him, "Joe Clark, our foreign minister, is coming to town. Maybe you could receive him at breakfast, with your colleagues on the committee. This has been done for us in the past."

Claiborne: "I am awfully busy right now."

Me: "Well, surely you and your colleagues would want to talk to the Canadian foreign minister."

Pell: "Maybe he could deal with the chairman of our regional subcommittee. That's the usual procedure."

"Who is it?"

"I'm not sure. Dodd[2] or maybe Biden.[3] Will you deal with the State Department?"

"No. I'll deal with your staff."

"Okay."

February 24, 1987 Today I called on the diminutive Gary Bauer, as suggested by Don Regan. I gave him a powerful pitch on acid rain and went through the tortuous history of the subject, beginning with the Trudeau era. Surprisingly, Bauer seemed sympathetic, and he said one thing significant. He pointed out that the president needs a foreign-policy success in Canada

---

[1] (b. 1946) Undersecretary of Education and Domestic Policy Adviser to President Ronald Reagan 1985–1989.

[2] Christopher Dodd (b. 1944) Democratic Senator from Connecticut 1981 to present; Chairman of the Democratic National Committee 1995–1999.

[3] Joseph Biden Jr. (b. 1942) Democratic Senator from Delaware 1973 to present.

and that if the summit goes badly, people here will say that it is further evidence that the Reagan era is over. We agree that both leaders badly need a foreign-policy victory.

Just before leaving for cocktails, I got a call at home from Don Hodel. "Let's not quarrel anymore – don't reply to my letter, as then I'll have to reply to yours. Allan, you'd be surprised at the support I have received for my remarks [about a Canadian acid rain conspiracy]." I said, "Don, I am not surprised. This country is full of people who want to zap the foreigner and blame everything on someone else."

Then I got a call from Jack Valenti. He informed me they were low-keying their response on film distribution, but he doubted that approach would continue. He is discussing his strategy with Bentsen. There is trouble looming.

February 26, 1987 At dinner at Kay Graham's, given for Mrs. Gardner Cowles[1] and her art dealer son, Kay said how happy she was for Deaver that he got a delay in the indictment. She is pro-Deaver, one of the few in the Georgetown set who is. I complimented Kay on her diplomatic handling of Don Regan the other day. She was pleased. "I don't admire that man!" she said. "I have never invited him for dinner."

February 27, 1987 The Stratford Theatre is in town performing *The Mikado*. We took fifty guests to see it at the Kennedy Center and had a reception for them and players at the Residence afterwards. Everyone lingered at the reception: Alan Simpson and Anne, Paul Volcker, Ed Derwinski[2] and his wife, the Brzezinskis, Safires, Fritcheys, Clare Booth Luce, Bernie Kalb, the Mirvishes[3] – father and son – from Toronto, Joe Alsop, Bill Webster, and more. Many of the guests said they like our cultural events best of all. Maybe there is value in cultural diplomacy, after all.

February 28, 1987 Reports appear in Canadian newspapers saying senior embassy officials recommended cancellation of the summit. Most embarrassing. Is there a mole in the embassy?

---

[1] Gardner Cowles Jr. (1903–1985) A U.S. publisher and founder of *Look* magazine.

[2] (b. 1926) Appointed Counselor to the Department of State in 1982; Undersecretary of State for Security Assistance, Science, and Technology 1987–1989; Secretary of Veterans Affairs 1989–1992.

[3] David Mirvish (b. 1945) Canadian art collector, art dealer, theatre producer, and son of "Honest" Ed Mirvish.

March 1, 1987 I went for a walk with Joe Alsop along the Potomac. It was a beautiful, brilliant, warm day, the first of the year. Joe saluted the little children and congratulated their parents. It was a voyeur's walk, watching the young on their bikes and lying around taking in the sun. Joe was as enthusiastic as a child himself, as he approached the black mothers and cooed at their babies.

Got back from briefing Canadian businessmen and received a call from Mulroney. He asked me to pass a very upbeat message to Reagan, which I promised to do through Frank Carlucci. It was a good idea, this – be nice to a guy when he's down. And the world is mightily down on Ronald Reagan. Mulroney is convinced Reagan is going to come back strong. I hope he's right, but I fear this might be another case of Irish optimism, as diagnosed by Conrad Black. The odds are against an effective presidency this late in the game, although it need not be a disaster. All the advice I gave Mulroney in the past few months about no one being home in the White House is proving to be correct. But Mulroney remains upbeat.

We chatted about Don Regan and Howard Baker's appointment as his replacement. Don Regan, I said, had undergone a public execution. The media led a drooling public to the central square to witness a public hanging. It was pretty disgusting. The prime minister asked me to pass a message to Regan saying that he was thinking of him.

Mulroney also asked me to pass on a personal message to Bud McFarlane. This is one of Mulroney's finest qualities: he is sympathetic to people when they are having a rough time.

March 11, 1987 Today marks the end of a three-day Joe Clark visit to Washington. The trip was a success, but Clark is still suspicious of his officials, even after all this time in office. Add to this that his chief of staff, Jodi White, makes them feel nervous and not liked. The visit was marred by unnecessary tension between White and Burney. The issue was who would accompany Clark during his visits on the Hill. The group had to be small, and when Clark chose White over Burney, Derek went into a rage. Understandably.

Clark's calls on Bentsen, Moynihan, Mitchell, Dodd, and Simpson provided him with his first (long overdue) taste of the Hill. The highlight of the visit was his call on Simpson, who was funny, corny, full of fun. "Our system is goofy. It does outrageous things. We don't understand it; how could foreigners do so?"

In all our calls – including on Bush, Baker, and Shultz – Clark got the same message: no breakthrough on acid rain. "We'll honour our commitments to the envoys' report, but we will not go beyond." This was useful because, as I had told Clark over and over, it is essential to lower expectations for the Ottawa Summit. Lower the hurdle and we may succeed. Raise it and we'll fail.

We are also going nowhere on our claim to Arctic sovereignty. Shultz seemed more negative today than at our previous meeting. Once again, the Tories set their sights too high. Urged on by a public that does not understand the limits of sovereignty in today's world, the government is overshooting the mark and may have to pay for it.

Shultz told me at lunch how badly he felt at the disgraceful behaviour Deaver was receiving from the Washington press.

At our dinner for Clark at the Residence, the crowd was as good as it gets: Webster, Volcker, Kampelman, Nitze, Whitehead, Armacost, Adelman, Lugar, Evans, Gibbons, Reston, Grunwald, Schlesinger, Brzezinski – some fifty in all. After dinner I got everyone into the living room, and after toasting Clark, I told the crowd we had a surprise. They were to see a videotape of a new threat to Americans, something of great concern to the officials and media in the room. No one had a clue what I was talking about. Some thought they were going to see a videotape of themselves, since CBS cameras were present (they were doing a piece on us for their morning program).

What they saw was a five-minute clip from *Saturday Night Live*, called "Amerida," a tale of a takeover of the United States by Canada. After scenes of the takeover (the Maple Leaf flag flying on top of the Capitol building, etc.), there was a Ted Koppel panel starring Henry Kissinger. A brilliant parody and the guests loved it.

March 12, 1987 Another crisis day in Washington. This time it's corn. When we won the recent corn countervail in Canada, there was an eruption in the Senate Finance Committee. I arranged to call on Dave Durenberger, the fomenter of the trouble and sponsor of a nasty, retaliatory resolution against us, which is to come up in the Finance Committee next week.

I found Durenberger in a mean mood. "You Canadians made a bad mistake," he said. "You shouldn't have picked on a big guy."

Durenberger then pulled a real dirty one. He told me a group of Minnesota corn growers were in the next room, whom he had promised I would meet with. I asked if the press would be present, and he said yes. I told him that was dirty pool, that I was being snookered. "If I see them, I will get bad publicity," I said, "and if I don't see them, I will get bad publicity." But there was really no way out, so I met with the group, defended the Canadian legal tribunal decision, got pounded, and left. Durenberger will be in political trouble in '88 in his home state, but this does not merit unprincipled behaviour.

I then called on Max Baucus, the great champion and instigator of the lumber countervail against Canada. I thought he would be able to see the absurdity of the U.S. position – eleven countervail actions against us, one against them. But he didn't give me any solace.

I put through calls to three cabinet secretaries: Baldridge, Yeutter, and Richard Lyng[1] in Agriculture. The point was to urge them to testify before the Senate in a responsible manner. I was annoyed at how ill informed Yeutter was. Lyng was even more unreasonable, and he knows nothing about U.S. countervail law and practice. Baldridge perceived the silliness of the U.S. position immediately, but I don't know if he'll be called to testify at the Senate hearing. The U.S. corn industry is upset because the Europeans are likely to imitate us and initiate agricultural countervails.

Later, I received a call from Derek Burney. Mulroney has asked him to become his chief of staff. What did I think? Take it, I told him. You might get in some trouble for crossing lines by being a public servant in the PMO, but you can do a lot of good there. There are precedents – Pearson had a public servant as head of the PMO in the late 1960s.

I called Fred Doucet to express my concern at media reports of his demotion. Whatever his faults, they are very few in comparison with the value of the service he's given the prime minister. He told me he did indeed feel burnt by the events of the past days. He knew he was being offered as a sacrifice to the Tory caucus, and so he underwent the public spectacle of being demoted when he really wasn't being demoted.

March 14, 1987 I spoke at the Vancouver Institute this evening, giving my Seven-Deadly-Myths-about-the-U.S. routine. Amazing that this organization could get a thousand people to come out on a Saturday night to the university campus, to hear a speech on Canada-U.S. relations.

---

[1] (1918–2003) Secretary of Agriculture 1986–1989.

I had dinner with Liz and John Nichols[1] prior to the speech. Liz took me to Bill Reid's[2] studio, where I saw his maquette of the *Spirit Canoe*, the statue he is making for our new embassy. It looks magnificent, and it will be a marvellous centrepiece for the building, where it will sit in the entrance to the lobby. But we have no money to pay for it (six hundred thousand dollars is the latest price), because Ross Johnson hasn't yet gotten off his backside to raise funds for the ill-starred Festival of Canada.

Now there is a new problem. Reid doesn't want to make the statue because he's angry over the logging of South Moresby Island in the Charlottes. I phoned him at the Charlottes and had a depressing conversation with him. I urged him to consider that not to build the statue as a protest was wrong-headed, because it would stand for a thousand years, reflecting and honouring Canada and his people. Aside from this minor fact, the federal government was opposed to logging on the island.

March 17, 1987 Bush called Mulroney to tell him that the administration will go for the full $5-billion acid rain program. Good news. But they won't go any further. Bad news. I'm not sure the PM fully realizes this bit. Still, it is a dramatic reversal, and he has reason to be pleased.

March 18, 1987 Called the prime minister in the evening. (There is a standing instruction at the PMO switchboard to put me through when I call. This gives me a sense of empowerment.) I said that he should feel he accomplished a great deal in reversing the U.S. stand on the envoys' report. The reversal resulted from his own personal intervention with Bush, which led to the Ottawa visit and reconsideration.

March 19, 1987 I received a telephone call from Mulroney late afternoon. He is pleased at the acid rain funding decision. But he must not come on too strong in praising it. Certainly it will be belittled by U.S. and Canadian environmentalists, who would much prefer Reagan do nothing than do a little. Mulroney urged me to try to get as much media support as

---

[1] (b. 1924) John was a Liberal Senator 1966–1973. Liz was the majority owner of the Equinox Gallery in Vancouver.

[2] (1920–1998) Canadian jeweller, sculptor, and artist. His best-known works are two large bronze sculptures: *The Spirit of Haida Gwaii*, at the Canadian Embassy in Washington, D.C., and *The Jade Canoe*, at Vancouver International Airport.

possible. I spoke to key people at the *Post*, *Wall Street Journal*, and *Globe and Mail*, while John Fieldhouse did a good job with the *New York Times* and other papers.

No sooner had I completed briefing the *Wall Street Journal* on corn when the story of Deaver's indictment for perjury broke. I spent several hours working on a press line with the embassy people. I tried to bring out that the grand jury exonerated Canada. My message: there was no indictment of Deaver for improper lobbying, so Canada was off the hook (so to speak).

March 21, 1987 Met with Burney and Campbell in Ottawa to hear a presentation on the furnishing of the executive rooms of the new chancery. The External decorators are making a mess of these key offices and rooms. I shocked them by saying they were doing violence to the architect and his building. I said that Erickson had to be consulted and given the right of veto.

It was a depressing experience. The executive dining room is to be supplied with the recycled dining room set of our ambassador to the Organization of American States, a job now abolished. It looks like a page out of the Eaton's catalogue. We'll be a laughingstock if we finish these elegant rooms in the manner these chaps want.

March 23, 1987 Scotty Reston called me about the interview I arranged for him with Mulroney in Ottawa tomorrow. What should I cover? he asked. I gave him a strong pitch on Mulroney's courage in proposing a free-trade agreement with the United States and on publicly standing on a pro-U.S. foreign policy.

I informed the prime minister of the conversation and suggested he aim at hitting Reston's sympathetic cord for North America being a privileged continent. I thought Mulroney seemed somewhat nervous about Reston, given Scotty's unvarnished admiration for Trudeau. But I reminded him that Reston was the only U.S. columnist who had written a pro-Canada-U.S. free trade column. I also said to Mulroney that I told Reston, "You should be aware that Mulroney is an admirer of Trudeau."

March 25, 1987 Problems are also brewing on the auto front. Ottawa is about to announce subsidies for General Motors at St. Therese. The Tory strategy: let's make a free-trade agreement our number one priority for the next election, then let's make sure it doesn't happen.

March 28, 1987 I called on Lee Thomas (asbestos) and Paul Volcker (state of the economy) and went to a *New York Times* reception in the evening. The American political world was there in its entirety. Chatted with Baker, Whitehead, Strauss, and Warren Phillips. I kept being warned that Valenti was present and on the warpath. Alas, we fell into conversation.

"That was a fine inflammatory speech you wrote for Lloyd Bentsen – the one he gave the other day – denouncing Canada for its new film distribution policy," said I.

Valenti responded with all guns blazing. "I'll never accept your policy. I'll fall on my sword before I do. It's monstrous, a disgrace, and now the French minister of communications says if you people get away with it, they're going to introduce a similar licensing scheme. You people are far worse than the French. I've got no quarrel with them. Frenchmen watch French films because they are good. Your problem is your films are no damn good, so that's why Canadians don't watch them."

Over on the Hill, the idiots in the Senate passed the revised Durenberger corn resolution impugning our countervail decision, by the close vote of ninety-nine to zero.

March 29, 1987 At Sunday brunch at Evangeline Bruce's (given for the visiting Nicko Henderson), I chatted with Cap Weinberger about the upcoming Ottawa Summit. He gave me the usual Defense position about Arctic sovereignty: the United States cannot accept our claim because of the precedential effects it would have on other areas of the high seas. I got the same story from Cobb in the White House this morning. It seems that the NSC meeting convened yesterday to crunch this issue went badly – all this as more or less predicted.

In the late afternoon I received a call from Mulroney. He wanted to hear what Reston felt about his interview with him in Ottawa this week. I told him I hadn't been in touch with Scotty as yet. But I gave him an account of my last conversation with Valenti, whose message was: "You won't get a free-trade treaty through the Congress as long as you have your new film policy on the books."

"Of course," I said to Mulroney, "Valenti's position is grossly excessive. He is always overreacting. But the U.S. government won't stand up to a lobby like Valenti's. So how can Canada expect to beat such a lobby?"

In the evening I attended the Gridiron dinner – my sixth. George Bush, speaking for the Republicans, bombed badly. His text was lousy and his delivery was worse. On the other hand, Reagan was outstanding. He sat through four and a half hours of insults and then got up to wow everyone with an upbeat and exceptionally funny performance. As he spoke, everyone fell silent. I saw the waiters and security people and other attendants all stand and listen in awe and with the utmost attention. And he was hilarious. After one of his last lines, everyone just cheered. "I've been investigated and probed," he said, "I've been operated on in my prostate, I've had my colon cut up, I've had cancer of the skin, I've been shot at, and I've never felt better in my life."

April 4, 1987 On the way to attend a black-tie dinner raising money for cystic fibrosis (Mila's charity, so I thought we should be there), we stopped to have a drink with John Whitehead and Nancy Dickerson[1] on her birthday. John told me, when I asked him point-blank, that he had never heard of or seen the letter the president sent to Mulroney yesterday, which rejected our negotiating document on Arctic sovereignty. I said I found this unbelievable. We negotiate a document for one year based on what the president offered the prime minister at the Washington Summit. Our differences are narrowed to one square-bracketed word. On the eve of the summit, the United States rejects the whole document and the agreement it was based on. The president repudiates his own words.

April 5, 1987 In the late afternoon I was informed that the prime minister will be sending a reply to Reagan's letter of April 3. It has torpedoed the Arctic talks on the eve of the summit and created a potential crisis.

At dinner I got a call from Ottawa saying Mulroney wants me to deliver the letter personally to Howard Baker or Frank Carlucci, and to do so immediately. "On Sunday night, on a few minutes' notice?" I moaned. The letter arrived at 8 p.m., and it was a mess. I managed to get it revised. Baker is out of town and Carlucci allegedly unavailable. After much abuse from Cobb, I managed to pull off a brilliant coup: I delivered it to Weinberger, Powell, and Cobb at a party Powell is having at his home that same Sunday night.

I pulled Weinberger out of the party. After reading the prime minister's letter, he said, "I've never even heard of the president's conversation at the last summit." After much discussion, he astonished me again by saying,

[1] (1927–1997) Television broadcaster from Texas. Married John Whitehead, deputy secretary of state during Reagan's second term. They met at our table at the Canadian embassy.

"Well, maybe we can agree to your sovereignty, but not to the need for consent." Washington is an Alice in Wonderland world – everything is upside down.

Imagine: Weinberger never heard of the president's commitment to Mulroney a year ago – the basis of one whole year's negotiation. Imagine: the president managed to reverse that stance on the very eve of the summit, thereby creating a confrontation and possible crisis at the summit. Imagine: Reagan didn't understand the significance of what he was saying.

April 6, 1987 I was supposed to leave for Ottawa last night but couldn't because of the need to deliver the PM's Arctic letter. Sondra and I got on a presidential backup plane. Without it, we would not have arrived at the summit for the first day. There wasn't, in any event, that much for me to do, Derek having graciously excluded me from today's tête-à-tête. In the late afternoon I attended the uneventful Shultz-Clark bilateral meeting. I found myself talking too much and worrying whether Clark resents my intervening so regularly.

In the evening we attended the state dinner at Government House. I sat between Nicky Eaton and Hilary Weston,[1] with John Turner "hosting" our table. We discussed Bill Reid's recent announcement that he would not build the *Spirit Canoe* for the new embassy, as a protest against the logging of South Moresby Island. John said he would call Reid to urge him to change his mind, if I thought this would be helpful. I encouraged him to do so.

Before I left Washington this afternoon, Mulroney telephoned and asked me how he performed on *Meet the Press* today. I thought he looked a bit nervous, but his answers were okay. He wanted reassurance, and I gave him what he wanted. On the eve of an important summit, I'm sure I was right to do so.

April 7, 1987 Day two of the Ottawa Summit. The highlight of the day came during lunch at 24 Sussex. While we were discussing South Africa and going on to arms control, Reagan stopped the conversation. "I always think that at such a meeting we should show we accomplished something, have some results." Turning to his team, he asked, "Can't we do that?"

This was a show stopper. The faces of the U.S. officials – Shultz, Weinberger, Carlucci, Baker, Cobb, and Niles – registered astonishment. After

[1] (b. 1942) Lieutenant-Governor of Ontario 1997–2002. Wife of Galen Weston.

all, the White House and NSC had been telling us for months that there would be no surprises and no results. Then the Americans spun off to a separate session in a room at 24 Sussex to discuss possible "results." During this break, Mulroney told me Reagan made this same point to him just as he arrived at lunch.

Carlucci then met with Burney and me, and we worked up language on acid rain and the Arctic. Carlucci amazed us by saying Reagan would put these points in the speech he was about to deliver to Parliament. The language on Arctic sovereignty didn't really signify anything, but it did suggest a commitment to keep the discussions going, and it did represent a withdrawal of the ridiculous Reagan letter of April 3.

The acid rain language, on the other hand, represented something more substantial. It was Reagan, at Mulroney's importuning, who decided that the United States should now say that it was willing to consider an acid rain accord. Here Reagan demonstrated as clearly as he has ever done that he is a leader, not a follower or just someone who reads his script. All of American officialdom going one way, and he decided to go the other.

Why did he do it? To help Mulroney? I believe so, absolutely. But also, perhaps, because his instinct told him that with all the effort we've put into this summit and all the fanfare and media hordes, he should try to make some news.

Reagan was incredibly robust. Despite the hectic schedule, he was always chipper, never more so than at the lunch with Mulroney, when he was in his best anecdotal form. After telling a couple of Russian stories, he said he "collects stories that the Russians tell on themselves."

Mulroney was on a great high during the visit. I met with him in the airport for about five minutes after Reagan left, and he was exuberant. But there are dark clouds over our head. The president raised film policy, using very strong language. Mulroney's free-trade initiative will break over this rock.

April 8, 1987 I paid a farewell call on Dick Darman today, who is retiring. We discussed an elaborate strategy to outflank Baldridge and his deputy, Bruce Smart, on an obscure issue in the softwood lumber agreement. I am going to miss Darman. He's probably the smartest of the gang still around (he certainly thinks so) and one of the most helpful in my efforts to work through the labyrinthine U.S. system. He has praised me as a modern de Tocqueville, but I am one of his disciples.

April 9, 1987 Spoke to the Empire Club in Toronto on my favourite theme: "Some Canadian myths about the United States." Before speaking, I was interviewed on *Canada AM*. Interviewer hostile. "What about Mike Deaver? Doesn't the whole affair prejudice the chance of getting anywhere on acid rain?" "Nonsense," said I. "How much longer are you going to be in Washington, anyway?" Press scrum after the speech. Lots of paparazzi, all hostile. "Everyone knows the summit was a waste of time. Wasn't it?"

I flew back to Washington on Garth Drabinsky's plane. We discussed "cultural sovereignty." He knows that much of it is hokum. The Canadian government, he said, is making much of the point that only 3 per cent of films shown in Canada are Canadian. "This is a dangerous point to make. This fact has nothing whatever to do with distribution. All Canadian films worth showing are fully exhibited in Canada."

This man's rise to commercial success is phenomenal. Private plane, limos, secretaries, flunkies, assistants everywhere. Phones, dictation, plugged into the world while in constant motion. He showed me his statement of earnings. From a few million in receipts to a billion in a few years. Now the biggest film distributor in the world. A gambler, an innovator, a risk taker. Ladies and gentlemen, Garth Drabinsky.

April 11, 1987 We went to dinner with the Colemans at their Jockey Club in the Ritz-Carlton, of which he is the proprietor. He told me that there was one simple reason for Mike Deaver's failure to disclose the truth about his contacts with me and others, leading to the perjury charges. The reason was not a mystery, although it was a secret. Deaver is an alcoholic, and during the entire period in question, he was deeply under the influence. He was taking treatment during the key period that he was charged with perjury. Could this be true? I never dreamed.

After dinner we joined Vernon and Ann Jordan and listened to Peggy Lee. At her age she was miraculously good. One song, which she rendered beautifully, seemed to be my own theme song: "Just Keep Holding On."

April 14, 1987 I got a call from Bruce Phillips this afternoon. Ken Taylor told him that Ross Johnson has decided to back out from the Festival of Canada. No explanations. Thus ends a glorious project, terminated by a lack of interest and commitment on the part of all, and especially the bureaucratic hands of Ottawa.

April 16, 1987 Don Hodel, secretary of the interior, came to the embassy to see me, an unusual reversal of protocol. He came to brief me on what he plans to say next Monday regarding the Arctic Natural Wildlife Reserve. He will propose drilling for oil in the area, to the likely detriment of the Porcupine Caribou herd. He will not back down. He will propose full development. Bad news for Canada.

April 24, 1987 We had Robertson Davies and Antonine Maillet[1] over for drinks before going to dinner with them at George and Liz Stevens's house this evening. The writers are here for a conference sponsored by something called the Wheatland Foundation, a fund created by Ann Getty at the behest of George Weidenfeld. The conference is terribly organized, and everyone is angry at each other about who goes to what party. I exchanged views with Robertson Davies about the Canadian national character. We agreed on everything, but especially on how Canadians like to put down achievers and people who stand out. He told me this story: In the late 1950s he was at a cocktail party in Vancouver and someone came into the room and said, "Did you hear the news? Lester Pearson was just awarded the Nobel Peace Prize." A woman at the party commented, "The Nobel Peace Prize! Lester Pearson! Who does he think he is?" From all accounts, Davies stole the show at the conference.

April 25, 1987 We had a dinner party for George Shultz, to watch a Fred Astaire–Ginger Rogers movie, *Shall We Dance*. Glen Bullard was in as our old-fashioned projectionist. Other guests were Hannah Gray, president of the University of Chicago, Ed and Judy Ney from New York, Les Gelb from New York, Meg Greenfield, the Kirklands, the Bradens, and the Schlesingers. This was the third time we've had an old Fred Astaire movie to show Shultz (or is it the fourth?). He gave a very fine toast: "I come here because I like Canada, I like the Gotliebs, and I like Fred Astaire and Ginger Rogers."

The evening illustrated the problems of overzealous staff. We called the dinner at 7:30 p.m. Shultz comes back, it's a Saturday, why don't we start earlier? We changed it to 7:00. Everyone comes at 7:00, except Shultz. At 7:05 Connie says to me, "The security people (there were a handful at the Residence) say the secretary is arriving at 7:25. He will want to sit down right

---

[1] (b. 1929) Canadian novelist, playwright, and scholar who taught at the Université de Montréal 1971–1976.

away. They must know when it's over because the secretary doesn't want to stay too late. The movie lasts one hour and fifty-five minutes. We must finish dinner by 8:30." I told Connie that was impossible, as did Sondra. "Funny," I said, "he wanted it early, and I know he likes a Manhattan before dinner." "I'll offer him one," Connie says, "but the secretary wants to sit down right away."

Shultz arrives at 7:30, looking surprised to see the whole crowd gathered. I gave him a Manhattan. 7:45: Connie tells Sondra we must sit down, the chef says everything will be overcooked and the secretary cannot stay up too late. Sondra tells Connie, "Between the chef and George Shultz, I choose Shultz." But I yield to Connie and call everyone in. Shultz, only partway through his Manhattan, is irritable.

As we go in, Shultz says to me, "Did someone tell you I was in a hurry? Did my security people say that?" Gotlieb: "We understood you wanted to sit down right away." Shultz, red with anger. "I'm going to talk to my security people right now." Gotlieb: "Hold on, the mistake might be with my staff, not yours. Take another drink to the table."

We watch the film. Shultz lingers after with a cognac, leaving around 11:30 or 11:45. On the way out, Shultz says to me, "Was this party called for 7:00 or 7:30? I want to know. I was told 7:30." Gotlieb: "It must have been our mistake." Shultz: "I don't like to keep people waiting."

Casualties of the evening: Mrs. Gelb got ill and had to leave – an allergy to raspberries, it seems. Archie, our new dog, started to barf on my lap in the middle of the movie. Jim Schlesinger got bored at all the trivia and halfway through the film walked out with his wife, Rachel, reluctantly in tow.

April 27, 1987 First thing this morning, a phone call from George Shultz: "I wanted you to know I checked my folder for your party, and I see that it was called for 7 p.m., not 7:30. I apologize. I don't like to keep people waiting."

I called on Ty Cobb at the White House. He was bitter about the Ottawa Summit. He felt the U.S. side had been double-crossed on acid rain. I did my best to disabuse him of this idea. We did not push Mulroney to push Reagan on this subject, I told him. Mulroney did it all himself, and Reagan had agreed – all by himself. Isn't this what summits should be about? Real discussions among men who are not puppets?

Cobb was fascinating on Arctic sovereignty. He said Reagan raised the subject at the U.S. delegation meeting at 24 Sussex following the PM's luncheon. He wanted to say something encouraging about it when he addressed

Parliament. Frank Carlucci, NSC adviser, warned him, "The secretary and Department of National Defense, the chairman of the Joint Chiefs of Staff, the secretary of transportation, the coast guard, the attorney general are all of the view that to agree to the Canadian position would be against the best interest of the U.S." Reagan insisted, "I'd like to say something positive."

April 28, 1987 Saw Bill Bradley today. I'm trying to get the message across that we are not greedily seeking exemption from U.S. free-trade laws. We want the free-trade treaty to lay down North American rules about what is a subsidy and create a binational tribunal to settle disputes. Bradley surprised me by coming on very strongly about films. He called our policy discriminatory, anti-American, and plain stupid. He is being flooded with telephone calls from lobbyists. Another example of industry capture of the political process, just like softwood lumber.

April 29, 1987 An article appeared in the *Washington Post* today stating that Deaver will plead impairment; he was an alcoholic at the time of the alleged perjury. This follows articles in the *New York Times* yesterday that Deaver was addicted to prescription drugs. John Coleman proved to be correct. Our lawyers say I will get a preliminary request from Seymour to testify next week, or maybe this week.

Telephoned Scotty Reston to discuss the column he wrote today about the Nixon-Kissinger article opposing an INF deal unless it's connected with the reduction of conventional forces. Reston said it was disgraceful for a former president and secretary of state to be offering advice to a successor government through a newspaper column.

Scotty told me he got a call from Kissinger to say, "You are right. I am the greatest admirer of George Shultz, the man most qualified to be president. But since I advised him that the Reykjavik proposals on nuclear disarmament went too far, he won't speak to me anymore. This is my only route."

May 1, 1987 Fred Hall, new deputy assistant secretary of state for Canada, was my guest at lunch at the Metropolitan Club. During the past week, he told me, he has spent 80 per cent of his time on Canadian film policy.

Reagan called Mulroney the other day when he read Lee Thomas's silly testimony in the papers on acid rain. He thought Mulroney would be upset. This speaks volumes about Reagan's concern for Mulroney. Canadians don't understand the depth of the personal relationship Mulroney has established with Reagan.

The Brinkleys invited us to an informal dinner, along with the Kirklands. We talked about Deaver, alcoholism, people who never reciprocate, how damaging the Iran-Contra revelations will be (not very), and the nobodies who want to be president.

May 2, 1987 Just before leaving the office yesterday evening, I learned that a cabinet committee had passed the film legislation and was pushing ahead. Joe Clark is right behind the push. As I walked out of the office, I got word that thirty-four of the thirty-five members of the House Ways and Means Committee (the most powerful congressional body on trade matters) wrote Mulroney to protest the film legislation. We are not shooting ourselves in the foot – just the heart.

May 6, 1987 In New York trying to relax but not succeeding. Spending most of the time lobbying senators on the telephone about the dreadful omnibus trade bill. Talked with Norm Jewison about the Festival of Canada. I hate to borrow a phrase from Don Regan, but so far as the Festival of Canada is concerned, I'm the shovel brigade. I told Jewison the Kennedy Center production was off, and he was unpleasantly surprised. Fortunately, he had only just begun to prepare for the spectacle and had entered into no financial commitments. Damn Ross Johnson for walking away. The Festival of Canada would have been a landmark event for Canada in Washington.

May 7, 1987 Briefed a group of state legislators and attended their banquet this evening. I certainly wouldn't have gone if Alan Simpson wasn't the guest speaker. He's the Will Rogers of contemporary America. Simpson talked about congressional staffers. "You get someone on your staff – he had an idea in high school. He still had it in college. Then he comes to Washington and he still has it, and he won't let go until you embrace it. Then he goes to a Georgetown bar at night and boasts to his friends that I got my idea passed in the Senate. When I came here, the farmers received 3 billion from the U.S. government. Thanks to a staffer, now it's 27 billion and they all hate the government."

Some of his one-liners: "In Washington, one week you're on the cover of *Time*. Next week you're doing it. . . . Congress shouldn't do a number on Canada, just a little selective bashing."

May 8, 1987 Spoke recently to Paul Tellier to urge him to take charge of a policy review on film. "I don't run the PCO like Pitfield used to," he said. "I let the department concerned take the lead." I told Paul this had to be an exception to his (imaginary) rule – otherwise there would be no free-trade agreement. He rose to the occasion. He would appoint Glen Shortliffe,[1] his number two in the PCO, to preside over such a review.

The light is dawning in Ottawa – or should I say they see the darkness descending? No doubt the letter to Mulroney on our film policy signed by thirty-four of the thirty-five members of the House Ways and Means Committee has helped concentrate the political minds up here.

May 12, 1987 The Southam papers and the *Toronto Star* carry a story (prominently) about how I called Mulroney twice to warn him to back off film policy. The *Citizen* account said there was consternation about me in the Department of Communications, I was out of tune with the government's cultural nationalism, and I bypassed Clark, who was in favour of the policy. Just before Question Period, I got a call from Mulroney. He wants to deny the report. I told him my preference was otherwise, but I could see no great harm in his doing so. The fact is, I never called him for that purpose, although I have often warned of the dangers of our policy.

Working closely with the creative Len Legault, we sent off yesterday an alternative proposal I developed for achieving our goals regarding film. The essential point was that our regulations have to be framed in a non-discriminatory fashion.

Tonight we gave a dinner party in honour of Calvin Trillin,[2] one of Sondra's favourite writers. She wrote him some time ago inviting him and tonight, finally, was the night. We had the Lehrers, the Christopher Buckleys, Chris Wallace[3] and his wife, the Laughlin Phillipses, the George Stevenses,

---

[1] (b. 1937) Canadian Ambassador to Indonesia 1977–1979; Assistant Secretary to the Cabinet, Deputy Minister of Transport, and Deputy Secretary to the Cabinet Operations 1982–1990; Clerk of the Privy Council and Secretary to the Cabinet 1992–1994.

[2] (b. 1935) American journalist, humorist, and novelist, best known for his writings about food and eating, and his humour column in the *New Yorker*.

[3] (b. 1947) Network journalist who began his career with NBC in 1975. He was chief White House correspondent, anchor of *Meet the Press* and the Sunday edition of *NBC Nightly News*, and is currently host of *Fox News Sunday with Chris Wallace*.

and Michael Kinsley.[1] Sondra arranged to have some smoked Winnipeg goldeye flown in, and we served it as a first course. Trillin spends his summers in Nova Scotia, so we joked a lot about the Maritimes – and especially fish.

Sondra toasted Trillin. She cleared her throat several times. This, she said, is the Winnipeg hork. Everyone in Winnipeg goes around horking, or clearing their throats. This is because they have goldeye bones stuck in them.

May 13, 1987 We gave a reception for the Washington Zoo (they are honouring Canada this year) and then attended a dinner at Jennifer and Laughlin Phillips's in honour of David Hockney.[2]

Hockney gave a half-hour lecture prior to dinner. During the meal, everyone at our table was thrilled by what he had to say, which appeared to be a continuation of his lecture. But no one could explain to me what he said. Something clever about images and Xerox machines. He even drew a diagram on a piece of paper to illustrate his thinking. I couldn't follow it but kept thinking I'd like to grab the paper off the table and put it in my pocket.

Chatted before dinner with Walter Mondale. He was, as usual, witty, charming – precisely the opposite of the image he projected as a politician. He was in an ebullient mood. The fall of Hart must have elated him, as, no doubt, have Reagan's woes.

May 14, 1987 Another dinner given by the Phillipses, this time at the Ritz-Carlton – their annual fundraiser for the museum. Mike Deaver was there. He looked more at ease than I have seen him recently. "Just think," he said, "my trial starts in a few weeks, and then it will all be over, thank God. Only I'll still have a million dollars in legal fees to pay." Congressman Scheuer, across the table, urged Canada to take the United States before the International Court of Justice over acid rain. "It's just as if we sent a truck across the border carrying garbage," he said. I explained that since we're trying to negotiate a treaty, suing the United States would be difficult.

---

[1] (b. 1951) Editor of the *New Republic* 1979–1981 and 1985–1989. He wrote that magazine's famous "TRB" column for most of the 1980s and 1990s. Kinsley also served as editor at *Harper's* and as managing editor of *Washington Monthly*. Co-host of CNN's *Crossfire* 1989–1992; Editor-in-Chief of *Slate Magazine* 1996–2002.

[2] (b. 1937) English artist, based in California. Important contributor to 1960s British pop art.

May 19, 1987 Pittsburgh. The Presbyterian University Hospital. Rebecca is here for surgery. The day before yesterday, Tom Starzl, who invented the liver transplant and is now the world's greatest liver surgeon, dropped by to discuss Rebecca's operation. It is the most difficult organ transplant to perform. We sat around the dingy, crowded lobby of our ghastly hotel having an unbelievable conversation in unbelievable circumstances with an unbelievable man.

May 20, 1987 Rebecca's operation lasted fourteen hours. Starzl, the miracle worker, tells us her prospects have greatly improved. He has removed most of the tumour and recommends radiation for what remains. He is hopeful she can return to normal life.

May 21, 1987 Another day in Pittsburgh at the Presbyterian University Hospital. Rebecca is recovering from her ordeal in the intensive care unit. Starzl, godlike, walks the corridors, followed by armies of assistants. The idol worshippers draw back as he passes. Sondra and I stand around in a surreal scene surrounded by distraught families awaiting news of their liver-transplanted loved ones.

In the midst of this, I receive news that Deaver's prosecutor, Whitney North Seymour, is trying to subpoena me as a witness for the prosecution. Our lawyers are astonished at his aggressive, rebarbative behaviour. Jim Judd at the embassy described him as a rabid moose. Seymour fears he cannot get a Deaver conviction on acid rain without my testimony. On being informed today that the government would not waive my diplomatic immunity, he has gone on a rampage. He seems to have assumed I would be allowed to testify.

May 22, 1987 The rabid moose continues to run wild.

May 23, 1987 We all agree Seymour is behaving very shabbily. In the papers he sent to our lawyer, he accuses the Canadian government of frustrating the U.S. legal process. He told our lawyer, Stuart Pierson, he would do all he can to embarrass Canada publicly.

Seymour is betraying me. He knows I used my influence to get the government to co-operate by filing detailed replies to his questions. By now asserting that we have thereby waived immunity, he is being more than disingenuous: he is being dishonest. McPherson says Seymour fears press criticism from the Bill Safires of this world for being weak in his prosecutory zeal, so he's looking for a scapegoat. That's where I come in.

But there is good news. We finally got the State Department to issue a letter to Seymour fully supporting my diplomatic immunity.

May 26, 1987 Seymour tried to subpoena both Sondra and me. All the servants, drivers, guards, and officers at our premises have been told not to accept any papers for me. As Marc was driving into Washington from Pittsburgh with Rebecca and Sondra, I telephoned Sondra to warn her that process servers would be trying to give her a document at the Residence and that she shouldn't accept it. All this while Rebecca was lying in the back seat of the car, recuperating after her massive day-long surgery.

At 3 p.m. an FBI officer turned up at the embassy with subpoenas for Sondra and me. Judd went down and told him I had immunity, as did Sondra, that he would not accept service, and attempts to serve us were an infringement of international law.

Seymour's conduct is prosecutorial harassment at its most extreme. It's obscene. Is this America? Is this us? Is this real?

May 27, 1987 Page 1 story in the *New York Times* on the subpoena affair. It accurately reflects our position. So far so good, but tomorrow the rabid moose will charge again. He has informed us that he is making a motion before the judge to serve both Sondra and me. State has issued a statement supporting us. Meanwhile, back home, the Liberal MPs want to get me before a parliamentary committee, but Clark pointed out that Seymour alleged no wrongdoing on Canada's part.

In the afternoon I called on Ken Duberstein[1] in the White House, now deputy chief and managing the whole operation. He intimated that the White House was not pleased with Seymour's behaviour. They regard it as unfortunate.

Our conversation was productive. We were all impressed, I said, with Reagan's new sensitivity to our concerns about acid rain, Arctic sovereignty, and trade, which top officials like Shultz shared, but there appeared to be a disconnect with the bureaucracy at lower levels.

---

[1] (b. 1944) Deputy Assistant to the President for Legislative Affairs 1981–1983; Deputy Chief of Staff to President Ronald Reagan 1987; Chief of Staff 1988–1989.

May 28, 1987 Got a huge shock this morning when I woke up and saw my puss on page 1 of the *New York Times*, above the fold, and an article immediately under stating that Seymour was accusing Canada of thwarting his prosecution and behaving duplicitously. I'm famous, or more accurately, infamous.

Ken Taylor told me Nabisco would give a million dollars for *Spirit Canoe* and the furnishings of the executive offices. Hallelujah. I passed on the news to Erickson.

May 29, 1987 Page 1 of the *New York Times* three days running. This morning's account was highly sympathetic to Canada. Great quotes citing various eminent lawyers calling Seymour's behaviour "quite astounding," "incredible," something that could "bring the whole office of the special prosecutor into disrespect."

Seymour has made a major tactical error. By infringing international rules, he has made himself the issue. If he had simply wailed, moaned, and criticized Canada, he would have had all the media on his side. Instead, he shot himself in his nether regions.

May 31, 1987 A Sunday lunch in Middleburg at Pamela Harriman's. International courtesan she may be, as Joe Alsop calls her, but she is also the perfect hostess and warm and welcoming to the Canadian ambassador and his wife. Subject of discussion: Deaver, the subpoena, moi. The *Washington Post* carried an editorial condemning Seymour's behaviour. Some at lunch thought he had destroyed his career over this ill-fated move and endangered the institution of special prosecutor. I found all this talk delicious. I'm the man of the hour – I'm a victim.

The Harriman estate in Middleburg, Willow Oaks, was previously called Journey's End. Pamela said she would never live in a place with that name. She is cultivating an English garden on the beautifully landscaped grounds, but the climate is a deadly enemy. The heat was torrid and the humidity worse. Glasses steaming up, mosquitoes unbearable. Nevertheless, Pamela was cool and elegant in what Sondra said was a "perfect cotton dress."

June 1, 1987 Reagan held a ceremony in the White House on the fortieth anniversary of the Marshall Plan. I had my fifteen minutes of fame on the great stage, thanks to Whitney North Seymour Jr. Ed Meese:

"Ambassador, I've got the subpoena right here in my pocket. Har, har, har." Scotty Reston: "I go away for a week, and you get into a mess of trouble." Lloyd Cutler: "If Meese wasn't so damaged by being under investigation himself, he could have fired Seymour for his conduct." Carlucci: "I told the president about Seymour's actions, and the president was very angry."

June 2, 1987 Before the Rockefeller dinner for the Americas Society in New York, we attended a cocktail party at the apartment of Paul Nitze's son, who is coming to the State Department to be an assistant undersecretary (responsible for the environment). Everyone stood watching television as the appointment of Alan Greenspan to replace Paul Volcker was announced. Volcker's departure is a big loss for me. He would always see me on the shortest notice and was a regular at our table. Sondra and I both grew to admire him enormously. We've met Greenspan a number of times with either Barbara Walters or Andrea Mitchell,[1] and he's been to the Residence on a couple of occasions. I have a connection with him that we joke about. His first wife, Joan Mitchell, was from Winnipeg, an Ayn Rand disciple at the time. I used to date her.

Sondra told me David Rockefeller, whom she sat next to at the Americas Society dinner, spent considerable time telling her how outraged he was about the behaviour of Seymour North Whitney Jr. I talked to his wife, Peggy, whom I sat beside, about the recent political assassinations in Washington. She told me that her husband, who didn't know Don Regan well, went to see him when he was appointed chief of staff. "You have to face it," Regan said, "I'm the prime minister."

Ken Taylor and I discussed the Nabisco-embassy fiasco. Bruce Phillips called me yesterday to tell me the PMO is worried about the idea of accepting $1 million from Nabisco as sole sponsor for Reid's *Spirit Canoe* and upgrading the executive offices. It seems Stevie Cameron[2] wrote a critical piece in the *Globe and Mail* about Johnson's recent Order of Canada. So now

---

[1] (b. 1946) American journalist, television commentator, and writer. NBC White House Correspondent 1981–1988; Chief Congressional Correspondent 1988–1992. Married Federal Reserve Chairman Alan Greenspan in 1997.

[2] Stephanie "Stevie" Cameron (b. 1943) Canadian author, investigative journalist, and commentator for the *Ottawa Journal*, *Toronto Star*, *Globe and Mail*, and *Maclean's*. She was a commentator for *CBC Newsday* in the 1980s and host of the *Fifth Estate* 1990–1991.

they're all flapping over the possible intimations of bribery, payoff, and a new furniture scandal. Now I am placed in the ridiculous position of saying to a potential donor to the government of Canada, "Please be less generous and give only about half of what you offered. But also, please find some others who will contribute what we don't want to take from you."

June 3, 1987 I flew back from New York at a very early hour and received Pat Carney, who is visiting Washington. I arranged an early breakfast between her and Bob Strauss, whom she wanted badly to meet (as does everyone in Canada). He told her if we thought we'd get Congress to renounce the U.S. unilateral right to resort to trade remedies, we were dreaming in technicolour.

Carney and I called on Senator Bentsen. They were on different frequencies. He mistook her legitimate probing about the Senate's willingness to get involved in the free-trade dispute as implicit criticism of himself and the Senate. Strauss called me later to say he had phoned Bentsen to soften him up for Carney's visit. I told him Bentsen was as cold as an icicle, although polite. Bob said, "Well, if he wasn't cold, he'd be president of the U.S."

Carney's call on Spark Matsunaga went much better, as he was in a talkative mood for a change. He kept feeding her chocolate-covered macadamia nuts from Hawaii, which she devoured like a bear. He gave her four boxes to take home.

Throughout the day we were treated to vintage Carney. What am I doing here? What should I say? What's the purpose of all this? She was walking badly, complaining of lack of sleep and everything else. At the huge dinner for forty-seven people we gave her in the evening, she turned to Sondra on the way out and said, "Where's my staff? Find them."

June 4, 1987 There is a nasty piece in *Maclean's* about Deaver and me, co-authored by the hate-driven Marci MacDonald.[1] She quoted Liberal Member of Parliament John Nunziata[2] as stating that the Canadian government "aided and abetted Gotlieb in the breach of the U.S. law." On checking, I discovered Nunziata never said any such thing. *Maclean's* has

[1] Freelance journalist. A former bureau chief for *Maclean's* in Paris and Washington.

[2] (b. 1955) Member of Parliament for York South–Weston, Ontario, 1984–2000, initially as a Liberal and later as an independent. Ran for mayor of Toronto in the city's 2003 municipal election.

libelled me. I got hold of Ian Binnie[1] of McCarthy and McCarthy, a former Justice official and friend of Len Legault, to serve notice of defamation. *Maclean's* has accused me of violating the law, and of course they don't have a leg to stand on. But I'm not happy about going this route again. This week I received Lorne Morphy's[2] bill for my lapsed suit against the *Star* and *Sun* – 7,200 bucks. I suppose it was worth it, as Hepburn and Hoy have since laid off. But it's an expensive burden for a public servant.

June 5, 1987 Lloyd Axworthy sent a letter to a parliamentary committee asking for an investigation into the Deaver affair and calling me as a witness. What motivates this man? He knows there is nothing to investigate – no breach of Canadian law, no breach of U.S. law, no impropriety. I trust the government will oppose this. Am I naive?

The *New York Times* this morning had a long list of precedents of foreign waivers of diplomatic immunity in the United States, including Fiji ambassador (running over Washingtonians while drunk) and the son of a Brazilian ambassador (shooting someone at a bar in town). Some company.

June 6, 1987 Received a note in the mail regarding Whitney North Seymour Jr. It informs me that his father was an eminent lawyer and senior partner of a prominent New York firm. His son was made a member of the firm. The father was known to the partners as Whit, the son as Half-Whit.

June 8, 1987 I called on Weinberger today to deliver a copy of our new defence white paper. Paul Heinbecker and General Younghusband accompanied me. Weinberger expressed disappointment at the commitment to only 2 per cent real growth and quizzed me about the plan to build nuclear-powered submarines. He questioned me repeatedly as to whether the submarine plan was related to our Arctic waters sovereignty claim. I replied in the negative, explaining that we claim the waters regardless of whether we have, or could have, submarines. On the other hand, it's ridiculous to have territory if you can't even participate in its defence. I told

---

[1] (b. 1939) Justice of the Supreme Court of Canada 1998 to present; previously Associate Deputy Minister of Justice.

[2] Senior trial and appellate counsel at Davies Ward Phillips and Vineberg LLP; appointed Commissioner of the Ontario Securities Commission in 2001.

Weinberger that the emphasis on the ability to protect our own borders was a sound thing, because it would lend greater public support in Canada for our defence efforts. Until recently, Canadians thought of their country as a fireproof house, of the "threat" being a threat to Europe or elsewhere but not on our own soil. In the long run, there would be great benefit flowing from a defence policy made in and for Canada. Weinberger was skeptical. What he liked best about the paper, understandably, was the emphasis on the Soviet threat.

In the afternoon I received a disturbing call from Si Taylor on the secure line. He told me Flora MacDonald called him last Friday and said her problem was me. There was no way that Canada could get its film policy accepted in the United States as long as I was ambassador. I was telling people that the government would not introduce the legislation. I was saying Canada would cut a deal. She had spoken to Clark and would speak to the prime minister.

I sent a report of a disastrous resolution introduced into the Senate by Alan Cranston[1] and Bentsen to the PM and Clark in Venice (attending the economic summit). The resolution calls our film policy discriminatory and states that it would be an absolute bar to a Canada-U.S. free-trade agreement. Sad but predictable. Flora is trying to shoot the messenger.

June 9, 1987 We went to a huge privately sponsored dinner in honour of Mark Fowler, the strong-minded retiring chairman of the FCC. Sitting next to me at the head table, he said apologetically that he was sorry there were no FCC commissioners present. "Why aren't there?" I asked. "Because they can't accept a gift for a dinner valued at over thirty-five dollars, unless it is from a 'friend.' I brought in that regulation just before I left," he said proudly. "That," I told him, "is an unusually silly policy. I can't believe you're serious." "I am," he replied.

"Well," I commented, "why didn't they come and just skip a course?" Fowler thought that was funny enough to quote in his remarks.

June 12, 1987 Derek Burney, back from Venice, called on the secure line to give me a report on the Reagan-Mulroney meeting following the economic summit. Mulroney made a strong pitch for a new approach to

---

[1] (1914–2000) Democratic Senator from California 1969–1993; Senate Majority Whip 1977–1981 and 1987–1991; Senate Minority Whip 1981–1987.

dispute settlement. It seems Howard Baker and Frank Carlucci, who were with the president, were skeptical about the possibilities. But the president undertook to get Jim Baker, Mac Baldridge, and Howard Baker to meet and study this as a matter of priority so Mulroney can know if it's a possibility. It seems the U.S. team also said, "The bad-mouthing of Murphy in Washington has got to stop." I told Burney no one at the embassy was bad-mouthing Murphy, although a lot of people in this town certainly were.

As expected, the president raised film policy. Mulroney mentioned that the legislative agenda in Ottawa was quite crowded and told Reagan he would get back to him prior to the introduction of legislation.

I received a call from Conrad Black. He has decided to buy *Saturday Night*. Do I know any good writers? Editors? Great news, I told him. I would try to think of someone controversial. Black asked if I could line up Mulroney for the Bilderberg steering committee meeting in Toronto on October 1. He wants him to speak. Black is pro-Mulroney and says if he achieves all his objectives, his will be the most creative government since St. Laurent. He was critical of Trudeau's constitutional stance.

June 15, 1987 *Maclean's* apologizes for its libel. Pretty good apology. (*Maclean's* unreservedly retracts any suggestions of impropriety by Ambassador Gotlieb and apologizes to him.) But I may continue with the libel action. When you accuse someone of breaking the law, the courts take it seriously.

June 16, 1987 Hosted a dinner under hot skies for Paul Nitze, the Evanses, Brandons, and Laughlin Phillips. It was an exhilarating evening of talk about arms control and change in the Soviet Union. To the always skeptical Nitze, Gorbachev's moves were for the purpose of saving the party, not the economic improvement of the Soviet people. I didn't agree with him, but at eighty plus, there is no one more impressive in Georgetown.

June 18, 1987 Washington's fixation on the Iran-Contra hearings continues. But it's not about morality, or even bad foreign policy. It's about a power struggle between the administration and Congress. Congress wants to micromanage foreign policy.

At the time of the McCarthy hearings, people who were watching did not understand their significance. They did not know that they were seeing McCarthy being destroyed. They thought the very opposite to be the case.

So it will take some time – perhaps years – before one can assess the true significance and effects of the current hearings.

June 22, 1987 Spoke with Glen Shortliffe to check on the status of film policy. Big news. The bill has been heisted until the fall. The prime minister put it on hold and told Flora as much.

I then spoke to Simon Reisman about the new U.S. proposals on dispute settlement. I told him I thought they were a good start, although probably not sufficient to build adequate machinery. He would have none of it. "It's all or nothing. Compulsory arbitration or no deal. We'd be giving too much to get too little." I told Simon that this was a good negotiating stance, but again, he would have none of it.

"It's not a negotiating stance," he barked, "it's the bottom line. The prime minister agrees with me," he added.

June 27, 1987 This evening we attended a cocktail party given by the mysterious Judith Miller,[1] former girlfriend of Rick Burt and others, in honour of Yves Montand.[2] A mix of left and right, *Times* and *Post*, Jew and gentile. I just missed Jack Valenti, which was fortunate. I didn't have to hear him crow.

It's Kay Graham's seventieth birthday party on Tuesday. Lally Weymouth, Kay's daughter and the hostess, thought I was attending. She hadn't received my regrets, although I know Connie told them a month ago I had a commitment in California and Sondra would attend alone. It looks like a bad decision on my part, even though six hundred are attending, including the president. Because of the screw-up in communications, my refusal sticks out. Jennifer Phillips told Sondra a while ago, "Kay doesn't notice who comes, just who refuses." She was dead right. When I saw Kay tonight, she said to me, "Traitor!"

June 28, 1987 We went to a huge Sunday brunch at the new Potomac Restaurant on a beautiful, cool, windy day. A large crowd of mostly B-list people were on hand. Jack Valenti caught my eye and said, "Allan, it's victory."

---

[1] (b. 1948) Reporter for the *New York Times*, starting at the Washington bureau in 1977, and retiring from the newspaper in 2005. Washington Bureau News Editor and Deputy Bureau Chief 1987–1988.

[2] (1921–1991) French-Italian actor, notably in *Jean de Florette* (1986).

"Don't be too damn sure, Jack," I told him. "It's postponement, not cancellation, and a lot will depend on how the free-trade negotiations go."

July 4, 1987 On Martha's Vineyard we attended a Fourth of July brunch at Milton Gordon's, the Phillipses' neighbour, who now owns Katherine Cornell's[1] magnificent beachfront estate. Hot dogs, hamburgers, a band, singing, American patriotism, a bevy of genuine liberal artifacts, including Art Buchwald, Bill and Rose Styron, Walter Cronkite, Beverly Sills,[2] Henry Grunwald, Louise Melhado, and other Vineyard celebrities. Art Buchwald came up to me in his chummy way and said, "Seymour was really stupid in what he tried to do to you. I know Seymour well, and he is a good guy."

"I'm glad to hear someone speak well of him," I responded. "You're the first."

As we strolled into the living room, Buchwald added, "Deaver will never be convicted."

"Why not?" I asked.

"Because Seymour can't call you as a witness," he replied.

"Asshole," I wanted to say, but suppressed it.

July 6, 1987 Dinner at the Laughlin Phillipses' house, where we are staying. Their friends the Styrons were there, plus a few others, including Claudette Colbert. I was seated next to her and wasn't particularly thrilled at the prospect of having to act interested in a celebrity talking about herself.

How wrong I was. She was as radiant in life as in the movies. She recounted to me tales of being stuck for months in Australia with Rex Harrison[3] in a two-person play. Harrison was soused the whole time.

I asked her how close she was to Ronald Reagan. "He is a lot younger than me," she said, "so we weren't in the same set, but I knew him well. When I was playing at the Kennedy Center on Christmas Day, I felt I had to call Nancy, in view of how bad things were on the Iran-Contra front. She said to me, 'Oh, if only Poindexter and North would agree to testify. How I wish they would.'" Or wondrous words to that effect.

---

[1] (1898–1974) German-born actress nicknamed "The First Lady of the American Theatre."

[2] (b. 1929) Coloratura soprano and well-known American opera singer in the 1960s and 1970s. In 1980 she became the general manager of the New York City Opera.

[3] (1908–1990) British theatre and film actor.

July 7, 1987 Back from Martha's Vineyard to attend a Canadian dinner convened by Peter Lougheed and old friend Don MacDonald at the Washington Four Seasons. Its purpose was to discuss with the private sector how to advance the free-trade negotiations. I described the emotive, anti-foreign mood on the Hill, now peaking because of the intense Senate debate on the new protectionist trade bill.

As I was speaking, Don MacDonald broke in with an impassioned plea for our film policy. He said if he couldn't tell the Americans exactly what he thought and if he had to pull his punches, he was going to go home. I then said, "If you want my honest advice, pull your punches." MacDonald replied, "Okay, I'm going home." He gathered up his papers and walked out. I eventually went upstairs, found him in the lobby, and spent ten minutes trying to convince him to return to the talks. I think I finally got to him when I said, "Don, you'll catch more bees with honey than vinegar." He came back to the meeting, but it was the shambles.

July 8, 1987 Canadian Press reports that MacDonald said in Toronto before he came to Washington that Mulroney doesn't know how to deal with Americans – you have to kick them in the shins from time to time if you want to get anywhere. I doubt he said this, but if he did, I understand better why he reacted as he did last night.

I spent the day with Perrin Beatty. At a meeting with Weinberger in the morning, the U.S. naval brass ridiculed our plans to build ten or twelve nuclear submarines. The meeting was perhaps the most fascinating I've attended in the Mulroney years. The U.S. Defense Department wants to scuttle our program. They want us to act like a little boy, not a big one. This makes me all the more convinced that the idea of going for nuclear submarines is a good one.

We are facing a serious situation. The U.S. navy chiefs don't want Canada to have nuclear subs. They don't need or want our presence. This is bad. It will be easy for them to subvert our effort with the media and Congress. Our nuclear intentions have provoked more interest than any defence or foreign-policy initiative of ours since the Trudeau "peace proposal."

Beatty was pleased that I was aggressively pushing the policy. I think it is a good one. If we go ahead, we will end the we-they situation that now prevails in the Arctic. It's our Arctic, but they protect it. Now we can have a maritime NORAD, with ourselves participating realistically in our own defence. And now we too will be using nuclear power for defence – not just the dirty Yanks. We will lose our nuclear virginity. I discussed this at length with Beatty and Bob Fowler. They are nervous about my "loss of virginity" analysis. God forbid I should mention it publicly.

July 9, 1987 *Globe and Mail* headline: "U.S. Senators Reject Compulsory Free-Trade Arbitration." So the Canadian business group got out of this ill-timed and ill-conceived visit exactly what I predicted they would get: embarrassment.

July 10, 1987 Had breakfast with Bob Strauss at the Metropolitan Club and told him he may be the man who can save the Canada-U.S. free-trade agreement. I showed him yesterday's *Globe and Mail* headline about Bentsen's and Danforth's pronouncements that compulsory dispute settlement was out of the question. "The time is at hand," I told him, "for a Jew from Texas to start trying to put things together." There was a risk, I told him (borrowing his line about shingles and shakes), that the whole effort was likely to collapse "because of some assholes on both sides of the border."

July 12, 1987 Former NASA administrator James Beggs on news of the withdrawal of an indictment against him for alleged fraud: "There's no experience more exhilarating than being shot at and missed." I think of Seymour and his subpoenas.

July 13, 1987 While I am sure Joe Clark will not love me the more for it, I waded into deep waters today, sending a telegram of advice on the United States' prospective request to test the advanced cruise. I realize there are domestic political factors in play, I said, but we in the embassy have to point out that there could be heavy deleterious consequences flowing from further significant delay. Were we not to co-operate, the consequences would be greatest for the defence sector, where the white paper has created the prospect of a more equally balanced relationship. Nor could we exclude negative effects on the attitudes of senior officials whose active co-operation will be needed on other top items on the bilateral agenda (trade negotiations, acid rain). I reminded Clark that Trudeau agreed to test the cruise, despite strong public opposition.

July 14, 1987 The dog days of summer. Another barbecue on our terrace (for sixty-two) and more staff farewells. Among the departing, alas, are Jim Wright[1] and Jim Judd, the two big Jims, long, lean Anglo-Saxons who have been powerful gun-slingers defending our honour and reputation on the Hill. Judd is a stand-in for Clint Eastwood, a man of few words, and, so far as I can tell, even fewer sentiments. The best shot we have on our side. Jim Wright is everything a diplomat should be – discreet, intelligent, tough, and smooth. His beautiful wife, Donna, is my favourite among the officers' wives. If I've had any success here, I owe much of it to the two Jims.

July 18, 1987 Day two of protesting the sugar duty provision of the terrible omnibus trade bill. I placed eight calls to eight senators.

The Canadian position is that this is an export subsidy contrary to GATT, and other countries will demand compensation or retaliate. A few agreed – Nancy Kassebaum, Bill Roth, and Mark Hatfield. But what I got from the others was very different. "I grow sugar in my state, and I promised my vote to Bennett Johnston[2] of Louisiana," declared Tim Wirth of Colorado, one of the brightest of the younger senators. Fritz Hollings of South Carolina and John Warner of Virginia explained to me, "I don't have sugar in my state, but I have tobacco. Sugar supports tobacco because tobacco supports sugar."

In other words, good old-fashioned log-rolling. Once again, dealing with senators proves to be a remarkable experience. The provision passed on the floor of the Senate by a close vote. The only consolation is that the small margin will help attract a presidential veto.

Warner said he'd like to talk to me about submarines. It certainly hasn't taken the navy long to start lobbying the Congress. I alerted Defence and External in Ottawa that they should be slightly alarmed. I urged Beatty to get a letter off immediately to Weinberger informing him that we would be delighted to consider procurement in the United States if they have the right product.

July 18, 1987 We had a small dinner at the Residence with the Lane Kirklands, Edmund and Sylvia Morris, and Mary Jane Wick. We ate under the stars, drinking an excellent claret (the head of the AFL-CIO is the only oenophile I know in Washington). Sondra's garden was looking magnificent

---

[1] Canadian foreign-service officer in Moscow 1978–1980 and in Washington 1983–1987; High Commissioner to the United Kingdom 2006.

[2] (b. 1932) Democratic Senator from Louisiana 1972–1997.

and I believe is among the most beautiful in Washington. The conversation was difficult, because we talked (we had to talk) about the Iran-Contra hearings. Everyone in Washington seems to come at this experience from a different angle, and everyone seems to have deep feelings. Thank God for dogs, wine, and vacations. They saved our conversation, and the evening.

July 19, 1987 A letter from Big John Dingell arrived on my desk. Copies were sent to Shultz, Herrington, members of his Energy and Commerce Committee, and various coal, electrical, and labour lobbies. On the day of my heavy lobbying on the Hill, his closing paragraph states, "I believe that Canada's lobbying effort aimed at the Congress and our system is inappropriate. Both nations would be better served by resorting to the traditional diplomatic approach as suggested by your Prime Minister when he and President Reagan met last April."

How ironic. If I followed his advice, I would be unemployed.

As I was leaving the office yesterday, I got a call from the prime minister. He wanted to know about my contretemps with Don MacDonald, whom he admires, and he wanted all the details. We talked for about half an hour. He was hurt by Don's remarks about him not knowing how to negotiate with the Americans.

July 20, 1987 Sunday. We spent seven hours talking to Arthur Liman,[1] counsel for the Senate committee investigating Iran-Contra, whom I had not met before today.

Muffie and Henry Brandon had asked us to brunch in their summer place in Middleburg. There was one other couple there – the Limans. We got back about 5 p.m. and went to an early dinner at Vernon Jordan's, and there was one other couple there – the Limans. I did not expect to like or be impressed with Arthur Liman. I was surprised. He was not heavy on the moralizing side and seemed dubious about holding these hearings in public.

Liman came out with one novel twist. He suggested the real reason Poindexter didn't tell Reagan of the Contra funds diversion was not to protect the president but to avoid the information leaking out. They didn't trust him to keep a secret.

---

[1] (1932–1997) U.S. attorney. A partner at Paul, Weiss, Rifkind, Wharton, & Garrison LLP and Professor of Law at Yale Law School.

July 21, 1987 Had a tête-à-tête lunch at the Residence with Admiral Crowe, chairman of the Joint Chiefs of Staff. He's the only man in the navy with a Ph.D. to reach so exalted a position. The purpose of my lunch was to try to convince him to get behind our nuclear submarine policy, to restrain Admiral McKee[1] and the navy to stop lobbying against us.

He was displeased to learn from me that McKee was lobbying Congress, but he dwelled on the enormity of the task we had undertaken and said that McKee's warnings of financial, technical, and environmental horrors downstream were all justified. "What should we do?" I asked Crowe. "If you make it absolutely clear," he replied, "that you intend to persist, the U.S. will not risk the defence relationship with Canada, if that is the cost of blocking the submarine program."

July 22, 1987 Jim Baker and I had an hour-long tête-à-tête on the Canada-U.S. free-trade agreement. My pitch was that if the United States fails to conclude a treaty with Canada, this would go down as one of the three or four biggest political blunders in modern U.S. history. And if we are not successful, there would be a profound change in Canada. Now only the fringes are anti-American. Mainstream Canadians see their destiny linked to that of the United States and favour close relations. But if these negotiations fail, Canadians will see the United States as having rejected us. This could wreak havoc with our psyche for a generation, and many Canadians might believe that they need more distance from the United States. "Hell hath no fury like a woman scorned."

Baker said, "I agree with your analysis. The president wants this agreement. Indeed, we want it even more now than six months ago, given what has happened in the Iran-Contra affair. But I thought the negotiations weren't going too badly."

The central problem, I replied, was dispute settlement. Bentsen's and Danforth's statements were appalling. It was ridiculous to think that if we had a comprehensive treaty governing all our trade and a lot more, each side could unilaterally interpret its provisions. This made a mockery of the negotiations.

In all great moments in U.S. history, I went on, whenever anything important needed to be accomplished, a consensus was forged with the

[1] Kinnaird McKee (b. 1929) Commander, Third Fleet, and Director of Naval Warfare in the Office of the Chief of Naval Operations 1978–1982; Director of Naval Nuclear Propulsion 1982–1988.

Congress. Think of the Marshall Plan, the Truman Plan, the Baruch Plan. You must get a key group of players together in one room, drawn from both the Congress and the administration, to forge a basic consensus on this issue. I suggested the two Bakers, Carlucci, Bentsen, Strauss, Shultz, probably others, such as Bradley, and one or two from the House. "And you must have the lead role."

Baker asked me to call him in ten days to discuss the matter further. The lack of vision on the Hill is appalling. However, Baker is the most effective member of the Reagan team. If anyone can do anything, he can.

The Senate, by a big majority, passed the terrible trade bill. More trouble for us on the free-trade front.

In the evening we went to the opening performance of the Bolshoi Ballet at the Kennedy Center, an event much anticipated in this town. Never, in six years in Washington, have I seen such a gathering of senators. I spotted Max Baucus and said in a loud voice, "Hi, Senator." Four people turned around and said, "Hi, Ambassador." "They sure as hell aren't here to catch the culture," I said to Paul Volcker, who came with his daughter. "It's obvious the Russians are drawing them – Soviet power." Paul replied, "Well, I don't think you're right. It's the sponsor, Allied Signal. I'm sure they contribute to all their PACs."

July 23, 1987 Frank Carlucci came to lunch at the Residence today. A big deal – Carlucci does not see ambassadors, let alone "do lunch" with them.

I asked him how the White House planned to regain credibility. "We are going to have some foreign-policy successes," he replied. "The Soviets are having a very bad time in Afghanistan, especially with our stingers now in rebels' hands, and Gorbachev wants out badly, although of course on his terms."

"In the Gulf," he commented, looking at his watch, "our ships are at precisely this [X] position. If we get through these reflagging measures without a hitch, we'll have a great foreign-policy success. We will have demonstrated our will to protect a vital area, and Congress will have to be supportive."

I switched over to two big bilateral issues: free trade and submarines. When we got to Canadian defence policy, I pulled out a copy of a telegram from our military at the embassy to our defence headquarters in Ottawa. Our informant said that the U.S. navy was closing ranks, was determined to block Canadian access to U.S. nuclear technology, and was actively lobbying against us on the Hill. Carlucci was shocked and said he would put an end to this at once. "However," he said, "we have real doubts about your capacity to implement this program. The pitfalls are enormous, and I doubt your military have explained this to your ministers." But he acknowledged my warning about the awful impact on our defence partnership if the navy were allowed to scuttle our program.

July 24, 1987 Mac Baldridge's funeral. One of Canada's best friends. It's hard to believe he was killed by his own horse falling on him in rodeo practice. What a tragic – and absurd – way to die. I saw more of him than any other cabinet secretary. There were times when I called on him a couple of times a week, usually alone. I almost set up camp outside his office. The most thoughtful man in the cabinet, he always listened patiently to me. As I had to be in Toronto for lunch and St. John for dinner, I couldn't attend the funeral. The prime minister sent a special envoy, Pat Carney. How ironic. Mac couldn't abide her.

July 27, 1987 In Toronto I got a call from Mulroney at the Park Plaza, where we are staying. He had been watching television and saw Reagan on a trip to Camp David and thought he looked terrible, as did Nancy. He had me track down Carlucci to see if the president would welcome a call. I set it up for tomorrow afternoon. I found Mulroney very subdued. The continuing bad polls have dispirited him.

Mulroney told me a story of a supporter who liked his policies. He read the *Toronto Star* and noted that it called Mulroney an asshole. Well, that's a liberal paper, the supporter observed. Then he read the *Globe*, and it called Mulroney an asshole. That's an independent paper, he said. Then he read the *Sun*, which called him an asshole. And the *Sun* is a conservative paper. Well, the supporter said, I guess you're an asshole.

July 30, 1987 "Speaking of the omnibus trade bill that just passed the Senate, one man has been warning Canadians for several years now that they can no longer take for granted their free access to the U.S. market. That man is Canada's Ambassador to Washington, Allan Gotlieb. . . . The prophet has proved dead right, as we discovered." William Johnson in the Montreal *Gazette*. Very gratifying. And ego-boosting.

August 3, 1987 We end a three-day visit to Fishers Island, as guests of Polly and Clayton Fritchey. A couple out of Washington's past – the era of Bohlen[1] and Kennedy, Harriman and Acheson.[2] No Jews on this island. She has the use of Mrs. Jock Whitney's's[3] house during the summers, and it is most beautifully situated on a corner of the island. I asked Fritchey who he thought was the most impressive of the Wise Men. He knew them all. Clayton said Harriman. Polly interrupted with disbelief – Kennan, she asserted. Clayton exploded with anger. He's a volcano.

We are leaving for Newport, where we are to spend the night with Fitzhugh Green and his Newport friends.

August 5, 1987 Called on Bill Bradley to fire him up on the free-trade front. I gave him my number one spiel: if the United States misses this opportunity, it will go down as one of the three or four biggest foreign-policy mistakes in U.S. history. I urged him to be a white knight. "I know your leadership capabilities," I exclaimed. He replied, "I get your point, and I'll think about your appeal." For my money, Bradley is the most impressive legislator currently on the Hill.

August 6, 1987 Ottawa is madly upset at statements yesterday by Danforth, Baucus, and Heinz that compulsory dispute settlement is out of the question.

Lunched with a few key sympathetic senators in the Senate dining room – Chafee, Evans, and Moynihan – to discuss our strategy to deal with this threat. I described deep negative consequences of a failed negotiation. If the Canadians perceive that the United States is rejecting Canada, the history of the continent will never be the same.

As we were talking and plotting, Danforth came up to our table, looking pretty sheepish. Moynihan leaped up and asked him to sit down. Danforth said, "I know what you're talking about," stood there for about ninety seconds, and then said, "No, I'd better not."

---

[1] Charles Bohlen (1904–1974) U.S. diplomat. Ambassador to the Soviet Union 1953–1957, to the Philippines 1957–1959, and to France 1962–1968.

[2] Dean Acheson (1893–1971) Secretary of State 1949–1953. He served as an unofficial adviser to the Kennedy, Johnson, and Nixon administrations and was known for his brilliant and acerbic wit. Not widely known are his Canadian family origins.

[3] John Hay "Jock" Whitney (1904–1982) American industrialist, movie producer, and philanthropist. Ambassador to the United Kingdom 1957–1961; Publisher of the *New York Tribune* 1961–1966.

Dick Rivers of the Strauss firm is advising the U.S. coalition supporting our free-trade agreement. I asked him what the hell is going on. He tells me the strategy is to wait until an agreement is in place before starting to lobby the Hill. "You'd better reconsider," I said. "Start lobbying right after Labour Day. A vacuum is forming, and the naysayers will occupy centre stage. This could kill prospects for a successful conclusion to the negotiations."

August 20, 1987 A few minutes after we arrived at Keltic Lodge in Cape Breton Island, where we are taking a two-week holiday, I got a call from Don Campbell in Ottawa. I knew it wouldn't be good news, and I was right. A couple of months ago, I accepted an invitation from Garth Drabinsky to attend a lunch honouring him during the Montreal Film Festival on August 27. "If you ever do me a favour," he said to me in the grand Drabinsky style, "let this be it." My name then appeared in the Montreal papers as an "honoured invitee" at the forthcoming lunch, along with Jack Valenti, among others. Flora was furious. The idea of me appearing at a lunch with Jack Valenti! She went to Clark, who sent a note to Don Campbell telling me not to go.

August 22, 1987 I'm fuming over this Flora and Joe act. I've thought a lot about resigning but decided in the negative because (1) the issue is too trivial and (2) the Canadian cultural clique would say good riddance.

August 24, 1987 Back in Washington, I learn that Jodi White managed to neutralize Clark. While not agreeing that I should go, he seems to have softened up. She passed on the message – in effect, a *nihil obstat*. I'll fly to Montreal for the day.

August 26, 1987 Lunch today with Ty Cobb at the Metropolitan Club. I asked him why the president failed to mention the free-trade agreement in his public comments two weeks ago and why the briefing on the administration's priorities, emanating out of Santa Barbara, totally ignored our negotiation. He said Yeutter and others thought that since the negotiation was in a crucial stage, the U.S. side shouldn't appear to be eager. "An analogy," Cobb said, "is our INF negotiations with the Soviets. We can't appear too eager. That's a bad negotiating ploy." I had a hard time believing my ears. What dwarfs there are in the White House.

August 27, 1987 I flew to Montreal for the Drabinsky testimonial. About six hundred were there, with a head table of a couple of dozen. Michael Caine and a few other movie heavies were at the head table, along with Valenti. I concentrated on avoiding a photo op with the Great Satan.

September 2, 1987 A new round of life in Washington begins. We near completion of six years. On Monday I spoke to a crowd – six hundred motor vehicle regulators – about Canada-U.S. trade and trucking. Sondra gave a tea for a couple of hundred spouses. We met all day yesterday with the Canadian consuls general to discuss how to sell the free-trade agreement, assuming we have one. This morning there was a bomb threat at the new embassy site and the Residence. It was a beautiful morning, and we evacuated on the lawn. Familiarity causes boredom. If I didn't have the free-trade challenge at hand, with the prospect of a six-month lobbying campaign, this would be a good time to jump.

September 10, 1987 "Canada As a Major Power" was the theme of my luncheon speech to the Canadian Club of Ottawa. I am so fed up with all this talk about Canada as a middle power. Pearson talked about being a middle power, but that was a long time ago. Trudeau talked about it but shouldn't have. Now Mulroney is using the phrase – it seems irresistible to the Canadian mind and mouth. It contributes to the "poor little Canada" mentality and affirms the "you are the elephant and we are the mouse" attitude vis-à-vis the United States. I outlined how ridiculous it is for Canadians to think that way, we who have the eighth or ninth highest GNP in the world, the highest annual growth rate among the Western industrialized countries, including Japan, we who are a resource superpower, the world's biggest exporter of wheat and lumber and so on, with an economy bigger than that of over 150 other countries.

September 11, 1987 Saw the prime minister yesterday in his office in the Centre Block. He was hurting from two recent events.

The first was the shabby treatment he received in the press (*Globe*) and on TV (CBC) about Mila allegedly interfering in the immigration process to get landed immigrant status for her children's French teacher. Nothing wounds a person in public life more than an attack on the spouse. It was deliberate and, so far as I can tell, wholly unjustified, because everyone in

Parliament tries to get immigration officers to use their vast discretion to help particular individuals. I found this out when I ran the damn service.

The second is the Americans are signalling that they're not going to accept our reasonable demands on dispute settlement and subsidy definition in the free-trade talks. The attitude seems to be forming in the White House that our demands are too high.

Mulroney is bitter about this. If the United States turns their back on us, they'll feel our wrath, he said. He vowed to use every occasion over the next few months to ensure that those people in the Congress, including Bentsen and the like, feel our anger. "Let Jim Baker and George Shultz know that when you see them," he told me.

My response to Mulroney was that although our prospects looked poor at the moment, we could still succeed. Putting out a message of the sort he has in mind was premature and would not be productive. "Let's wait a few days or a week," I suggested, "but no longer. Then, if they won't meet our position in a reasonable way, we should tell them the negotiation is over. Period." The idea is to create a crisis just before the October 5 negotiating deadline. "We must cause a crisis and make creative use of it." Mulroney agreed – or said he did.

The prime minister was talking more loudly than I can remember him doing before, although we were the only two in the room. He stood up, so I did too, and we remained standing throughout our discussion. I could feel the intensity of his wrath. He stood more and more closely to me as he spoke.

Sitting in my hotel at the end of the day, I got a call from Jon Fried,[1] our congressional liaison officer at the embassy. Although an experienced lawyer in his thirties, he was as excited as a bar mitzvah boy. "Do you know what Lugar did?" he asked. "During a hearing in the Foreign Relations Committee on Central America, where Shultz was testifying, Lugar said they should talk about the Canada-U.S. free-trade agreement before getting on to Central America. He made some fine remarks: 'If we're unable to work out an agreement with our closest friends, I think this could be a very serious deficiency.'"

Lugar described the October 5 deadline for a deal as "the most critical

---

[1] Jonathan Fried (b. 1953) Counsellor for Congressional and Legal Affairs, Canadian Embassy in Washington 1987–1991; Associate Deputy Minister in the Department of Foreign Affairs and International Trade 1997–2000; Foreign Policy Adviser to Prime Minister Paul Martin 2003–2006.

date in this continent and perhaps in the Western Hemisphere." A marvellous message. This is exactly what I've been saying to Baker all along.

September 12, 1987 In the late afternoon we went to the wedding of Joan and Tom Braden's daughter. It was a thin crowd. Everyone in town is furious at Joan for her remarks – written in her leaked book proposal – about her affairs or near affairs with a lot of important people in Washington. Joe Alsop and his brother Stewart's widow came, even though Joan wrote some frightfully indiscreet things about her. Joe looked heavy and white. We talked briefly. "I have lung cancer," he said. He was smoking even as he told me and clearly had had his share of vodka. I felt terribly saddened. He is taking radiation, he said. Susan Brinkley came to the reception, but not David, although they are – or were – close friends of the Bradens. Joan has been indiscreet about David as well.

September 13, 1987 A brilliant Monday morning in New York City. I open the *Wall Street Journal* to read a lead editorial entitled "Go Canada," everything I could have wished for from my interview with the *Journal*. The only thing missing was my signature. This puts me in a buoyant mood for my call at midday on the editorial board of the *New York Times*. Maybe this effort is worthwhile.

September 14, 1987 Strauss tells me Murphy is freewheeling. No one knows what's he's doing, including Yeutter. He's disconnected from everything in Washington. But shortly after talking with Bob, I had lunch *à deux* at the Residence with John Whitehead, who sang a different tune. "The cabinet is fully engaged," he said, "as we are meeting continually. We have just made a significant new proposal on a trade dispute mechanism. Murphy is a fine negotiator and is doing an excellent job." I like Whitehead, but I believe Strauss.

In a call at the White House, I complained about the slow U.S. response on acid rain to the diminutive, perky Gary Bauer, known as a formidable ideologist. Bauer seemed to accept our impatience as justified. He said there are even people in the administration saying we've only got one more summit with Mulroney to get through, so we must hold the line. "This is not," he assured me, "the view of the president or senior members of the administration." I wonder who he is talking about.

I informed the White House that Mulroney does not want a bilateral meeting with Reagan in New York next Monday. This after I told the White House the opposite last week. I feel ridiculous. Both the process and the decision reflect the mood of pessimism and confusion that is taking hold in Canada.

September 15, 1987 In Ottawa Don Mazankowski, Joe Clark, Mike Wilson, Pat Carney, Paul Tellier, Stanley Hartt, Gerry Shannon, Simon Reisman, Gordon Ritchie, and I met in the PMO boardroom. Burney was the chair. The atmosphere was grim. Reisman gave a gloomy report on the negotiations, and I gave a gloomy report on the Washington political atmosphere. Apparently, what I said to the prime minister last week about the need to create a crisis is what prompted him to call me to this meeting. I repeated my advice: Reisman, on instructions, should break off the negotiations. To use my term, we should apply "electric shock treatment." The U.S. side, I said, especially the president, will go very far to avoid failure. Otherwise, what will they have left to show as foreign-policy successes? Arms control, that's it.

September 17, 1987 After rude treatment from Cobb (as usual), I contacted Frank Carlucci's and Howard Baker's secretaries to request appointments for Burney and me. (Derek has been added to the delegation, on the prime minister's instructions.) No luck. Instead, the White House made a counter-offer: call on Jim Baker. According to the NSC, Jim Baker is now running the show; he has been designated by the president to take complete charge. I repeated this to Burney, recommending, of course, that we meet with him instead.

My chores prevented us from having to attend the two-hundredth-anniversary ceremonies on the Constitution in Philadelphia. At a National Gallery dinner tonight, we saw the French ambassador, Bobby de Margerie, who attended the opening part of the twenty-four-hour ordeal.

"You had a miraculous escape," he told us. "First we almost died of the heat, then we were rained on as we stood for hours in an open enclosure, and at such a distance we couldn't see a thing."

At the dinner I sat between two immensely rich old females, Enid Haupt, Walter Annenberg's sister, and Mrs. Mosbacher of Texas. Mrs. Haupt, who collected what is regarded as the finest portion of Walter's impressionist collection, commented that "everyone says the pictures looked better in my house than on Walter's wall."

Got a call from John Turner. He inquired about Rebecca, of whom he had heard positive news from Barbara Frum,[1] which I confirmed.

September 19, 1987 Wilson, Burney, and I called on Jim Baker. It's a Saturday morning, and according to Whitehead, Baker gave up his participation in a celebrity tennis match for this meeting. No greater sacrifice. Peter McPherson[2] joined him. The main message from us: Murphy, your negotiator, is backsliding. The moment is slipping away. The main message from Baker: if you don't back off on your binding-mechanism demands, we will have no agreement. This is not good news.

Mulroney called me in late afternoon. "I'm not calling you on free trade. Call Alan Simpson. Tell him for me he was magnificent during the Bork hearings this afternoon. His performance was in the finest tradition of the U.S. Senate. When the founders framed the Constitution, this is what they must have had in mind." I passed the message at once to an appreciative Alan Simpson. He sensed that Mulroney's own experiences heightened his response to what he had said at the hearings.

We went to Germaine's for dinner with Jennifer Phillips and Polly Kraft. The food is always mediocre, but the scene is not. It was a wet night ending a dreary day. While we were eating, Arthur Liman, Abe Sofaer, and their wives came in and we kibitzed. Then came Chris Wallace and his wife, then Bob Hormats with Richard Cohen's[3] abandoned wife, then the producers of *Meet the Press*, then Johnny Apple[4] of the *New York Times*. Sofaer put his arm around a man at the next table, and Liman whispered to me, "Abe doesn't remember he sent this guy to jail for three years."

Animated, crammed with clever and accomplished people, conversations sprouting everywhere, all sorts of unexpected encounters, drama, humour, pain . . . an endless political circus. This is the Washington we will miss.

---

[1] (1937–1992) Canadian journalist and CBC news anchor. Co-host of the CBC Television newsmagazine series *The Journal*.

[2] (b. 1940) Administrator of the Agency for International Development 1981–1987; Deputy Secretary of the Treasury 1987–1989; Bank of America Executive Vice-President 1993 and Michigan State University President 1993–2005.

[3] Columnist for the *Washington Post* who received national syndication in 1981.

[4] Raymond Walter "Johnny" Apple (b. 1934) Highly experienced reporter with the *New York Times* since 1963, a gourmand and gourmet.

September 21, 1987 I took Colin Powell, deputy national security adviser, for lunch at the Metropolitan Club. An exceptionally able man. I'll be surprised if he isn't chairman of the Joint Chiefs of Staff someday. He told me this was the first lunch he had had outside the White House in six months. I said I was flattered. We talked Arctic sovereignty and nuclear subs. Powell said that the policy review group, over which he presides, is now looking at the fortieth or forty-first draft of an agreement on the Arctic, and there is still ferocious opposition from some agencies (the coast guard, no doubt). He will submit a draft to the president soon, with or without consensus, he said.

On the subject of nuclear submarines, he is convinced we are stepping into a financial morass. That's a better argument, I told him, than the one the navy gave us. They stressed technical competence, or lack thereof, I said, and are thus treating us like a Third World country. I explained that the nuclear submarine program originated with our own military people and was perfectly logical when you considered our territory and defence needs.

Powell told me a tale about Yukon Erik, when he flew down to see Cap Weinberger. During the meeting, Neilson said to Weinberger, "We would like to rent some of your submarines." The Americans were dumbfounded.

September 22, 1987 The trade talks are awfully close to breaking up. We met in my office at about 7 p.m. with Reisman, Ritchie, and others, sitting in a circle around a large bottle of Black Label. At the same time, I was dressing for a black-tie fundraising event for multiple sclerosis. We had agreed to be a sponsor, but I kept debating whether to go, given the crisis point we were at. As compulsive as usual about keeping commitments, I went. Good move. I saw Frank Carlucci at the next table. My instinct was to leave him be – after all, the guy did pretty well to avoid us last weekend.

The lady sitting next to me noticed my distraction and inquired after it. I told her in a general way and she said, "Don't be a hesitant diplomat."

I took her advice. I approached Carlucci while he ate and said to him, "The talks are about one inch from breaking up."

"What?" he exclaimed. "We've been showing more flexibility since meeting last Saturday."

"No," I said, "you've become more rigid on subsidies and dispute settlement. You're pulling back. The talks are about to collapse."

"We're going to have a full cabinet review the day after tomorrow," he responded. "It could be too late," I told him.

"I have a crisis management group at 8 a.m. tomorrow. We'll go into it," he said.

No longer the reluctant diplomat, I then had a similar conversation with Clayton Yeutter, who was also attending the ball. Yeutter urged us to remain at the negotiating table and hinted at future flexibility. "We're out of time," I told him.

After the dinner we dropped by for coffee with Dwayne Andreas in his new apartment at the Hay-Adams overlooking the White House and the monuments. I told Strauss, who was there, that we were an inch from failure. "You exaggerate," he said, "as you usually do." I replied, "We're an inch and a half from failure."

September 23, 1987 I spoke to Reisman just after waking this morning. "Are you still of the view I should walk?" he asked. "Yes," I replied, "unless you see new light." At 1 p.m., Simon walked.

Strauss called soon after to tell me we had done the right thing. Late in the night, Tom Niles reported that Reagan wants to call Mulroney tomorrow at noon. Is our strategy working already? I argue that if the Americans offer us something really new, we should go back to the table, but we should make some changes in our negotiating teams. I stick my neck out and propose each side form new three-man teams. On their side: Jim Baker, Murphy, and someone from the White House. On ours: Wilson, Reisman, and Burney. Wilson is very restrained but has excellent judgment and understands the issues. He would be bolstered by Reisman and Burney.

September 24, 1987 A day of panic and confusion.

It's Rosh Hashanah, and I decided to go to synagogue for a couple of hours in the morning. I have a lot to be thankful for.

Burney called Howard Baker at the request of cabinet to tell him to ask the president not to call the prime minister unless he has some good news, new ideas. By the time I got out of synagogue, Burney was calling me to say that Baker had apparently misinterpreted his message. So the shovel brigade was called into action. I am to contact the White House immediately and try to clarify that the prime minister would like to hear from Reagan, but that a message of "let's get together and talk" would be worse than no message. Also, the prime minister wants me to see Bush.

I told Derek I could do both, but he had to understand that since he is being used as the authorized channel, I could be regarded as more or less kibitzing. One of the costs might be some weakening of my own credibility as interlocutor. He didn't dispute this.

In the middle of all this, Sam Gibbons called me with an idea of his own. If we couldn't agree on new joint rules on subsidy and countervail, we could set up a joint tribunal to apply the existing trade law of each country in settling disputes. I said immediately that I thought this was a new idea not previously discussed and was well worth examining. But there was danger, I thought – either side could subsequently change their law to the detriment of the other. Gibbons agreed that for the idea to work, the trade laws of each country would have to be frozen until new rules were jointly worked out. I immediately passed the idea to Ottawa. Officials there confirmed this was a new approach that had not been considered. They showed interest.

Chafee told me that our walkout was being interpreted by his colleagues on the Hill as a sign that Mulroney is weak – frightened of an agreement. How wrong can they get?

September 25, 1987 Everyone is scrambling to put humpty dumpty back together again.

There is interest in Ottawa in the idea Sam Gibbons discussed with me yesterday, but we've learned that Jim Baker is throwing cold water on it. I called on Bill Bradley and Pat Moynihan and urged them to get involved. "Don't let Baucus and Danforth and the likes be the only voices the administration is hearing." Bradley was sympathetic, but I don't think he'll do much. Moynihan asked me what he could do. "Phone Jim Baker," I said. He did, right then and there, with me in the office. Great. Except Baker wasn't in.

I spoke to Strauss a few times today, but he remains pessimistic. He recounted that when Reagan was told of our walkout, he asked, "Why can't we have free trade with Canada like between New York and Pennsylvania?"

"That's good," I said to Strauss. "No, it isn't," he replied. "Reagan thinks U.S. law would apply. Still, your walkout was a good ploy. If you break the back of the problems, it will be because of this."

September 26, 1987 More toing and froing on the telephone between Ottawa and Washington. Baker sent a written proposal to Ottawa, but they don't like it.

At midnight I received instructions to personally deliver to Jim Baker a reply to his proposal. I believe it's negative, but there is a suggestion for a meeting. My instructions were clear: the prime minister wants me to deliver the message, not Wilson. He wants me to say that he went over the text word by word between 10:15 and 11:10 this evening and that he drafted the last paragraph himself, the purport of which is that he believes that if we get an agreement, it will be because Jim Baker wants one.

September 27, 1987 Another wild and weird day in Washington.

I called a meeting at 2 a.m. in the library of the Residence to look at the reply that Derek Burney was planning to send to Jim Baker. The letter's tone was so negative it would have had the opposite effect to the one intended by Mulroney and would have assured that the Americans would not resume discussions. I called on Wilson at the IMF office at 7 a.m. and convinced him on this point.

Together, we then telephoned Burney and had a rough time persuading him to alter the letter, given that it had word-for-word approval from the prime minister, deputy prime minister, and other ministers. He finally agreed to the cleanup. In particular, he agreed to my key change: we would be prepared to have a meeting to clarify not our draft, as stated in the original message, but the position of both sides.

We met Baker in our IMF office at 8:30 a.m. He was very critical of the Murphy show. When we walked out of our negotiations, his first reaction, he said, was that this was a ploy on our part for domestic consumption. His second reaction was different. When he understood what Murphy was proposing that day, he changed his mind. He realized Murphy was operating on the basis of the consensus in his team of officials. He was following, not leading, them.

I went directly to the point by urging that there be a meeting at the political level tomorrow to try to avoid the impasse, and he agreed. We discussed participants with Baker, who said it would be himself and Yeutter, whom he had to have if his support were to be maintained. It was agreed on both sides that the negotiators themselves should not be at the meeting. Later in the day I was told our team was to be Burney, Wilson, and Carney. Throwing modesty to the winds, I urged Burney to ask the prime minister to add me as a fourth man. I told him that, my role aside, I thought I had a close and special relationship with Baker and could communicate with him more effectively than anyone in Ottawa. I know this to be correct. Burney called me back (our twentieth conversation of the day) to say the prime minister had agreed.

In the late afternoon the prime minister called me for my assessment. I said we faced a long shot but could still pull it off. He asked me to tell our interlocutors that the FTA is like SDI – a foolproof defence against charges that the United States was protectionist.

Bruce Phillips said I was the hero of the day in Ottawa because of my role in getting a political dialogue established. Oh yeah?

September 28, 1987 The negotiating sessions with Baker and Yeutter that began at 1:30 p.m. and were supposed to last until 4 p.m. went on until 9:30 this evening, leaving us all exhausted. After that, the Canadian team came back to the chancery and met in my office to assess the day. I started off by saying we made real gains and should push on. Carney said the arguments in favour of continuing were marginal, and Wilson seemed to be in the same frame of mind. I came on strongly – as is my want. "You may be snatching failure from the jaws of victory." Burney, who led the talks, did not show his cards.

At 11 p.m., as I was drafting a telegram in my office about the talks, I got a most unusual call from McPherson. According to him, Baker thinks the U.S. position on regional development is stupid. McPherson said we should press harder. That's what I call good intelligence. The message seems to be that a deal can be done, but Yeutter's nose is seriously out of joint, and he has become a problem. Home at 1:30 a.m.

September 29, 1987 Called on Alan Simpson. We discussed acid rain, and I told him I got an optimistic reading on congressional action at the lunch I gave today at the Residence for private environmentalist groups.

Simpson said, "You've got a bill before the committee that is an environmentalist's dream. If it became law, it would give them all they want. But the bill will be about as useful as an ossified turd."

Jean Chrétien came to the chancery, flanked by two lobbyists from Alaska. They want the U.S. government to break their commitment to Canada to bring Alaska gas south on the Alaska Gas Pipeline. How can we get Canada to go along with this? Chrétien asked. Surely, I said, you could work this out with your good friend, Mr. Pipeline himself, Mitchell Sharp.[1] He worships you.

---

[1] (1911–2004) Minister of Finance 1965–1968; Secretary of State for External Affairs 1968–1974; President of the Privy Council 1974–1978; Commissioner of the Northern Pipeline Agency 1978–1988.

How odd to see two old friends apparently on opposing sides of this issue. Moral: lawyers will do anything to maximize income.

The cabinet in Ottawa debated all day whether to continue the negotiations. I waited in my office to receive instructions. None came.

In the middle of dinner, I got a call from the Prime Minister's Office, asking me to deliver a letter to Jim Baker tonight, conveying a revised proposal on regional subsidies. The letter will say that if they are satisfied with our proposal, we can resume discussions. This sounds pretty good to me. I left dinner in the middle of the main course and went back to the chancery. When I saw the proposal, my spirits sunk. They sent a ten-page document describing, with full technical details, our proposal. This will surely get summarized and analyzed by the U.S. experts, and they'll say Canada is standing pat. All this is too technical to discuss at the political level.

Do our ministers in Ottawa want an agreement? I believe they can get what they want, including a binding dispute-settlement mechanism. But they seem to be frightened at the prospect of having to discipline themselves as the price for getting the mechanism.

September 30, 1987 We delivered the foolish subsidies document to Baker's office at 7:30 a.m. Baker called Burney shortly thereafter, very depressed. The document doesn't reflect yesterday's discussions. We've stepped backward.

Once again we have misunderstandings. What can we expect when we are nutty enough to send a ten-page document that Baker and Yeutter would not read or understand but would turn over for summary and analysis to the same "experts" who have been screwing us all along.

3:30 p.m. Burney to Gotlieb: "They're giving us a new paper at 5 p.m." Gotlieb to Burney: "Get down here with the ministers. This has to be done face to face. You are snatching defeat from the jaws of victory."

8:30–11:05 p.m. No word from Ottawa.

11:05 p.m. Burney (hoarse, almost voiceless): "Can you get hold of Jim Baker? Can he see us tomorrow at 11 a.m.? Same team."

Baker to Gotlieb: "We're ready."

October 1, 1987 It is exactly two years to the day since Mulroney first proposed a free-trade agreement with the United States. But we've reached the end of the road. It looks like it's all over. Why, I don't know. I thought it was still doable. I said that to Burney, Wilson, and Carney during our last round of talks with Baker and Yeutter. But this time they came down from Ottawa with a Dunkirk mentality. They act like they want out. Baker thought they were coming down to negotiate, but when they brought no experts with them, I think he sensed it was over. Ottawa has kept me in the dark for the past twenty-four hours. I've been blanked out. I was shocked by Burney's prepared statement at the outset.

He gave a brutal speech, basically seeming to close the door on the talks. I don't know if this is what he was instructed to do. I think he was told to leave a crack open, but he didn't. I know Mulroney does not want this agreement to fail. But he has been let down by Americans and to a large extent his own cabinet.

The Yankees behaved abominably. Assholes on the Hill – today's Hickenloopers, Borahs, and Judds – pressured the administration, and the administration lost its way. It showed no sense of history. Baker is the only man of larger spirit. As for the Canadians, we had more to lose than the Americans, and we blew it. Burney was like a tank, and he drove it deep into enemy territory. At the end of today's discussions, we talked of minor agreements, mini-agreements, mini-mini-agreements, two-stage agreements, extensions, and all that. Nothing will come of it.

Blame cannot be allocated to one side or the other exclusively. Trying to understand why the negotiations failed is like trying to account for why a marriage fails. Too many reasons, too many nuances, too many mysteries, too much history. One thing is clear: aside from Baker, there were no Americans of vision and on our side none, except Mulroney. He had a better grasp of the situation than his foreign minister and cabinet did.

If this thing fails – and this now seems inevitable – it will be two years of commitment and effort turned to dust. The Americans showed themselves to be shallow-minded and leaderless, the Canadian ministers to be divided and erratic.

I am sunk in gloom, disappointment, and regret.

October 2, 1987 The corpse is revived. The United States has reconsidered its position and will go with the Gibbons-Gotlieb formula (as it now seems to be called in Washington). Cabinet decided to resume negotiations. On a beautiful, clear, cool autumn morning, I found myself back at Andrews airport waiting for the Challenger with the Wilson-Burney-

Carney trio. This time Reisman was with them. We went right to Treasury.

I saw Jim Baker alone for a few minutes. "I had to break a lot of china," he said. "I had to overrule Clayton. He was against it. I had to call a half-dozen senators and various congressmen. I know I'm in deep trouble proposing this. I've taken a big risk for Canada." He is right. Without his having taken charge, we would be nowhere.

At our first meeting, we got good news and bad. The good news was their support for the new formula. The bad news was that the United States could not "freeze" the existing countervail and dumping laws. "Absolutely impossible," Baker said. "We can't bind the Congress." This leaves us exposed to the omnibus trade bill and every future change in U.S. trade law, with no protection whatsoever. Baker's solution was to require new legislation to be GATT compatible, with a binding approval process, either by a GATT panel or the bilateral mechanism.

There were several other problems about dispute settlement to be addressed. The United States wanted the right to terminate the whole mechanism in five years if there was no agreement on joint countervail and dumping rules. We wanted a longer period. We wanted a tribunal, they a panel. (My own preference is for the U.S. position. With ad hoc panels you get less bureaucracy and better people. I've argued with Ottawa before about this, and they regard me as traitorous for it.)

We worked throughout the day on the whole gamut of subjects – tariffs, intellectual property, safeguards, autos, agriculture, standards, investment, financial and other services. Progress was slow but evident. The atmosphere turned bad early on because Wilson would not go higher than $100 million for a ceiling on direct and $500 million for a ceiling on indirect investment. He also refused to agree to a rule for U.S. financial services that Baker thought Wilson had already conceded. This made Baker angry. He felt he had moved the United States to a breakthrough on the dispute mechanism and Wilson was offering nothing new on investment or the service package. Wilson wouldn't show his cards and held firm.

So we ploughed through texts on virtually every aspect of the trade negotiations, eliminating or isolating remaining differences, knowing all the while that the issue of a binding dispute mechanism was the overriding one. We reached that point just as Yom Kippur eve set in. Our experts provided us with a paper dumping on the Baker version of the Gibbons formula, saying it was a pact full of holes, a hollow agreement. They argued that GATT rules on subsidy were so vague that applying them to limit future

U.S. legislation would be meaningless. The U.S. Congress would be left free to do virtually anything it wanted. Baker rejected the freeze-the-law concept once again – out of the question, because Congress won't bind itself.

For about an hour we sat around and faced the impasse. We are in a cul-de-sac. Our two approaches have failed. We spent fourteen months on approach one – define new subsidy rules – and we couldn't do it. Then we moved to approach two – the Gibbons formula: each side keeps its own law, which is applied by the bilateral mechanism in a binding manner. The Baker breakthrough Thursday night was to accept approach two.

We are told by the Americans that there is no legal way to limit the right of Congress to change U.S. trade laws and thus greatly impair the benefits of the agreement. On the Canadian side, all our "experts" are being negative, not creative.

October 3, 1987 Yom Kippur and the final day of trade talks. Yes or no by midnight tonight. I'm still fasting.

Baker demonstrated real flexibility, while playing hardball most of the time. He showed that he had extraordinary authority to negotiate – he was in full command. At a morning meeting I had with him in his office alone yesterday, an aide brought in a document prepared by an official of the Department of Justice, stating that a dispute-settlement mechanism was unconstitutional. Baker said – in my personal presence in his office – "This is nonsense. Get me the attorney general." He immediately spoke to Meese. The statement proved to have been a cooked-up move by protectionist Commerce officials.

But his willingness today to reverse his earlier stand on our last compromise approach was even more impressive. I had proposed to the Canadian team that we give the new mechanism the right to review any new legislation to see if it is compatible with the spirit, object, and purposes of the agreement (the liberalization of our trade). The Canadian group jumped at this, and in our first restricted meeting with Baker, Burney put it forward, along with a suggestion for resolving our differences on the duration of the mechanism (extending to seven years from five). Baker made no comment.

Our two teams spent the next seven or eight hours ploughing through the agenda. Wilson showed his goodies – which were fascinating and should be very meaningful to Baker – and we got a lot of problems out of the way. At about 4 p.m. Baker pushed Wilson so hard on an element of financial services that Burney lost his cool and we adjourned.

We went back to our assigned room in Treasury to caucus. Burney and Reisman were shouting, angry and jumping all over the place. Burney said, "The reports from our people in the working groups are that the U.S. is tightening up all over. They're squeezing, squeezing. Baker believes that the negotiations are going to fail, and he has decided to put the onus on us – on agriculture, financial services, and intellectual property." I said this was wrong. "The U.S. wants an agreement, Baker wants one, and Reagan wants one, and we're going to get it." This is what I have been saying over and over again, like a broken record.

Our side eventually cooled down in the early evening, and we met Baker and Yeutter again on the dispute-settlement mechanism, only to have them completely reject our new proposal! I pressed Baker very hard. "We can't do it," he said. "Congress would never agree to such a vague approach and any limits on its power."

We adjourned and the Canadians caucused again. It was about 9 p.m. Those in the room were polled – Wilson, Carney, Burney, Gotlieb, Reisman, and Hartt – and all agreed we could not go forward; the deal was off. The negotiations were over. Finished. Burney telephoned the prime minister in Toronto and Clark in cabinet. They accepted our conclusion that it was all over.

We then prepared to announce failure. Burney went back in to see Baker alone to convey the news that the grand game was terminated and that we had failed. Our decision seemed to come as a thunderbolt to Baker. He pulled back and asked to be given more time. Burney agreed. An hour later, with only a few hours to go, Baker came back to us with a *volte-face*. He accepted our earlier proposal on dispute settlement. He had gotten the U.S. side to agree to meet our fundamental requirements. Unbelievably, we had a deal.

We ironed out the remaining issues in a wild atmosphere, everyone running up and down corridors trying to keep up with the speed of developments. Baker kept popping into our caucus room saying, fifty minutes to go, forty to go, and so on down to the wire. The deal was done and completed at ten minutes before midnight. Baker then dispatched a messenger, and notice was received in Congress at a minute before the deadline.

If it were not for Baker, there would be no agreement.

Midnight The Canadians came back to the Residence. We drank. And we drank. The mood was ecstatic. The night was cold, so we had the first fire of the year. Everyone praised everyone for two hours non-stop, and we toasted the prime minister for his leadership and his courage. Sondra joined us and was very gay.

At 2:30 or 3 a.m., just as everyone was filing out, I got a call from Mulroney. I went over the events of the day. He was buoyant, in a state of absolute elation. I congratulated him and told him his finest hour was when he reversed his earlier decision to accept failure and an hour later accepted the new solution. You could have hesitated, I said, and it would have all been over. Maybe, I added, this is what Mackenzie King would have done. But you were bold and took a risk.

Mulroney told me how he had made his decision. When on the line with Burney at eleven o'clock, Mulroney asked him what the team's final recommendations were. When he learned that the people he put there and respected the most were all of the view that he should go with the accord, he determined to go. And thus it was done.

Mulroney told me he knew only two people in the country who were convinced a deal could be struck: he and I.

By the time we signed off the telephone conversation, it was past 3:30 a.m. I had yet another drink and went to bed, euphoric.

October 4, 1987 Terribly hungover, I got up after three hours' sleep to go to the Madison to meet the gang. The happy gang. We all proceeded to the trade office to vet the final text and resolve the few outstanding issues. At lunch I went off with Burney, Carney, and Reisman to the Mayflower Hotel nearby. Our lunch was interrupted by news that the United States wanted to conduct a press conference this afternoon. This was done, although Burney was furious because the U.S. side started the press conference without him. Wilson and Carney ditched him and got to the stage themselves. It was amusing to hear Reisman and Carney coo with each other this morning, saying how much they really do like each other. Carney actually said to Reisman, "You must tell me sometimes about your negotiating triumphs." I don't know what I find more wondrous to behold, Simon in a nasty mood or Simon in a sentimental one.

The prime minister called me in the early afternoon to get an account of the mood in Washington and to go over the tumultuous events of the past two days. He is still euphoric, as he well deserves to be.

We ended the day at the Treasury, cleaning up issues, working conditions no better than before – no food, drink, or secretaries.

Around 9 p.m., just as we were nearing the end, we got into a furious argument with Baker and Yeutter about the cultural exemption. They wanted some language that was totally inconsistent with the exemption, but after sharp words, bitter debate, and acrimony, we settled on a formula that basically recognizes the U.S. right to retaliate for cultural measures in certain circumstances. A tempest in a teapot that will, alas, lead to a genuine tempest back home when people read the words and ask, "Was culture on the table?" It wasn't. All we did was recognize that the United States reserves its rights. But that kind of fine point will be difficult to get across.

The last issue we had to cope with was the damnable film issue. We told Baker and Yeutter that the current bill was not going forward, that we could work with industry for a solution, and that if a bill did go forward, it would be non-discriminatory. This didn't seem to satisfy either of them, who know little about the substance of the problem and don't really care. What they do know was the free-trade agreement would go nowhere in Congress if the film issue wasn't diffused. Having 98 per cent of the market won't satisfy Hollywood and their lobbyists.

Midnight I went with the group to the airport and got home, only to receive a frantic call telling me that their aircraft had returned to Andrews airport because of problems with the hydraulic system. In a state of absolute fatigue, I dragged myself back to Andrews, taking with me a supply of liquor and mixes. Carney was barely fit for human company, nor was I. Everyone else was overwhelmingly exhausted. We transported Carney and Reisman to a nearby hotel and then spent two hours trying to get another aircraft. I got to bed at 2 a.m.

October 5, 1987 At the free-trade press conference today at the embassy, I was so damn tired I didn't think I could get through it. The library was chockablock full of journalists and officials, and John Fieldhouse distributed copies of the "Elements" of the agreement.

As I was sitting at the table before the mikes, along with Len Legault and embassy officer Jon Fried, the latter sent me a note with some terrible news. Close to the end of the lengthy document, there was an initialled sheet on intellectual property, which contained a clause that should not have been there, because it was not agreed upon. The clause was on pharmaceuticals and provided that the Canadian government agreed to pass the pending legislation. When we saw this text last Sunday, we caught the error and asked that it be deleted, which the United States agreed to do.

Unfortunately, the earlier version (the mysteriously incorrect one) must have floated into the embassy's hands last night, and whoever was assembling the package didn't realize that the later version was not the same as the earlier one. Hence the embarrassing error.

Fieldhouse stopped the show, told the journalists that there were errors in the text, and asked for their co-operation in getting them back. All present grumbled but complied. Or so we thought. But after the press conference, we noted that only twenty-five of the twenty-six copies circulated were returned. Trouble . . . this spells trouble. It will only be a matter of days before the discrepancy comes out. If not from this source, then another.

It's trivial all right, but it is just the sort of thing the media and the opposition will make a lot of. Especially because the government has been saying for months – absolutely correctly – that pharmaceuticals were not part of the free-trade negotiation. Some damn gremlin got into the system.

In the evening Sondra and I dined at Russell Train's.[1] It was a party given in honour of Bill Nitze,[2] who has been appointed to a high environmental job in State. It was a heavy environmental affair, the guests being rich Mayflower types, very committed. Curious to see so many bluebloods in one place. In the six years I've been here, I would not recognize the face of Nitze's predecessors in the job at State.

Russell Train gave a long and earnest toast to Canada and our mutual custodianship of the environment. I replied without any forethought, but Rowly Evans thought I scored. "We've got no border now for trade, but we've also got no border for acid rain. So please," I said, looking at Lee Thomas, "clean up your act. When Trudeau appointed me here and Mulroney confirmed it, each told me I should not come home until we resolve the acid rain problem. Well, I love the U.S. but would like to go home soon."

October 6, 1987 I had breakfast at the Residence with Irving Layton[3] and his current wife, a sturdy Acadian. We talked of Montreal and books. He admired my eyebrows.

---

[1] Environmental Protection Agency Administrator 1973–1977; President of the U.S. World Wildlife Fund 1978–1985.

[2] President of the Gemstar Group. Assistant Administrator for International Activities at the Environmental Protection Agency.

[3] (1912–2006) Canadian poet raised in Montreal's St. Urbain Street neighbourhood, later made famous by Mordecai Richler's novels.

I talked to Strauss in the afternoon. He told me that after I had alerted Dick Rivers on Thursday to the dire situation, Strauss sent a message to Baker to the effect that he'd better think long and hard before he rejected the Gibbons proposal, because that was all that was left. Success has many authors, etc.

We've been getting some beauties from the Hill about the free-trade deal:

Byrd: "I would look with concern, for instance, upon any provisions which reduce U.S. sovereignty to make and adjudicate final decisions in trade disputes."

Bentsen: "It has to be an agreement that benefits both sides. Up to this point since the Canadian walkout all we've been hearing about are U.S. concessions."

Good old Max Baucus: "No free-trade agreement is worth its salt if it isn't fair. America is not going to let itself be taken advantage of. . . . Only after Congress has an opportunity to review the specifics will it be able to determine whether this trade agreement is fair, or if the American consumer is being asked to pay too high a price for what amounts to a political deal."

Also some beauties from the administration:

Yeutter in top form: "I would give you a personal estimate that, had Canada not selected Mr. Reisman as their chief negotiator, we would have had this agreement six months ago."

His statement would be accurate if you substitute the name Murphy for Reisman.

October 7, 1987 Senator Bradley gave me an account of the events of last Thursday. He was the missing link. In the afternoon he called Baker and told him that Congress was not as negative about binding dispute settlement as he might think. Baker said, "Show me." Bradley then organized calls from four solid senators (as he said) and about eight others. So I wasn't wrong in singling out Bradley for a white knight role.

October 12, 1987 Canadian Thanksgiving Day, and the night of a surprise party on Charlie Wick's seventieth birthday. It was black tie at the Watergate for about eighty people.

Shultz was full of congratulations about the free-trade agreement, not that he did a hell of lot for it. The president told me he was delighted with the agreement. He then commented that we had this enormous common frontier without a single gun defending it. He thought our border should not be different from the border between states of the union! I told him the new agreement goes far in that direction from a trade standpoint. This is the same remark that Strauss told me the president had made to Jim Baker. The president looked extraordinary for a man of seventy-seven.

What made this evening so different was the California crowd, warm, friendly, besieged, an island in hostile Washington, true to their own friendship, loyal to each other to the end, and above all, loyal to Reagan.

October 14, 1987 I received a surprise call today from Arthur Liman. He told me he thought Seymour's letter to me amounted to "extortion" and constituted unprofessional conduct. If he were not fully engaged in writing the Iran-Contra report, he would write an op-ed piece for the *New York Times*. If this happened in New York, Seymour would have been brought before the bar for professional misconduct.

Called on Tony Coelho[1] in the afternoon, the Democratic whip. He kept me waiting in his office for close to forty minutes after setting the appointment back a half-hour. A rising congressional star, he struck me as a little slippery. He was coy on our trade agreement, unconvincing in predicting the passing of an omnibus trade bill by Thanksgiving.

October 15, 1987 My nemesis-friend Fotheringham had a full column, with a picture of me, describing the screw-up at the embassy press conference a week ago Monday. He twisted it into a "the government-is-duplicitous" theme, although he was kind in crediting (wrongly) the discovery of the pharmaceutical error to my eagle eye. He described the press conference and the gathering up of the copies of the earlier incorrect document, me looking awful and very fatigued and more of that kind of bumph in the best-worst Fotheringham tradition – all colour, few facts, and many perverse interpretations.

October 16, 1987 Another great day in the Deaver-Gotlieb-Seymour triangle. Last night, just before I left the office, I received a copy of a Department of Justice brief at the trial on the Deaver case, due to begin Monday. The *Wall Street Journal* also got it and went to town. It had both an editorial entitled "Seymour in North America" and major extracts from Seymour's letter to my lawyer, Stuart Pierson, our diplomatic note to State, and the

[1] (b. 1942) Democratic Representative from California 1978–1989; House Majority Whip 1987–1989.

Justice brief. The last was all we could have wished for. "The U.S. asks the court . . . to order that all future communications between Seymour and Canada be conducted through diplomatic channels [and to] admonish Mr. Seymour to desist from any effort to threaten, embarrass or punish the Canadian government for asserting diplomatic immunity in this case." The *Wall Street Journal* editorial refers to Seymour's letter as "blackmail."

I could have written every word of this editorial. It would give me a curious notch in U.S. constitutional history if I were to end up playing a role in the decline and fall of this institution.

In Montreal today, for a PBS panel on free trade. A large part of the questioning concerned the pharmaceutical fiasco. This isn't a tempest in a teacup. It's a tempest in a thimble. It illustrates the principle if you can't get hold of a big theme, get hold of a little one.

October 19, 1987 We sent a further diplomatic note to State. "Mr. Seymour's actions with regard to a friendly sovereign state are intolerable and the Government of Canada expects that the Government of the United States will continue to assert its responsibility for the conduct of relations with Canada in keeping with the established norms of international law and practice that Mr. Seymour has so wantonly disregarded."

It was only a matter of time, of course, before the Canadian nasties would emerge from the woods.

"When the trial opens," a Canadian journalist wrote, "Canada must be prepared for nastiness. Washington insiders are betting Seymour will attempt to show that Gotlieb suborned Deaver while he was a White House official." Interesting. He could with equal justice write that I conspired to murder the pope.

October 21, 1987 I am urging Clark and the prime minister to try to put some sort of a lid on Tom MacMillan and his acid rain campaign here in the United States. So far he has achieved three things. First, he called Byrd a "neanderthal," making a total enemy of him. Then he called the recent U.S. science report (NAPAP[1] report) "voodoo science," although all scientists in the United States agree with it (it was the summary that was misleading and unfortunate). And now Dingell is alleging "illegal" Canadian lobbying on

[1] National Acid Precipitation Assessment Program.

acid rain. Quite an accomplishment. In the politics of this country, *illegal* is a very ominous word.

MacMillan's approach risks making Canada the issue rather than acid rain. We cannot manipulate some of the most powerful leaders in Congress into taking a position they oppose. We can, though, accidentally play into the xenophobic mood of Congress and alienate some people whose sympathy we will need in order to make progress on acid rain.

At a small reception at Evangeline Bruce's, I chatted with Mrs. Dean Acheson. She is close to ninety but erect, alert, and sharp. We talked at length about the friendship of her husband and herself with Hume Wrong. She says her husband used to drop by the embassy to talk with Wrong when he was ambassador here. Wrong's father was a professor of history at the University of Toronto at the same time as Dean Acheson's father was at the university. It's a rare occasion when one makes contact with Canadian diplomatic history in Washington.

October 23, 1987 Joe Clark seems reluctant to defend me against media attacks in the Deaver affair. After all, I had wanted to testify at the Deaver trial. I have absolutely nothing to hide, and all Seymour wanted me to testify to was the fact that I had lunch with Deaver – for which he had no other witness. For sound public-policy reasons, Ottawa said no to the waiver, and inevitably, and most predictably, the story now emerging was that we had something to hide.

Clark implies he doesn't want to raise the profile of the issue further! (Could it be any higher?) And he seems to hint that maybe Seymour knows something he doesn't know! (A nice vote of confidence.) So he wants to let Gotlieb swing in the wind. Before I appeal to the highest authority, I want his support for sending a rebuttal letter to the *Toronto Star*.

October 27, 1987 The papers are full of a disastrous (for me) development in the Deaver case. The judge, Thomas Penfield Jackson,[1] backed Seymour in his fight with Justice and State and us.

Sondra and I sat around after breakfast this morning in our downstairs sunroom talking about it. We both had just read the *Washington Post*

---

[1] (b. 1937) Appointed U.S. District Court Judge for the District of Columbia in 1982 after serving as President of the District of Columbia Bar Association. Perhaps best known as the presiding judge in the *United States v. Microsoft* case (filed in 1998).

report of Penfield Jackson's decision. It was pouring rain outside, matching our depressed mood. The only way I can vindicate myself, I said to her, is to resign and testify. I would then blast Seymour out of his boots, because neither I nor Sondra can even remember the lunch. So how can Deaver be said to be perjuring himself for a similar lapse of memory? But I fear that resignation would be a stupid thing to do. It would be taken as an admission that I was guilty of something awful and therefore had to vacate my office.

Lunched with Bob Strauss at the Metropolitan Club. We talked about the Deaver affair. Right off the top, he said, "Alas, the guy you are having lunch with has not got the biggest brain in this town. The guy you're lunching with is not the richest. But you are lunching with the man with the finest judgment in Washington!" Vintage Bob. He said, "No one in Washington is following it except Mr. Deaver, Mrs. D., Mrs. G., and yourself, and you shouldn't exaggerate its significance."

Sam Gibbons was his old self when I visited him in the late afternoon, in the middle of a driving rainstorm. He handed me a big bag of sugar. The package read "US Sugar," produced by "US Sugar Co.," and was decorated in red, white, and blue. In tiny letters at the bottom of the package, the label read "Made in Canada from pure sugar cane."

"Now, where did you get all that cane, Mr. Ambassador?" he asked. "Do you grow it in hothouses up there?"

No doubt he had Cuba on his mind.

October 29, 1987 In Toronto to give a couple of speeches, I am surprised at the changed atmosphere of this city. Politics are discussed everywhere, free trade is on everyone's lips, and one can feel tension in the strangest places. One senses the city and the huge country are in the grips of a historic debate. Some vignettes. Last night, addressing a huge agricultural conference, a few members of the media scrummed me. "Are you here to sell the government's line on free trade?" asked one. Another: "What are you doing here, anyway? Your job is in the States, not here. Ontario doesn't want a free-trade agreement. Why are you here pushing it?" Yet another: "The Auto Pact is not free trade. You don't know what you're talking about. You have no business citing it as a free-trade agreement."

After addressing a group of CEOs this morning, I dropped into a second-hand bookstore nearby. By the cashier's desk, posted on a little bulletin board, was a heavily underlined copy of the article by Fotheringham, accusing

Canada, the embassy – and me – of duplicity on pharmaceuticals and of cheating the public.

October 30, 1987 The *Toronto Star* continues to love me, especially Bob Hepburn. Up in Canada I read, "Canada has hired an alcoholic to perform a controversial lobbying role at the White House – what did Canada get for its $106,000? Whose idea was it to hire Deaver? And why aren't Canadians outraged? It is clear Americans are."

November 2, 1987 Lloyd Cutler, with whom I breakfasted at the Metropolitan Club, continues to express doubts about the constitutionality of our dispute-settlement mechanism. If, he says, a decision were challenged for fraud or lack of due process, there would have to be an appeal to the U.S. courts. He is possibly the leading U.S. expert in this area, and if he's right, then we're in for trouble. Called on Bill Frenzel in the afternoon. I doubt if there is a Canadian MP as knowledgeable about U.S. politics as he is about Canadian issues. He is also a great free-trader, a strong rod of support. He, like Gibbons, is convinced the opposing special interests can be stopped.

November 3, 1987 Richard Gwyn is in town. He's doing research on East-West relations, so we invited a few Washington gurus to lunch: Ken Adelman, Hal Sonnenfeld, Edward Luttwak,[1] and a Professor Feshbach of Georgetown University. Luttwak was on some sort of high and never stopped talking, principally about sex, discos in Toronto, and famous people who entertain him. In the few moments we managed to talk sense, all agreed there would be no START agreement next year. I dissented mildly. There was also much talk of Weinberger's abdication. Much surprise. Was his wife mortally ill? Or not at all? The town is awash in contradictory reports. But everyone agrees his departure strengthens Shultz.

A reception at the White House and dinner at State for the Friends of Art at U.S. Embassies, an organization so quintessentially American. A substantial proportion of the Forbes 400 was in attendance (post-crash), including five Annenbergs. The crowd from New York and Los Angeles was thick. All of this was in aid of bestowing antiques and art on U.S. embassies. I saw Ron

[1] (b. 1942) U.S. military writer and theorist.

Spiers[1] at the reception and joked that the buildings were doing fine, but they had been hit by a neutron bomb, so that there were no people inside. Mrs. Spiers contradicted me: the buildings are not doing fine – they may be filled with art, but the foundations are rotting. Everyone lined up for a half-hour to shake hands with the president and have a photo op (Nancy is recovering from her cancer operation), and having done that, we were transported to State to line up for another half-hour to be welcomed by Shultz. Very few foreign diplomats were invited, except the usual inner half-dozen.

November 4, 1987 In New York Sondra and I attend a gala for the fiftieth anniversary of the Guggenheim Museum. Sat next to Angie Biddle Duke, wife of the chief of protocol during the Kennedy era. She told me, in some detail, how she adored her trip to Israel some years ago and then enumerated the Israelites she knew. In a deft move, I impressed on her some minutes later that I represented a certain other country.

At the next table was H. Kissinger. I don't know why he was there, but then I don't know why I was either.

Later in the day, the president gave a press conference in Washington on the Canada-U.S. free-trade agreement. It seems the president of AT&T is on the warpath because no one told him he would have to be patient and wait five years to see the end of tariffs on his products. I got a frantic call from Strauss at the Pierre, but I explained, and he agreed, that if anyone made a boo-boo, it was the United States, not us, and that AT&T was perhaps just being a little greedy.

November 5, 1987 At lunch I reviewed Canada-U.S. relations with Ty Cobb, the last vestige in the White House of earlier times. Ty gave me the good news: the president approved our Arctic sovereignty agreement this morning. Then I gave him the bad news: the Canadian government was not keen on announcing it until January. Cobb understandably was very upset. But he would have been a lot more upset if I had told him that I wasn't sure Mulroney would ever sign the agreement, given that many of his ministers seem to have gotten cold feet on the matter.

---

[1] (b. 1925) U.S. foreign-service officer. U.S. Ambassador to Turkey 1977–1980; Undersecretary of State for Management 1983–1989; Undersecretary-General of the United Nations for Political Affairs 1989–1992.

I also didn't tell him that the political situation in Canada is such that the Mulroney team couldn't give away gold bricks without being attacked.

November 8, 1987 Dinner in Vancouver with Arthur Erickson at Liz and John Nichols's. We spent most of the evening talking about the mess affecting the official opening of the chancery. Bill Reid still hasn't received a nickel for *Spirit Canoe*. He has spent tens of thousands of his own dough, and he's laid down his tools.

November 9, 1987 I flew to Edmonton and called on Don Getty.[1] He had just hung up the phone as I arrived, having been called by Peterson, who apologized for his minister's remark that what's no good for Ontario is no good for Canada.

Dinner took place at Government House, with about a half-dozen ministers presided over by Jim Horsman, minister responsible for intergovernmental affairs. They were anxious to hear what they could do to sell the free-trade agreement in Washington. I explained that this was the Americans' job, and they would resent foreigners telling them what was good for them. On the other hand, quietly working the state governors on a personal basis could be useful. I invited Getty to visit Washington but not, I underlined, to sell free trade.

November 10, 1987 The *Edmonton Journal* reports this morning that Getty said "he was invited by Gotlieb to visit Washington to help sell the deal." A politician's trickery?

And now I'm in the middle of another upsetting development at the Deaver trial. Paul Robinson, former U.S. ambassador, not known for subtlety, was asked by Seymour to relate my conversation with Deaver and Robinson in the limousine in Quebec City on December 17, 1984. Robinson proceeded to disclose diplomatic conversations that had nothing to do with the case against Deaver – but whose revelation constituted a serious breach of diplomatic courtesy and protocol.

"Trudeau Aims Called Stupid by Gotlieb, Court Told" was the headline on page 1 of the *Globe*. I can only imagine what the *Star* is carrying. Robinson: "Ambassador Gotlieb began by pointing out that the Canadian

---

[1] (b. 1933) Premier of Alberta 1985–1993; Leader of the Progressive Conservative Party of Alberta 1985–1992.

government had done many foolish things, including the NEP and FIRA, which he characterized as stupid." He then told the court that he considered my position to be a "remarkable change" from my attitude in 1981 and 1982, when I defended both policies in the face of strong U.S. objections. At the time, the *Globe* report continues, I was the top civil servant in External Affairs. "When he subsequently became ambassador and made his plea [about acid rain] to Deaver, I thought it was a remarkable transformation . . . to call these stupid," Robinson said.

Yes, it was a transformation. A new government had just been elected. Mulroney announced in New York a week before that both FIRA and NEP were ruinous to Canada, and his government was going to abolish them as a matter of top priority. I was selling the new government's principal objectives. But I doubt I used those words. Unfortunately, we were in a car, so there could be no transcripts.

Dinner was a distraction – given by the French Smiths at the Jefferson. Bill French Smith organized a round-table quiz on who each guest would want as president, current candidates aside. The most favoured names were Alan Simpson (Sondra's and my choice) and, surprisingly enough, Bill Webster. I put forward the proposition that the absolute requirement was to get someone as president who understood and could work the system, which was more complex than the Kremlin.

A former congressman, Frank Ikard,[1] put it well. "The problem in America," he said, "is the Congress. Congress is not a legislative body; it's a mob."

Tom Braden shouted out, "The problem is not with the Congress. The country has had a president who's been asleep in the White House for seven years."

This exchange neatly sums up the two prevailing views of Washington.

November 12, 1987 At a farewell for Cap Weinberger at Anderson, I used the opportunity to chat with John Herrington about our submarine program. "You can count me against it," he said. Given his responsibility for Admiral McKee's nuclear submarine unit, we'd better get Herrington up to Ottawa fast to see our nuclear facilities and show him we're not a bunch of nuclear yokels.

[1] (1913–1991) Republican Representative from Texas 1951–1961; Vice-President of the American Petroleum Institute 1961–1963 and President 1963–1979.

Then we hosted a small dinner for Edmund Morris and Sylvia, Alexander Chancellor of the *Independent*, the Phillipses, and Judith Miller of the *New York Times*. We played a game: the social occasions it was most essential to avoid. The winners:

1) The Soviet National Day (this year was the worst yet – huge crowds of hungry Eastern Europeans),
2) Israeli receptions for visiting politicians, featuring huge throngs of hungry Jews, and
3) Any boat trip on the Potomac – especially Marshall Coyne's.

November 17, 1987 Any day when I see Big John Dingell makes me nervous. This was one of them. I tried the high road on free trade, but he ran through a whole list of unacceptable provisions in the agreement, running from culture through energy to autos, trucking, and anything else he could think of. He was by turns menacing, prosecutorial, and adversarial. I barely had the stomach to go on to acid rain.

In all my discussions of trade on the Hill, I make only one point that seems to have an impact. I use the Andreas-Brinkley approach. I say that since the Europeans have given themselves the world's largest preferential system, why shouldn't we have our own. Dingell responded with some enthusiasm.

November 20, 1987 Friday night at 6:30, I got a call from Elliott Abrams[1] at State. Joe Clark is leaving for Central America tomorrow, to visit Nicaragua, among other lands. He plans to visit a co-operative there. The point of Elliott's call was to say that Clark's life would be endangered if he went there – the Contras consider it a base, and there has been fighting in the area. It is safe, he said, neither by road nor by helicopter. The United States has been in touch with the Contras, and it appears Clark's personal security cannot be assured. I passed the message on to Ottawa, but it seems Clark regards these warnings as part of a U.S. plot to discourage him from visiting the Nicaragua co-operative.

He's foolish to go. There is some reason to believe that the Sandinistas wouldn't be too unhappy if the Contras knocked off a friendly foreign minister.

---

[1] (b. 1948) Assistant Secretary of State for International Organization Affairs 1981, for Human Rights and Humanitarian Affairs 1981–1985, and for Inter-American Affairs 1985–1989.

November 23, 1987 I delivered an invitation to John Herrington and Admiral McKee to see our nuclear installations. He and McKee had one refrain: you're not serious, you're going about this in an amateurish fashion, you don't show evidence of having made the commitment. Both emphasized that our experience in the commercial nuclear reactor field did not carry over into the submarine field, as the technologies were entirely different.

November 25, 1987 The *Toronto Star* printed my "protest" letter about Paul Robinson's statements. "I did not switch song sheets in December, 1984: I followed a new conductor. This is the way we do things in Canada. Under the United States' system, ambassadors resign with a change in government. Under the Canadian system, they continue in office but defend and promote the policies of the new government. A Canadian ambassador is required to be a man for all seasons. An American ambassador, in principle, has only one season." I hope Robinson reads this.

November 26, 1987 Our Thanksgiving holiday in New York was interrupted by frantic calls from a lawyer-lobbyist in Washington. Lloyd Hand[1] said, "We are about to be screwed by the British in the low-level air defence deal. They are making a political intervention at the White House at the highest political level. Do something!" (Last week it was the French that were interfering politically.)

So last night, Thanksgiving eve, I managed to get hold of a key contact in the NSC – he had never heard of a British intervention. Then I got hold of William Taft, deputy secretary of defence.

"Well, Allan," he said, "there's been no high-level British intervention in the White House that I know of, and I'm the point man here. The only intervention I'm aware of is yours."

"Yes," I said to Taft, "but I'm arguing against political intervention, the others are arguing for it." That one startled him. (How's that for Canadian high-mindedness?)

This information only half assured the lobbyists. Thanksgiving Day, I got a call from Derek Burney in Ottawa. "Do something" was the message.

"I've done it," I replied.

---

[1] Washington attorney. In 1957 he was assistant to Senate Majority Leader Lyndon B. Johnson. When Johnson became president in 1963, he was appointed U.S. chief of protocol.

November 29, 1987 Back from New York, I followed my usual ritual. As soon as I get home, I go to the upstairs sitting room and open my office security briefcase. Then I go through all the material that arrived while I was away. I always do this with a sense of urgency, nervousness, and trepidation. I feel, know, there are some explosives inside. This time there were two: one was a letter to Sondra from the Canadian Cattlemen's Association or some such group, complaining that according to a recent U.S. news broadcast, she said she does not serve red meat at parties. What a piece of shit.

Then I opened a personal and confidential letter from Si Taylor, the undersecretary, that expressed unhappiness on the part of him, Sylvia Ostry, and Gerry Shannon that in my free-trade speeches in the United States and Canada, I seem to be critical of GATT. It seems I should be praising GATT, not pointing out its weaknesses. Well, if it was so good, why are we entering into a bilateral trade agreement with the United States?

But there was also a nugget in the briefcase. It was a notice from Government House that I am being promoted from Officer to Companion of the Order of Canada. Unless I'm mistaken, a Companion hasn't been named from the public service in many years. I don't know to whom I owe recognition – probably the committee's chairman, Brian Dickson. It may help wipe away some of the accumulation of dirt that has cleaved to my skin over the past couple of years.

December 1, 1987 My standing is high in the arms trade. I'm flooded with thank-you calls from grateful Canadian arms manufacturers and their lobbyists. We won a very big one in the low-level air defence systems for the U.S. army. It means thousands of Canadian jobs. The president and the chairman of Martin Marietta phoned me, along with the president of Litton Industries – there is joy all around. It seems to be recognized that my intervention with Weinberger was the key to victory.

December 3, 1987 Ken Adelman invited me and a few others to a farewell luncheon for himself, and he arrived an hour late. This annoyed the hell out of me, as I had to cut short my efforts to try to get the White House to deny the accuracy of a ghastly *Star* article saying that the White House was laughing at Mulroney's demands to stage a border extravaganza on January 2, on signing of the FTA. I'm furious at the White House, because the idea was theirs, not ours, they asked us to consider this and other options, and they had better get that story out to the media. I dictated the press line to Cobb, which was released in the early afternoon.

I'll miss Adelman. He has a lot more depth than people give him credit for, and he is communicative, lively, and cares what others think. He is one of the last of my useful interlocutors from the early Reagan era.

December 4, 1987 I spent the day in continuing discussion with Elliott Abrams about the awful mess in Haiti. Just before leaving to attend a dinner hosted by Shultz, I said to Abrams on the phone, "Whatever you do, don't do the same thing you did on Grenada. If you're going to go in to rescue your citizens, let us hear first. Don't do unto Mulroney as you did unto Trudeau."

We'll see. He wasn't too happy with some of Joe Clark's pronouncements while on his Central American trip.

Shultz could not stay long at the British North American dinner at State. It was remarkable that he even came, given that he is buried in preparations for Gorbachev's visit. He gave a short speech in which he lavishly praised Thatcher but did not mention Mulroney or, for that matter, our free-trade agreement, except in response to a question from Paul Martin Jr.

December 5, 1987 Dinner hosted by Alan Greenspan and Andrea Mitchell at her delightful house. The Cheneys were there, David Gergen,[1] Brent Scowcroft, and Margaret Tutwiler.[2] Shultz played a large part in our conversation. I seemed to be the only pro-Shultz person there. Scowcroft, who was on the White House–appointed Iran-Contra commission, was particularly critical of Shultz's role. There was much talk of his insistence on travelling with a grand retinue and of always expecting head-of-state treatment.

We sat around the table until midnight. Greenspan was, as always, polite and a good listener. We talked at some length of his connection with Ayn Rand and his relations with the ex-Winnipeg Ayn Rand mafia. Greenspan said he was one of the few individuals who could argue Rand out of a position. He made some corrections, he said, in the manuscript of *Atlas Shrugged.*

---

[1] (b. 1942) Political consultant and presidential adviser during the Republican administrations of Ford, Nixon, and Reagan.

[2] Assistant to Chief of Staff James A. Baker III 1981–1985; Assistant Secretary of Public Affairs for the Treasury Department 1985–1989.

Although it was very late when we left the dinner, we dropped in at Judith Miller's pre-summit party. We chatted with her and Richard Perle about the two subjects dominating Washington conversation these days: who would be the best Democratic and Republican candidate and can Gorbachev really succeed in altering Soviet policies. Perle doesn't think Bush can choose good people. All agreed Ford chose the best cabinet.

December 7, 1987 On the eve of the Gorbachev-Reagan summit, the embassy sends a message to Ottawa assessing the mood and the prospects for disarmament. After much arcanery, it concludes: "Adelman concerned with Gotlieb interpretation that administration goal on ABM/SDI is for the two sides to agree to disagree. Bottom line, if this not possible, is for the two sides to agree not to disagree, rather than agree to disagree."

Such is the absurdity to which arms control is reduced.

December 8, 1987 There is a strange feel about Washington today . . . a sense of history. In the American psyche, the Soviet Union has a unique place. They view it with a sense of wonderment, fear, dislike, respect. All of those sentiments collect themselves into a sort of special ether and permeate the town.

Huge portions of Washington are blocked off for security. As a result, there are far fewer cars on the street. There is wall-to-wall television blather about Reagan and Gorbachev, Nancy and Raisa. And of course, we ambassadors perform our prop role. Ambassadors from the NATO countries were invited to the White House to witness the signing of the INF treaty and to hear Reagan's and Gorbachev's signing statements. The Americans do this sort of thing well. All the powerful senators and congressmen lined up on one side of the room, ambassadors on the other, cabinet secretaries, high officials, and Russians in the middle, 180 in all – and cameras, cameras, cameras.

I spotted Alexandre Yakovlev, our old neighbour from Lisgar Road, then in exile as Soviet ambassador, now in the politburo. He is an architect of glasnost, one of the most powerful men in Moscow and a man of history. He greeted me warmly but not overly so. I wonder if he still resents my having called him into my office in 1980, when I was undersecretary, to inform him of the imminent expulsion of more than a dozen spies in his embassy, including members of his personal staff. To my dying day, I will remember the look of complete astonishment on his face.

"You mean . . . you mean . . ." questioning me about this and that name on the list, asking me to repeat the names, etc., shaking his head in disbelief. You knew exactly what he was thinking.

As I left the White House, I experienced the most pleasant part of the ceremonies – joking with Alan Simpson, Pat Moynihan, Tom Foley, and Bobby de Margerie. I feel I am a part of the great Washington scene. My seniority gives me a front-row seat – next to the formidable Turk and the Italian Casanova. But I know it's only an illusion. On the very big issues, foreign ambassadors here are voyeurs, kibitzers. The greatest challenge for a foreign diplomat is to be more than that.

December 9, 1987 During an hour-long tête-à-tête with Clayton Yeutter today, we talked about the congressional timetable for the now finally agreed-upon Canada-U.S. text. We'll be lucky, Yeutter said, to have the agreement and bill into Congress before June 1, 1988. That means the clock with ninety legislative days won't begin ticking until then and won't even run out before the expiry of the one hundredth Congress. As a result, we will lose our leverage for a final up-and-down vote as the debate runs smack into the American and possibly Canadian elections. I told Clayton this spells real trouble.

When I called on the great, distinguished, elegant, and lordly Lloyd Bentsen, senator of the mighty Texans, I went over the same ground and urged him to use his office and influence to expedite the passage of the FTA. Bentsen said he was in favour of the agreement and wanted it to pass. He blamed the administration for the mess but said he would do all he could to ensure passage before the summer recess, whenever that might be. I couldn't expect much more.

Yeutter was right in saying that Bentsen has a real sense of grievance against the administration. He is critical of their trade policy and since 1983 has been pushing for a new one. He is deeply committed to passage of the omnibus trade bill before he gets our FTA. So our agreement, and the national interests of both countries, get subordinated to domestic and political rivalries. Bentsen doesn't want to be the spoiler of the FTA. But if he subordinates the consideration of our bill to his own protectionist agenda, he will indeed spoil it all.

December 10, 1987 Last evening we went to a black-tie dinner honouring David Brinkley at the National Press Club, followed by drinks with Roone Arledge. Lane Kirkland and Strauss spoke, as did George Will, and, of course, Brinkley. I gave Lane nine out of ten, Strauss ten out of ten or one out of ten, depending on how well the listener enjoys a cruel roast. His best line: "I've been in Washington many years, but being here speaking to you tonight is the greatest honour of my life. (Pause) This is not an exaggeration. It's a downright lie."

December 11, 1987 The jury is out at the Deaver trial. The overreaching Mr. Seymour goes for the kill. Deaver's attorneys seem confused and weak. He will be convicted on one or two or three of the perjury charges but probably not on acid rain, where it seems to me that the case is not strong. I never could understand this persecution, but having just finished Tom Wolfe's *Bonfire of the Vanities*, I do now. His book is the most savage satire I have read in years, Swiftian in its indictment of the U.S. prosecutorial system. In reading how politicized and manipulative it is, I can understand how Seymour managed to bring indictments. The Deaver trial is a political trial.

At the Braden dinner tonight for the Bradshaws, Tom Braden said to me, with apparent satisfaction, "Deaver's going to jail."

It was a blue-ribbon crowd tonight, as Joan re-enters respectable society following her recent revelations in the *Post*.

Tom gave, as usual, a genuinely repulsive toast. He recited all the Reagan "scandals" – Iran-Contra, Wedtech/Meese, Deaver – and then proclaimed, "But we're all free from any taint of scandal, so let's drink to us." Washington humour. The truth is, he and Joan have contributed more than their share to what passes for Washington scandal. The curious thing is, he was serious. Brinkley, however, was not, when he jumped to his feet to announce that Strauss was about to announce his presidential candidacy. Strauss beamed all over. He was in heaven sitting next to Nancy and across from Gorbachev at the Gorbachev banquet earlier this week.

December 12, 1987 An active Sunday at Joe Canzeri's huge annual Christmas party. I got an earful from Lloyd Cutler about Simon Reisman's remarks, reprinted in the *New York Times* yesterday, on how "negotiating with the Americans was like negotiating with a developing country" and how he got five times back for every nickel spent. This is going to hurt us, Cutler said. Chatted with Rowly Evans, who, like Braden, is looking forward to Deaver going to jail. Ah, Washington.

December 13, 1987 Yesterday's *Washington Post* carried a nasty article by Sally Quinn on the theme of the end of the Washington hostess. She wrote that although the "Golden Age" is now over, the Gotliebs practically single-handedly revived it. She then showed how I managed to save my political neck by entertaining Mulroney in a glittering way. Then came the slap, and then the only socially viable embassy in Washington closed down.

Her piece was very unfair, but I fear the Canadian papers will reprint it. The true story is that the embassy is closed to Sally Quinn since she made her unfortunate remarks about Rebecca's illness over the airwaves in Canada, causing Rebecca much pain.

December 15, 1987 Cobb was frank with me when I called on him today. He said there was no planning being done in the White House regarding our agreement and the White House coordinating committee under presidential aide Nancy Risque had never met; a vacuum had formed. He urged me to tell Duberstein to get his White House committee cracking.

Cobb was as disgusted as I that there would be no signing ceremony on January 2. It seems Bob Hope is giving a party on that day, and Nancy laid down the law; Ron can't go to Canada and sign the agreement. Having just seen this town go bonkers over the Gorbachev-Reagan signature of the INF agreement, it depresses me that the administration could be so casual about the signing of another agreement of such great importance.

It seems that Colin Powell went ballistic when he heard that our Arctic agreement had not been signed. I had explained to him that Mulroney wants to postpone signature until after the new year so as to avoid creating a new issue prior to the FTA signature on January 2. The United States interprets this – unfairly, I think – as typical Mulroney waffling. Powell put an enormous amount of effort into ramming a controversial and unpopular agreement through the interagency process and was most concerned that the uneasy consensus in Washington could be overturned if signature were delayed. The opponents of our nuclear submarine program are beginning to create problems.

December 16, 1987 In the early afternoon my highly competent secretary, Nicole St. Pierre, came into my office and said, "Mr. Gotlieb, a registry clerk just came to my office and told me he heard on the radio that Deaver was found guilty on all five counts." I was at first incredulous and then simply stunned. My initial thought was how awful and terrible this was for Deaver. But beyond feeling sick about Deaver, I immediately began to think about the trouble some people in Ottawa – like Lloyd Axworthy – would try to make for me. I could hear it already: "Deaver lied and covered up, and you participated in the cover-up. We must have a parliamentary investigation."

I should feel ashamed that my thoughts began to dwell on my own possible difficulties rather than on Deaver's impending misery. But after all, I said to myself, we contracted with him in good faith. Why did he have to be so dumb as to lie? Then Ray Boomgardt, our legal officer, came into my office, looking white, sad, and shaken.

"Deaver was found guilty on all five counts," he reported. "It's all over the radio and TV." Fieldhouse, our press officer, then popped into my office to get me to sign off on our agreed contingency press line: "This is a matter between Mr. Deaver and the U.S. government, and we have no comment." I signed off.

As I was sitting there, totally depressed, Fieldhouse stepped back into the office and said, "Hold it, I've just got an AP report saying that Deaver was convicted on three counts and acquitted on two." "Is it possible?" I asked. "We're checking it out," Fieldhouse replied.

Five minutes later, he brought in the news: the verdict was guilty on three counts, not on five, and of the two accounts on which Deaver was acquitted, acid rain was one. Hurrah. Hallelujah. I felt like a patient who had been diagnosed on the basis of the wrong X-rays. I had believed all along that the perjury case on acid rain was flawed.

At a buffet reception given tonight by Paul Laxalt, the Deaver conviction was the only subject of conversation. Many seemed genuinely distressed. The conviction of someone so close to them and recently so powerful seems unbelievable. In the hearts of so many of these "formers," they know that either they are guilty or the conviction was wrong. They are right on both counts.

December 17, 1987 Breakfast at the Residence with Garth Drabinsky. He has purchased a pack of theatres in Washington, front-page news in the *Post*. We co-hosted a reception for one thousand people at his new palace on Wisconsin Avenue. Sondra and I engaged in Garth's ribbon-cutting exercise. He hands me a pair of giant scissors, I try to cut, the scissors don't cut, the ribbon remains, and there is confusion, horse laughs. Garth pulls out his own, very small scissors and cuts. The joke is on me. Darth Grabinsky (as the *Post* article called him) saves the day.

Just before departing for the ceremony, I got a whiff of Whitney North Gasbag Jr. on the TV screen, denouncing Shultz for defending Deaver, denouncing the president and the White House for lax moral standards, denouncing immorality in Washington. I wanted to barf.

December 18, 1987 The Canadian papers screech "Prosecutor Raps Gotlieb over Deaver Trial" (*Gazette*), "US Attorney Blames Deaver 'Perjury' Acquittal on Envoy's Refusal to Testify" (*Citizen*), "Canada Aided Deaver Defense, Prosecutor Says" (*Star*). Actually, Seymour never even mentioned my name. But all these papers, including the *Washington Post*, speak of my "claiming immunity," never "Canada" claiming immunity – thus conveying the impression that it was a personal dodge on my part.

The *Star* yesterday carried yet another salacious piece by Hepburn insinuating that I cut a deal with Deaver at our lunch on January 5, 1985. I spent a good part of the afternoon trying to get Ottawa to issue some sort of statement. What I want is a denial that my testimony was relevant to the particulars on which Deaver was acquitted. Clark is away in Hawaii, and his office, a.k.a. Jodi White, knows he wants the issue to just go away. My request to be defended is falling into the black hole of External Affairs.

December 20, 1987 A cold, sunny Sunday, and our thirty-second wedding anniversary. Sondra and I dined at home alone (pâté de foie gras, pheasant, Pichon-Longueville '76) and realized that out of our last thirty-one wedding anniversaries, we can barely remember what we did on more than two or three.

Bill Safire's piece on "Our Deaver Lessons" in today's *New York Times* was a pleasant surprise. Among Seymour's list of sins, "the power-dippy prosecutor all but declared war on the government of Canada for standing on its sovereign rights." Looks like being friendly with him over the past six years didn't do any harm.

December 21, 1987 Christmas season and my outer office is stuffed with goodies I am giving away. Jim Baker sent me a hand postscript to his card: "There would be no US-Canada FTA without your leadership."

December 22, 1987 At an extended lunch at the Residence, I entertained the high navy brass from Ottawa, here to promote our nuclear submarine program. Defence took my advice: they have now appointed Admiral Thomas, top officer in our navy, to head the program and have sent him here to show the flag.

From the Canadian defence officials, I learned that Clark is continuing to oppose missile testing, behaving just as he does towards the nuclear submarine program.

December 23, 1987 Dinner at Vernon Jordan's. Of all the people I've gotten to know in Washington, he is the one with the biggest heart (that may not be all that significant, considering how heartless a town Washington is). It was a small dinner, an almost all-black evening, the other guests being Bill Coleman, outstanding lawyer and former secretary of transportation under Ford, and Congressman Charles Rangel of New York and his wife. I was surprised to learn, talking quietly with Vernon after dinner, that his view of the media was as critical as my own. He recently had an unrewarding experience with Meg Greenfield and complained that he never really knows where he stands with her. I described her in the phrase used long ago by some dinner companion in New York: "She is a hooded figure."

In the six years we have been here in Washington, this was our first evening where blacks outnumbered whites.

December 24, 1987 We gave a buffet for "all ages and stages" at the Residence. We thought of doing this because our children were visiting. The formula worked. There were about eighty at the party, and the injection of youth into the recipe made it a different Washington evening.

Bill Webster, Sandra Day O'Connor, my old student and new solicitor general Charles Fried, were there, along with Jim Schlesinger, Abe Sofaer, John Whitehead, Evangeline Bruce, Susan Mary Alsop, the Kirklands, and many others with their families. In my biased opinion, it was the best Christmas party of the season.

December 31, 1987 We flew into Miami just in time to attend Dwayne and Inez's New Year's Eve party. I carried on my arm several of Eliz Dole's dresses. It was a nuisance, but what the hell – her husband could be the next president of the United States. It was the usual black-tie affair, starting in Dwayne's penthouse at the Sea View and continuing with dinner in the dining room dungeon. But we enjoyed this affair more than its predecessors. The caviar (Iranian) was better than I have had in years – unlimited quantities of beautiful, grey, pearly, moist beads, and I ate at least one pound of the stuff, as did Sondra. At dinner Dwayne omitted the kitschy entertainment he is prone to offer, and the guests seemed to us more and more like old friends – the Strausses, Brinkleys, Howard Bakers, the Doles, among others. Maybe it's an illusion, but it feels good.

Talked to Howard Baker about the free-trade signature schlemozzle. He told me there was simply no way Reagan would interrupt his vacation at Palm Springs to sign the agreement. As a Canadian, I felt wounded by this remark.

January 1, 1988 A beautiful New Year's Day at the Sea View, and I am, for a change, feeling good – almost relaxed. Bob Dole met with Kissinger here for three hours, preparing himself for the presidency. We sat around the Strausses' cabana and talked to Bob, Dwayne, and Dole. The senator was on a high, rolling from handshake to handshake, having twenty-second conversations, several of them with me.

Yesterday I tried to talk to him about free trade, but he rolled on. So today I took a slightly different tack. What do they think in Kansas of the Canada-U.S. free-trade agreement? I asked. He said he didn't hear much at all in Kansas but was getting some negative reactions in the northern states, mainly about agriculture and resources. When I mentioned Max Baucus's self-appointed leadership of the negative brigade, Dole seemed surprised and said he had a very high regard for Baucus. The politician speaking, no doubt.

I suggested he see the initiative as Canada and the United States forming the biggest free-trading zone in the world and thus responding to the European preference to trade amongst themselves. Andreas has been urging me to use this argument as a selling point, and Dole responded positively. But he is a man to whom Canada is irrelevant at this time. The next six weeks, he told me, are make or break for his presidential campaign.

In the evening we went with the Strausses and Andreases to a Chinese-cum-steak restaurant in Bal Harbour. Bob did not think the prospects for Bush were bright. I explained to him why I thought Bush would get the nomination.

Strauss then told me a story about Averell Harriman and Churchill in London after the war. Harriman talked non-stop about British politics, leading Churchill to observe that in his experience people rarely understood the politics of their own country, let alone those of a foreign land. I congratulated Strauss on his brilliant put-down.

January 2, 1988 I joined the Department of External Affairs thirty-one years ago today. Should I announce soon that we will leave Washington in the summer or fall, right after the free-trade agreement is done in Congress? Should we stay on longer? I am intrigued at the idea of Dole as president, Strauss as secretary of state or treasury, Andreas as secretary of agriculture. I am intrigued by the idea of the Sea View as the southern White House. But then I say to myself, so what's the big deal? So you're plugged in. Isn't it time to unplug and make a living?

January 6, 1988 Back in Washington, Henry Grunwald was sworn in as ambassador to Austria, and we attended the ceremony in the State Department. Nancy Reagan came, as did Shultz, and she stayed and stayed. As it was unprotocol for us to leave before her, she kept a few dozen of us prisoners as she chatted with her pals.

Ken Duberstein, deputy chief at the White House, called to say the president had meant to tell Mulroney when they spoke earlier this week that he was counting on him to do something about our film policy. Duberstein asked me to pass on the message. I told him I would, but I emphasized that Ottawa was now well aware of Congress's capacity to frustrate the free-trade agreement if the film issue was not properly resolved. Duberstein said that wasn't the point of the call. Ottawa should be aware that the president is personally concerned.

January 7, 1988 Called on Howard Baker and Ken Duberstein in the inner sanctum of the White House – thanks to the Sea View connection. I was not surprised, but I was concerned, to find the number one and the number two at the White House poorly informed of congressional attitudes and strategies vis-à-vis our free-trade agreement. Baker had little to say other than that he'd get back to me soon.

I had given the president's message about film to Mulroney, I informed them, "personally," as requested. The prime minister now asked me to ask them to pass a personal message to Reagan: could they possibly explain how, after nine months from the time of the president's commitment to consider an acid raid accord, the administration had still not given us their response? Baker went on about how extraordinarily difficult, contentious, and divisive this issue was in the United States. We really had to appreciate this. "I do have some knowledge and experience with regard to the subject," I told him. I opened my shirt and asked, "Do you want to see my wounds?"

On the way out of the White House, I bumped into John Negroponte,[1] whom I had called this morning to complain of an impending decision on the Alaska natural gas pipeline. As I passed him in the hall, he said, "My God, do you have an office here?"

January 8, 1988 Strauss called me from the Sea View to say that he'd heard from Valenti that the meeting yesterday in New York between the film people and our man from the PMO (Glen Shortliffe), was "the shambles." According to Jack, "it's war." Even Strauss, who represents the MPPA, is getting fed up with Valenti's overreactions. I asked Strauss, "How can you have a guy represent an industry in their largest foreign market who is *persona non grata* in that market?"

January 9, 1988 Four inches of snow and Washington closes down. People in government were saying on Thursday, "See you Monday." All government offices are shut. I had an appointment to see the new secretary of commerce – cancelled. I called Clayton Yeutter to get his view on how the congressional picture looked concerning the omnibus trade bill – USTR switchboard closed. Called Ty Cobb in the NSC – closed. Imagine – NSC closed down because of a few inches of snow. A good day for the Russians to bomb Washington. Another illustration of my point that for all the talk of the importance of productivity, the nation's capital, thanks to snow, has a calendar year of around 360 days or less.

Even the intrepid Scotty Reston cancelled lunch today. I'm sorry he did so. He always gives me interesting tidbits. Scotty, who likes George Bush, recently told me that Bush should never attack anyone. He sounds ridiculous when attacking others. He also told me that, according to good authority, Dole doesn't read books. I can believe that. Reston said, "It's a mistake to choose a president with no sense of the rest of the world."

---

[1] (b. 1939) Career diplomat. U.S. Ambassador to Honduras 1982–1985; Assistant Secretary of State for Oceans and International Environmental and Scientific Affairs 1985–1987; Deputy National Security Advisor 1987–1989; Ambassador to Mexico 1989–1993, to the Philippines 1993–1996, to the United Nations 2001–2004, and to Iraq 2004–2005; Director of National Intelligence 2005 to present.

January 10, 1988 I flew to Ottawa to attend a briefing for Joe Clark in preparation for the Shultz visit tomorrow. We spent a lot of time on the cruise missile issue. Clark gave us his reasons for wanting to say "No testing." It would be politically destabilizing, go down badly in the country, and prejudice the free-trade debate in Canada. I was surprised at how pliant the External officials were in his presence. I think he spooks them all. I told Clark it was probably not my place to say so, but if he pressed his nuclear stance, he would be handing his colleague the minister of national defence two heavy losses: one, the testing program, which he favours, and two, the nuclear submarine program, which is the centrepiece of our maritime defence policy. The government could find itself, I said, in a situation comparable to the Diefenbaker fiasco of 1963 when the minister of defence resigned.

Curiously for a former prime minister, Clark does not seem to see himself as someone who speaks for the government as a whole. The divisive conflict between Beatty and Clark has been going on for close to a year. I'm told Mulroney keeps saying he won't resolve this conflict; the two ministers have been instructed to present a joint recommendation to him. They can't agree, the dispute festers, and our foreign policy suffers.

January 11, 1988 At the bilateral meeting with Shultz, Clark pleaded with him not to press a request for cruise testing at this time. Maybe, he said, after a START agreement we would be more responsive. The inscrutable Shultz was taken aback. Shultz then took a hard line on acid rain, predictably. We're in real trouble here, as I told Clark yesterday. We must plan for the management of failure.

Another downer was the discussion of Central America at lunch. Clark was critical of the U.S. policy of support for the Contras. Shultz pinned him against the wall. "Why do you think the Soviets are trying to get out of Afghanistan?" he asked. He answered his own question. "Because we armed the rebels, and they're winning the war. That's why we are arming the Contras – to pressure the Sandinistas to negotiate." Clark repeated that he didn't agree but did not explain himself adequately. Shultz can be intimidating.

January 12, 1988 Joe Clark is planning a "think-in" on Canada-U.S. relations in Toronto next Saturday. Don Campbell told me I was invited, but no one else in the embassy was. It seems that Clark's new chief of staff, a callow young man who replaced Jodi White, believes that the embassy is the tail that wags the dog. It's ridiculous to have a dozen officials from Ottawa and not invite the deputy chief of our operations in Washington, one of the most senior officers in the department. Campbell agreed, but we both know he really can't influence Clark, nor can any other officials.

January 13, 1988 The president and Nancy attended a farewell banquet at the Four Seasons for Roger Stevens, retiring director of the Kennedy Center. We, along with about 250 others, were there. It was a select and glittering group, most of whom had some connection with the Kennedy Center at some time. Ted Kennedy was there, of course, along with the usual Georgetown crowd and an assortment of stars. Isaac Stern[1] played a couple of tunes, and that was the highlight. Although sick with a cold, Sondra enjoyed herself because she sat next to Herman Wouk,[2] who talked a lot about his writing.

The Reagans sat through the affair from start to finish, and at the very end of the banquet, the president gave the longest speech of the event. He did this in spite of the fact that he was reported to have been sick this morning with an upset stomach and had an official visitor today – the new prime minister of Japan.

I thought of my colleague the Japanese ambassador trying to explain to his boss why Reagan was at the Four Seasons and not at the official dinner in honour of the prime minister. Reagan chooses to be with the movie and theatre crowd, rather than with the second or third most important political leader in the Western world.

January 15, 1988 Called yet again on Ty Cobb at the White House to discuss the next Reagan-Mulroney summit. I predicted it would be a difficult one, because Mulroney will press Reagan on acid rain until the last minute of the meeting. Mulroney won't cut his losses and accept failure on this issue. He will keep pressing for further steps, even though few believe the administration will deliver. It was important for the president to realize this.

Cobb urged us to regard this as a working visit and – predictably – place the emphasis on multilateral issues, especially the Toronto Economic Summit. I replied that Mulroney will want it to be an official visit, and he will

---

[1] (1920–2001) Ukrainian-born American violinist, widely considered one of the finest violin virtuosi of the twentieth century.

[2] (b. 1915) Bestselling American author of a number of novels, including *The Caine Mutiny* (1951).

want to emphasize the bilateral issues, especially acid rain. I warned Cobb of trouble on the film front and pressed for speedy action on submarines.

I've got no stomach at all for the great battles that will be waged in preparation of this summit. More demands, more litmus tests, and more unrealizable expectations as the event draws nigh.

January 16, 1988 A day of low inspiration. Seven hours on planes just to get to Toronto and back. Purpose: to attend the think-in session on Canada-U.S. relations ordered up by Joe Clark. Legault, Heinbecker, and Osler from the embassy were finally invited, after great whining on my part.

Unfortunately, I find myself disagreeing more and more often with Clark. We are simply not on the same wavelength. I increasingly realize how frustrating this must be for him. I suspect he finds me overbearing at times. With some justice. And I do have to respect the stoicism with which he accepts or tolerates my unwelcome dissents.

Some impressions: Joe C. insisting he was now going to take charge of Canada-U.S. relations; Joe C. spending the first hour endlessly pounding his finger on the table; Joe C. being suspicious of officials; Joe C. showing little understanding of the United States. His greatest concern was to organize and martial Canadian lobbying in Washington for the free-trade agreement. Only with great insistence did I manage to dissuade him, explaining that the last thing Canada should do is appear too eager for the accord and that our real job was to get the White House to give the agreement the priority it deserved. Extraordinary that Clark was giving us the "I'm in charge now" refrain when the uninvited-to-the-powwow Pat Carney has the prime role. His approach to her is like his approach to his colleagues at National Defence – ignore or oppose what they want to do. He seems to expect the embassy and departmental officials to carry out his policies, not those of the cabinet.

We spent most of the remaining time hearing Clark explain why he was opposed to advanced cruise tests. I outlined the costs to the defence relationship. Heinbecker courageously outlined the technical and strategic reasons for a positive response. Clark would hear none of this. On Central America, another Clark hobby horse, which he is riding more each day, Derek Burney took him on. "What interests does Canada have that leads you to put so much time and emphasis on Central America?" Clark could give no answer other than the rather strained one of "refugees." (We have far more refugees from other, vastly greater, areas.)

Before the meeting got under way, Clark spoke to me privately in order to administer a rebuke, albeit a rather mild one. "I am still not kept fully informed by you," he said. "The last time you were in town I wasn't informed. Also, I did not know you were seeing Derek Burney."

Dark shadows everywhere, green monsters at work. On the plane back I read Epictetus: "If a man will have only two words at heart, his life will be tranquil and serene – bear and forbear."

January 18, 1988 Leading story in the *Post* about an auction sale in Texas of the goods of the now bankrupt John Connally.[1] I picked up the Saturday *Post*, and it carried a similar story about the auction of Mike Deaver's goods. *Sic transit gloria mundi*. Hundreds of souvenir hunters swarm through Deaver's office during the sale, ghoulishly looking, snooping, gloating, seeking pleasure in his pain. Of course, the *Post* reported it as if it were a fun affair, which I'm sure it was for its reporter.

I managed to complete my reading of Richard Ellmann's[2] enormous and depressing biography of Oscar Wilde. Reading of the disgraceful conduct of the British judges, press, and public, I have to think of Deaver as a sort of Washington Oscar Wilde, *mutatis mutandis*, first bestriding Washington like a royal prince, the darling of Georgetown and the media, then beaten by the overreaching special prosecutor, then reviled by the elites of Washington. The English people, Ellmann wrote, liked to beat a beaten man. That's Washington today.

January 21, 1988 Three items of bad news for the free-trade agreement. Shortliffe phoned to say his talks with the U.S. film industry had broken down.

The second piece of bad news: according to congressional legal advisers, the ninety-day approval period of the FTA could run into the next Congress (the 101st) without the clock stopping. This means the Democrats could stall the accord until after the next election and thus deny the Republicans the benefits of their victory. It is amazing how the administration keeps

---

[1] (1917–1993) U.S. Secretary of the Navy 1961; Governor of Texas 1963–1969; Secretary of the Treasury 1971–1972. He filed for bankruptcy in 1986 as a result of a string of business losses in Houston.

[2] (1918–1987) Literary critic and biographer.

offering up surprises about the legal situation affecting passage of the legislation. This information will shock Ottawa. The free-trade debate in Canada, with all its debilitating effects on our own unity, could be prolonged for another half-year or more!

And finally, the third shocker: a U.S. trade journal reports that Senator Alan Simpson, Republican whip, announced that he was going to oppose the FTA. I could hardly believe that Simpson, one of my congressional heroes, would allow some special interest – uranium producers – to cause him to depart so far from principle. For the first time, I begin to fear we could lose the vote in Congress.

To borrow a phrase from Lyndon Johnson, if the report on Simpson is true, I will henceforth be able to hold him only "in minimum high regard."

January 22, 1988 I drank too much at our dinner last night. Sitting around the table – Scotty Reston and Sally Quinn, Les Aspin, Walter Pincus, the Phillipses, David Brinkley – until close to midnight, talking about the candidates.

I got up early to meet Sol Linowitz for breakfast at the Metropolitan Club. He is close to Shultz and often meets him one-on-one. We talked about what one constantly hears these days from his bad-mouthing White House critics – that Shultz likes to travel like a king, sit next to movie stars, etc. Yet his dogged support for arms control and better relations with the U.S.S.R. has been of decisive importance. I told him Shultz has been good to us and good for Canada. Also, he is a serious person who sticks to his agenda and knows how to get results. The balance sheet, I told him, is unquestionably in Shultz's favour.

At the end of the afternoon, Whitehead asked me to call on him in his office. I met an intimidating lineup – Whitehead, Lee Thomas, Roz Ridgway, Bill Nitze, and a few more officials lower on the scale. He informed me of the official U.S. position on our proposal for an acid rain accord. I told him the government would be very disappointed. It fell short of our needs and expectations, and I was surprised that the administration would not go further. Whitehead said it would be impossible for the United States to agree to negotiate specific reductions of acid rain as long as Congress had not passed control legislation.

In the evening we attended a black-tie dinner down at the Ritz-Carlton that Paul Nitze gave for himself. Eighty-one years old – sharp, cerebral, handsome, rich, newly widowed, and he danced all night. I saw his son Bill on the way in. I think of him as an ally, or sort of, at State. "Bill," I said, "to be undiplomatic, your proposal to us on acid rain is a dead duck, it croaked on arrival, d.o.a." Seated next to me at the dinner was David Acheson's wife, Dean Acheson's daughter-in-law. She told me she was friendly with all Canadian ambassadors in Washington and then observed, correctly, that we have never invited her to the embassy.

January 23, 1988 The *New York Times* and the *Washington Post* carry major page 1 stories on the striking down by the U.S. Court of Appeal of the special prosecutor law. Hurray. One of the great strengths of this country is that injustices, in time, get corrected.

January 25, 1988 My seventh State of the Union, and I am now number nine in the precedence world. Some accomplishment.

Reagan made a reference to the Canada-U.S. free-trade agreement in his speech, but it will probably go down badly in Canada. He talked first of a Canada-U.S. accord, which would then extend to Mexico, then to the Americas from Tierra del Fuego to the Arctic. As Sondra said, it sounded like an exercise in American imperialism. I am surprised at the insensitivity of the people in the White House who write this stuff and at the president himself for embracing it. I think this weakens the notion of a special Canada-U.S. trade relationship.

I was furious this morning to read the record, prepared by External, of our think-in in Toronto. I found references to my comments about the Americans having a "mad system," about the film policy conflict being a "gruesome issue," and about my advice to Joe Clark "not to shoot the messenger." The memorandum was marked for circulation to about thirty people! I spoke to Campbell in a fury. This was the very stuff of leaks, and it was irresponsible to circulate it. The idea of a verbatim account of a think-in was itself preposterous.

Although verbatim, the drafter left out an exchange that apparently has caused some amusement in Ottawa.

Clark: We need to convince senators friendly to us to support the FTA.

Gotlieb: They are moved not by goodwill but special interests in their constituency. George Mitchell of Maine loves Canada, but his vote on the issue is controlled 100 per cent by a small group of potato farmers.

Clark: Surely not 100 per cent. Some part of him rises above potatoes.

Gotlieb: You are right. Potatoes only count 80 per cent. The other 20 per cent is lobster.

January 26, 1988 I called on Alan Simpson to tell him how disappointed I was by his attack on our free-trade agreement. He tried to play it down. "It was just something I said in Wyoming. I am not taking a high profile on it or a leadership role." He added, "My only problem is uranium and your subsidies." Gently, I replied, "Alan, you issued a release right here in Washington. The news was carried in national energy journals, and your statement criticized the FTA provisions not only on uranium." He seemed very embarrassed. Then I gave him the "high road" treatment. "Alan," I said, "you're a national figure, number two Republican senator, next senate majority leader, a statesman, a man of principle – how could you do this? The day Congress rejects this agreement will be one of the blackest days in U.S. history." I pulverized the poor fellow. He said, "The door isn't closed. I have room."

There was a bit of the old Simpson flash. The Japanese ambassador, he said, came to see him after a disastrous vote in the Senate concerning Japan and trade. The ambassador said to him, "Senator Simpson, you are very helpful and intelligent, tell me how should I interpret this to my government?"

Simpson replied, "Mr. Ambassador, tell them we're trying to fuck you."

January 29, 1988 In the afternoon Fred Doucet called me, just like in the old days, before Derek Burney became chief of staff. "Allan," he said, "the news on acid rain looks bad. Is it as bad as it seems?" he asked. "Worse," I replied. "The U.S. has taken a step backward, not forward." "The prime minister wants your views," Fred said. "Should we send an emissary to call on the White House?" I had a vision of Doucet coming down to plead our case. "Fred," I told him, "nothing could be more useless. The whole system is opposed. The only way to reach the president is for Mulroney to call him."

January 30, 1988 I attended the annual dinner of the remarkable but bizarre Alfalfa Club. The event was so typically American. So typically awesome. In one room, all the business and governmental elite of the nation were gathered: the president, the cabinet, the congressional nobility, former everything and everybody, CEOs from all over the country. No press and no media whatsoever. It was America celebrating itself – something they do very well.

I was seated at the head table, three seats away from the president, and between Chief Justice Rehnquist[1] and former Chief Justice Burger. Heavy lifting for me. We talked about abortion, legal advertising, the Constitution, and other light topics. I was impressed with Rehnquist's sense of humour, but Burger's range of mind and interest was greater. He is very opposed to the excesses of legal advertising and is trying to get the public concerned about it. I told him he won't succeed.

Before dinner there was a small head table reception, and I chatted with the president. "The free-trade agreement will set a wonderful precedent for the rest of the world," he said. The president became encircled by Senator Bentsen, new president of the club, Senator John Warner, outgoing president, Senator Alan Simpson, and Congressman Tom Foley. In walked the secretary-general of the United Nations, Perez de Cuellar.[2] These barons had no interest in talking to the secretary-general and did not move to introduce or present him until their circle broke up. Not that they were rude. Maybe it's just that for them the rest of the world isn't real.

January 31, 1988 Had lunch at Joe Albritton's[3] for a crowd attending the Alfalfa Club. The owner of Riggs Bank can draw anyone he fancies to his table. It was a phenomenally warm day. We sat around with the Neys, Bill Webster, Nancy Dickerson, and a few others. Everyone agreed that the one uniting factor in the huge chunk of the American establishment last night that included such people as David Rockefeller, Kissinger, Ross Perot, and hordes of other leading business and political figures was fear and loathing of the media.

---

[1] (1924–2005) Associate Justice of the Supreme Court of the United States 1972–1986; Chief Justice 1986–2005.

[2] (b. 1920) Peruvian diplomat. Secretary-General of the United Nations 1982–1991.

[3] Member of the Albritton family that controlled Riggs Bank in Washington, D.C., serving many members of the diplomatic corps and foreign countries. In recent years the bank was plagued with scandal and intrigue, and Albritton was forced to divest.

Tonight was the Super Bowl, and the Redskins trounced the Denver Broncos in San Diego. There is Redskin fever here. Worship of the "Skins" is the one thing that unites Washington, the one civic phenomenon that creates something in common between the 80 per cent black and 20 per cent white populations, the haves and the massive number of have-nots, the street dwellers and the cave dwellers. I hate the sport, but I went over to Lane Kirkland's to watch the game together with the Safires. In the line of duty.

February 1, 1988 Spoke to Dan Rostenkowski, chairman of Ways and Means, about the free-trade agreement and the omnibus trade bill timetable. Elusive, busy man, no respecter of foreign representatives. After trying to see this super-satrap for four or five months, the best I could get was a phone conversation. "We can't rush the free-trade agreement," he said. "We have to iron out bumps first, if things are to go successfully." "If you reopen issues," I replied, "the whole thing will unravel." "I'll do my best," he said, "but I've got the omnibus bill on my plate, the FTA, and catastrophic insurance." And on he went. I thought to myself, what power for a representative of Illinois. And where's the accountability?

If our agreement goes down the tube, as well it might, he'll be re-elected in Chicago with the same huge majorities. That's the trouble with the U.S. system. Great power and damn little responsibility.

The trouble with the U.S. system was the subject du jour at a small dinner at the Residence, with Rick Burt, visiting from Bonn, the legendary Lee Atwater,[1] who is running the Bush campaign, Rowly Evans, Judith Miller of the *New York Times*, and David Ignatius[2] of the *Post*. Atwater recounted seemingly endless minor variations on figures that could spell triumph or despair in Iowa next week. If Bush loses Iowa or New Hampshire, he is dead meat.

I have never met anyone quite like Atwater before. With his southern drawl, his thespian flair, his wit, and his earthiness, he kept us spellbound all evening.

---

[1] (1951–1991) Republican political consultant, strategist, and adviser to President Ronald Reagan and George H.W. Bush. Played a key role in the defeat of Michael Dukakis in the 1988 presidential election.

[2] (b. 1950) Reporter, editor, and columnist for the *Washington Post*.

February 2, 1988 Accompanying Jim Kelleher, now solicitor general, I called on Bill Webster and then Ed Meese, the purpose being to sign a drug enforcement accord with the latter, who also offered us a lunch. Yesterday Kelleher's office called to inquire whether he should come. He was worried about media embarrassment in view of the avalanche of reports of new investigations regarding allegations against Meese, this time in connection with alleged bribery in some mad scheme involving an Iraqi pipeline, instigated by his very bad-news pal Bob Wallach.[1] I told Kelleher's office there was no way he could cancel. The true reason would be immediately apparent, and not coming would embarrass and prejudice our relations in the judicial sphere.

Ed Meese was his old bluff, vigorous, jolly self. He acted as though he had no worries, although he is under endless attack ("Meese Is a Pig" signs hang all over town) and has been convicted in the minds of all of Washington's splendidly impartial elite.

Rushed from lunch to see Peter Murphy and Alan Holmer,[2] who called me to complain about our recent plan for textile duty remissions. They told me it's curtains, game over, for the free-trade agreement if we make this move. Holmer said we already have about twenty-five or twenty-eight negative votes in the Senate on the FTA. The textile people will push us over the cliff – fifty negative votes easily. Knowing the legendary clout of the textile lobby, it is difficult to be skeptical about this assessment.

February 3, 1988 Saw Howard Baker this afternoon. The president's chief of staff was relaxed, cool, and friendly in his fire-lit office in the East Wing. I handed him a letter from Mulroney to the president on acid rain. It was polite, I told him, because Mulroney has so high a regard for the president. But the message is clear. He is vastly disappointed, and unless the president reconsiders – which he urged Reagan to do – he is unlikely to authorize negotiations to continue. Quoting the president's words on arms

---

[1] (b. 1934) Attorney and long-time friend of Attorney General Edwin Meese. Appointed by President Ronald Reagan as U.S. representative on the Human Rights Commission of the Economic and Social Council of the United Nations in 1986.

[2] (b. 1950) Deputy Assistant to the President for Intergovernmental Affairs 1981–1983; Deputy Assistant Secretary for Import Administration at the Commerce Department 1983–1985; General Counsel to U.S. Trade Representative Clayton Yeutter 1985–1987; Deputy U.S. Trade Representative 1987–1989.

control, Mulroney's letter said a bad agreement is worse than no agreement.

Baker took the hard line very well (I made it harder than the letter). "I don't think our position will change, but I will brief the president tomorrow morning. He is, as you know, very sensitive to Mulroney and Canadian issues." Another useless appeal, I thought to myself, but so pleasant to deal with such a civilized and graceful man.

Just as I was leaving, Baker said to me, "I was pleased at the call I got from Burney the other day and the good news he conveyed." "What good news?" I asked, after hesitating for a moment. "Well, Allan," he replied, "I don't know much about protocol, but it seems to me that if your government didn't tell you, it's not up to me to do so." "You're dead right, Howard," I replied, and left mad as hell.

Later, I picked up Sondra and went to the State Department, where the Shultzes asked us to dinner, along with the Israeli ambassador, Moshe Arad, and U.S. Ambassador Glitman, the INF negotiator. We ate in Shultz's private dining room, but it was a difficult dinner as Shultz got up every five minutes to telephone the Hill to lobby House members on the Contra aid bill. I steered the conversation in the direction of Israel and reports of a new U.S.-Israel peace mediation. I asked Arad if the government he represented was in favour of the peace initiative. Looking at Shultz, he replied that Shamir would not even think of negotiating if Shultz were not secretary of state. So high was his regard for Shultz that that factor alone was responsible for his willingness to talk.

February 4, 1988 I called Burney on the secure line. Ottawa must get its act together. There must be no more wild initiatives like the textile one. We must put a clamp on all initiatives vis-à-vis the United States until the free-trade agreement is in the bag. He said he would raise this at once with Mazankowski.

I then gave him living hell over my embarrassment with Howard Baker. He was apologetic. He would not repeat the reason for his call, and his excuse was lame. He said he was embarrassed and did not want to tell me about it. "Did the subject of the message start with an *O*?" I asked. Yes, he replied. I explained that Colin Powell had already told me about it at the Alfalfa Club. (Story: the PM directed that Daniel Ortega,[1] on a recent visit to give a speech in Halifax, not be invited to Ottawa.) "Big deal," I said to

[1] (b. 1945) President of Nicaragua 1985–1990 and leader of the Sandinista National Liberation Front.

Derek. "The message was a useful one to send down here, and appropriate. You should have told me."

February 5, 1988 I called yesterday on the House minority leader, Trent Lott[1] of Mississippi. My appointment was for 11 a.m., and I arrived at 11, along with Jon Fried. As I went into the congressman's office, he came out. "I'll be with you in a minute, Mr. Ambassador," he said as he strode down the hall to make, as he explained, a short speech on the floor of the House. At 11:40 he returned, just as I completed my third cup of coffee and was about to leave. After the usual apologies, we had a fifteen-minute meeting that showed he knew nothing about our free-trade agreement.

If I ever write a book about my adventures in Washington, I think I'll call it *I'll Be with You in a Minute, Mr. Ambassador*.

February 6, 1988 Called on Senator Melcher,[2] Democrat from Montana. The man behaved like an ass from beginning to end. Yeutter, he said, should not have been negotiating the FTA with Canada, he should have been negotiating the elimination of your $20-billion trade surplus. I could stand it no longer. I told him his facts were wrong, his theories of trade were wrong, and he was completely ignoring the benefits of Canada-U.S. trade. The only reason I called on this man was that his state is contiguous to Saskatchewan. It was more than a waste of time. It was a waste of emotion.

February 8, 1988 We held the regular Monday morning meeting of our embassy steering group on free trade. We agree that the odds are increasing against its implementation by Congress, although they are still better than even. But if Ottawa keeps indulging in foolish initiatives, we will blow it. The government can't seem to keep its priorities in view. First textiles, then salmon and herring, and now, it seems, chicken parts. There appear to be a lot of gnomes in Ottawa going through the agreement with a fine comb, looking for loopholes they can fill by unilateral action before the agreement takes effect. It seems that chicken legs are more important than the chicken. We sent a telegram to Ottawa, drafted by Legault, stating quite

---

[1] (b. 1941) Republican Representative from Mississippi 1973–1989; House Minority Whip 1981–1989; Senator from Mississippi 1989 to present; Senate Majority Leader 1996–2002.

[2] John Melcher (b. 1924) Democratic Representative from Montana 1977–1989.

simply that if Ottawa persisted in its duty remission scheme for textiles, it was game over for the agreement. Legault's draft was brilliant. (He is the best writer in the department, author of Trudeau's celebrated phrase about Canada being more than a loose association of shopping malls.)

The present controversy accentuates the need to impose total control on all decisions in Ottawa that might prejudice the American approval process over the next few months. "Almost any trade dispute is guaranteed to make the front page," the telegram said, "and the distance from the front pages to the obituaries could prove to be a short one indeed for the FTA."

In the evening Christopher Plummer and Glenda Jackson[1] came to dinner. They are doing *Macbeth* in Baltimore, a city they find rather depressing. (I know because I visited them there.) We invited about thirty-two guests, including Chief Justice Rehnquist and his wife; Federal Reserve Chairman Alan Greenspan; the newly appointed head of the Kennedy Center, Ralph Davidson, and the outgoing one; the Wicks; and many of the familiar suspects. There was the usual frustration. Colin Powell called at the last moment to say he couldn't make it. A gentleman, he called personally. The Dubersteins distinguished themselves in a somewhat different manner. The White House deputy chief of staff first refused. Then late last week his secretary called to accept. This morning his secretary called again to refuse. Reason: his wife couldn't get a babysitter.

Plummer and Jackson were marvellous guests, relaxed, amusing, and enjoying themselves hugely. In a gutsy move, Bill Webster asked Sondra if he could sit beside the actress, known for her radical opinions. She and the director of the CIA hit it off amazingly well, the two lingering at the table after all the others left.

Background entertainment was the Iowa caucuses. We stood about watching the tube in the library. Looks like Bush may be going down the tube himself.

February 9, 1988 I gave a lunch today for Doug Roche,[2] our deeply idealistic ambassador for disarmament, the most high-minded politician I know. I invited a handful of opinionated arms control think-tankers, who

---

[1] (b. 1936) Academy Award–winning British actress and Labour Member of Parliament for Hampstead and Highgate 1992 to present.

[2] (b. 1929) PC Member of Parliament for Edmonton-Strathcona 1972–1984; Canadian Ambassador for Disarmament 1984–1989; Independent Senator 1998–2004.

provided lively entertainment by denouncing each other's ideas. The prize for the most obnoxious went to Bill Arkin,[1] nephew, he said, of Alan Arkin, the actor. I will be more famous than he, Mr. Arkin assured us.

Roche led off the discussion by stating that, admittedly, the United States seemed to be getting on well with the U.S.S.R., but he wondered why the Americans refused to negotiate seriously in any multilateral forum. Since our disarmament ambassador deals with issues in multilateral forums, it appears this is his frame of reference. The Canadian obsession with multilateralism over the top?

In the early evening I dashed home to put on my white tie for a White House diplomatic reception. This was the first time the Reagans have held a white-tie affair for diplomats (or for anyone?), and no one knows why Nancy decided to do it now, in the Reagans' eighth and last year. But everyone agreed that it was ludicrous to put on a white tie for the sake of an hour-long affair, consisting of a long lineup of waiting diplomats, presented one-by-one with spouses to the Reagans for a photo opportunity. There was a short reception after the photo lineup, which the Reagans did not attend. I chatted briefly with other diplomats, as there were no Washingtonians and few officials present.

February 10, 1988 I flew to New York this morning to speak at the Americas Society. The theme of my speech was how de Tocqueville would see the United States today if he returned. I wove this into the Canada-U.S. relationship and the significance of the free-trade agreement. My basic message was that the U.S. congressional system is so prone to manipulation by special interests, and economic conflicts are occurring at such a rate, that we now have to change our approach to management of this relationship. We need to try shared institutional arrangements, a major innovation in our relations.

February 11, 1988 Our telegram about the short distance from the front page to the obituaries has ruffled feathers in Ottawa. More accusations that the embassy is a mouthpiece for the Americans, or alternatively, that we exaggerate and get carried away in assessing the consequences of Canadian political initiatives. But we are dead accurate in our reporting. Emphasis on the dead.

---

[1] Columnist for the *Los Angeles Times* and military analyst for NBC News. He was an army intelligence analyst in West Berlin in the 1970s and a nuclear weapons expert in the Cold War.

February 12, 1988 Yesterday Clark called Shultz directly to tell him that we would not test the advanced cruise missile, bypassing the embassy entirely. Well, almost entirely. He called Heinbecker to get Shultz's phone number. When Shultz asked what the call was about, the minister's office declined to tell him.

The decision will come as a bombshell to the Americans. Joe Clark's foreign policy, which has little to do with Mulroney's, prevails. Beatty, true to form, backed off. Later today, the PMO instructed Heinbecker to tell State that we would like to test, but we need more time. This was a softer message than the letter Clark sent to Shultz, but it is still a negative.

February 14, 1988 Spoke to the Canadian Club of the Desert in Palm Springs. Biggest crowd they've had. Lots of very old people jumping up and down with questions about free trade. Everyone is affected, one way or the other, by the agreement.

Question from a concerned Winnipeg lady: I bought a popcorn cooker in Palm Springs for nineteen dollars. At home the same popcorn cooker costs fifty-five dollars. I just priced it. Will this agreement eliminate the difference in price? Best question I've heard on free trade.

February 15, 1988 The intelligence community in Ottawa has begun to focus on developments in the United States – a complete waste of time. Last week the bureau concerned sent a message asking the embassy to comment on the future of protectionist forces in the United States. This after my speech in Toronto a few days ago analyzing those forces and predicting their continuation far out into the future. A *Globe* editorial summarized the speech.

In my absence, the embassy sent a cutting reply to Ottawa. "Ambassador Gotlieb's speech 'The Politics of Protectionism in the USA,' delivered before the Institute of Corporate Directors in Toronto on January 28, makes it clear that protectionism is alive and well in the USA, that it is not a short-term phenomenon and that the omnibus trade bill is not its only manifestation or vehicle. Speech provides comprehensive review of protectionism as a systemic phenomenon here. Copy available from US bureau. Suggest you read it and then put to us any questions you may still have."

I can't think of anything more useless than an assessment of the United States done by Canadian intelligence. Unless it an assessment of Canada done by U.S. intelligence.

February 16, 1988 This afternoon the PMO called me on the secure line to tell me about the advanced cruise decision. I learned nothing I had not surmised. The PM wanted to do it and all that, but later. I should get that message across to the White House.

The department's failure to pre-notify the embassy was a disgrace. If I didn't have a critical job to perform in the next few months (selling the free-trade agreement), the government would have my resignation. The fault can be attributed mostly to Joe Clark and, to a lesser degree, the department, which is very weak. The Japanese foreign office notified their embassy in Washington before they bombed Pearl Harbor.

It looks to me more and more like we have two foreign policies in Canada, one directed by the prime minister, the other by the foreign minister. In turn they reflect two versions of the national interest – one to enhance our relations with the United States, the other to distance ourselves whenever we can get the chance.

February 17, 1988 The decision to refuse the cruise continues to reverberate in Washington. The president has written to Mulroney urging reconsideration. On short notice, I saw Colin Powell to deliver Mulroney's reply. I gave him the PMO line – the PM really wants to do it, but he needs time. I explained to Powell that the government in Ottawa is suffering from political overload. With scandal allegations and the personal attack on the prime minister for not reporting the party loans for renovating his Residence, the Conservatives have suffered a major dip in the polls and are in poor shape politically.

Powell said the decision was deeply upsetting, and Carlucci could hardly believe it. I suggested – very privately – that at the NATO summit in Brussels next month, the United States should get Kohl and Thatcher to explain to Mulroney how important this issue is to them (and not just to the United States) in the post-INF environment. He thought this a good suggestion.

Later in the day, I briefed Axworthy, Herb Gray, and Jack Austin, who are in town, ostensibly for the purpose of observing the trade situation in Washington but in reality to lobby against the free-trade agreement. I find their action unprecedented in my long experience in External, but everything goes these days. It was a strange feeling, talking with "Herb," "Lloyd," and "Jack." On the surface, camaraderie. In reality, distrust on their part, anger on mine. Jon Fried accompanied them on their calls on the Hill – to Bentsen, Gibbons, and others. He concluded that the Liberal tactic is to delay the approval process as long as possible, stretch it out until the current session of Congress expires, delaying parliamentary action at the same time, and then go to the polls in Canada, without the Conservatives having an agreement to show for their efforts.

February 18, 1988 Spoke to Duberstein to urge an early answer to the prime minister's letter asking the president to reconsider the U.S. position on acid rain. He was very frank: the United States will not change its position.

He asked me whether the next summit in Washington should, in our view, be an official or working visit. I said it was their call. He asked what our preference was. I replied, "Well, why not make it official, since that would make it unique, inasmuch as you never have two official visits of the same leader in the same term. But then if we ask for this, we'll probably see an item in the papers saying, Canadians begging for special treatment. So you call it."

Saw Alan Greenspan at the Federal Reserve, for the first time in his official capacity as chairman. I told Philip Somerville[1] it was going to be a short visit, as this was a man of few words, Greenspan being even more taciturn than Volcker. I was wrong. Greenspan was talkative, open, perceptive, and impressive. He gave me a novel theory about our free-trade agreement, on which he is very keen. It will go through because it is so broad and wide that the special interests will more or less neutralize themselves. This, he says, is what happened in the case of the tax bill. No one, including he, can figure out how the tax bill passed. The very enormity of it was the key to its passage. Same with the FTA. Listening to him talking about the economy was like listening to Heifetz play the fiddle, an effortless, flawless performance.

Just as I came home, I learned that our textile telegram (short distance from front page to obituaries) leaked and will appear in tomorrow's *Toronto Star*. It will create a storm. Along with "scorched earth," these words will help immortalize me.

Legault, who drafted the message, was extremely upset. Ottawa was critical both of the bluntness of the telegram and its wide distribution. I told Legault to relax. I've been through this before, on books, film, and other topics. There will be a frenzy of headlines, anger, bitching, and then it will

[1] Economic Minister-Counsellor for the Department of External Affairs in Washington 1986–1991.

all blow over. Our telegram told the tale correctly. We were right to send it.

We will not tell our masters what they want to hear. We will not tell our masters that Chiang Kai-Shek will prevail.

February 19, 1988 Jack Valenti called just as I was rushing out to have lunch at the Maison Blanche with Karen Elliott House[1] of the *Wall Street Journal*. Frank Wells of Disney had called him, consequent on my chat with him in L.A., and Valenti said he wanted to talk things over.

"Allan," he said, "Flora MacDonald should proclaim victory. We are willing to accept a separate Canadian market and an affidavit system, but we can't agree to licensing as we are about to hit Switzerland and London with reprisals for the same thing. You people got what you want – proclaim victory. We're willing to talk, we're ready to meet in New York next week."

I called Shortliffe, who thought the call was a breakthrough. He and Derek were highly pleased with the news.

February 23, 1988 Still in New York, staying at the Pierre, having the first relaxing day in a while. I attended a reception today at our consul general's, Bob Johnstone, to launch a Canadian cultural program and had a long chat with Hume Cronyn,[2] whom I had not met before. He told me with considerable poignancy how he had been consistently ignored by his Canadian homeland, even though he had retained Canadian citizenship all his life, was Canadian through and through, and always maintained close contact with Canada. He had never been invited to Government House, to any function involving the PM, nor had he received any Canadian honours. He was never appointed to the Order of Canada. He saw this as a display of the characteristic Canadian resentment of Canadians who "make it" in the United States. I agreed with him – Canadian resentment is a mixture of dislike of success, preference for mediocrity, and a very unhealthy dose of anti-Americanism.

I am going to try to see if he can get the Order of Canada.

---

[1] (b. 1948) Joined the *Wall Street Journal*'s Washington, D.C., bureau in 1974. Named diplomatic correspondent in 1978, moved to New York in 1983 as assistant foreign editor, and became foreign editor in 1984. In 1989, was named vice-president of Dow Jones's international group.

[2] (1911–2003) Canadian stage and film actor noted for his successful career on Broadway and in Hollywood.

February 25, 1988 Item in *Financial Post*: "Carney, who oversaw Canada's trade negotiating team [*sic*], did not deny the leaked cable was written by Canadian Allan Gotlieb [it wasn't], which puts considerable weight on the warning [not to implement the textile duty remission scheme]. She downplayed the memo: 'I attach as much significance to the telex as I do every one that I receive every day from Washington.'" Nice *shtip*.

February 26, 1988 Global TV did a three- or four-minute segment on my Americas Society "de Tocqueville" speech, interpreting my remarks as a brutal indictment of America, heralding my early retirement. *Meshuga*, I would say.

The more I think about it, the more I believe we are running a two-track foreign policy. One track: Joe Clark's foreign policy, fearful of the self-styled peace groups, anxious to distance Canada from U.S. defence policy and unwilling to test the cruise; second track: Mulroney different to the core. Clark was telling Shultz and Duberstein one thing (withdraw the request), I was telling Powell another thing (Canada wants to test but needs more time), and Burney was to tell Howard Baker the same thing at the NATO summit in Brussels next week. What was our foreign policy? Was it Clark's or Mulroney's? Was there to be a repetition of the last months of the Diefenbaker era, with cabinet ministers determining their own policy? Burney told me the PM's policy would prevail; he just talked to him about the whole situation. I replied that I feared Clark was running foreign policy and Mulroney wasn't.

Carney has finally decided to comply with the GATT decision against us on salmon-herring processing but plans to announce a substitute technique for doing so. It's a problem in her constituency, and she is sneaking through a policy that will enrage the U.S. Senate at the worst possible time – especially the likes of Senator Stevens of Alaska, a very tough customer. I urged caution in a message – thus risking further leaks, further accusations of being in U.S. pockets, and further criticism from Carney. Last line of my telegram: "To cite an old Indian proverb quoted by John Diefenbaker (and repeated to me by Prime Minister Mulroney), 'big game hunter going for bear doesn't chase rabbit tracks.'"

February 28, 1988 Andrea Mitchell of NBC gave a surprise birthday party for her "friend" Alan Greenspan – his sixty-second. This being my sixtieth birthday, we both got cakes. Andrea arranged for chamber music to be performed before dinner – by a group that contributes their fee to the hungry – and then there was a buffet for about thirty or so, mostly media. I sat with Chris Wallace, Elizabeth Drew, and David Gergen. Everyone's very excited about the uncertainties of super-Tuesday. Gergen asked my view as to presidential candidates. Bush over Dole, I said, as Dole had no knowledge of the world offshore. Anyone over Gephardt.[1]

March 4, 1988 Dinner at the Knickerbocker Club in New York for Dwayne Andreas's seventieth birthday. Happy Rockefeller,[2] the hostess, sat me beside her. She flattered me shamelessly – marvellous student of American society, all that. I loved it. The Kissingers were there, along with Barbara Walters, the Mosbachers, the Strausses, and Bill Luers (now chairman of the Metropolitan Museum). Kissinger was in a tense mood. There's an awful piece coming out on him in the *New York Times*, quoting what he said at a private party with Jewish leaders to the effect that Israel should throw the media out, get tough with the Palestinians, and then negotiate. After dinner the toasts began and went on and on – family toasts, friends' toasts, etc. After Dwayne replied, Happy leaned over to me and said, "You know, my secretary had a call today from the Soviet ambassador, Dubynin [sitting next to Inez]. He wanted to know if he was expected to make a speech." I said, "Tell him no, he's not expected to but can certainly do so if he likes." (We all know the Soviets love Dwayne.)

A few minutes later she said to me, "If you say something, he'll say something. He's shy and doesn't know what to do. So will you please make some comments? Do you mind?" I leaped to my feet. I said some nice things about Dwayne but prefaced my remarks by commenting, "I can't speak for the Soviet ambassador. I know he would like to make some remarks himself."

Dubynin read a carefully prepared statement on the state of Soviet-American relations.

---

[1] Richard Gephardt (b. 1941) Democratic Representative from Missouri 1977–2005; House Majority Leader 1989–1995; House Minority Leader 1995–2003.

[2] Margaretta "Happy" Rockefeller (b. 1926) Widow of Nelson Rockefeller (1908–1979), the forty-first vice-president of the United States and former governor of New York.

March 5, 1988 We had a black-tie dinner for eighty guests for my sixtieth birthday. Sondra was host. Jim Baker came, as well as Colin Powell, Senators Lugar and Evans, Conrad Black, Garth Drabinsky, and Barbara Frum from Canada, Marietta Tree, Ed Ney, Dwayne Andreas, Dick Gardner from New York, and a grand cross-section of Washington – the Strausses, Kay Graham, the Vernon Jordans, the Brzezinskis, Schlesingers, Stevenses, Phillipses, Kirklands, Brandons, Tafts, Whitehead, and so on.

After endless debate, Sondra and I decided we would not have toasts, except for a very short one from her and a quick reply from me. We stuck to the script. Kay muttered after that there should have been toasts and she would have made one. But I thought it was more of a class act not to have them – following the Joe Alsop school of good behaviour.

Table arrangements were hell. We had to move virtually all the furniture out of the living room and set up six of the ten tables of eight there, with cocktails held in the dining room. Two tables each were set up in the library and sunroom. I put Kay and Bob Strauss together at the same table but not close to each other, as Bob is upset about a nasty article about him on the *Post*'s editorial page. Evangeline Bruce and Joe Alsop were not happy with their tables. We put Meg Greenfield beside Vernon Jordan. I think neither was happy. Diplomatic life in Washington, what's it all about? Knowing who's mad at whom.

March 6, 1988 Feeling ghastly, hungover and exhausted, we struggled our way to the Four Seasons to have Sunday brunch with Ed and Judy Ney, Kay Graham, Cynthia and (the Manchurian Candidate) Dick Helms. (June Callwood could find out, but I decided to live dangerously.) Kay came into the lobby at the same time as us, after having parked her car a few blocks away (Sunday is the democratic Kay – no driver). I couldn't resist wisecracking as the valet-parking man moved my car away, "Too cheap to spend five bucks for valet parking, Kay?" She wasn't greatly amused. "Well," she said, "I was glad to see Bob Strauss thawing just a little and actually beginning to talk to me at your party."

At brunch in the beautiful, sunny hotel dining room, the conversation was inconsequential, until at some point an opening arose as Kay repeated her comments about Bob's overreaction. Sondra moved quickly. "Really, Kay, Michael Kinsley's article about him was ghastly. It went beyond all bounds and should never have been published." Silence, except for grunts of approval from the Neys and Helmses. Kay looked embarrassed and then delivered her classic Kay exculpation. "Well, frankly, I didn't really read the column."

March 7, 1988 I fired off a short message for the prime minister in response to the PMO request for feedback on Mulroney's pro-American speech at Brussels. Colin Powell, I wrote, told me the PM's presentation was "wonderful," "marvellous," and "stunning." I know he meant it, because he told the same thing to Kay Graham at our dinner the other night.

March 8, 1988 Travelled ten hours yesterday to get to Saskatoon and had a terrible night's non-sleep in the Holiday Inn. Spoke to the western free-trade conference this morning at breakfast. Tried like the devil to get out of this, but I promised Grant Devine I would do it, and he wouldn't let me off the hook. I spent most of those ten hours working on my speech – Heinbecker did a good draft, but it didn't get to the heart of what I wanted to say. I observed the basic paradox at the centre of the American mood, politics, and the presidential campaign. The economy is booming, far outdoing most industrial countries, unemployment is way down, job creation bursting, yet the national mood is resentful, anti-foreign, fearful, and fretful about American decline. I warned of the dangers for Canada.

March 9, 1988 A free-trade speech in Toronto, a brief interview on *Canada AM* (how long will I remain in Washington?), and then a Garth Drabinsky celebration – the opening of the Toronto production of *Macbeth* at the O'Keefe Centre.

I went up to Trudeau as soon as I saw him at the black-tie reception before the play. I'd heard earlier today from Sondra's lawyer, Michael Levine, that Trudeau was angry with me because of my critical comments about his nationalist policies, as reported during the Deaver trial. He was with a young constitutional lawyer we know, Debbie Coyne, and looking quite sour. "I hope you didn't believe Paul Robinson's account of my alleged remarks in the limousine in Quebec City back in 1984," I said. "I didn't use those offensive words about FIRA or the NEP. Surely you would recognize that those words sounded like Robinson's, not mine." He looked at me dubiously.

Conrad Black waved to me and said, "I had lunch with Brian today in Ottawa – just the two of us. He was very pleased with your report of Powell's appreciation of his pro-American intervention at the summit in Brussels, as well as a letter from Shultz."

Conrad was very upbeat about the United States. I told him of the theme of my Saskatoon speech yesterday, "Some falling star." I reminded Conrad he was one of the first to tell me about the revival in manufacturing and the new export boom in the rust belt. He spoke of his gamble in buying up small local newspapers in the U.S. industrial heartland. "In rust we trust," he told me – our new motto.

After the play we headed for Drabinsky reception number three, where Hugh Hanson, my old tormentor – now, he says, admirer – pulled me aside to try to sell me some far-fetched PR idea for the ears of Gorbachev and Reagan (how I was supposed to get it to them, I don't know, but he seems to have faith in me). As we chatted, all of a sudden a full-flowering Flora stood in front of me, in sparkling attire. "I want to talk to you about your friend Jack Valenti," she said. I then got the full spiel: if her film policy is not implemented, there will be a national eruption; if Canadian film policy is sacrificed for free trade, the industry will explode.

Perversely, I made myself seem more chummy with "Jack" than I am and tried to explain to her that while I knew what political brouhaha there would be if we were seen to back off our film policy, if we don't come to an accommodation, we will lose the free-trade agreement. I said that I told Valenti sharply many times that if he gets Congress to scuttle the FTA, he and his industry will be the biggest loser. "Nevertheless," I said, "we need one more round of talks with the industry to complete the bridge we are building." "There won't be any more discussions," she replied. "Flora, there has to be," I argued.

As I walked out of the reception an hour later, she called out to me, "Remember what I told you."

March 10, 1988 Note received from Joe Alsop on my sixtieth birthday: "If I did not have a private aversion to 'jump-upness' I should have yielded to temptation last night. The temptation was to tell all and sundry at dinner that you and Sondra were about the most successful diplomatic couple, serving and representing your country better, and giving us pleasure too, than I've seen in Washington in donkey's years. At any rate, here it is for the record. Joe."

As Maurice Bowra used to say, "Praise, praise, I can never get enough of it."

March 11, 1988 Bud McFarlane pleads guilty to withholding information from Congress. Stories blare on television. His face is plastered on the front pages of the press. What kind of crime is it not to tell Congress something? In Canada it is a crime – a breach of the Official Secrets Act – for an official to pass confidential information to Parliament. I've never heard of a more phony crime. This man is a political victim.

March 12, 1988 At 1:15 a.m. the telephone rings. Another wrong number, I mutter to myself. We seem to get disturbed by such calls a few times a month. Not this time. Marc was in a serious accident in Baltimore, struck while in the back seat of a car by a kid jumping a red light. He is badly hurt – broken ribs, serious internal injuries. The nurse on emergency at the Mercy Hospital says come now. We arrive at 3 a.m. while he is in surgery. The doctors remove his spleen, but a few hours later it is clear that he is still hemorrhaging internally. In the afternoon he comes close to the end. Amidst great confusion, panic, and shouting, I manage to get him moved to a Baltimore hospital specializing in shock and trauma. In the evening he is operated on once again to address the internal bleeding. The doctors in shock trauma tell us he is in a very critical state. "He nearly bit the biscuit," one of them tells Sondra. We go home at midnight, in a deep state of disbelief.

March 13, 1988 Marc holds his own. Mulroney called in the evening to express his concern.

March 16, 1988 Burney and Campbell are in town to plan the prime minister's visit to Washington next month. I arranged a call on Jim Baker, who took the opportunity to criticize us for eight trade actions – yes, eight, he counted them – that the United States considers run counter to the spirit of the FTA and that, if we persist in them, will easily sink the agreement (according to Baker). He cited textiles, film, plywood, yoghurt, and ice cream, among others. Indeed, textiles has become a real crisis, and we finished the day with a further session with Baker where he produced a half-dozen proposals to water down our textile duty remission schemes. It looks like the FTA goose will be cooked if we don't back off even further than we had initially planned.

March 18, 1988 We invited the Deavers for dinner tonight. We had heard that they were hurt because they were not invited to my birthday dinner in March. I should have asked them, but I didn't for cowardly reasons. If we had, there would have been articles in the Canadian papers rehashing tales about me and my pal Deaver, his rise and fall, my rise and fall. But it was craven of me to omit him from the list, and I hate myself for it. The Laughlin Phillipses, Edmund and Sylvia Morris, and Carolyn Peachy joined us this evening, all of whom are friends of Mike and Carolyn. Irony of the day is the announcement of the indictment of John Poindexter in the Iran-Contra affair.

Deaver, McFarlane, Poindexter – all key colleagues and contacts, all friends of Canada. Now they are all broken or being broken on the Washington wheel.

March 22, 1988 The British ambassador, my old Christ Church fellow student, Anthony Acland, came to breakfast with his number two and number three. Six of us spent an hour discussing our common interest in pushing the United States to amend the Canada-U.S. nuclear agreement of 1959 so as to allow us the choice of buying British-made nuclear-powered submarines. I initiated these monthly breakfasts to discuss common problems. This might be the first time the Canadian embassy has done such a thing since the days of Vincent Massey.

Called on Yeutter and then James Baker to persuade them to try to influence Valenti on the film issue. Shortliffe and the Gulf and Western industry representatives reached an agreement last Friday in New York, *ad referendum*, on a compromise formula on licensing and appeal.

March 25, 1988 Talked to Howard Baker about the upcoming Mulroney visit. The chief of staff told me his soundings on the Hill about a Mulroney address to Congress were positive. Now all I have to do is persuade Mulroney. Baker doubted whether we should proceed on Mulroney's idea of appointing special representatives to try to resolve the current impasse on acid rain. He thought the idea would not produce results, would leak, would raise expectations, and all that. We're better off facing the reality of our differences squarely instead. I told him I leaned towards his view and would recommend to the PM that he drop the idea.

March 27, 1988 In the afternoon Sondra and I flew to New York to get ready for the Mulroney visit. As his PMO people put the final touches to his speech, it was sad to see the conceptual framework, the structure, and the connecting points stripped from the drafts that Heinbecker and I had prepared. "All we have left now are one-liners," I told them. "Everyone knows that's the PM's style" was the response.

March 28, 1988 The prime minister requested me to try to interest the *New York Times* in his speech tonight. I called some of my closest contacts. I told Judith Miller for the second time that his speech carried a big news story: his exasperation at the U.S. failure to move on acid rain. I called Les Gelb with the same message. I don't blame Mulroney for believing that Canada counts and his speech should be well reported. After all, Canada does count. But you don't get anywhere pleading with the press.

Mulroney was excellent at the *Wall Street Journal*. Bob Bartley[1] presided, and Karen Elliott House was chief questioner. They like him and his policies. And well they should. Mulroney was never better. On free trade he was outstanding, as he denounced protectionism. On acid rain he was superb, bearding the lions in their den. On the bilateral issues he was a ten. When asked his objectives as host of the forthcoming summit – a predictable question – he replied: first, policy coordination; second, Third World debt; third, trade. When Bartley gently asked him what he meant by "policy coordination," my heart sank. After the interview he asked me how he did. "Excellent on the bilateral side, but you might have to review your comments on your role at the summit. To refer to policy coordination is not much of an answer. It sounds technical, even bureaucratic, a little like the words of Sylvia Ostry." He smiled sheepishly. "Yes, Sylvia is always harping on this."

March 29, 1988 I met alone with Mulroney for a half-hour in his suite at the Pierre prior to his departure for Ottawa. The miserable coverage of his speech in the *New York Times* was painful to him. Better no coverage at all, he said. We agreed the *Wall Street Journal* coverage was good, although we both knew it wasn't great. We then spoke of his upcoming visit to Washington. He told me he was worried about addressing Congress and doubted he should ask to do this. The congressional chamber will not be filled, in all probability, he thought, and the Canadian TV networks will zoom in on the empty seats. The story will not be about the speech Mulroney gave, or its reception, but about a snub by Congress. His concern is, of course, very legitimate.

---

[1] (1937–2003) *Wall Street Journal* Editorial Page Editor 1972–2002. He became editor of the *Journal* in 1979 and vice-president of Dow Jones and Co. in 1983.

I tried to convince him that the congressional chamber would be full – the Congress would see to that. If he ignored Congress at a time when it addresses two vital issues to Canada, this could be the subject of adverse comment. I underlined that this was his second official visit to Washington, a unique situation, as no other leader was given two official visits in one presidential term, according to the NSC. To ignore Congress twice would be a mistake.

We discussed whether personal representatives of Reagan and himself should be appointed to review the acid rain impasse. I explained Howard Baker's negative reaction and said I agreed with it. The worst thing that could happen would be for us to get sucked into some feeble step that we would have to try to sell as "progress." The critics would say, there's Brian, Ron's friend, snowed again. Mulroney agreed entirely.

March 30, 1988 In Toronto to deliver a lecture at York University's Faculty of Administrative Studies. At a small dinner with the faculty at the Toronto Club after my lecture, Jim Gillies[1] asked me to explain to the dinner guests what I saw as my principal accomplishments in my public-service career. I replied, "Jim, I got old too soon and smart too late. Looking back, it seems to me I spent most of my efforts fighting useless bureaucratic battles, the issues seeming of great importance then but not now. Worst of all, a lot of them were over turf. How happy I was every time my departments – Communications, Manpower – were given increased responsibilities.

"My accomplishments were perhaps three: (1) working with Trudeau and Cadieux in the sixties to uphold Canadian federal principles against separatist assaults in the field of international affairs; (2) restoring the foreign ministry to a central role in foreign policy after years of neglect; and (3) helping Canadians understand the U.S. congressional system and the ways in which we had to conduct ourselves to promote and protect our interests."

April 1, 1988 Called on the ex-husband of Elizabeth Taylor, the influential Senator Warner, to give him a pitch on submarines. He and Exon[2] of Nebraska are establishing themselves as troublemakers in the Senate on this issue. They are warning about the dangers of proliferating nuclear

[1] (b. 1924) PC Member of Parliament for Don Valley, Ontario, 1972–1979. Served in the cabinet of Prime Minister Joe Clark, and as a senior policy adviser to Clark.

[2] John Exon (1921–2005) Governor of Nebraska 1971–1979; Democratic Senator from Nebraska 1979–1997.

powers. I told Warner bluntly – I hit him right between the eyes – that a lot of Canadians in the Department of National Defence and in the navy were keen on the French boat, and even preferred it to the British. With the French boat, we would not need U.S. permission, as its technology was not involved. If the Congress blocked amending our nuclear agreement, this would make a lot of people happy in Ottawa, although obviously not the British. Warner seemed very surprised, as he was not aware of the French Amethyst class of nuclear-powered subs. It's clear he's acting as Admiral McKee's mouthpiece, as is my friend John Herrington, who has declined to meet with me to discuss the issue.

April 4, 1988 I said farewell to Joe Clark and Maureen McTeer at the airport after their four-day holiday here, where they visited with Jack Osler. I briefed Clark on plans for the PM's visit. I had to tell him that Mulroney, contrary to advice tendered, had decided not to be accompanied by any ministers. "This was a mistake," I said. "But you understand the PM as well as anyone," I added (lying). Clark wondered whether Wilson and he could nevertheless meet for a small working dinner with Shultz and Baker at the same time as the State dinner. I explained that was out of the question. Shultz and Baker would never be more than three feet away from the president during an official visit.

Clark was very negative about the idea of Mulroney addressing a joint session of Congress. I gave him a dozen reasons why he should.

April 5, 1988 I flew to New York to meet John Crosbie, who has just been appointed minister of trade, replacing Pat Carney. There is joy all around in Ottawa and a pretty good feeling in Washington too. This man is a gentleman, a wit and a free-trader – who can ask for anything more? I met with him for about an hour and a half in his hotel and gave him an account of the rocks and shoals on the road to free trade – plywood, lumber, ice cream and yoghurt, textiles, films, and now aircraft (it seems Air Canada is about to award a giant deal to Airbus in return for industrial goodies). This compilation is the agenda of U.S. grievances against us, the list of our sins that could doom the FTA. We are being targeted, I explained, by many special interests and many lobbyists. Gucci Gulch is getting very crowded.

April 7, 1988 Arthur Erickson gave a brilliant lecture at the Washington Design Center, and we then met at the embassy to discuss problems and delays in the construction of the new embassy. There is much evidence on the files of External Affairs to suggest that officials want to blame me and Arthur for cost overruns. Whenever they mention overspending, they cite "the ambassador's suite" as a cause. Malicious nonsense. The reference is to the floor of executive offices, not mine personally. Any overruns have nothing to do with any personal requirements of mine, as I will never occupy them. These memos will all be requested under the Access to Information Act and are no doubt designed for the readers of the *Globe and Mail.*

April 11, 1988 I called on Speaker Jim Wright[1] to request an invitation for Mulroney to speak to Congress. I was delighted by Wright's courtly and attentive manner, at his warm reaction, and at how he seemed unconscious of the clock. We talked about the timing of a speech on the first or second day of the visit. He studied his calendar, made phone calls, and discussed the specific details, such as whether to meet beforehand or after with the leadership, whether to meet both Houses at once or sequentially, and who among the leadership should be invited – name by name. This forty-minute conversation in his elegant office reminded me of my first (and only) call on his predecessor, Tip O'Neill, who received me for a moment or two as a petitioner in a large chamber containing about thirty beggars, all standing around, waiting their turn to ask for favours, as if in a medieval court – or a Boston backroom.

April 12, 1988 John Crosbie arrived this afternoon to meet with Clayton Yeutter. I met him at the airport for half an hour to discuss the current impasse on film. As expected, Crosbie was stormed by the Canadian media on the steps of the Trade office as we began our meeting. They were reacting – negatively, of course – to his freshly minted, marvellous remarks about the Canadian opponents of free trade – "CBC-type snivellers," he called them. "Toronto literati, fakirs, encyclopedia salesmen." Crosbie was very effective in his meeting with Yeutter, talking film and aircraft. Yeutter complained about alleged offsets in the Air Canada purchase of Airbus. Crosbie won the Americans over when he said, "As minister of transport I looked at this closely, and there was no hanky-panky. I wish there was,

[1] (b. 1922) Democratic Representative from Texas 1954–1988; House Majority Leader 1977–1987; Speaker of the House of Representatives 1987–1989.

because I don't like the French. I would like to do them one in the eye. They've given us a lot of trouble in Newfoundland."

I held a working dinner for Crosbie and the team from Ottawa in the evening – no Americans present. I drew a disturbing picture of the state of governance in Washington. No one is home in the White House. Congress is a battleground for special interests locked in permanent conflict. The administration increasingly acts like an agent for these special interests in international relations. It was essential to tread carefully in the months ahead. We already had a potential coalition of thirty or more senators opposing us in the free-trade vote and could not afford to add more.

Crosbie reacted emotionally. "If they don't want us, they can stuff it," he said. "Who is they?" I asked. I answered my own question. "There is no 'they.' 'They' are just a band of fragmented interests, represented by lobbyists. The issue is do we want the agreement or not. Obviously we do, because it helps to substitute laws and institutions for a political morass." "You're too worked up," he said. "Take a month off."

It's curious how people react to the realities of Washington. They don't want to accept the fact that it is a vast political battleground requiring the most calculating strategies and strictest self-discipline.

April 13, 1988 Sam Gibbons and Bill Frenzel came to breakfast at the Residence to meet Crosbie and fill him in on the bad state of affairs in Congress. They told him the same thing I told him last night. Maybe they should take a holiday too.

I had a difficult conversation with John Whitehead. I warned him of what we were hearing on the Hill – that if the White House vetoes the omnibus trade bill, there could be a bad Democratic backlash against the Canada-U.S. free-trade agreement. I told him of my conversation with the Democratic deputy whip, David Bonior,[1] an impressive, partisan congressman who put it to me succinctly – "If the president vetoes our trade bill, many Democrats will say, okay, you denied us our initiative, we'll deny you yours." So I found myself in the ridiculous position of trying to save the infamous omnibus trade bill. Thankfully, it has been defanged and there is little left in it to hurt Canada.

Whitehead was not at all receptive. "It's true that Shultz and I are totally opposed to the bill. It would be wrong to let bad legislation go through."

---

[1] (b. 1945) Democratic Representative from Michigan 1976–2002, a senior Democratic leader in Congress.

"But," I replied, "isn't it more important to pass our free-trade agreement than to veto a bill that means so little."

April 14, 1988 Just before briefing the National Defence College at the Sheraton chancery in the morning, I got an urgent phone call from Fred Hall, deputy assistant secretary at State. "I've got good news to tell you and then great news." "Wonderful," I said, in high expectation. "The good news is that the president agrees to have lunch with the prime minister at the White House on the second day of the visit. The great news is that Nancy wants to join them and invite Mila Mulroney as well. When Mrs. Reagan heard of the lunch, she said it would provide a wonderful occasion to show the world, before the visit of the president to Moscow, that Canada was America's closest friend."

April 15, 1988 Early morning meeting with Frank Carlucci today, my first since his elevation to defence secretary. He is a person of deep influence in the town. My purpose was to try to salvage our nuclear sub initiative.

He got my number one spiel: a U.S. refusal to co-operate on nuclear technology would be regarded as insulting and would pollute the defence atmosphere for many years, given that this is the most important Canadian defence initiative since NORAD. A refusal could be based on only one of two reasons or both: "You think we are not competent, or you want to monopolize the defence presence in the Arctic. Either would be objectionable to us."

"No," Frank said. "There's a third possibility. We could turn you down because we think the program is a bad one and is not in NATO's interests or that of Western defence." "That reason," I said, "would be no better. It would be equally condescending."

When I told him the French boat was very attractive to us, dropping the broadest possible hints of the direction of our thinking, he didn't seem to believe me. I left the meeting irritated and disappointed. Carlucci said he hadn't yet decided what position to take, but he is hard-boiled and not sympathetic to Canada.

April 16, 1988 Kay Graham was at her most gracious at the dinner party she gave tonight for Charles Adams,[1] an old Bostonian from the

[1] (1910–1999) President of the Raytheon Company 1948–1974; Chairman 1960–1975.

distinguished family. The usual crowd was in attendance: Joe Alsop, the Fritcheys, John Whitehead, the Bradleys, Evangeline, together with the Neys from New York, the Danforths, and about thirty others. Kay put me on her right, principally, I suspect, because she wanted to show Sally Quinn the correct protocol. Lots of talk about Afghanistan at our table among Whitehead, Bob Silvers[1] of the *NYR Books*, and Peter Reddaway.

Chatted with Andrea Mitchell about former Winnipegger Barbara Weidman's book on Ayn Rand, which I had suggested she read. She told me she now had but that Alan Greenspan was reluctant to discuss the book with her. He had glanced at it, but he doesn't seem to want to read it. She is obviously very attached to Greenspan and so is trying to better understand this rather incomprehensible side of his life. I told her about his first wife, Joan Mitchell from Winnipeg, whom I dated as an adolescent. She wondered why their marriage lasted so short a time. A very legitimate question for her. I couldn't explain it.

April 17, 1988 Attended a dinner for Lee Hamilton. The guests were rich and old Washington: Kay Graham again, the Cattos (rich, rich), Michael Strait[2] (former spy), Joan Bingham (newspaper heiress), Clayton Fritchey, and others. Hamilton was very pro-FTA and doubted very much that the Democrats would wreak any revenge against it were the president to veto the omnibus trade bill. Talked to a young, attractive historian, Michael Beschloss,[3] writing a book about Kennedy and Khrushchev. He told me he is reading the cables of Arnold Smith, then our ambassador in Moscow. "Weren't those the ones," I asked, "that always started off 'I told Khrushchev.'" "Yes," he replied, "but they are very good."

My Democratic hostess assured me that if the Democrats won, Lee Hamilton[4] would be secretary of state.

---

[1] (b. 1929) Associate Editor of *Harper's* magazine 1959–1963; Co-Editor of the *New York Review of Books* 1963 to present.

[2] (1916–2004) American magazine publisher, novelist, and a member of the prominent Whitney family. Deputy Chairman of the National Endowment for the Arts 1969–1977. In the 1930s Strait worked for the Soviet Union as part of a spy ring whose members included Donald Maclean, Guy Burgess, Kim Philby, and KGB recruiter Anthony Blunt.

[3] (b. 1955) Historian of the U.S. presidency. Author of *Mayday: Eisenhower, Khrushchev and the U-2 Affair* (1986).

[4] (b. 1931) Democratic Representative from Indiana 1965–1999.

April 18, 1988 The cornerstone plaque for the embassy ceremony arrived today, after a lot of badgering on our part. It reads that the prime minister laid this cornerstone to commemorate the friendship of the United States and Canada. The texts, of course, are in both English and French. The only problem: the United States is spelled with a hyphen.

April 20, 1988 Called on the Senate aristocrat, Jay Rockefeller from West Virginia, to pitch free trade. As I arrived for my meeting with him at 2 p.m., we crossed paths in the hall. A big man with a broad smile, he said, "I'll be with you in a minute, Mr. Ambassador." When he returned at 2:25, I told him the title of the book I will be writing on my dealings with the Congress: *I'll Be With You in a Minute, Mr. Ambassador*. Rockefeller did not smile.

I came loaded with facts about his state's big surplus with Canada, future plans of Hydro Ontario to buy more coal from his state, and all that. What I got back was, "I'm not sure . . . I don't know . . . the coal people are very upset about your electricity exports." "But you're a free-trader," I said to him. "No, I'm not," he replied. "I seem to recall you told me you were when I called on you last year." "No, no, I have a poor, weak state," he replied. Weak state, weak man, I thought to myself.

As the summit approaches, the PMO is fussing about the PM's friends being invited to the White House (five couples filling in the official delegate slots at the White House dinner, the rest for dancing afterwards) and the Shultz lunch at State. So I called Linda Faulker, White House social secretary, to ask her to expedite instructions to Chief of Protocol Lucky Roosevelt, to ensure that she invited Mulroney's list, not Canada's officials, to the State lunch. I'm not sure if there is some resistance here.

April 21, 1988 At a lunch I gave at the Residence for Barbara McDougall,[1] new minister of employment and immigration, I sat Fred Hall next to me. A political appointee, he is nice, inexperienced, and a little naive. I told him what I'd told Taft earlier: that a reasonable Canadian could suspect that the U.S. navy preferred we buy a French boat because if there was any trouble from a safety standpoint, it would not prejudice the U.S. program.

---

[1] (b. 1937) PC Member of Parliament for St. Paul's 1984–1993; Minister Responsible for the Status of Women 1986–1990; Minister of Employment and Immigration 1988–1991; Secretary of State for External Affairs 1991–1993.

When I told Hall that Taft strongly denied this, Hall literally began to choke. His face went red, and he seemed to have a spasm of some sort in his throat. Recovering, he said, "You hit the nail on the head. The navy does not want U.S. fingerprints on the Canadian boat." It was good to have confirmation of what seemed to be a far-out theory.

In the evening we attended the White House Correspondents' dinner, as a guest of Judith Miller, *New York Times* deputy bureau chief. Every year this event gets sillier. After a coarse monologue by a Russian émigré comedian, we had some vintage Reagan. "America is a wonderful land," he said, "and unique. You know a person cannot become a Frenchman and he can't become a Greek, even if he lives there. But anyone can become an American."

The French ambassador, the civilized Bobby de Margerie, flushed with surprise and annoyance. "Four million Frenchmen have been naturalized. That's equivalent to twenty million Americans. Should I try to get this point through to the president?" he asked me. "Save it for the next one," I told him.

As I entered the ballroom of the Washington Hilton, I bumped into Barbara McDougall, and as we were chatting, Congressman Jim Scheuer of New York approached. "Meet a great friend of Canada," I said (standard line), "very helpful on acid rain." "I have a solution to the acid rain problem," he said, "but when I tell people from Canada, they don't agree." "Well, what is it?" I asked.

"Your nine counties should join the U.S.," he replied. "Then you'd have lots of congressmen and senators, and we could join in doing something about the problem."

These remarks left Barbara reeling.

April 22, 1988 Called on John Negroponte at the White House (Colin Powell is in Moscow) to make a *démarche* about submarines. Mulroney met yesterday with officials and stiffened the already stiff instructions I wrote for myself. He wanted me to add that a U.S. negative on transfer of the technology would be a crippling blow to him personally, his senior ministers, and his government.

In the talking points I left with Negroponte, I asked a specific question: did the United States want a partner in the north – or a protectorate? I added that never before in my experience had Canada been treated with such condescension by the United States.

Meanwhile, Negroponte asked a very pointed question: how could we avoid putting the president in the embarrassing position of asking Congress to authorize a transfer of technology if this was unnecessary, that is, if we bought French. We explored the idea that if the president could say yes in the next few days, we could let the United States know our choice before the drop-dead day for the president's notifying Congress, around May 15.

We had a quiet dinner at Evangeline Bruce's with Washington socialite Oatsie Charles and an English bookseller, Saumarez Smith,[1] who owns a smart bookstore in Mayfair. He knows everybody alive and dead. I told Evangeline hers was the most beautiful house in Georgetown, indeed in Washington. Oatsie muttered, how would I know?

April 23, 1988 At Jim Schlesinger's for a buffet, along with the Brzezinskis, the de Borchgraves, and others, including Fritz Kraemer,[2] Kissinger's mentor. He is a remarkable man of eighty, vigorous in mind, strong in experience, monocle dropping, intellectually intimidating. He said he has not seen Kissinger since 1976, when he walked out of the secretary of state's office. He will not talk to the man.

According to Kraemer, Kissinger's strong personal sense of vulnerability causes him to make compromises that betray his conservative principles. Kraemer said he heard Kissinger refer to Dobrynin as Anatoly. He asked Kissinger how he could do this. "I had no choice," Kissinger said. "Dobrynin was ill, so I went to his bedside to see him. Dobrynin said, 'We know each other so well we must call each other by our first names.' How could I refuse?" "But," Kraemer said to Kissinger, "don't you understand, you talk to him because of your office and his. You can't personalize it. You are a state representative dealing with another state representative. You violate the very nature of the relationship if you indulge in the Anatoly-Henry routine."

"Would you see him again?" I asked. "No," he replied. "If I were to lunch with him, he would tell everyone the next day, and it would be as if I was endorsing his views."

April 24, 1988 At midday the boss called. He wanted a rundown on progress in preparing for the summit, and I gave him a frank assessment. On submarines he told me I could assure the White House that the president

[1] John Saumarez Smith. (b. 1954) Has been running the Heywood Hill bookstore in London since 1974.

[2] (1908–2003) Senior Civilian Adviser to the U.S. Army Chief of Staff in the Pentagon from the 1950s to the late 1970s.

wouldn't have to lift a finger unnecessarily, that his political responsibility would not be engaged without cause, his credibility would not be wasted. I passed this on immediately to the NSC.

I informed Mulroney that I had persuaded Erickson to come back from Asia to attend the embassy opening. Mulroney was pleased. "Trudeau was right," he said, "to appoint Erickson. He was right to ignore the bureaucrats' advice." "You saved the building," I told him. "Clark told Shultz we were putting it on hold, but you saved it."

He asked me if I could find out if Reagan knew Henry Fonda well. "I want to tell Reagan that the 'Golden Pond' in Massachusetts is dead, thanks to acid rain." My guess was that he didn't like Fonda, certainly not his daughter, but I promised to investigate. He also wanted any and all material relating to Dukakis and acid rain.

We talked a bit about whether the congressional chamber would be full and whether the right people would be there. He is absolutely right to be worried about the media preoccupation with these points. The CBC has already asked me who will be there. I assured him I'd personally touch base with key senators – Kennedy, Moynihan, Bradley, and others.

Late in the evening I began to brood about the PM's speech. At 1 a.m. I picked up a book by Robertson Davies and found a good quote: "Sometimes when I think of the great world family of English-speaking peoples, I think of Canada as the daughter who stayed at home." From there I took off with three pages of noble prose, but I know the PM won't use it. His speech writer is a sausage-maker who will slice my piece into little bits, little morsels, one following the other, beaded together but with no unity.

April 25, 1988 A day of intense activities preparing for tomorrow's summit.

I started with breakfast with Jeffrey Simpson at the Metropolitan Club. I was enhanced in Simpson's eyes because of Bill Safire's word column in Sunday's *New York Times*. Safire wrote about meeting me at an antique book dealer's fair and my asking about the origins of the phrase "the level playing field," so extraordinarily in vogue these days. (Safire failed miserably to throw light on its origins.)

There is some good news. Valenti is finally supporting the film compromise worked out by Shortliffe in Ottawa and the Gulf and Western gang. We've had to back off a lot, but we also got something – a separate Canadian market. This is an achievement, but William Randolph Hearst's *Toronto*

Star will assuredly accuse Mulroney of a sell-out. This in spite of the fact that the *Star*'s beloved Liberals achieved nothing in this field over a twenty-year period.

I've been working continually on the PM's congressional speech and trying to keep the sausage-makers at bay. I have suggested a passage praising the only other Canadian prime minister who spoke to Congress: Pierre Elliott Trudeau, for his role in bringing about unity in Canada. The PM will gain himself a lot of credit here and in Canada, I said, if he gives some credit to Trudeau for his accomplishments.

Even the submarine file is looking better, and we may get a green light tomorrow.

The PM is adamant that he is going to press Reagan at their lunch on Wednesday (when Nancy and Mila are present), and on every other occasion, to agree to an acid rain treaty. Burney, Taylor, and Campbell met this afternoon and were concerned that the United States not be taken by surprise. They suggested I call Colin Powell and let him know about the prime minister's plans so as to avoid the impression that we were not candid and misled them. Mulroney is convinced the issues have not been fairly put to Reagan. Maybe he is right. I got through to Powell in the late evening and left him an angry man. He was particularly irritated at the notion that Reagan was holding back because officials had not explained the issue clearly to him.

The events of the day reflect Mulroney's personality well. He has been remarkably determined to convince Reagan to do something on acid rain. Going back to his time as president of the Iron Ore Company of Canada, he is convinced decisions are made in head office. He believes Reagan will come through for him. He is alone in this view. The question is, is there a head office in this country at this time?

April 26, 1988 The day of the prime minister's arrival and a day of surprises, notwithstanding months of meticulous planning. While we sat in my office going over names for the embassy cornerstone ceremony, Glen Bullard rushed in to say that the Pennsylvania Avenue Development Corporation had just cancelled the ceremony. Great panic all around, diplomatic manoeuvres abound, the chairman of the commission is stroked, and it is back on. I called Moynihan, Chafee, Bradley, Simpson, Hatfield, Warner, and others to try to get a good turnout. I pitched Carter Brown and lined up a congressional crowd. Very hard slogging. The text of the PM's congressional speech arrived. He didn't use a word of my fine prose, nor my words in praise of Trudeau.

As the day wore on, I sensed trouble developing. The *Washington Post* Canadian correspondent, the mean man Herb Denton, filed a piece, based on the interview he and other U.S. journalists had with Mulroney yesterday, reporting that he had said he was disappointed with Reagan's failure to fulfill promises to curb acid rain pollution. Mulroney proclaimed, however, that Dukakis and even Jackson would have a lot to say about acid rain, as would Bush. In the afternoon Cobb was in a rage, yelling about Mulroney's terrible conduct in saying such things. He told me Baker, Shultz, and Powell were bouncing off the wall. I discounted a lot of this as the usual Cobb overreaction. Nevertheless, I reported this to Ottawa just before Mulroney got on the plane for Washington.

I was wrong. When I met Shultz at the reflecting pool to take the helicopter to Andrews airfield, he was beside himself. "This," he said, "is totally unacceptable behaviour on the part of Mulroney. He is interfering in our political campaign. His references to Dukakis and Jackson are outrageous. This is gross misbehaviour. I'm going to tell your prime minister that if that's the way he intends to behave down here, he should not get off the plane. He should go right home. Howard Baker is upset, the president is upset, everyone is upset." Shultz kept up this tirade all the time we were in the helicopter and did so in the presence of his wife, Sondra, Lucky Roosevelt, and U.S. officials.

I said a few times, "I haven't seen the transcript, wait till you see the transcript, remember the bumper sticker 'I don't believe anything I read in the *Washington Post*.'" It was useless.

When Mulroney landed, Shultz repeated his remarks in the helicopter while flying into town with him. The prime minister, prepared, pulled out a transcript. Shultz spent several minutes going through them line by line, and it was evident that Mulroney didn't make the remarks attributed to him about Reagan – in fact, he praised Reagan – and the context of his words about the Democrats was totally changed. Shultz became contrite and indeed sheepish. He said he would go over these remarks with Baker in the morning, but everything looked okay.

Mulroney called me and Derek into his room later in the evening to express his irritation at Shultz's behaviour. The later in the evening it got, the madder he got. I promised to pass the word in high circles that he was upset because he wasn't given the benefit of the doubt. What a start to an official visit.

April 27, 1988 I got up at 6:30 and – this wasn't easy – contacted Howard Baker, Colin Powell, Roz Ridgway, and John Negroponte and conveyed the message that "Mulroney was not amused." However, by the time the welcome ceremony kicked off at 10 a.m., everyone was in a sunny mood, matching the temperate, sunny day. Mulroney's opening remarks on the White House lawn used humour, high rhetoric, light-heartedness, and self-deprecation, all to great effect. He was in top form.

At the outset of the official discussions in the White House, the talk focused on the political situation in Canada. Mulroney spoke of the Senate, stating that he had several options, including "pulling the plug" politically. After hearing Mulroney speak critically of "the socialists," Reagan interjected. "You're lucky your socialists call themselves socialists. Ours call themselves Democrats."

Mulroney made a great emotional pitch for an acid rain accord. He described the acid rain problem as "tarnishing an otherwise impeccable relationship." "A treaty is inevitable, so do it with me, not my successors" was his *cri de coeur*. He was persuasive, and all at the table seemed taken aback. The president agreed, in effect, to look at it again.

After the meeting Howard Baker and Colin Powell told me that it was remarkable how Mulroney could move the president. We saw this clearly at today's meeting when the president told him that the United States would agree to request a transfer of technology on nuclear subs if we decided to buy British. This was an astonishing development. Reagan's commitment ran heavily against the military's advice, as well as that of the Department of Energy. We have also achieved something from the United States on Arctic sovereignty. Who can reasonably say, in the light of this, that summitry is not useful or that good personal chemistry doesn't count?

The answer is, of course, that the media can say it and do. Indeed, they have created the fiction that on Arctic sovereignty the two sides agreed to disagree. The truth is that Mulroney used summitry to extract the greatest concessions we have achieved from the United States on Arctic sovereignty.

Mulroney was in superb form before a packed Congress. He delivered his speech in a brilliant manner, filling the chamber with his huge personality. Senator Wirth told me it was the best speech he had heard in the chamber given by a foreigner in the last ten years. Moynihan went even further. At least a dozen senators and congressmen came up to me after to praise his remarks, a point I stressed on *The Journal*, responding to a hostile

CBC interviewer. The meeting with congressional representatives again reflected Mulroney at his best, politician-to-politician style.

The only disappointment was the White House dinner – to me but not to the PM or Mila, who seemed pleased. It wasn't really an A-list, but more importantly, there was once again no Canadian connection, no Canadian content. Just some of Nancy's "W" friends – the usual Hollywood and media performers – and no businessmen other than Mulroney's friends (Ross Johnson and Paul Desmarais and wives). I saw someone who looked like Red Skelton. It was Red Skelton.

In the exchange of toasts, Mulroney spoke movingly and admiringly of Reagan and brought tears to Nancy's eyes.

April 28, 1988 The embassy cornerstone ceremony was a glorious affair. The clouds opened and the sun beamed down. Almost everyone I buttonholed managed to show, including Senators Moynihan, Evans, Stafford, Warner, Lugar, and more. Tom Foley also came, as did Bill Webster, Byron White,[1] Chief Justice Burger, Bill Sessions,[2] and Bill Verity.[3] In my opening remarks at the outdoor podium, I welcomed all the guests and saluted Moynihan and Howard Baker for their support, reminding Baker that he referred to the building as being the "signature of Canada" on America's most important street. Mulroney followed and handled the crowd of around three hundred superbly. He poured schmaltz on "the two unofficial leaders of Washington" sitting in the front row: Kay Graham and Bob Strauss. Kay's face lit up like a bonfire. She looked just like a schoolgirl whose father had presented her with a pony on her birthday. Mulroney, whose remarks were cleverly crafted by Len Legault, departed from his text and blew some hyperbole my way. I was intoxicated. He called me one of Canada's greatest public servants. I was very moved and so was Sondra, who bent over to kiss me as we both sat on the dais. Erickson, who flew in from Hong Kong, was surrounded by admirers, while Bush and Mulroney worked the crowd.

I am not sure what inspired Mulroney's eloquence about me. It was a repeat of what he told the U.S. reporters who interviewed him last weekend

[1] (1917–2002) Former NFL running back. Associate Justice of the Supreme Court of the United States 1962–1993.

[2] (b. 1930) Director of the FBI 1987–1993.

[3] (b. 1917) U.S. administrator and steel industrialist. Secretary of Commerce 1987–1989.

prior to his departure. Among the half-dozen was Herb Denton of the *Post*, who asked him if the reason why there was no return entertainment during the visit was to avoid embarrassment. Mulroney angrily denied this and went on to praise me, saying I rank with the "finest ambassador any country has ever had represent them." I loved it.

Denton was not satisfied with this and so made a specific reference to the "slap" incident, asserting that Sondra had upset social Washington.

Mulroney shot back, "No, I don't think Mrs. Gotlieb tarnished Canada's image [Denton's words]. I think Mrs. Gotlieb, over the years, has done a tremendous job herself in helping promote Canada's interests. It happens that this was the kind of incident that can occur in the very stressful and demanding life of someone called upon to fulfill these important functions. My responsibility as prime minister is to judge what is important for Canada's interests and what is not important. And if I, as prime minister and leader of the Progressive Conservative Party, am unable to see beyond personal incidents, regrettable though they may be, that could happen to all of us, then I'm not capable of dealing with the large issues and am directed by the small ones. And I made the decision that night that Allan Gotlieb would stay in Washington and that there was nothing at all that prevented him from continuing to serve as effectively and as honourably, as well as he has for such a long period of time." He continued, "So, look it, I wish I could tell you that none of us ever make mistakes, but I can't say that about myself, and I suppose I can't say it about too many others. I wish that incident had not happened. It wasn't pleasant for Mrs. Gotlieb, for the young lady involved, who was also a most effective public servant of Canada, and for myself – it wasn't the highlight of my political career. But you know, in life, these things happen. Small things sometimes take on undue importance."

At the meeting with the senators that followed the embassy event, Mulroney continued to be in top form. Some twenty-five came into the chamber to see him, after his tête-à-tête with Majority Leader Byrd. He handled Byrd, our greatest enemy in the Senate on the environment, masterfully, telling him we would never put his coal miners out of work. He even praised Byrd as a brilliant politician. With the senators as a group, Mulroney handled himself with gusto and style. Again he stated that there would be a treaty between us to reduce acid rain. The question was would it be with him or his successor. The discussions on the free-trade agreement were very muted, and he got a standing ovation. Then, in a ceremonial gesture, Byrd led him onto the floor of the Senate and presented him.

At the reflecting pool waiting for Mulroney to arrive for his official departure, I said to Shultz that perhaps there was a chance of progress on acid rain now, given Mitchell's Senate leadership aspirations and his efforts to find a compromise with Simpson's bill. Shultz responded, "You mean it might be easier than a Middle East settlement?" "I wouldn't exaggerate the prospects," I shot back. "But why don't you get in touch with Mitchell and attempt to work out a compromise approach?" Shultz was intrigued by the idea. This is new; up to now his interest has, I think, been more or less pro forma.

A great day for Mulroney.

April 29, 1988 Up at dawn to give an interview to *Canada AM*. I'm feeling good, since the PM seemed so pleased with his visit. He called me last night and was full of unvarnished praise.

I am trying to galvanize the acid rain players by urging them to take some action and putting them in touch with each other. I asked George Mitchell to make a statement on what Mulroney had done to move things forward on the issue. He did so immediately. "In his eloquent address to the joint meeting of Congress, and in private meetings as well, Prime Minister Mulroney made a forceful, effective, and persuasive presentation on the need for acid rain controls. I know first-hand that he made a powerful impression on many members of Congress . . ." I also urged Mitchell to call on Shultz soon. Shultz, I told him, may believe he can get credit for a great achievement here. He's a broker. Mitchell agreed to write to him.

I then contacted John Whitehead and suggested he get himself briefed on a really major development this week: a statement by the newly appointed director of the National Acid Rain Precipitation Program. When asked about the agency's recent report that most lakes in the northeast United States were not likely to become more acidic in the near future, he said, "I will not subscribe to that statement at this time." Bingo. The biggest break we've had in a long time. I said to John, "There goes the scientific foundation for your political stance on acid rain."

Dingell, the great champion of the report, didn't even have the courtesy to come and hear Mulroney when he addressed Congress or when invited by Jim Wright to meet with him afterwards.

April 30, 1988 Peter Calamai's article in the *Ottawa Citizen* on the new embassy ceremony carries the headline "Homeless Displaced by New Embassy." He writes about the plight of the homeless, allegedly displaced by the Canadian government. He makes no mention of the architecture, the symbolism, the honour, or Erickson's achievement. "While the government ate croissants, the poor roamed nearby."

Wrong – it was in 1979 that a hostel on the site was torn down, not 1988, and it was under the Trudeau regime, not Mulroney's. A sickening example of how Canadians put down their own, how they denigrate achievement. Norma Greenaway of the Canadian Press asked me, "Doesn't the embassy, so close to Congress and facing it, suggest subordination and cringing before the Congress?" Sick.

May 1, 1998 In Dallas Sondra and I dined on catfish at Bob Strauss's condo in the huge, luxurious, and somewhat empty new building owned by his son Rock. This was actually the first time in my life that I ate catfish. I've somehow managed not to do so until now. For years I've listened to Bob eulogize these ghastly things. I got through it by drowning it with ketchup.

At the Ambassadors' Ball we marched in first under the banner of the Canadian flag and sat with the mayor, Annette Strauss, her husband, Ted (Bob's brother and sort of clone), and Bob and Helen. I say clone because he has Bob's sense of humour.

"You're Bob's brother," I said on meeting him. "No," he replied, "he's mine. I hear you had catfish last night at his place." "Yes," I replied. "Well, I hope you drowned it in ketchup."

The evening went down easily. We listened to the Three Hot Tamales singing old rock songs.

May 3, 1988 Item in the *Washington Post* gossip column. At the annual Press Club dinner (Canada's Gridiron) last Saturday in Ottawa, Mulroney got a big laugh when he said that on his recent trip to Washington, "there was no flap at the embassy. But then, there was no dinner." This hurts us a lot.

May 4, 1988 Lunched the other day at the Metropolitan Club with David Acheson, Dean's son. I asked him why Dean seemed so out of sympathy with Lester Pearson in his later years. I found this surprising, given Acheson's long friendship with Hume Wrong and Pearson and his Canadian origins. David said his father had one prominent quality: he found it easier to get along with enemies than friends. His father became very unhappy if a friend only agreed with him 80 per cent, rather than 100 per cent. Friends had to be completely onside. This is why Acheson liked Truman so much. He was always with him, all the way. Pearson, on the other hand, had doubts about U.S. foreign policy, especially in Vietnam. Hence the discord. Dean always thought that at heart Canadians were neutralists. I wonder why he thought that.

May 5, 1988 I have been growing rather pessimistic this week about the progress of events on the Hill. The odds on approval of our free-trade agreement have gone from about sixty-forty to fifty-fifty, notwithstanding the fact that we have got the film issue out of the way. Ottawa is about to make a decision on Airbus that will be badly received in Washington (Boeing territory) and Missouri (MacDonald-Douglas country). There's a strong belief that offsets were a condition of the deal, offsets that run counter to the GATT procurement code. Maybe yes, maybe no, but the perception remains strong. Four senatorial votes are at stake.

May 9, 1988 Colourful ceremony on the lawn in front of the Pentagon for retiring NATO Secretary-General Peter Carrington.[1] Beautiful sunny day. I was the senior NATO ambassador. God, I feel old. Found him now as I always did: supremely confident, effortlessly superior, sardonic, wondrous in the perfection of his manners, deeply and perpetually ironic, faintly suggesting at all times distance, remoteness, and a certain condescension towards one and all. Not much of a speaker, but he did tell one good story. To the suggestion that he would be welcomed back to NATO, he recounted: George V and Queen Mary visited a naval installation at Bournemouth, and the presiding admiral urged the King to go down in a submarine, not a terribly safe experience at that time. The Queen was reluctant about it, but the King wanted to go. The sub went down, and it stayed submerged as the Queen and admiral waited on shore. After a while the imperious lady said, "If His Majesty does not come up again, I shall be very disappointed."

[1] (b. 1919) British Foreign Secretary 1979–1982; Secretary-General of NATO 1984–1988.

May 10, 1988 Peter Carrington ceremony at the White House. Some words and a medal hung on the peer. We were in a small room in the White House, about thirty invited guests, including the NATO ambassadors and in the rear a slew of TV cameras.

After the short ceremony, as the president is leaving through the front door into the hall, a voice behind the camera booms. "Mr. President, have you ruled out pardoning Poindexter and North?" The president stops, turns, and says vigorously, "No. Not me."

This little event sort of sums up America. Obsessed with its own agenda. Who indeed is Carrington? What is Carrington? What happened to good manners? To borrow a phrase Rowly Evans used last week, this country is experiencing a catastrophic failure of discipline.

We attended a dinner given by the Shultzes for Carrington and his wife. I sat beside Obie Shultz, who said, "George and I agree that you and Sondra are the best ambassadorial couple in Washington. We like you the best of all the ambassadors here." I was deeply moved and touched her hand. "You know, it hasn't been an easy time for the Gotliebs." She replied, "No, and it hasn't been an easy time for the Shultzes."

May 12, 1988 Shultz says to me, "I'm getting into the acid rain files. I'm really getting into the subject. But I'm not ready to meet yet." This is more encouraging than the conversation I had earlier this week with Lee Thomas of the EPA, who confided to me, "I can't talk about it. It's too sensitive. I really wanted to say in the White House when Mulroney was there that we can't agree to a Canada-U.S. acid rain accord, because then we would have to agree to domestic control legislation, and we can't." I found this statement unbelievable, except I could believe it coming from him.

May 13, 1988 Working closely with key officers of the embassy, we have completed our assessment of the free-trade vote. Based on my discussions today with Peter McPherson, Strauss, Bentsen, and Yeutter, plus heavy input from Hill staffers and lobbyists, we have concluded that prospects for success are strengthening. Lots of worrying fixes in the making, but in all probability negative votes can be contained.

I put the assessment into a highly restricted letter to Clark. Votes in the Finance Committee are critical. If the agreement is voted down there, the game is over. Four positive votes are certain – Moynihan, Packwood, Chafee, and Bradley; a half-dozen others seem probable – Matsunaga, Roth,

Bentsen, Dole, Riegle, and Armstrong. Undecided include Durenberger (currently incensed about ice cream and yoghurt), Rockefeller (thinks only about coal), Danforth (might be influenced by Airbus), Heinz (steel and textiles), and Pryor (yoghurt again). Four senators in the committee must for the moment be counted in the negative columns: Baucus, Mitchell, Wallop, and Boren. Their ranks could be augmented from among the thirty-nine senators who told the president the Canadian textile program jeopardizes the agreement. The decision on Airbus could turn Danforth into an opponent and also undermine Packwood's support. It would not take very much to get a negative vote against the agreement.

Conclusion one: "We are facing a highly unstable situation demanding extreme prudence and discretion on our part. Actions that in normal times would go unnoticed or be taken to dispute settlement can rapidly become issues on which votes depend. Logic, law, and negotiating history count for little. Politics is all."

Conclusion two: "We must do everything we can that might help the approval process. More important still, we must do nothing we can avoid doing that might hinder it. Otherwise the FTA implementing bill may be defeated outright. The up-or-down vote may be seriously delayed; or the bill may contain so many fixes in response to Canadian actions as to make it unacceptable to Canada. If this be pessimism, it is hard-earned pessimism that has been bought and paid for many times during my years in Washington."

May 17, 1988 Spent most of the day chasing people on the Hill. The Senate Finance Committee and House Ways and Means are considering their "non-markup" of the bill. Fixes, tricks, manoeuvres, and skulduggery are the order of the day. A lobster fix for Mitchell and a potato fix too. Shabby dealings. You want a favour? Sure, no problem. Just do this for me.

The worst development is a move by eminent Senator Bentsen to transfer some wide-ranging retaliating language from his beloved, ill-fated omnibus trade bill and stick it in the free-trade bill. The effect would be an omnibus trade bill directed against Canada – a special retaliatory clause devoted against us if we misbehave.

May 18, 1988 The Bentsen manoeuvre continues to be the target of my lobbying. I spoke to Moynihan, Packwood, and others and got them onside. The result was Bentsen didn't move. He knew he was outvoted.

(Packwood went into the Finance Committee with five proxies against Bentsen.) Amazingly, we conducted a successful lobbying operation against one of the most powerful senators in the United States!

May 19, 1988 I received a blast from Simon Reisman. "You don't know how to deal with these goddamn Americans. The Baucus-Danforth language is completely unacceptable.[1] The last thing I will have to do here is make a recommendation to Mulroney on how to proceed. I may recommend against signature, and I'll go public. I know you don't want to stand up to the Americans. I know how to deal with them."

Simon, in his last days with the government, hasn't yet decided, I would guess, whether he wants to go down in history as the builder of a great agreement or the wrecker of a bad one.

May 20, 1988 I spent the day trying to calm the waters in Ottawa. Everyone is panicking. A multiplicity of channels has been opened up – Crosbie and Yeutter, Wilson and Baker, Ritchie and Holmer – all, no doubt, carrying different messages, or at least messages with different meanings. The Congress has left us with a half-dozen fixes: the bad Mitchell lobster regulation, the meaningless Mitchell potato proposal, the unilateral plywood solution, the "override" problem (does federal law prevail over all previous laws or not?), and the Baucus-Danforth language. A few of these are reversible, and a few may not be. I urged Ottawa not to paint ourselves into a corner.

May 22, 1988 It's a brilliant Sunday, and the house has never looked more beautiful, with our new pink rug installed in the living room and our green glass antique birdcage dominating the far end of the room. The garden is bursting with roses of all colours, and all the other spring flowers are blossoming. We had thirty-six for Sunday brunch, almost all the people we like – the Brinkleys, Strausses, Lehrers, Schlesingers, Freedbergs, Morrises, Susan Mary Alsop, Evangeline Bruce, Bobby de Margerie, Elizabeth Drew, Happy Rockefeller.

Everyone is talking about the Russians, the Russians, the Russians. The

---

[1] The Baucus-Danforth formula, aimed at protecting U.S. workers from the impact of the Canada-U.S. free-trade agreement, provided for trade measures against Canada that would not have been in effect against other countries. It would thus have been discriminatory against Canada.

Washington Post today is *Pravda* from cover to cover. Why the big obsession? I asked a couple of the guests. It's obvious, they said. The Soviet Union is the only country in the world with the capacity to destroy us.

May 24, 1988 The Governor General and her husband, Maurice, arrived this morning on a "private" trip to Washington and are staying with us. Horrid time for a visit. But one benefit has been that I have spurred and spooked and provoked Glen Bullard to make habitable the two guest bedrooms they are about to occupy – paint, new mattresses, clean carpets. We met them at Andrews Air Force Base, where their Challenger arrived, and arranged to get to the Residence just before the arrival of the twenty-four guests we asked for lunch. It's one of these late-spring broiler days in Washington, but we ate outside anyway – four tables of six on the upper terrace. We got out an exceptionally good group – Charlie Wick, Gilbert Grosvenor,[1] Sandra Day O'Connor, Jim Schlesinger, John Negroponte, Bill and Ann Nitze, Will and Julia Taft, Susan Mary Alsop, Tom and Joan Braden, and more. We let the two Excellencies host their own tables. In the evening we took them to Germaine's eatery with a few embassy officers.

Hell is breaking loose on the Hill as the House Ways and Means and Senate Finance Committee begin conferencing on the free-trade bill. I've been very frustrated trying to figure out what I can do to try to dilute the Baucus-Danforth "administrative" language, having failed to get USTR to acknowledge that they buggered things up by agreeing to it in the first place. On the House side, Gibbons and Frenzel – known in the administration, I am told, as the second and third Canadian ambassadors – will help, but the Senate is also a key problem.

I decided to contact Bradley again, because he may be the only one with the sense of commitment or the mental equipment to help us. I spent about a quarter of an hour explaining specifically in what manner the Baucus-Danforth formula went beyond existing U.S. trade law. I thought I convinced him. A half-hour later he called back, and we went over the issue once again. He doubted our concerns were all that well founded. But by the end of the discussion he said, "Okay, I've got it, I'll go to bat over this." I learned later that he circulated a memo to his colleagues on the Finance Committee criticizing the formula.

---

[1] Gilbert M. Grosvenor (b. 1931) Became Editor of *National Geographic* in 1970. President of the National Geographic Society 1980–1996; Chairman 1987 to present.

May 25, 1988 I remind myself to tell Glen Bullard tomorrow about His Excellency Maurice Sauvé's parting shot at the goodbye scene at the Residence. "You have no cold water in the bathroom of the bedroom I occupied. The water was so hot I haven't had a bath in two days. I'm looking forward to having one when I get home."

May 26, 1988 Started today with an early breakfast at the chancery, briefing an all-party group of miffed Canadian senators visiting Washington on a fact-finding (that is, trouble-making) tour related to the agreement. Miffed because no one at the embassy greeted them when they arrived at the chancery (I was in Chicago). The Liberals were all chanting the same refrain: protectionism is waning, we don't need a free-trade agreement to protect ourselves, the problem is not with Congress but with the administration, and on and on (inspired, it seems, by their interview with Julius Katz).[1] I'm glad they raised these canards, as it allowed me to go into full flight and expose them for the nonsense they are.

I flew with the Governor General on her aircraft to Ottawa before going on to Montreal for a speaking engagement. I talked to Mme. Sauvé extensively about the political scene in Canada, submarines, free trade, appointments. She is a sharp person, quite quick, somewhat opinionated, no fool. I never left any subject with any sense that there was more to be said, discussed, or understood. Moreover, she has the appearance of graciousness, of being a grande dame, but in truth, I think she is not.

On arrival at noon, I went to the Pearson Building, to see the prototypes of the furniture designed by Erickson for the new chancery's executive floor. External has held up approval for some time, finding an enormous amount of fault with them, especially the dining room tables, which they considered too low, slightly tipsy, and so on. Erickson had already agreed to correct these problems, but I was not prepared for what I saw. The chairs and tables were elegant and handsome, made of beautifully designed chrome and glass. I urged the department to move full steam ahead. This furniture will look cool and splendid in the glass-enclosed, light-saturated offices of the new building.

My stay in Montreal was punctuated by strident, anxious calls from

---

[1] (1926–2000) Trade policy specialist and State Department negotiator. Chairman of the Government Research Corporation in Washington 1987–1989; Deputy U.S. Trade Representative with rank of Ambassador 1989–1993.

Washington and Ottawa. The experts in Ottawa have decided that the Baucus-Danforth formula is unacceptable and want me to meet with Baker, Yeutter, and Strauss to tell them so. I replied that, thanks to the embassy, the language had been brought into complete conformity with the existing law. But I undertook to do my best. I got hold of Yeutter and gave him an aggressive sell. All I got back was that the formula was no big deal, nothing really. Arguing with Yeutter is, as Crosbie says, like pissing on a duck. It just washes off.

May 27, 1988 Peter McPherson called me at 7:15 a.m. at the Ritz-Carlton, waking me after a terrible night's sleep. I told him a heavy tale about Baucus-Danforth and how upset the cabinet was, how much more difficult it would now be to get approval in Canada. He said he'd talk to Baker right away but commented that Yeutter and the administration had both committed themselves to a difficult position for us, and they didn't really know what more they could do. This was followed a half-hour later by a call from Jim Baker himself, and I gave him an even heavier sell.

I told Baker of my call yesterday to Clayton and how he whitewashed their deal with Baucus, saying, in essence, it was a nothing-burger (borrowing a phrase from the vocabulary of Anne Gorsuch about acid rain).

Baker's comment was quick, sharp, and right on. "I know what you're saying," he interjected. "It's a nothing-burger in the U.S., but it's a Big Mac in Canada."

May 28, 1988 Back in Washington for the Memorial Day long weekend, feeling ever so glad that we have no commitments over the weekend and can relax by the pool in what promises to be a broiling few days. However, we got a last-minute invitation to have dinner at the Brzezinskis at their home in MacLean, with Jim and Rachel Schlesinger and another couple. It was one of those rare informal Washington evenings when we sat around outside, drank a lot, discussed the world, and let our hair, and our guard, down. Zbig and Jim, two of the best minds in Washington, expressed much misgiving about the theatre, or circus, going on in Moscow at this very time. It was strange to sit there and all agree that "the Cold War is over." What they see clearly, however, and what most Americans do not, is that the two countries remain adversaries and competitors in many ways, and if Gorbachev succeeds, the Soviet Union could become an even more powerful adversary.

June 1, 1988 This morning, while I was briefing John Crosbie on the congressional "fixes" – lobster, plywood, and the Baucus formula – Crosbie said, "I've got to go, we've got an emergency." "What kind?" I asked. "Film," he replied. "We're being pushed around by the bully boys."

Apparently, the deal blew up in the past twenty-four hours because the Gulf and Western negotiators refused to agree to a licensing provision. They said it was a double-cross on our part, and the deal was off. I told Campbell and Shannon that there was no such licensing provision in the deal struck during the negotiations. It could therefore be seen as a double-cross. Shannon didn't agree and suggested I put pressure on the administration to accept it.

I reached Burney with only an hour to go before Flora's bill was to be introduced in Parliament and a press conference convened. I told him if this film deal collapsed in these circumstances, we would have a revolt on the Hill, probably counter-retaliation, and then no FTA. I quoted him a comment from Treasury and USTR officials to that effect. Derek said, "We've got an impossible situation. The bill is to be tabled in an hour. Clark, Mazankowski, and others are all supporting Flora. Cancelling it could be disastrous." I said, "Yes, but losing the free-trade agreement will be a far bigger disaster."

As I hung up, I figured it was all over except the big disaster. But ten minutes later I got a phone call from the PM, who was with Maz and Burney. Mulroney asked, "Tell me if you think the administration can handle the Congress on this issue, and if not, what is likely to happen." I told him in a half-dozen sentences. The conversation lasted less than five minutes.

Back at the office in mid-afternoon, I learned rather casually from an officer in External that the tabling and news conference had been postponed. Also that Glen Shortliffe, now deputy minister of transport, was mandated to negotiate these issues and not Flora's people. That Flora threatened to resign (again).

Thus did we come within a whisker of selling the interests of Canadians downstream in order to line the pockets of a few Canadian distributors.

June 3, 1988 Lunched with Norman Webster, editor-in-chief of the *Globe and Mail*, and an editorial colleague of his. We talked mostly free trade, and they pressed me for an opinion on what would happen if Canada backed off the FTA. I painted a dark picture. I said the politics of free trade in North America are as follows: only Canada could propose a FTA; only the United States could reject it.

At the opening Stratford performance of *My Fair Lady* in Niagara-on-the-Lake, where we are guests of honour, we sat with the Petersons, Frums, and our host, the chairman of Mutual Life Insurance, and saw many faces from the past – and present.

Watching David Peterson was an experience. His magnetism was extraordinary. For each and all, he gave some greeting or comment that seemed intimate or amusing. He has vivacity and vitality, and when he talks to someone, he creates an air of excitement. It is sad that the policies he has adopted for Ontario – rent control, increased taxation, opposition to the FTA – are abominable.

June 6, 1988 Monday morning. I had to take the ghastly round trip to Ottawa to attend a high-powered meeting to discuss counterstrategies for dealing with the Baucus-Danforth anti-subsidy formula. Baucus has made matters so much worse by a statement quoted in yesterday's *New York Times*: "The Administration heard the dog's growl and gave it a good meal."

Ottawa invited up three trade lawyers from different firms (Hertztein, Horlick, and Morgan), all of whom, as could be anticipated, gave conflicting advice. One said the formula was a nothing-burger, one said it was a small mess, and the other said it was a big mess. The meeting, attended by Wilson and Crosbie and a few officials, was awful. Everyone wants to hit back hard. But not so hard as to lose the FTA. It was agreed that Burney should come down as soon as tomorrow, acting as Mulroney's emissary, to see Baker.

Flora's threatened resignation is all over town and the newspapers. I've learned that only Mulroney stood up to Flora – all the other ministers, including Clark, supported her.

June 8, 1988 After a briefing lunch at the Residence, Derek and I called on Baker and Yeutter at Treasury and Colin Powell in the NSC. The Baker meeting produced the predictable results – there's no chance whatsoever that the Baucus formula could be dropped. But they agreed to try to clean it up further.

We then called on Powell to discuss the economic summit in Toronto at the end of the month. Mulroney wants leaders to give Reagan his due at this,

his final summit. I wonder if Mulroney is making a political mistake by trying to link his own success with that of Reagan. The Canadian media, led by a fawning *Maclean's*, are declaring Dukakis a messiah and the Democrats the likely big winners.

June 9, 1988 I continue to lobby the Senate and the House on the Baucus formula. The uranium package has unwound, and the administration and congressional committees are scrapping over the constitutionality question. Yeutter called to say our own lobbying was useful (wonder of wonders!) and asked us to continue with our efforts. So I placed more calls, including to Roth, Rockefeller, and Matsunaga. Jon Fried is doing a brilliant job lobbying the staffers.

June 10, 1988 The Finance Committee gathers, and there is a chorus of criticisms led by Senators Bentsen and Mitchell about Canada's "paranoia," overreactions, and double standards. Bentsen said that Burney should stay home. Burney called me, somewhat agitated, and I told him to relax. All this is hot air. I quoted the Treasury assessment, "It wasn't done today, but it will be done."

June 13, 1988 Flew to New York, lunched with Larry Eagleburger, now a political consultant, both of us bemoaning the ungovernability of the United States, and then met Joe Clark prior to the get-together with Shultz at the end of the afternoon. Clark was looking shaky, having just been operated on for a hernia.

The meeting was called to deal with acid rain, more particularly to receive Shultz's new proposal on the subject. It shows progress. For the first time the United States would accept the reduction of transboundary flows as the object of the negotiation, but they are prepared to discuss only *criteria* for specific targets, rather than *targets* themselves. I had already briefed Clark to the effect that the proposal did not go far enough, but if he could get Shultz to consent to negotiating substantial reductions in a specified timeframe, he should agree. If he were to agree to less, we could be accused of impeding progress in the Congress, where there were some signs of forward movement.

Shultz made his proposal but would not go one inch further and would not agree to conclude negotiations within the lifetime of this administration.

He then proposed that each side appoint a special representative, such as Derwinski or Burney, to negotiate under his and Clark's direction.

I was sure Clark was going to be cautious. I was stunned when he told Shultz to go ahead and inform Senator Byrd (with whom he had discussions) that we would proceed on this basis and the two representatives should meet. Shultz, Vernon Walters, Fred Hall, and the other U.S. officials all looked very pleased. Shultz especially, having described this effort as a personal one by him. The two ministers then went on to discuss free trade.

I was upset. I wrote a note to Clark, who was sitting next to me, and stuck it in front of him. It read: "Acid rain. Don't you think you should *study* [the Shultz proposal] with your colleagues *before* he talks with Senator Byrd. You then get back to him *directly* in a few days."

At the end of the meeting, Clark said to Shultz, "My ambassador has a problem." He then presented the essence of my remarks and concluded, "So I guess you should hold this until I get back to you." Shultz looked astonished. His officials looked astonished. I also must have looked astonished. Clark accepted a proposal he should only have agreed to take into consideration. Then he backed off and fingered me as the bad guy. As I walked out I muttered to Shultz sheepishly, "We have to look at this carefully."

June 14, 1988 Jim Schlesinger called to ask if I would be interested in an appointment as Mackenzie King professor of Canadian studies at Harvard next year. Not many people around this town will go out of their way on behalf of others. Harry Truman's nostrum about friends in Washington still applies.

June 15, 1988 I flew to Newport to address at lunch the New England Governors and Atlantic Provinces Premiers' Conference.

I got back from Ottawa in time to attend a party at Marc Leland's in honour of Arianna Stassinopoulos's dreadful new biography of Picasso, now being hyped by the media from one end of the country to the other. Judith Miller of the *New York Times* co-hosted. There was the usual Georgetown turnout, and I hadn't been there very long when I felt ill. I bolted and then felt well enough to go to a black-tie dinner honouring Clayton Yeutter and John Crosbie. I sat at the head table, started to shake, got up, and went home, where I shook for several more hours. I don't know what's the matter with me.

June 16, 1988 Am sick with some form of bacterial infection, according to my doctor. Sondra has been in agony for weeks with a pain in her leg and needs surgery tomorrow. Diagnosis: herniated disk. We cancelled all our engagements this week, except for breakfast with Lloyd Cutler this morning, which I barely got through. We've had our share, as everyone tells us. They mean well, but it makes us feel worse.

June 18, 1988 Sondra's operation went well and I am feeling better, so I attended the wedding of Vernon Jordan's daughter today, the first black wedding I have ever been to. Even though his daughter was beautiful, the clothes superb, and the crowd exciting, Vernon stole the show. Colin Powell chatted with me about the Mulroney-Reagan bilateral at the beginning of the economic summit in Toronto tomorrow. "Acid rain and submarines," he said, "that will be about it, won't it?" Sure, I said, not wanting to tell him that this was the first I had even heard of the meeting.

At the Jordan wedding, Strauss urged me to contact Mulroney and ask him to avoid any comments that could be construed as favouring Bush. The Dukakis folk are upset about a comment by the British foreign secretary to that effect. I told him not to worry but sent a message anyway to Phillips in Toronto.

June 19, 1988 Seven years ago I was head sherpa for the economic summit in Montebello, with Trudeau my boss. On this occasion I wasn't even asked to come up. How I feel out of it. I spend a lot of time looking at pictures I can't afford to buy, and will never be able to afford to buy. Up to now never a man of melancholy, I am becoming one.

June 20, 1988 As I was entering Parliament to see Mulroney, someone said to me, "Did you hear the news? Turner and MacEachen just announced the Senate will block the passing of the free-trade agreement until the election is called."

I saw Mulroney in his Centre Block office. I told him that if I were him, I would be tempted to call the election tomorrow on the issue of Senate usurpation of power. Seize the opportunity, I suggested, in the great Mackenzie King tradition. Mulroney seemed contemplative. He wanted to take a few days to digest this development, he said. My guess is he'll pull the plug in mid-August. He emphasized the importance of getting both houses of Congress to pass the FTA by that time. I assured him there would be no problem with the House, but the Senate could decide to delay until our own Senate acted. I told him I might recommend he call Senator Byrd, with whom he'd established a good rapport.

Mulroney was very complimentary about my work in Washington. It sounded like a symbolic gold watch. I discussed my future with him and told him I didn't want to be bounced out on three weeks' notice this fall (having made the same point to the likely cause of my bounce – Burney). I was ready to resign at the end of the year or as late as April, but did prefer a decent exit, one that would allow me the privilege of celebrating the coming into force of the free-trade agreement and the move to the new embassy. Paul Tellier told me I'd find him noncommittal, and he was right.

I had previously called Joe Clark's office to say I was coming into town to see some people – I named them – and would, of course, be available to see him. Message back: he was going out of town in the afternoon. I said I was available for lunch. No invitation. But Clark did call Burney to ask why I was seeing the PM.

June 21, 1988 Conrad Black asked me to attend the annual Hollinger dinner in Toronto to hear Margaret Thatcher. As she was speaking right after the summit, I informed Burney that I was attending the dinner, which led him to say, graciously, well, you'd better also attend the earlier dinner at the Empire Club, where Reagan is speaking. So I flew up for the club dinner and sat at the head table to hear Reagan. He was full of praise for Mulroney, who had, in introducing Reagan, laid it on thick for him. Prior to the dinner, at the head table reception, I chatted with Shultz about acid rain. He was disappointed that Clark had finally turned thumbs down on the U.S. proposal. I told him he should make no mistake: the government did appreciate that he took the U.S. position further than it had ever been taken before. The problem was it would be seen as an insufficient move at this stage in the life of the government.

Black's dinner was amazing. Never have I seen such a gathering of the Canadian establishment. At the small head table, Black had Mrs. Thatcher and himself seated, as well as the PM, Turner, Peterson, the chief justice, Cardinal Carter,[1] and Kissinger. Every round table was star-studded with leading businessmen and bankers. He even had Kay Graham. It was a night

[1] Gerald Emmett Carter (1912–2003) Bishop of London, Ontario, 1964–1978; Archbishop of Toronto 1978–1979 and Cardinal 1979–1990.

for hyperbole. Black introduced important guest after important guest, summoning up their names with great authority, praising some (I am "the best ambassador Canada has ever had in the United States"), throwing barbs at others. Never, he said, in our history, have we had two leaders, Mulroney and Turner, subject to such unfair criticism and personal attacks – not Diefenbaker, not Pearson, not Trudeau.

Black introduced Thatcher with praise that exceeded all bounds, calling her the greatest British leader in a thousand years. Thatcher took all the praise as her due and then lectured the audience for a half-hour on how she personally saved Britain. "Others imitate our solution," she said, "but it doesn't work, because one has to believe in my approach. I believe in it." Indeed, she is a true believer. Her greatness appears to lie in her will and in her absolute confidence in herself. There is no doubt that as egotistical as she sounds at times, one is in the presence of a great person. Kissinger thanked her in a long Kissingerian ramble, so we had three speeches by three of the greatest egos of our time.

June 22, 1988 Back in Washington, Sondra is recovering from her back surgery. We held, however, to a small pre-arranged dinner at home that worked out to be one of the more memorable evenings we've had – fourteen people sitting at one round table in the sunroom, all journalists, including the Johnny Apples, Al and Pie Friendly,[1] Hedrick Smith[2] and spouse, Elizabeth Drew and spouse, and Ken Adelman (now writing a column). Apple, a bon vivant and tireless talker, held forth on the Toronto Summit, absolutely raving about Toronto as a city and extolling Mulroney's handling of the summit.

After allowing him to dominate the conversation for an hour or so, I steered the lead over to Hedrick Smith, who had just returned from Moscow, his first visit since the publication of his highly regarded book *The Russians*. He gave us a detailed account of how differently and openly some of his old contacts behaved and how extraordinarily accessible everyone was. Some of the guests tonight said it was the best conversation they'd had in Washington in years. I was struck by how Apple and Smith were so superior in learning and experience to people serving in the administration. It is remarkable that one must look to journalists now for this level of conversation.

---

[1] Alfred Friendly (1911–1993) Managing Editor of the *Washington Post* 1955–1965.

[2] Pulitzer Prize–winning journalist and twenty-six-year correspondent for the *New York Times*, serving in Washington, Moscow, Cairo, Saigon, and Paris.

June 26, 1988 A stay in Toronto breaks my free-trade promotional tour most conveniently. Friday my pitch was in Winnipeg, and tomorrow it will be in St. Catharines. I couldn't make Vancouver. Crosbie was anxious I do this tour, and I agreed, although some think this is too political a matter for a public servant to be engaged in. This is the opinion of various foreign-service officers in External who are deeply opposed to the FTA because they don't like Americans and because they are a small-minded lot.

June 27, 1988 Went to the farewell reception for Howard Baker, where he spoke a few words. He is one of the most sympathetic persons in public life, as well as wise and always sensible. "Reagan," he said, "is the most presidential president we've had, and I've known six. . . . Don't kid yourself, the president still has great powers, notwithstanding congressional encroachment. . . . The Canada-U.S. FTA is the most important economic agreement in history," a statement he then qualified by saying, "modern history." "It is awesome in its implications." They threw away the mould.

June 29, 1988 The Strausses, Jordans, and Rick Burt came to dinner and to see Sondra convalescing. The general opinion is that Bush is doomed and Dukakis is next president. Burt said he tells the Germans that Bob Strauss is likely to be secretary of state under Dukakis, but Bob says he is too old. And Bob acknowledges that he is not that close to Dukakis, spotting his virtues rather late in the day. Indeed, if Dole teams up with Bush (this is the heavy rumour) and if Bush wins and Jim Baker is secretary of state, as everyone then assumes, Strauss will be closer to the Republicans than to the Democrats.

Vernon quoted a good Strauss line tonight, of which he has an endless supply. "I don't care about manure unless I step in it." Dominant theme of the conversation: whatever happened to George Bush. Strauss says this about Bush: in his closest circles – up to 250 people – everyone is deeply committed to him and believes in him, more so than with most candidates. Outside the circle, opinion of him falls off a cliff. All agree he'd choose a damn good cabinet.

June 30, 1988 After weeks of protest, I've lost a major battle with Ottawa. They have produced an acid rain video that is condescending to the Americans, an unnecessary provocation, and boring at the same time – quite a feat. In a showdown of who's in charge, the department, encouraged by

Environment and supported by the PMO, said we're going ahead with it. I managed to hold it up a month but didn't stop it. They've already spent a mint on it, it's been distributed in Canada, and they are afraid if they back off or revise it, the story will leak. This video was produced as a domestic political response to "do something." In the United States the only "something" it can possibly "do" will be to make Canada the issue, rather than acid rain. We will thereby play into the hands of our enemies, of whom we have plenty.

As a gracious concession, Ottawa did agree to tone down the letter to be used by our consulates in lobbying for acid rain. They are to remove the phrase "please write your congressman." (!) It is amateur night in Canada. Officials did not even ask us to check out the legality of this activity, in this, the most litigious country on earth. We did anyway and got back an opinion warning us to proceed in a very specific and cautious way, if we are to avoid the Foreign Agents Registration Act and the labelling of the video as propaganda. I told Ottawa that no one in Canada is more familiar with the pitfalls of lobbying for acid rain controls than I am. Deaver's hiring triggered the Dingell investigation (even though we didn't hire him to lobby for us on acid rain or anything else), and my earlier activities led to a proposal from a midwestern congressman that I be declared *persona non grata*. In the old days – under Trudeau – we lobbied through the instrument of a non-governmental institution, the Canadian Coalition on Acid Rain. We had some cover.

July 1, 1988 I spent Dominion Day, as I still like to call it (why do we hate our past so much?) on the telephone with Treasury and officials in Ottawa. The burning issue is the "globalization of the Baucus-Danforth formula." What a phrase. I have spent the past few days lobbying the Democratic members of the Finance Committee to make sure that the foolish, irritating Baucus formula aimed at our subsidies applies to all countries. This is so we do not appear to be receiving "least-favoured nation" treatment. Bradley, Matsunaga, Rockefeller, and Riegle will all, I think, be helpful, but support for globalization is soft, and the chairman, the aloof Mr. Bentsen, thinks we are making a fuss about nothing. It's interesting that the administration encouraged us to lobby the Hill. They recognize their own limited effectiveness.

My most memorable conversation was with the highly intelligent and ambitious Senator Mitchell of Maine, and most likely the future Senate majority leader.

Me: "George, we've got a problem with the Baucus proposal. I know you have some problems with the FTA, but you're a leading Democrat figure, statesman, and a friend of Canada [ha]. Would you support globalizing the Baucus formula? Can we count on you? This is important to Canada."

Mitchell: "Allan, we have a frank relationship. Your people wouldn't do a thing for me on my problem with lobsters. How can I help you?"

Me: "George, we're willing to look at lobster sizes as an environmental issue. We can't put an import restriction into the agreement."

Mitchell: "Allan, this is what I'm going to do. I'm going to vote against the agreement, and I'm going to try to stiffen Max Baucus to make his proposal as difficult as possible for you. That's my plan. But Allan, we're friends. I can be straight with you."

Me: "George, that's a big help. It's nice being friends. I'm glad we're not enemies."

July 3, 1988 We gave a party for Rachel, who is visiting us. Sondra and Connie managed to round up about a dozen people in their twenties, and we added "old folks" to create an all-ages mix – Alan Greenspan and Andrea Mitchell, the Kirklands, just back from Europe, the Brzezinskis, the Morrises, and the Schlesingers. We ate under the stars. Conversation was dominated by the shooting down by the U.S. navy of an Iranian Airbus civil airliner, with all on board killed. We agreed tonight that the story will turn very nasty as U.S. critics begin to create doubts and condemn the U.S. role in the Gulf. In an election period, the issue will come down to a patriotic one.

This should have been a quiet weekend, but I've been on and off the phone with Treasury and Ottawa over the silly "globalization" business. I find the negotiating team in Ottawa instinctively comes up with the wrong answers. It's very frustrating.

July 6, 1988 Ed Meese resigns. This comes as no surprise to anyone. The guy was ground up in little chunks by Congress and the media, who acted in league with each other. Meese was extraordinarily accessible to me, took helpful positions on difficult issues when in the White House (for instance, on the steel quota), was a champion of Canada-U.S. police cooperation (he adored the RCMP). He was, however, a relentless ideological opponent of acid rain controls, which was a particular problem given his chairmanship of the Social Policy Cabinet Council. My view on Meese: not as bad as he was made out to be; a lot better than the image of him that the media has created. A man who will swim against the tide.

July 7, 1988 Hepburn (why does he despise me so much?) publishes a piece in the *Toronto Star* entitled "Gotlieb Ignores Canada's Birthday." "Allan Gotlieb," he writes, "might be the Grinch who stole Canada Day." He doesn't point out that (1) there hasn't been a Canada Day party since at least the 1950s; (2) government guidelines discourage use of public funds for this purpose; (3) there is no place available where we could entertain the myriads of Canadians living here; and (4) a selective list of Canadian invitees would be condemned as elitist.

July 8, 1988 I got an urgent request from Ottawa to call John Whitehead, who is acting as secretary of state, to make representations about an issue that has totally dominated Question Period the past two days: a hare-brained scheme by Governor Jim Thompson[1] of Illinois to divert water from Lake Michigan into the Mississippi (running dry because of the horrendous drought in the West). I delivered a letter to Whitehead requesting consultation that Whitehead described as "sharp." As I left State I was summoned by a dozen hacks of the Canadian press to deal with this issue, which the Liberals have dramatized because it deals with water. The excited reporters allege that Mulroney has given away our control over this resource in the FTA.

Visited Moynihan late in the afternoon. "You people should agree to drain Lake Superior. This would give you a lot of goodwill and a lot of new land." Later he phoned to tell me that he had just been briefed by the U.S. Corps of Engineers, who told him that if Governor Thompson's diversion were implemented, it would raise the water levels of the Mississippi in New Orleans by one inch!

July 9, 1988 In the afternoon I penned a personal letter to John Crosbie assessing the state of affairs concerning the passage of free-trade legislation. My theme was set by the opening questions: "What is the matter with Lloyd Bentsen? And why do his views matter so much?" I got my point across by describing a conversation I had with Bob Strauss.

---

[1] (b. 1936) Republican Governor of Illinois 1977–1991.

According to Strauss, Bentsen believes that Canada got the better of the free-trade deal, that USTR did a poor job of negotiation, and that the United States, as a result, did not achieve its objectives. Bentsen is known to have negative constituency interests, but this analysis has hardened his opposition.

There is another factor that Strauss put to me bluntly. "Virtually everyone in Washington, both on the Hill and in the administration, has become allergic to Canada's complaints and alleged overreaction to various matters. There is a growing sense of exasperation with Canada; this erupted at the recent Finance Committee hearing when Bentsen spoke harshly about Derek Burney's visit to Washington and intervention." Strauss, in telling me of this attitude, spared me the trouble of reply. "Allan," he said, "I know that the same thing has happened in Ottawa with the U.S. Nevertheless, I am describing what is felt down here, which you must appreciate."

Strauss said, "I think the free-trade agreement will prove to have been worth the enormous effort. But the first year may be difficult here because of attitudes towards Canada. When I describe the reaction here to Canadian worries, anxieties, and interventions, I include you, Gotlieb. They're fed up with you."

Strauss's observation conforms to an attitude on the Hill that we have been reporting for some time. Bill Bradley (who has gone to bat for us more than any other senator) told me recently, "I have to say that I don't understand what is going on in Ottawa. Why are they overreacting to everything?"

I know Crosbie will hate this letter, as will Clark and Mulroney. But why worry? I'm history in a few weeks or months.

July 10, 1988 In Maine the potato and fish interests have prevailed, and the two senators – Mitchell and Cohen – are determined to oppose the free-trade agreement. I learn that they have informed the pro-free-trade interests in Maine that they were well aware of the opportunities that the agreement offered the paper and lumber industries and other Maine companies. However, the senators say they find it politically prudent to pay more attention to constituencies that would be injured by the agreement than to those that would benefit. Both indicate they were driven by the opposition of the lobster fishermen and potato farmers.

So further lobbying of the lumber interests would be useless. This experience confirms my view of a basic U.S. rule of lobbying: the negatives carry more weight than the positives. The narrowly focused interests outweigh the general ones.

July 12, 1988 Big news today: Lloyd Bentsen has been chosen to be Dukakis's running mate. Strauss sees him as one of the best minds in Washington. I see him as a protectionist, isolationist, America-centric Texan who has little sympathy for the world beyond U.S. shores. For years he has plugged the "blame-the-foreigner" line. Strauss loves him, Cutler thinks he is great, and Baker does too, it seems. He is elegant, a gentleman, soft-spoken, courtly, and polite. Maybe we all have it right.

Congress is trying to coordinate consideration of the free-trade bill this week. But the stupid so-called globalization issue is unresolved. Yesterday I met with McPherson, and this morning with the key players of the USTR. They are really going to bat for us now. We looked at every possible option, from good to bad to impossible, with me making it clear that I could not necessarily deliver Ottawa. By mid-afternoon, the king staffers on the Hill worked out a formula that was better than I could ever have expected.

I sent the text up to Ottawa expecting joy and got shit back. Each official in Ottawa vies with the others to see who can be more negative. I spent hours on the telephone with Ottawa trying to convince them. They are going to have a big powwow tomorrow morning and formulate a response. If the meeting fails to signal a *non-obstat*, we're going to see the bill postponed for weeks at least.

July 13, 1988 My tolerance level is breaking, as is the tolerance level of my American counterparts. Strauss is dead right. Both governments have become allergic to each other. Derek Burney called with a list of nitpicking changes, which I passed on to Holmer at USTR in the expectation they would not fly. They didn't.

I was finally authorized to tell officials here that we don't like the whole business of the Baucus-Danforth formula, but we won't put a kibosh on it. In other words, let her rip. Canadian ministers and top officials seem to have put more time on this trivial issue than on whole chunks of the free-trade agreement, such as the far-reaching energy package. The problem is that Ottawa has gotten traumatized by the media critics; they are now afraid of their own shadows. It's a good thing that my job is coming to an end. I don't seem to be able to exercise influence in Ottawa as I used to in my prime.

I spoke to Fred Doucet in Ottawa, who still has not fully recovered from his recent serious heart attack. He says he is quitting government and going into the private sector as a consultant. Sick and bruised. He did a good job as adviser to Mulroney and deserves credit for it.

July 14, 1988 Huzzah. Bastille Day. The day of liberation for me. Three years' toil on behalf of free trade, and the end is now in sight. The gates of the Promised Land are opened. We are at the end of the journey. We have succeeded. We have a done deal.

Moynihan was the first to call. It was he who moved unanimous approval of the free-trade agreement in the Finance Committee. "A day in history," we both agreed.

I drafted and fired off a message to Ottawa, the essence of which was "you have won."

The largely ungovernable U.S. political system has disciplined itself. What many astute people believed over the past few years could not be done is virtually achieved. The skeptics have been dumbfounded, the doubters silenced, the naysayers no longer in evidence.

I asked a member of the embassy staff to draft a letter to Bentsen on his selection as vice-presidential candidate. I sent him the following letter, without the staff member's footnotes:

> Dear Mr. Chairman,
>
> As a foreign diplomat, of course, I cannot intervene in the domestic affairs of my host country.[1] Nonetheless, I may surely be permitted to offer you the warmest[2] congratulations on your selection as Democratic nominee for the vice-presidency of the United States.[3] I am confident in the knowledge that your long and meritorious service to your country is recognized[4] by all Americans[5] and internationally as well.[6]
>
> I also wish to take this opportunity to thank you – on my own and on behalf of Prime Minister Mulroney – for your valuable contribution to the success of free trade negotiations[7] and for ensuring expeditious consideration of the agreement by the Finance Committee.[8] It is an honour for me to have been associated with you and your colleagues in this historic enterprise.[9] I know that you share my desire to move quickly to final adoption of the implementing package[10] and that you too look

forward to the new era in Canada-U.S. trade relations that will begin on January 1, 1989.[11]

[1] Although I will pull out all the stops necessary to defend Canadian interests, including dealing with the Administration, Congress, lobbyists, the private sector, and U.S. media.
[2] I have always found you to be cold, distant, diffident . . .
[3] It might at least have the benefit of removing you from the chairmanship of the Finance Committee.
[4] And . . . by special interests.
[5] Jesse Jackson considers you to be to the right of Attila the Hun.
[6] As one of America's great protectionists.
[7] You voted against the fast-track authority.
[8] You held up the entire committee by resisting the Baucus-Danforth changes.
[9] It has been excruciatingly painful for me to try to have you understand Canadian interests and perspectives.
[10] You may still hold the FTA hostage to domestic political imperatives, including the timing of the omnibus trade bill, the Republican Convention, etc.
[11] You believe that the U.S. was out-negotiated on the agreement, and are concerned that U.S. and Texas industries will come out losers.

July 15, 1988 Could barely drag myself out of bed this morning because of our party last night. Ten of us sat around a table until very late – Vernon Jordan, Kay and Rowly Evans, the Kirklands, Mary Jane and Charles Wick, Meg Greenfield, and Sondra and me. It was one of the most animated evenings I can remember – everyone argued for hours about Dukakis and Jesse Jackson[1] – what does Jesse want? What will he do to/for Democrats? I argued that Jackson wants to stay outside the party until he can capture the top or second job. Everyone disagreed. I said Dukakis's choice of Bentsen could hurt his presidential prospects. It muddies his identity. Lane mumbled, "Identity – you sound like Woody Allen."

At the end of the long dinner, I said, "Let's stop this endless talk about the Democratic prospects – don't you Americans know how important this day is? The day that the U.S. did the deal on free trade with Canada?"

Kirkland: "Oh, you mean the *Anschluss*?"

---

[1] (b. 1941) Politician, civil rights activist, and Baptist minister. Candidate for the Democratic presidential nomination in 1984 and 1988.

I said the real significance of this day for Americans was that they could show themselves and the world that the U.S. system was not ungovernable – it could produce results.

Meg Greenfield: "I'm tired of people saying the U.S. system is ungovernable. We have a governable system. We have the best system in the world."

Tonight we went to a cocktail-buffet given by the president of the National Association of Manufacturers. Had a long talk with a dispirited Frank Carlucci. He was visibly upset by the Defense Appropriation Bill voted in by Congress yesterday – a collection of boondoggles, arbitrary actions, wrong-headed requirements, and constituency fixes. "You have twenty-four-year-old staffers ordering around generals," Frank said. "But I had to tell the president, veto this bill and you'll get a worse one."

I told him my comment about the FTA showing that the U.S. system is not completely ungovernable. I recounted Meg's riposte last night. Frank said, "I think our system is close to ungovernable and in deep trouble. I'm going to go public on what's happening in the defence field."

July 22, 1988 The diplomatic elite of Washington – about one hundred ambassadors – were flown to Atlanta to watch the Democratic National Convention. Of all my political days in the United States, this was one of the emptiest. We were on the margins of marginal events. Navigated from building to building by three large buses, the best part of our trip was the good-natured banter among the corps about our fate. One of the only memorable moments was when, during a briefing to us, Fritz Mondale said, "The only quality that counts today in presidential politics is strength, and that means projecting the image of strength on television." This explains Dukakis?

The intrepid Bobby de Margerie manoeuvred himself and myself onto the convention floor as part of the Arkansas delegation. So we were the only two ambassadors to witness, from the floor of the convention, Lloyd Bentsen's feeble vice-presidential address and Dukakis's show of his family, his immigrant roots, and his "strength." For his handlers, the message was "strength, strength, and more strength." My clearest impression was of a political group that wanted power, wanted it badly, but was going about getting it in a self-defeating way.

July 30, 1988 We joined Secretary of Commerce Bill Verity on his rented paddle-wheeler to celebrate the upcoming Republican Convention.

One hundred and fifty guests, terrible so-called Creole food, unbearably loud so-called Dixie band, and stifling heat in Washington's worst summer since 1936. Sondra heard tales about life with Nancy by the first lady's former chief of staff while I chatted – in between free-trade exchanges – with former CIA chief Dick Helms about the agency. (Forgive me, June.) Among my strongest memories of the nation's capital will be withering with heat on slow-moving boats on the Potomac on hot summer nights.

August 1, 1988 Dinner with David and Susan Brinkley at Nora's, the "liberal" restaurant off Dupont Circle owned in part by Ben Bradlee.

When we arrived I noticed the small restaurant was surrounded by several tough-looking men, obviously security – the signal to the world that someone very important was inside. Within was indeed none other than vice-king Lloyd Bentsen, just the man I'd been trying to reach for the past week. I gave Bentsen the quick lobby treatment: "For the sake of Canada, get the free-trade bill passed and out of Congress by August 12. This is of critical importance to the fate of the agreement up north. It will greatly simplify the issue during the upcoming Canadian election." Bentsen's response was surprisingly positive. I think he wants to get the agreement out of the way before he begins his big political campaign.

This is the second time Bentsen surprised me these past few days. The first was when I received an acknowledgement of my congratulatory note to him. Given the supposedly thousands (tens of thousands) sent to him, I was amazed to receive, almost immediately, a courteous letter in return, acknowledging the importance of the free-trade agreement and my comments about his role. Must have been signed by his staff, I said to myself. But when I saw him tonight, he thanked me again for the note. So he is certainly strong on organization as well as courtesy. Also, there is a moral. It pays to send letters of congratulation.

August 3, 1988 My number one challenge these days: continue the push in Congress for an accelerated vote on the free-trade agreement. I feel like a bit of a hypocrite pleading with the U.S. legislators to do something (pass the bill) that our Parliament cannot or will not. But many of the legislators want to help Mulroney – they like him. They consider him a friend. Rostenkowski told me just that. I talked to the entire Democratic House leadership, Foley, Coelho, and Bonior. I had very successful results with

Foley: he told me he intervened in the House today to bring our bill to a vote on Tuesday of next week, rather than Thursday. This is good news because it now gives the Senate more time to act. Duberstein told me the president had urged the Republican senators to push and that Majority Leader Bob Dole was being helpful.

In the afternoon Dole gave me the bad news. "Byrd is being difficult. He wants to give priority to other bills, such as defence appropriations and textiles. You'll need to work on him." I told Dole the problem is Byrd won't answer my phone calls. He's the only one with whom I can't connect. "Try Strauss," Dole said. "He has more influence with Byrd than anyone else." The amazing Mr. Strauss. Dole warned me that George Mitchell was urging a full twenty-hour debate on the floor. "It seems he needs time to talk about the bad deal for Maine lobsters." I don't think Dole was kidding.

August 5, 1988 While I've spent the week successfully lobbying the Hill to vote on the bill next week, Ottawa is threatening to wreck the show. Crosbie has tabled a controversial rule about copyright for cable transmission programs. The effect of this proposed rule is to make Buffalo's signals "local" in Toronto, and consequently free. This may be very fair – I suspect it is – but its timing is terrible and will lead to yet another confrontation on the Hill. Predictably, Yeutter telephoned Crosbie and told him the likely result is no Senate approval this week. If it works out this way, the government can be seen to have taken a totally unnecessary risk and undermined their main goal. The gang can't shoot straight.

A new national survey shows 58 per cent of Canadians back John Turner's use of the Senate to delay the government's free-trade legislation until an election is called. I don't believe Mulroney is going to win a majority. In that event, there will be no free-trade agreement. That will mean several years of work down the drain. I feel very emotional.

Amidst all the grand battles going on regarding the future of Canada, I am dealing again with a small poisonous one. Arthur Erickson called me three times to tell me that the External Affairs decorators have insisted on substituting a different shade of red from the one he chose for all the upholstery in the executive offices. The External decorator czars said the upholstery had to be the same colour as the flag. Arthur said that conflicts with the limestone wall and floors that dominate the building. Arthur lost. He had every reason to be upset.

I called the associate undersecretary in Ottawa and told him that to substitute the taste of the departmental decorators for that of the architect was an affront to the architect. The guerrilla warfare goes on and on. The anti-Erickson feeling in the department still runs high.

August 7, 1988 The House of Representatives passes the FTA 366 to 40. The big issue is will the Senate move too. Ken Duberstein called me from the White House and said, "We're trying to get a vote. We have a lot of balls in the air. The president has worked on Dole and Simpson. We've done everything we can. I suggest you call Strauss in California and ask him to work on Byrd." "I already did that," I replied, "but I'll do it again." I reached Bob in California and once again asked him to do a little pro bono work. Bob called back shortly after to say that Byrd assured him, "It will be done. The bill will pass."

The Finance Committee formally passed the bill today. Moynihan, moving the vote, said that "special recognition" should be given to me as a valuable interlocutor who has served his country well. Bentsen chimed in, "His country, yes." Stu Auerbach of the *Post* got a good quote from Rostenkowski: "The Ambassador should spend less time lobbying the Congress and more time lobbying the Parliament."

August 10, 1988 Burney called me on behalf of the PM. "Can't you do more to get the Senate to vote? Tell the senators that if the vote is in September, we could be in an election."

"I've told them, I've told them," I said. "I moved Congress so far. I can't move it any further. I've done everything that could be done. I've made a monumental pest of myself."

September 8, 1988 In New York we attended a black-tie dinner given by Marvin Traub[1] in honour of Robert Campeau,[2] in the Temple of Dendur at the Metropolitan Museum. Campeau is the toast of New York. Wealth (Forbes, Trump, the Lauders, Sulzbergers, Si Newhouse,[3] Ron

---

1 Prominent retail business executive. President of Bloomingdale's 1978–1992.

2 (b. 1923) Canadian real estate tycoon and businessman who ran into financial difficulty.

3 Samuel Irving "Si" Newhouse Jr (b. 1927) Chairman and CEO of Advance Publications and Chairman of Conde Nast Publications, which owns *Vogue*, *Vanity Fair*, and the *New Yorker*.

Perelman)[1] was there en masse, as well as a few star Canadians (Paul Reichmann,[2] Mortimer Zuckerman,[3] etc.). In a tasteless, rambling speech, Campeau, after praising Reagan at length, told the crowd that he estimated the wealth in the room at over $30 billion, "enough to eliminate the Canadian deficit."

September 9, 1988 Called on Whitehead to present a new acid rain initiative, inspired by Mulroney, who never gives up. "Why not go back to the Americans," said the PM, "and ask them to reopen negotiations on an acid rain agreement. Now that Bush and, of course, Dukakis have come out for controls, why shouldn't the administration reconsider?" It's hard to fault this reasoning, except that logic might suggest that negotiations with one or other of the candidates, once elected, would be more fruitful than trying to negotiate with what is left of this team. But I gave a hard sell to Whitehead, who seemed somewhat apathetic. I mentioned the idea to Colin Powell at the opening of the Cirque du Soleil tonight (he and two hundred others were our guests). Powell was cautious. He commented that Bush had been saying a lot of things recently, implying that one couldn't take them all that seriously. Also, Ronald Reagan would have to reverse himself – an unpalatable prospect.

September 14, 1988 More rumours of our imminent departure and Burney's appointment to replace me. I can't get anything out of Ottawa about when his appointment will be announced and when he wants to arrive. We are sitting on our suitcases. Burney wants out of Ottawa, because Peter White, now head of the PMO, is crowding him (at least that's the word on the street). I want to stay until the end of the year. As Mulroney delays the election from day to day, this seems likely to happen.

---

[1] (b. 1943) Wealthy American investor and businessman who appears ninety-fourth on the *Forbes* list of the world's richest people. He has been involved with numerous companies, including Revlon.

[2] (b. 1930) Canadian real estate billionaire. He led the development of Canary Wharf in London, England.

[3] (b. 1937) Canadian-born billionaire magazine editor, publisher, and real estate magnate in the United States. Editor-in-Chief of *U.S. News & World Report* and Publisher/owner of the *New York Daily News*.

Joe Clark is in town for probably his last quarterly meeting with Shultz. Clark used the occasion to handsomely attribute the idea of quarterly meetings to Shultz, and Shultz acknowledged this gracefully. Clark warned Shultz that there could be a delay of a few weeks in passing the free-trade legislation in Parliament, but the Tories are confident of re-election. Clark also pitched for reconsideration of the U.S. position on acid rain negotiations. Shultz refused.

Shultz said, "We won't ask you during the elections for your agreement to test the advanced cruise." Clark emitted a sigh of relief. "But we'll be back," Shultz said. "It's terribly important to us." At the formal lunch of the two sides, Shultz gave a handsome prepared toast, and Clark was irritable because he hadn't been warned (by me) that toasts were being exchanged. Regrettably, I don't have any time left to improve my performance.

I have never seen Shultz so fully in command of his data, so sensible in his judgments. About to leave office, his perspective was long-term.

In the evening, exhausted, we went to a dinner the Bradens gave for Kirk Douglas, here on a book tour. Sat next to Pamela Harriman, who was not optimistic about Dukakis's prospects. "He doesn't listen to people, that's his problem – stubbornness," she said. Jack Valenti queried me about Mulroney's prospects. As I was explaining that Mulroney was likely to win a majority at the next election, I suddenly became quite ill. I felt dizzy and nauseous and bolted in the middle of a sentence. I made it to the bathroom but was badly shaken. Mary Jane Wick, sitting at my table, ran after me and kept saying I was white as a sheet. She told Sondra, and there was alarm in the air, but I recovered and went home. I think it was exhaustion.

Paul Tellier called me. Do I want to be chairman of the Canada Council. Mulroney was offering it to me. I said I'd think about it and let him know. On the one hand, I hate the idea of working for the government, even though only part-time. On the other, I am fearful of holding no public office after more than three decades.

September 15, 1988 Called on a number of senators and asked that they acknowledge the PM's leadership when the final Senate debate on our free-trade agreement takes place on Monday. The friendly senators told me that while voting for the bill, they don't know whether they should criticize the agreement, thereby making it more palatable for public opinion in Canada, or praise it. I told them to praise it. Packwood, Chafee, and Bradley all responded with enthusiasm.

September 17, 1988 John Holmes[1] dies. The obituary in the *Globe and Mail* is a collection of dry biographical facts. There was no sense of his role in the glory days of Canadian diplomacy. A comparable U.S. figure would have received at least a half-page notice. He wrote a very good book about Canada and the United States called *Life with Uncle*. Now forgotten, of course.

I can see him now, walking down the corridors of the UN delegates' lounge in 1957. I was on my first foreign assignment, as an adviser to the Canadian Delegation to the General Assembly. Holmes was dressed in a sporty, checked brown suit, and his face was bright and ruddy as he loped down the corridors with his own special stride. Delegates and others, black and white, jumped up to shake his hand, banter, have a word, exchange information, give a compliment, touch his sleeve, or whatever. He was the prince of the UN, as well known and popular as the great Lester himself.

September 18, 1988 I got some further sense of the dominant protectionist sentiments in play when I accepted an invitation, along with a half-dozen other ambassadors, to lunch with Madeleine Albright,[2] Dukakis's foreign-policy adviser. From her I heard much more than I had expected about the "level playing field" and about how the new omnibus trade bill will help redress foreign "unfair trade" practices. I was negatively impressed. I told her that many U.S. friends were not too convinced about how level the grounds are on which trade is played in her country.

The lady was very disturbed about the reaction to Dukakis being photographed in a tank. "All of his professional foreign-policy advisers are being ignored," she said. She seemed discouraged, as well she should be.

September 19, 1988 The bill enacting the free-trade agreement passes the Senate. Only nine votes against: Mitchell and William Cohen, both of Maine; Kent Conrad[3] and Quentin Burdick, both of North Dakota;

---

[1] (1910–1988) One of the key architects of postwar Canadian foreign policy. Assistant Under-secretary of State for External Affairs 1951–1953; Director General of the Canadian Institute of International Affairs 1960–1973, when he became Counsellor and Research Director.

[2] (b. 1937) Senior Fellow in Soviet and Eastern European Affairs at the Center for Strategic and International Studies 1981–1982; U.S. Ambassador to the United Nations 1993–1997; U.S. Secretary of State 1997–2001. Now a Distinguished Professor at Georgetown University.

[3] (b. 1948) Democratic Senator from North Dakota 1987 to present.

Jeff Bingaman[1] and Pat Domenici of New Mexico (uranium lobby); Carl Levin of Michigan (autos); Wendell Ford[2] of Kentucky (coal); and John Melcher of Montana (antediluvian). Packwood, Evans, and Chafee, among others, praised the PM's leadership.

There was an expected undercurrent of criticism of Canadian subsidies and allegations that Canada got the better deal. What was not expected – at least not until recently – was the extent of the support for the agreement. How I recall worrying about the perilous state of the treaty – the fifty-fifty odds. In the end, even some of the worst critics and complainers, such as Jack Danforth and John Heinz, swung behind the deal (groaning and criticizing all the way).

The turning point came when it became obvious that the opponents could not achieve a blocking coalition of fifty votes; the coalition then began to unravel. In the final analysis, the U.S. Senate wanted this agreement, so the United States could stand taller in the world, especially in relation to the Japanese. They do not see us as the fifty-first state, but they believe in the mysterious notion of American "exceptionalism," and they see Canada as more or less falling under the U.S. psychic umbrella of exceptionalism.

We are moving into a world of enormous trading blocs. That is why we have to be part of something larger. We couldn't do it with the British and the Europeans – we tried and they wouldn't have us – and we can't sell manufactured goods into Japan, whatever treaties we may have, because they have the worst trade barriers of all, the invisible ones. So U.S. and Canadian interests came together.

September 21, 1988 We flew to New York and had dinner at Ed and Judy Ney's. The event – a small number sitting around one table – was in honour of the ubiquitous Lord Weidenfeld. Felix and Liz Rohatyn, super-agent Mort Janklow, and Kay Graham and her daughter, Lally Weymouth, were there. Ed is close to Bush, so we discussed what embassy Ed would like to collect. It seems he can have his pick.

Without meaning to be offensive, I told him the story of Jack Kennedy and his dog. A good friend of Kennedy used to walk the dog on the campaign

[1] (b. 1943) Democratic Senator from New Mexico 1983 to present.

[2] (b. 1924) Democratic Governor of Kentucky 1967–1971; Senator from Kentucky 1974–1999; Senate Majority Whip 1991–1995; Senate Minority Whip 1995–1999.

trails. When asked by a reporter why he did so, he replied, "It's not a dog, it's an embassy." Then I pitched Canada to Ney.

Much talk about the pending or expected demise of Mike Dukakis, the reborn Jimmy Carter. Two months ago, king; now, bum.

Bumped into Lew Wasserman on the shuttle back to Washington. Like Katharine Graham, he's worth half a billion and travels by cattle car rather than by private plane.

September 22, 1988 Derek Burney's assignment came through today. Ottawa was pretty pushy about getting agrément in forty-eight hours rather than the average two-week period. I suppose this is to allow an immediate announcement. Ottawa has kept me badly in the dark. The PMO has been dealing directly with the White House on this issue. My phone calls aren't answered.

I flew to Toronto to attend a black-tie farewell dinner for Don MacDonald at the Toronto Club, on the eve of his departure for London. Among the speakers was John Crosbie, who joked, "Don, follow Allan's example in Washington – avoid publicity. Keep a low profile."

September 28, 1988 In New York to attend a dinner at the Metropolitan Museum to mark the opening of the big Degas exhibit, in which the National Gallery of Canada (and Jean Boggs[1] especially) played a large part.

We got up early to return to Washington in time for the president's signing of the free-trade bill. Colin Powell asked me a couple of weeks ago about holding the signing ceremony at the new Canadian embassy. After talking to Ottawa, I told him that we regretfully had to decline. The embassy wasn't ready yet, I said. I suggested they hold the signing ceremony at the White House in the normal way. What I didn't tell him was there was nervousness in Ottawa about his idea (something about mixing up our two sovereignties, that sort of thing). The Canadian pathology at work.

The ceremony unfolded on the Rose Garden on a sunny, warm day, in the presence of about two dozen of the major congressional players and most of the cabinet. I stood on the dais next to the president as he gave his remarks, with Yeutter and Baker on my left. The president paid tribute to

[1] (b. 1922) Canadian art historian and civil servant. First female director of the National Gallery of Canada (1966–1976).

the "visionary" Canadian prime minister (he chose this adjective himself, Duberstein told me) and the "able" Canadian ambassador (I'd rather be visionary). After the ceremony I talked to the president, Baker, and Duberstein and told them things were looking good for Mulroney (a majority was in the offing) and for the passage of the agreement in Canada.

I doubt that any Canadian will participate again in a U.S. domestic ceremony in this manner, unless we join them in a political union. I was profoundly moved, even choked up. I thought, this is the culmination of my career in Washington.

But I was quickly brought back to reality. After the ceremony I was besieged on the White House grounds by reporters who wanted to know (1) what I thought of the Ben Johnson affair; (2) when I was leaving Washington; and (3) what could happen to Canadian culture under the free-trade agreement.

September 29, 1988 The *Globe and Mail* runs a front-page photo of the president and myself at the signing ceremony, and the *Washington Post* carries it on the front of their business section. The CBC featured the ceremony on the evening news. My little flame of glory flickers for a moment.

I got a message that Burney's appointment will be announced tomorrow, but my appointment as chairman of the Canada Council will not. Who cares when it is announced? But I wonder if a storm is brewing in Canada. Peter Roberts, outgoing director of the Canada Council and one of my oldest friends from Oxford days, says he thinks Flora may be going ballistic. Old colleague Jeremy Kinsman, picking up the rumours, called Roberts to ask what he thought the reaction of the Canadian cultural community would be, given my cardinal association with the alleged sellout of Canadian culture. Roberts said the reaction would be good, as I would use my high profile to push aggressively for Canadian culture. Kinsman reports that Margaret Atwood might issue a statement attacking the appointment. Go ahead, Margaret, make my day.

September 30, 1998 In Hilton Head giving one of my last speeches on U.S. soil. Jack Manion[1] called to explain the delay in the announcement of my appointment to the Canada Council. The prime minister wants to separate it from the Burney appointment to Washington, to be made later

[1] Deputy Minister of Employment and Immigration 1977–1979; Deputy Minister of the Treasury Board 1979–1986.

in the day, so the press release could be fulsome about me. I explained to Manion that the correct meaning of fulsome was "hypocritical."

At 4 p.m. my office called to say Derek's appointment as my replacement had been announced, effective January 1. An era ends – for me. We went out on the beautiful beach, took a long walk, came back to the hotel, had an unspeakably bad pizza, watched TV, and went to bed.

October 1, 1988 Our first visit to Savannah, and we are sorry we never visited here before. This is the loveliest city in the United States, even surpassing Charleston and New Orleans for the grandeur and elegance of its historic quarters.

Back at the hotel in late afternoon, the beautiful old Gastonian Inn, we switched on the local TV to learn that Mulroney has called an election. Pretty impressive that Canadian news (other than Ben Johnson's steroids) travels this far.

October 3, 1988 Two more chapters in my life in Washington close. Deaver was not sentenced to jail, just a fine and community work. Maybe there is still an ounce of humanity left in Washington, if you're lucky enough to find it. Over the weekend the papers printed stories of Whitney North Seymour Jr.'s latest activity – writing to universities offering to lecture on the lack of ethics in Washington for a mere $2,500 to $5,000. Most of the papers have gently mocked him. He deserves worse.

The other chapter to close is the Orlikow case. The CIA will settle out of court. I'm happy for the plaintiffs, although their lawyer, that McCarthyite of the left, Joe Rauh Jr., viciously attacked me, Clark, and Mulroney. The truth is we have been very helpful to Orlikow and his co-plaintiffs. The only credit we received were insults.

Tonight we went to dinner at Kay Graham's for Kitty Carlisle Hart.[1] Kitty responded to Kay's toast to me by quoting George Bernard Shaw: "Every seven years a man must change his life." I couldn't think of a more appropriate comment.

October 4, 1988 Three hundred people came to our reception to mark the passage of the free-trade agreement in Congress. The crowd

[1] (b. 1910) U.S. singer, actress, and spokeswoman for the arts. Widow of theatrical director Moss Hart.

consisted mostly of congressional staffers and administration officials who worked on free trade – a thank you to everyone. Jim Baker – now heading the Bush campaign – not only came but stayed and stayed. Clayton Yeutter, just returned from Pakistan, also came and stayed and stayed. It was one of the most memorable receptions of my time here. A sense of accomplishment, history, and optimism radiated throughout the evening.

An encounter with Bogdan Kipling, he who told the press that I was the worst Canadian ambassador ever to serve in Washington. I noticed him hovering, and then he came up and said, "I want to tell you, you have done a remarkable job in Washington. During the past few years, your work has been outstanding. What I said about you before was wrong."

But the tensions in Canada-U.S. relations never end, not even for a minute. Colin Powell came to the reception and pulled me aside to alert me to a problem. A U.S. coast guard vessel, the *Polar Star*, is in trouble in the Arctic and needs to enter the Canadian archipelago for repairs and transit. Ottawa was aware of this and was not helping. Powell was in a rage. "We have an Arctic agreement covering precisely this issue," he said, "and we will seek your consent. The boat is in trouble. Ottawa's attitude is awful."

I tried to explain that the last thing we needed in Canada was a revival of the "sovereignty" issue during a federal election. Mulroney has said, "We own the Arctic, lock, stock, and iceberg," so if a U.S. vessel comes in, the cry will go out, why doesn't the United States first recognize our sovereignty? I did my best to calm Powell. The truth is there would be no justification whatsoever for refusing entry to the vessel.

October 6, 1988 Yesterday I flew to New Brunswick, New Jersey, to speak to 1,200 businessmen about free trade. Meanwhile, the flap over the *Polar Star* continues to upset the powers that be in Ottawa. I spent a night in New York, and this morning I was awakened by a call from Colin Powell. "We are going to present you with a request today," he said. "The vessel is in trouble. We must go in to refuel." I told the PMO we will have no choice but to say yes, provided proper procedures are followed. The only memorable aspect of this affair has been Powell's tight handling of the issue. The White House clearly doesn't want to hurt Mulroney in any way during this election period.

October 7, 1988 The *Financial Post* carries a profile of me. Jim Baker is quoted: "Allan is the most outstanding ambassador this city has seen in a long, long while." I'm deeply moved, because of all the people I've met in my sojourn here, Baker is the most impressive.

October 11, 1988 After days of fear and trembling and suffering in Ottawa, and arrogance and irritability in Washington, the voyage of the *Polar Star* through the Northwest Passage is resolved. Marlin Fitzwater[1] really bungled, confusing notification and the granting of consent. I spoke immediately to Powell and urged a statement of clarification. The embassy officers worked on it, along with the NSC. Then the White House came out with a very fine statement. It couldn't have been better and makes great progress in attaining our aims of sovereignty over Arctic waters. It's good to see another difficult issue virtually resolved as I end my term. The statement said simply: "The U.S. asked for and obtained consent from the Canadian government for transit of the icebreaker *Polar Star*. The icebreaker will transit water covered by the agreement only after the U.S. government explicitly requests and receives the consent of the Canadians for such transits. [This] will be the procedure in the future." A hell of a statement.

Ken Adelman interviews me for the *Washingtonian* and cable TV on "what I have learned in Washington." His closing question: What single piece of advice would you give your successor? I have an easy answer: "Forget everything you have ever learned about diplomacy. It has no value here."

October 12, 1988 As I came into the Washington world, so I leave it – a lobbyist. I continue to lobby. It's the classic type of case: U.S. Congress invokes new legislation to deal with a big domestic problem – drugs.

The legislation is overreaching and contains several extraterritorial elements (it would apply to Canadian banking, drug testing in our workplaces, and our trucking industry). I make representations to the administration. It is powerless. I contact leading members of the Republican College of Cardinals – Senators Dole, Simpson, and Chafee – pleading with them to drop the clauses. "What clauses?" they ask. "The extraterritorial clauses," I reply. "Never heard of them," they say.

October 16, 1988 At Western to inaugurate a lecture room in the name of the new chancellor, Grant Reuber. I spoke on U.S. foreign policy in the 1980s. When I got back to the office, I received the good news from

---

[1] (b. 1942) State Department spokesman and White House Press Secretary 1987–1993.

Philip Somerville at the embassy that most of the extraterritorial provisions we were objecting to in the anti-drug bill before Congress are being dropped. This was a textbook case of how the U.S. system works, and how to work it. Rules:

1) Work the Hill, not just the administration.
2) Decode the process by which the decision is made. Find out who are the key instigators on the Hill. This is not easy.
3) Lobby by telephone or in person. Letters are unread.
4) Call *all* key players. You might hear back from three or four.
5) Good personal relations are a must. You have to know the perpetrator.

Dole and Moynihan told their staff to "fix this Canadian problem." They gathered only a limited idea of our worries from my hurried conversations with them, but it was enough.

October 17, 1988 At dinner last night at Evangeline Bruce's, in honour of Lord Quinton, the British librarian of Parliament and an old Oxford acquaintance, I chatted with author Larry McMurtry[1] (*Lonesome Dove*) about books. He owns several rare bookstores and explained that when he fills up a house with books, he adds a new one to his collection (of houses). He told Sondra he recently attended a small dinner given by Richard Helms for the president. The president spent considerable time explaining to McMurtry his theory about acid rain: it comes from trees. McMurtry says the president blames it mostly on all the underbrush beneath the trees that prevents the rain from hitting the ground and dissolving the sulphur – or something like that. The problem with the underbrush, says Mr. McMurtry, is that it prevents the president from riding his horse through the forests.

Evangeline Bruce and Joe Alsop, looking very fragile, told me they both wanted to give us farewell parties. Evangeline: "Let's make it as late as possible. I can't stand the thought of you going." I can't stand it either.

October 18, 1988 We attended a big black-tie dinner for Bob and Helen Strauss, in honour of their seventieth birthdays, held in a tent behind

[1] (b. 1936) American novelist, essayist, and screenwriter, author of *Lonesome Dove*.

the F Street Club. Dwayne and Inez Andreas were hosts for one hundred and twenty-five of the Washington crowd, including Jim Wright (bumptious as ever, attacks on his reputation notwithstanding), Shultz, Baker, Bradley, Jay Rockefeller, the Brinkleys, the Kirklands, Clark Clifford[1] (I sat next to him), and on and on.

As we walked into the dinner, we were handed a little pamphlet called "The World According to Strauss" or "It ain't bragging if you done it." It contained vintage Strauss. Some samples: "The Democratic Party opened the doors – and let all the votes out. . . . Damn right, I'm riding first class – till something better comes along [on austerity] . . . I'm a professional. I can teach it round or flat. . . . Hell, I'm not going to participate in any Poor Peoples' March. Set up a Rich Peoples' March. I'll lead it. . . . I look out my window at the swimming pool and say, 'Strauss, you is one rich som'bitch.' "

My tribute in part: "Mind you, if you feed him, you have to give him what he likes to eat. He goes for the high nitrates and high cholesterol: sausages, kidneys, smoked meat, tongue (centre-cut), and steaks, with a potato pancake or two thrown in. If you want to find him in New York, call Kaplan's delicatessen: 643-8191. He'll eat fish as long as it is catfish and fried. If you want to make an enemy of him, give him poached bluefish. If you want to work out with him, go with him to the racetrack and watch the horses run. Whatever you do, don't give Bob a rowing machine for his birthday."

October 19, 1988 The anti-drug bill continues its weary way through the dying days of the one hundredth Congress. Now Jesse Helms has a provision to require the inspection of diplomatic bags if guns or drugs are suspect. State Department officials suggest to the embassy that it would be appreciated if I called Lugar and Evans to ask them to fight this. I told both that, really, I was doing this pro bono. The United States would be hurt by such a violation of international law and the Vienna Convention, far more than any other country. Every state in the world would reciprocate by opening U.S. bags on "suspicion" of trafficking. Exit confidentiality.

We gave a going-away farewell lunch for John Fieldhouse, who has done a fine job here dealing with the press. Among the guests was Marlin Fitzwater, a true gentleman who manages to muck up every question at his

---

[1] (1906–1998) Influential lawyer, adviser, and high office-holder under several presidents. His reputation was severely damaged as a result of a banking scandal at the end of his career.

daily noon briefing as regards Canada (recently announcing the date of the Canadian election before it was decided in Canada). Fitzwater recounted that there is now a standard routine in the White House. He gets a question on Canada at the noon briefing. He answers. Fieldhouse then calls to say he muffed it. Then I call Powell to demand a correction. Powell calls Fitzwater. An hour or two later, a correction is issued. Powell then tells Gotlieb. Fitzwater calls Fieldhouse to let him know. The circle, and the cycle, are completed.

October 23, 1988 We are in Los Angeles to attend the annual dinner and dance last night sponsored by the Canada-California Chamber of Commerce, our farewell visit to the coast. Arthur Erickson was the honouree.

I made a speech in praise of him, and he had the kindness to reciprocate, saying that without my support, the new embassy in Washington would not have been built. This meant a lot to me.

We had Sunday lunch with Arthur and his friend Francesco in their Beverly Hills home. Arthur is very tired of being harassed by External's decorator crowd, but as I pointed out to him, we managed somehow to win all the battles. I was shocked to learn the decorators went to see Derek Burney shortly after the announcement of his appointment to ask him to reverse the decision to commission Arthur to do the embassy executive furnishings. Will the assault on Arthur ever end?

October 28, 1988 Alan Simpson sends me an eloquent letter on a dismal subject: the acid rain impasse in Congress. Regrettably, there will be no solution in my time.

October 31, 1988 Sunday night and we had a dinner for fourteen – one of our last, probably our very last soirée or salon dinner. Our guests were the new attorney general, Dick Thornburgh, and his wife, the Strausses, Jim and Kate Lehrer, Greenspan, the Brzezinskis, and the Schlesingers.

As I sat there it struck me as strange that in spite of all our close contacts with the Republicans, and the criticisms of us for being cozy with them, there we were, with three top members of the Carter administration at our last small dinner.

November 2, 1988 In Toronto to give a couple of last speeches. Mulroney finally announced my chairmanship of the Canada Council. The

NDP and arts community are starting to howl. The NDP critic, Ian Waddell,[1] calls my appointment "an insult to the Canadian cultural community." The Conference on the Arts says, "We wanted an artist." Civility has gone to the winds. The Conservatives look like they are going down the tube – and taking the FTA with them.

November 3, 1988 Called on David Peterson and we chatted for an hour or so. I told him Toronto will be hurt badly if the free-trade agreement goes down the drain. Toronto is getting to be to Canada what London is to England. It needs an open system to flourish. Peterson knows it and didn't argue with me, but he made a few highly nuanced arguments about why "institutionalization" with the United States is bad. He should know better. But as a politician, he has that very necessary ingredient that most – including Dukakis – lack: likeability. I told him that. He took it well.

November 6, 1988 Len Legault's "legal" farewell for us. Among the guests: Chas Fried, Bill Webster, Steve Schwebel,[2] Harvey Poe, Thad Holt, Lloyd Cutler, Elliot Richardson, Abe Sofaer, and John Stevenson, among many others. Sandra Day O'Connor couldn't come because of recent surgery. Ditto for Rehnquist (his wife's surgery). Richardson gave a fine toast. He said to me afterwards that no one would ever really know or fully appreciate my accomplishments here. I'm deeply moved.

Lane gave the best toast. He said that in this town you could respect people even when you disagreed with them totally. I was trying to promote an *Anschluss* with the United States, and he and his unions were fighting this manoeuvre, even appealing for solidarity and help from their northern brothers. But through all this we had remained good friends.

November 7, 1988 Burney called twice for my opinion as to whether we should ask Shultz or someone even higher up the pole for a clear statement to confirm U.S. understanding that the free-trade agreement does not allow it to interfere with Canada's social programs. I was very negative.

---

[1] (b. 1942) NDP Member of Parliament for Vancouver-Kingsway 1979–1988 and for Port Moody–Coquitlam 1988–1993.

[2] (b. 1929) Burling Professor of International Law at Johns Hopkins University 1967–1981; Deputy Legal Adviser, U.S. Department of State 1974–1981; Judge of the International Court of Justice, The Hague 1981–2000.

The United States will expose itself to the charge of interfering in the Canadian election.

In the late evening Burney returned to the charge. Pressure in Ottawa is big and growing. Still a bad idea, I said.

Burney shocked me by saying that a number of Tory members wanted Mulroney to say flatly that a Tory government would take its time proceeding with the FTA, that it would study it further. Others in the Conservative camp wanted Mulroney to drop it altogether. Do that and the Mulroney government will most assuredly end up on the ash-pit of history.

November 8, 1988 The Canadian election is unbelievable. Henry Adams in 1907: "Politics, as practised, whatever its pretensions, has always been the systematic organization of hatreds." That's what's happening to Canada. The Liberals seem to be organizing a systematic hatred of the United States.

At lunch with Abe Sofaer we analyzed the social program dilemma: how do we get clarification that social programs are not covered by the free-trade agreement without Uncle Sam stepping in to the election to say so? He suggested we file a unilateral instrument or reservation stating that they are not covered. We developed the idea further, and I explored the notion of the International Court of Justice settling any disputes under the protocol. Later in the day, working with Legault and Dymond in the embassy, we drafted a Protocol of Interpretation (to be referred to as the "sovereignty clause").

In the evening we watched the U.S. elections at Marianne Stoessel's and then at the Madison at a party given by Marshall Coyne. We witnessed the unexciting and predictable triumph of George Bush.

November 9, 1988 The PMO, Burney (after discussion with Lowell Murray[1] and the War Council), authorized me to proceed to try get a favourable reaction to our unilateral Protocol of Interpretation. I asked to see Shultz and informed Sofaer, who at first agreed that Shultz was the right channel but later called me back to say we should talk.

I was surprised to be met by Sofaer at the front door of the State building. It was as if he didn't want me to come in. "Let's take a walk in the woods,"

---

[1] (b. 1936) PC Senator 1979 to present; Leader of the Government in the Senate 1986–1993; Minister of State for Federal-Provincial Relations 1986–1991; Minister Responsible for the Atlantic Canada Opportunities Agency 1987–1988.

he said. He told me he had talked to Shultz, and Shultz's reaction was that I shouldn't see him, and I shouldn't seek prior U.S. acquiescence in the protocol. If we did it this way, it would leak out and look like a cooked-up scheme – the very consequence we are seeking to avoid. Shultz's view was that Mulroney should just do it. Once again, Shultz shows his good judgment.

November 13, 1988 We attended a Sunday-night farewell party for us given by Judith Miller of the *New York Times* at her little Georgetown house. Ken Adelman shouts at Rick Burt, Rick at Ken, and we all shout at each other. Burt is anxious for a job with the Bush team and was gnashing his teeth because he doesn't seem to be getting one. Adelman was canvassing names all evening for the VP's chief of staff and foreign-policy adviser (revealing how close his relationship is with Quayle). He's been unique in his commitment, public and private, to Quayle but told me he doesn't want a job. We stayed until midnight. This is the Washington we will miss so much.

November 14, 1988 Throughout the weekend I explored the idea of Baker making a statement to a U.S. journalist saying that the United States considers that the free-trade agreement does not impinge in any way on our social programs, environmental policies, or water. The beauty of this approach is that it would be said by an authoritative American to other Americans, so it wouldn't be contrived as "interference." Niles told Burney that Baker was going to call me in next Tuesday to set this up. The State Department duty officer even called on the weekend to alert me to the secretary of state–designate's intentions. Today no one seems to have heard of it.

We seem to be dealing with two weak U.S. governments instead of one. And I can't figure out how to make contact with the government-in-waiting. Danzansky[1] in the White House has never heard of the scheme and thought Baker would not meet foreign ambassadors at this time. He offered to try to contact Bob Zoelick,[2] Bush's campaign "issues" manager. No word back. McPherson at Treasury said he was not part of the loop. In the

---

[1] Stephen Danzansky. Washington lawyer. Special Assistant to the President and Senior Director for International Economic Affairs on the National Security Council Staff 1985–1988.

[2] Served at the Department of the Treasury in various positions, including Counselor to Secretary James A. Baker III, Executive Secretary of the department, and Deputy Assistant Secretary for Financial Institutions Policy 1985–1988. Served under President George H.W. Bush as Undersecretary of State for Economic and Agricultural Affairs.

evening, with still no news from anyone, I spoke to Colin Powell at Vernon Jordan's farewell dinner for us. Colin said, somewhat grudgingly, "I'll see what I can do. But it's a minefield. Things often don't work out as one would expect." Amen to that, I said to myself.

Speaking to Colin Powell earlier in the day, I expressed my astonishment that the administration would not lift the shakes and shingles tariff. A statutory review had been completed, the decision of the Trade Commission was split, so why, I asked, can't the president lift the ban? The PMO is, understandably, very keen to get it lifted. This could, after all, influence the outcome of several ridings in British Columbia. I said to Powell, "Tom Niles calls the PMO every day and repeats that the U.S. administration is most anxious to be helpful. So why don't you help and lift this silly damn tariff?"

At the Jordans' farewell dinner, Powell told me there were problems doing so. After all, we were being unreasonable about giving access to our cedars and logs. Well, I suppose they'll enjoy dealing with the Turner government; they'll be a lot more reasonable.

In addition to Powell and his wife, the Jordans had the Strausses, Kirklands, Alan Greenspan, Andrea Mitchell, Nick Brady, Ralph Davidson, Lloyd Cutler and Polly (soon to be married), Bill Coleman, Eliz Drew, the Fritcheys, Bill Webster, Carolyn Peachy, and Dick and Cynthia Helms. Lane gave the best toast. In this town, he said, you could respect people even when you disagreed with them totally. I was trying to promote an *Anschluss* with the United States (he just loves this line and keeps repeating it) while he and his fellow workers were fighting free trade, even appealing for solidarity and help from their northern brothers. But through all this we had remained good friends.

I said in my toast that years ago, when some unfortunate scene was being displayed on the Washington stage, I made some critical comments about this town. Bob Strauss said to me, Gotlieb, you fool, don't you realize that, notwithstanding all the theatre and rough play, there is at the centre of Washington a solid core of decent, loyal people who could be counted upon. Well, tonight, I said, in this room, there were gathered a substantial number of people from that core, who were to us loyal and steadfast friends, and at the heart of the core were Vernon and Ann Jordan. I could go around the room and comment – but I wouldn't – on everyone who was there who we counted in this very special way, including some whom we had not met before tonight (laughter).

November 15, 1988 No success with Alan Holmer and Peter McPherson. I urged them to have the administration lift the tariff on shingles and shakes. Got a reserved response. "The president would have to go back on a commitment to the industry if he did," they said. "Besides, it would be interference. And what good would it do?" "It could merely affect the outcome of a few seats in British Columbia," I said, "and ergo, the election."

November 16, 1988 Last night we attended a black-tie dinner at the National Gallery on the occasion of a magnificent Paul Veronese exhibition. By an excellent stroke of good fortune, I sat near Isaiah Berlin and was saved from a dull evening talking to Ford executives at the same table. Berlin is close to eighty years but in remarkable shape, his mind still working like light energy. We talked of Bowra. Wadham, he said, had forgotten him. No, Bowra was not exclusively homosexual. He had affairs with women too. It was fashionable then to be homosexual. His obscene poetry was the best thing he wrote. But the meanings are obscure. He, Berlin, is one of the few living people who could unlock the hidden meanings. No, he couldn't think of anyone who could try to get his poetry together, edit it, analyze it, and prepare it for print. We agreed the best hope was an American Ph.D. student.

November 17, 1988 Yesterday we ambassadors spent an interminable amount of time waiting to be ushered into the chamber of commerce meeting room to hear the president make his anodyne remarks on free trade and the FTA. As soon as he left the room, several members of the Canadian press rushed at me for comments. Were we consulted? Why were his comments so short? Was it interference? When I got out of the building, I was again scrummed by a mob of Canadian journalists. God knows where they all came from – some of them must have been flown down from Canada specially for the event. Many asked me questions about the likely course of events down here if the free-trade agreement were rejected by Canada. I spoke of the strong and growing protectionist pressures and the enhanced security the FTA offered us. Then a couple of reporters accused me of interfering in the Canadian election. One asked, "It's unprecedented for a public servant to be interfering in an election, isn't it?" Another: "Don't you think that John Turner will denounce you on television tonight?" I told them my comments related to the U.S. scene, which I am paid to cover and observe.

November 19, 1988 The *Globe and Mail* wakes me in my hotel room in the Pierre in New York. "Mr. Timothy Findley[1] wrote to the *Globe* today to say that you were appointed by Mulroney to preside over the dissolution of the Canada Council. What do you say to that?" I was speechless.

Last night we attended the opening of Christopher Pratt's[2] exhibition of paintings at the 49th Parallel in New York and the Maple Leaf Ball, put on by the Canadian Club of New York, which was honouring Norm Jewison. Chris and Mary Pratt[3] looked downcast. They have taken much abuse by the artistic community for having the courage to support free trade.

November 21, 1988 A huge crowd, maybe five hundred, filled our offices in the NAB building to watch the sensational news: Mulroney wins. Victory for free trade. The course of history is changed. There will be no champagne bottles opened in the *Toronto Star* building tonight.

November 22, 1988 We are all euphoric at the embassy. All of us are getting calls from friends, well-wishers, former skeptics and doubters. I dashed off letters of congratulations to Darman, Baker, Burt, and Scowcroft – all those who have gotten or are about to get jobs with Bush. It's sad to leave when all one's contacts are being elevated to higher office. But so it goes. My cycle is complete.

November 23, 1988 Mulroney telephoned me in the late evening to chat and thank me for my role in the free-trade affair. "How sweet it is," I said to him, borrowing Jackie Gleason's famous phrase. "You did it," I said. "I know that had it been for your cabinet, the free-trade agreement would never have been proposed, negotiated, or done." I also said, "The papers and screens here are awash with news of you and Canada. You gave them some real drama." Mulroney said, "Well, I had to win it twice." He told me he was going to telephone a number of senators and thank them for their support. I suggested Bradley, Moynihan, Chafee, Packwood, Lugar, Evans, and Bentsen as well as Congressmen Gibbons and Frenzel.

---

[1] (1930–2002) Canadian novelist and playwriter. Winner of the Governor General's Award for Fiction for his novel *The Wars* (1997).

[2] (b. 1935) Canadian painter. He designed the flag of Newfoundland and Labrador.

[3] (b. 1935) Canadian painter specializing in still-lifes.

December 6, 1998 Suffering from a hideous cold and having just returned from Cambridge, where I rented the house of the tough-minded Sovietologist Richard Pipes,[1] we flew to Toronto to attend a dinner Conrad Black gave for Lord Carrington. Marietta Tree accompanied us from New York, but the rest of the guests were mostly Toronto establishment. Robert Campeau bet me that within two years the U.S. deficit would disappear, because Gorbachev's announcement of unilateral defence cuts would lead quickly to very heavy cuts in the U.S. defence budget. This will bring interest rates tumbling down. He was extremely unconvincing, but for him it's both an act of faith and necessity. (They say if interest rates don't come down sharply, he's finished.)

December 7, 1988 Susan Mary Alsop gave us a farewell dinner, for which Alan Simpson flew in. After seven years' experience, I am convinced that she is the most polite, attentive, and animated hostess in Washington. She, Evangeline, and Joe represent, more than anyone we know, the cultivated, worldly Washington that is a unique part of its mystique. No one will replace them.

December 11, 1988 Sunday lunch at the Brzezinskis, a big brunch in a cold house on his farm in the country. It was very political, with everyone discussing and arguing about Gorbachev. Brzezinski is a good host, and one of the few in Washington not corrupted by absence of power.

In the evening we had a dinner, one of our very last, in honour of George and Obie Shultz, and showed a James Bond movie, *Diamonds Are Forever*. A great crowd – the Brinkleys and Strausses, Evangeline, Susan Mary, the Schlesingers, the Neys from New York, Charles Wick, and the Jim Lehrers. Also asked Brent Scowcroft, but he called me personally to say he'd better not come because Shultz was still angry with him over his role in the Iran-Contra investigations. A true gentleman, saving us from a Washington boo-boo.

December 13, 1988 The Bradens gave us a dinner packed with the usual crowd, and many toasts celebrating Sondra and myself. Tonight is a

---

[1] (b. 1923) American specialist in Russian history. Director of East European and Soviet Affairs on the National Security Council 1981–1982.

virtual repeat at the Brinkleys', inaugurating their new house, with the same cast of characters plus the Kissingers. Can we stand up to the march of dinners in our honour?

December 14, 1988 Received from Joan Winser[1] in Los Angeles a copy of a eulogy about me in the *Los Angeles Times*. Two lines meant more to me than all the others: "Allan Gotlieb can explain Washington to the average American as well perhaps as anyone in that confusing power center, and surely better than most." More than a eulogy. An epitaph maybe?

December 15, 1988 My last press briefing to Canadian journalists – a farewell breakfast for about thirty of them. I am glad to wish them goodbye. Most were well behaved except, appropriately, Bob Hepburn of the *Star*, who went on about Mike Deaver. "Did you get your money's worth?" he asked. Another journalist put this question: What was my greatest mistake during my more than seven years in Washington. I answered, "No way will I tell you." But Peter Calamai came up with the answer: "You never bought a house in Toronto."

December 16, 1988 At night another farewell, this time a dinner at Ken and Carol Adelman's. They had the Kampelmans, Brzezinskis, Irving Kristol,[2] and his wife, Gertrude Himmelfarb.[3] Even as we leave, our intellectual horizons widen.

December 18, 1988 One of our last weekends in Washington and a very hectic one. Alan Greenspan and Andrea Mitchell gave us a farewell dinner party, with Brent Scowcroft, the Vernon Jordans, Al Hunt,[4] Judy

---

[1] Canadian Consul General in Los Angeles 1985–1991.

[2] (b. 1920) Considered the founder of American neo-conservatism. Managing Editor of *Commentary* magazine 1947–1952; Co-founder of *Encounter* and Editor 1953–1958; founder of the political and cultural journal *The Public Interest* (Co-Editor 1965–2002) and the foreign-affairs journal *The National Interest* (Publisher 1985–2001).

[3] (b. 1922) American historian known for her studies of the intellectual history of the Victorian era, and as a conservative cultural critic.

[4] (b. 1942) Worked for the *Wall Street Journal* for thirty-five years (1970–2005) in the Washington bureau as a congressional and national political reporter, bureau chief, and executive editor. Wrote the weekly column "Politics and People."

Woodruff,[1] and a few others attending. For a taciturn man, Greenspan gave a toast that was moving and articulate. I was, he said, the best foreign ambassador in Washington in all his experience.

In the late afternoon we rushed to our new embassy on Pennsylvania Avenue, where we held a Christmas reception for about four or five hundred of our embassy staff and their families. This was our very first use of the building, and beautiful as it is, my heart sinks at the banality, no, downright ugliness of the large all-purpose reception room on the main floor. Did the great architect nod off when he designed the room?

December 19, 1988 After breakfast with Roy Pfautch, my favourite Washington lobbyist, I gave an interview to CNN on "What I Have Learned." The toughest question was "What was my worst moment in seven years?" I replied, "Moynihan's phone call the night before the Senate Finance Committee's vote on fast-track authority. 'There's a revolt,' he told me, 'the free-trade agreement is in deep, deep trouble.' "

In the evening Polly Kraft and Lloyd Cutler, now a pair, gave us their farewell party with about two dozen guests, including the Shultzes and Kay Graham. Very short speeches – everyone is drained of material. God, how they must be sick of saying goodbye to us.

December 20, 1988 Gave a farewell luncheon address at the National Press Club – the first ambassador to do so in many years.

There was a large crowd of working journalists and their guests, including some pretty mean types. I gave my "Decalogue" of propositions about what I learned: the U.S. system is the only one in the world with two executive branches, every country is famous for twenty minutes, a foreign country is just another special interest in Washington and isn't very special at that, in the U.S. Congress it's never over till it's over and it's never over. In answer to a question about my attitude to Bourassa's new legislation to replace Bill 101, I said, "I never interfere in the domestic affairs of my own country."

After the speech the government sent a plane for me to get up to Ottawa in time for a celebratory "free-trade dinner" hosted by the Canadian Business Alliance Supporting Free Trade.

---

[1] (b. 1946) American television news anchor and journalist. NBC Chief White House Correspondent 1977–1982; host of *Frontline* since 1984.

The prime minister didn't show at the free-trade dinner, and it was pretty heavy going among the forty or so black-tie invitees who were the backbone of the FTA process. Reisman was asked to speak. He warned that he would be "watching" to see how the implementing process was conducted, and if anything were done wrong, he would publicly denounce those responsible. After dinner he came up and asked if I was writing anything. Yes, I said, at Harvard I intend to write a book. "What about? Free trade?" he asked. "No," I said, "the U.S." He then smiled, and I think I detected a look of relief spreading across his face. We are all a little obsessed about our place in this chapter of Canadian history, if we have one.

December 23, 1988 I desperately need all my time to pack up thirty years of personal papers, but the pressure of work continues. It's never over; the lobbying goes on and on. I'll lobby until the last hour. All very banal except for one event.

I signed a diplomatic note informing the United States that all Canadian obligations under the free-trade agreement have been met, and the Canadian House of Commons and the Senate have completed their work. A historic note it is, and I wanted to be able to sign it personally. It will be delivered to the State Department today, and a similar note on the U.S. side is to be delivered by Tom Niles. They will close the chapter and make history.

December 24, 1988 As I pile up my boxes, throw away papers, and sort through seven years of accumulated junk, I receive a copy of the *Globe and Mail*. No one has summed up my odyssey better than the editorialist who wrote about the "Canadian caped crusader on Capitol Hill": "He began his stint in Washington in 1981 as a brusque defender of the Trudeau government's National Energy Program and Foreign Investment Review Agency, not exactly fab favourites of the new Reagan administration. The techniques he acquired there in trying to vary the Republican disposition towards Pierre Trudeau were relentlessly applied later to help win the day for free trade." How gratifying that someone saw the big picture and got it right.

December 26, 1988 All the kids are here. It's our last Christmas together at Rock Creek Drive. The house is empty, our pictures and photographs are gone, leaving Eaton's furniture and our barren walls. We dropped in at Eliz Drew's annual Boxing Day party, which is growing bigger and bigger. So she's buying a big new house, right around the corner from the embassy.

December 28, 1988 Kay Graham gave a dinner for us, the last in our honour. It expanded from about ten guests to thirty. The Kirklands were there, Mike Deaver (deeply scarred, I fear), Jim and Rachel Schlesinger, Lloyd Cutler and Polly Kraft, Edmund and Sylvia Morris, Polly Fritchey, Brent Scowcroft, Evangeline Bruce, Susan Mary, and a few of Kay Graham's friends, including Jane Wrightsman, a relatively unknown face to me, but not her fame as a furniture collector and New York social arbiter. A poor listener, I thought, but then why should she listen to me? Kay's meal, with its trademark extra course, began with a delicious duck liver accompanied by a Sauternes-type wine. Everyone gobbled it down except the anorexic Susan Mary, at whom Kay glowered with her famous, terrifying glower. This will be the last time I bear witness to it.

December 29, 1988 Rebecca and Keith departed for Toronto, taking our beloved Archie, leaving Sondra and Teodora sobbing.

We flew to the Sea View at Bal Harbour and collapsed into bed listening to the ocean, exhausted.

December 30, 1988 I gave an interview to ABC on the free-trade agreement for a segment it is doing on the national news on Sunday, January 1, the day the agreement comes into force. They sent a TV crew to the Sea View, as I wouldn't budge. I didn't give enough of a damn. Is this freedom I am experiencing?

January 1, 1989 It's appropriate we end our assignment in America with Dwayne and Inez's New Year's Eve party. Of course, it followed the same formula of earlier years – loads of caviar upstairs in their penthouse and then downstairs in the dining room for poor food and lots of noise. The same guests too – Strausses, Brinkleys, Howard Baker, Bob Dole and Elizabeth, the cement mixer,[1] Ross Johnson, and so on. After midnight we followed the old routine. We dropped in on the Brinkleys, and the four of us gossiped until 2:30 a.m.

---

[1] James Stewart. CEO of Lonestar Industries Inc., one of the largest cement corporations in the United States.

This closes our Sea View Odyssey. We go out in style. We will never think of the Sea View as just a hotel. We will remember it as an extraordinary political salon in Washington that just happens to face the sea in Bal Harbour, Florida.

January 7, 1989 A couple of nights ago, we gave our own farewell dinner at the Residence, now entirely stripped of our personal possessions. A large slice of George Bush's incoming cabinet was on hand, along with Majority Leader Tom Foley, leading senators (such as Bradley and Chafee), and congressmen (including the champions of our free-trade agreement, Sam Gibbons and Bill Frenzel). Yes, as the Canadian press reported, it was "a display of all the social power and contacts the Gotliebs acquired over the years." Among the mix of some sixty black-tie guests were Alan Greenspan, Katharine Graham, Bob Strauss, Jim Schlesinger, Brent Scowcroft, David Brinkley, and Christopher Plummer. And many more of the usual suspects to be found at 2521 Rock Creek Drive.

In remembrance of things past, we served Manitoban caviar. And gossiped about who is in and who is not. Many flattering words were spoken, many compliments exchanged. As parties go, it was a good one. But for us it was a melancholy occasion.

I thought long and hard about what I should say in my farewell to the guests. I decided to give Thackeray the last word. "Come, children, let us shut up the box and the puppets, for our play is played out."

January 9, 1989 On Saturday night we held our very last farewell, our very last official activity. We hosted a reception for people we dealt with or have known over the years. It was a vast assembly.

"The Ambassador's Adieu" occupies much space in the *Washington Post*. "They've thrown hundreds of parties honoring everyone else in town during their seven years in Washington. Saturday night the Gotliebs threw one themselves."

This one was different in another way. We entertained at our new embassy on Pennsylvania Avenue, our first – and last – official entertainment in this glorious structure created by Arthur Erickson. I was so glad he was on hand for the event.

Borrowing from Sondra's vocabulary in her "Dear Beverly" columns, the *Washington Post* reported that "the Serious Media were there. And Powerful Jobs and Wives of" – and other figures from "Powertown."

And indeed they were. From current Powerful Jobs, such as William Rehnquist, Sandra Day O'Connor, and Frank Carlucci to former men of glory: John Poindexter and Bud McFarlane. And the upper media in droves and the denizens of the Hill – over five hundred guests in all.

It was a night (to borrow again a phrase from the *Post*) for "serious gushing only." Andrea Mitchell's gush to the press meant the most to me: "I cannot remember another ambassador who has had as much effect on the Hill as Allan. And his secret is Sondra . . ."

Sondra wore the same long violet velvet dress with the multicoloured sequined collar that she did at our first important dinner party seven years ago, when Haig and Weinberger, rather warily, dined together under our roof. The dress still fit her. She was very pleased.

January 10, 1989 Last day of my assignment. Winston Churchill describing Lord Curzon: "The morning was golden; the noon was bronze; and the evening lead." My evening arrives.

January 28, 1989 No more diaries. I'm quitting the habit. This is my last entry.

A private citizen, I'm in Berkeley with Sondra to give a course of lectures over the next two weeks. I'm trying to learn how to live without infrastructure. As I walk down Telegraph Avenue and see the headlines announcing the arrival of the "Bush Era," I feel very distant from Washington and irrelevant.

A batch of obituaries, including a very flattering one in the *New York Times* describing my style of diplomacy, is sent on to me by the embassy.

Newsday has published the entire text of my speech to the National Press Club, "A Diplomat's Rules for Washington's Power Games." Barbara Bush writes Sondra, "We all agree that you brought wonderful Canada into the frontline of all American thought." The eponymous president-elect sends a personal farewell.

Two obituaries were especially gratifying. One from a historian, Michael Beschloss: "There is little question that you have been the most effective Ambassador in Washington in the past 25 years." The other from Mike Armacost at State: "The professionals know how dazzling your performance has been – your diplomatic colleagues are paying you the ultimate tribute: emulating your method (as best they can)."

Sheer vanity leads me to record these remarks. But I tell myself there are worse sins.

INDEX